THE REIGN OF K
STEPHEN, 1135–1154

Pearson
Education

We work with leading authors to develop the
strongest educational materials in history,
bringing cutting-edge thinking and best learning
practice to a global market.

Under a range of well-known imprints, including
Longman, we craft high quality print and
electronic publications which help readers to
understand and apply their content,
whether studying or at work.

The find out more about the complete range of our
publishing please visit us on the World Wide web at:
www.pearsoneduc.com

THE REIGN OF KING STEPHEN, 1135–1154

David Crouch

An imprint of **PEARSON EDUCATION**

Harlow, England · London · New York · Reading, Massachusetts · San Francisco · Toronto · Don Mills, Ontario · Sydney
Tokyo · Singapore · Hong Kong · Seoul · Taipei · Cape Town · Madrid · Mexico City · Amsterdam · Munich · Paris · Milan

Pearson Education Limited
Edinburgh Gate
Harlow
Essex CM20 2JE
England
and Associated Companies throughout the world

Visit us on the world wide web at:
http://www.pearsoneduc.com

First published 2000

ISBN 0 582 22658 9 CSD
ISBN 0 582 22657 0 PPR

British Library Cataloguing-in-Publication Data
A catalogue record for this book is available from the British Library

Library of Congress Cataloging-in-Publication Data
A catalog record for this book is available from the Library of Congress

Set by 35 in 10/12pt Bembo
Printed and bound in Singapore

Contents

List of Maps and Genealogical Table

Acknowledgements

There are many debts to remember in writing a book like this. Firstly I must acknowledge the help of those academics with whom I have discussed aspects of Stephen's reign over the years, among them Marion Archibald, David Bates, Jim Bradbury, Paul Brand, Marjorie Chibnall, Charles Coulson, David Cox, Richard Dace, John France, John Gillingham, Judith Green, John Hudson, Edmund King, Chris Lewis, Graham Loud, Patrick McGurk, John Meddings, Heather Tanner, Kathleen Thompson, Claire de Trafford, John Walker and Graeme White. In mentioning Edmund King, I have to record my regrets that time constraints meant that I was unable to incorporate his revised edition of the *Historia Novella* into this work, much to its loss. A considerable debt is owed to Nicholas Vincent of Christ Church College, Canterbury, for his great generosity in sharing the fruits of his archive work. There have been others who have helped down the years, and I hope those I have not mentioned in person will accept that it is memory and not gratitude which is at fault. There have been others too who can only be thanked in piety, as they have died. I must particularly mention John Brand, Ralph Davis, C. Warren Hollister and Tom Keefe. It is to the memory of the last two scholars, *altero magistro altero alumno*, that I dedicate this book.

There are other people and institutions who have helped this project on its way. I have to mention here especially the staff, students and library of University College, Scarborough; the Brotherton Library of Leeds University and the Institute of Historical Research, University of London. Some of the preliminary work done on this book was made possible by the generosity of the Leverhulme Trust, the Twenty-Seven Foundation and the British Academy. Lastly I must thank my wife and children for their support and their tolerance of my abstraction while working. Lately too I have had to trespass upon the good nature of the clergy and people of the parish of St Martin-on-the-Hill, Scarborough, while adding the duties of assistant curate to those of husband, father and teacher.

David Crouch
June 1999

Abbreviations

ANS	*Anglo-Norman Studies* (before 1982, *Proceedings of the Battle Conference on Anglo-Norman Studies*).
ASC	*The Anglo-Saxon Chronicle* (citation by year) the edition used by the author was *The Peterborough Chronicle*, ed. C. Clark (Oxford, 1970).
BL	British Library
Brut	*Brut y Tywysogyon: Peniarth MS. 20 Version*, ed. T. Jones (Cardiff, 1952); *Red Book of Hergest Version*, ed. T. Jones (2nd edn., Cardiff, 1973) (citation by year).
CDF	*Calendar of Documents preserved in France* i, *918–1206* (London, 1899).
EHR	*English Historical Review*.
EYC	*Early Yorkshire Charters*, vols i–iii, ed. W. Farrer (Edinburgh, 1914–16); vols iv–xii, ed. C.T. Clay (Yorkshire Archaeological Society, Record Series, Extra Series, 1935–65).
GC	Gervase of Canterbury, *Opera Historica* (2 vols, Rolls Series, 1879–80).
GS	*Gesta Stephani*, ed. K.R. Potter and R.H.C. Davis (Oxford, 1976).
HH	Henry of Huntingdon, *Historia Anglorum*, ed. D. Greenway (Oxford, 1996).
Historia Pontificalis	*The Historia Pontificalis of John of Salisbury*, ed. M. Chibnall (Oxford, 1986).
HN	William of Malmesbury, *Historia Novella*, ed. K.R. Potter (London, 1955).
HSJ	*Haskins Society Journal*
JH	*Symeonis Historia Regum Continuata per Johannem Hagustaldensem*, in *Historia Regum*, ed. T. Arnold, ii (Rolls Series, 1885).
JW iii	*The Chronicle of John of Worcester*, iii, *The Annals from 1067 to 1140*, ed. P. McGurk (Oxford, 1998).
LCGF	*The Letters and Charters of Gilbert Foliot*, ed. A. Morey and C.N.L. Brooke (Cambridge, 1967).

Liber Eliensis	*Liber Eliensis*, ed. E.O. Blake (Camden Society, 3rd ser., xcii, 1962).
Monasticon	W. Dugdale and R. Dodsworth, *Monasticon Anglicanum*, ed. J. Caley and others (4 vols in 8, London, 1795–1815).
OD	Odo of Deuil, *De Profectione Ludovici VII in Orientem*, ed. V.G. Berry (New York, 1948).
OV	Orderic Vitalis, *The Ecclesiastical History*, ed. M. Chibnall (6 vols, Oxford, 1969–80).
PL	*Patrologia Latina*, ed. J-P. Migne (221 vols, Paris, 1844–64).
PR	Pipe Rolls.
PR 31 Hen I	*Magnum Rotulum Scaccarii vel Magnum Rotulum Pipae de anno tricesimo-primo regni Henrici primi*, ed. J. Hunter (Record Commission, 1833).
PRO	Public Record Office
Red Book	*The Red Book of the Exchequer*, ed. H. Hall (3 vols, Rolls Series, 1896).
Regesta	*Regesta Regum Anglo-Normannorum*, ed. H.W.C. Davis and others (4 vols, Oxford, 1913–69).
RH	Richard of Hexham, *De Gestis Regis Stephani et de Bello Standardii*, in *Chronicles of the Reigns of Stephen etc*, ed. R. Howlett, iii (Rolls Series, 1886).
RHF	*Recueil des historiens des Gaules et de la France*, ed. M. Bouquet and others (24 vols, Paris, 1869–1904).
RT	Robert de Torigny, *Chronica*, in *Chronicles of the Reigns of Stephen etc*, ed. R. Howlett, iv (Rolls Series, 1889).
TRHS	*Transactions of the Royal Historical Society*
WN	William of Newburgh, *De Rerum Anglicarum*, in *Chronicles of the Reigns of Stephen etc*, ed. R. Howlett, i–ii (Rolls Series, 1884–5).

Introduction: Feudalism, Anarchy, the Baron de Montesquieu and Bishop Stubbs

England is a lucky nation. It has experienced only two long-term civil wars in the past nine hundred years. The first of these was the series of wars of succession during the reign of King Stephen (1135–54). The wars have been commonly called (since the late nineteenth century) 'the Anarchy'; a bad choice of name. This introductory chapter is going to dispute strongly its suitability as a label for the civil wars of Stephen's reign. Wars are terrible events and horrific for those who live and fight through them, but they are only rarely anarchic. When wars are begun in order to pursue political rather than social ends, they generally have a clear objective, and those objectives inform strategies. Wars involve reason and logic, and are not devoid of a sort of morality. Stephen's civil wars were no exception. There were two parties contesting the succession to the kingdom of England and the duchy of Normandy, and each knew precisely what its objectives ought to be. Having those ends in view, they manoeuvred, fought, argued and disputed to achieve them.

The twelfth-century civil war could indeed be considered a 'modern' war. To call Stephen's civil wars 'modern' is not to make a judgement on the military technology of the times. It is to comment on the amount of thought that people of the time devoted to the meaning of the conflicts they were witnessing. The wars split the nation. By 1135 England had long been a stable nation with a well-defined idea of itself as an entity. It was an idea that the Norman Conquest had not troubled in the slightest. The collapse of the nation into warring factions caused a number of people to think hard about the reasons why they were suddenly fighting amongst themselves, and then to argue about them. In the mid-twelfth century, people of influence (not just churchmen) had begun to commit their speculations to writing. If there is anything that marks out the twelfth century from those that preceded it, it is the amount of argument that we can discover that was going on. It produced a world beginning to resemble our own: keen to pin down ideas, blame and definitions. So the fighting of Stephen's reign was given something that might be described as a journalistic treatment by contemporaries. The rights and wrongs of either

1

side were pondered and argued. Manifestoes were written and positions taken. We are not ignorant of the reasons why people thought they were fighting in England in the middle of the twelfth century, and, as historians, we have the materials at hand to form our own theories.

For all these reasons it is contentious to label the twelfth-century civil war in England an 'anarchy'. The warriors fighting it were not moral imbeciles. Time and again throughout the conflict they showed themselves willing to discuss peaceful solutions for the violence that was plaguing their lives, and the political problems which were causing it. At no level did the conflict involve the dissolution of the social or political order.[1] It is only by the reading of a few selected texts written as polemics by clergymen that we can get that impression. How therefore did we end up with the label of the 'Anarchy' of Stephen's reign? The answer is complicated, and involves some very deep-rooted presuppositions about the nature of medieval society. The great sweep of time in which these presuppositions have dominated the work of historians has allowed them to become more deeply rooted in our understanding of the past than the most stubborn weed in an unkempt garden.

The first self-consciously analytical history school in Britain was the circle of William Stubbs and his pupils at Oxford in the late nineteenth century.[2] It was this school which identified the problem of Stephen's reign in the 1860s. It was Stubbs himself who dubbed the reign 'anarchic'. He did so because it met his ideas of what happened to a land when the aristocracy got out of hand, and overbalanced the stabilising power of the king. Stubbs had read the Baron de Montesquieu's analysis of forms of government published in 1748, *De L'Esprit des Lois*, and had fitted Montesquieu's analysis of what went wrong with Carolingian France into his own English scheme of things. In France, what Montesquieu called 'feudal government' had evolved, when rising aristocrats had developed the military resources to defy their king and lord, and society fell into a chaos of violence. Montesquieu despised this state of society, and used it as an argument in support of strong monarchy, for he was an ardent supporter of the Bourbon *ancien régime*. He was particularly arguing against the Comte de Boullainvilliers, who saw the monarchy as the usurper of the customary rights of the aristocracy.[3]

1 Studies which highlight the degree of morality and ideology inherent in the conduct of the conflict are, R.B. Patterson, 'Anarchy in England, 1135–54: the theory of the constitution', *Albion*, 6 (1974), 189–200; C.J. Holdsworth, 'War and peace in the twelfth century: the reign of Stephen reconsidered', in *War and Peace in the Middle Ages*, ed. B.P. McGuire (Copenhagen, 1987), 67–93, esp. 75–83.
2 Such was Stubbs's own view, in his inaugural lecture at Oxford in 1867, where his debt to French and German scholarship is very evident, see the comments on this by his friend J.R. Green, printed in *Letters of William Stubbs, Bishop of Oxford*, ed. W.H. Hutton (London, 1904), 117–18. On the existence and ideals of this school, D.S. Goldstein, 'History at Oxford and Cambridge: professionalization and the influence of Ranke', in *Leopold von Ranke and the Reshaping of the Historical Discipline*, ed. G.G. Igges and J.M. Powell (Syracuse, N.Y., 1990), 141–53.
3 Charles Louis de Secondat, baron de Montesquieu, *De L'Esprit des Lois*, ed. R. Derathé (2 vols, Paris, 1973) i, 65, ii, 403. See on Montesquieu's political allegiance, M. Hulliung, *Montesquieu and the Old Regime* (Los Angeles, 1976), 58–71. For the view against which he reacted see especially, H. de Boullainvilliers, *État de France* (3 vols, London, 1727) iii, 37.

It is within this wider perception in the eighteenth and nineteenth centuries about the nature of early medieval society that the narrow idea of the 'Anarchy' of Stephen's reign arises. It is intriguing to see now from a distance of over two and a half centuries how the basic assumption of Montesquieu has colonised the historiography of the middle ages. Montesquieu's successors, writers such as David Hume, Adam Smith and François Guizot, although admirers of constitutional and limited monarchy, did not contest the idea that the feudal baron was egotistical, violent and socially disruptive. Guizot saw the only virtue in the feudal period and feudal aristocracy as being that of resistance to over-enthusiastic royal oppression, an idea fervently advocated by Boullainvilliers a century earlier.[4] It is from this thought-world that we derive the basic perception of the 'feudal' medieval period in two dominant nineteenth-century historical schemes. It is the perception of both the Marxist school of socio-economic philosophy, and also that of Stubbs and his Oxford constitutionalist school. Both schools saw the feudal aristocracy as a historical obstacle in their various schemes of 'progress'.[5]

Stubbs's motive for decrying the 'feudal anarchy' of Stephen's England was not, of course, the same as that of Marx in criticising the feudal order. Stubbs was a passionate Tory (which was how he acquired Disraeli's nomination for his regius chair at Oxford), but had what has been called a 'Liberal Anglican' outlook on English history. He was a priest and for him history, as the place in which God's plan was acted out, must tend to a merciful outcome. He saw nations as therefore tending to advance but vulnerable to powerful people, both good and bad, who were raised up within them. Stephen's reign was for

4 I mean these writers to be understood as 'successors' in the sense that they were all universalists, formulating general theories out of their studies of history. David Hume, *The History of England* (new edn., 8 vols, London, 1823) i, 253, talks of feudal law as 'the foundation both of the stability and of the disorders in most of the monarchical governments of Europe'. On Hume's ideas of feudalism, see N. Phillipson, *Hume* (London, 1989), 130–6. Adam Smith, *The Wealth of Nations*, talks of medieval government as 'too weak in the head and too strong in the inferior members'; François Guizot, *The History of Civilisation in Europe*, trans. W. Hazlitt (Harmondsworth, 1997), 64–81, gives an extended treatment to the contradictions of feudal society in his Fourth Lecture.
5 For the historicist tendencies in the universalists' treatment of history at the turn of the eighteenth century, see J.G.A. Pocock, *The Ancient Custom and the Feudal Law* (Cambridge, 1957), 246–7. This was translated by their nineteenth-century readers such as Thomas Arnold and A.P. Stanley, and to some extent Stubbs, into what has been called the 'Liberal Anglican' framework of history, a sort of intellectualised Whig interpretation, in which nations were perceived as capable of a degree of advance, but which believed that nineteenth-century England was about as far as advance could go, see D. Forbes, *The Liberal Anglican Idea of History* (Cambridge, 1952). Stubbs's Whiggish idealisation of 'the nation' and his belief in its ability to determine its destiny was noted by Powicke and explored in H. Cam, 'Stubbs seventy years after', in *Lawfinders and Lawmakers* (London, 1962), 195. For the strangely congruent basic supposition of Marxists and Whigs, see the comment of C.J.W. Parker, *The English Historical Tradition since 1850* (Edinburgh, 1990), 4, that they were both stuck 'between determinism and freedom'. For a stimulating study of the evolution of the term 'feudalism' into the nineteenth century from a decidedly Marxist perspective, see S.N. Mukherjee, 'The idea of feudalism: from the philosophers to Karl Marx', in *Feudalism: Comparative Studies*, ed. E. Leach and others (Sydney Studies in Society and Culture, no. 2, 1984), 25–37, and from a nominalist, pragmatic perspective, S. Reynolds, *Fiefs and Vassals: the Medieval Evidence Reinterpreted* (Oxford, 1994), 7–14.

him an example of what happened when a weak king upset the process, and was unable to hold in check the anti-constitutional and anti-centralist forces of a feudal aristocracy. Stubbs was to that extent the bridge by which French ideas of feudalism entered the mainstream of English historiography, even though he and Montesquieu hardly shared much other common ground.[6] For Stubbs (unlike Montesquieu) the monarchy was not the end, but a means to an end: one side of the balanced forces of king and aristocracy which would eventually spark off Magna Carta, cause the evolution of parliament, and start the long march through history which would eventually produce the triumph of the limited, constitutional monarchy of Palmerston, Disraeli and Stubbs's friend and admirer, W.E. Gladstone.[7]

So for Stubbs, Stephen was a weak king and therefore a warning of what would happen when feudal forces were not kept under control by the balancing forces of royal centralism. Stephen was one of those occasional royal incompetents whose pathetic ineptitude led to those crises which produced desirable change. If there was not much else good to say about his rule of England, Stephen's failures were redeemed because he was the catalyst which produced the reign of one of Stubbs's great medieval constitutional heroes, King Henry II. Stubbs was a historian of great industry but not great originality. He adopted the views of the medieval past that he found to agree with his own (occasionally polemical) prejudices.[8] His devoted disciples consolidated his ideas. It is not surprising that one of the first 'scientific' studies of the reign of an English king – John Horace Round's treatment of Stephen's reign, *Geoffrey de Mandeville* (1892) – was produced under Stubbs's inspiration. In Round's great work, Stephen appears as Stubbs would have him: a decent mediocrity at the mercy of an unscrupulous and treacherous aristocracy (of which the defining type was his alleged arch-enemy, Geoffrey de Mandeville, earl of Essex), out for everything it could get. For Round, as for Montesquieu, the aristocracy was tied into a cycle of acquisition and violence.

As a result of Stubbs and his school, historians have talked for a century and more of the 'anarchy' of Stephen's reign. Since J.H. Round's use of it in

6 For Stubbs's reading of Montesquieu, *The Constitutional History of England* (3 vols, Oxford, 1874–8) i, 254–5n, and for his sharing of the basic equation of feudalism and anarchy, Cam, 'Stubbs seventy years after', 194. One should point out that Henry Hallam's *View of the State of Europe during the Middle Ages* (London, 1818), esp. ch. 2, shows plenty of evidence of acquaintance with French ideas of feudal society, and (as Dr Graeme White points out) does use the word 'anarchy' of Stephen's reign (see below, n.9). On the other hand, Stubbs drew little of his historical thinking from Hallam and his generation of historians; his independence of them is noted by Cam, 'Stubbs seventy years after', 190–1.

7 Although we call this a 'Whig' interpretation of history, Stubbs was rather more subtle and diffident in his expression than Macaulay, see Cam, 'Stubbs seventy years after', 195; Parker, *English Historical Tradition*, 1–4. Nonetheless, despite his diffidence, he assuredly did view the history of England as the story of the progress to perfection of its constitution, as noted by C. Petit-Dutaillis, *Studies and Notes Supplementary to Stubbs's Constitutional History* (Manchester, 1930), 307.

8 A point made brutally by H.G. Richardson and G.O. Sayles, 'Stubbs: man and historian', in *The Governance of Medieval England* (Edinburgh, 1963), 2–7.

4

1888, the word has been dignified with a capital letter.[9] Round was not him-self convinced that England fell into a *complete* Anarchy: he knew too much about the original sources to make that mistake. He was in fact quite generous to the memory of Stephen and made much of the particular circumstances that disabled his full exercise of power: a rival claimant, the unpopularity of his predecessor's methods and the 'feudal reaction' that followed. Round also knew that the warfare was confined to certain places and certain times. But he did believe that Stephen's weak rule led to a collapse of the strong kingship imposed on England by the Conqueror and his sons and to 'feudalism run mad'.[10] It was Round's younger contemporary, H.W.C. Davis who, in con-sidering the evidence of the early pipe rolls of the reign of Henry II, argued strongly that Stephen's reign saw a *national* breakdown of order.[11]

The elder Davis – whose son was R.H.C. Davis, the biographer of Stephen – focused on the evidence of the appearance of the word 'waste' (Lat. *vastum*) in the sheriff's accounts between 1154 and 1160. He noted that it was not just the shires of the southwest which showed large proportions of land written off as waste for tax purposes, but those also of the north, the midlands and east. If you interpret 'waste' as land made unproductive by the exigencies of war, then it naturally followed that Stephen's reign saw a far greater disrup-tion than even Round had visualised. But is that what 'waste' actually meant? Historians took a long time to get around to reassessing this assumption, and as a result the real presence of anarchy, of the complete collapse of civil order in the mid-twelfth century, was long considered to be proved. Between Round's assumptions of the nature of medieval society and the analysis of waste by the elder Davis, the feudal Anarchy of Stephen's reign was taken for granted for three-quarters of a century. Rather unfortunately, this long-lived presupposition about medieval society has meant that the idea of the 'Anarchy' has acquired the characteristics of a *Ding an sich*, a critical term meaning 'a phenomenon capable of being studied and analysed'. It will be the argument of this book that to subscribe to such a view is to handicap oneself in studying Stephen's reign. In fact there was nothing inevitable about the civil war of 1139–47 and indeed there was nothing either generic (or anarchic) about the war as it happened, any more than there was anarchy in the seventeenth-century civil war. The civil disorders that accompanied the war of succession between royalist and Angevin parties were not fought without regard to morality or order, and (as will be demonstrated) many areas of the kingdom – and perhaps the bulk of it – saw little military violence, although many people

9 For the use of the term 'Anarchy' see G.H. White's analysis in *The Reconstruction of Eng-land, 1153–65* (forthcoming). Dr White finds the first capitalisation of 'Anarchy' in J.H. Round, 'Danegeld and the finance of Domesday' in *Domesday Studies*, ed. P.E. Dove (2 vols, London, 1888–91) i, 112. I must thank Dr White for generously allowing me to see a draft of the introduc-tion to his new work before publication.
10 J.H. Round, *Geoffrey de Mandeville: A Study of the Anarchy* (London, 1892), 35–6.
11 H.W.C. Davis, 'The Anarchy of Stephen's reign', *EHR*, xviii (1903), 630–41.

within these otherwise tranquil areas may have experienced constraint and threat.[12]

These old presuppositions of Round and H.W.C. Davis have only been seriously contested in the past quarter-century. In 1974 Edmund King broke fully with the – by then – venerable notion of feudal 'anarchy' as being innate in the medieval social order. He suggested that the magnates were forced into independence of the king, rather than quite consciously aiming at it.[13] As for the supporting evidence introduced by H.W.C. Davis about the wasting of the kingdom, it has been heavily attacked by successive generations of scholars. Poole in 1951 noted some inconsistencies in Davis's argument and league table of devastated counties, but had no alternative theory to account for the waste entries.[14] In 1975, W.E. Wightman demonstrated that the word 'waste' applied to land in the return for Domesday Yorkshire could be a fiscal term; it signified land not assessed for taxation, for whatever reason.[15] Judith Green, Graeme White and Edmund King have since concluded in separate studies that the 'waste' of the early pipe rolls of Henry II may indicate only that the sheriff was unable to collect money for particular lands, possibly because he could not establish who must pay, rather than because the land was unproductive. Waste may even have been a convenient term by which the mid-twelfth-century exchequer wrote off unrecoverable debts.[16] Emilie Amt has subsequently made the point that in certain instances 'waste' in the pipe rolls of

12 E. King, 'The Anarchy of Stephen's reign', *TRHS*, 5th ser., 34 (1984), 151–2, somewhat surprisingly maintains that 'anarchy' is a usable term for the warfare in Stephen's reign; Professor King gives a definition of Stephen's anarchy as 'a failure of central control', notably in the area where there previously had been strong control, the coinage. In thus defining the term, it is difficult to take issue with Professor King's use of 'anarchy'. The problem is that he then goes on to use it to describe the disorder that the magnates were creating in the countryside, ibid., 135.
13 E. King, 'King Stephen and the Anglo-Norman aristocracy', *History*, lix (1974), 180–94, esp. 185. It is true that historians had realised that 'feudal' medieval society actually possessed its own ideas of social order long before 1974, cf. the comments on private charters of Stephen's reign originally made in 1929 by F.M. Stenton, *The First Century of English Feudalism, 1066–1166* (2nd edn., Oxford, 1960), 245, 'these passages give no support to the view that a state of general war was agreeable to the baronage as a whole'. But Professor King's article was new in its exculpation of the aristocracy.
14 A.L. Poole, *From Domesday Book to Magna Carta* (Oxford, 1951), 151–4, notes how Davis's top county for 'waste', Warwickshire, was never a principal theatre of war and the counties that indubitably suffered heavily, Gloucestershire and Wiltshire, are eighth and fourteenth on his list; Poole also pointed out that Rochester (untouched by war) had liberal allowances for waste, and Worcester (devastated in 1150–51) paid its tax in full. The attempt of Emilie Amt, *The Accession of Henry II in England: Royal Government Restored, 1149–59* (Woodbridge, 1993), 135, to account for the Rochester anomaly by saying that Kent was crippled by taxation under royal demands itself undermines the use of the term 'waste' to establish war damage. Amt's point about the Gloucestershire town of Winchcombe's tax being written off in 1156 because it was damaged in war by the putative rebellion of Earl Roger of Hereford in 1155 is lost if (as I have suggested elsewhere) there was no violence in Gloucestershire in 1155 as Henry II did not oppose Earl Roger; see D. Crouch, 'The March and the Welsh kings', in *The Anarchy of King Stephen's Reign*, ed. E. King (Oxford, 1994), 284–6.
15 W.E. Wightman, 'The significance of "waste" in Yorkshire Domesday', *Northern History*, x (1975), 55–71.
16 J.A. Green, 'The last century of Danegeld', *EHR*, 96 (1981), 252; E. King, 'The Anarchy of Stephen's reign', 143–5; G. White, 'Were the Midlands "wasted" during Stephen's reign?', *Midland History*, x (1985), 26–46.

1155–56 must have referred to the damage done in war, and she is right to do so.[17] But what cannot be accepted now is that Davis's original thesis about waste entries justifies any belief in an anarchy. The arguments in its support by Warren Hollister urge that we should trust the chroniclers' accounts of mayhem, but he skims over the big cracks in Davis's argument.[18]

Leaving aside deterministic models of history, this book will take the other obvious avenue in dealing with Stephen's reign: it will focus on the character of Stephen as an explanation for the problems of his reign. Stephen's character has long been seen as an important cause of what happened and I see no particular reason to be contrary and dissent from this view. I would not go so far as some recent contributors to the debate, who have looked for explanations for the civil war in underlying social developments which would have floored Stephen even had he been far more efficient than he was (for which see Chapter 6). But even they (as we shall see) would not queue up to exonerate Stephen from his share in the blame. So it is to Stephen that we will first look. It may seem rather pointless to try to assess the capacities and character of a man who was born nine centuries ago, but the evidence of his actions testifies to the degree of reasoning behind them, and there were besides no shortage of contemporaries willing to give their opinion of Stephen as king. Providing we avoid the mental hermeneutics of 'psycho-history' (that is, assessing past lives and characters in the light of twentieth-century patterns of behaviour) we will find sufficient material to discover quite how competent or incompetent was Stephen of Blois.

17 Amt, *Accession of Henry II*, 134–6.
18 C. Warren Hollister, 'Stephen's Anarchy', *Albion*, 6 (1974), 233–9, and idem, 'The magnates of Stephen's reign: reluctant anarchists', *HSJ*, 5 (1993), 82–6. In the later article Professor Hollister focuses on Warwickshire, the anomaly in Davis's original argument according to Poole, and notes in support of Davis *père* the observation of R.H.C. Davis that Duke Henry had campaigned through the midland shires in 1153: in fact, all we know of that campaign is that Warwick fell without a fight to the duke – hardly an indication of widespread fighting and certainly no basis for a belief that it was wasted to a degree beyond that of any other shires in England!

PART ONE

The Causes of the Civil War

Stephen as Count and King, 1113–1139

CHAPTER 1

The Count of Mortain

Stephen of Blois was born around the year 1096; it is impossible to be sure exactly when.[1] He was named after his father, the count of Blois-Chartres and Meaux, the ruler of one of the key regional principalities of northern France. Blois-Chartres was in fact the boss-stone of the power structures of northern France: a compact principality wedged between Normandy to the north, the French king's domain around Paris to the east, and the county of Anjou to the west. From his accession in 1089 his father, Count Stephen (sometimes called Stephen-Henry), had used the natural advantages of his position well, and was a successful ruler. He had consolidated his power by military means and by an excellent political marriage – made at some time between 1080 and 1084 – to Adela, daughter of King William the Conqueror and elder sister of Kings William Rufus and Henry I of England.[2] In this way he allied with the powerful king of the Anglo-Norman realm to the north, as a means of pursuing his ambitions against his dangerous neighbours, whether Anjou to the west or the French king to the east. Count Stephen did rather less well when, in 1096, he was seduced by the nobility and glamour of the Crusade to recover Jerusalem. He became the principal leader of this great expedition as it entered Syria, but, while besieged in Antioch in 1098, the count panicked and fled the city. This was a piece of bad judgement, for the city in the end held out against the Turks. He returned home in disgrace the same year. He died at the battle of Ramlah in May 1102 while attempting to recover his reputation in a further expedition to the Holy Land.

Stephen the boy cannot have grown up with much memory of his father. His childhood was lived out in a court dominated by his mother: a woman of grand connections (and not shy about mentioning them), admired for her piety, and quite capable of ruling everything and everyone around her. Her sons were no exception. The eldest of them was naturally brought forward as his

1 For the rough calculation of his birthdate, see R.H.C. Davis, *King Stephen* (3rd edn., London, 1990), 1n, 7n.
2 For the date of the marriage, see K.A. LoPrete, 'The Anglo-Norman card of Adela of Blois', *Albion*, 22 (1990), 572n.

father's successor. The young William, named after his grandfather, the conqueror of England, was accepted and designated as count of Blois even before his father's departure on his second crusading venture in 1102. In 1104 this William married the heiress of the lordship of Sully, in northern Berry. By now he must have reached or was approaching adulthood, and was still being referred to as count in 1105. But in 1107, it was the second son, Theobald, who was finally and formally installed as count of Blois.[3] There is no knowing the reason why this happened, although there is every reason to believe that Countess Adela was behind the exclusion. Count William had certainly been hot-headed enough to get into trouble with the Church in 1103, in his violent support of his mother against the bishop of Chartres in a dispute over chapter appointments. However, that was a sin of which many a greater man than he was guilty. After 1107 Count William settled in the lordship of Sully, and produced children who were later to join their uncle, the younger Stephen, in England.

Stephen, the third son, was involved in the family settlement. It seems to have been his mother's intention that the number of her sons should not lead to the weakening of Blois-Chartres, by dividing it up to provide for each. So William, although overlooked for the big prize, was provided for by a strategic marriage outside the ancestral lands. The third son, the young Stephen, also had to be found opportunities outside Blois-Chartres, and no better place could be found than the distinguished household of his mother's brother, Henry I of England. It is not known with any certainty when Stephen entered his uncle's household. One writer implies that it was soon after the battle of Tinchebray (1106) when King Henry defeated his brother, Duke Robert of Normandy, and took over the duchy.[4] The battle (almost the reverse of Hastings, forty years on) led to the deprivation of the Norman magnates loyal to Duke Robert. One of them was the king's rebel cousin, Count William of Mortain. The writer, Orderic Vitalis (a monk of the abbey of St Evroult on the southern Norman frontier), gives the impression of believing that William was immediately replaced at Mortain by Stephen of Blois, who would still then only have been a boy of about ten. There is no way of confirming the date of 1106 for the grant. But the fact that Stephen's mother settled the succession to Blois at about this time makes it possible that she prevailed on her royal brother (and now neighbour) to provide for the boy Stephen by at least a promise of Mortain and by adopting him into his household, hence Orderic's confusion.

---

3 For Count Stephen and his disgrace, see Davis, *Stephen*, 1–4. For William's mysterious relegation from Blois to Sully, and his mother's apparent part in it, see LoPrete, 'Anglo-Norman card', 580; K.A. LoPrete, 'Adela of Blois and Ivo of Chartres: piety, politics, and the peace in the diocese of Chartres', *ANS*, xiv, ed. M. Chibnall (Woodbridge, 1990), 147–8; Davis, *Stephen*, 4. However, note that Robert de Torigny, writing in the 1130s, believed that the marriage alliance between William and the daughter of Gilo de Sully had been planned by his father, Count Stephen, before his departure to the Holy Land in 1102, William of Jumièges, *Gesta Normannorum Ducum*, ed. E.M.C. van Houts (2 vols, Oxford, 1992–95) ii, 263.
4 OV vi, 42.

Adela of Blois also had a fourth son, Henry, a few years younger than Stephen and born after his father returned from the Holy Land.[5] This, the youngest surviving boy, was provided for by placing him in the Church, another way of avoiding cutting into the core patrimony. Adela's wide network of connections included the abbot of the great Burgundian abbey of Cluny; she was to retire to a Cluniac priory on the Loire. This vast house had dominated Benedictine monasticism in western Europe since the tenth century. Its reputation for liturgical elaboration and excellence was high, and its monks were frequently recruited to provide abbots for other great monasteries in England, Italy and France. On occasion Cluny took direct control of other houses, which were subordinated to it as dependent priories under its monarchical abbot; eventually there were well over 1,500 of them. By the time of King Henry I of England, Cluny had long been powerful at the papal court also. Pope Urban II (1088–99) was a Frenchman and a Cluniac and under him and his successor the papacy's finances were reformed under a fellow monk, Peter. Henry of Blois was professed as a monk and was cloistered in the mother house itself.[6] Thus he was educated in a great centre of Church politics and papal ideology, at a time also when the great abbey church at Cluny was being rebuilt in grand Romanesque style. The young Henry was a novice monk in a house that was the very apex of ecclesiastical power, art and architecture, and the mixture left its mark on him.

In 1126, when he was probably in his mid-twenties, his royal uncle offered Henry of Blois the abbacy of the great royal Benedictine abbey of Glastonbury in Somerset, one of the wealthiest in England. In 1129, when he must have reached the canonical age of thirty, he was nominated by the king to the wealthy see of Winchester, and permitted to continue to hold Glastonbury in plurality. His relative youth may have been a slight embarrassment to him. It was observed by John of Salisbury at the papal curia in 1149 that Henry affected a full patriarchal beard, and he appears bearded in the portrait of him on a dedicatory plaque (now in the British Museum) which was once attached to some object or reliquary that he donated to one of his churches, and he also is bearded on his seal.[7] Since the seal would have been cut in or soon after 1129, he must have grown a beard before his promotion to Winchester, when

---

5 *English Episcopal Acta* viii, *Winchester, 1070–1204*, ed. M.J. Franklin (British Academy, 1993) xxxv suggests that Henry was born as early as 1090, a line followed also by N.E. Stacy, 'Henry of Blois and the lordship of Glastonbury', *EHR*, 114 (1999), 4 (who has Henry arriving at Glastonbury in his 'mid-thirties'). But Ralph Davis's persuasive argument is that Stephen, his elder brother, was born around 1096. Their father returned from Crusade late in 1098, and it is possible that Henry of Blois, born in 1099, was the result of the passionate reunion of his parents. This date of 1099 could also be supported by the observation that if Henry was nominated to a bishopric at the earliest possible age (thirty), then 1129 would have been that year.
6 Henry himself said, when writing of the troubles he met at Glastonbury, 'I would far rather have been a poor man at Cluny with the rest, than to lord it over others under such a burden', Adam of Domerham, *Historia de rebus gestis Glastoniensibus*, ed. T. Hearne (2 vols, London, 1727) i, 305.
7 *Historia Pontificalis*, 79; *English Romanesque Art, 1066–1200*, ed. J. Alexander and others (London, 1984), no. 277a–b; Stacy, 'Henry of Blois', 4 and n.

he was an abbot in his twenties. The nature of the man was already apparent by then. He has left a series of autobiographical memoranda about his steward-ship of Glastonbury (written at some time between 1139 and 1141 during the period of his political eclipse at court) which demonstrate that he was in-secure, acquisitive and politically very alert. These two latter qualities were to be deployed on his brother's behalf in due course, and the insecurity and self-importance were to be the devil in the relationship between them.

THE ANGLO-NORMAN REALM

Because of family circumstances Stephen, and later his brother, Henry, were both sent to their uncle, the king of England, to further their careers. There was no better place than his court to make a career in the early twelfth century. King Henry had succeeded his brother, William Rufus, in 1100, after Rufus's accidental death in a hunting accident in the New Forest. The then Count Henry had been living at his elder brother's court in England, and, by making key friends in Rufus's household, was able to seize power in the brief period of uncertainty that followed the king's death. He was able to survive the challenge to his rule in 1101 by his remaining elder brother, Duke Robert II of Normandy. By 1103 he had so consolidated his power that he was freely intervening in the affairs of Normandy, where he sponsored a party of dissid-ent magnates against his brother. In 1106, Henry was powerful enough gra-ciously to invade the duchy at the invitation of his supporters so as to restore order. At Tinchebray he and his army defeated and captured Duke Robert and seized his principality. Robert spent the rest of his life in honourable captivity, dying at Cardiff castle in 1134. Robert's son and heir, William, called 'Clito', spent most of the rest of his young life as a refugee in the courts of his uncle Henry's political enemies. Henry became duke and king of the realm he had forcibly united.

Under King Henry after 1106 the great artificial condominium of the king-dom of England and duchy of Normandy which had existed under the Con-queror between 1066 and 1087 (and briefly under Rufus from 1096 to 1099) was restored. Modern historians call this political entity the 'Anglo-Norman realm', echoing the phraseology of the so-called 'Hyde abbey chronicler' (actually more likely to have been a secular clerk connected with the earls of Surrey). The word 'Anglo-Norman' is a convenient label, although it does not comprehend the full breadth of King Henry's influence. He inherited from his Anglo-Saxon predecessors a claim to overlordship of the kings of Wales, and the Scottish king also had to be wary of his power. In France, as duke of Normandy, he claimed rights to intervene in the affairs of Brittany to the west and Maine to the south; and Henry soon extended his power to ally with many of the lesser princes around his borders: Flanders, Boulogne, Ponthieu, Perche and Meulan.[8]

---

8 The adjective 'Anglo-Norman' is first found used at the beginning of this century in connec-tion with the sort of Norman French spoken in England, see J. Le Patourel, *The Norman Empire* (Oxford, 1976), 252. For the extent of Anglo-Norman influence, ibid, 319–54.

The Anglo-Norman realm at its widest extent had little resemblance to a modern state, but was a continuation of the sort of tributary over-kingship which had been a political feature of western Europe since the end of the Roman empire. Yet within it, England and Normandy formed two nuclei of organised lordship which were developing new forms of administration. As we will see later, King Henry's remorseless drive to accumulate power and wealth, when combined with the growth of literacy in society, produced innovation. His government's need for information and control produced greater centralisation on the court in matters of finance and justice. This was so much so that in those long periods when Henry was out of England, government demanded and created an alter-ego, a justiciar, to occupy his empty, central place. The chief symptom of incipient centralisation of government was the biannual financial accounting session at the treasury, called the 'exchequer'. It may have had antecedents under Henry's predecessors, but the earliest traces of it appear in the middle of his reign. There is some reason to believe that it was produced out of a household reorganisation following the conquest of Normandy in 1106. It generated records, the famous pipe rolls (so called because they have the physical shape and dimensions of Victorian earthenware drainage pipes). The pipe roll for 1130 actually survives and is a unique glimpse into a sophisticated world of profit and account in Anglo-Norman government. But this roll itself carries debts that can be traced back over twelve years, notably the continuing debt still being collected in 1130 for the farm owed for the minority of the heirs of Count Robert of Meulan, who died in 1118. We have less information about the organisation of Normandy, but we do at least know that its officers also answered to an exchequer in the duchy, and its government, too, generated a need for a justiciar figure.

King Henry became the dominant monarch of western Europe; his wealth and prestige dwarfing the Capetian kings of France, whose power was confined to the region of Paris, and who were at constant odds with their notional dependants: particularly the counts of Vermandois to the north, and the counts of Blois to the southwest. It was not an effortless rise. King Henry found that Normandy would not stay conquered, and fought a protracted series of campaigns between 1118 and 1124 against powerful internal rebels who allied themselves with his threatened neighbour, Louis VI of France. But his edge in resources, his disciplined and well-organised military household of hundreds of paid knights, and his own personal gifts of astuteness and cool judgement pulled Henry out of every difficulty. The last ten years of his life were an unparalleled period of peace, order and economic expansion in the history of England and Normandy. In those ten years he consolidated an ideology of remorseless administrative kingship unique in the Europe of his day, which had a long-term impact not just on the development of England, but also on Scottish, French and papal government.[9]

9 For the significance of the reign of Henry I, see generally, R.W. Southern, 'The place of Henry I in English history', reprinted in *Medieval Humanism and Other Studies* (Oxford, 1970), 206–33; C. Warren Hollister, 'Henry I and the invisible transformation of medieval England',

But despite his achievements, King Henry was not a 'modern' monarch, and although his England and his Normandy were changing, they remained early medieval realms. Royal agents got everywhere under his rule, but they monitored more than they ordered. Civil order and the lives of most people were focused on superiors other than the king. Power remained mediated in Henry's realms by aristocracies. In England there were something in excess of two hundred dominant secular magnates who could overthrow the king with ease had they ever united in a common agenda. Henry's good fortune was that these men never could unite entirely against him. In 1100–01 he was saved by the fact that a significant magnate faction was prepared to sponsor and support him against his elder brother. He was careful thereafter to enlist the most dangerous and talented magnates in his own interest. He was not vengeful in how he did this. One of his great opponents at the beginning of his reign was William II of Warenne, earl of Surrey in England and lord of Bellencombre in Normandy. By 1110, William was one of the great pillars of Henry's rule, won over by favours and the profitable rewards of office.[10] The king had great gifts in assessing men's usefulness to him. To these men, he offered 'good lordship', access to him and great favours at court, so that they could raise themselves in the world's eyes. In this way the king turned one of the great potential dangers in his situation into one of his greatest assets. He was not always wise in those men he excluded; the troublesome rebellions of a talented soldier and politician, Aumary de Montfort, count of Evreux, proved this. But such was his success that he never again had a majority of the magnates against him or indifferent to him, as he had in 1101.

Henry of England is not the subject of this book, but his personality and his achievements cannot but be part of it. The past two generations of historians have come to realise something of the measure of the man. Once only remarked upon personally as a monster of adultery and his reign as lacking policies and important events, Henry I is now seen to be a king and warrior of rare distinction and his reign a key one in the formation of English government. There remains something monstrous about him, or as Judith Green puts it with more subtlety, 'he was complex and in many respects highly unpleasant'.[11] He was, as a young count, capable of personally executing a dissident by throwing him from a castle tower. He could be merciless to traitors and was not above deceit when it suited him. His sexual appetite was formidable. He fathered more bastard children than any other English king apart from Charles II. But severe as these defects were, they need to be qualified. The young Count Henry showed a rather touching attachment to his mistresses,

---

in *Studies in Medieval History Presented to R.H.C. Davis*, ed. H. Mayr-Harting and R.I. Moore (London, 1985), 303–16; idem, 'Anglo-Norman political culture', in *Anglo-Norman Political Culture and the Twelfth-century Renaissance*, ed. C. Warren Hollister (Woodbridge, 1997), 1–16.
10 C. Warren Hollister, 'The taming of a turbulent earl', repr. in *Monarchy, Magnates and Institutions in the Anglo-Norman World* (London, 1986), 137–44, esp. 141–3.
11 J.A. Green, *The Government of England under Henry I* (Cambridge, 1986), 1.

the two earliest of whom he selected from respectable English landowning families in the southern midlands. He was a man who needed a home, and home for him was his favoured resort of Woodstock in Oxfordshire. He was deeply devoted to furthering his illegitimate children's fortunes, and in return they loved him. In short, Henry was one of those strong medieval men who acknowledged moral duty and affections to a limited circle of family and dependents and who was remorseless to those outside it.

Stephen was not like his uncle. He was a man of much more diffuse good nature, and of a genuine humanity. He was always at a loss when faced with children and women. Stephen's personal morality and spirituality were of a higher standard than those of his uncle. As we will see, his sexual partner before marriage was decently put aside after his wedding, although he acknowledged their son. Henry had qualities that elevated him to greatness. His capacity for detail and his energy were positively Napoleonic, as also was his gift for assessing individuals at his court. Stephen himself was by no means devoid of these qualities but what Henry also had was a breadth of political vision and a grip on the processes of power in his own day that were unsurpassed. While very much a monarch of the old school – jealous of his rights and warlike – he still developed a new and remorseless view of kingship, founded on close control of finances and justice, that amounted to centralisation of government on the royal court and household. In time, this idea of kingship and order was Henry's legacy to Stephen, and both an advantage and a source of difficulty to his nephew. Stephen had to live with the fact that his uncle lived on in the minds of his courtiers and magnates as the ideal of what a king should be.

STEPHEN AND KING HENRY OF ENGLAND

Stephen remained invisible in the historical record for a good six years after Tinchebray. But he emerges into historical daylight in Normandy in February 1113, touring the duchy (with his brother Count Theobald) in his uncle, the king's, entourage.[12] This appearance must have been just after his coming of age and knighting by the king. Knighting was an event which could take place as early as sixteen years of age in northern France at that time. Stephen had grown up at an exciting time and in a royal court that set the tone for Europe in courtly and military culture: a place of wealth and administrative innovation unheard of elsewhere in Christendom, and peopled by a singularly devious and talented population of courtiers and clerics. Although the sources

---

12 OV vi, 174, where he is not in fact called *comes*. What might be interpreted as an earlier instance of Stephen as count of Mortain is provided by a charter of King Henry confirming *per petitionem Stephani comitis Moretonie* to one Ernald Ruffus a grant by Count Stephen in the honor of Eye, *Calendar of Charter Rolls* i, 47. As is pointed out by the comments on it in *Regesta* ii, no. 783, the charter's witness list dates it to a time when Waldric was royal chancellor (i.e. before February 1107). Yet on the other hand, Stephen did not obtain Eye until *c.*1113. The charter may therefore be disregarded as a fabrication of a time after 1154, designed to bolster title to an estate which otherwise depended on an unsupported grant from the 'usurper' Stephen (itself probably doctored so as to record the then king's part in the transaction).

for Stephen's activities in the 1120s and early 1130s may not be overwhelming, there is more than enough to tell us of his success in this dangerous, edgy and dazzling little world, which (to contemporary eyes) was the centre of everything that represented power and patronage.

As has been said, King Henry was not much of an example of sexual morality to his courtiers. He had been involved with a series of mistresses since the mid-1080s, showing a particular liking for women from English landholding families of modest means, such as the mother of Robert of Gloucester. Stephen was happy to follow his example, and formed a long-term liaison with a woman known as 'Damette' (the 'Little Lady') with whom he had a son, Gervase, at some time in the mid- to late 1110s and possibly also a daughter. He acknowledged his son, arranged for his entry into a monastery and made him abbot of Westminster in 1138. Abbot Gervase used his good fortune to settle on his mother the perpetual lease of the abbey's manor of Chelsea at a preferential rent. The grant caused some little scandal, and may have been used later by King Henry II to oust Gervase from Westminster in 1157.[13] Damette, the mistress of Count Stephen, seems (from what little we know about her) to have lived quietly with him and been decently put aside on or before his marriage in 1125. But she seems to have been left with some endowment, for she able to produce forty shillings in cash and a silk cloth worth 5*li* as a payment on entry into her lease on the manor of Chelsea.[14]

Stephen of Blois was not alone in seeking to better himself in King Henry's military household: he had several high-born rivals for attention. The Anglo-Norman royal household was a great school of fortune, and it attracted a good number of young aristocrats on the make. Some of these other young men were likewise destined for great things, and were to be Stephen's life-long rivals. Chief among them was his contemporary, David of Scotland, the queen's brother, who had joined the court some years earlier and for exactly the same reason. He was the youngest of several brothers, and he also had little expectation of inheritance at home. It is most likely that Stephen and David were raised jointly to comital status (respectively of Mortain and Huntingdon) in the Christmas court held at Windsor in 1113/14.[15] There were

13 On Gervase, see generally, H.G. Richardson and G.O. Sayles, 'Gervase of Blois, abbot of Westminster', in *The Governance of Medieval England* (Edinburgh, 1963), 413–21, and see below, p. 301. For the daughter, *GS*, 108.
14 *Westminster Abbey Charters*, ed. E. Mason (London Record Society, 25, 1988), 127. The reference to Damette's 'heirs' in this document may indicate that Stephen had arranged for a marriage for her after he set her aside, but might also refer to her siblings or collateral relatives.
15 For David of Scotland's arrival at court and elevation to an earldom, J.A. Green, 'David I and Henry I', *Scottish Historical Review*, lxxv (1996), 2–3, 6. As has been pointed out, a charter of the priory of Eye tells us that Stephen held the honor for twenty-two years as count and king, which would confirm that (since he transferred it in 1136 to William of Ypres) he had obtained it in 1113 or 1114, *Calendar of Charter Rolls* v, 366–7. See also comments on the significance of the passage by C.P. Lewis, 'The king and Eye: a study in Anglo-Norman politics', *EHR*, 104 (1989), 579–80. Stephen's first undeniable appearance as *comes* is not until the end of 1115 at St Albans (*Regesta* ii, no. 1102).

other home-grown rivals for Stephen to take account of: the king's eldest and favourite bastards, Robert and Richard; the twin sons of Count Robert of Meulan (d. 1118), Waleran of Meulan and Robert of Leicester; Richard, earl of Chester; and Brian, bastard son of Count Alan of Brittany and Richmond. Most were in their teens or early twenties, a 'brat pack' of able youths of lineage and ambition. This conjunction of young stars was no accident. They made perfect companions for the young heir, William the Atheling. But Henry I, by this time in his late forties, himself rejoiced in such company, which gave his court tone and (in its excesses of costume and libido) an enviable notoriety. But the king complemented his thoroughbreds with a supporting cast of hard-working and reliable mongrels: his so-called 'new men', cool-headed and sometimes remorseless administrators drawn from the lesser aristocracy on the make, the likes of the Clintons, Bassets, Ridels and Veres.

During the period before his uncle's death, we begin to get some measure of Stephen. We cannot know a great amount about the first forty years of his life, but we do know that the chances of his life developed him into a most accomplished courtier. This was partly through his natural disposition, and partly through alertness to the culture of the court. He was even-tempered and good-humoured, the necessary basic survival qualities for a courtier. He had, and retained throughout his life, a confident amiability that secured him easy popularity. He absorbed the dominant culture of the day – although how deep it went is hard to say. He became conversant with the intellectual circles that touched on the court, and had works dedicated to him by appreciative or flattering authors, who considered his protection worth securing. We can never be quite sure that he was literate, as were many of his running mates brought up at King Henry's court, but it is not unlikely that a young prince of his expectations would have been educated, at a time when men of far less lineage were being taught their letters and the elements of grammar, philosophy, poetry and history. His mother was a generous patron of the arts and letters, and friend of two scholarly archbishops, Baudrey de Bourgeuil of Dol and Anselm of Canterbury. His parents had corresponded (touchingly) by letter while separated by the Crusade. Stephen had spent his boyhood in a sophisticated and lettered court, and moved into the even more eminent literary environment of his royal uncle's household.

A critical year for Stephen and his young colleagues at Henry's court was 1120. In that year, the king broke the back of the first serious rebellion aginst him in Normandy, and in the glow of the aftermath of a victory over Louis VI of France, he embarked with the court for England, on 20 December. The ship carrying the heir to the throne, known as the *White Ship*, foundered on the submerged rock called Quilleboeuf outside the harbour of Barfleur and sank with all but one of its passengers. The passengers included Richard, the king's bastard, and Earl Richard of Chester, and had almost included Stephen himself, but he had not liked the overcrowding on the ship, and was in any case suffering from diarrhoea, so he stayed ashore.[16] When the king, a widower now for two years, finally recovered his composure, he found himself in a most uncomfortable situation. He was a widower; he still had plenty of sons, but none legitimate, and the generation of magnates who had sponsored his bid for the throne two decades earlier and who had been his main support, were fast disappearing into monasteries or into eternity. Henry's response over the next two years was to remarry (to a daughter of the duke of Brabant) and to restructure power in his realm, by bringing forward into positions of power those of his young favourites he felt he could trust. So, around 1121, he promoted his bastard, Robert, to the earldom of Gloucester, and Robert of Leicester was given by marriage the great inheritance of Breteuil in Normandy.

Stephen had already secured his appanage, and it was a great one. The forfeited Norman county of Mortain brought him a compact and strategic western lordship in the duchy, with several formidable castles (Mortain, St-Hilaire du Harcouët, Le Teilleul, Tinchebray and Gorron) and a notable collegiate church, and what was later assessed as the service of $29^{1}/_{2}$ knights' fees (which in English terms would have translated into as many as a hundred).[17] We have seen that late in 1113 he had secured in England the confiscated honor of Eye, in Suffolk. At the same time Stephen must also have had a grant of the lordship of Lancaster, which made up most of the northwest of England, from Cumbria south to the Mersey. Eye and Lancaster together had previously been held by Count Roger of La Marche, a member of the powerful southern Norman dynasty of Montgomery, until his deprivation in 1102.[18] This Montgomery link may have been one excuse for King Henry to add the Montgomery lands on the southern March of Normandy (confiscated since 1112) to Stephen's Norman estates: a good way for the king to enhance painlessly the power of the house of Blois on the borders of his realm. In 1118, the king granted the former Montgomery strongholds of Alençon, Séez, Le Mêle-sur-Sarthe, Almenèches and La Roche-Mabille to Count Theobald, on the apparent understanding that Theobald should grant them on to his brother, Stephen. This was so that Theobald could use the lands to buy off any future claim by Stephen against the paternal estates in Blois-Chartres. Unfortunately for the brothers, at the end of 1119 a conspiracy between the inhabitants of Alençon, Arnulf de Montgomery (Count Roger's brother) and the count of

---

16 See Le Patourel, *Norman Empire*, 177–8 on the location. J. Bradbury, *Stephen and Matilda* (Stroud, 1996), 1–3, gives a recent collation of the contemporary sources. Evidence that Stephen really had intended to cross in the *White Ship*, and that Orderic's is not merely a retrospective 'narrow miss' story is in the number of barons of the honor of Mortain who actually did drown in the wreck, OV vi, 306.

17 For the extent and strategic significance of the county of Mortain, J. Boussard, 'Le comté de Mortain au xie siècle', *Le Moyen Âge*, 58 (1952), 253–79, especially map on p. 270 and 273–5.

18 Lewis, 'King and Eye', 576–80. Lewis establishes that Stephen was holding components of the honor of Lancaster in 1115 × 1116, ibid., 571n. J.A. Green, 'Earl Ranulf II and Lancashire', in *The Earldom of Chester and its Charters*, ed. A.T. Thacker (Journal of the Chester Archaeological Society, 71, 1991), 103–4, has some pertinent observations as to the grant and suggests that Ranulf le Meschin may have been Count Stephen's immediate predecessor in that division of Lancashire north of the Ribble.

Anjou, led to Stephen's ousting from the region, despite the military assistance of Count Theobald and the king. The next year, the king solved the problem by restoring Alençon and the other Montgomery lands to a member of the family whom he was obliged to trust. They did not return to Stephen.[19]

It may be that after the loss of Alençon, the king felt that he owed some sort of compensation to his nephew. It took the form of a handsome marriage. But Stephen's marriage to the heir of the county of Boulogne in 1125 was just as much likely to have been a strategic bid to strengthen the northern defences of Normandy, and tighten links with the rising house of Blois.[20] Count Eustace III of Boulogne had decided to retire into the abbey of Cluny. He stayed to preside over the marriage between Stephen 'to whom I have given my inheritance with Mathilda my daughter', at some time early in 1125. He then laid down his authority, took the vows of profession into the Cluniac order, and took leave of the newlyweds at a public ceremony in the priory of Romilly, where he surrendered himself to the prior of Cluny.[21] The late R.H.C. Davis noted how this marriage made Stephen something out of the ordinary way of courtiers. He meant that it exposed Stephen to the political and economic realities of an economically expanding and politically turbulent region of northern Europe. It was certainly to be an education for the young count (still not thirty years old) and perhaps the learning was at another level too. Boulogne (linked with the county of Lens, north of Arras) was a small state hemmed up to the Channel coast by the power of the counts of Flanders and Vermandois. It nonetheless maintained a certain independence, and its count was the only power in his own land. In his county of Boulogne, Stephen got a scent of that unsupervised power denied to most courtiers.

---

19 OV vi, 194–6, 204–6, 224. Orderic (followed by Davis, *Stephen*, 7, and also C.W. Hollister, 'The Anglo-Norman succession debate of 1126: prelude to Stephen's Anarchy', *Journal of Medieval History*, 1 (1975), 23) harshly condemns Stephen for ineptitude at Alençon, but the point needs to be made in his defence that – in the time given to him – Stephen had little chance of counteracting generations of allegiance to the Montgomery family, especially when representatives of it were still powerful at the court of neighbouring Anjou. The Montgomery lands (or most of them) were restored to William Talvas, count of Ponthieu, son of Robert de Bellême and nephew of Arnulf, see K. Thompson, 'William Talvas, count of Ponthieu and the politics of the Anglo-Norman realm', in *England and Normandy in the Middle Ages*, ed. D.R. Bates and A. Curry (London, 1994), 169–84, esp. 171–2.

20 It was William of Malmesbury's belief that the Boulonnais marriage was initiated and arranged by King Henry, *HN*, 57, and this assumption is followed by Hollister, 'Anglo-Norman succession debate', 25. If William was right, the king was acting as overlord of Count Eustace for his English lands – he had no overlordship over Boulogne itself, which had theoretical tenurial links with Flanders. However, both the evidence of Eustace's own act of 1125 (see below) and Robert of Torigny, *Gesta Normannorum Ducum*, ed. van Houts, 262 ('Having no son because his wife was barren, Eustace appointed Stephen heir to the county of Boulogne and his father-in-law's possessions in England') imply that there was at least an appearance that Eustace was free to choose his successor. Another possible factor in Stephen's marriage might have been the succession to Champagne in 1125 of his elder brother, Theobald of Blois: thus much enhancing Theobald's wealth and influence in Central France. Arranging for Stephen to succeed to Boulogne would have increased the obligation of the house of Blois to King Henry.

21 *Recueil des chartes de l'abbaye de Cluny*, ed. A. Bernard and A. Bruel (6 vols, Paris, 1876–1903) v, *1091–1210*, 340–1, allows us to reconstruct this sequence of events.

By the year 1126, Stephen was count of Mortain and Boulogne, the most considerable landowner in Suffolk and Essex, and master of the northwest of England. But although great, his landed wealth and influence were by no means unprecedented in the Anglo-Norman realm. The elder statesman of Henry I's court, Robert of Meulan (who had died in 1118) had controlled a far-flung complex of lands and interests which spread from the suburbs of Paris, down the Seine, and as far north as the Trent (including, like Stephen, a semi-independent county from which he took his title). The new earl of Chester, Ranulf, controlled estates on the Norman–Breton frontier, the compact county on the Welsh March from which he took his title, and estates widely spread across the north midlands of England. These great men, and others like them, were the grid of iron that stiffened and stabilised the structure of King Henry I's Anglo-Norman condominium. Like the king, they had to have an understanding of lordship which spanned the Channel, rather than stopped at it, and so shared the king's ambitions to maintain the links between England and Normandy. To do otherwise would be to risk serious loss.[22]

It is worth dwelling on Count Stephen's material position in 1126. At the age of thirty he was one of the principal supports of his uncle, the king of England, with whom he was closely identified. He was also ruler of one of the near-independent counties that lay around the fringes of the realm of the king of France. He was already fulfilling his role to be one of those magnates who bound together politics and patronage in England to Normandy and France. For example, in 1126 he was negotiating the foundation of what was intended to be a prestigious reformed abbey of Savignac monks, eventually moved to Furness in 1127, in his lordship of Lancaster. Savigny, its mother house, was located in his Norman county of Mortain and it spread its network of foundations across the Anglo-Norman world by means of cross-Channel magnates like Stephen.[23] Around the same time, the monks of Canterbury cathedral priory obtained from Stephen, as count of Boulogne, an exemption from toll at his port of Wissant (from where the monks shipped their wines to England).[24] Stephen's mobile world is conjured up by one or two of his charters. One in favour of the priory of Eye is addressed to his justices and barons in England, but it comes from France during the Norman campaigns of 1118–24, for it safeguards the priory's possessions as they held them: 'on the day when I took over the land of Robert Malet from the king and on the day when I last crossed the sea . . . until I return to England and hear by what reason they have [them]. They are to defend a plea in my absence on behalf of

22 For an analysis of the place of the aristocracy in binding together the Anglo-Norman realm, see D. Crouch, 'Normans and Anglo-Normans: a divided aristocracy?', in *England and Normandy*, ed. D. Bates and A. Curry (London, 1994), 51–67, esp. 51–3. This view is first to be found in, J. Le Patourel, *Normandy and England, 1066–1144* (Reading, 1971), 8. For a critique see also D.R. Bates, 'Normandy and England after 1066', *EHR*, 104 (1989), 871.
23 *Sir Christopher Hatton's Book of Seals*, ed. L.C. Loyd and D.M. Stenton (Oxford, 1950), 294–5. On Stephen and Savigny, B. Poullé, 'Savigny and England', in *England and Normandy*, ed. D. Bates and A. Curry (London, 1994), 159–68, esp. 164–5.
24 Canterbury D & C, Carta Antiqua, F 129.

no writ or man, as I wish there to be no plea on the matter except in my presence.'[25]

This introduces another important aspect of Stephen's life as count and travelling magnate. His widespread lands and interests meant that he had to delegate responsibilities to officers who could act with his authority. When he was in Normandy or Boulogne, there had to be people managing his affairs in England, and vice versa. We know that those of his contemporaries who rivalled him in power and influence had just such ministers.[26] Stephen's principal officer seems to have been Robert de Sauqueville, one of his Essex tenants, whom Orderic records as a knight in Stephen's household as early as 1120, and who features as his seneschal before and after 1125. But there was also his principal baron of the honor of Eye, Robert fitz Walter. Robert acted as sheriff of Suffolk throughout the 1120s, until removed by an exchequer reform in 1129.[27] The relationship between the count and these officers was noticeably close. Robert de Sauqueville named one of his sons, Stephen (perhaps an indication that the count had stood godfather to the boy). Two of Robert fitz Walter's sons went on to serve Stephen as king. Stephen was later to draw another of his comital servants into his service after he became king; this was his Norman officer, Adam de Beaunay, who was to become one of the principal royal justices in Essex and Middlesex.[28]

These men and his other 'justices' were responsible for keeping watch on Stephen's interests in England and Normandy. Some indication of their efficiency can be found in the exchequer pipe roll for 1130. Stephen had at that time been out of the country since (it seems) 1126. Nonetheless, officials of his had been hard at work in Lancashire enforcing his rights on at least eight of his principal tenants; so hard in fact that one of them, Robert Grelley, lord

25 Charter printed in F.M. Stenton, *The First Century of English Feudalism, 1066–1166* (2nd edn., Oxford, 1960), 265–6.

26 Ralph, the butler of Robert II of Leicester, was his chief minister in England, D. Crouch, *The Beaumont Twins: The Roots and Branches of Power in the Twelfth Century* (Cambridge, 1986), 26, 142–3; David of Scotland could rely on his seneschal of Huntingdon, Robert Foliot, *Regesta Regum Scottorum* i, *The Acts of Malcolm IV*, ed. G.W.S. Barrow (Edinburgh, 1960), 100–1; Robert of Gloucester could delegate to his seneschal, Geoffrey de Waterville, E. King, 'The knights of Peterborough abbey', *Peterborough's Past*, 2 (Peterborough Museum Society, 1986), 36–50.

27 OV vi, 306. For Robert de Sauqueville, *dapifer comitis*, see Cartulary of Merton, BL ms Cotton Cleopatra, C vii, fo. 78v; Stenton, *First Century*, 266; *Cartularium monasterii sancti Johannis baptiste de Colecestria*, ed. S.A. Moore (2 vols, Roxburghe Club, 1897) i, 49. For the Sauqueville family in general, J.H. Round, 'The Essex Sackvilles', *Archaeological Journal*, 64 (1907), 217–26. For Robert fitz Walter, J.A. Green, *English Sheriffs to 1154* (HMSO, 1990), 76–7. He attests a charter of Count Stephen before 1125, *Calendar of Charter Rolls* i, 46–7. Both Roberts appear together with Stephen in a charter datable to 1125 × 29, *Roberto vicecomite, et Roberto de Sacheuill'* . . . , Cartulary of Castle Acre, BL ms Harley 2110, fo. 67v.

28 For Stephen, son of Robert de Sauqueville, *Cartularium de Colecestria* i, 131; for the sons of Robert fitz Walter, John fitz Robert le Vicomte and William de Chesney, see below. Adam *de Belnayo* attests a late writ of Count Stephen of Boulogne and Mortain for the nuns of Moutons, see C.H. Haskins, *Norman Institutions* (New York, 1918), 127n. These examples do something to contradict the view of G. White, 'Continuity in government', in *The Anarchy of King Stephen's Reign*, ed. E. King (Oxford, 1994), 119, that Stephen did little to advance the careers of those who had served in his household before his accession.

of Manchester, had – for a large sum of money – secured the king's assistance in coming to an agreement with the count.[29] Elsewhere, in Essex and Bedfordshire, Stephen's officers had secured refunds at the exchequer board from fines imposed for pleas, in addition to the blanket exemption from Danegeld that Stephen enjoyed with other court magnates. Apart from these officials, there were others who had aligned themselves with Stephen in court and country. It is not possible to list or quantify the 'affinity' of well-wishers and supporters of the wealthy and affable count of Mortain, but its importance is beyond doubt (for the technical term 'affinity' see Appendix to Chapter 9). One contemporary commentator believed that these supporters, and other men who were tied to his brothers' interests, were crucial in overawing opposition in England to Stephen's bid for the throne in December 1135.[30]

COUNT STEPHEN AND THE SUCCESSION TO ENGLAND

Already at such a height of wealth and power in 1126, what was to become of Count Stephen? What more might he not achieve? Increasingly from that year, that question (which he himself must have often pondered) was bound up with the other question of the succession to his uncle, King Henry. Stephen could not have expected the succession himself in 1126. Expectation of succession then lay with two other young people: the king's last legitimate child, Mathilda, who called herself the 'Empress', the widow of Henry V of Germany; the other was William, called 'Clito' (the young) the only son of King Henry's elder brother, Robert, the dispossessed duke of Normandy (in 1126 a long-term prisoner in Sherborne Castle – and then Bristol – with no expectation of parole).

In 1126, King Henry had made it perfectly clear that he intended his daughter to succeed him. This was after his return from Normandy to England on 11 September, bringing Mathilda back with him. Her succession to England had clearly been on the dynastic agenda even before her husband had died in May 1125. Between 1122 and 1124 Henry V of Germany had consistently manoeuvred and campaigned in the Low Countries with an eye to securing a place of embarkation for England – Utrecht – in case he had to intervene in the struggle between the king and William Clito. It was the right to the Anglo-Norman realm that he had acquired through his wife which had drawn the emperor there.[31] It might be suggested that Stephen's marriage to Mathilda of Boulogne was part of the dynastic chess game designed to make the empress her father's successor. Mathilda of Boulogne's mother was Mary, the empress's aunt, younger sister of Henry I's late queen. If Stephen married Mathilda, it was bringing under King Henry's control another blood line

---

29 *PR 31 Henry I*, 33, 114. The eight tenants paid a total of 280 marks (186li. 13s. 4d) to settle with Stephen.
30 *GS*, 8.
31 K.J. Leyser, 'The Anglo-Norman succession, 1120–1125', *ANS*, xiii, ed. M. Chibnall (Woodbridge, 1991), 235–7.

descending from the Old English monarchy and grafting it safely into the Norman family tree.[32] Professor Hollister found more evidence of this process of assuring the succession in the shifting of state prisoners from custodian to custodian in late 1126. We can see through all this a party developing or being developed behind the empress's candidature.

King Henry affirmed the Empress Mathilda's status as designate heir in the great council held at Windsor at Christmas, which later shifted in a body to London. On 1 January 1127 all the assembled magnates swore to support the empress's succession to England and Normandy conditional on the king's death without further legitimate male children. The occasion was very grand. King Henry had gone out of his way to draw into the council rulers of principalities around the fringes of his dominions to endorse the settlement publicly. Chief among them was David of Scotland (king since the death of his brother, Alexander, in 1124). King David – according to *The Anglo-Saxon Chronicle* – was working hard in the interests of his niece, the empress, throughout the autumn of 1126. Also present were the duke of Brittany and the count of Perche, both married to Henry's illegitimate daughters, as well as Count Stephen of Boulogne. William of Malmesbury and John of Worcester describe Stephen as being present and taking the oath (and later accusations by other writers against Stephen as a perjurer in taking the throne confirm that he was indeed there).[33]

Malmesbury describes a highly symbolic scene at the oath-taking when, after David of Scotland had led the way, the first magnates of the kingdom jostled as to who was to be next in line. Stephen and Robert of Gloucester seem to have politely disputed as to who between them had the degree of honour to follow King David: each a count, but one a nephew and the other a natural son to the king of England. Stephen, it seems, won, by which we must assume that he was judged by his uncle to be a greater man in dignity than the earl of Gloucester.[34] That this incident rankled with the Gloucesters is evident from Malmesbury's harping on it several years later. It is also some evidence of a rivalry between Gloucester and Stephen before 1135. But doubtless in retrospect this courtiers' tiff took on greater significance, for the winner proved disloyal to the oath and the loser (ultimately) loyal. To Malmesbury, looking back from the early 1140s, the spectre of civil war was already gathering shape in the dark corners of the court eight years before King Henry died.

---

32 Hollister, 'Anglo-Norman succession debate', 148. Hollister, however, notes that the empress was at the time of the Boulogne marriage still married to Henry V, so his interpretation is that the Boulogne marriage could have been calculated to strengthen Stephen's candidacy for the throne of England in 1125 rather than pave the way for Mathilda.
33 *ASC s.a.* 1127; *HN*, 3–4; JW iii, 166; HH, 700; *Regesta* ii, no. 1466.
34 *HN*, 4. JW iii, 178–80 has a similar account, although he says that Earl Robert wanted Stephen to swear first as *maior natu*. The author is mistaken if he meant that Stephen was the elder of the two: Robert of Gloucester has to have been born at least as early as 1090. The same account records another dispute as to precedence on the same occasion between the secular magnates and abbots. For the king as final arbiter of matters of dignity and status in the royal court see, D. Crouch, *The Image of Aristocracy in Britain, 1000–1300* (London, 1992), 65–75.

William of Malmesbury's assessment of the situation might well be disputed. The phantom at the feast early in 1127 was surely not Stephen but William Clito – openly recognised as count of Normandy by the Capetian court. It was Clito who was to throw several of the king's plans into confusion several months after the oath-taking, when he secured from King Louis VI investiture as count of the troubled realm of Flanders. The murder of King Henry's ally, the childless Count Charles of Flanders, on 2 March 1127, led to the collapse of public order in that wealthy and strategic realm, which dominated the north of France.[35] Neither King Louis VI nor King Henry of England were slow to appreciate the opportunity. Louis wanted to disrupt the long-standing alliance between Flanders and England, and Henry wanted to maintain it. Louis was, however, first on the scene, encamping at Arras in the south of the county by 9 March, and summoning (as overlord) the magnates of Flanders to elect a new count. On 23 March they elected William Clito, and, in doing so, much furthered King Louis's plans.[36] William Clito had been taken up by Louis at his Christmas court in 1126 and in January 1127 had married Louis's sister-in-law, being given the Capetian possessions in the Vexin as dowry. The intention must have been to place in Flanders the prince most likely to ally with Louis against the Anglo-Norman realm.[37]

King Henry of England could hardly miss the implications of King Louis's actions. He was prompt in doing something about the threat. There were rivals for the countship of Flanders, and King Henry immediately began to manoeuvre around and behind them. Walter of Therouanne, a contemporary observer, believed that the king himself had plans at this point to claim Flanders (by right of his mother), and that Count Stephen of Boulogne had been sent from England to Flanders as the chief of his agents to flatter, intimidate and bribe so as to secure the county. However, Walter also thought that the king's pursuit of a claim to Flanders was more to undermine support in Flanders for William Clito than a serious bid for power there.[38] We may see further evidence of King Henry's deviousness in that before Clito's election, another possible claimant, Count William of Ypres, a grandson (though through an illegitimate liaison) of Count Robert I of Flanders (died 1093), was apparently claiming English support for *his* candidature. In March and April 1127 William of Ypres managed to seize much of Flanders adjacent to the

---

35 For events of Flanders in 1127–28, on which we are singularly well informed, see Galbert of Bruges, *Passio Karoli comitis*, and Walter de Therouanne, *Vita Karoli Comitis*, ed. R. Köpke (Monumenta Germaniae Historica, Scriptores, 12), 537–61, 561–619; Herman of Tournai, *Liber de restauratione monasterii sancti Martini Tornacensis*, ed. G. Waitz (Monumenta Germaniae Historia, Scriptores, 14), 284–9. Especially valuable is the translation of the first named source, *The Murder of Charles the Good*, trans. J.B. Ross (Columbia, 1967).
36 William Clito was descended from the ancient line of counts of Flanders through his grandmother, Mathilda, queen of William the Conqueror and daughter of Count Baldwin V (died 1067), but there were other claimants descended through the male line, most notably Baldwin IV, count of Hainault.
37 OV vi, 370.
38 *Vita Karoli comitis*, 557–8.

counties of Guines and Boulogne (to which Stephen had returned). On 14 April Stephen is to be found in conference with King Louis and William Clito at or near St Omer. But on 26 April the situation changed when William of Ypres was unlucky enough to get captured when King Louis and Clito assaulted Ypres. This undoubtedly hampered King Henry's further efforts at destabilising Flanders.[39]

William Clito was not unaware of the source of danger to himself represented by England and its political satellites, not least Boulogne. First he established his friend and former tutor, Helias de St-Saens, in garrison at the castle of Montreuil on the southern border of Boulogne, and then in August 1127 he launched his forces into the county, and inflicted considerable damage on Count Stephen's lands.[40] Stephen seems to have resisted the Flemish invasion with some stubbornness. Count William had returned to Flanders by early September, and – swamped by other problems – later agreed to accept a three-year truce with Stephen. By early 1128 harsh English and Boulonnais sanctions against the northern Flemish towns, and the bribes of King Henry to their castellans, incited them into open rebellion against Clito's rule.[41]

The principal contender for the county of Flanders was now Thierry, son of the duke of Alsace and a legitimate grandson of Count Robert I through his daughter, Gertrude. Thierry secured the recognition of the cities of the north of Flanders in April 1128, and despite the renewed intervention of King Louis, supported by the princes of the Rhineland, William Clito was enveloped in warfare during which, on 27/28 July 1128, he was wounded and died. Count Thierry was then universally accepted as his rightful successor in Flanders (the north of which he already controlled) and was eventually recognised as count by both King Louis and the emperor. Thierry's victory would seem to have been regarded with some satisfaction by King Henry, for he renewed the Anglo-Flemish alliance with the new count, who duly did homage to the king of England. As part of the arrangements, Orderic Vitalis reports that Count Stephen – under his uncle's persuasion – recognised the dependent relationship of Boulogne on Flanders.[42]

39 A. Giry, *Histoire de la ville de St Omer* (Paris, 1877), 373, ch. 17.
40 Montreuil-sur-Mer was a castle, bourg and abbey in territory between the Canche and Authie rivers held by the counts of Ponthieu, but disputed by the counts of Boulogne. Ownership was not finally settled until 1208, when Philip Augustus awarded it to Count William II of Ponthieu, who married his daughter to Simon, brother of Count Reginald of Boulogne, *Recueil de documents pour servir à l'histoire de Montreuil-sur-Mer, 1000–1464*, ed. G. de Lhomel (Compiègne, 1907), 8–11. By occupying Montreuil in 1127 in order to attack Boulogne, it looks as though William Clito was artfully playing off the count of Ponthieu against Stephen. Thompson, 'William Talvas', 172–3, does not notice the move of Clito against Montreuil, but sensibly suggests that the resignation of Ponthieu by Count William I to his son, Count Guy, happened at this time due to the complications of allegiance that he, as a Norman magnate, would otherwise suffer.
41 OV vi, 370–2; *Murder of Charles the Good*, 277 and n. Davis, *Stephen*, 10 states that Stephen invaded Flanders, but Orderic does not suggest that, nor is there any real evidence that Stephen was defeated by Clito, only that his lands were savagely handled.
42 OV vi, 378. For a later reference to Count Thierry's homage to King Henry I, viz. '*et quia comes Teodoricus hominium [fecerat] regi Henrico avo istius regis Henrici . . .*' see *Diplomatic Documents preserved in the Public Record Office*, ed. P. Chaplais, i, *1101–1272* (HMSO, 1964), 11.

Stephen might well have been happy with the outcome of the Flemish wars of succession. He had, in effect, passed over the body of William Clito in war. He may not have regarded himself as the rival to Clito for the succession of England before 1127, but the war between Flanders and Boulogne must have changed his view. He had been his uncle's able auxiliary in King Henry's great game in northern France. He had aided his uncle's victory, and was one of the chief players in the destabilisation of Flanders during the critical months of the spring and summer of 1128. This was – for the first time in his life – a taste of grand politics: it is worth considering that Stephen would from now on have regarded his place in the game of the Ango-Norman succession differently, especially now that his cousin, William Clito, was fortuitously removed from the board. The board was now singularly empty of key pieces. But did other people see the situation in the same way?[43]

The position of the Empress Mathilda was naturally strengthened by the death of William Clito. He had been her most obvious male rival. His particular appeal to a section of the Norman nobility meant that his sudden death left open new potential support, or at least enfeebled potential opposition. But all was not good news. The king her father had decided, in the emergency of 1127–28, to use her to reinforce his French alliances. She was formally betrothed to Geoffrey, son and heir of Count Fulk V of Anjou, at Rouen in May 1127, fulfilling her father's long-held dream of linking the two successful and aggressive Norman and Angevin dynasties, and so strengthening them both against what he saw as their common enemy, the Capetian royal dynasty. Therefore, the Flemish crisis of 1127–28 had materially changed the empress's position as much as that of her cousin Stephen, and not all for the better.[44]

King Henry's vision of future security had its costs. Firstly, there was the personal price that his proud twenty-five-year-old daughter, so fond of her royal and imperial status, had to pay in being united to a fifteen-year-old boy, the son of a count. There is some evidence of her resistance to the plan.[45] Second, and less obviously, there was the abrupt change of direction it signalled in Anglo-Norman dynastic (I hesitate to say 'foreign') policy. Throughout his reign, Henry I had developed links with the dynasties along the southeastern Norman march, the houses of Bréval, Montfort, Perche and Gouet, but most notably the dynasty of Blois-Chartres, which had been, since the early eleventh century, the natural and persistent enemy of Anjou, with which it still disputed control of the Touraine.[46]

43 John of Ford, *The Life of Wulfric of Haselbury*, ed. M. Bell (Somerset Record Society, xlvii, 1933), 117, has the story of Stephen, while still count, visiting the famous hermit with his brother Bishop Henry and being greeted prophetically as king. The story's point that Wulfric charged Stephen particularly to protect the Church shows retrospective tampering, but it may reflect a perception in the last years of Henry's reign that Count Stephen was a likely successor.
44 *HN*, 2, 5.
45 M. Chibnall, *The Empress Matilda* (Oxford, 1991), 55.
46 Chibnall, *Matilda*, 54, neatly disposes of the myth of the Angevins as hereditary enemies of the Normans.

No chronicler tells us how Count Theobald IV of Blois-Chartres and his brother and ally, Count Stephen, regarded the Angevin match of 1128, other than that Malmesbury tells us (indirectly) that Stephen had not been consulted about it. What we can say, however, is that it robbed the alliance of Blois with the Anglo-Norman realm of any local use to Theobald. It meant that, for Theobald, the death of Henry I and the consequent succession of the count of Anjou to England and Normandy would be a disaster for his independence in northern France; his choice was either dependency on Anjou, or submission to Paris.[47] We can only think that Theobald and his brothers knew this and debated how to get around the problem. Theobald and Stephen must have worked out well before 1135 a policy for dealing with King Henry's death. The event – when it finally happened – proved that this was so.

---

47 J. Bradbury, *Stephen and Matilda* (Stroud, 1996), 15; M. Chibnall, 'Normandy', in *The Anarchy of King Stephen's Reign*, ed. E. King (Oxford, 1994), 95, explore this aspect of the succession question.

CHAPTER 2

Succession

Henry I of England died quickly. Falling ill after hunting at Lyons-la-Forêt on 25 November 1135, he was dead within a week, passing as the sun went down on the evening of 1 December.[1] Yet he died lucidly, aware of death's approach and in command of himself and his intellect almost (it seems) to the end. His deathbed was conducted with great propriety. He was attended from 28 November by Hugh, archbishop of Rouen, former abbot of his own foundation of Reading, who daily confessed and absolved him, and enjoined measures of penance, to which the king agreed. He made arrangements for his own burial. Watches of courtiers surrounded his bed, day and night; they were sworn at the king's own command not to abandon his body, but to escort it to its burial. He received the rites of anointing and last communion.

The dying king is reported by all sources as being able to dispose verbally of the future of his realm. The problems are firstly that the sources – for their own reasons – differ as to what that disposition was, and secondly that no written testament was made, or one side or the other would assuredly have produced a copy to support their case. William of Malmesbury tells us that King Henry affirmed that his daughter was to succeed him; although he did not want his son-in-law, Geoffrey of Anjou, to rule with her, because of a frontier dispute which had lately soured relations between them.[2] But Malmesbury's probable source was Robert of Gloucester, the king's illegitimate son and (after 1138) commander of the empress's armies. Another writer, the anonymous West Country prelate who wrote the *Gesta Stephani* (the 'Deeds of Stephen') puts forward the view that the king had a deathbed change of mind, and decided to release his magnates from the oath imposed on them in 1127. The author of the *Gesta* was a confirmed royalist well into the 1140s, so it is perhaps significant that he did not go so far as to suggest that Henry

---

1 OV vi, 448 gives the chronology.
2 *HN*, 12–13.

actually nominated Stephen as his successor (although others were not so shy).[3] The royalist view would seem to be simply that the old king had withdrawn his endorsement of his daughter on account of her husband's unfitness. Since we will later see that Geoffrey made no attempt to put himself forward as a potential ruler of England, we could thus find a reductionist agreement between the rival sources: both sides agree (the Angevins, tacitly) that the old king equivocated about his succession at the end.

There are accounts of the deathbed in two letters, one from the archbishop of Rouen to the pope, and the other by Peter the Venerable, abbot of Cluny, to the king's sister (and Count Stephen's mother), Adela.[4] Both were written soon after the king's death, but both studiously avoid questions of state and confine themselves to the pastoral side of the death. It may, however, be that neither had anything to say on the succession, because the dying king, although lucid and communicative to the end, had chosen not to make any public declaration as to who should succeed him. In his cloister at St Evroult, Orderic Vitalis had all the details about the course of the king's illness, yet knew nothing of what he might have said about the succession; indeed, he describes the Norman magnates, without guidance, in furious debate over the next few weeks as to who they were to support.[5] In view of the silence of the *Gesta Stephani* it is most likely that King Henry had said and done nothing publicly on his deathbed about the succession: neither affirming Mathilda, nor naming an alternative. This does not (of course) mean that he said nothing about the question *privately* to those closest to him, notably those whose privilege it was to support his dying head. It may even be that at different times during his week of suffering he had discussed – and came almost to the point of endorsing – several candidates. But it seems beyond question that he chose to die without committing himself to any successor.

Count Stephen was not with the court when his uncle fell sick. He had been with his uncle earlier in 1135 at Rouen, and possibly also Argentan, in Normandy.[6] But in late November 1135 Stephen was in his county of Boulogne, and here news of the rapid collapse of his uncle's health found him out. Who brought it? John Prestwich has recently demonstrated the way information was collected, marketed and spread through Anglo-Norman society.[7] Doubtless,

3 *GS*, 10–12. However, the independent account of the succession in *Liber Eliensis*, 285 – written within the reign – agrees with John of Salisbury (*HP*, 84) in stating that Stephen had Henry's nomination on his deathbed, and it is alleged that this deathbed change of heart was part of the case for his succession made before Pope Innocent II early in 1136. We may therefore suggest that the 'official' line amongst Stephen's supporters was no more than that the dying king had absolved his men of their oath to Mathilda, but that hard-line Stephanites went further and maintained that the old king had specifically nominated Stephen. See below for Hugh Bigod's part in promoting this view.
4 For the text of Archbishop Hugh's letter, *HN*, 13–14. For Peter's letter, *The Letters of Peter the Venerable*, ed. G. Constable (2 vols, Cambridge, Mass., 1967) i, 22.
5 OV vi, 454.
6 *Regesta* ii, nos. 1757, 1761, 1794–5, 1908 (Rouen), 1934 (Argentan).
7 J.O. Prestwich, 'Military intelligence under the Norman and Angevin kings', in *Law and Government in the Middle Ages: Essays in Honour of Sir James Holt*, ed. G. Garnett and J. Hudson (Cambridge, 1994), 1–30. One possible candidate for the role of Stephen's 'spymaster' at court is

Count Stephen had his sources at court, even while absent, and Boulogne was within two days' courier ride of Lyons-la-Forêt. Stephen could have known of his uncle's serious illness days before his death actually occurred, and had time to prepare his response.

The nature of Stephen's response to the news of his royal uncle's death indicates that he had been giving it some measured thought for a while. How else to account for the mixture of calculation and speed that he displayed? The *Gesta Stephani* says that he did not cross to England until he had certain news of Henry's death, and this might not have been until 3 or 4 December. He took few attendants with him and sailed from his chief port of Wissant, taking the short crossing to Kent. Canterbury sources say that he had trouble at both the city and at Dover. Quick as he had been to move, news of Henry's death had been quicker, and the castles closed their gates to him, for their commanders and garrisons looked to Robert of Gloucester as their lord. Clearly, the antagonism of Earl Robert to Stephen was already well recognised in the kingdom. Nonetheless, Stephen reached London rapidly, quite possibly within four or five days of the old king's death and found things there more welcoming. The city magnates (with perhaps one eye to trade with Flanders and another to the count's dominance over neighbouring Essex) welcomed him with enthusiasm and adopted his cause, and in a spontaneous assembly were the first to accord him the title of king, by acclamation.[8] We may see in this success some influence of Stephen's courtly education. Several contemporaries record how his practised ease, affability and charm, and the confidence of lineage and life-long power, had a devastating effect on those lesser folk with whom he came into contact.

Stephen had come to the point of committing himself, and seems to have laid claim to the throne with a frankness and courage that disarmed opposition. There were those in England who were quite prepared to help: not just the Londoners, but in the kingdom at large, we are told of large numbers of lesser men who had embraced the fortunes of the Blois party. Even more significantly, the greatest of the court magnates were still in Normandy, Robert of Gloucester among them. The dying king had prevailed on the archbishop to swear them to stay with the corpse till its burial. So, as Stephen entered London to cheers and celebration, the greatest magnates of the realm were manoeuvring and plotting in the duchy, to little lasting effect. Orderic reports that they were acting in cautious concert. Within two days of Henry's death, the senior magnate present, Earl William II de Warenne of Surrey, was delegated by his fellows to assume command of the capital, Rouen (where the king's

---

King Henry's butler, William Martel. William was in Normandy with the royal court throughout 1134 and 1135 and yet turns up with Stephen in England at his coronation (his subsequent prominent career in Stephen's service may well speak volumes), *CDF*, no. 1009; *Regesta* iii, no. 270. Not being a magnate, Martel was not bound by oath to stay with the dead king.

8 *GS*, 5; *HN*, 14–15; *GC* i, 94; *OV* vi, 516–18. It is likely that Stephen was at this point consciously copying the actions that the late king had taken to secure the throne in 1100. Henry had hastened from the New Forest direct to London.

body was resting) and the surrounding province. Two lesser magnates, Hugh de Gournay and William de Roumare, were sent with a force to secure the frontier towards France. Then, while the body was taken under escort to Caen, to await shipping to England, the great magnates applied themselves to a serious discussion as to what on earth to do next.[9]

All the sources make it perfectly clear that, oaths notwithstanding, the Anglo-Norman aristocracy was reluctant to consider Mathilda as a successor to her father. There are reports of several interregnum meetings in Normandy in the week or so between the king's death and the arrival of news of Stephen's coup. Torigny talks of Count Theobald of Blois being hastily summoned to Normandy by the Norman magnates to receive the duchy from them. In what seems to have been leisure born of misplaced confidence, he met them first in council at Rouen and later at (or more likely near) Lisieux to negotiate terms. Orderic talks of only one meeting of Theobald with the Normans, at Le Neubourg, which is undoubtedly the same meeting as the second one discussed by Torigny, for both he and Torigny say that it was in the final meeting that Theobald heard by a messenger from England that his brother had been accepted as king by the English.[10] Torigny says that the meeting heard that Stephen was already king (that is, anointed), but this cannot be right as it would put the meeting as late as 24 December 1135. Orderic must be correct, and Theobald's discomfiture is much more likely to have been earlier, in the second week after the king's death (that is 8–14 December). Perhaps the news came by way of the earl of Gloucester's men in Kent. It needs little effort to believe that Count Theobald was discomfited (although not necessarily enraged) to hear that his younger brother had beaten him to the crown of England, when Normandy was already in his grasp. If anyone felt that he had been betrayed in December 1135, it may have been Theobald rather than the empress. His younger brother's quick reactions had secured the succession of a member of the house of Blois to the Anglo-Norman realm, but it was the wrong succession and not the one Stephen himself may have discussed and decided with Theobald in earlier days.

So as Theobald – the only man who could have controlled it – quit Normandy in disgust, other claimants moved in. Geoffrey of Anjou and Mathilda had crossed the southern borders of the duchy in force, probably even as Count Theobald was in discussion with his would-be subjects. The couple speedily secured the upland march of Normandy towards Maine, including the strategic castles of Exmes, Argentan and Domfront, which had been assigned as marriage portion to Mathilda by her father. They also assisted their ally, Count William Talvas, in reclaiming his family's possessions of Séez and Alençon.[11] But although the pair were able to establish themselves rapidly in this strategic salient on the southern edge of Normandy, they found themselves unable to

9 OV vi, 448–50.
10 RT, 128–9; OV vi, 454.
11 M. Chibnall, *The Empress Matilda* (Oxford, 1991), 66–7, analyses the Angevin incursion.

proceed any further. Significant Norman support for Mathilda and her husband simply did not appear when they crossed the border, and their campaign (if campaign of conquest it was intended to be) ground rapidly to a halt. Geoffrey's forces encountered strong local opposition as they quartered themselves on the population and Orderic reports something like a local guerrilla campaign, which shut them close in their corner of the duchy. Count Geoffrey in any case found that internal troubles made a stay in the north dangerous, for his absence had provoked a baronial rising which had cut him and his army off from Angers.[12] Mathilda was left behind with a strong garrison to maintain herself in that small part of her father's empire over which she had been able to establish control.

Historians, in retrospect, bring forward for discussion only one other figure in the succession crisis at this point: Robert, earl of Gloucester, Henry I's eldest bastard. One contemporary plays with the idea that Robert himself was a possible contender for the throne. The author of the *Gesta Stephani* had heard a story that unknown advisers urged Earl Robert to claim the throne. He had also heard that the earl, well aware of his compromised descent, refused and expressed a preference for the rights of his nephew, Henry, the empress's eldest son, still then only a small boy.[13] It is difficult to accept that this happened. Earl Robert had come out as a leading supporter of Count Theobald in the first week after King Henry's death, not for the empress nor for the young Henry. Nonetheless, it is intriguing to find such a pro-Stephen writer acknowledging Robert as a potential contender: had William of Malmesbury come out with such a story, we would be much less likely to believe it.

The *Gesta*'s interest in what Earl Robert might or might not have claimed in the critical weeks of December 1135 lies more in hindsight than anything else. In December 1135 it was a matter of concern which of the claimants the earl would support: the earl's own claims were not relevant. Hence the Canterbury source notes the opposition of Earl Robert's men in Kent to Stephen's arrival, and Robert de Torigny is concerned to place the earl in Count Theobald's camp. The *Gesta* wished to make the point that whoever Robert did support in the aftermath of King Henry's death, it was not Mathilda. The problem for William of Malmesbury, the earl's great apologist, is just this fact. The earl's dedication to the empress's cause after 1138 is very much a contrast to his apparent indifference to it before 1138. Malmesbury's solution to this difficulty is simply to repeat the explanation which was doubtless that which the Gloucester party had adopted: the earl was dubious about Stephen in 1135 and inclined to Mathilda because of the solemnity of the oath sworn

---

12 OV vi, 456 reports that Geoffrey had to face a major internal rebellion led by Robert of Sablé, which seems to have involved all of the Sarthe valley between Le Mans and Angers, and which – according to the later account of John of Marmoutier – could not be resolved without long and complicated military and diplomatic manoeuvres, *Historia Gaufredi ducis*, in *Chroniques des comtes d'Anjou et des seigneurs d'Amboise*, ed. L. Halphen and R. Poupardin (Paris, 1913), 206–7. Geoffrey was unable to return to the Norman border for nearly a year.

13 *GS*, 12–14. William of Malmesbury (*HN*, 17) notes that the interests of his nephews, as much as his half-sister, informed Earl Robert's actions in December 1135.

in 1127, but the strength of support for Stephen was such that he had to go along with the new king until circumstances allowed him to appear in his true colours.[14] The only other hint we have of what Earl Robert thought in December 1135, after the disappointment of the candidature of Count Theobald, is that he 'gave up' his control of the ducal fortress of Falaise (we suppose to supporters of Stephen) but not before stripping it of a good deal of the great deposit of royal treasure kept there, presumably so that he could honour his father's request to pay off his debts.[15] After that we lose sight of him for quite a while.

It is perhaps only in retrospect that Robert of Gloucester looks important in December 1135. He had misjudged the situation, thinking that the next monarch would be made in Normandy and had left England and Stephen out of his calculations. In the meantime, Stephen seems to have reciprocated by leaving the earl out of *his* calculations, and with more reason. Hindsight (and Malmesbury) persuade us that Stephen and Robert were naturally antagonistic and rivals even before 1135. However, Stephen might not have seen things quite like that. He was less at court than Earl Robert before the old king's death, and rested in the security of having been (with David of Scotland) the first and greatest of King Henry's creations. From Stephen's exalted perspective, Earl Robert might have looked rather smaller than he has done to modern historians: a bastard and Marcher earl of moderate wealth (compared to others at court), a career soldier and administrator; the tallest head in the patch of nettles that was Henry's coterie of new men. The fact that the only person whom Stephen felt he needed to deal with promptly after his succession was David of Scotland ought to tell us how the new king assessed the risks facing him, and that to him Earl Robert was at first only a secondary concern.

FROM WESTMINSTER TO OXFORD: CHRISTMAS 1135 TO EASTER 1136

After London had acclaimed Stephen as its chosen king in the second week of December, Stephen still had some way to go up the steps of the throne.[16]

---

14 *HN*, 17–18. For the involved historiography of the question of Gloucester's motives, see R.B. Patterson, 'William of Malmesbury's Robert of Gloucester: a re-evaluation of the *Historia Novella*', *American Historical Review*, 70 (1965), 983–97; J.W. Leedom, 'William of Malmesbury and Robert of Gloucester reconsidered', *Albion*, 6 (1974), 251–63; D. Crouch, 'Robert of Gloucester and the daughter of Zelophehad', *JMH*, 11 (1985), 227–43.
15 OV vi, 448; RT, 129.
16 *GS*, 8, calls Stephen 'king' before his coronation and after his acclamation at London. The author is determined to exaggerate the significance of what happened at London: in fact his own account demonstrates that Stephen's royal status was not accepted before his anointing by the archbishop. On London and the succession generally, see M. McKisack, 'London and the succession to the crown in the middle ages', in *Studies in Medieval History presented to Frederick Maurice Powicke*, ed. R.W. Hunt and others (Oxford, 1948), 76–89, esp. 88–9. One should note the view of the new king's chancery as stated at Reading *c.* 4 January 1136, in an act which said that the abbey there should have their goods as on 'the day on which [King Henry] was alive and dead and the day on which I undertook the responsibility of the kingdom and the crown', *Regesta* iii, no. 678. That this ambiguous phrase meant there was a gap of three weeks between those two days is indicated by another early act, probably dating also to January 1136, which pardons a

The ideology of kingship had advanced by the 1130s to the state where the all-important act was the anointing and coronation rite in the recognised English investiture church: Westminster abbey. The acclamation of London was more a useful political endorsement than a necessary preliminary, and Stephen's chancery itself recognised that his kingship depended on the act of anointing, which signified the consent of the Church.[17]

The main outlines of Stephen's success in securing coronation from the Church are well understood and uncontentious. Moving down to Winchester, he found he had the all but instant support of the two most potent English bishops: his brother, Bishop Henry of Winchester, and the great administrator, Bishop Roger of Salisbury. It is difficult to know which of the two was the more influential supporter.[18] Bishop Roger's adherence to Stephen brought with it not just the widespread influence of his clerical family, but also control of the exchequer, the treasury and many of the sheriffs – in effect, the nascent English civil service. Bishop Henry's endorsement also had its uses. Henry was wealthy, and influential at Cluny and Rome. Still young, he was a vigorous and astute politician, of whom the rest of the Church in England stood somewhat in awe. But perhaps most significant was that his support represented some family endorsement of what he had done in twitching the Anglo-Norman realm out of the grip of their elder brother, Theobald. William of Malmesbury, whose account is valuable in view of his closeness to both bishops, believed that it was Bishop Henry who was able to win over the archbishop of Canterbury, William de Corbeil. Archbishop William had some scruples about setting aside his oath to support Mathilda, according to the author of the *Gesta*, who was another friend of Bishop Henry.[19]

The *Gesta* pictures the encounter between the archbishop and Stephen's supporters as something of a trial of his claim to be crowned. We have no way of knowing whether anything so formal really happened. But the *Gesta*'s report of the debate is interesting enough, however artificial it is, in the way it was resolved. In this account the oath of 1127 is the main issue. The king's

murder committed between 1 December and 22 December, apparently on the grounds that Stephen's majesty could only be offended after he was crowned king, *Regesta* iii, no. 428. The views as to when precisely Stephen became king are an interesting sidelight on the slow development of the 'Two Bodies' theological-legal doctrine of uninterruptible kingship, whose canon law foundation was being laid in the twelfth century, see E.H. Kantorowicz, *The King's Two Bodies: A Study in Medieval Political Theology* (Princeton, 1957), 314–450, esp. 385ff.

17 For useful recent overviews of the understanding of medieval kingship, see J. Le Goff, 'Le roi dans l'occident mediéval: caractères originaux', in *Kings and Kingship in Medieval Europe*, ed. A.J. Duggan (London, 1993), 1–40; J. Le Goff, 'Aspects religieux et sacrés de la monarchie française du xᵉ au xiiiᵉ siècle', in *La royauté sacrée dans le monde chrétien*, ed. A. Boureau and C-S. Ingerflom (Paris, 1992), 19–28.

18 *GS*, 8, says (ineptly) that Stephen's 'highest hopes' (*summa*) hung on his brother. HH, 700 talks of the 'great bishop of Salisbury' who delivered the crown and the weight of his assistance to Stephen (and does not mention Bishop Henry); naturally, *Liber Eliensis*, 285 agrees with the importance of Bishop Roger ('on whose say-so depended the whole running of the country') in the consecration.

19 *HN*, 15; *GS*, 10–12; GC, 94.

supporters pointed out that the oath was forced on them against their will, and that King Henry himself did not expect it to be kept, but imposed it for the sake of unity in his realms in his own lifetime. They further said that, at the end, the dying king repented of the whole business, and (according to the Canterbury source) there was an unnamed English magnate present who was willing on oath to say that he had heard the old king release his men from the oath. In view of all this, together with the support of London, the alleged unrest in the kingdom, and Stephen's military reputation and close kinship to the dead king, the archbishop found that there was every reason to set the oath aside, and proceed to crown him. The anointing and coronation of Stephen occurred on 22 December, three weeks after his uncle had breathed his last.

The *Gesta*'s account is important in the way that it concentrates so closely on the oath of 1127 as the main obstacle in accepting Stephen. Another source brings a yet closer focus on the problem. It would be unwise to dismiss entirely the idea that Henry really did at some point nominate Stephen as his successor (despite the significant fact that the *Gesta Stephani* makes no mention of it). John of Salisbury may be a later writer but he had himself heard the story of Stephen's nomination being repeated at Rome in 1139 before the pope. John mentions that Henry's former steward, Hugh Bigod, was the magnate who swore to the change of mind in the dying king (supported by two household knights). A similar story appears in the *Liber Eliensis*, whose compiler may have derived it from Bishop Nigel of Ely, son of Bishop Roger.[20] It was therefore a story widely accepted amongst royalists in the aftermath of the succession, not merely that King Henry had released his men from the oath to support his daughter, but that he had chosen Stephen to be his successor in the hearing of several of his household. A way to reconcile these conflicting stories might be to suggest that what we may be seeing here is evidence of the way that the dying king was willing to discuss privately the succession with those physically closest to him at the end, but unwilling to make any public declaration. Since there was no public declaration of his intentions to the assembled magnates, then it was possible for all parties to argue a case. Hugh Bigod may or may not have been telling his story to get in the new king's good books, but it would be unwise to assume that he was lying.[21]

So on 22 December 1135 Stephen was crowned king at Westminster with the support of the Church. As yet he had little in the way of a court around him: all we know of his companions in what must have been a near-deserted palace is that they included those bishops who had crowned him, the riding

20 *HP*, 84; *Liber Eliensis*, 285.
21 J. Bradbury, *Stephen and Matilda* (Stroud, 1996), 18–19; J. Bradbury, 'The early years of the reign of Stephen', in *England in the Twelfth Century*, ed. D. Williams (Woodbridge, 1990), 20, strongly argues for the veracity of Hugh Bigod, and makes the additional telling point that Archbishop Hugh of Rouen, who was closer than anyone else to the dying king, did not contradict Hugh's story.

retinue he had brought from Boulogne, some officials of the old king who had escaped to England (Martel and Bigod) and a few alert political animals who had raced to greet him at his coronation banquet (such as the monks of Bath who got him to promise their abbey a charter 'on the day of his consecration at Westminster'[22]). But the mechanisms of Stephen's kingship were beginning to gear up. The dies of a double-sided great seal in silver must have been commissioned almost immediately (the workshops which produced them were in London): it was in use by February 1136. The seal pointedly imitates that of the late King Henry, although it is more accomplished in execution. It identifies Stephen not just as king of England, but on the obverse, as duke of Normandy (although he was not formally invested as duke then, or perhaps ever).[23] London workshops were also very soon issuing to the licensed moneyers new official dies from which to strike silver Stephen pennies, and a national recoinage must have been under way even before Stephen moved north in February 1136.[24] Stephen was adopting the powerful ideology of bureaucratic kingship which his uncle had fostered in his thirty-five year reign. Henry had remorselessly moulded a new image of kingship with recognisable symbols of control and power, and Stephen and his advisers were as prompt to lay claim to them as Stephen had been to seize the political initiative earlier.[25] There is little doubt that at Winchester within a month of the coronation, the clerks and barons of the exchequer would have met in January for the half-yearly audit of the accounts, and notes would have been compiled for the drafting in September 1136 of that most intimidating royal document, the Pipe Roll of 1 Stephen, which, although it does not now survive, does not need a ghost to tell us that it once existed.

Things were going remarkably well for the new king, and his luck continued to hold. In council at Westminster after his coronation, he would have already asserted control over the bureaucracy. He had the support of the Church and had identified himself as its advocate and protector. The trappings of the English monarchy were being transferred to him, and he had secured its incomparable wealth. In Normandy, his most serious rivals had accomplished little, while the Norman aristocracy had declared for him as a body on hearing of his acceptance in England. There were rumours of general unrest in both England and Normandy, it is true, and there was a worrying situation

---

22 *Regesta* iii, no. 45.
23 The seal first appears on a writ issued at York in February 1136. Doubtless, the king carried it north with him, so it may have been delivered to his seal-bearer as early as the previous month, see for date *Regesta* iii, no. 99; T.A. Heslop, 'Seals', in *English Romanesque Art, 1066–1200*, ed. J. Alexander and others (London, 1984), 303.
24 M.M. Archibald, 'Coins', in *English Romanesque Art*, 335–6; M. Blackburn, 'Coinage and currency', in *The Anarchy of King Stephen's Reign*, ed. E. King (Oxford, 1994), 194–6.
25 On the particular contribution of Henry I to the understanding of kingship in England, see R.W. Southern, 'The place of Henry I in English history', repr. in *Medieval Humanism and Other Studies* (Oxford, 1970), 127–70; C.W. Hollister and J.W. Baldwin, 'The rise of administrative kingship: Henry I and Philip Augustus', *American Historical Review*, 83 (1978), 867–905; J.A. Green, *The Government of England under Henry I* (Cambridge, 1986), esp. 1–18.

developing in southwest Wales. But Stephen remained singularly uncrowded by circumstances as yet, with room for manoeuvre and space for reflection; quite unlike his uncle's situation in 1100. Thus he was able to begin a royal progress westwards to Reading, to preside over the solemn obsequies of his late uncle. This was an occasion of no small significance. What better occasion to be hailed as the new Henry than at the burial of the old? No expense or symbolism was spared in the solemn festivities, carried out before a great crowd. Stephen put his royal shoulder to the bier on which the late king's body was borne to the abbey church. And as he sat enthroned on 4 January with the corpse of his predecessor (and the abbey's founder) resting under its pall before him, no better demonstration of the way power had shifted was necessary to impress those of his people who were most alert to the symbolism of power, his aristocracy. As his clerks took pains to state at the time, or very soon after, when Stephen confirmed the late king's privileges to his royal mausoleum, 'however general is my obligation to safeguard royal alms, it is more pressing and particular towards the abbey of Reading, for good and sufficient reason.'[26]

But after Reading, ceremony, symbolism and display had to give way to action, and rapid action at that. Stephen moved to Oxford on the day after the funeral, according to Henry of Huntingdon, and there he heard news of the first serious opposition to his rule, with the hostile activity of the king of Scots in the north in favour of the Empress Mathilda.[27] For all that monarchy had acquired a particular vocabulary of power by Stephen's time, military and diplomatic success talked louder. Two events followed on from this bad news. The first was the inevitable confrontation with that former colleague of his, whose power and prestige appears to have most obsessed him, David, king of Scotland. The second would have been the first great crown-wearing of his reign to be held at Easter, for which we know that summonses were issued directly to the great magnates.[28] Since it appears that the king had decided that the first great court of his reign would not be until the end of March 1136, it

---

26 *Regesta* iii, no. 637. The best source for the funeral of Henry is JW iii, 214–16, which states that 'because of his [Stephen's] love for his uncle, putting his own royal shoulders to the bier with his barons, he caused the body to be carried to Reading'.

27 HH, 706.

28 The existence of these summonses may be deduced from mention by *GS*, 14 of the many 'royal instructions and letters' (I prefer this translation to Potter's of '. . . *regiis mandatis et scriptis*') sent from the court to Robert of Gloucester requesting his presence. If Robert was so pressed to come to the king at Easter, so were others (the author, if a bishop, would himself have received such summonses), and so we learn from the mention in *GS*, 22, 24 of the '*scripta regis*' by which a number of Henry's 'new men' were summoned to court (which sounds like individual writs) and of the '*edicto per Angliam promulgato*', by which the lay and ecclesiastical magnates were summoned (which sounds like the later general summons through the sheriffs). For the early writ of summons to the king's council, see G.B. Adams, *Councils and Courts in Anglo-Norman England* (repr. New York, 1965), 39, 110–11, 117, who notes what William fitz Stephen says of the prerogative of the chancellor in the 1150s '. . . *ut omnibus regis assit conciliis et etiam* non vocatus *se ingerat*', *Vita sancti Thome*, in *Materials for a History of Thomas Becket*, ed. J.C. Robertson iii (Rolls Series, 1877), 18. See also *LCGF*, no. 26, p. 63, which in the 1140s refers to barons customarily summoned 'by their names' to council.

is little surprise to find that he moved north to meet King David in February with no great following of magnates, but with a notably large force of knights. Stephen and his advisers seem to have been calculating on success and a profitable meeting in the north: a diplomatic coup that they could bring south to display as a trophy before the great council. If this deduction is correct, the new king's first steps look both assured and enterprising.

Stephen's progress was again leisurely, almost confident. He spent a month on his march to the north, collecting troops and settling some civil disturbances (such as that at Pontefract, where a *curialis* of the late king had been first imposed, and then assassinated, when news of King Henry's death reached the north).[29] On the way he added to his entourage some significant supporters: Walter Espec and Robert de Ferrers of Tutbury.[30] The north had suffered a serious attack by King David around Christmas 1135: the border fortresses of Carlisle, Wark, Alnwick, Norham and Newcastle-upon-Tyne had fallen, and only Bamburgh continued to put up resistance. What made it particularly pressing for Stephen to confront this danger first was that King David was believed to have moved into England in the interests of his niece, the empress. He had imposed oaths of loyalty to her on the northern barons who submitted to him.

In the event, it seems that by the time Stephen reached York, King David had come to realise that he had moved too quickly into England, and was not very confident about his ability to maintain his position in Northumbria or to extend himself south of the Tyne. The approach of Stephen with a large force soon produced an offer of an amicable conference at Durham, which in the end spanned a full fortnight, 5–20 February 1136. Following this conference, King David's heir, Henry, acknowledged Stephen's kingship by doing homage at York, before the end of the month, while David withdrew to Newcastle. There is no surer indication of the strength of Stephen in his first months as king than that his chief rival capitulated so quickly.[31]

The court held at York may well be regarded as the high point of Stephen's reign to date.[32] It was held in some state (with a small host of bishops and abbots) as was appropriate to the occasion, for it marked the solemn resolution

29 For the problem over Pontefract see RH, 140, which talks of the succession settled 'soon' after Henry's death. Stephen had himself come to Pontefract and received Ilbert de Lacy and his men into his peace 'for all the forfeits which they committed after King Henry's death up till the day I was crowned, namely the forfeit for the death of William Maltravers', *Regesta* iii, no. 428.

30 *Regesta* iii, nos. 99, 255. J.H. Round points to the early adherence of the several magnates of the house of Clare to his side from early January at Reading: notably, Robert fitz Richard, Baldwin and Walter fitz Gilbert, J.H. Round, *Geoffrey de Mandeville: A Study of the Anarchy* (London, 1892), 13–14n. Robert fitz Richard accompanied the king on his northern campaign.

31 RH, 146; JH, 287. HH, 706 believed that Stephen's northern army was the largest anyone could recall seeing in England.

32 The court was marked by solemn confirmations made out in the chancery to some great northern religious houses of which a good number survive: those to York minster, Beverley minster, Ripon minster, Whitby abbey, Fountains abbey, and Walter Espec's two foundations of Rievaulx and Warden abbeys (*Regesta* iii, nos. 99, 335, 716–17, 919, 979). Attestations reveal also the presence of the baron, William de Percy, in York with the king, among all the bishops.

of one of Stephen's most immediately pressing problems. Stephen's concessions were politic and economical.[33] He gained the acquiescence of the Scots by confirmation of the earldom of Huntingdon to Henry (which David already held by right of his deceased wife, Mathilda[34]) and by grants of the royal fortresses and estates of Carlisle and Doncaster. There was – according to some – discussion of the revival of an earldom of Northumbria at the conference, but Stephen promised no more than to consider Henry's claim in his court, should the subject ever arise. As if recognising that a new order had been established, King David's cousin, Gospatric of Dunbar (who was another claimant to the earldom of Northumbria) also settled his claims in Northumberland with the new king, being content with a confirmation of the lands his family had from King Henry.[35] King David then withdrew his forces and returned the hostages and pledges he had taken, and so in effect abandoned his niece's cause.

Henry of Huntingdon believed that David would not himself do homage to Stephen, because of the oath he had taken to support Mathilda, but if this was so, that refusal was as much as he could now offer.[36] Did he have any choice? From his own perspective, probably not. In acting against Stephen in December he had moved too fast, before the full situation in Normandy could have been known to him. Unfortunately for him, the pragmatic Norman nobility had accepted Stephen, and rejected Mathilda. By February he knew that his niece's cause in Normandy had stalled, and that in England Stephen was not merely unchallenged but increasingly formidable. He might also have reflected that his other niece, Stephen's wife, Mathilda of Boulogne[37], would be crowned queen of England at the forthcoming Easter festivities, that favouring one niece would slight the other, and that there was more to gain by favouring Mathilda of Boulogne in February 1136. But that his actions were regarded as a betrayal by Mathilda's few remaining partisans is clear from the faintly sneering comments of William of Malmesbury on his apostasy, blaming David's age and his 'mildness' (*lenitas*).[38]

---

33 H.A. Cronne, *The Reign of Stephen: Anarchy in England, 1135–54* (London, 1970), 31–2, launches into a polemic on Stephen's 'unnecessarily lavish' concessions to David, especially the 'insult' given to Ranulf of Chester by the cession of Carlisle (which his father had given up in 1120): it should be noted, however, that the offence was not so great as to drive Ranulf from the Easter court a month later.

34 J.A. Green, 'David I and Henry I', *Scottish Historical Review*, LXXV (1996), 16–17.

35 *Regesta* iii, no. 373a.

36 RH, 146; HH, 706.

37 Mathilda of Boulogne was the daughter of King David's younger sister, Mary, who had married Count Eustace III; the empress was daughter of his elder sister, Edith-Mathilda, who had married Henry I of England.

38 *HN*, 16. Modern commentators point by contrast to what they see as King David's single-minded energy in pursuit after 1135 of a vision of an Anglo-Scottish *regnum* in the north, G.W.S. Barrow, *David I of Scotland, 1124–1153* (Reading, 1985), 18; idem, 'The Scots and the north of England', in *The Anarchy of Stephen's Reign*, ed. E. King (Oxford, 1994), 245–7; P. Dalton, *Conquest, Anarchy and Lordship: Yorkshire 1066–1154* (Cambridge, 1994), 203–4. See particularly the thoughtful critique of Scottish policy in K.J. Stringer, *The Reign of Stephen* (London, 1993), 28–37.

THE EASTER COURT OF MARCH 1136

And so south to Westminster for what was intended to be the set-piece demonstration of Stephen's kingship, the Easter court and queen's coronation of 22 March 1136, after which the court moved to Oxford. The king came south, bearing with him Henry of Scotland as evidence of his successful resolution of the northern problem. Just so that everybody realised this, he carefully placed Earl Henry in the position of honour on his right hand at the banquet which followed his crown-wearing and the coronation of Queen Mathilda (who was Earl Henry's first cousin).[39] Since John Horace Round in 1892, the significance of this court has been well recognised by historians. Round regarded it as Stephen's attempted revival of the grandeur of the great festive crown-wearings of the eleventh-century Norman kings, which Henry I had allowed to lapse in his first years. There is some sense in Round's idea, although Oxford was not one of the traditional places favoured by the Norman kings: nearby Woodstock was, however, used for three Easter courts by Henry I.[40] Stephen and his advisers might well have been looking for precedents by which to illustrate the strength and confidence of the new kingship: and what better way than for Stephen to recast himself as a king after the mould of the already legendary conqueror of England? Besides, as Round said, the hasty and poorly attended anointing of the previous December had to be eliminated by an event of remarkable grandeur.

A very great number of magnates appeared, each name adding its measure of reality to the balance of Stephen's kingship. In total, the charters of the Easter period issued by Stephen record in attendance on the king three archbishops (Canterbury, York and Rouen) and sixteen English, Welsh and Norman bishops, five magnates of comital rank (including Henry, son of King David) and more than two dozen significant barons. The rather primitive attendance register represented by the contemporary royal charters gives only a minimum number; clerks would only have recorded the names of those whose presence added obvious lustre to the occasion. There would have been others: abbots and priors, archdeacons, lesser barons and officers present too, but unrecorded. Henry of Huntingdon's glowing description of the court that 'never was there one to exceed it in England in numbers, in greatness, in gold, silver, gems, costume and in all manner of entertainment', seems justified. But the court was more than just a stage on which Stephen could display

---

39 RH, 146, says that this seating arrangement caused something of a problem over precedence with the archbishop of Canterbury, but it is difficult to believe that Stephen lost much sleep over the archbishop's discomfiture: once he was anointed, the archbishop's annoyance was a matter of limited concern. Queen Mathilda's coronation at Westminster at Easter 1136 is noted by the St Augustine's Canterbury chronicler, *Ungedruckte Anglo-Normannische Geschichtsquellen*, ed. F. Liebermann (Strasbourg, 1879), 79–80, copied by GC i, 96. *Regesta* iii, no. 341 reveals that the queen had brought their son, Eustace, with her from Boulogne for the court.
40 J.H. Round, *Geoffrey de Mandeville: A Study of the Anarchy* (London, 1892), 16–19; M. Biddle, 'Seasonal festivals and residence: Winchester, Westminster and Gloucester in the tenth to twelfth centuries', *ANS* viii, ed. R.A. Brown, (Woodbridge, 1985), 51–63.

his royalty, for the court included a great council of the Church, in which the implementation of the king's coronation promises was debated, amongst other things.[41]

But even among those names which were recorded, some were more politically significant than others: names which had been the pillars of Henry's rule now acknowledged Stephen's. One significant group was represented by Count Waleran of Meulan, with his stepfather and sometime guardian, Earl William de Warenne, and Earl William's son-in-law (who was also Waleran's first cousin), Earl Roger of Warwick. Earl William and Count Waleran had been leading magnates at the deathbed of King Henry in Normandy, and Earl William had taken charge of the capital and the Pays de Caux while the court magnates debated the succession (fruitlessly) in council. Now they were in England. Count Waleran was the key Norman magnate, as far as Stephen was concerned: the greatest Norman landowner after the duke, his castles and estates controlled Central Normandy south of Rouen. Waleran's younger identical twin brother, Earl Robert of Leicester, was the greatest Norman lord on the southern march of the duchy, and Earl Robert was known to be the faithful auxiliary of his elder twin. We do not know what relations between Waleran and Stephen had been like before 1135. The fact that Waleran had spent the years between 1124 and 1129 imprisoned in various castles – the result of an unsuccessful rebellion in favour of the Clito – more than likely meant that relations between them were more distant (and perhaps less fraught) than those, say, between Stephen and Robert of Gloucester.[42]

Despite this, Count Waleran had moved more quickly than most to meet the new king. Before the Easter council he had already had a grant of the royal manor of Steeple Morden, Cambridgeshire, from King Stephen; one of the earliest grants the king can be proved to have made to an individual.[43] So Waleran had made the crossing to England some time – probably weeks – before Easter. The king's urgings might well have spurred him on. The king, and his advisers, well knew that the 'Beaumont' group of magnates (the grandchildren of the Conqueror's baron, Roger de Beaumont) were incontestably the single most influential magnate group in the early 1130s. They can be demonstrated to have worked to a common purpose too, on occasion. If he were to control Normandy, and if he were to secure a hard core of midlands supporters in England, Stephen needed the Beaumonts. Waleran's gains from the previous reign were confirmed to him. These included the keeping of the lands of his imprisoned brother-in-law, Hugh, lord of Montfort-sur-Risle in Central Normandy, which was a key lordship for Waleran's control of the

41 HH, 706; *GS*, 26–7. Round, *Geoffrey de Mandeville*, 262–6, compares names in the principal relevant charters (*Regesta* iii, nos. 46, 271, 944).
42 See generally, D. Crouch, *The Beaumont Twins: The Roots and Branches of Power in the Twelfth Century* (Cambridge 1986), 24–30.
43 *Regesta* iii, no. 944. At Westminster at Easter 1136 Stephen gave Bishop's Sutton, Hants, to Winchester cathedral priory in return for Morden '. . . which I have given to Waleran count of Meulan'.

Risle valley: the dividing line down the centre of the duchy. Stephen kept Hugh in prison, proving that he was just as able to put pragmatism above justice as his late uncle had been. More was offered to the count of Meulan. Waleran, who was thirty-one at this time, was betrothed to Mathilda, the two-year-old daughter of Stephen. With this arrangement appears to have gone the keeping of an ample marriage-portion which included several royal manors across England (including Steeple Morden, and Lessness in Kent) but principally royal forest and holdings in Worcestershire, undoubtedly including the borough and salt-works of Droitwich, and perhaps considerably more. A form of marriage apparently was undertaken, but the arrangement lapsed when the little girl died in 1137, to be buried at the priory of Holy Trinity, Aldgate in London, and it seems that she never reached the age to leave the custody of her mother.[44]

With Waleran, Stephen was being generous indeed, but it should not be assumed that the king was recklessly profligate with gifts and promises at the outset of his reign. He has been accused of this by some modern writers, notably the Birmingham school as represented by Davis and Cronne.[45] The exact opposite seems true: Stephen was accused by contemporaries of being irritatingly parsimonious in the face of hopeful demands by his new courtiers. One baron who had expected much from the Easter court was Richard fitz Gilbert, the marcher lord of Chepstow and Ceredigion, lord of Clare in Suffolk, the most potent member of the Clare family. His brothers and cousins had been among the first to join Stephen. The *Gesta Stephani* tells us that 'when he had made great demands on the king and not obtained them according to

---

44 Reconstructed in Crouch, *Beaumont Twins*, 28–9 and n. 53. J. Bradbury, 'Early years of the reign of Stephen', 29, citing E. King, 'Waleran, Count of Meulan, Earl of Worcester, 1104–1166', in *Tradition and Change: Essays in Honour of M. Chibnall*, ed. D. Greenway and others (Cambridge, 1985), 165–76, appears to suggest that the Beaumonts were not promoted against Robert of Gloucester till 1139. But he does not take account of the evidence for Stephen's earlier generosity to Waleran presented in Crouch, *ut supra*, published after King's article. King's daughter, Mathilda, '*quondam uxorem comitis de Medlint*', is mentioned as being buried in the priory church of Aldgate on the south side of the high altar (her brother, Baldwin, being buried on the north), *The Cartulary of Holy Trinity, Aldgate*, ed. G.A.J. Hodgett (London Record Society, 7, 1971), 232, a reference I owe to the generosity of Dr Heather Tanner. From charter references, the deaths of both children must have occurred before 1138, *Regesta* iii, nos. 508, 511–12.

45 Cronne, *Reign of Stephen*, 31; R.H.C. Davis, *King Stephen* (3rd edn., London, 1990), 18. This idea of Stephen's profligacy and weakness at the beginning of his reign seems to have arisen ultimately from Malmesbury's remark about his excessive favour towards mercenaries (*HN*, 17) and Round's analysis of Stephen's charters to Miles of Gloucester issued at Reading in January 1136 (*Regesta* iii, nos. 386–7), seeing one (no. 387) as a treaty 'between equal powers', Round, *Geoffrey de Mandeville*, 14. What Round did not say (although he must have noticed) was that the charter granted Miles nothing that he had not held in the reign of Henry I, other than an exemption from pleas arising from those lands. This attitude has been adopted by modern writers such as Edmund King in 'Dispute settlement in Anglo-Norman England', *ANS*, xiv, ed. M. Chibnall (Woodbridge, 1992), 120; 'Introduction', *The Anarchy of King Stephen's Reign*, ed. E. King (Oxford, 1994), 12, who sees what are properly confirmations as 'grants', and talks then of Stephen's 'generosity'; nonetheless, Professor King is perfectly aware that, as he also says, 'the king was not uniformly generous'. For a critique of the Reading acts, D. Crouch, 'A Norman *conventio* and bonds of lordship in the middle ages', in *Law and Government*, ed. G. Garnett and J. Hudson (Cambridge, 1994), 313n.

his desire [he] went away, as they said, to stir up war against him'.[46] If Richard fitz Gilbert was denied how many more lesser men must have been disappointed? Such a man was Baldwin de Redvers, a West Country magnate of substance, but not particularly close to the court of Henry I. It is Richard of Hexham this time who says that the baron in question had petitioned Stephen for 'a certain distinction (*honor*)' and been denied. Baldwin retaliated by seizing the city of Exeter as a bargaining counter.[47]

These few high-profile cases were perhaps the tip of quite a large and discontented iceberg: those who believed that they might exploit the insecurities of a new king, only to discover that he felt confident enough to smile and ignore them. The king's confidence at Easter 1136 is hardly to be wondered at. There is a certain triumphant exuberance in the charters of his first months, many of which solemnly and pointedly record that they were issued 'in the first year of my reign': dating by regnal year is barely to be found in earlier reigns. The only group he now needed to conciliate was that which had given him the crown, the English Church. Around the beginning of March, the Church delivered its final benediction on his accession when a letter from Pope Innocent arrived, confirming the archbishop's decision to anoint Stephen king. Copies of this letter were soon (prudently) in wide circulation: a text had certainly reached as far north as Hexham within the year.[48]

It only remained for Stephen to consummate the promises made to the archbishop in December, the promises of obedience and reverence to which the pope pointedly referred in his letter. This he proceeded to do, when he moved his court from Westminster up the Thames to Oxford, sometime at the end of March 1136. Here, still surrounded by a great gathering of magnates and bishops, Stephen announced that he was king 'by God's grace, chosen (*electus*) by the assent of the clergy and people of England, consecrated by William, archbishop of Canterbury and legate of the Holy Roman Church, and afterwards confirmed by Innocent, pontiff of the Holy Roman See', and as such went on to confirm its liberties to the Church within his kingdom.[49] Stephen's clerk was emphasising how his master was beholden to God, the archbishop and pope in his assumption of power. The reference to his acclamation by clergy and people is also a vaguely sacerdotal formula, for bishops of old were also acclaimed by their clergy and people. Again, multiple official copies of this grant were put into wide circulation, probably being sent to all the cathedrals

46 *GS*, 16. Richard does not turn up in the attestation lists to Easter 1136 royal acts, however since he left Stephen to be murdered in the Welsh mountains on 15 April, there is little reason to doubt that he had been there.
47 RH, 146–7. See the analysis of Baldwin's motives and background in R. Bearman, 'Baldwin de Redvers: some aspects of a baronial career in the reign of Stephen', *ANS* xviii, ed. C. Harper-Bill (Woodbridge, 1996), 20–24, which suggests that the honor in question was the shrievalty of Devon. Bearman also (p. 22) makes a good case that the Somerset landholder, Robert of Bampton, rebelled because he had been disappointed in his expectations of the manor of Uffculme by Stephen (who favoured his brother Bishop Henry over Robert).
48 RH, 147–8. For some observations on this, see C.J. Holdsworth, 'The Church', in *The Anarchy of King Stephen's Reign*, ed. E. King (Oxford, 1994), 209–10n.
49 *Regesta* iii, no. 271. See Chapter 15 below.

and greater religious houses of the land. The Church meant to have his promises on record, and for his part Stephen intended to keep them. Certainly there is evidence that he did his best throughout his reign to keep the promise he made not to subject the Church to pleas for hunting and assarting (clearing woodland for agricultural purposes) in areas that King Henry had added in his reign to the royal forest.[50]

From the text we have, Stephen's promises to the Church seem to have fulfilled its limited hopes of the new king. He did not surrender any of his traditional prerogatives, but he did publicly distance himself from the practice of simony: taking money or gifts in return for ecclesiastical appointments. He also made positive noises about being responsible in his use of his right to the wardship of ecclesiastical sees in times of vacancy; he promised freedom to episcopal courts in dealing with clerics; and liberty to clergy to dispose of their goods by testament. Perhaps his most material concession was to exempt the Church from forest exactions in the forests which Henry had made. As we have seen, he tried his best to keep that promise, and there are indications that he meant to do the same in his custody of vacant sees. When Canterbury and Salisbury were vacant in 1136–38 and 1139 he appointed a cleric to their wardship, in accordance with his written promises. The fact that the cleric was his brother may have detracted from his generosity, but he kept to the letter of the agreement. His episcopal appointments were not without merit, and he usually allowed himself to be guided in them by his advisers, as we see early on when Henry of Blois promoted the candidacy of his vicegerent, Robert of Lewes, as bishop of Bath. Robert was a Cluniac monk closely connected with Henry of Blois, as his intendant in the abbacy of Glastonbury and John of Worcester believed the appointment to have been Henry's.[51]

There were undoubtedly other statements made at this time by Stephen in his court about his future intentions as king, made as much to the laity as the

---

50 Henry of Huntingdon says that Stephen made such a promise to both the barons and the Church in April, and that at a forest eyre held at Brampton (on 29 September 1136) he broke his promise to the barons (*proceres*), HH, 704, 708. However, Huntingdon does not say that the promise was broken to the Church. A writ in favour of the see of Hereford survives which shows he certainly took immediate measures to implement his promise for one diocese, *Regesta* iii, no. 382; see also for Barking abbey, ibid. no. 32. A charter to Wenlock priory, Shropshire, datable to 1146 x 48 (not in *Regesta*) demonstrates that he was still then reinforcing this pledge when he quitclaimed to the priory 'all assarts which the monks and their men made after the death of King Henry from their demesne woodland . . . which my uncle King Henry had afforested (*adforestavit*)', D.C. Cox, 'Two unpublished charters of King Stephen for Wenlock priory', *Shropshire History and Archeology*, lxvi (1989), 58–9. J.H. Round, *Geoffrey de Mandeville*, 378, makes the obvious point that if Stephen had to repeat and reinforce the grant for individual houses (he was considering Barking abbey) then the blanket exemption had lapsed, but he does not take account of the known overenthusiasm for royal rights exhibited by farmers of revenues, such as royal foresters, which continually needed to be checked. I must thank Dr Nicholas Vincent for his help on this vexed subject.

51 JW iii, 212 and n. The *Historiola de primordiis episcopatus Somersetensis*, a work written in the later twelfth century, informs us that Robert had been Bishop Henry's agent in his house at Glastonbury, *Ecclesiastical Documents*, ed. J. Hunter (Camden Soc., 1840), 23, and see GS, xxxiv–xxxv.

Church. For what they were we have only some sketchy, if evocative hints. Henry of Huntingdon gives a list of what he believed Stephen's promises to have been, and says they were 'recorded', although it might be that Huntingdon was misled by the charter to the Church into thinking that there was also a corresponding charter to the kingdom at large recording the king's general promises in council.[52] But Henry must be considered a good source for these promises, considering his curial connections with the family of Roger of Salisbury. According to him, Stephen had promised speedy elections to vacant sees in the run-up to the Oxford Easter court and extended his pledge about the unjust exploitation of King Henry's afforestations to laity too. Henry also reports that the king pledged to abolish Danegeld, a national property tax that was unpopular because it was selectively levied, with broad exemptions to leading courtiers and their friends.[53] John of Worcester confirms that Stephen had made a statement about abolishing Danegeld, and that he did not stand by it. One other statement that Stephen might have made at this time, or soon after, was that when a man died leaving female heirs, the property should be divided between them, rather than go to the eldest. This would have much increased the number of marriageable women with property, and so answered the clamour for patronage.[54]

With the Easter court a great success, Stephen now had every reason for full confidence. Not only did he have the pope's blessing, the pope's letter itself revealed that Innocent had received since Christmas letters supporting Stephen's claims to the throne from both King Louis VI of France and Stephen's elder brother, Count Theobald of Blois, who seems to have got over his immediate anger at being thwarted of the succession. Someone (perhaps Bishop Henry) had masterminded embassies and concentrated diplomacy at Chartres, Pisa, Paris, and perhaps also Bruges, which had swung what might pass for international opinion behind Stephen. We know the name of at least one cleric

---

52 HH, 704. In her recent edition of the *Historia Anglorum*, Professor Greenway questions whether Henry's account is indeed (as has been assumed) a 'garbled version' of *Regesta* iii, no. 271, or whether it is an account of promises made at another and earlier Oxford court, when Stephen went there at the 'close of Christmas', that is, the day before the feast of Epiphany (6 January). Since Stephen's promises to the Church in the *Historia* are a little more generous than those we know were written down at Easter, there is good reason to take this suggestion seriously. His position in March 1136 was much stronger than it had been in January, and he could afford to be more guarded. But if we accept this idea, then it does not necessarily follow that we should accept that Stephen made promises in January that were stated more than verbally. The Easter charter to the Church is then evidence that what was said in January was no more than an agenda for a final discussion in March, when the results were recorded in writing. The summonses issued in January for a meeting in March, and the king's small retinue of magnates in the north in February indicate that the meeting at Oxford in January was not a great court and had little purpose except as a forum for decisions. Henry of Huntingdon chose to read more into the January meeting than he had a right to do, for his own hostile purposes.

53 J.A. Green, 'The last century of Danegeld', *EHR* 96 (1981), 241–58.

54 JW iii, 202 mentions a *regale decretum* of Stephen's; for the *statutum decretum* concerning partition of inheritance, mentioned in a document of *c*.1145, see F.M. Stenton, *The First Century of English Feudalism, 1066–1166* (2nd edn., Oxford, 1960), 40–1, 260. It has to be said though, that this last reference to a *statutum decretum* might very well refer to a decision in the *curia regis*, or some other pronouncement than a coronation promise.

consulted on the planning of the Italian mission, Abbot Geoffrey of St Albans, who had knowledge of and contacts in the papal Curia, but whose place in the embassy was withdrawn just before it set off.[55] Stephen was therefore supported by clerical statesmen of some weight and experience in his initial contact with the Curia. As Christopher Holdsworth has recently pointed out, the distant Curia, residing at Pisa since the anti-pope held Rome, would have viewed Stephen's succession with equanimity. He was supported by the English hierarchy and the king of France. The empress, on the other hand, had failed to establish herself, and her late marriage had identified her with the imperial party which had promoted the schism. Innocent II was still suffering from the results of this split in the Church, and he may not have looked kindly on the wife of the papacy's late enemy.[56]

Crossing the Channel from Normandy in Easter week, while the celebrations of the great court were still under way at Westminster, Earl Robert of Gloucester landed in England. For whatever reason, he chose to avoid the court and did not join it until it moved to Oxford at the beginning of April.[57] But he was there when the king swore to uphold the liberties of the Church, and was the first layman to attest solemnly to the charter, swearing fealty to the king after the bishops. We have every reason to believe that he was received with honour at court. The *Gesta Stephani* says that 'he was received with favour and distinction and obtained all he demanded in accordance with his wish', and notes that with his adherence almost all of England had gone over to Stephen.[58] If the *Gesta* is correct, then Gloucester was one of the few to receive appreciable rewards for their allegiance. Unfortunately, we do not know if the reward was anything more than what Miles of Gloucester had obtained in January: confirmation of what he held in Henry's days, with exemption from pleas for past offences. Moreover, the *Gesta*'s concern to highlight Robert's adherence in such a way may unduly flatter the (by now limited) importance of the earl. When its author wrote, in the 1140s, Robert of Gloucester had long assumed leadership of the Angevin cause in England,

---

55 *The Life of Christina of Markyate: a twelfth-century recluse*, ed. C.H. Talbot (Oxford, 1959), 160–2, says that, 'In the year when Stephen was first elected king of England, he decided on the advice of wise counsellors to send *nuncii* to Pope Innocent II at Rome in order to obtain from this supreme authority the confirmation of his election.' OV vi, 514 mentions negotiations early in his reign between Stephen and his old ally, Thierry, count of Flanders, over a marriage between the count's daughter and a son of the king. Whether or not Orderic is right that the two parties did reach the point of a betrothal, there is every reason to see this, too, as part of the charm offensive.
56 C.J. Holdsworth, 'The Church', in *The Anarchy of King Stephen's Reign*, ed. E. King (Oxford, 1994), 208–9.
57 Crouch, 'Robert of Gloucester and the daughter of Zelophehad', 229–30, suggests that the deteriorating Marcher position in Wales may have forced him to head first for his lands in southeast Wales. For this, see Chapter 3 below. There remains some question as to whether there had not been a previous meeting between earl and king, for the *Anglo-Saxon Chronicle, s.a.* 1135 states that 'his son and his friends' took his body to be buried at Reading (but then, the late king had other sons than Earl Robert), R.B. Patterson 'Stephen's Shaftesbury charter: another case against William of Malmesbury', *Speculum*, 43 (1968), 487–92, fails to date conclusively *Regesta* iii, no. 818 to before 22 March 1136.
58 *HN*, 17–18; *GS*, 14.

so it was important to highlight the moment when he had committed himself to the king. But in April 1136, with the news of the support of the pope and king of France public, Robert's appearance may have seemed no more than the last delicate piece of icing on Stephen's royal cake, and a matter of only limited significance.

The peace and complaisance of his realm was the target of Stephen and his episcopal advisers in the spring of 1136, and they spared no pains to establish it. Diplomacy and pressure secured peace with the Scots and with the Church. Those of the old king's *curiales* who petitioned for it, secured a blanket exemption from prosecutions for offences during the previous reign. The murderers of the lord of Pontefract were pardoned and their deed tacitly condoned, as it was done between the old king's death and the new king's coronation, and so his majesty could not be offended. A great curial bandwagon had begun to roll, which in the end dragged Robert of Gloucester on board. The new king found a realm at his feet with an ease which must have gratified him. The problem for him was going to be those who had no need of his peace, and who were not amenable to negotiation. The summer of 1136 was therefore to be more of a trial.

CHAPTER 3

Wales and Normandy

Something went wrong early in Stephen's reign. Nobody would deny that. That 'something' may not have seemed much at the time, but it grew and unbalanced the whole governance of England. Deciding what it was has been one of the oldest questions in English medieval historiography, and we will be returning to the question in later chapters, for the cause of the problem was in no way simple. But I will deal with one particular and key aspect of the problem here: when things *began* to go wrong. Previous studies of the reign have been Anglocentric; they have concentrated unduly (but understandably) on England and English affairs, and therefore on English causes for the problem. But if there is one thing that needs to be recognised about Stephen's reign above all else, it is that England was but one factor in a large equation.[1] Stephen himself failed to recognise that; a mistake which his predecessor had never committed. Here lies the beginning of his problems. Two areas in particular had always engaged King Henry's immediate attention: Wales and Normandy. These two were the very areas that broke into the most serious unrest soon after Henry's death. My contention is that these were the areas which quickly unmasked Stephen's most serious weaknesses, and perhaps not merely Stephen's, but those of his advisers also.

We do perhaps sometimes assume all too readily that Stephen was the only deviser of the policies and responses which got him into such trouble. Yet part of the king's problem may have been to put too much trust in the judgement

1 The key importance of the 'British' dimension of many episodes of English history is slowly being recognised, whether in the period of the 'English' Civil War, for which see C.S.R. Russell, 'The British problem and the English Civil War', *History*, 72 (1987), 395–415, or in the Middle Ages, see R.R. Davies, *Domination and Conquest* (Oxford, 1990); R. Frame, *The Political Development of the British Isles* (London, 1990). But of course from the eleventh to the fifteenth century there was equally well a Franco-Norman dimension to English affairs, see amongst others, J.J.N. Palmer, *England, France and Christendom, 1377–99* (London, 1972), 256–7; J. Le Patourel, *The Norman Empire* (Oxford, 1976); J.C. Holt, 'The end of the Anglo-Norman realm', *Proceedings of the British Academy*, lxi (1975), 223–65; M. Vale, *The Angevin Legacy and the Hundred Years War, 1250–1340* (Oxford, 1990); D.R. Bates, 'The rise and fall of Normandy, c.911–1204', in *England and Normandy in the Middle Ages* (London, 1994), ed. D.R. Bates and A. Curry, 19–35.

of those around him whom he found most impressive. In the first critical five months of his reign there is little reason to doubt that it was his episcopal brother, Henry, and Henry's colleague, Roger of Salisbury, who were most often prompting him: contemporaries and lists of attestations tell us as much. The masterminding of Stephen's strategy at the papal Curia and Paris, in the handling of Archbishop William and the Church, were doubtless the work of Henry, his brother, the Cluniac prince-bishop with wide contacts and an international reputation. In the rapid rebuilding of the image of royal power around Stephen, in writs, seals, coinage and careful patronage, we see the work of Bishop Roger, the justiciar.

Both bishops were well rewarded for their work. Patronage was skewed in their interest.[2] At the Easter court of 1136, Bishop Henry claimed and obtained on behalf of his abbey of Glastonbury several prizes: several valuable manors alienated by the Conqueror and – more contentiously – the hundredal manor of Uffculme, Devon. Whatever was claimed on Glastonbury's behalf, Uffculme belonged by right to someone else. Robert of Bampton, a prominent land-owner in Somerset and northern Devon, and his father, had held Uffculme unchallenged at and since the time of the Domesday survey.[3] For his part, Bishop Roger is known to have secured from the king in 1136 the borough of Malmesbury and a manor in Wiltshire.[4] It was later recorded by William of Malmesbury that Stephen was so far carried away by gratitude to Bishop Roger that he publicly gushed, 'By the birth of God! I would give him half England until the end of time if he asked for it: he will grow tired of asking before I do of giving.'[5] But apart from some promotions for his relations, it seems that Roger's demands were not so extreme.

The two bishops were together with the king until the break-up of the Easter assembly at Oxford, and indeed Stephen went on to celebrate the feast of Pentecost with Bishop Roger at Salisbury, a pretty compliment to

2 This is explicit in what Bishop Henry himself said in his account of his tenure of the abbey of Glastonbury, in the matter of his frustrated claim on Uffculme 'I bore with it for the time being cheerfully and deferred my claim' while his uncle was on the throne, but as soon as his brother, Stephen, became king, he obtained the homage owed for the place, Adam of Domerham, *Historia de rebus gestis Glastoniensibus*, ed. T. Hearne (2 vols, London, 1727) ii, 310.

3 For the reclamation of Uffculme, *Regesta* iii, no. 341, which may be dated to the week after Easter 1136 (as it features Mathilda as queen). For the resulting alienation of Robert of Bampton, see H.P.R. Finberg, 'Uffculme', in *Lucerna* (London, 1964), 212–21; *English Episcopal Acta* viii, *Winchester, 1070–1204*, ed. M.J. Franklin (British Academy, 1990), 208; R. Bearman, 'Baldwin de Redvers: some aspects of a baronial career in the reign of Stephen', *ANS* xviii, ed. C. Harper-Bill (Woodbridge, 1996), 22. For the identification of Robert, see J.H. Round, 'Robert of Bampton', *EHR*, 5 (1890), 746–7. For the reclamation of royal alienations (and Henry of Blois's conscience over Uffculme) see now, N.E. Stacy, 'Henry of Blois and the Lordship of Glastonbury', *EHR*, 114 (1999), 16.

4 For Bishop Roger's rewards, E.J. Kealey, *Roger of Salisbury, Viceroy of England* (London, 1972), 159 and n.

5 *HN*, 39. I have not adopted Potter's translation of '*donec tempus pertranseat*', as his choice 'until his time shall pass' seems unnecessarily ominous and does not fit the apparent sense of the preceding clause. Malmesbury's use of the quotation against Stephen is ironic enough, as it is.

the justiciar.[6] Since this was a period of success for the king, we may as well make the obvious connection that he was relying on the advice of two informed and talented men, with secular and ecclesiastical world-views which were highly developed. There is every reason to think that these men added depth and perspective to Stephen's own undoubted military gifts, and that between all three they triumphantly established Stephen as king in England; undermined and overawed King David's attempts to manipulate the succession, and staged the brilliant success of the Westminster–Oxford council. They may also have jointly masterminded the next phase too. Well before the Easter court had broken up – and there is reason to believe the intention was made public as early as the Easter session at Westminster on 22 March – the participants would have heard that the king was to cross to Normandy after the celebration of Pentecost on 10 May (apparently at his palace of Clarendon).[7]

Waleran, count of Meulan, had already been sent ahead into Normandy from the court at Westminster, with authority to begin moves for the establishment of Stephen's effective rule in the duchy, and was beating down the doors of the rebel castle of Vaudreuil on the day Stephen himself began celebrating Pentecost at Salisbury.[8] But Stephen did not cross to Normandy, apparently because while awaiting the crossing he heard false rumours of Bishop Roger's sudden death, and returned immediately to Salisbury. For the first time, Stephen had not done what had been sketched out for him and agreed in council, and the consequences were to be dire. For he *had* to go to Normandy in person, but having failed in his attempt, he decided to postpone the trip for the best part of a year. Why was this so? If there is a reason, we can find it – of all places – in the contemporary chronicles and their obsessive concern with disorder in England and Wales.

How disorderly was England in the spring of 1136? It had been in the interests of Stephen and his advisers to paint the picture of England sinking into a chasm of social disorder once news of King Henry's death broke: a 'pseudo-Anarchy'. They had taken care in December 1135 that this was the view the pope had received, and when he came to recite the reasons why he supported Stephen's coronation, the first was that, '. . . on [King Henry's]

---

6 HH, 706, notes that the king had first to make a long detour across England to Norwich, so that he could reclaim the castle in person from Hugh Bigod, who had panicked and seized it in the last week of April, hearing a rumour of the king's death. Hugh's later appearance at Exeter in the royal army indicates that he was soon forgiven, *Regesta* iii, no. 592, and there is no warrant for Davis's belief that he had rebelled in April against the king, R.H.C. Davis, *King Stephen* (3rd edn., London, 1990), 18n. See comments in A. Wareham, 'The motives and politics of the Bigod family, *c.*1066–1177', *ANS* xvii, ed. M. Chibnall (Woodbridge, 1994), 23.

7 OV vi, 462 is alone in directly mentioning Stephen's plan to cross to Normandy, but it is implied also by an otherwise inexplicable error by RH, 150. The celebration at Clarendon is also implied by Orderic's assertion that Stephen returned to Salisbury after his failed crossing. Clarendon is the great royal palace which overlooked the city, and *Regesta* iii, no. 32 given at Clarendon, can be dated to 1136 (as it benefits a relation of Payn fitz John, it is most likely to belong to Stephen's first year).

8 D. Crouch, *The Beaumont Twins: The Roots and Branches of Power in the Twelfth Century* (Cambridge, 1986), 31. Waleran is absent from all the Stephen charters dated at Oxford, and Orderic said he was sent over by the king *post Pascha mox*, OV vi, 456.

being taken from our midst, as was reported to us, the affairs of the Church in the realm of England were thrown into confusion. No legal writ was put out from the royal chancery, and the horror of such crimes was attended by no punishment.'[9]

Yet how much horror could logically have been perpetrated in the three weeks between the news of Henry's death reaching England, Stephen's ascent of the throne and the despatch of ambassadors to Italy? Certainly, contemporaries produced little evidence of England's collapse into chaos in December 1135. There are only two firm instances cited in the record. The first was the murder of William Maltravers by the knights of Pontefract, and the second was the *Gesta*'s vague story of Stephen's apprehension of a minor royal officer (whom the author would not or could not name) who was allegedly oppressing a district through which Stephen passed on his march from London to meet his brother at Winchester. The *Gesta* is nonetheless full of the English 'throwing off the reins of justice' on Henry's death and indulging in rebellion, wickedness and violence. But, echoing the version of events given later to the pope, the *Gesta* says 'It was therefore worth their [the Londoners] while to appoint as soon as possible a king, who, with a view to re-establishing peace for the common benefit, would meet the insurgents of the kingdom in arms and would justly administer the enactments of the laws.'[10]

I would myself believe that what afflicted England on Henry's death was insecurity and nervousness, causing castle and town gates to be closed and knights to be called to the banners of their lords, but not widespread violence. Yet Stephen's supporters found it useful nonetheless to promote a view that England had trembled on the edge of chaos until preserved by the prompt action of their man. It is no coincidence that neither of the contemporary writers who are remarkable for the vigour of their opposition to Stephen have anything to say about unrest in England before or immediately after his coronation. Indeed, Henry of Huntingdon says Stephen's succession (however regrettable) was quick and trouble-free '*sine mora, sine labore*' and England became his 'as in the blink of an eye'. He also talks in retrospect of Stephen's first two years as being 'very prosperous'.[11]

But the view which was generally adopted as the official story as early as the spring of 1136, was otherwise, and it is the view which has come down to us. The problem with such official versions of history is that even the people who promote them come to believe them, and Stephen in May 1136 was quite ready to believe that England was simmering with discontent and seems to have been prey to any rumour that came his way. The political demonstrations of Robert of Bampton and Baldwin de Redvers in the West Country

9 RH, 147.
10 *GS*, 2–8. JW iii, 216 says much the same, but points to Wales as the real centre of trouble.
11 HH, 702, 710. William of Malmesbury in *HN*, 17–18 also says nothing of violence at the succession, only that Stephen's predilection for employing both home-bred and foreign mercenaries encouraged oppression. He leaps from the events of April 1136 to those of March 1137 with no comment on the intervening year.

that broke out soon after his decision to defer his voyage to Normandy were the more serious in his eyes as a consequence, and not to be shirked.[12] So he diverted much of his time into destroying two dissidents with little broad support amongst their contemporaries, even Robert of Bampton, who at least had genuine cause to complain. Robert's unsupported rebellion collapsed rapidly when the royal household, led by the king, arrived to blockade Bampton, and he took himself off to exile in Scotland at the court of his long-time friend, King David. Indeed, it may be that King Stephen had decided to deprive him of Uffculme precisely because Robert had been a supporter of the king of Scotland in December 1135.[13]

WALES AND THE MARCH

But the real tidal wave was already rising above the ripples that were distracting Stephen, and it was coming from the direction of the March of Wales. On 15 April 1136, returning by stages from Oxford to his domain in west Wales, the baron, Richard fitz Gilbert de Clare, also known as Richard 'of Ceredigion', was waylaid by the military household of the south Welsh king, Morgan ab Owain, and murdered in the deep and forested pass of the Grwyne Fawr between Abergavenny and Talgarth.[14] The act itself was perhaps no more than an opportunistic strike at an exposed and hated opponent, but the results could not have been more catastrophic for the March had it been calculated. It is from this event that the Welsh chronicles date the collapse of English power in Wales.[15]

Under the shrewd manipulation by King Henry of the native dynasties, the English had come to disregard any danger represented by the Welsh. Memories were by now long gone of the time when Gruffudd ap Llywelyn had dominated Wales as high king in the 1050s and forced the Confessor and his earls to take a hand in Welsh affairs or resign the borderland to him. Norman barons had built upon the success of Earl Harold of Wessex in breaking Welsh

12 J.A. Green, 'Family matters: family and the formation of the empress's party in south-west England', in *Family Trees and the Roots of Politics: The Prosopography of Britain and France from the Tenth to the Twelfth Century*, ed. K.S.B. Keats-Rohan (Woodbridge, 1997), 158, regards Robert of Bampton and Baldwin de Redvers as allies, but *GS*, 28–30 (which she cites) does not support any assumption that the two barons were working together.

13 As has been said above, Robert of Bampton suffered for the sake of the need to reward the king's brother, Bishop Henry. There is, however, the point to be made that Robert can be identified as an English supporter of King David of Scotland, being a member of his entourage in the 1120s, see G.W.S. Barrow, *The Anglo-Norman Era in Scottish History* (Oxford, 1980), 100. This being the case, it may be that the king singled him out for unfavourable treatment early in 1136 as a prominent member of the hostile affinity of King David; one possible interpretation of the very hostile account of Robert's activities after King Henry's death in *GS*, 28 might be an attempt by Robert to support David from a distance.

14 *GS*, 16–18; Gerald of Wales, *Itinerarium Kambriae*, in *Opera* vi, ed. J.F. Dimock (RS, 1868), 47–8, gives the traditional site of the murder as still remembered in the 1180s. Richard's body was recovered and buried in Gloucester abbey.

15 For most of what follows, see D. Crouch, 'The March and the Welsh kings', in *The Anarchy of Stephen's Reign*, ed. E. King (Oxford, 1994), 255–89.

power, and by 1100 had whittled away at two of the great kingdoms of Wales, Gwlad Morgan and Deheubarth, until their hereditary rulers were little more than upland fugitives. Then Henry had added his own distinctive genius to Welsh affairs (to which he gave a remarkable amount of attention). From 1106 onwards, he populated the March with his loyal curial magnates (including Bishop Roger in Cydweli) and even when at a distance, managed and monitored the Welsh through his justiciar at Shrewsbury, Bishop Richard de Beaumeis of London. It was Henry's particular luck that during his reign, the most powerful Welsh kingdom, Powys, turned in on itself in a merciless and bloody dynastic war. Another, the kingdom of Gwynedd in northwest Wales, was preoccupied for the first half of his reign, as its king, Gruffudd ap Cynan, endeavoured to establish firmly his own parvenu dynasty. Everywhere, the keeps of new Anglo-Norman castles, some even in masonry, arose like headstones on the graves of native lordships.[16]

King Henry's success was more momentary than it appeared from England, however. By the 1130s, Powys had done all that it could to itself, and a new king, Maredudd ap Bleddyn, was putting the pieces of the kingdom back together again. More significantly, the sons of Gruffudd ap Cynan (who, although aged and blind, had outlived his enemies) were beginning to exert military pressure on their neighbours, including the lands of the earl of Chester to the east. Less visibly, but more critically, the Welsh magnates had by now mastered those elements of Anglo-Norman culture that most interested them – the military ones. By 1130, Welsh noblemen had had several decades to observe at close quarters how the Anglo-Norman armies fought in the field and in siege: a number of them had accompanied King Henry's court around England and France. Castles and keeps were being built routinely by Welsh lords and kings in south and north Wales. But the Welsh political system was itself formidable if turned against outsiders. Welsh royal power depended on no ideology, only the coercive force represented by the military household (*teulu*). The households were made up of mercenary troops and encouraged an élite ethos, they seem generally to have travelled and fought on horseback, and (for the right king) they were quite as formidable as any force of English household knights, even if not as heavily armed. They were a permanent part of the royal household, always available to fight.

It was partly because of this military danger that King Henry was concerned to keep the Welsh butchering each other. But his system was already breaking down even before his death. As Henry lay dying in Normandy, the Welsh magnates in the Tawe and Tywi valleys had combined against his Marcher lords. Here, where the lands of the earl of Gloucester in Glamorgan met the lands of the earl of Warwick in Gower, and where Miles of Gloucester attempted to exert a vague overlordship from Brecon, was an area difficult to

16 For studies of Henry I in Wales, I.W. Rowlands, 'The making of the March: aspects of the Norman settlement in Dyfed', *ANS* iii, ed. R.A. Brown (Woodbridge, 1980), 142–57; R.R. Davies, 'Henry I and Wales', in *Studies in Medieval History presented to R.H.C. Davis*, ed. H. Mayr-Harting and R.I. Moore (London, 1985), 132–47.

control. The Welsh here had some sympathy and contact with neighbouring Welsh dynasties still struggling to maintain their kingly status. To the west was Gruffudd ap Rhys, who claimed the kingship of Deheubarth (although most of the kingdom was under English lordship); and to the east was Morgan ab Owain, head of the family which claimed the kingship in Gwlad Morgan.

On 1 January 1136, as Stephen was progressing from his Christmas court at Westminster towards Reading for his uncle's funeral, the Welsh of eastern Glamorgan decisively defeated an English force which had ventured into northern Gower, and killed hundreds, much to the shock of the Marcher community. Writing over a decade later, the *Gesta* took this defeat in Gower as the start of the great Welsh rising, and traced its beginnings to the great boost given to Welsh morale by news of the dreaded Henry's death.[17] But in fact this promising campaign rapidly petered out when the Welsh attempted to repeat their success in neigbouring Cydweli, and were defeated in turn by a Marcher force. The Welsh chronicles themselves make no mention of this campaign, which apparently so unnerved the Marcher community. For Welsh writers, the key event was to be the death of Richard fitz Gilbert of Ceredigion over four months later.

The fact is that – for all the ominous signs it was throwing out – Wales provided no exception to the unbroken success of Stephen's first months as king. Wales did not rise against him as soon as his uncle's death was known; on the other hand, Wales was to give him the first great test of his ability to rule, had he but realised it. While Stephen and his magnates were encamped around Exeter from June to August 1136, intent on flushing out Baldwin de Redvers (whose ostentatious defiance really had gone too far) the situation in the Welsh March first got out of hand, and by the end of summer had become irreversible without a huge commitment of cash and manpower.

King Henry had personally intervened twice in Welsh affairs, the second time in 1121 to chastise an attack by the Welsh of Gwynedd on the borders of the earldom of Chester, then in royal wardship. Henry's intervention was decisive, and the Welsh refrained from offending him thereafter. The death of a prominent Marcher lord would have certainly brought Henry himself in force, but it did not bring Stephen. Stephen was not unaware that a response was necessary, and cannot be convicted of failing to provide one, but it proved inadequate because he did not come himself. He despatched two lieutenants to the March; the first was Richard fitz Gilbert's younger brother, Baldwin. Baldwin had established himself at King Stephen's court in the first month of the reign, and his reward was the grant of his dead brother's Welsh lordship of Ceredigion. With substantial support in money and mercenaries, he entered Wales, but got no further than Brecon, where he encamped and stayed, apparently daunted and disconcerted by the size of the task he had taken on. For in the month after his brother's death, the Welsh lords of Gwynedd, Deheubarth and Maelienydd had united and overrun much of west Wales, except for

---

17 *GS*, 14–16.

isolated garrisons and coastal Pembrokeshire. But what must have discouraged Baldwin from moving beyond Brecon was the fact that the Welsh of southeast Wales had also united and under the leadership of Morgan ab Owain (the architect of his brother's murder) had seized control of the strategic Usk and Tawe valleys, which made any campaign deep into Wales dependent on one narrow corridor, through Herefordshire and the upper Wye valley into Brycheiniog. Little wonder that Baldwin thought twice about moving unsupported into the mountains beyond his base, and stayed there till his money ran out.

Stephen's first response was followed by another, a smaller force under the minor Marcher lord, Robert fitz Harold of Ewyas, who showed more daring than Baldwin and managed to do some useful local work in garrisoning the royal castle of Carmarthen and maintaining himself for a while in support of the Anglo-Flemish settlers of Pembrokeshire and Cemaes. But he also proved how accurate had been Baldwin fitz Gilbert's strategic assessment of the situation: he found himself unsupported and isolated, and although he fought his way back to the border with a small escort, was unable to raise more funds and troops and to return.[18] All this time the major Marcher barons were notable by their (apparent) absence. King Henry's principal military agents in dealing with the Welsh had been his son, Robert of Gloucester, and the sheriffs, Payn fitz John (sheriff of Shropshire and Herefordshire) and Miles of Gloucester. These great men may or may not have been in their border lordships at some time during the critical summer of 1136, but the only evidence for their activities that we actually have is their presence at the great siege of Exeter.[19]

While it would go beyond the evidence to say that King Stephen had deliberately detained the three leading Marcher lords at Exeter for the duration of the siege, it does not go beyond it to say that he had deliberately *not* used them to lead the counter-thrust against the Welsh. We can only speculate why this was. Did he expect Exeter to fall quickly, and to lead an army promptly into the March in person, and so kept them with him? Did he distrust these great men of the last reign who had (as the *Gesta* puts it) 'raised their power to such a pitch that from the Severn to the sea, all along the border between England and Wales, they involved everyone in litigation and oppressed them with forced services'?[20] Or did he simply misread the situation? The last explanation is the least likely, because those actions he did take showed an awareness of a need for a quick response and a heavy commitment of resources in the March.

By the end of the siege of Exeter, as Stephen single-mindedly pursued Baldwin de Revers across southern England to the Isle of Wight, cornered him at Southampton, and celebrated the fact by exiling him from England, the real fight had been lost in Wales. Stephen did not then turn west to the

---

18 For the reconstruction of his mission, see Crouch, 'The March and the Welsh kings', 262 and n.
19 *Regesta* iii, nos. 337, 592, 952, locate the three at Exeter during part at least of the siege.
20 *GS*, 24.

March. So far as can be told, he spent what was left of 1136 touring England, moving to the palace at Dunstable in Bedfordshire for his second Christmas court. Stephen's apparent failure to comprehend the significance of the situation in Wales is the first symptom of his inadequacies, and not his alone. His two principal advisers from before Easter were with him at Exeter, and Bishop Henry is recorded as the one most hotly in favour of prosecuting the siege to the bitter end.[21] R.H.C. Davis, in his study of Stephen's first years, pinpointed Exeter as Stephen's mistake; he considered it such because the king had listened to those of his army who wanted the garrison released on easy terms. Stephen had proved himself soft.[22] But for me the mistake was a very different one. The barons who came to the king and argued that 'it was more to the advantage of his kingdom to have done with that wearisome siege by which they were so much distressed, that he might . . . gird himself more readily and more eagerly to perform other tasks,'[23] were those of his advisers who were talking sense, and may well have had other motives than covert sympathy for the besieged. They might have sensed the sudden alarming drift in the direction of the king's strategy, and the lack of that informed and confident world-view so characteristic of his late uncle. Stephen should have gone to Normandy, but he had instead become obsessed with a protracted siege at the edge of his kingdom. He should have gone to Wales, but he had instead sent two agents inadequate to the task.

The consequences for Stephen were very serious. In October 1136, as Stephen was startling his English barons with a comprehensive forest eyre, the battle of Cardigan destroyed the last Marcher field army in west Wales, and much of Deheubarth was reclaimed by its royal dynasty. The episcopal community of St David's (whose Norman bishop had stayed with the king through the siege of Exeter) submitted to King Gruffudd ap Rhys as their new advocate. Gwynedd was established as the leading Welsh power by its successful invasions of Ceredigion and Powys and by the defeat of Earl Ranulf of Chester's attempted intervention in the north. It would be a century and a half before English power reclaimed the position Stephen had so nonchalantly resigned. He was indeed nonchalant. There is some evidence for a deliberation in Stephen's council about what to do with the Welsh situation late in 1136. The *Gesta* talks of the king coming to a point where he decided that he could not afford

---

21 We might note the parallel obsession of the author of the *Gesta*, a sympathiser of Bishop Henry, with the siege of Exeter and its aftermath (it makes up seven *capitula* of his text, as opposed to three for the Welsh wars).

22 Davis, *Stephen*, 24. This particular argument of Davis is criticised by J. Bradbury, 'The early years of the reign of Stephen', in *England in the Twelfth Century*, ed. D. Williams (Woodbridge, 1990), 27–8, on the grounds that clemency was the better policy at Exeter. Whether or not this view is valid, there is no justification for either Davis or Bradbury to treat as fact their assumption (with no warrant from the text of the *Gesta*) that Robert of Gloucester was one of 'those at whose instigation Baldwin had taken up arms against the king, and who were then serving in the king's army with treacherous designs' (*GS*, 40), which is itself no more than an untestable assumption by the *Gesta*. This makes Bradbury's argument (p. 29) that Stephen 'not only consulted' Robert at Exeter 'but followed his advice', circular and unsustainable.

23 *GS*, 42.

the resources in money and men to reclaim the Welsh situation, and took advice to do nothing, counting on the Welsh to fall out amongst themselves, as the Powisians had done in the last reign. John of Hexham may locate this decision for us in time when he records at the end of 1136 that 'the Welsh, laying waste the border areas of England killed two barons . . . but then speedily made peace with King Stephen'.[24] This would seem to refer in part to the actions of Earl Robert of Gloucester, who we know went down into south Wales and – before the end of 1136 – concluded a series of peace treaties with the Welsh magnates on his borders, surrendering large areas of land in return for their adherence and (in the case of King Morgan ab Owain) formal homage. It was his only real option without effective royal support.[25]

Earl Robert would seem to have taken Stephen's decision to cut his losses as a *sauve qui peut*. So also might Miles of Gloucester, who put himself at the head of a raiding column and rode down from Brecon to Cardigan at the end of the year, relieving the garrison at great risk and his own expense, and carrying off Richard fitz Gilbert's trapped wife to safety. Payn fitz John's apparent attempt to relieve the garrison at Carmarthen in July 1137 had a less happy result, and he died in an anonymous skirmish as a result of a javelin blow to the head. Earl Robert, Miles and their fellow Marchers knew they were now on their own. They cannot have acquitted Stephen in their minds of indifference (either lackadaisical or deliberate) to the situation of themselves and their men. The Marcher community (like border communities in general) was self-reliant and antagonistic to the centre of power. Stephen had given it a grievance around which to unite, yet at the same time failed to neutralise it as an internal threat. He was to learn the full extent of his failure on the field of Lincoln less than five years later.

NORMANDY

By the end of 1136, the Norman magnates may well have had similar feelings about their new king to those of the Welsh Marcher lords. It may be denied that England was on the edge of civil unrest in the first year of Stephen's reign, but there is no doubt that Normandy was falling to pieces. Again and again, Orderic Vitalis bewails the fact that the duchy was without a ruler in 1136, and it is he (not an English chronicler) who sadly notes Stephen's postponed crossing to Normandy in May. The Normans' idea of themselves was that they were a turbulent and martial people, difficult to bring to heel.[26] They were doing their best to prove it that year.

---

24 *GS*, 20; JH, 287.
25 Events reconstructed in D. Crouch, 'The slow death of kingship in Glamorgan, 1067–1158', *Morgannwg*, 29 (1985), 32–4.
26 OV vi, 454, 456 '. . . the Normans, who are innately warlike and bold', 'if the Norman people . . . be united under a good prince they would be as invincible as were the Chaldaeans under Nebuchadnezzar'. See on this, R.H.C. Davis, *The Normans and their Myth* (London, 1976), 31–2; G.A. Loud, 'The *Gens Normannorum*: myth or reality?', *Proceedings of the Battle Conference, 1981*, ed. R.A. Brown (Woodbridge, 1982), 104–16, esp. 111–12.

59

What should have brought Stephen to Normandy in the spring of 1136, not the spring of 1137, was the danger represented by the Angevins. The military danger was not the principal problem; although that was bad enough. The main danger was that the southern March of Normandy was a place where a viable rival had been allowed to establish herself; so she became a focus and rallying point for any and every dissident, playing the same part as her first cousin, the Clito, had done in the previous reign. We have a first-hand witness to the consequences of this in the *Ecclesiastical History* of Orderic Vitalis, senior monk of St-Evroult, a wealthy Benedictine abbey right in the heart of the unstable border region, not a day's travel from the nearest Angevin garrison. In theologically coloured language, he bewailed the way that Normandy was troubled by her inhabitants, like a woman in labour with her children; he saw them as devouring each other with their own teeth. His own abbey and its bourg came under attack on 11 May 1136 from the neighbouring lord of L'Aigle, when the townspeople of St-Evroult defended themselves vigorously against his mercenaries, who were collecting exactions to provision his bourg and fortress.[27]

Richer (II), the lord of L'Aigle, was not entirely to be blamed for his actions, however. He was in the middle of a region disintegrating politically and had to take what measures he could for his defence. It was not merely that the empress and her supporters had established themselves a day's march away to the south and west of L'Aigle. They had in fact done very little since arriving from Maine in December 1135 and securing the border screen of castles; Count Geoffrey was not to return to Normandy until September 1136. But all over Normandy, private rivalries and grudges were precipitating the breakdown of the civil order so relentlessly imposed on the duchy by King Henry. Although this was most severe in the area where the Angevin presence complicated matters, more distant areas became unstable.

After the failure of the scheme to promote Theobald of Blois as duke, the chamberlain of Normandy, Rabel de Tancarville, fortified his powerful castles on the right bank of the Seine below Rouen, seized the neighbouring ducal stronghold of Lillebonne, and refused to recognise Stephen, for whatever reason. Even more catastrophic were the unrestrained ambitions of Roger de Tosny and William de Pacy in the lower reaches of the Iton and Eure valleys, again, well away from the Angevin incursions. Like Rabel, Roger de Tosny seized a ducal castle (Vaudreuil) at the beginning of May 1136 but widened the local conflict by allying with his neighbour, William, lord of Pacy-sur-Eure, in a private war against the lord of Breteuil, Robert of Leicester. William de Pacy was reviving the claims of his father (who had died in February 1136) to the great border lordship of Breteuil, of which his father had been deprived

---

27 OV vi, 460–2. For Richer see now the study by K. Thompson, 'The Lords of L'Aigle: ambition and insecurity on the borders of Normandy', *ANS*, xviii (1995), 177–99, esp. 186–91. Dr Thompson notes the undoubted antagonism between Richer and his neighbour Robert of Leicester in 1140, but it cannot be automatically assumed they were at loggerheads earlier, in the period 1136–38.

by King Henry in 1119. Roger's motives were less simple. He and Count William Talvas had both been under suspicion of Angevin sympathies in the months before King Henry died, and Roger's principal castle of Conches had been seized by royal troops. This had kept him quiet for a while, but with the old king gone he was free to express his sympathies in any way he could.[28]

Into this increasingly chaotic situation came Count Waleran of Meulan, twin brother of Robert of Leicester, in the last days of March 1136, direct from King Stephen's Easter court. He must have brought some very convincing authority from the king, for we find that by the end of April he had levied a significant military force from the city of Rouen, sufficient to march to the ducal fortress of Vaudreuil and retake it from the garrison put there by Roger de Tosny only three days before. For his brother's sake, no doubt, he concentrated his power against Roger, and on 11 May 1136 he mounted a punitive expedition against the Tosny castle of Acquigny, which was completely destroyed. But the coup was not conclusive and Roger immediately took the war into Waleran's own lands.[29]

Waleran had arrived in Normandy as Robert of Ewyas had arrived in Wales, bearing King Stephen's authority to do what he could to master a difficult situation. The fragmentary sources allow us an instructive glimpse of Waleran in action, showing that Stephen had at least selected a promising lieutenant, even if he had not himself come to Normandy. When the fight began against Roger de Tosny, there was one week left of a truce that Count Theobald of Blois, Stephen's brother, had made with Geoffrey of Anjou the previous Christmas. Waleran's priority was to bring Count Theobald back into Norman affairs. His brother Robert negotiated Theobald's assistance in prosecuting the war against Roger de Tosny, and in mid-June 1136 a considerable force from Blois arrived in the duchy, set about wasting the Tosny lands and settled into a long seige of the Tosny castle of Pont-St-Pierre, across the Seine from Vaudreuil, which eventually fell to Theobald and was handed over to Robert of Leicester.[30] While Count Theobald was holding down the Seine and Eure valleys, Count Waleran (for no-one else seems capable of having done it) mobilised such of the Norman magnates as would go on the offensive against the Angevins and their supporters, and was also able to bring into the fight from outside the duchy Count Alan of Brittany and his forces. Richer de L'Aigle attacked both Roger de Tosny in one direction and Gacé (a castle under ducal control which seems to have been taken by Mathilda) in the other, and Gilbert fitz Gilbert, lord of Orbec (brother of Stephen's great supporter, Baldwin) led a determined assault against nearby Exmes.

The assault on Exmes was no great success, for Count William Talvas was quick to bring support. But the attacks show some sort of direction and

28 OV vi, 444–6, 456–62. For the competing claims to Breteuil, Crouch, *Beaumont Twins*, 108–12.
29 OV vi, 456–8.
30 Although Orderic believed that Theobald's siege of Pont-St-Pierre failed, OV vi, 464, Robert de Torigny recorded the success of the siege, RT, 131, and charter evidence proves that Robert of Leicester obtained it before 1140, Crouch, *Beaumont Twins*, 32 and n.

aggression emerging amongst the Norman supporters of Stephen. Count Geoffrey of Anjou must have thought so too, for on 21 September 1136, he reappeared in Normandy in great force with several distinguished supporters from amongst the greater French nobility. His intention is clear from Orderic's account of the expedition. He intended to move north, taking strategic castles on the way, and to seize the city of Lisieux, so hemming in his opponents towards Rouen. But for various reasons, what was expected to be his decisive expedition collapsed. Hardly any Normans supported it, and some of the Norman-held castles in the Hièmois on his planned route proved stubborn. After a week, the disconcerted Angevin army reached Lisieux, to be faced by the main Norman field army under Count Waleran, which encamped beyond the city, feeling itself unable to prevent the siege. But when the Breton garrison deliberately set fire to the city outside the castle, the Angevin army suddenly lost confidence and withdrew abruptly to Le Sap back down the valley of the Touques, where it encamped and amused itself in besieging a small castle. But even here the garrison put up an exemplary resistance, and on 1 October Count Geoffrey was seriously wounded in the leg as he led his army's attempts to storm the castle.

The Angevin army withdrew rapidly to the frontier, despite the arrival of the empress with reinforcements. If you believe the somewhat partisan Orderic, it collapsed into a shambles, the troops afflicted with severe dysentery, and fled the next day for the border in a way the Normans found wonderful to behold, even losing Count Geoffrey's personal baggage.[31] To cap it all, on 3 October, Roger de Tosny and his own French mercenaries were overwhelmed by Count Waleran, fresh from the defence of Lisieux. Roger and his allies were imprisoned to general satisfaction. Normandy spent the winter of 1136–37 in relative peace (although Rabel de Tancarville remained unreconciled), and Waleran of Meulan established himself as its master in default of the king, lesser magnates flocking to join his court.

One can see Henry of Huntingdon's point about Stephen's lucky first two years. For when he finally crossed to Normandy in late March 1137 he found a duchy still mostly loyal to him, with a degree of peace re-established, and the Angevin threat dormant: Mathilda was now confined only (it seems) to her base at Argentan. Despite the lateness of his coming, Stephen's situation in the duchy was nonetheless still relatively sound, largely through the successful efforts of his lieutenants and the failure of Geoffrey and Mathilda to establish themselves with the Norman magnates as real alternatives as rulers. Historians are very much undecided as to the success or not of Stephen's long stay in the duchy in 1137, and indeed it is difficult to assess. With hindsight, of course,

31 J. Bradbury, *Stephen and Matilda* (Stroud, 1996), 39–40 rightly points out the gleeful bias in Orderic's account, but Bradbury's verdict that the campaign had 'generally been a success for Geoffrey' is difficult to sustain in view of his failure to achieve any significant Norman support, even in a duchy Orderic describes as leaderless. M. Chibnall, *The Empress Matilda* (Oxford, 1991), 72–3, points also to the evidence from Orderic that the campaign created a long-term alienation of most Normans from the Angevin cause.

we know that Stephen was to lose Normandy in a few years, so we tend to look to 1137 for the causes of failure. Contemporaries do not help much, for the two principal Norman writers (Orderic and Robert de Torigny) were not enthusiastic about the campaign, and William of Malmesbury, for his own reasons, ridicules Stephen's efforts. On the other hand, Henry of Huntingdon – although decidedly not a royalist – still talked of Stephen's stay in Normandy in glowing terms. My own feeling is that Stephen and his advisers were successful in the targets they set themselves in the duchy, and that Stephen did not compromise the modest achievements of the previous year; nor did he make Geoffrey and Mathilda seem any more attractive as alternatives. The true measure of the campaign, however, is in what Stephen should have done, but did not do, and by considering those things we get a more three-dimensional image of his success or failure.

Stephen's brother, Bishop Henry of Winchester, crossed to the duchy in December 1136, well in advance of the king. Orderic believed that he was stationing himself in a place more accessible to the papal Curia in northern Italy, so that he could negotiate the confirmation of his election to Canterbury (Archbishop William had died on 21 November).[32] But it would also have signalled the beginning of a characteristic diplomatic offensive in his brother's interests. Bishop Henry's targets were the courts of King Louis VI, Theobald of Blois, his elder brother, and the lesser counts of the frontier. In the case of King Louis and Count Theobald, contact had been established at the beginning of the year, for both of those great men had been persuaded to write to Pope Innocent in support of Stephen's claims to England early in 1136. Theobald had (with monetary inducements) been active in the field on Stephen's behalf for the better part of a year. Now meetings were to be arranged to seal the respective alliances. Bishop Henry seems to have spent time during the winter touring the duchy and, by Orderic's account, was mobbed by petitioners, complaining about the state of affairs since the old king's death.

So Stephen's arrival in Normandy, at the beginning of the third week (14–20) of March 1137, was well prepared. He made the longer crossing (probably from Portsmouth) and landed at St-Vaast-la-Hougue, on the Cotentin peninsula of Lower Normandy.[33] Stephen may have deliberately chosen to land in the west of the duchy: it was the area of Normandy traditionally less tied to ducal control from Rouen, and it does not seem that Waleran of Meulan had made any attempt to extend his activities even as far west as Caen. It was more important that Stephen show himself there first than at Rouen. But the king nevertheless headed rapidly east, and had clearly decided that he must deal with the leading Norman dissident, the chamberlain of Tancarville, at

---

32 OV vi, 478.
33 OV vi, 480. Unfortunately, Orderic's account of the 1137 expedition after the landing is inaccurate (he put down his pen in the winter of 1136, and did not resume his narrative until after a significant break, OV vi, p. xviii) and the sequence of events given by Robert de Torigny is now preferred by historians as more demonstrably accurate, RT, 132–3. See for this, R. Helmerichs, 'King Stephen's Norman itinerary, 1137', *HSJ*, 5 (1995), 89–97, who radically revises the itinerary favoured in *Regesta* iii, p. xl (which was reliant on Orderic).

once. He marched through Bayeux (by which time he had been joined by both Waleran of Meulan and Robert of Gloucester)[34] and came upon the western Tancarville outpost of Mézidon (halfway between Caen and Lisieux). It must have fallen without much of a fight, for Stephen's army passed on rapidly to the Seine estuary, crossed the great river, recovered Lillebonne and circled around to seize the lesser inland Tancarville castle of Villers, leaving Rabel with only his ancestral fortress (with its great square keep overlooking the lower Seine valley) to defend. Prudently, Rabel made his quick submission to the king and was received at court. Stephen was rapidly justifying his reputation for military skill, and now opened the way for his brother to stage-manage the diplomatic coup which would assure him of the duchy.

The focus of operations now switched to Evreux, for several good reasons. The ancient city and its great ducal castle lay in the centre of the area devastated the previous year by the warfare between the Beaumonts, the Tosny and William de Pacy. It was close to the frontier towards Blois-Chartres and France[35], and a day's journey from the remaining Angevin outposts within the Norman borders. Moreover, it had a cathedral and ducal hall suitable for the holding of Stephen's second Easter court and the proper reception of visitors. There could be no better place in 1137 for Stephen to assert and parade the image of his kingship before the Norman aristocracy, and he had brought Queen Mathilda and his young son, Eustace, with him in order to stress the point that he was not just in Normandy as a war-leader. There were also two minor but practical considerations. The small castle of Grossoeuvre, 9 km south of Evreux, still held out as a lonely rebel centre, and needed to be suppressed in a symbolic show siege. The second was that Amaury de Montfort, the count of Evreux and friend of Geoffrey of Anjou, was dying, with two small sons as heirs; his strategic county, which spread north and east of the city, had to be secured promptly.

Stephen was established at Evreux before 24 March 1137.[36] It was here that he formally received his elder brother, Count Theobald, and undertook to pay him an annual fee of 2,000 marks (1,333*li*.13*s*.4*d*) 'because', as Robert de Torigny claims, 'he was annoyed that Stephen, who was younger than him, had assumed the crown which belonged to him, as he said'. This was a common belief at the time, for Orderic also repeats it.[37] In fact, whatever grudge Count Theobald harboured could not have lasted long, because he had caused letters to be written in support of his brother's coronation early in

---

34 *Regesta* iii, no. 594

35 By 'France' I mean what contemporaries called *Francia*: the area ruled directly by the king of France.

36 *Regesta* iii, nos. 69, 843 are charters of the king and queen dated at Evreux in the year of the Incarnation 1136. Years of the Incarnation ought to be reckoned either from Christmas or from the feast of the Annunciation (25 March) and the latter is only possible here. The possibility that the year reckoned from Easter is intended, as in Helmerichs, 'Norman itinerary', 95, is unlikely; it was apparently a form of reckoning introduced into Normandy by Philip Augustus, see *Handbook of Dates for Students of English History*, ed. C.R. Cheney (RHS Guides and Handbooks, no. 4, 1978), 4–6.

37 RT, 132; OV vi, 454.

1136, and had allied with the Beaumonts against Stephen's internal enemies in Normandy in the summer. Stephen's generosity to his brother may have been formalised as a treaty. Stephen was very urgent that his brother should assist his cause. We know that in the 1140s Theobald was in possession of 'two gold basins of huge weight and marvellous workmanship, in which were set most precious gems, which King Henry of England, his uncle, used to have placed on the table before him at his crown-wearings (*in solemnitate coronae suae*) to show off his wealth and glory'.[38] These were suitably royal gifts which Stephen had (no doubt) made to assist a reconciliation. There is also evidence that he further rewarded Theobald with estates in England at this time.[39]

There was a lot at stake in the meeting of brothers, for upon it depended a new political order in northern France. Following it – and following the surrender of Grossoeuvre, according to Torigny – there was a meeting on the Norman frontier with the ailing King Louis VI. The kings greeted each other warmly, and by prior arrangement, the young Eustace did homage for the duchy of Normandy on behalf of his father. The needs of King Stephen and King Louis happily coincided. Louis must have dreaded the possibility of a great condominium under Theobald of Blois, incorporating England, Normandy, Blois-Chartres, Champagne and several satellite statelets. Now that was not to be, and the favourable situation of the last years of King Henry survived, with the additional benefit of an irreversible alienation between Normandy and Anjou. For this reason, Louis VI was happy to welcome Count Theobald into his inner circle of advisers in 1137 and offer him the prestige of the revived title of 'count palatine'. Louis could look upon Theobald and Stephen together as twin anchors of his southern frontier against Anjou and counterweights against the power of the counts of Flanders and Vermandois in the north.[40]

The similarity of Stephen's first months in England to his first months in Normandy is striking. Once again we see a meticulously organised military and diplomatic campaign, producing an economical and triumphant assertion of rulership. Significant new adherents were received at court. One such notable was Robert du Neubourg, a first cousin and long-term opponent of Waleran. He was the son of King Henry's warmest friend, Earl Henry of Warwick, and through his mother's sister he also had another first cousin and mediator in the royalist camp, Richer de L'Aigle. Robert demonstrates the complexity of personal relationships in cross-border Norman politics, for he was a friend of Geoffrey of Anjou through their mutual ally, Count Amaury of Evreux. In September 1136, Robert had supported Geoffrey and surrendered his border castle of Annebecq, directly south of Falaise, to the Angevins. Count Amaury's

---

38 Ernald, abbot of Bonneval, *Vita sancti Bernardi: Liber Secundus*, in *PL*, 185, cols. 301–2. As Abbot Ernald was both a subject and contemporary of Count Theobald, the source is a good one.
39 *Regesta* iii, no. 274 reveals that £100 of the rents payable to Theobald were drawn from the boroughs of Newport and Maldon in Essex, and the payment thence was stopped by the empress when she occupied London in 1141.
40 M. Bur, *Suger: Abbé de St-Denis, Régent de France* (Paris, 1991), 160–1.

terminal illness, and Count Geoffrey's failure seem to have persuaded him to cross into Stephen's camp before Easter 1137, doubtless with the welcome assistance of his cousins Waleran and Richer. Other significant border lords appeared at Stephen's court: William Gouet and Count Rotrou III of Mortagne, the leading magnates of the Perche and both great allies of Count Theobald, were with the king at Evreux, as well as Richer de L'Aigle, Count Rotrou's nephew.[41] Stephen reached a treaty with Rotrou, granting him the ducal fortress of Moulins-la-Marche, with the intention of strengthening Rotrou against his great rival, Count William Talvas, the Angevins' ally, with whom he disputed the lordship of Bellême. The twin fortress of Bonsmoulins was confided to the loyalist Richer, thus extending his power up the Iton valley and giving him a forward base on the frontier towards Maine.[42] In the general euphoria of what must have seemed a continental rerun of the triumph of Easter 1136, Stephen magnanimously released Roger de Tosny from the prison in which Count Waleran had put him.

As King Stephen concluded the festivities at Evreux and moved away north, affairs must have seemed promising. His next move was clear: he had to mount a conclusive campaign against the empress and the Angevins. This was recognised by everybody, and we can see some of the preparations which were made. Few Norman magnates, and none of any weight other than William Talvas, now supported the empress. Her supporters were isolated and confined to a few of the lesser barons – like the brothers Engelger and Alexander de Bohon from the Cotentin – who had joined her force at Argentan. Stephen at this point expanded his mercenary squadrons by recruiting a sizeable Flemish force, which had arrived by Easter in Normandy under the command of William, late count of Ypres, in alliance with whom Stephen had campaigned in Flanders in 1127.

Stephen was poised for the final campaign against his dynastic rival, but for some reason the stroke did not fall on her head. All the sources talk of dissension breaking out in the royal camp. At the root of it (as William of Malmesbury, Robert de Torigny, John of Marmoutier and Orderic all agree) was the arrival of such a large force of Flemish knights in the king's camp, and the king's apparent intention to rely on it rather than on his subjects.[43] The

41 *Regesta* iii, no. 69; OV vi, 484. For William Gouet (III) or (IV) and his family's dependency on Blois-Chartres, see K. Thompson, 'The formation of the county of Perche: the rise and fall of the house of Gouet', in *Family Trees and the Roots of Politics*, ed. K.S.B. Keats-Rohan (Boydell, 1997), 300–14, esp. 305–6, 312–13.
42 For the L'Aigle lands and connections see Thompson, 'The Lords of L'Aigle', 181, 183, 188.
43 RT, 132; OV vi, 484–6; *HN*, 21; *Historia Gaufredi ducis*, 225, describes the quarrel as between William and the Anglo-French baron, Reginald de St-Valery, and talks of internecine slaughter breaking out between the Normans and Flemings. For a discussion of Malmesbury's claim of an assassination bid against Robert of Gloucester, D. Crouch, 'Robert of Gloucester and the daughter of Zelophehad', *Journal of Medieval History*, 11 (1985), 232. The inaccuracy of Malmesbury's account of 1137 is to be seen in his mistaken claim that Robert crossed to Normandy in pursuit of the king at Easter (whereas a royal charter places Robert at Bayeux with the king over a fortnight before Easter). When precisely Stephen began extensive recruitment of Flemings is debatable.

Norman magnates, affronted, suspicious and alarmed, withdrew their support for the campaign. There are tales of internal skirmishes and plots against the Flemings; Hugh de Gournay (a magnate from the Norman Vexin) was named by both Torigny and Orderic as close to the centre of trouble. Orderic has Hugh leading a mass walk-out from the camp without the necessary royal licence to depart. Malmesbury repeats an unlikely story he had heard that William of Ypres plotted (with the king's agreement) to ambush and murder his hero, Robert of Gloucester. Stephen managed to master his recalcitrant army, but had clearly lost confidence in it, and maybe it had lost confidence in him. When in late May or June Geoffrey of Anjou reappeared on the Norman frontier in support of his wife, with an even bigger force than the previous year, Stephen and his advisers decided to negotiate. A truce of three years was ironed out, to commence at midsummer (24 June) 1137 in return for an annual payment of 2,000 marks. The truce was advertised positively in England, where Henry of Huntingdon believed that the count had been overawed by the king's power and military and monetary resources.[44]

Nonetheless, the year concluded less positively than it had begun. True, Stephen had established his claim to the duchy and brought peace even to the border areas of the south. He had created a solid block of support to the east of Count Geoffrey's principality and bought off Geoffrey himself. Stephen may even have considered that he had now neutralised the empress as a threat, and confined her to her dowry of Argentan. He seems to have spent the rest of the year in ducal centres such as Lyons, Caen and Rouen, doing very little other than itinerating as duke, apart from a military demonstration in the Norman Vexin, perhaps as a way of asserting his lordship after King Louis died in August.[45] But in fact he was being as mistakenly overconfident as he had been towards Wales and the March. There is no trace, for instance, that the king personally asserted himself in the Cotentin and Avranchin, where the exiled Baldwin de Redvers and his allies, Reginald, the empress's half brother, and Stephen de Mandeville, were conducting a campaign of banditry against his peace. They were probably based at the castle of Néhou, in the centre of the Cotentin peninsula, where William de Vernon, Baldwin's brother, could offer them shelter. The Bretons also were restless beyond the frontier and there were other brigands on the loose; the Avranchin was much troubled by raiding.[46]

William of Ypres is first associated with the king in Norman sources for spring 1137. William of Malmesbury (*HN*, 17) says that Stephen made use of the royal treasure to recruit Flemish and Breton mercenaries in great numbers, but although he observes this while talking of Stephen's profligacy with money and the Easter court of 1136, he does not specifically say that the recruitment happened then.

44 HH, 710.

45 OV vi, 490.

46 *Historia Gaufredi ducis*, 225 (cf. OV vi, 510–12) describes the ability of Mathilda's supporters to roam at will in lower Normandy, see further on this Chibnall, *Matilda*, 74; Bearman, 'Baldwin de Redvers', 35. See also, OV vi, 490–2.

THE GROWTH OF FACTION, DECEMBER 1137

At last, King Stephen sailed for England, taking back the large household he had brought with him, and bringing in addition Waleran of Meulan, who had done so much to establish his rule, Waleran's twin, Robert of Leicester and their cousin, Robert du Neubourg. The king landed at Portsmouth on or around Advent Sunday (28 November) 1137, to be greeted by Bishop Roger of Salisbury, and he itinerated around the west midlands until settling down for a second Christmas at Dunstable.[47] But although Stephen began the third year of his reign in England in apparent peace and stability, a quiet revolution had occurred in his last few months in his court in Normandy, the effects of which were to poison the rest of the reign.

Since Robert Patterson in 1965, modern historians have increasingly come to view the early years of Stephen as a descent into political infighting that eventually broke out into warfare in the countryside. Patterson's idea was that Robert of Gloucester left the court in Normandy in 1137, not so much in support of his disinherited sister, the empress, but in discontent at the way the Beaumonts and their allies were monopolising royal favour.[48] Other historians, including myself, have adopted this idea, and examined potential opposing factions: most notably clerical ones. As I have already speculated, the decisive influence of Bishop Roger of Salisbury and Bishop Henry of Winchester is clear enough in the consistency we see in the policies of King Stephen until the end of 1137: the reliance on diplomacy and treaty backed up by heavy expenditure on threateningly large mercenary forces is evident in the north and in Wales in 1136, and in Normandy in 1137. There is something of a continuity here with the methods of the late King Henry, but there is also something lacking: neither Stephen nor his episcopal advisers had quite that persistence and strategic vision so characteristic of King Henry. As a result, business was begun, but not always fully concluded.

After 1137 this distinctive policy of Stephen's first years disappears. What subtlety there was evaporates; direction disappears. Stephen's decisions become reflexive; he was at the mercy of circumstances and lost the appearance of being in control of events. My belief is that the sudden decline is because he began to entrust himself to those whose ideas were limited simply to self-aggrandisement. The principal seducer of the king was undoubtedly Count Waleran of Meulan, and it was he who had begun to exert a fascination over Stephen in the Norman months of 1137. Waleran was as noble as it was possible for an aristocrat to be in the mid-twelfth century. Rags of the glamour

---

47 *Regesta* iii, nos. 312, 579, 827; RH, 151; HH, 710. For his Christmas court in 1137, JW iii, 234. HH, 710, says that Stephen began the siege of Bedford on Christmas Eve and it occupied the whole Christmas season, and that 'it seemed to many to have displeased God that he reckoned this solemnity of solemnities as little or nothing', but *GS*, 47 agrees with the Worcester chronicler that Stephen was holding court elsewhere than Bedford, although the surviving manuscript does not say exactly where.

48 R.B. Patterson, 'William of Malmesbury's Robert of Gloucester: a re-evaluation of the *Historia Novella*', *American Historical Review*, 70 (1965), 990–2.

that clung to him in life still hang about his reputation today.[49] He was literate, a noted Latin poet and a trend-setter in current fashions (such as the growing fascination with the colourful symbols of lineage we now call 'heraldry'). He was the centre of an extensive network of family and magnate connections that far exceeded his territorial power, which was itself large enough (he personally controlled central Normandy from the sea nearly south to the March). He had great wealth, rooted in his control of the wine trade down the Seine through his French county of Meulan, his numerous towns and markets, and the agricultural wealth of his demesne estates and fisheries. Then there was his descent. He was the son of that Count Robert of Meulan and Leicester who had fought at Hastings, and who had played a great part in making William Rufus and Henry kings of England, and who in his day was regarded as the wealthiest man in western Europe after the sovereign princes. Through his father, he had a claim to cousinship with the royal family of England. Through his mother, Isabel or Elizabeth of Vermandois, he was first cousin of King Louis VI of France, and a direct descendant of Charlemagne (as his flatterers knew only too well). R.H.C. Davis said (a touch cruelly) 'he was just the sort of friend one would have expected Stephen to make'.[50] Grandeur doubtless spoke to grandeur, but there was also the practical point that Stephen had good cause to be grateful for the younger man's military talents in holding Normandy down in 1136 (Waleran was in his early thirties during the Norman campaigns, Stephen now just past forty).

Waleran had already been singled out at Easter 1136 for betrothal to a child of the king and the wardship of (what I assume to have been intended to be) the eventual marriage-portion in Worcestershire. But he had been engaged for a year away from the court thereafter. It is tempting to suggest that the bishops had suggested the deployment of his talents to keep him at a safe distance from the king, although that suggestion depends rather on hindsight. But his reunion with the king in Normandy did spark further extravagant gestures, which may have something to do with the premature death of the count's child-bride, Mathilda, who seems not to have survived 1137, dying in London, much to her parents' evident grief. Waleran was rewarded (or compensated) with the keeping of the city of Evreux, its castle and viscounty. Count Amaury of Evreux had died on 18/19 April 1137, an event which would have made Waleran master of the Evreçin, for the county entered a long minority which lasted until *c*.1146.[51]

It did not seem to occur to anyone that Waleran should carry on in Normandy after the king's departure. Not only did Waleran cross to England with Stephen, but so did his brothers (Earl Robert and Hugh) and his cousin,

---

49 For what follows, Crouch, *Beaumont Twins*, esp. 207–12.
50 Davis, *Stephen*, 27.
51 Crouch, *Beaumont Twins*, 34 and nn. For the death of Waleran's infant wife, Mathilda, see above, p. 44n. The successive heirs to the county (Amaury II and Simon) seem to have come under the wardship of Amaury de Maintenon, leading baron of the honor of Montfort-en-Yvelines in France, A. Rhein, *La Seigneurie de Montfort-en-Iveline* (Versailles, 1910), 57–8.

Robert du Neubourg. The peace of Normandy was left to several justiciars, of whom the leaders were William de Roumare, a lesser magnate of the Caux and half-brother of Earl Ranulf of Chester, and Roger II, viscount and leading magnate of the Cotentin, lord of the honor of St-Sauveur. It was Roger's unfortunate fate to have to try to do what King Stephen had failed to do, and pacify Lower Normandy. He campaigned in the west throughout the winter, but was ambushed and murdered by Stephen's opponents some time in January 1138, which effectively ended Stephen's influence in Lower Normandy, as by then it was beginning to be recognised that Robert of Gloucester – still in control of the castles of Bayeux and Caen – was contemplating defection.[52]

Stephen should not have left Normandy in November 1137. He had not finished the job he had started to do, and, in leaving, he took with him the only other person who had accumulated sufficient prestige to maintain the king's cause in the duchy. There were doubtless reasons why the king was anxious to get back to England. King David of Scotland had taken advantage of Stephen's absence and massed an army on the borders of Northumberland soon after Easter 1137, but, on the king's instructions, an amy was summoned to Newcastle-upon-Tyne impressive enough to deter the Scots from proceeding, and negotiation by Archbishop Thurstan of York at Roxburgh had achieved a truce to last until December.[53] A more pressing and personal reason might have been the death in England of two of Stephen's infant children, Baldwin and Mathilda, if we knew at precisely what point in the year they had died, but a precise date is lacking and they might have died before he left, for all we know. Then there were the continuing troubles in Wales. Payn fitz John, one of King Henry's most effective agents on the March, was killed in a skirmish in July 1137, and the fortress of Carmarthen had at last fallen to the dynasty of Deheubarth, finally severing the land route into the royal demesne lordship of Pembrokeshire from England. Orderic talks also of troublesome rumours of plots and conspiracies which had seeped across the Channel to the king in Normandy, and since this sort of thing was more or less the norm in Anglo-Norman politics, we can well believe it. But whether England itself was in civil turmoil, as Orderic believed, is another matter; it is more likely that he was referring to the kingdom in its widest sense.[54]

Stephen need not have left Normandy, or at least need not have left it for long; he had agents in England sufficient to deal with the problems there. He should not have left Normandy because the duchy remained (as King Henry had known) the key to the kingdom. As long as Stephen was undisputed lord of both England and Normandy, the Anglo-Norman aristocracy would be obliged to maintain him or face the difficult situation of serving two lords.[55]

---

52 OV vi, 494, 512.
53 RH, 150–1; JH, 288.
54 OV vi, 494.
55 This is the thesis of the cross-Channel baronage expounded first in print by J. Le Patourel, *Normandy and England, 1066–1144* (Reading, 1971) and developed later in his *Norman Empire*, 190ff., and also by C.W. Hollister, 'The Anglo-Norman civil war, 1101', *EHR*, 88 (1973), 315–43. It

Should Stephen lose Normandy the political logic broke down, and it became a persuasive argument for the higher aristocracy that the ruler who replaced him in Normandy ought to replace him in England too. But just as compelling was the argument that the empress should not be allowed to gather dissidents and support in her salient in the southern march of Normandy unopposed. As long as Stephen was in the duchy, the war of succession was confined there, for his continental enemies dared not attack England while he was on the borders of Anjou. Stephen's failure to understand and resolve the problem eventually caught him out; indeed, it followed him home when – within two years – the empress gathered enough Norman support to stage an invasion of England from the duchy and directly challenge Stephen for his crown.

---

has been subsequently criticised by D.R. Bates, 'Normandy and England after 1066', *EHR*, 104 (1989), 853–61, J.A. Green, 'Unity and disunity in the Anglo-Norman state', *Historical Research*, 62 (1989), 128–33; eadem, *The Aristocracy of Norman England* (Cambridge, 1997), 15–16, but the aristocratic dimension of Le Patourel's work has still a certain validity, see D. Crouch, 'Normans and Anglo-Normans: a divided aristocracy', in *England and Normandy in the Middle Ages*, ed. D.R. Bates and A. Curry (London, 1994), 50–67. For views of the importance of Normandy in Stephen's early reign, Davis, *Stephen*, 28; Chibnall, 'Normandy', in *Anarchy of Stephen's Reign*, ed. King, 104.

CHAPTER 4

The Summer of Rebellions, 1138

Stephen at Dunstable at Christmas 1137 might well still have considered his position with a certain satisfaction, but as the year developed he would soon have found less and less to congratulate himself upon. His vigorous promotion of the Beaumont connection was already causing problems. Not far from Dunstable was the town and castle of Bedford. The castle had been committed to Simon de Beauchamp, the leading magnate of the shire and lord of the considerable honor of Eaton. Simon had joined Stephen as his steward early in the reign, and his family had a long-standing link with the town and castle of Bedford. His lineage included the Conqueror's sheriff of Bedfordshire. But Simon de Beauchamp had died at some time in 1137, leaving a young daughter as heir, and according to the *Gesta Stephani*, at the Christmas court the king had decided to use her as a piece of patronage to provide for Hugh Poer (that is, Hugh 'the Young') younger brother of the Beaumont twins, who was to be created earl of Bedford.[1] Hugh had been left after his father's death in 1118 with no English or Norman lands, just a substantial rent charge on his father's Parisian properties. Waleran, it seems, had applied himself to advance Hugh at no further cost to the family.[2]

---

1 *GS*, 46–8. For the earlier generations of the Beauchamp family, C.G. Chambers and G.H. Fowler, 'The Beauchamps, barons of Bedford', *Bedfordshire Historical Record Society* i (1913), 1–8. Simon de Beauchamp was present as a loyal supporter of Stephen and a royal steward at Westminster and Oxford in March–April 1136, when he must have obtained a confirmation of the keeping of Bedford castle, *Regesta* iii, nos. 271, 944. There does not seem to be any warrant for believing that the Bedfordshire Beauchamps had any hereditary grip on the shrievalty, as H.A. Cronne, *The Reign of Stephen: Anarchy in England, 1135–54* (London, 1970), 141 and R.H.C. Davis, *King Stephen* (3rd edn., London, 1990), 132 assume. J.A. Green, *English Sheriffs to 1154* (HMSO, 1990), 25, has Hugh de Beauchamp (Simon's grandfather) as sheriff in the reign of the Conqueror, and none of his family subsequently; the only known sheriff for Stephen's reign is one William Bacon.
2 For Hugh Poer and his inheritance from his father, D. Crouch, *The Beaumont Twins: The Roots and Branches of Power in the Twelfth Century* (Cambridge, 1986), 9 and n. There is a debate as to whether there was ever more than an *intention* to make him earl, as *GS*, 46 may imply as argued by G.H. White, 'King Stephen's earldoms', *TRHS*, 4th ser., xiii (1930), 77–82. The negative evidence is marshalled by E. King, 'Waleran, Count of Meulan, Earl of Worcester, 1104–1166', in *Tradition and Change: Essays in Honour of M. Chibnall*, ed. D. Greenway and others (Cambridge,

Stephen, it has to be said, seems to have been behaving reasonably in the way he carried out his response to what we must assume was Waleran's request. He promised ample compensation to the Beauchamp woman's male kinsfolk, led by the eldest surviving nephew of Simon de Beauchamp, Miles, who was keeping her and Bedford castle in wardship by the king's grant, in succession to Simon. Yet the Beauchamps still chose to resist. Why they did so is something of a mystery, but then, the similar fruitless protests of Robert of Bampton and Baldwin de Redvers in 1136 are just as unaccountable if we leave out of the reckoning the inexhaustible suspicion, litigiousness and combativeness of the twelfth-century aristocrat. The *Gesta* and Orderic say that Miles de Beauchamp was concerned that the male Beauchamps were about to lose their hold on the castle of Bedford.[3]

Orderic had heard that Bishop Henry was dead set against the siege of Bedford, and that the king acted against his advice in pursuing it. The Beauchamps in the end submitted on terms, but arranged the submission through Bishop Henry, in early February 1138, after the king had departed on urgent affairs elsewhere.[4] The Beauchamps' behaviour implies that it was now recognised that the king and his brother were pursuing different ends, and we can assume also that the Beaumonts were at least in part the cause of that. If so it was only in part, for the failure of Bishop Henry to secure translation to the vacant archbishopric of Canterbury must by now have been becoming obvious to everyone. We cannot in fact attribute that failure directly to any hostility of Waleran of Meulan towards Bishop Henry. Waleran did not come into direct contact with Stephen until five months after the death of Archbishop William, by which time the bishop had long been in Normandy attempting to make bridges to the pope for his translation to Canterbury. If anyone was opposing Bishop Henry's translation, it is most likely to have been the pope himself.

The next of a mounting series of crises (and in some ways the most revealing) was the resurgence of the Scottish problem. King David and his son, Earl Henry, had kept the terms of the truce through 1137, but it had run out in December and David followed up by sending ambassadors to address his demands on Stephen. David's intention would seem to have been subtle: a delicate threat to prompt a negotiation. What he and his son were asking was that the question of the earldom of Northumbria, shelved at Durham in February 1136, be reopened. Unfortunately, the ability to respond with delicacy had been bleached out of Stephen's council. Stephen and his new advisers simply rejected the demand, and war promptly followed. The refusal would have had to provoke war or David would have looked extremely foolish.

1985), 177–8, but although Hugh never appears in his family's acts in the 1130s as '*Hugo comes*', but always as '*Hugo pauper*', it is hard to explain away *GS*, 116, which states that after losing Bedford he moved from being an 'earl' to being a nobody.
3 JW iii, 234–6 indeed directly compares what happened at Bedford in 1137–38 with the affair at Exeter in 1136.
4 *GS*, 48–50; OV vi, 510.

King David, his son, and his nephew, William fitz Duncan, crossed the border with their army and besieged Wark. But the castle this time proved stubborn, and the king's army suffered heavy losses. After three weeks, at the end of January 1138, King David let loose his army on a chevauchée down through the north of England, pillaging and murdering in a trail through inland Northumberland down to the Tyne, where he halted at Corbridge, while part of his army raided freely through St Cuthbert's land, or County Durham, opposite.[5]

Stephen moved rapidly up from Bedford, and he and a great army approached the area of devastation soon after 2 February 1138. The sudden absence of the use of moderating diplomacy in the conduct of campaigns (which we saw in 1136 and 1137) is striking. No attempt was made to contact King David. Count Waleran was detached to relieve Wark and rout the Scots besiegers, which he had achieved by mid-February, while King Stephen made immediate retaliation in kind on coastal Lothian. He then returned abruptly to England, so abruptly that John of Hexham speculated that the king doubted the loyalty of some in his army. Passing back through Northumberland he relieved Eustace fitz John (brother of that Payn fitz John he had not trusted in the March of Wales) of the keeping of Bamburgh castle. King David and his army would not oppose so great an army as that which Stephen could deploy, but withdrew inland to Roxburgh until the English departed after a fortnight, and then planned the renewal of the campaign of plunder and waste. The intention this time was to devastate coastal Northumberland and County Durham, which the Scots began to do on 8 April.[6] A harsher period of Stephen's reign had opened, and as his strategy hardened so, naturally, did that of his opponents.

THE LIONS ESCAPE THE ARENA

As militancy and exclusivity grew at the court, corrosive factionalism grew along with it. This brought the danger that – if the battle for favour and patronage was lost in the arena of the court – the competition for survival would move out into the country. It is perhaps a measure of King Henry's achievement in domesticating the higher aristocracy that it was so reluctant, even under provocation, to take the struggle for promotion on to the streets.[7] Had Stephen had no viable rival – or had not Stephen left some credibility to her – then it is possible that this domestication would have prevented them

---

5 RH, 151–4; JH, 288–9.
6 RH, 155; JW iii, 252; JH, 289–91. Ailred of Rievaulx in *Relatio de Standardo*, in *Chronicles of the Reigns of Stephen etc*, iii, 191, accuses Stephen of violating the peace of his court by arresting Eustace and not releasing him till he surrendered the castles King Henry had entrusted to him, but the similarity to later charges against Stephen in his relations with Geoffrey de Mandeville and others makes this later claim dubious.
7 E. King, 'King Stephen and the Anglo-Norman aristocracy', *History*, lix (1974), 180–94, remains the best brief for the defence of the aristocracy against Round's charges of wilful anarchism, and his essential point is that Stephen failed his aristocracy in the matter of even-handed patronage, he did not offer them good lordship (see pp. 192–4).

moving against him at all. Stephen then would have been remembered as a moderately successful, if not outstanding, king – and, despite upsets, be counted among the royal sheep and not the goats. But the existence of a credible rival in arms within his realm allowed the disgruntled and dissident a way to pursue their own interests against an unsympathetic king, and not expose themselves as mere self-servers.[8]

Mathilda's first great convert was just such a man. Earl Robert of Gloucester claimed later – if William of Malmesbury is reporting his views – that he believed that in Normandy in the summer of 1137 he was the subject of an (apparently) murderous conspiracy promoted by his enemies, and sanctioned by the king. Whether or not we choose to believe him, what we can reconstruct of the events of that summer supports the idea that Earl Robert was being squeezed out of any influence in a realm in which he once had enjoyed great power. Malmesbury accuses Stephen of never showing his earl 'an entire friendship', of suspecting his power and working to diminish his possessions.[9] Without easy access to the king and without a share of favour the earl's personal prestige and reputation were compromised, for he could not then attract lesser men on the strength of his reputation for closeness to the king. But this was not everything he had against Stephen. The March of Wales was where Robert's chief power was located, and it had collapsed under a Welsh resurgence about which Stephen had done very little. If Stephen's reaction to the Welsh crisis had shown anything, it was that he preferred to keep the established Marcher magnates at a respectable distance, and trust his own men. The favour offered William of Ypres and Waleran of Meulan in Normandy in 1137 would have confirmed for Robert – who seems from Malmesbury's account more than a touch paranoid towards the king – that he had little to look forward to from the king except further indifference.

Malmesbury says that Robert of Gloucester kept his inner turmoil to himself throughout Stephen's Norman progress, but used the king's return to England as a way of separating himself from the court without suspicion. He remained quiet in the duchy, but gossip was certainly rife as to his views and future intentions because he does not seem to have kept them to himself. Malmesbury says that he consulted widely about the moral case for supporting his sister, and we can well believe it, for he was – as we can tell even at this distance – a strange mixture of man of action and ardent controversialist. The oath he had taken in the previous reign was once more brought to the centre of the debate, the same oath from which others had alleged that the late king, his father, had released him on his deathbed; a release he had not denied at the time that it was first debated in 1136. He is said to have had the support of the numerous clergy (*religiosi*) he had consulted in his decision about whether

---

8 Whatever his suspicions of the innate anarchism of the aristocracy, and his belief in the weakness of Stephen's claims, Round's assessment of the problems presented by a rival is similar to mine: 'had he enjoyed better fortune, we might have heard less of his defects', J.H. Round, *Geoffrey de Mandeville: A Study of the Anarchy* (London, 1892), 35–6.
9 *HN*, 21.

the oath was still valid.[10] But there are echoes in other writers that the oath was not the single point of debate for him and his circle. A text that we know that he consulted was the book of Numbers, the fourth of the five books of the Jewish law, one which particularly concerned itself with the way that Moses was said to have regularised the priestly affairs of the Hebrews in the years they travelled in the wilderness. Moses did, however, make one pronouncement in it concerning inheritance, and since it concerned female inheritance, someone brought it to Earl Robert's attention, and, as significant texts tend to do, it stuck in his mind.

Gilbert Foliot, abbot of Gloucester, wrote a letter to Brian fitz Count, lord of Wallingford, at some time in 1143 or 1144 reflecting favourably on a tract dictated by that remarkable baron in support of the empress's claims to the throne (which has not survived). He added some reflections of his own on the subject, reflections to which we will later return, but the significant passage for present purposes runs,

> Divine law provides this answer to that [viz. the argument based on scripture that royal succession pertains only to sons and not to daughters]. In the last chapter of the Book of Numbers, *you find that which we often heard quoted by the earl of Gloucester: Zelophehad was a jew of the tribe of Manasseh who had many daughters and no son.* It seemed to some that women ought not to succeed to their father's goods, disqualified by their sex. The Lord devised a law because of this case – that everything their father owned should come entire to the daughters of Zelophehad.[11]

The exegesis of the passage is, however, Gilbert's, and not Earl Robert's. If you read the Book of Numbers you find that the point at issue in the last chapter was not whether the daughters should succeed – that was uncontentious – the problem was whether they should be allowed to marry outside the tribe of Manasseh and so take land away from it and into another tribe. The earl's use of the passage might well have been very different from that of Abbot Gilbert.[12] An unavoidable issue for any Anglo-Norman baron in supporting Mathilda was the man to whom she had been married. We have good evidence that Count Geoffrey and the Angevins had made themselves deeply hated in southern Normandy in the two years since King Henry died. It was this hatred that had allowed Count Waleran to mobilise the aristocracy against Geoffrey and Mathilda and erode what little support they had found. To support Mathilda in 1138 was to align with a discredited invading power – no wonder then that Earl Robert put himself in the place of the elders of the tribe of Manasseh, unwilling to see a daughter of the tribe carry what was theirs to an alien race. For him, the decision would have been so much easier had Mathilda never married an Angevin, and he must have wished that he had

10 *HN*, 23.
11 *LCGF*, 61–2.
12 D. Crouch, 'Robert of Gloucester and the daughter of Zelophehad', *Journal of Medieval History*, 11 (1985), 232–3.

never been amongst those in 1127 who had supported King Henry in making the match.[13]

A great struggle and deep doubt lay behind the earl's defiance of Stephen in late May 1138, six months after the king left him behind in Normandy. We see this in the evidence that Earl Robert took so long to decide to embrace the empress's cause; that he took great care in constructing a religious and moral brief to defend his change of side; and that he cultivated in William of Malmesbury and his circle an almost paranoid obsession with Stephen's capacity for treachery. Even the means by which he did it – a formal act of 'defiance' which Malmesbury believed was 'according to custom' – is further evidence of Earl Robert's singular obsession with the appearance of the thing.[14] The legal circus of debate around the theoretical rights and wrongs of Stephen's accession to the throne began in Earl Robert's household in Normandy in the winter of 1137–38. It started a long-running aristocratic seminar on the subject which did not end until 1153, and which is a remarkable characteristic of the eventual civil war. In the arguments, the synods and the conferences of the intervening years, we see the stirrings of the effect of literacy on the closed group of the Anglo-Norman aristocracy: its developing tendency intellectually to justify its pragmatic actions, which will be later seen at its finest flower in the future generations which lived through the civil unrest of the reigns of John and Henry III. Those at the top of society had begun to feel that they also needed to occupy the moral high ground.

In the meantime, the consequences of Earl Robert's disaffection began to show themselves, even before he had formally stated his intention of opposing the king. It seems that – with Earl Robert's defection at hand – the pro-Angevin party began to develop some perception of strategy other than Count Geoffrey's cautious and unsuccessful nibbling at the Norman frontier. The *Gesta Stephani* mentions communication between the empress and her uncle, King David, in the form of a letter which reached Scotland reciting her dispossession and asking him to honour the oath he had sworn.[15] In the week after Easter, King David responded by reopening – on 8 April – his campaign in Northumbria, this time with no intention of temporising with Stephen (he had learned his lesson there). Other messengers must have been at work in England. Orderic Vitalis and Henry of Huntingdon both give lists of prominent

13 C. Warren Hollister, 'The Anglo-Norman succession debate of 1126: prelude to Stephen's Anarchy', *Journal of Medieval History*, 1 (1975), 154n. Suspicions about Earl Robert's self-interest in supporting the empress are not new: note W. Stubbs, *The Constitutional History of England* (Oxford, 1874–8), i, 328–9, 'Even the fidelity of Robert of Gloucester to the interests of his sister was an after-thought, and resulted in no small degree from his distrust of Stephen.'

14 J. Gillingham, '1066 and the introduction of chivalry into England', in *Law and Government in the Middle Ages: Essays in Honour of Sir James Holt*, ed. G. Garnett and J. Hudson (Cambridge, 1994), 48–9, suggests that Earl Robert invented the formulaic act of defiance for the occasion. However note that in 1119 Reginald de Bailleul went in person to the king at Falaise and '. . . *fidelitatem regi reliquit*', OV vi, 214; he, too, refused to return the lands he had from the king, doubtless because (like Earl Robert) he believed he held them from a rival claimant.

15 *GS*, 52. Orderic talks of the '*fraudulenta invitatio factiosorum*' which was one factor in causing David to move, OV vi, 518.

magnates of the West Country and March who fortified their castles against the king soon after Easter (3 April 1138). The movement shows signs of awareness that Earl Robert was intending to defy Stephen, although the messengers bearing the defiance itself did not reach England until over a month later.[16] King Stephen in April 1138 found himself with his first serious domestic crisis since taking the throne: co-ordinated trouble in the north and west of England, and also in Normandy.

The way that the king responded to his sudden onset of troubles does him some credit, and confirms that, whatever his inadequacies in some departments, he could formulate and execute quite complex military strategies. The quality of his council at this time needs to be taken into account, too. At the time the troubles began the Beaumont twins, and Count Waleran in particular were firmly established as favourites, but William of Ypres and Queen Mathilda were also close to him. When news of the troubles began to break in Easter week, the king was in council at Northampton, and moved thence slowly down to Gloucester, which he reached on 10 May.[17] The royalist strategy evolved during that period was not unfamiliar, and again involved delegation of responsibilities: the king himself moved into Herefordshire to deal with the troubles in the March; the queen made use of her connections with Flanders and Boulogne, and herself took responsibility for containing the rebels in Kent.[18] Count Waleran and William were despatched to deal with Earl Robert and Count Geoffrey in Normandy. The threat of King David in the north was apparently left to Archbishop Thurstan of York and the northern barons to contain, until the king could come.

In the end, the summer of 1138 saw the defeat of the anti-royalist forces on all fronts by a mixture of good luck and military enterprise. Also, there was some bad judgement on the rebel side. This was nowhere clearer than among the western rebels. Their professed leader was far away in Normandy when they put their castles in defence against the king, and there was no-one in England who could offer direction in Earl Robert's absence, so they were dealt with piecemeal. The Gloucester contributor to the Worcester chronicle goes

---

16 *GS*, 52–4; HH, 712; RT, 134–5; OV vi, 516–18. For an analysis of the lists of rebels in Earl Robert's interest, see D. Crouch, 'The March and the Welsh kings', in *The Anarchy of King Stephen's Reign*, ed. E. King (Oxford, 1994), 276 and n. Orderic explicitly calls the rebels he lists supporters (*faventes*) of Earl Robert. Ralph Louvel and William fitz John of Harptree are said by *GS*, 66 to have been linked to the earl '*fide et iureiurando firmiter*'. Geoffrey Talbot is referred to as his household knight, see below. William fitz John was brother to Eustace, whom Stephen had insulted by removing Bamburgh from his keeping the previous February. William fitz Alan, who held Shrewsbury against the king, had recently married Earl Robert's niece, OV vi, 520.
17 JW iii, 240–2.
18 Davis, *Stephen*, 35, suggests that Walchelin Maminot held Dover for the earl in order to secure him a port of entry, and that the naval blockade of the port confined Earl Robert to Normandy. However, Dover would be possibly the worst port for Robert's entry, since he had to sail from the Bay of the Seine. Wareham was the port later used by the Angevin party in the West Country to communicate with Normandy, and Robert of Lincoln was holding it open for the earl in 1138. There is every reason to believe that the earl's intention in 1138 was to do his best to loosen Stephen's hold on the duchy.

out of his way to describe pointedly how loyal Miles of Gloucester was at the time, humbly greeting Stephen after his ceremonial procession into Gloucester abbey, and ushering him to the royal hall next door.[19] Some of the rebels were brought to heel by negotiation. Walchelin Maminot, himself an early convert to Stephen, but linked to Robert of Gloucester in both Kent and the March, was closely blockaded in Dover Castle by sea and land by forces commanded by the queen. He was eventually talked over by his father-in-law, Robert de Ferrers, who had witnessed both the defeat of the Scots and the fall of Shrewsbury, and who had then joined Queen Mathilda in Kent to convince Walchelin of the futility of further resistance. Apparently Ralph Louvel of Castle Cary was also brought to surrender by threats and persuasion rather than force.[20]

But Stephen's victory over the rebels could not be won this time without a significant campaign, involving more than one siege. The king was more than equal to the problem. His first target was Hereford, seized in April by Geoffrey Talbot, a baron with close links to the household of Robert of Gloucester who may have been the ringleader in the western rebellion.[21] The king summoned a feudal army to the city, and determinedly besieged the powerfully defended castle in its southeastern corner between 13 May and 15 June. It was here that messengers reached him from Normandy bearing Robert of Gloucester's written statement of defiance: no doubt Stephen by then would have thought the formality unnecessary. He gained Hereford castle's surrender on easy terms, although not without extensive fire damage to the city's suburb across the river Wye opposite the castle. Talbot escaped the siege and had to be pursued to the Lacy castle of Weobley, which another, briefer siege delivered to the king. Unfortunately for the king, Talbot escaped once more, with his cousin Gilbert de Lacy, and made for Bristol, where the

---

19 JW iii, 242.

20 OV vi, 520; RT, 135. Ralph Louvel held Castle Cary by the king's grant (it was a former possession of Robert of Bampton). His defiance of the king was therefore foolhardy, for if the king had been overthrown in 1138, the Bampton family (sheltering with King David) would have reclaimed the castle, see GS, p. xxviii n.

21 Geoffrey attended the Easter court of 1136 as a *baro*. JW iii, 248 calls him the *commilito* of the earl of Gloucester's garrison at Bristol, which indicates that Talbot was attached to the Gloucester household. Sources from Neath abbey (founded by Earl Robert's constable) note Geoffrey as grantor of land in Somerset *c.*1130, *Cartae et alia munimenta quae ad dominium de Glamorgancia pertinent*, ed. G.T. Clark (6 vols, Talygarn, 1910) i, 77. *GS*, 58 calls Talbot a cousin (*cognatus*) of Gilbert de Lacy (he was in fact Gilbert's first cousin, son of Gilbert's aunt, Agnes, wife of Geoffrey Talbot senior) which explains why he was using the Lacy castle of Weobley as a base. Both Geoffrey and Gilbert were in opposition to Roger, son of Miles of Gloucester, who had inherited through his wife, the eldest daughter of Payn fitz John and Sibyl de Lacy, the lands of Hugh de Lacy, Gilbert's uncle; see R.H.C. Davis, 'Treaty between William earl of Gloucester and Roger earl of Hereford', in *A Medieval Miscellany for Doris Mary Stenton* (Pipe Roll Society, new ser., xxxvi, 1960), 140–1. The Lacy genealogy of W.E. Wightman, *The Lacy Family in England and Normandy, 1066–1194* (Oxford, 1966), 168–90 disagrees with that of H.A. Cronne, *The Reign of Stephen: Anarchy in England, 1135–54* (London, 1970), 157–8, and Cronne is validated by B. Coplestone-Crow, 'Payn fitz John and Ludlow Castle', *Transactions of the Shropshire Archaeological and Historical Society*, lxx (1995), 171–83. Sibyl de Lacy was not the daughter of Hugh de Lacy, as Wightman assumed, but daughter of Hugh's sister, Agnes.

supporters of Earl Robert in the West Country were rallying for a final stand, under the earl's eldest son, William (still in his late teens), and his cousin and perhaps tutor, Philip Gay.[22] The king, it seems, attempted negotiation with the Bristol garrison at this point. But on his withdrawal to London, the situation rapidly got out of hand, with royalist Bath threatened and northern Dorset and Somerset terrorised. The king returned and deployed a large army to blockade Bristol, while successfully reducing the outlying rebel strongholds of Castle Cary and Harptree and systematically wasting the lands of the earl in the vicinity. The author of the *Gesta*, who had very close connections with the cathedral priory at Bath and who may well have been the bishop himself, sneered that the king had listened rather too much to those in his army who had covert sympathy with those in Bristol: but the writer's quivering hatred of the town and its people does not encourage much faith in his judgement on this point.[23]

Thinking that Bristol had been contained, the king moved back in July to Gloucester and up through the middle March to secure more rebel outposts: Ludlow, Bridgnorth and Shrewsbury. The Shropshire barons, Ralph Paynel and William fitz Alan, had embraced Robert of Gloucester's cause and seized the royal castles in the shire. Ludlow was bypassed in the following campaign, for reasons not altogether clear but probably to do with the fact that it was commanded by a woman, the widow of Payn fitz John (its former lord) and the action concentrated in the north and east of the shire, at Shrewsbury, Bridgnorth and Dudley.[24] Shrewsbury castle put up a considerable fight, being unusually stubborn for that day and age in refusing to negotiate with the besiegers. This was even stranger as William fitz Alan and his family had escaped before it was invested, and found their way to Normandy to join the empress and the earl of Gloucester. Yet the castle garrison fought to the death, even though there was no hope of relief.

The siege of Shrewsbury continued some days after the news of the defeat of the Scots at Northallerton (22 August 1138), which was brought into the royal camp by Robert de Ferrers, fresh from the victory. Heartened by this, the royalists overwhelmed the garrison (led by fitz Alan's uncle, Arnulf de Hesdin) by concentrated artillery fire and a mass assault on the gate under cover of smoke. For once, King Stephen did not lift his hand to save the garrison; its leaders and many of their followers were hanged and the rest butchered, as the customs of war allowed, either as they stood or as they attempted to run out. Soon afterwards, the royal army moved eastwards to Bridgnorth, also

22 JW iii, 242–4, 248–50. The account here is fragmentary due to the misplacing of the arrest of Roger of Salisbury in the events for 1138.
23 *GS*, 56–70; JW iii, 250.
24 Coplestone-Crow, 'Payn fitz John and Ludlow castle', 180, 183n. suggests that Gilbert de Lacy, rival of Roger fitz Miles of Gloucester, had seized Ludlow in the summer of 1138. But the only certain evidence is that the Lacy castle and honor of Ludlow was at the time the dower portion of Sybil de Lacy, widow of Payn fitz John, ibid. 183n. It is a likelier suggestion that she herself had declared for Robert of Gloucester, as had her two ex-brothers-in-law and her brother, Geoffrey Talbot (II). For the honor of Ludlow, see Wightman, *Lacy Family*, 134–6.

held by rebels, and received its prompt surrender. Magnanimously, the king allowed Ralph Paynel at Dudley to make his peace. In this way, the king concluded the bloodiest and most disruptive campaign that England had seen for over sixty years: Wareham in Dorset, and Dover in Kent and other lesser rebel strongholds capitulated within days.[25] The chroniclers in the area concerned (the *Gesta* and the Worcester chronicler) were overwhelmed by what they witnessed, and their writings reflect this in their anxiety and anguish. Nonetheless, the king had – with determination and skill – broken the back of the premature rebellion of 1138: the Welsh border counties were reclaimed and only massively fortified Bristol remained defiant in England.

The northern campaign, in the meantime, had developed in a way that put little heart into the empress's cause. Sources for the Scottish discomfiture are very full, for it inspired several northern chroniclers with something resembling glee. We cannot do much more than survey the high points, however, for, in its failure, the northern campaign of summer 1138 proved of less long-term significance than the campaign of the previous winter (which had revealed Stephen's new refusal to negotiate, and willingness to be confrontational).

King David's armies crossed the border into England once again on 8 April 1138. As we have seen, there are some grounds to believe that he did so in concert with the dissident English barons attached to Robert of Gloucester. Certainly, one obvious link is represented by the brothers Eustace fitz John, lord of Alnwick and Malton, and William fitz John, lord of Harptree, who joined respectively the northern and southern campaigns.[26] The Scottish army divided: a force under the king besieged Norham castle, and another under William fitz Duncan pillaged Craven, the Pennine district of Yorkshire, reaching as far as Furness abbey on the west coast. There they laid waste to the abbey's lands (and there was a certain satisfaction in this, as it was Stephen's own foundation) and on 10 June defeated a force of local knights at Clitheroe. Norham rapidly fell, and after threatening Durham, King David chose instead to besiege the troublesome fortress of Wark in the second week of May, which was unfortunate as its stubbornness slowed him down. Nonetheless, around this time, Eustace fitz John joined David – whom it was believed he had long favoured – and prompted him to leave the siege of Wark to a holding force and to assault Bamburgh, whose custody Eustace had lost earlier in the year. But the king – perhaps concerned to put pressure on Stephen – chose to move

25 JW iii, 250, 256–8; OV vi, 520–2. Two charters of the king reveal that the numerous royal army at Shrewsbury, and later at Bridgnorth, included the earls of Leicester and Northampton, Miles of Gloucester, Robert de Ferrers (who had fought at Northallerton) and numerous bishops, see *Regesta* iii, no. 132, validated by D.C. Cox, 'Two unpublished charters of King Stephen for Wenlock Priory', *Shropshire History and Archaeology*, lxvi (1989), 57, dated '. . . *apud Brugg' in reditu obsidionis Salop*' (a charter of Stephen not in *Regesta*). On the taking of Bridgnorth after Shrewsbury, I was helped by the generous advice of Dr Patrick McGurk, whose new edition of John of Worcester includes a reference to the event which is not in Weaver's edition. According to HH, 718, however, Leeds castle in Kent did not surrender to the king until he came in person just after Christmas 1138.
26 For the fitz John brothers, *GS*, p. xxix.

further south, it being apparently said in the Scottish army that the plan and purpose was to devastate not just Yorkshire but much of England.[27] Bypassing Durham, the great army crossed the Tees and entered Yorkshire at the end of July.

The magnates of Yorkshire were left to defend themselves, although since Archbishop Thurstan had been in council with King Stephen at Northampton at the beginning of May, before he marched off to engage the rebels in the southwest, it would seem likely that the archbishop had been conceded some formal authority to organise the defence of the north. Nor was the king uninformed of the progress of events. He despatched Bernard de Bailleul and certain north midlands barons (Robert de Ferrers, William Peverel of Nottingham and Geoffrey Alselin) with a force of knights to reinforce the Yorkshire magnates. When negotiations proved fruitless, the Scots and the northern royalists met at Northallerton, where the English army blocked the road south to York, which was King David's target. Here on 22 August, on a typically foggy Vale of York summer's morning, was fought the famous battle of the Standard, which the Scots lost due to the indiscipline of their infantry, which broke itself by a wild assault on the armoured and disciplined English knights, who had dismounted and lined up with the archers. King David was escorted from the field by his household knights barely in time to escape capture, and although he and the household rallied and retreated in good order to Roxburgh, and then Carlisle, the bulk of the army was massacred. This is perhaps the reason why the Yorkshire army did not feel it necessary to pursue King David beyond the county boundary (for which its leaders have been criticised by modern writers). It was reputed that Earl Henry, the king's son, had to make his way with only one companion on foot, to meet his father at Carlisle. Eustace fitz John fled for Alnwick, and his Yorkshire castle of New Malton promptly surrendered. David, having recovered from the defeat, moved to Wark, where he maintained the siege within a safe distance of his own frontiers, eventually starving the castle into surrender around 11 November before the truce with Stephen was set to begin. He made no attempt to move back down into Northumberland.[28] Doubtless, he became progressively gloomier as Stephen pacified first the southwest and then Kent, and began to wonder what sort of punishment would come up from the south.

The crisis of 1138 in England was resolved in Stephen's favour by the end of August. What of Normandy, to which Count Waleran and William of Ypres had been sent in May? Here, too, Stephen's luck held, despite Earl Robert of Gloucester bringing over to Count Geoffrey the strategic castles

---

27 RH, 159. P. Dalton, *Conquest, Anarchy and Lordship: Yorkshire 1066–1154* (Cambridge, 1994), 150–1, argues that Eustace fitz John's defection was principally due to his concern to protect his Northumbrian estates, but notes the counterargument that Eustace had more to lose in Yorkshire (p. 150n).

28 The principal accounts are RH, 155–77; JH, 291–5; Ailred of Rievaulx, *Relatio de Standardo*, 181–99; JW iii, 252–6; HH, 712–18. A good modern synthesis of the campaign is to be found in Dalton, *Conquest, Anarchy and Lordship*, 148–52, and see also 205–6; the account by J. Bradbury, *Stephen and Matilda* (Stroud, 1996), 33–6 gives a very useful tactical reconstruction of the battle.

of Bayeux and Caen and so cutting the duchy in half. But not everything was running against the king-duke. On King Louis VI's death in August 1137, Stephen's brother, Count Theobald of Blois, along with Count Ralph of Vermandois, had become the principal ministers of the new young king, Louis VII. Count Theobald's assistance could be guaranteed, and it so happened that Count Ralph was Waleran's uncle, his mother's brother. When in June 1138 Geoffrey of Anjou crossed into Normandy and sought to link up with Robert of Gloucester, Waleran negotiated major reinforcements from across the French frontier, and an imposing mercenary force joined him in July. Together with Waleran's own connections, the Norman army was too forbidding for Count Geoffrey to confront, and he retired to the border without offering battle, leaving Robert of Gloucester to be blockaded at Caen.

Fortunately for Earl Robert, Waleran and his great allies were too badly distracted by the civil disorders created by the renewed Tosny problem in the Evreçin to give him their undivided attention. Count Waleran was unable to do more than lay waste the earl's estates around Caen. He then went off to defend his brother's lordship of Breteuil, where the complicated situation had become more complicated when an internal rebellion of a powerful tenant family added itself to the external threats. Earl Robert of Leicester seems to have hastily crossed over to Normandy after the conclusion of the siege of Shrewsbury, but neither he nor his twin brother were able to prevent the sacking of his town of Breteuil on 7 September 1138.

In October Count Geoffrey once more reappeared, and this time devoted his attention to the seizure of the great fortress of Falaise, which blocked the direct route between his wife's base at Argentan and Earl Robert's centre at Caen. The siege was not successful, but a good deal of damage was done to the regions of the Hiémois and Lieuvin as far north as Bonneville-sur-Touques on the Channel coast, where in November a fortuitous rebuff convinced Count Geoffrey that he had overextended himself, and he abruptly closed the campaign, having achieved little other than to have reassured Earl Robert of his support. At the same time, for unknown reasons, Roger de Tosny decided to make peace with the Beaumont twins, and crossed with them back to England to offer his submission to King Stephen.[29] In this way the year's problems ended with the campaigning season, leaving Stephen no less a king-duke in November 1138 than he had been in November 1137. Were we to argue that his need to overcome such powerful and multiple challenges demonstrated his weakness, then we would have to take account of similar years in the previous reign where Henry I had been as seriously challenged. Henry had had just as busy a time in both England and Normandy in the third year of his reign as Stephen had in his.

29 OV vi, 516–18, 524–8, see also Crouch, *Beaumont Twins*, 37–8.

CHAPTER 5

Radicalism and Conspiracy

It may be no coincidence that King Stephen's last major act before the onset of full-blooded civil war in England, was radical administrative reform. The winter of 1138–39 was notable for wide-ranging changes in the structure and balance of government as handed on to Stephen by his predecessor, changes which were without clear precedent and therefore can be truly called radical. Lack of a precedent may suggest desperation on the part of the reformer or at least a lack of insight. Reforms which most easily catch the imagination are those which are designed to get back to what is perceived as a better time. These were no such reforms, they were radical and unprecedented, and disturbed people.

THE CREATION OF NEW EARLS

At the end of 1138 Stephen shrugged off the mantle of administrative kingship which had been so carefully tailored for him out of his uncle's wardrobe. It would not do to underestimate the importance of the image of kingship handed on to him from King Henry. Henry's kingship had much to do with the annual routine of exchequer administration, with the monitoring of sheriffs and the local work of justiciars, and the imposition of the idea of criminal offences and injustice as being an affront to the exalted majesty of kingship. The promises of peace and justice expressed in the coronation oath were taken seriously.[1] The public image of King Henry even in the first half of his reign was formidable both at home and abroad. The Welsh chronicler writing in Deheubarth went so far as to say that he believed that only God could prevail against him.[2] As for the people of his own land, the author of the legal tract known as the 'Quadripartitus' could write in the aftermath of the conquest of Normandy (1106),

1 On Henry's reputation as the 'lion of justice', and the extension of royal control over local courts, see J.A. Green, *The Government of England under Henry I* (Cambridge, 1986), 95–117.
2 *Brut, s.a.* 1116.

Yet when we were worn out and almost done for, the peaceful times of the king and duke of Normandy, our lord Augustus Caesar, Henry son of King William the Great, brought back the longed-for joys of peace and our former happiness. He looked with pious mercy on the liberty of the Church, the security of the country, reward for virtues, favour for labours, joys to the deserving, and help to those asking . . . who triumphed over the provoking follies of many and put an end to rapine.

It is with a certain prescience that the panegyrist goes on to state what must indeed have come to seem the bane of Stephen's kingship, that people came to believe that under Henry they had never had it so good.

. . . he so far excels other men in the unique prerogative of his merits that the descendants of our descendants through the infinite course of the ages will seek after his law with public satisfaction.[3]

This was the inheritance which Stephen had to live with, and against which he was measured. It is no surprise to find that several of Stephen's early ecclesiastical benefactions were granted 'for the peace and security of the realm' ('*pro statu et incolumitate regni*') in a way that links king, subjects and the prayer of the Church into a common purpose.[4] Kingship in England in 1136 was understood as much by stable administrative and judicial routine as by rituals evoking the divine charism. Therefore, to redesign the image of his uncle's kingship which he had inherited into a model of his own ideological conception in the disturbed circumstances of autumn 1138 was a risk, and (from what happened next) a far bigger risk than he and his advisers seem to have realised. The late King Henry's achievement was a frail structure when the robust and domineering king around which it had been built was taken out from the middle of it.

Stephen created numerous new earls at the end of 1138. The numbers were unprecedented: the three previous Norman kings had developed a tendency to limit the dignity to a very few favoured followers. When King Henry died, his England had only seven earls whom he recognised (Buckingham, Chester, Gloucester, Leicester, Surrey, Huntingdon and Warwick). Stephen carried on this tradition in his first years as king. Apart from Bedford for Hugh Poer at Christmas 1137, Stephen made (or promised) no new creations to reward any supporters: in fact, as his succession was more or less unopposed in England

---

3 R. Sharpe, 'The prefaces of "Quadripartitus"', in *Law and Government in the Middle Ages: Essays in Honour of Sir James Holt*, ed. G. Garnett and J. Hudson (Cambridge, 1994), 165, 167.
4 *Regesta* iii, no. 591 (Jan. 1136) '. . . *pro salute et incolumitate mei ipsius et statu regni mei*'; no. 335 (Feb. 1136) '. . . *pro statu regni mei*'; no. 716 (Feb. 1136) '. . . *pro statu regni mei*'; no. 341 (Mar. 1136) '. . . *pro statu et incolumitate regni mei*'; no. 592 (c. June 1136) '. . . *pro salute et incolumitate mei et statu regni mei*'. See also the reference in the Plympton Annals for 1141 that the empress obtained the '*status regni*' after the victory of Lincoln, *Annales Plymptonienses*, 28. The Latin word *status* had little of the connotation of the English word 'state' and in this context signified something like 'extent', 'situation' or 'good standing', see for a detailed treatment, G. Post, 'Status regis', *Studies in Medieval and Renaissance History* i (1964), 1–103.

he did not need to do so.[5] At York in February 1136 he had adroitly banished the idea of the revival of the earldom of Northumbria, for which he had been petitioned, into the land of remote contingency. This is why the sudden torrent of high aristocratic patronage at the end of 1138 is so notable. Two of the new titles were awarded to men who already enjoyed the comital dignity across the Channel. Count Waleran was created earl of Worcester on his return from Normandy with Roger de Tosny and news of the duchy's pacification under his leadership.[6] Count William of Aumale, the lord of Holderness in Yorkshire's East Riding, who had been one of the baronial leaders at the battle of the Standard, was granted the earldom of York in a similar gesture. The count's fellow commander, Robert de Ferrers, lord of Tutbury, who had been a very early adherent of Stephen, was created earl of Derby (or Ferrers).[7] Gilbert fitz Gilbert (younger brother of the late Richard fitz Gilbert of Ceredigion) who had recently married Count Waleran's sister Isabel, was elevated to the earldom of Pembroke. William d'Aubigné the younger, lord of Buckenham in Norfolk, son of the butler of Henry I and another early adherent of Stephen obtained an earldom (initially of Lincoln, later of Sussex) when or soon after he was married to the dowager queen Adeliza late in 1138.[8] These last two acts were not military rewards; Gilbert had fought for his brother-in-law in Normandy but had led no known campaign, and neither had William.

5 An exception could be the recognition of the comital status of Simon (II) de Senlis, the dispossessed son of the elder Simon, earl of Northampton (who died *c*.1109) and Mathilda, who had been remarried to King David of Scotland, and whose inheritance formed the basis of the earldom of Huntingdon David and then his son, Henry, enjoyed. Simon was received at court by Stephen in 1136 and is pointedly called '*Comes Simon de Silvanectica*' in royal charters (in a manner comparable to the 'Earls Warenne' or 'Earls Giffard') but no English county is specifically allocated him; his dignity until 1139 was probably a personal one (comparable to the comital status of Arnulf de Montgomery in Henry I's reign).

6 Waleran founded Bordesley abbey in Feckenham forest in Worcestershire on 22 November 1138, at which time he had received the overlordship of the Beauchamps of Elmley, hereditary sheriffs of the county, and a block grant now of all the royal assets in the county. My argument is that the foundation was linked to the grant of the earldom. His second seal, not in use until after April 1139, but likely enough commissioned earlier, has him as COMES WIGORNIE on the reverse, see D. Crouch, *The Beaumont Twins: The Roots and Branches of Power in the Twelfth Century* (Cambridge, 1986), 39–40. A single act of Waleran dating to 1139 x 41 has him using the double style '*G[alerannus] dei gratia comes Mellent[i] et Wigornie*', Northamptonshire Record Office, Montagu of Boughton Deeds, Box 7, no 3/(2), a reference I owe to Professor Nicholas Vincent. E. King, 'Waleran, Count of Meulan, Earl of Worcester, 1104–1166', in *Tradition and Change: Essays in Honour of M. Chibnall*, ed. D. Greenway and others (Cambridge, 1985), 168 favours a later date for the creation of Waleran's English earldom, linking it with the royalist activity in Worcester in the summer of 1139.

7 RH, 165; JH, 295, and see for Count William, P. Dalton, *Conquest, Anarchy and Lordship: Yorkshire 1066–1154* (Cambridge, 1994), 146–7. Robert was still not earl in September 1138, but was enjoying the title by Christmas, see M. Jones, 'The Charters of Robert II de Ferrers, Earl of Nottingham, Derby and Ferrers', *Nottingham Medieval Studies*, xxiv (1980), 16–17n. Only two charters of his as earl ('of Ferrers') survive: he died early in 1139 and was succeeded by his son, Robert (II). Although he himself used a personal style as earl, contemporaries refer to him territorially, as earl 'of Derby'.

8 William d'Aubigné was not an earl in a royal charter dated at Arundel in autumn 1138, although the grant that the king confirms in that charter was assented to by him as the queen's husband, *Regesta* iii, nos. 679, 697. He was certainly earl before the summer of 1139, ibid., no. 493.

Furthermore, the elevation of Gilbert was of a piece with the advancement of Waleran's brother, Hugh, to the earldom of Bedford – uncomplicated nepotism.

By Christmas 1138, the king was on his way to doubling the number of earls in England. There was more than one reason why he had done this, but one stands out above all else; it soon became clear that these new earls were to be earls such as post-Conquest England had not previously seen; their titles were more than honorific, they were not merely to be the king's 'companions' (*comites*) in dignity, they were also to work in his interest. The earls of the Norman period had not been government officials in any strict sense. The Conqueror had begun by perpetuating the regional earldoms which had been a part of the pre-Conquest state apparatus, but by 1071 he began to cut his Franco-Norman earls down to size. So far as one can tell, his model seems to have been the contemporary counts of Normandy. The Norman counts were simply magnates who bore an hereditary title (like those of Evreux, Eu, Aumale and Mortain) whose positioning around the borders of Normandy preserved no more than a memory of the time early in the eleventh century when they were counts in the Norman march with military responsibilities. But their dignity was nonetheless prized and regulated: no new count could be created in Normandy without the duke's say-so. The English earls of the reigns of Rufus and Henry were little different. The only vestige of earlier responsibilities they still retained was the tendency of the Chancery and royal justices to assume that they stood at the head of the county from which they took their title, that they were its first lay citizens, comparable to the bishops. The only privilege they formally received was the annual gift of the third penny of the profits of justice in their shire, a survival of an ancient pre-Conquest piece of royal patronage.[9]

What Stephen's new creations were intended to be at the beginning is not firmly established. There was undoubtedly an element of patronage in the bestowal of titles: that would be true of Bedford, Lincoln and Pembroke. Also there was an element of reward: Waleran of Meulan, William of Aumale and Robert de Ferrers were all successful commanders. Robert de Ferrers is a particularly interesting case, from his early military support for Stephen (he had accompanied the king north in January 1136) and from the way he brought the news of the victory at Northallerton south to the king at Shrewsbury and then to the queen before Dover. Robert's elevation seems comparable to that of a Napoleonic English general bringing welcome despatches of victory to St James's.

But patronage and reward were only part of these promotions, there was a novel military and administrative dimension to them. When Waleran became earl of Worcester, he not only acquired the royal demesne assets in Worcestershire, but also the lands of William de Beauchamp of Elmley (the

---

9 This survey is derived from the detailed treatment in D. Crouch, *The Image of Aristocracy in Britain, 1000–1300* (London, 1992), ch. 1.

shire's greatest lay landowner). Along with these came William's hereditary office of sheriff. Retrospective evidence from other counties confirms that sheriffs there eventually came under the earl too.[10] Certainly, this was already the case with the Marcher *comitatus* of Cheshire and Pembroke. In Cheshire the sheriff maintained a subordinate relationship with the earl, established in the earliest days of the Conquest (as can also be demonstrated for Shropshire and Herefordshire in the early part of the Conqueror's reign).[11]

The Conqueror's emergency actions in the Welsh borderlands in the 1060s and 1070s really are the nearest precedent that can be established for Stephen's actions late in 1138. Stephen's new earldoms might be classed as emergency measures: he had just survived the first serious challenge to his kingship, and he and his council might well have been looking to stiffen their regional sinews. But he did not simply choose to create the new earls in areas where he felt vulnerable (as arguably were York, Pembroke and Worcester) but in other places too: neither Lincoln, Nottingham nor Derby were front-line areas. As further creations were made in 1139 and 1140, what developed was something which resembled nothing so much as the much later system of Tudor lord-lieutenancies: an attempt to tie some (although not all) of the higher aristocracy into the security and administration of the shires where their influence was concentrated.[12]

Was this initiative of Stephen and his advisers a sign of desperation in government? The later Tudors feared that they faced a serious social breakdown too, but the comparison between Stephen's and Edward VI's governments does at least go some way towards absolving Stephen from the charge of being a weak king, pottering his way into reckless and heedless experimentation. It indicates that an imaginative king who had a titled aristocracy with little formal role in the exercise of local power (but much real and potential power in the localities) might well seek to tie that local influence to the government by giving it a degree of formal control over local government. As royal interference in the localities had grown in the reigns of the Norman kings, so the local power of the aristocracy would be more likely to be seen as a threat by the centre. What Stephen and his advisers were doing, was attempting to transform the potential threat into a further buttress to royal power. Looked at in those terms, it was, as has been said, a rather imaginative leap to have made in administration. The problem for Stephen was that both circumstances and personalities frustrated him in the execution of the scheme.

This last, structural, explanation can bear more weight than explanations formed by a glance across the sea to France. The manifestations of comital power in the French kingdom and principalities in the early twelfth century were many and various, but none show much resemblance to the national

10 R.H.C. Davis, *King Stephen* (3rd edn., London, 1990), 127–8.
11 D. Crouch, 'The administration of the earldom', in *The Earldom of Chester and its Charters*, ed. A.T. Thacker (Journal of Chester Archeological Society, 71, 1991), 90–1.
12 The cosmetic Vere earldom of Oxford is one clear exception: the Veres held no land in the shire, their lands were concentrated in Essex and Suffolk, which already had earls.

reorganisation which King Stephen attempted in England. In the French king's 'principality' there were certain counts (like those of Beaumont-sur-Oise, Vendôme or Dammartin) who ruled within the framework of a royal administration: but they were not integrated into the administration, being merely, like the English earls of Henry I's reign, magnates who happened to carry a hereditary title. Elsewhere there were individual counts scattered all over France (like Count Waleran of Meulan himself) who exercised their own local power through subordinates called in Latin *vicecomites* (viscounts, translated into English as 'sheriffs'). Indeed, certain magnates in Normandy, even those who were not counts, such as the lord of Montfort-sur-Risle, used local judicial deputies called *vicecomites*.[13] It may have been such arrangements of 'count' and 'vicecount' which in part suggested such a tidy rearrangement of local administration in England to Stephen. But such arrangements were by no means to be found systematically in any French principality. In fact the only directly proveable example of foreign innovation in adminstration in England in Stephen's reign is to be found in Sussex, where the dowager Queen Adeliza established her younger brother, Joscelin, on his arrival in England from Brabant as 'castellan of Arundel', which was part of her dowry. This implies that the queen had adopted the Brabazon method of local government at Arundel, confiding power to castellans (such as those at Brussels and Louvain).[14]

It was the way that Stephen dealt with King David of Scotland which goes some way to confirming that a new comital policy had been worked out by Stephen and his councillors. The peace process between King David and King Stephen was protracted, and took up much of the time between September 1138 and Easter 1139, just the period in which the new earldoms were being created. A truce to begin on 11 November had been established by the end of September in negotiation at Carlisle between King David and the papal legate, the Cluniac bishop of Ostia, Alberic. The legate then returned to Stephen to report on what he had seen and heard. The negotiations were taken up again after Christmas by Queen Mathilda (who was David's niece, and who was said to have cherished some personal regard for him) acting for her husband. The terms were eventually ratified in an assembly of English and Scots magnates at Durham on 9 April 1139. The centrepiece was the creation of an earldom of 'Northumbria' for King David's son, Henry. Henry was to have

13 For Count Waleran's underling viscounts at Meulan and Mantes and elsewhere, and for the viscount of Montfort, see Crouch, *Beaumont Twins*, 59–61, 170–4.
14 Joscelin first appears at Reading, with his elder sister, the widowed Queen Adeliza when on 1 December 1136 she made a grant to the abbey on the anniversary of King Henry's death, '. . . *Ioscelino fratre eiusdem regine*', *Reading Abbey Cartularies*, ed. B. Kemp (2 vols, Camden Society, 4th ser., xxxi, xxxiii 1986–8) i, 301–2. It seems likely that he had only recently come to England so that his sister might make his fortune for him. On his father's death in 1140, Joscelin had no portion of the paternal estate, which his elder brothers Duke Godfrey II (d. 1144) and Count Henry (retd. 1149) divided between them, for the family, see *Chroniques des ducs de Brabant*, ed. E. de Dynk, i, pt 1 (Brussels, 1854) *passim*. His usual title was 'the castellan', see *EYC* xi, 69–70, or 'the castellan of Arundel', see BL, ms Cotton Nero C iii, fo. 188r. To maintain Joscelin's status he had a grant of a large estate at Petworth in Sussex to which was attached twenty-two knights' fees.

Northumberland, and the homage of those barons of the county willing to perform it to him, their loyalty to the king of England excepted. Bamburgh and Newcastle, and the possessions of the bishop of Durham and the enclave of Hexhamshire were excepted in the agreement. Earl Henry then accompanied the queen south to meet Stephen at Nottingham, where the terms were ratified, and where he was formally espoused to Ada, teenage daughter of the late Earl William (II) de Warenne of Surrey, and (surprise) half-sister of Count Waleran of Meulan.[15]

From the way that the terms are reported to us by contemporary writers in the community of Hexham, it seems quite clear that Stephen was not acquiescing in the extension of the boundary of Scotland south to the Tyne. The barons of Northumberland remained his men in the same way that the men of Worcestershire remained the king's men after the county was subordinated to Waleran of Meulan. Also, it was asserted by the queen, and accepted by Henry of Scotland, that Northumberland would retain the laws and customs it knew in the previous reign. Northumberland therefore remained an English county, and its earl, though son of the king of Scotland, was an English earl. So we may well suggest that (in view of the pertinent comparisons offered by the other contemporary creations of earldoms at Worcester and Pembroke) Stephen intended no more than to extend his own policy of twelfth-century 'Thorough' into yet another border area. Whether his intentions and expectations were reasonable on the Scottish March is a different matter: the number and quality of hostages his negotiators felt it necessary to extract from the Scots indicates that they had their doubts.[16] Whatever Stephen intended it to symbolise, the conference at Durham could not in fact be any other than the negotiation between two independent powers. But it does not hurt to point out its domestic relevance.

BISHOP HENRY OF WINCHESTER AND THE NEW REGIME

We may very well believe that the sudden change of governmental direction in the aftermath of the crisis of the summer of 1138 upset people, especially those who had been brought up and educated in good King Henry's days. In view of the radicalism of the measures which Stephen and his new aristocratic confidants were taking, we might very well expect a conservative reaction. The sentiments expressed in the early 1140s to Brian fitz Count, the lord of Wallingford and Abergavenny, and one of Henry's greater creations, may well stem from this period; a time when it appeared that all that was familiar from the period of the previous reign was being dismantled. What was most frustrating for Brian (as well as for others) was how they – who had been used to being included in the consultative process of the court – were now being

---

15 JH, 300 carefully notes that Ada was 'sister of Earl William de Warenne, Count Waleran of Meulan, and Earl Robert of Leicester', for her see V. Chandler, 'Ada de Warenne, Queen Mother of Scotland', *Scottish Historical Review*, lx (1981), 119–39.
16 RH, 167–71, 177–8; JH, 297–300.

utterly excluded. So when the abbot of Gloucester wished to sympathise with Brian, he rhapsodised:

> The distinguished memory of the pious King Henry is still with you. He, whose prosperous reign and golden age being now past, the world mourns as a father. The wreck of our present time brings him frequently and mournfully back to mind. For you do not forget that he raised you from a boy, tutored you as a youth, and when he had bestowed on you the belt of knighthood, gave more besides in gifts and estates.[17]

The golden past was evidently a favourite theme of Brian. It may be that others, who were more keen to move on with the times, found him tiresome. After receiving one of his choleric letters, Bishop Henry of Winchester sharply rebuked Brian for being too keen to look back, like Lot's wife, and warned him to take note of her peculiar fate.[18] Yet the same Bishop Henry earlier, on 8 April 1141 at Winchester, is said to have warmed the hearts of a council by recollecting the time of his royal uncle when 'England had been the peculiar habitation of peace', a peace so remarkable that even neighbouring kings and princes were infected by its blessed spirit.[19]

For such men, former confidants of the great Henry, the time of choosing was fast approaching. The greatest of them, Robert of Gloucester, had already shown the way. His fate had not as yet proved to be a happy one, and the fate of those of his political affinity who had rebelled in England in 1138 was positively discouraging, but for those whom Stephen had ignored and slighted, Earl Robert showed there was an alternative to silent acquiescence. Most obviously slighted in the spring of 1139 were those two great bishops who had masterminded Stephen's accession, and who had been nudged out of his closest counsels during the previous year. Bishop Henry of Winchester had been harbouring hopes of translation to Canterbury since November 1136, and indeed the king, his brother, had encouraged him in them by confiding to him the keeping of the diocese during the vacancy – surely a tactless move if he did not intend to support his brother's candidacy? The monks of Canterbury certainly got the message, and promptly elected Henry as their new archbishop.[20] But the pope proved unco-operative, Henry got no joy from his vigorous lobbying at the papal Curia in 1137 and, for whatever reason, he surrendered his claims as archbishop-elect. When Alberic of Ostia arrived and was welcomed as legate by Stephen in 1138, the time had obviously come to resolve the Canterbury vacancy. On Alberic's return from Carlisle at the beginning of October 1138, the prior and community of Canterbury were ordered to proceed to an election on 27 November, and inform him of affairs in London in advance of a Church council summoned to be at Westminster a

---

17 *LCGF*, 61.
18 H.W.C. Davis, 'Henry of Blois and Brian fitz Count', *EHR*, 25 (1910), 300.
19 *HN*, 52–3.
20 OV vi, 478. See the evidence for the vicariate marshalled by A. Saltman, *Theobald, Archbishop of Canterbury* (London, 1955), 8 and n.

fortnight later.[21] The result was the election to the archbishopric of Theobald, abbot of Bec-Hellouin in central Normandy since 1136.

What Bishop Henry thought of Theobald's election is a question that it would be useful to be able to answer convincingly. He was absent from the proceedings of the Council of Westminster on the day (Christmas Eve 1138) that the election of Theobald was announced, and accepted by the king. But since the monks of Canterbury were supposed to have confided the result of their deliberations to the legate over a week before, the candidacy of Abbot Theobald could not by then have been a secret from anybody: strict confidentiality was not a twelfth-century virtue. Theobald, after all, was already in England on his abbey's business, so was most conveniently present to hear of his own elevation. Bishop Henry was several miles away in St Paul's cathedral in London at the time of the formal election, at an ordination of deacons. The Canterbury source states that 'fiercely enraged, he stormed out of the ordination which had only just begun'. It adds that it was believed that he felt that he had been defrauded of the archbishopric on which he had set his heart, and as a result 'not a few in the Angevin party' believed he began to temporise with Earl Robert and Miles of Gloucester.[22]

There is an idea in the sources that Bishop Henry fell out with his brother over the election to Canterbury. Though the story – as the sources report it – cannot be accepted, there is good reason not to discount it entirely. It seems that Abbot Theobald of Bec was at Westminster, almost as if he had been asked to be present in expectation of nomination. Bishop Henry knew of the candidacy and was sufficiently affronted to absent himself from the palace on the day of the formal proceedings to confirm the election. So, although it is difficult to believe – as some suggested – that by Christmas 1138 he had any expectation of Canterbury for himself, he still had grounds for ill-feeling in the candidate preferred over him: Theobald of Bec. Theobald was Henry's equal neither in birth, education nor ability. Although Bec-Hellouin was a distinguished Norman abbey deeply engaged in English affairs, and although two of its alumni had been consecutive archbishops of Canterbury under the Norman kings, Lanfranc and Anselm were already scholars of European stature before election to the see. Nobody could make similar claims for Theobald, whom his fellow monk of Bec, Robert de Torigny, described coolly as 'a sufficiently venerable man'.[23] What Theobald might have had, however, was the backing of the aristocratic connections of the Clare and Beaumont families.

Bec had been founded by a coalition of aristocrats of which an ancestor of the Clares (Count Gilbert of Brionne) was the chief, and Gilbert's descendants remained loyal to the abbey. The Bec priories of Stoke and St Neots in England were under the advocacy of Gilbert de Clare, son of the late Richard fitz Gilbert and nephew of Gilbert, earl of Pembroke. In 1138 the mother abbey

21 GC i, 106.
22 GC i, 109; Saltman, *Theobald*, 12–13.
23 RT, 135, *vir admodum venerandus*, a pen sketch Robert added to Henry of Huntingdon's brief notice of Theobald's election, HH, 718.

of Bec-Hellouin was situated in the heart of the domains of Count Waleran, who was advocate of the Bec priory of St Nicaise at Meulan (and who was to convert his collegiate church of Beaumont-le-Roger to a priory of Bec in 1142). This factional promotion of Theobald of Bec, and Stephen's acquiescence, ignoring his brother's opinions, may well have been enough to annoy and ultimately to alienate Bishop Henry.

However frustrated the bishop of Winchester was in December 1138, he did at least have one or two satisfactions with which to console himself. The pope had been instrumental in depriving Henry of the *pallium* of Canterbury, but he was in a position to offer very satisfactory amends. On 1 March 1139, when Alberic of Ostia had perhaps been able to report to Innocent II on the complexities of the English situation, a legatine commission was issued to Bishop Henry. The commission was an unusual measure. It elevated its holder into the supreme ecclesiastical authority within its area, and so Bishop Henry had the satisfaction of outranking the new archbishop, and exercising prerogatives that as a diocesan bishop he would not normally enjoy, such as the consecration of bishops and the calling of Church councils. No justification for the measure was offered, so we may assume that it was a measure of the pope's concern to soften Bishop Henry and stiffen the leadership of the English Church.[24]

But did Bishop Henry start to open communication with the opposition in Normandy, and those remaining of the late king's 'new men' whom Stephen seemed so keen to edit out of political life? Although the Canterbury source alleges this, it would not do to make too much of it. The bishop was a man of affairs with many contacts and agents. In the months after the Council of Westminster, and especially after his promotion to legate, he might very well have sought to develop a new role for himself as bridge between the court and the opposition without compromising himself in any way: such is the role he seems to be acting out during the next crisis to afflict Stephen's England, the arrest of the bishop of Salisbury and his clerical family.

THE FALL OF ROGER OF SALISBURY

Bishop Roger of Salisbury ceased to have any real influence over King Stephen after the Norman expedition of 1137. He was effortlessly squeezed out of any curial influence by the aristocratic clique which had colonised the royal council in Normandy. The negative evidence of the lack of his attestations to royal acts is not conclusive proof of his absence from the court in 1138, but it is remarkable when contrasted with his omnipresence two years earlier.[25] But on the other hand, other than ignoring him, there is not much evidence that Stephen acted against Bishop Roger and his family in any way that could give

24 *HN*, 29; Saltman, *Theobald*, 15–16. Alberic of Ostia had left England just after 13 January 1139, JH, 300, allowing plenty of time for consultation with Pope Innocent before issuing the commission.
25 Bishop Roger, and his nephew Bishop Nigel, and probably Bishop Alexander were (unsurprisingly) at the Council of Westminster of December 1138, *Regesta* iii, no. 638. GC i, 107 says that seventeen bishops were present, which indicates that both episcopal nephews were there.

him cause to rebel. In that way, his position was much the same as that of Robert of Gloucester before his defection. But if he had limited access to the king's ear, the bishop still had the running of the machinery of government, and the king's aristocratic council might well have resented that. It is likely that the scheme to introduce the influence of new earls into the localities was devised by its promoters partly to challenge, or at least diminish, Bishop Roger's otherwise unshakable grip on the treasury, chancery, exchequer and sheriffs (the mysterious creation of a Norfolk magnate as earl of Lincoln earlier in 1139 might possibly indicate a wish to counterbalance Bishop Alexander, Bishop Roger's nephew).

Did Bishop Roger really conspire with the king's enemies at this time when his influence on events was waning and the court was hostile? As with Bishop Henry, it is very likely that Roger had lines of communication open to the developing opposition. But talking is not necessarily plotting, and we will never really know whether Bishop Roger was genuinely planning to embrace the Angevin cause, or whether it was just that his enemies at court found it convenient to pretend that he was. Contemporaries pointed tellingly to the great castles Bishop Roger and his nephew Bishop Alexander held and had strengthened with masonry works[26] as good cause for suspicion about their intentions. The *Gesta* damned Roger for the large military household which he employed and took about with him.[27] But in the middle of the twelfth century, the great stone castle and the extensive household were two of the ways in which a great man projected his greatness on to the world, and Bishop Roger's castle at Devizes was reputed to be 'more splendid than any other in Europe' and Sherborne 'only a little less handsome than Devizes'.[28] Since Bishop Roger could rest his nobility on no claims of lineage – he began his career as an obscure priest in the Norman diocese of Bayeux – he had to excel in display: something that William of Malmesbury, who was friendly towards the bishop, recognised.[29] Unfortunately for Bishop Roger, his self-importance was made to look like self-accusation.

26 Bishop Roger's castles were at Old Sarum, Sherborne, Devizes and Malmesbury, see for lists, *Annales de Wintonia*, 51, *HN*, 25. Bishop Alexander's were at Sleaford, Newark (and Banbury), HH, 720–2. *Liber Eliensis*, 314, says that Bishop Nigel likewise spent a large amount fortifying the Isle of Ely with stone defences.
27 Strong allegations of conspiracy and imminent defection are to be found in *GS*, 72, and they are reported (but not credited) in OV vi, 530. *HN*, 25–6 states the allegations to be groundless. HH, 720 says nothing directly about accusations, but only that the ill-treatment of the bishops was groundless. See for assessments of the charges E.J. Kealey, *Roger of Salisbury Viceroy of England* (London, 1972), 177–8; K. Yoshitake, 'The arrest of the bishops in 1139 and its consequences', *Journal of Medieval History*, 14 (1988), 98; Davis, *Stephen*, 28–9, none of whom are convinced. H.A. Cronne, *The Reign of Stephen: Anarchy in England, 1135–54* (London, 1970), 38, and J. Bradbury, 'The early years of the reign of Stephen', in *England in the Twelfth Century*, ed. D. Williams (Woodbridge, 1990), 23–5; idem, *Stephen and Matilda* (Stroud, 1996), 51–3, are more willing to believe the rumours and that action against Roger was necessary.
28 HH, 720. Of course, the very great also built castles as a matter of display, as for instance, Henry of Winchester; for the social imperative in castle-building, see D. Crouch, *The Image of Aristocracy in Britain, 1000–1300* (London, 1992), 257–64.
29 *HN*, 25, '. . . Roger, wishing to seem magnificent in the buildings he erected, had built several [castles]'.

The court conspiracy against Bishop Roger and his family must have been relatively quickly set on foot. If it had been long in the preparation, the bishop and his widespread connections would have found out about it, for Bishop Roger was with the king at Oxford just after the Christmas court and again at and after Easter, with his son Bishop Alexander.[30] As it was, he went off to a great council arranged for 24 June 1139 at Oxford not suspecting any trap. William of Malmesbury, who was there to see him on his way, reported the bishop as saying (with, no doubt, a weary smile), 'By my blessed lady Mary, somehow I am disinclined to this journey! This I know, that I shall be as useful at court as a young horse in battle.'[31] William took that remark as an omen, but it sounds just like the remark of a man for whom the royal court had long lost what charms it had ever had, and who was expecting little joy of the meeting. He would have known that he would be coming face to face again with Count Waleran. The count had been absent from England since well before Christmas 1138. Elsewhere, I have set out the evidence by which we can reconstruct an embassy which he led to the Christmas court of Louis VII in the area of Paris. Count Waleran's main achievement in France would seem to have been the arrangement of a marriage between Eustace, the king's son, and Constance, King Louis's sister, which was secured by a substantial cash payment on betrothal. We know that he went bearing gifts to those who had influence with Louis VII. He took a grant of lands in the royal demesne in Northamptonshire to Count Ralph of Vermandois, his uncle, the seneschal of France.[32] He had taken with him on his mission his young half-brother, Earl William (III) de Warenne (still not twenty), and a select group of Anglo-Norman barons, including Walter de Beauchamp, the brother of his newly dependent sheriff of Worcestershire. Waleran and his entourage returned to Normandy at the beginning of March, and he crossed to England, probably with Bishop Ouen of Evreux, in Easter week (24–29 April 1139).[33]

So it was likely enough to have been only in May 1139 that the dominant aristocratic clique began its work to convince the king that Bishop Roger and his family were conspiring with the Angevin party to renew the civil unrest so expensively defeated the previous summer. The *Gesta* and Orderic identify Waleran as the principal conspirator 'and those other adherents of the king

30 *Regesta* iii, nos. 473, 667, 964–5.
31 *HN*, 26.
32 Northamptonshire Record Office, Montagu of Boughton Deeds, Box 7, no. 3/(1), a charter of Count Ralph dating between 1139 and 1141 concerning his lands in Weekley, Northants, as granted him by King Stephen, discovered by Professor Nicholas Vincent.
33 Crouch, *Beaumont Twins*, 42–3. The evidence is a series of closely datable charters which plot an itinerary for Waleran and his entourage up the Seine to Paris at Christmas 1138 and back to Normandy by March 1139, see *Chartes de l'abbaye de Jumièges*, ed. J-J. Vernier (2 vols, Société des historiens de la Normandie, 1916), i, 160–1 (18 December 1138, Rouen); *Cartulaire général de Paris*, ed. R. Lasteyerie (Paris, 1887), 281–2 (midwinter 1138/9 at Paris); *Recueil des chartes de St-Nicaise de Meulan: prieuré de l'ordre du Bec*, ed. E. Houth (Paris, 1924), 13–14 (5 March 1139 at Beaumont-le-Roger). See also OV vi, 530. HH, 720 mentions the betrothal in describing the events of June 1139, for confiscated treasures from Roger of Salisbury's castles went towards the down payment.

who were on terms of the closest intimacy with him'.[34] The king spent much of May and June in the Beaumont-controlled areas of Worcestershire and Warwickshire. He was entertained at Worcester between conducting a siege of Ludlow (unfinished and rather tedious business from the previous year's campaign) and meeting Henry of Scotland at Nottingham.[35]

The poison was duly poured into the king's ear, and (despite reservations) the king – tacitly or otherwise – permitted the count and his supporters to arrange for their men to look for ways to implicate the bishops in a disturbance within the peace of the king's court when it moved to Oxford on or about 24 June 1139. Malmesbury believed that Count Alan's knights offered the conspirators just the opportunity they wanted by coming to blows with the bishops' men over claims to lodgings in the town. According to the *Gesta*, the conspirators had other men standing by to finish the fight, but the authors differ as to who came off worst. The fight achieved its purpose, however, and Bishops Roger and Alexander were apprehended and taken before the king. Also arrested was Roger Poer, the chancellor, Bishop Roger's son. Bishop Nigel of Ely evaded capture and rode off to take shelter at Devizes, which he put in readiness to defend, finding Mathilda of Ramsbury, his uncle's wife, in residence there.[36]

The bishops' influence was systematically broken. The king moved his forces to Devizes, which was surrendered under pressure after three days. The rest of Bishop Roger's castles surrendered with less resistance. A similar strategy delivered Sleaford and Newark castles when the consecrated person of Bishop Alexander was threatened if his garrison did not surrender. The fact that the king entrusted Bishop Alexander's castles to Earl Robert of Leicester demonstrates his involvement along with that of his twin brother. Once Bishop Alexander was in prison, the earl took further advantage of the situation by seizing episcopal estates near Leicester which had been in dispute between earl and bishop during the previous reign. His opportunism matches what we know of the stripping of Bishop Roger's castles by the king's agents, which, according to Henry of Huntingdon, raised a sum sufficient to finance the betrothal of Eustace, the king's son, to Constance, the sister of Louis VII.[37]

---

34 *GS*, 74–6; OV vi, 530–2. Orderic adds the names of Waleran's brother, Robert of Leicester, and Count Alan of Brittany to the principals in the conspiracy.
35 For the king's movements after Easter 1139, see *Regesta* iii, p. xli; JW iii, 266. John of Worcester describes the king resuming a blockade begun earlier with two siege castles. He also has an interesting account of what seems to have been a regional tournament organised by the besiegers and besieged to liven up the tedium of the siege itself. Stephen sternly forbade it.
36 *GS*, 76–8; *HN*, 26–7.
37 *HN*, 27 says that Bishop Roger fasted until Devizes surrendered, and that Bishop Alexander surrendered his castles in return for his freedom. *GS*, 79 (supported by JW iii, 246–8) depicts a more brutal solution, with both bishops put on a starvation diet in front of Devizes, which was surrendered when the life of Roger Poer was threatened. HH, 720–2 gives a similar story, but says the king left Alexander in prison at Oxford, taking him thence so that he could be threatened with starvation before his own castles. Robert, earl of Leicester, obtained the keeping of Newark from the king, for which the bishop excommunicated him once free, *The Registrum Antiquissimum of the Cathedral Church of Lincoln*, ed. C.W. Foster and K. Major (10 vols, Lincoln Record Society,

Other government officials were removed, Adelhelm, the treasurer, another son of Bishop Roger, was dismissed and not replaced. The Beaumonts were able to take advantage of the changes, by securing the succession of Philip de Harcourt, a cousin and clerical follower of Count Waleran, to Roger Poer as chancellor. Philip had already risen far through his family connections. By Waleran, he had been made a prebendary and dean of the collegiate church of Beaumont-le-Roger, one of the ancient churches in the family's gift in Normandy. Through his mother's family, the Briouzes, he had secured the rectory of Sompting in Sussex. Waleran must have secured Philip an archdeaconry in the diocese of Evreux around this time, and he was also given the deanery of Lincoln to add to his clerical cornucopia.[38]

KING STEPHEN'S REPUTATION IN 1139

The 'arrest of the bishops' is notorious in modern historiography as very much the beginning of the end for Stephen. Such was the view of William Stubbs, who saw Bishop Roger and his family as the high priests of the administrative kingship set up by King Henry. When they fell, the arcane mysteries of the exchequer and the emergent constitution were beyond King Stephen (to whom, in the famous words of Ralph Davis, they were so much 'double-Dutch') and reasonable government collapsed into anarchy.[39] The Anglo-Norman bishops were alleged to have abandoned the court, and aristocratic suspicion is said to have driven the kingdom into instability. Davis's particular accusation was that, because he had broken the terms of his 'peace', no-one could in future trust Stephen's safe conduct and that the king had exposed his moral 'weakness and perfidy'.[40] Recently, historians have rapidly moved away from an apocalyptic view of the events of June 1139. If they had a significance (and they undoubtedly did have some) it was on a different plane from that suggested by the constitutional school of historians.

Kenji Yoshitake has been the historian who has principally taken issue with the views which ultimately derive from Stubbs. His careful studies have proved that the bishops were quite as assiduous in their attendance on King Stephen after June 1139 as they were before, and if there were any break, it was to be in 1141. Even Bishop Alexander was reconciled with King Stephen (despite the death in December 1139 of his uncle as a result of the stress of the events of June). Indeed, before 1141, there was something of a swing back towards

---

1931–73) i, 239–40. For the rivalry between the earl of Leicester and the bishop, D. Crouch, 'Earls and bishops in twelfth-century Leicestershire', *Nottingham Medieval Studies*, xxxvii (1993), 9–20.
38 For Philip's origins and his rise, Crouch, *Beaumont Twins*, 34, 45, 154, 220.
39 For Stubbs's views, W. Stubbs, *The Constitutional History of England* (3 vols, 6th edn., 1897) i, 326–7, 351–3; J.H. Round, *Geoffrey de Mandeville*, 100, was already differing from Stubbs's sweeping judgement in 1892. Kealey, *Roger of Salisbury*, 199–200, largely concurs with the view of Stubbs. For Davis's assessment of Stephen's administrative capacity, *Stephen*, 29.
40 Davis, *Stephen*, 31–2.

Bishop Roger's family, with Earl Robert of Leicester, his principal aristocratic persecutor, paying heavily for a formal reconciliation and to avoid papal excommunication because he held on to Newark castle by force. Furthermore, although evidence is not plentiful, there is sufficient to believe that both exchequer and chancery continued their routine under new management uninterrupted. The issue of royal writs remained constant in quantity in 1139–41 as had been issued before it. The fact that the chancery employed a new royal seal after the fall of Roger Poer does argue that its clerks (some at least of whom – including the keeper of the seal, the vice-chancellor, Baudrey de Sigillo – continued in employment) were being careful to monitor output under the new regime and differentiate it from the old.[41]

Davis's sideways swipe at King Stephen's understanding of the administration of his realm also needs a cool appraisal. It is impossible that Stephen was the aristocratic twit that Davis believed him to be. Although we do not know whether he was literate, he had at least moved in literate courts since his boyhood and it had its effect. It can be no coincidence that one of the first major administrative documents of his new reign was the *Constitutio domus regis*, a short manual describing the personnel of the royal household and laying down their rates of pay. It is believed that it was drawn up by the clerks of Bishop Roger for the information of the new king himself.[42] Stephen had been an Anglo-Norman magnate for over twenty years before he became king, and that meant that he had already learned to accommodate himself to the rhythms of royal and ducal taxation and administration. As we have seen earlier, Stephen's own administration when he was count of Mortain and Boulogne issued writs and worked within the framework of royal exchequer and justice in the 1120s. There is no reason to believe that Stephen was less instructed in the ways of King Henry's administration than was usual among his magnates, and, as has been established by Hollister and Prestwich, many of his magnates were indeed deeply engaged in the day-to-day business of Henry's government.[43] Moreover, as we will see later, King Stephen had a good eye for selecting competent and experienced servants. Two of the closest men to him between 1135 and 1141 were William Martel, his steward and close friend, and Roger de Fécamp, his chaplain (and perhaps confessor). Martel was the grandson and the nephew of Norman sheriffs of Dorset and had been Henry I's butler. Roger had been treasurer of Normandy before

---

41 K. Yoshitake, 'The arrest of the bishops in 1139 and its consequences', *Journal of Medieval History*, 14 (1998), 99–108. G. White, 'Continuity in government', in *The Anarchy of Stephen's Reign*, ed. E. King (Oxford, 1994), 122–3, summarises the case for any change in administrative practice, and apart from the change of seal, finds none.
42 *Dialogus de Scaccario and Constitutio Domus Regis*, ed. C. Johnson (rev'd edn., Oxford, 1983), xlix–l, 129–35. The key to its dating is that it refers to Ralph de La Marche, the king's cook, who died just before King Henry, and seems to indicate that his post was not yet filled.
43 If it were to be argued that Stephen was so grand a magnate that administrative routine would have been far beneath him, it is worth noting that the grandest of all of them, Count Robert I of Meulan, Waleran's father (who died in 1118), was the first known possessor of a private exchequer on his estates, and Count Robert's younger twin son was a most assiduous justiciar for Henry II, see Crouch, *Beaumont Twins*, 89–96, 163–6.

1135.[44] Stephen's closest household advisers were therefore men who were perfectly well informed as to how King Henry had governed his realm, and we know that Stephen was the sort of king who listened to advice from those around him.

Davis's view of Stephen's alleged weakness and perfidy is rather harsh – not because he did not do some foolish and underhand things, but because few politicians who exercised such power as he did could stand immaculate before the tribunal of history. The judgement has to be a balanced one, and there is a case to be made in his favour. Stephen's defence could point to many times when he was honourable in his personal dealings: to his honest attempts (for instance) to maintain the terms of the Oxford charter to the Church. Davis compares Stephen unfavourably to King Henry, who, he says, was confident enough in his possession of power to honour his safe conduct even to those who defied him; and he cites an example of 1119 given by Orderic where a man defied him to his face in his castle of Falaise. But if you wish to condemn Stephen by comparing him unfavourably to his uncle, then it is only fair to examine Henry's record more fully. Another example of 1119 might be given, reported this time by a well-informed household cleric of the Warenne family, a man less adulatory towards Henry than Orderic:

> [King Henry] ordered two Anglo-Norman magnates, the count of Eu and Hugh de Gournay, coming peacefully to him, to be arrested without warning in his court, and gaoled.

As a result of this, we are told, the king's name was mud across northern France and everyone from the count of Flanders to Louis VI moved against him. Count Stephen of Aumale (the father of William of York) on being summoned to King Henry's court, refused the invitation, and joined with the relatives and followers of the captured men in defying the king, until Henry backed down and released them.[45] The public measure of a politician's morality can only be whether his contemporaries routinely think the worst of him, and by that measure, King Henry was more severely criticised for inhumanity and abuse of trust than his nephew.[46] The Church's reaction to the arrest of the bishops demonstrates this admirably.

There was a hostile reaction to the bishops' arrest and the confiscation of their castles, but it was not by any means overwhelming or unmixed. William of Malmesbury was in the thick of the affair, and fairly reports the views of the royalist party, put forward strongly by Archbishop Hugh of Rouen, that

---

44 For William Martel's background, *Regesta* iii, p. xviii; *Gesta Normannorum Ducum* ii, 272–4; for Roger de Fécamp, *Regesta* iii, p. xii.
45 OV vi, 214; *Liber monasterii de Hyda*, ed. E. Edwards (Rolls Series, 1866), 313. On the custom of offences against the king's peace as understood in contemporary France and England, see J.O. Prestwich, 'The treason of Geoffrey de Mandeville', *EHR*, 103 (1988), 295–6.
46 C.W. Hollister's sympathetic reassessment of King Henry's contemporary reputation for barbarity is based on the case that he was no worse than his contemporaries, nonetheless, it does not obscure the fact that there was criticism of him, see 'Royal acts of mutilation: the case against Henry I', *Albion*, 10 (1978), 330–40.

the bishops had been in error in aggrandising themselves by building castles in disregard of canon law. Further away, in Normandy, Orderic picked up a view of events which characterised the arrested bishops as men drunk with power and wealth who oppressed their neighbours and plotted against their sovereign lord. The anonymous author of the *Gesta*, himself a churchman of high rank, and probably a bishop, had no doubts that Bishop Roger and his clerical clan were traitors. He, too, condemned them for a style of life and for ostentation quite incompatible with their office.[47]

It fell to the bishop of Winchester to publish his commission as papal legate at this point, and air the matter at an ecclesiastical council at Winchester on 29 August 1139, at which he had the momentary satisfaction of (in effect) putting his royal brother on trial for what had been done in his curia. The case for the defence of Bishop Roger and his nephews lay in the insult done to their episcopal office. Even the royalist author of the *Gesta* could not stomach the fact that consecrated and anointed bishops had been imprisoned and threatened.[48] His views on the matter were quite as trenchant as those of Bishop Henry as reported by William of Malmesbury: if the bishops had done wrong it was the Church's business to try them; only an ecclesiastical council had the right to deprive them of their secular possessions. They were bishops, and their persons were sacred.

The king sent an aristocratic delegation to the council. He let Aubrey de Vere, his chamberlain, skilfully intimidate the bishops with threats both veiled and open. When Archbishop Hugh of Rouen arrived on 1 September, his powerful advocacy on the king's behalf broke any chance of a common episcopal front against Stephen, for his argument was that there was nothing in canon law which could justify bishops holding castles, and even if they held them by an act of royal grace, they had no choice but to give them up when told to do so. One can only believe that this was a not-too-delicate swipe at the legate, who held, and had lavished money on, five very powerful fortresses.

In the end, there was little alternative for the legate and the archbishop but to leave the council and cross to the royal palace, where they fell dramatically at the king's feet and pleaded that he maintain the partnership between the crown and the Church, for (when it came to placing blame) they dared not censure him.[49] It seems that the king was gracious enough to the prelates at his feet, and he had reason to be. It looked as if he had come away victorious after a second summer of crisis. He had pushed through his reforms; broken an unreliable and powerful faction in his kingdom; confronted and beaten down the worst the Church could do to him, and made a lot of money. The *Gesta* may be right therefore in saying that he did public penance for the outrage

---

47 *HN*, 28; OV vi, 530–2; *GS*, 76–8.
48 *GS*, 81.
49 *HN*, 29–34, gives an eyewitness account of the council, though unsympathetic to the king. *The Life of Christina of Markyate*, 166, also mentions contemporary concerns about a rift opening between king and Church, with what would be perceived by contemporaries as the consequent danger to social order.

to episcopal dignity committed at his court. It was a politic gesture in a man who had come comfortably out of a potentially uncomfortable affair. A further politic gesture seems to have been his transfer – in due course – of the deanship of the great collegiate church of St Martin-le-Grand in London from Bishop Roger of Salisbury to Bishop Henry, his brother, the legate. The bishop seems to have reconciled himself to at least that much discreet advancement at the expense of his disgraced (and deceased) colleague.[50]

Yet the affair of the bishops was not forgotten. It deeply rankled in the higher echelons of the Church that the king had humiliated some of the greatest from amongst them. Though he came successfully out of the affair in the short term, there were consequences. Henry of Huntingdon, looking back on it, believed that the arrival of the empress in England soon afterwards was a divine chastisement on Stephen and his family. He was not alone in this. Abbot Gilbert Foliot of Gloucester, writing four years later, nursed among his reasons for loathing Stephen that he had 'dishonoured the episcopate'. Writing some years later, the author of the *Gesta Stephani*, for all that he was sympathetic to Stephen, adopted a guarded manner of describing his kingship, not least in his choice of biblical similes. Unusually for a royalist writer, he compared Stephen to Saul, whom God had first selected to be king of Israel. If you wished to flatter a contemporary monarch, the appropriate comparison would be with Saul's successor, David, the king who was faithful to God and established his line for ever. Saul was interpreted by medieval exegetes from the time of the Fathers as a compromised monarch, compromised by his refusal to obey the Lord and honour his priests.[51] It is most unlikely that the author of the *Gesta* was being anything other than deliberate in his comparison, bearing in mind his stated views on the arrest of the bishops. Even for him, Stephen had sacrificed the Church in his pursuit of security, and his fate would necessarily be that of the disobedient. This was a view which the author believed that Stephen himself shared, as he was led away into captivity after his defeat at Lincoln eighteen months later. The Gloucester continuator of the Worcester chronicle seems to have spoken for many when he delivered his terse verdict on Stephen's capture, that it was 'by the just judgement of God'.[52]

---

50 *The Life of Christina of Markyate*, 166–8, mentions threats of censure made against the king, who retaliated with threats of an appeal to Rome, but since it says that the proposed royal delegation to the Holy See was cancelled it may be that we find here some further evidence that Stephen backed down and submitted to a decorous degree of punishment. For the transfer of the deanship (presumably after Bishop Roger's death in December) see R.H.C. Davis, 'The college of St Martin-le-Grand and the Anarchy', in *From Alfred the Great to Stephen*, ed. R.H.C. Davis (London, 1991), 251.
51 *GS*, 5, 52, 112. For the exegetical use of King Saul by Ss Jerome and Gregory the Great see *Sancti Gregorii magni expositio in librum primum regum*, ed. P. Verbraken (Corpus Christianorum Series Latina, 144, 1963), 49. Walter Map in *c*.1180 compares 'the kind and merciful' Louis VII of France favourably to David, and his 'tyrannic' elder brother Philip (who predeceased him in 1129), to Saul, see *De Nugis Curialium*, ed. and trans. M.R. James, rev. C.N.L. Brooke and R.A.B. Mynors (Oxford, 1983), 456. On the use of exegesis as a critique of, or support for, monarchy, see P. Buc, 'Pouvoir royal et commentaires de la Bible (1150–1350)', *Annales*, 44 (1989), 691–713.
52 HH, 722; *LCGF*, 63. JW iii, 292 and HH, 738 both talk of the verdict of Lincoln as being a *iudicium*.

At the end of the summer of 1139, King Stephen maintained his political ascendancy in England, but he had alienated significant numbers of his subjects. As has been said before, one of the major criticisms of the king is that he lacked his uncle's confident ability to manipulate his court and his opponents. It is fair to say that even bishops and abbots who had been sympathetic towards him were now wary of what he might do and felt distanced from his regime. Abbot Geoffrey of St Albans, for instance, is said to have been perturbed by a royal summons to court in 1140 because 'he was afraid that the king's heart might be turned against him because of the plots and lies of others'.[53] The king's men had laid violent hands on leading members of the bench, and the bishop who as much as any other had put him on the throne, Roger of Salisbury, had been ruined and disgraced. The other great bishop, Henry of Winchester, was also distanced from his brother. Stephen now depended on one major aristocratic faction, and his own emerging party of 'new men', his selected officers and captains, men like Hugh Bigod, William of Ypres and William Martel. The older generation of King Henry's new men, the likes of Brian fitz Count and Miles of Gloucester, had been systematically excluded from influence. Some, like Eustace and William fitz John and Earl Robert of Gloucester, had already crossed over into active rebellion, and a Gloucester abbey source believed that Miles of Gloucester was in communication with the empress (if not in rebellion) well before she arrived in England.[54]

It has to be said that, at the end of the summer of 1139, King Stephen was still in nearly total control of England, and only isolated trouble spots remained. In the course of the summer he had removed several more problems. Ludlow, left over from the campaign of 1138 and commanded by Payn fitz John's widow, Sybil de Lacy, had surrendered in early summer 1139 after a systematically conducted siege in which the king distinguished himself by personally saving the life of Earl Henry of Northumbria, his new ally.[55] The southwest of England was still not entirely pacified, and Bristol, with its massive stone castle, water defences and access to the open sea, defied him. William de Mohun, the lord of Dunster on the Somerset coast, had broken out into rebellion, showing that support for Earl Robert of Gloucester's cause was still destabilising the region: and the earl's power in the southern March remained as yet unchallenged. But the region still had its loyalists too. Henry de Tracy, probably a connection of the king's cousin, William de Tracy (Henry I's bastard), was established at Castle Cary (confiscated successively now from Robert of Bampton and Ralph Louvel) as a regional commander with a permanent force of mercenary knights, and he successfully contained and punished Mohun and others. The king was punishing another dissident, his former

53 *The Life of Christina of Markyate*, 170.
54 JW iii, 252. For a comment on this conjecture, see M. Chibnall, *The Empress Matilda* (Oxford, 1991), 80n.
55 HH, 718; JW iii, 266. For the possession of Ludlow, see B. Coplestone-Crow, 'Payn fitz John and Ludlow Castle', *Transactions of the Shropshire Archaeological and Historical Society*, lxx (1995), 180, 183n. It would seem that the king then solved the Ludlow problem by marrying Sybil to the loyalist knight, Josce de Dinan.

close friend, John Marshal, beseiging him in Marlborough castle at the time when the first foreign reinforcements for the Angevin rebels arrived in England in August 1139.[56]

Stephen's position was therefore still very strong in England. It was by now quite understood that he was not the leader of assurance and vision that his uncle had been. It had been observed that his lack of assurance led him to rely overmuch on certain advisers to the exclusion of others: by 1139 that meant Count Waleran of Meulan and his aristocratic clique, as it had been the two great bishops before 1138. But the Beaumont and Clare barons were at least formidable men of some military talent. Stephen was not the sort of king who relied on flatterers and broken reeds; he had too much capacity in judging men for that. All might yet have been well for him, but on 30 September 1139 the whole game changed, for the Empress Mathilda and Earl Robert landed in Sussex, and civil war began in earnest in England.

---

56 *GS*, 80–2. Stephen settled on Henry de Tracy in 1138–39 the Bampton barony and other estates, including Barnstaple, confiscated from Alfred of Totnes, an ally of Baldwin de Redvers exiled in 1136. He was later to obtain the barony of Torrington, confiscated from another local rebel, William fitz Odo. For the siege of Marlborough in August 1139, JW iii, 268.

The Civil War, 1139–1147

CHAPTER 6

Civil War in England

On 30 September 1139, a squadron of ships from Normandy bearing the Empress Mathilda and Earl Robert of Gloucester arrived on the west Sussex coast near Arundel.[1] The landing point was not a matter of accident.[2] The empress, the earl and their not inconsiderable military escort (including some Angevin knights) were received openly at the castle, a formidable fortress in the possession of the queen dowager, Adeliza of Louvain, recently married to Stephen's stalwart supporter William d'Aubigné (created earl of Lincoln on the marriage). They knew, it is clear, that the queen would not arrest her step-daughter and hand her over to King Stephen, indeed William of Malmesbury believed that Adeliza had been in correspondence with the empress for some time before the crossing. The landing seems to have been part of a carefully co-ordinated military operation, for the empress and her half-brother were attempting a dangerous adventure: Stephen had ordered all the harbours of the south coast to be closed and watched.[3]

Several weeks before – probably to distract and to misinform the king – a formidable force had arrived from Normandy, led by the exiled Baldwin de Redvers, one of the leaders of the empress's military household. It had descended on the Dorset coast further to the west, had attempted to take the key port and royal castle of Wareham (perhaps to provide the empress with a

1 Accounts of the landing are in GS, 86–8; HN, 34–5; RT, 137; OV vi, 534; JW iii, 268; HH, 722. William of Malmesbury's account of the date and the size of the escort is preferred, as his sources – being close to Robert of Gloucester – are likely to have been more reliable on the detail. Robert de Torigny dates the crossing to August. Arundel was not a port, although there was a landing some miles south of it, at the mouth of the river Arun. It may be, however, that the actual point of disembarkation was elsewhere. The Worcester chronicler talks of a landing at Portsmouth – and any of the inlets east of Hayling Island might liberally be interpreted as 'Portsmouth', even as far as Chichester (then under Earl William d'Aubigné's control).
2 RT, 137 does, however, say that 'there was available no other port at the time'.
3 The closure and guarding of ports is mentioned by both JW iii, 268 and GS, 87. The king's reason for this is perhaps indicated by the Gloucester abbey source's allegation that as early as the previous year, Miles of Gloucester (still then nominally a royalist) was urging the empress to cross to England. Whether true or not, this allegation might represent a general belief in 1138 that the empress would attempt the crossing to support her failing cause, see JW iii, 252, a state of affairs also implied in GS, 84.

landing point) but had instead moved a few miles south and surprised the garrison of the royal castle of Corfe and seized the place.[4] By making such a military demonstration further west on the southern seaboard, the coast would be literally clear for Mathilda to slip into the country, and this was the case, for the king's army was drawn far to the southwest from Marlborough to blockade Baldwin in Corfe, and the king was apparently still there when the empress arrived. It is worth adding the observation that in first attacking Wareham, Baldwin had succeeded in insulting Waleran of Meulan (who was with the king's army), for the town was the possession of Waleran's twin brother, Robert of Leicester. The insult might well have been deliberate and have been calculated further to incite the royalist army to pursue him to Corfe since both Waleran and Robert had extensive estates in coastal Dorset.[5]

King Stephen knew what to do in the face of this emergency, and decamped east from Dorset as soon as he reasonably could, so rapidly indeed that he allowed Baldwin to escape his net. But he was not soon enough to prevent Earl Robert of Gloucester slipping out of Arundel with a small escort. Taking little-used country lanes, the earl evaded pursuit and came to the Severn valley, the heart of his own country in England. So the king found himself encamped around Arundel castle in the first week of October 1139 in a most difficult position, despite the fact that he had his dynastic rival most decidedly trapped in the castle he had blockaded. There he was soon joined by his brother, Bishop Henry, leading a large force of knights.

The king's problem was twofold. Since Earl Robert was on the loose in England, the main damage was now already done. He could not now prevent the earl rallying his affinity (his political connection) in the southwest and sharpening and worsening the military struggle in England, and every moment he wasted in front of Arundel increased his danger. He had apparently trapped the empress in Arundel castle, but that in itself was a problem. If he succeeded in capturing her, as eventually he would have, despite the strength of the castle, he would not have lessened the military threat posed by her party. By taking the empress prisoner he might have further compromised a reputation for probity already tarnished by the arrest of the bishops the previous year. The position of Queen Adeliza was the crux of his dilemma. The queen is reputed to have put her step-daughter, the empress, under her protection in receiving her into Arundel. To beseige Arundel was to insult a woman who commanded

4 For the strategic importance of Wareham in Anglo-Norman England, see J.A. Green, *The Aristocracy of Norman England* (Cambridge, 1997), 50, 66; for the Beaumont acquisition of much of the borough in Henry I's reign, D. Crouch, *The Beaumont Twins: The Roots and Branches of Power in the Twelfth Century* (Cambridge, 1986), 46n. For a notice of the strategic importance of Baldwin's mission, M. Chibnall, *The Empress Matilda* (Oxford, 1991), 80.
5 *GS*, 84 is our source for the arrival of an Angevin vanguard. The date of August 1139 might reasonably be suggested for this, firstly because the *Gesta* says that the king besieged Baldwin in Corfe 'for some considerable time' (*tempore diutissimo*), and secondly because Baldwin's earlier expedition was doubtless the reason why John of Worcester and Robert de Torigny believed the empress's expeditionary force had arrived in August (the Worcester source suggesting 1 August). For the reconstruction of this important incident, Crouch, *Beaumont Twins*, 46; Chibnall, *Matilda*, 80–1, 80n.

a high degree of respect in the kingdom and with whom Stephen had previously had good relations.[6] In the event Stephen's response was politic, even if it must have galled him intensely: he negotiated a safe-conduct for the empress and Countess Mabel of Gloucester (also left behind in Arundel) under escort to the rebel centre of Bristol. His nominated escorts were his chief adviser, Waleran of Meulan, and the legate, his brother Henry, and they duly delivered the empress and the countess to Earl Robert's representatives, she arriving safely in Bristol with the bishop (the count had stopped at Calne) 'as much by God's as by man's calculation' as a contemporary Lichfield cathedral clerk put it.[7]

A number of questions are raised by the events at Arundel in early October 1139. The first is about Stephen's judgement. There were contemporaries who condemned him: Henry of Huntingdon was ready to believe that the king had been persuaded to release Mathilda by 'taking deceitful advice' and another clerical writer, Orderic Vitalis, berated him: 'prudent men must deplore his lack of regard for both his own safety and the security of the kingdom', believing that the king should have taken the golden opportunity to destroy his enemies by acting ruthlessly 'after the fashion of his ancestors'. John of Hexham deprecated his action as stemming from 'rash naïvety'.[8] But others were generally understanding. The author of the *Gesta* considered that the king had acted rightly in refusing to waste time in front of Arundel, and attributed the good advice to concentrate on wiping out their enemies in the field to Bishop Henry of Winchester. Modern historians in general agree with the *Gesta* that Stephen had made the best of a bad job, and that his judgement in the matter had been sound.[9]

There is a fog of conspiracy about the whole business which also needs to be pondered, even if we cannot penetrate it. William of Malmesbury's theory was that Queen Adeliza was deeply implicated in the affair, and actually enticed the empress to come to Arundel. If this was so, it may well be because Adeliza had cherished hopes of acting as peace-broker between Stephen and Mathilda, with both of whom she had good relations; peace-making and intercession was the traditional activity of the great queen.[10] Others saw some of Stephen's

---

6 *HN*, 35. The Worcester chronicler agrees with this, though he also portrays Adeliza as later blaming anyone but herself for welcoming the king's enemies into Arundel, rather than risking her position with the king, JW iii, 268.

7 A charter dated '. . . *anno quo aplicuit prenominata domina ad castrum Arundel, de quo* tam providentia quam sapientia *venit Brist[olliam] et euasit de obsidione regis Stephani*', Cartulary of Lichfield, Brit. Libr., ms Harley 3686, fo. 35v. The translated phrase is rendered '*tam prudenter quam sapienter*' in the edition of this act in *English Episcopal Acta*, xiv, *Coventry and Lichfield, 1072–1159*, ed. M.J. Franklin (British Academy, 1997), no. 42, which seems to make less sense and is apparently drawn from the edition in *Collections of the William Salt Archaeological Society* xi, 322.

8 OV vi, 534; HH, 722; JH, 302.

9 GS, 88. See the favourable analyses of Chibnall, *Matilda*, 81; J. Bradbury, *Stephen and Matilda* (Stroud, 1996), 71–2.

10 L. Wertheimer, 'Adeliza of Louvain and Anglo-Norman queenship', *HSJ*, 7 (1996), 112–14, has a careful consideration of this episode. Stephen had been at Arundel at some time in autumn 1138, perhaps at the time of the queen's remarriage to d'Aubigné, when he had confirmed the queen's grants to Reading made by her at the late King Henry's anniversary mass in December

erstwhile supporters as having a conspiratorial hand in the affair. The *Gesta* has the extraordinary story that Earl Robert met Bishop Henry deep in the wilds of Hampshire as he was hurrying on to the Severn valley, and there the pair struck a secret deal to work to each other's advantage. The Gloucester abbey source is clear in his mind that Miles of Gloucester had secretly promoted the whole expedition. Like any conspiracy theory, none of these rumours can be confirmed and perhaps they ought to be discounted, but they do lay open the tortured and suspicious thought-world of England at the close of King Stephen's fourth regnal year. That sort of *Zeitgeist* did not promise well for what was to follow.

THE FORMATION OF THE EMPRESS'S PARTY IN ENGLAND

By the autumn of 1139, the embattled Gloucester affinity had only barely survived a savaging by King Stephen in the absence of their lord. Bristol had been the only major centre to survive the summer campaign, although there were lesser strongholds still scattered about Somerset which stubbornly held out, and the centre of the earl's power in Glamorgan and Gwent was quite beyond the king's reach. On the day the empress and the earl landed, an objective observer would have concluded that it was only a matter of time before the attempted rebellion in England would collapse. With no leader of any prestige openly exerting himself in the empress's cause in England, the end was clearly in sight. William de Mohun fighting from Dunster was an opportunist despised even by his own side (as Brian fitz Count openly reveals) and John Marshal fighting from Marlborough and Ludgershall was little better.[11] This might very well be why Queen Adeliza and her royalist husband had welcomed Mathilda into England, expecting perhaps that peace negotiations might well now open up.

But the rebel position was neither so poor as it appeared, nor the king's successes quite so overwhelming. The key to the sudden reversal in fortunes which followed on from the empress's arrival lay in that party of the late King Henry's new men whom Stephen had deliberately slighted and ignored since 1136. These men had always looked to Earl Robert of Gloucester as the greatest among them, and as political geography had developed in King Henry's reign, the landed power of the more considerable of these men just happened to be physically concentrated in Wales and the southern March: Earl Robert in Cardiff, Newport, Bristol and Tewkesbury; Miles of Gloucester in Brecon,

---

1136, *Regesta* iii, no. 679 (rehabilitated as a genuine charter in R.H.C. Davis, *King Stephen* (3rd edn., London 1990), 170). *The Waltham Chronicle*, ed. and trans. L. Watkiss and M. Chibnall (Oxford, 1994), 76–8 places the marriage between the queen and d'Aubigné 'after the death of King Henry', and places his creation as earl subsequent to the marriage.
11 For Brian fitz Count on William de Mohun, see H.W.C. Davis, 'Henry of Blois and Brian fitz Count', *EHR*, 18 (1903), 301; for John Marshal's dubious allegiance in the late 1130s, D. Crouch, *William Marshal: Court, Career and Chivalry in the Angevin Empire, c.1147–1219* (London, 1990), 14–15.

Caldicot, Dean, and Gloucester, and Brian fitz Count in Abergavenny. Miles had gone somewhat further in Stephen's reign than the others, and increased his hold on Herefordshire by securing for his son, Roger, much of the Lacy inheritance. However, Earl Robert alone of these three great men had rebelled. Miles and Brian had held aloof fastidiously throughout 1138 and 1139, their inactivity much helping King Stephen as he picked off those of the Gloucester affinity who had rallied to Gloucester's call from Normandy. But now, in October 1139, the great earl was among them at last, and that was enough to persuade Miles and Brian finally to abandon the king who had excluded them from the sources of power.

Earl Robert is said by the chroniclers to have made it his first business in England to search out Brian at his chief place of Wallingford and Miles in his great keep at Gloucester, and secure them for his cause.[12] With these two men, particularly Miles of Gloucester, came several other notable adherents. Earl Robert himself reopened communications with his Welsh ally, King Morgan ab Owain, and through him, and probably other contractors, he raised his own mercenary force of Welsh infantry and even some cavalry.[13] William of Malmesbury tells us that the collapse of the king's position in Wales and the west was very rapid. Leaving Arundel, the king struck out energetically at his new enemies but found the situation too confused to get a grasp upon. The confusion can be seen from the way that a Fleming mercenary captain called Robert fitz Hubert, whom Earl Robert had brought with him from Normandy, broke away from his force and only a week after the landing at Arundel had seized the castle of Malmesbury, avowedly for the earl.[14]

The king's plan seems to have been to press as far as he dared into the hostile core of his enemies' lands, to see what he could achieve. His first destination after leaving Arundel was Wallingford, Brian fitz Count's showpiece fortress, and the most exposed rebel centre, being detached from the core of the rebel lands by many miles of debatable land and the Cotswold hills. Because of his exposed position, Brian was to be nicknamed the 'marquis' by his allies.[15] Daunted by the strength of Brian's castle and his preparations, the king ordered Wallingford to be blockaded by long-term siege works, and led his army determinedly westwards up the Thames valley to find an ill-prepared garrison at Miles's new castle at his outpost of South Cerney, which fell into his hands.[16]

---

12 *GS*, 90–2; RT, 137. JW iii, 270 makes the point that Miles held his great fortress of Gloucester from Earl Robert.
13 OV vi, 536 decries Earl Robert's recruitment and employment in England of 'barbaric' Welsh mercenaries in 1139. For an analysis of the earl's novel use of Welsh troops in England see D. Crouch, 'The March and the Welsh kings', in *The Anarchy of King Stephen's Reign*, ed. E. King (Oxford, 1994), 276–7.
14 *HN*, 36; *GS*, 82.
15 *HN*, 51. See comments on this in D. Crouch, *The Image of Aristocracy in Britain, 1000–1300* (London, 1992), 99–100.
16 The loss of South Cerney was a significant blow against Miles, the manor was an old administrative centre of his family in the upper Thames valley on the Wiltshire–Gloucestershire border, see D. Walker, 'The "honours" of the earls of Hereford in the twelfth century', *Transactions of the Bristol and Gloucestershire Archaeological Society*, lxxix (1960), 198.

By 21 October the king had reached Malmesbury, which again was ill-prepared, and he drove off Robert fitz Hubert, seizing the town and the castle (and no doubt causing William, its librarian, the historian, to scribble some gloomy notes about his patron's declining fortunes). The king then turned south, meaning to reduce the castle of Trowbridge, the fortress of Miles's son-in-law and adherent, Humphrey de Bohun, who was interrupting communications with royalist Bath and Castle Cary. Here, however, he had less success, and a siege conducted with his usual energy had too little effect to make it worth prosecuting.[17] So, heavily garrisoning Devizes behind him, the king moved for London, having established some sort of perimeter against his new enemies running from Winchcombe down the Cotswolds south to Bath.

His enemies, in the meantime, had their successes. Miles of Gloucester mounted an unsettling raid against the siege works around Wallingford, to hearten Brian's garrison. But the most revealing move came elsewhere. Hereford was beseiged almost immediately after Miles's change of side with the aid of the veteran rebel, Geoffrey Talbot, now one of Earl Robert's household. For Miles to attempt Hereford was an act so flagrant in its opportunism, that we can assume that Miles's deepest purpose in his change of side was to consolidate his control over Herefordshire. He had not achieved much from adherence to Stephen; he was making sure that adherence to Mathilda would be more lucrative. Since he had met her in Gloucester on 15 October just before the blockade of Hereford, we may assume that she had given him permission to try to take over the most considerable royal asset remaining in the southern March.[18] It seems that she took homage from her new supporters in Gloucester and established herself in the castle as her temporary palace: preferring a show of independence to depending quite so obviously on the earl of Gloucester's hospitality.[19]

Within a month of landing at Arundel, Earl Robert and the empress had established a party, secured the lower Severn valley and southern March, and begun preparation for a long-term campaign. The achievement, despite its occasional setbacks, was impressive – and particularly so because their opponent, the king, had not made it easy for them. But Stephen had discovered now the fickleness of much of his support and been cruelly paid off for his early misjudgements. The sorry consequences of his overreliance on an aristocratic faction were exposed once an opportunity was given for those he had slighted to abandon him for an alternative ruler. The failure in 1136 to confront the Welsh crisis had come home to him: the neglected Marcher lords had now

17 *HN*, 36–7 indicates that the king also sent armed squadrons ranging through northern Somerset and Gloucestershire at this time to see what might be achieved opportunistically by chevauchée.
18 *HN*, 36–7 firmly dates the seizure of the city of Hereford and the beginning of the siege of its castle to the same time as the activity in the Vale of Gloucester, in October 1139.
19 JW iii, 270–2; Chibnall, *Matilda*, 83–4. In fact, she only succeeded in showing her dependence on another principal of her cause. Miles later was heard to make the claim that the empress was wholly dependent on him throughout her stay in England, ibid., 132–3, as noted by D. Walker, 'Miles of Gloucester, earl of Hereford', *Transactions of the Bristol and Gloucestershire Archaeological Society*, lxxvii (1958), 77.

abandoned the man who had abandoned them. Tellingly, among the new defectors were the border magnates Robert fitz Harold of Ewyas and his brother, John fitz Harold of Sudeley. Robert had commanded the king's vain attempt to regain west Wales, and John had, till now, been a close ally of his cousin Waleran of Meulan.[20] What was worse for the king was that the new dissidents were able to resist him the more bitterly because they were backed by the very Welsh kings whom Stephen had allowed to run riot in the hope they would fall out among themselves.

Finally, the king's utter failure to resolve the problem of a rival claimant within his domains, which he had ducked in Normandy in 1137, now had come to haunt him in England. The empress was at work constructing an alternative structure of government into which dissidents were invited to fit themselves. Her ideology – of right inheritance and keeping faith – would soon be vigorously promoted, and give her a moral eminence Stephen would find difficult to counter. The inherited structure of strong administrative kingship he had tried to use to buttress his rule was falling apart as a whole region of his kingdom simply defected to the pretender. Within all these circumstances and strategies lies the reason why the civil war in England was to last as long as it did.

However, the lightning successes of the new Angevin party in England in October 1139, promising as they were, had their flaws too. These were to be revealed in the very next month when Earl Robert of Gloucester unveiled his first major campaign in England. He assembled a very considerable force at Gloucester, and early in November he unleashed it against the city of Worcester. His choice of target was ominous, and echoed the strategy of Baldwin de Redvers's attack on Wareham as he entered England in August. Although Worcester was a royalist centre, an attack on it had the additional advantage of allowing Earl Robert to vent his particular animus against the man who had hindered and damaged his cause and his estates so badly in Normandy, Count Waleran of Meulan, who was also earl of Worcester.

The citizens of Worcester had some early intelligence of the coming disaster and hurried to stack their moveable goods in the cathedral, which became like a giant warehouse and refugee camp; as the chronicler of Worcester wrote: 'The clergy chanted in the choir, children screamed in the nave; the cries of babies and the grieving of their mothers gave the response to those singing the office.'[21] It was soon to be an all-too-common experience in some parts of England. The blow fell on the city in the early morning of 7 November, sending the monks of the cathedral scurrying into the castle bearing the relics of St Oswald (they had already concealed the contents of their treasury). The castle resisted the initial onset, but the enemy had clearly come to pillage the city and the surrounding countryside. An attempt was also made to burn the

---

20 For John fitz Harold's rapid defection once Earl Robert was in England, see Crouch, *Beaumont Twins*, 47. Robert of Ewyas appears to have abandoned the king with Miles of Gloucester, his neighbour, and he made a new career as Miles's household constable.
21 JW iii, 272 (my translation).

city down and a large number of the citizens caught in the streets were hauled off for ransom. It was a very sorry sight indeed, and the chronicler was talking in more than one sense when he referred to 7 November as 'that day on which winter began'. Some three weeks later, the city's earl, Waleran of Meulan, arrived to inspect the damage, and, says the chronicler, 'he grieved, for he knew that all this had been done to hurt him'. The citizens, too, had their theory: they believed that the whole disaster had been deliberately inspired by their commercial rivals in the town of Gloucester. As his enemies had served the count, so the count served them. To encourage the citizens of Worcester, and recover some prestige, he led his military household south from the city to Sudeley, the residence of his recent ally, John fitz Harold. There he did such things, as was said, that would bear no repeating, and returned on 1 December 1139, loaded with plunder and captives.[22]

CONTAINMENT

King Stephen spent Christmas 1139 at Salisbury, holding a solemn crown-wearing and taking possession of the city and cathedral following the death of the great Bishop Roger, whose fortunes he had shattered the previous summer, and his health too, as it had since become clear.[23] The council that accompanied his Christmas court would seem (from what happened next) to have concentrated on military matters, with the overriding item of the agenda being the comprehensive destruction of the empress's party.[24] In that respect the king and his advisers were following the same policy as they had done since the sidelining of the bishops in 1137: confrontation and not negotiation. Unfortunately, it does not seem that the king was able to find any overall strategy to master the rebel southwest. The next year or so shows him as striving with great energy to contain his enemies, but reacting to events and not in command of them. Once more we see traits we have already identified in Stephen's management of events: a lack of any internal map of power structures and personalities by which to pilot his way through to his desired end.

---

22 JW iii, 274–6.

23 For the deathbed and death of Bishop Roger, see E.J. Kealey, *Roger of Salisbury Viceroy of England* (London, 1972), 201–8, 262–9. He had some time to contemplate his approaching end, and (after confession) issued letters addressed to the king, the legate and the archbishop, restoring several properties he had abstracted from various churches in his power.

24 The *Gesta* and William of Malmesbury do both, however, give a complimentary account of the way Stephen settled the affairs of the chapter of Salisbury and the houses of Malmesbury and Abbotsbury after the death of their domineering patron, *GS*, 96–8; *HN*, 40. JW iii, 279–80, puts the freeing of the abbeys at a court held at Reading soon after Christmas. Stephen's treatment of the chapter is confirmed by the several charters he issued to it at this time, *Regesta* iii, nos. 787–90, although JW iii, 278 says that the canons bribed him with a gift of 2000*li*, and Kealey, *Roger of Salisbury*, 205 points out that the canons were having to secure from the king what the bishop had freely restored to them on his deathbed. Malmesbury also mentions a fine being paid by his abbey for the king's favour, but refuses to agree with Bishop Henry of Winchester that it was anything improper, *HN*, 40.

The death of Roger of Salisbury brought the bishop's most resentful and aggressive episcopal nephew, Nigel of Ely, to rebel in East Anglia. What he hoped to gain is impossible to say, for there were at that time no potential allies in East Anglia with whom he could operate. He acted out of anger, fear and frustration. Nigel was swiftly overwhelmed by the king in person early in January. He was betrayed even by his own monastic chapter (which had argued against his plan), and he took refuge in Gloucester with the empress's court. Most charitably interpreted, Bishop Nigel's stand was a moral one, a personal protest against the treatment of his uncle and the Church.[25] But no sooner was Bishop Nigel under control than trouble broke out at the opposite end of the kingdom, drawing the king down to the far southwest. This new agitation may have been a testimony to the activities of the likes of Baldwin de Redvers after the empress's landing. We last see him distracting the king in Corfe castle while the empress and the earl of Gloucester landed in Sussex. Although we lose sight of him in the historical record at that point, if he were to be of any use, we must assume that he would be as active as he could be in raising his tenants. Although no source mentions Baldwin at work in the southwest, we do know that his close companion, Reginald, the king's son, was very active in Cornwall in the empress's interests.

For reasons which it is impossible now to recover, William fitz Richard, lord of Cardinan and one of the principal magnates of Cornwall, joined the rebellion against Stephen early in 1140. As a token of his change of allegiance he married his daughter to Reginald, the king's son, and the two men combined to attempt to secure Cornwall for the Angevins. William of Malmesbury states that at this time Reginald was made earl of the shire and his regional lieutenant by Robert of Gloucester.[26] There was an energetic and apparently ferocious campaign, in which Reginald made the mistake of alienating the local church by imposing a tax. He was excommunicated and a counter-campaign by the king and Earl Alan of Richmond during January seems to have found local support. Reginald was confined to one castle (probably Launceston) and contained, while Earl Alan was given the title of Cornwall by the king so as to cancel out Reginald's new-found status. There is a reference to his later holding of a shire court on Bodmin Moor as a demonstration of his control over the county and Reginald's failure, and it appears that Count Alan maintained

25 *GS*, 98–100; *Liber Eliensis*, 314–15. HH, 722–4 says that Stephen 'drove Bishop Nigel of Ely from his see because he was the bishop of Salisbury's nephew', but this is an unsustainable accusation contradicted even by sources friendly to the empress. *Regesta* iii, nos. 261–3 show that, as at Salisbury, the king took care to act kindly towards the cathedral chapter at Ely having once disposed of the bishop; the monks therefore complimented him as being 'kindly and dutiful at heart' in his treatment of them, *Liber Eliensis*, 315.
26 Davis, *Stephen*, 136 and Chibnall, *Matilda*, 89, for different reasons question that Reginald could have been created earl by his half-brother, Robert of Gloucester (as William of Malmesbury says) but this doubt supposes that the twelfth century shared the later attitude (not established till the fourteenth century) that the king had sole sanction as to who was or was not titled, see Crouch, *Image of Aristocracy*, 59–75.

himself successfully and in force in the county until the debacle at Lincoln the next year.[27]

But while the king was being active and successful in Cornwall, the situation escaped his grasp in another part of the realm. Miles of Gloucester broke his winter camp (around besieged Hereford) and began a campaign against royalist outposts in the Vale of Gloucester, attacking the garrisons of Winchcombe and Sudeley at the very end of January, capturing Winchcombe, but being worsted at nearby Sudeley. The intention may well have been to reopen links with Wallingford, but instead it brought the king and the count of Meulan back to the Severn valley with a great force. The king seems to have hoped to draw the earl of Gloucester into battle through a formidable chevauchée through Devon and Somerset on his return, but the earl was too wise a soldier to risk battle on such terms, and withdrew to Bristol where, it seems, he stayed.[28] The king proceeded to the Severn valley to make a determined effort to recover the ground lost the previous year. Waleran of Meulan took his revenge for the sack of Worcester by proceeding to lay waste the Vale of Gloucester within a mile of the town itself; only the lands of Tewkesbury abbey were spared, Tewkesbury itself, with the earl of Gloucester's impressive hall and residence, was completely destroyed. The count returned to Worcester 'telling all and sundry that he had scarcely ever carried out such a burning in Normandy or England'.[29]

The king in the meantime had campaigned into Herefordshire with a great army, including at least five loyalist earls, determined to drive his enemies out of the north of the county and relieve the beleaguered garrison of Hereford, besieged since October 1139. Stephen set up a base at Little Hereford on the Shropshire border south of Ludlow, where he stayed for some time.[30] While there, just as he had done in Cornwall with Count Alan, he made moves to establish a regional governor. In this case it was Count Waleran's twin brother, Earl Robert of Leicester. A charter still exists – issued as the king's army was on the road between Leominster and the city of Hereford at Newton – by which the king granted Earl Robert the city and castle of Hereford (still firmly in Miles's grip) and the whole county (including, we must assume, Miles's lands and much of the disputed Lacy fee). The charter tells us that, as yet, the king still had the allegiance of the significant magnates in the north of the county: Osbert fitz Hugh of Richard's Castle, Hugh de Mortemer of Wigmore and William de Briouze of Buellt and Radnor were all to be exempt from

---

27 *HN*, 42; *GS*, 100–2; *The Cartulary of St Michael's Mount*, ed. P.L. Hull (Devon and Cornwall Record Society, new ser., 5, 1962) 6. For comments on Alan's earldom, Crouch, *Image of Aristocracy*, 67. For our ignorance of the doings of Baldwin de Redvers at this time, *Charters of the Redvers Family and the Earldom of Devon, 1090–1217*, ed. R. Bearman (Devon and Cornwall Record Society, new ser., 37, 1994), 7, although idem, 'Baldwin de Redvers', 25, 38, makes a case that he based himself in his eastern estates, in Dorset or Wight, rather than Devon in the period 1139–41.
28 *GS*, 104, see also *HN*, 41 on Earl Robert's general inactivity in early 1140.
29 JW iii, 282–4 (my translation).
30 I follow here the logic of the editors' dating of *Regesta* iii, no. 263, see also JW iii, 282.

the earl's obedience and so must have still been offering at least lip service to the king.[31]

Establishing the earl of Leicester as his lieutenant in the county was one way to ensure that the damage done by Miles of Gloucester was contained. It seems that the arrangement was reinforced with other grants: the earl was given control of Kidderminster in the upper Severn valley.[32] As it happened, the king's army nearly reached Hereford, but was then forced to retreat for some unknown reason. The castle fell to Miles and Geoffrey Talbot sometime in early spring after a determined assault with artillery which was mounted on siege works in the cathedral cemetery (graves being ruthlessly desecrated as the earthworks were thrown up by the besiegers). In the process, the rest of the city and the cathedral suffered considerable damage.[33]

King Stephen has been criticised by some modern writers (as well as one contemporary one) for racing about England from crisis to crisis at this time with little idea of what to do.[34] The criticism that Stephen was at the mercy of events has some truth in it. But the idea that he was unable to form a policy to deal with his problem of dispersed resources and many enemies is less easy to sustain. As we have seen in Cornwall and Hereford (and as we will also see in Wiltshire) the king early in 1140 began strengthening his policy of granting administrative earldoms into a policy of establishing regional military governors with the resources and soldiers to contain his enemies, while he himself could move from place to place wherever danger was greatest or the threats were new.[35] To some extent this seems to be prefigured in earlier moves (such

31 *Regesta* iii, no. 437. Whether or not this charter explicitly creates Robert of Leicester 'earl of Hereford' is a question difficult to answer as the Latin '*me reddidisse et concessisse . . . totum comitatum de Herefordisc*' . . .' can bear more than one interpretation. G.H. White, 'King Stephen's earldoms', *TRHS*, 4th ser., xiii (1930), 72–7 argued against it as a grant of an earldom. The context of the grant needs to be considered, however. Only weeks previously Alan of Brittany had been awarded a second county in Cornwall in a very similar situation. There are parallels here also with the creation of Henry of Scotland as earl of Northumbria in 1138 (the lesser magnates of the shire were exempted from homage to him) and Waleran of Meulan as earl of Worcester the same year (he, too, obtained the royal assets and rights in his shire). P. Latimer, 'Grants of "totus comitatus" in twelfth-century England: their origins and meaning', *Bulletin of the Institute of Historical Research*, lix (1986), 143–4, prefers a minimalist interpretation of the charter's evidence, and despite differing with him on points of detail, one has to admit that his is a position difficult to gainsay.
32 For the earl's possession of Kidderminster (formerly a possession of the earl's Norman enemy, William III de Breteuil) see J. Nichols, *The History and Antiquities of the County of Leicester* (4 vols in 8, London, 1795–1815) i, pt 1, app. I, 37–8.
33 *HN*, 36–7 seems to allude to the king's failure to relieve Hereford castle, and *GS*, 108–10 gives an incomplete account of the end of the siege. The letters of Gilbert Foliot, abbot of Gloucester since the previous year, include ones to the dean and to the bishop of Hereford at this time. They allude to the plundering of the cathedral church, and the intolerable situation which had led the dean to quit the city, much to the despair of the citizens, *LCGF*, nos. 1–2.
34 Davis, *Stephen*, 41–2; H.A. Cronne, *The Reign of Stephen: Anarchy in England, 1135–54* (London, 1970), 36, 39–41, which to some extent echo the scornful observation by HH, 724, 'does it matter where he was at Christmas or Easter [1140]?'
35 Another obvious candidate for such a regional military governor in early 1140 was Hervey de Léon, who (probably) married an illegitimate daughter of King Stephen, and who was deployed as earl in Wiltshire with a base at Devizes castle after its capture from Robert fitz Hubert in April 1140, *HN*, 43–4; *GS*, 108. Davis, *Stephen*, 45, includes Geoffrey de Mandeville among these regional satraps of 1140.

as the use of Robert of Ewyas on the March, Waleran of Meulan in Normandy and Henry de Tracy in Somerset). The campaign of spring 1140 in Herefordshire is the best indication how the minds of the king and his military advisers were adapting to the threat of the empress's party.

By March 1140 when the king moved out of the March back to London the military situation was stable, although hardly healthy. The marginal outbreaks in Cornwall and Cambridgeshire had been overcome. Miles of Gloucester had obtained his objective and at last regained Hereford (from which he had ruled the southern March in Henry I's reign), but otherwise the declared rebel party was still contained in the lower Severn valley. It would seem that the allegiance of a number of minor magnates in the region was shaken, and the king had cause to worry about them. A leading member of this dubious contingent was John Marshal, who until 1139 was the king's firm (and well-rewarded friend). The king had favoured him with the custody of two important royal castles, at Marlborough and Ludgershall. Yet in August 1139 the king and he had fallen out and it was from the siege of Marlborough that Stephen moved to confront Baldwin de Redvers's invading force. Yet was John a supporter of the empress? Nobody was quite sure whose side John favoured in early 1140. When he seized Devizes by an astute trick from Earl Robert of Gloucester's over-ambitious mercenary, Robert fitz Hubert, at the end of March 1140, William of Malmesbury and the author of the *Gesta* believed that John was in rebellion; the Worcester chronicler, on the other hand, thought that John was fighting for the king. John Marshal was certainly still keen to keep good relations with Stephen, for he did not hinder the handing back of Devizes to the king. John Marshal represents the new and unsettling appearance of the neutralist magnate, doing his best to profit from whatever opportunities the struggle between the parties threw up but keeping back from full engagement.[36]

John Marshal's uncertain allegiance was not unprecedented in March 1140, for a similar situation applied to another old and loyal supporter of the king: Hugh Bigod, a royal steward and lord of Framlingham in Suffolk. Like John Marshal he had benefited greatly from his support for the king, but that did not prevent him from striking a hostile attitude at the end of spring 1140. The king was forced to march an army into Suffolk at the end of May against Hugh and seize the castle of Bungay, and although eventually, in August, the two men met and returned to amicable terms, 'it did not last long', as the Waverley annalist says.[37] What was happening here? Despite Cronne's belief of Hugh that 'his was not a stable or reliable character', he had been unwavering in his support of Stephen since the new king's succession, in which he had played such an important role.[38] My feeling is that what we see in his sudden outbreak is yet another symptom of what had alienated the king both from his

36 *GS*, 106–8; *HN*, 44; JW iii, 286.
37 *Annales de Waverleia*, 228.
38 Cronne, *Stephen*, 88. Cronne was incorrect in his belief that Hugh Bigod controlled Bungay before 1140 (see on).

brother and from Robert of Gloucester, that concentration of influence at court in a narrow aristocratic clique headed by Waleran of Meulan.

Just before Hugh Bigod's outbreak, in mid-March 1140, there was a council at London at which Waleran of Meulan had secured the nomination of his cousin and follower, Philip de Harcourt, as the new bishop of Salisbury. This had aroused the anger of Bishop Henry of Winchester, who wanted his nephew, Henry de Sully, as bishop, and who therefore had refused to agree to the appointment.[39] But the anger may not have been limited to Bishop Henry. With the king more or less monopolised by the Beaumont clique, the likes of Hugh Bigod, who had dogged Stephen faithfully across England and Normandy since his first weeks as king, must have become as frustrated as the earlier generation of Henry I's new men who were now fighting for the empress.[40] The king's move to Bungay in May 1140 has a different significance than has been previously realised. Bungay was not in 1140 a Bigod manor, but it, and other lands in the Waveney valley, formed an isolated but important estate block of Robert of Leicester, Count Waleran's brother, himself only recently endowed by the king with the county of Hereford (see Appendix). Therefore, what has been portrayed as Hugh Bigod's revolt was aimed not so much at the king, but at the Beaumonts, in the same way that Baldwin de Redvers had struck at Wareham and Robert of Gloucester had struck at Worcester the previous year. That the king seized Bungay in the far north of the county and not the Bigod castle of Framlingham in the centre does indicate that he was intervening in a local Beaumont–Bigod dispute, not countering a Bigod rebellion.[41] Although troops had been moved around in haste, it is likely that the Bigod problem in Suffolk had involved little or no violence; its significance was not that Hugh Bigod was disloyal to the king (any more than Ranulf of Chester was disloyal later in the same year when he seized Lincoln) but that Hugh had lost faith in the king's will to favour him without forcible prompting.[42]

39 *Annales de Waverleia*, 228; OV vi, 536.
40 A. Wareham, 'The motives and politics of the Bigod family *c.*1066–1177', *ANS* xvii, ed. C. Harper-Bill (Woodbridge, 1994), 228, 235, suggests that Bigods and Warennes were regional rivals on the Suffolk–Norfolk border; accepting this, it would then be significant that Earl William III de Warenne was Count Waleran's younger half-brother.
41 For the political geography of the Bigod honor in Suffolk, see Green, *Aristocracy of Norman England*, 153. Judith Green, ibid., 375 and n, suggests that Hugh had some other cause for complaint in the fact that he had not inherited his father's and elder brother's shrievalty of Norfolk and Suffolk, held in the 1120s and 1130s by Stephen's follower, Robert fitz Walter. The shrievalty continued after 1135 in the hands of Robert fitz Walter's son, John de Chesney (for the relationship see above p. 23n). It is certainly true that Hugh later claimed the shrievalty from Duke Henry. Ralph Davis's arguments against Hugh Bigod's creation as earl of Norfolk in the settlement of August 1140, and in favour of his creation as earl by the empress, are convincing, Davis, *Stephen*, 138–9, but see Wareham, 'Motives and politics of the Bigod family', 234, for a restatement of the earlier argument, stemming from John Horace Round.
42 Hugh Bigod has an unjustified reputation as an untrustworthy supporter of Stephen due to his panicky seizure of Norwich at the end of April 1136 on hearing news of Stephen's alleged death (see above p. 52n). This is not sufficient warrant for believing, as Cronne, Davis and Bradbury assumed, that he was an inveterate trouble-maker from the beginning of the reign.

APPENDIX – BUNGAY, THE BEAUMONTS AND THE BIGODS

Bungay, Suffolk, largely royal demesne in 1086, had come to Count Robert of Meulan, the twins' father, perhaps as early as Rufus's reign, and had been inherited in 1118 by Robert of Leicester, the younger twin, as is evident from a charter concerning Bungay to Thetford priory, Brit. Libr. ms Lansdowne 229, fo. 147r (datable to 1121 × 35). Earl Robert of Leicester conceded his claim on it to his cousin, Earl Roger of Warwick, at some time in the decade after 1140 in return for two knights' fees in Warwickshire, *Red Book* i, 325. Earl Roger sensibly legitimised Earl Hugh Bigod's seizure of Bungay by marrying his younger daughter, Gundreda, to the earl and including Bungay as part of the marriage contract, as we learn from her enjoyment of the town as part of her marriage portion after Hugh's death, see a charter of hers dating from after 1177 in Bodl. Libr. ms. Dugdale 39, fo. 82v and her foundation of a nunnery there out of her *libero maritagio, Monasticon* iv, 338. *Complete Peerage* ix, 585–6 and n. demonstrates that to marry Gundreda, Hugh had set aside his previous wife, Juliana de Vere.

After Countess Gundreda's death, Bungay passed to her son, Hugh Bigod, but somehow by 1270 it had come to the Bigod earls (descendants of Hugh and Juliana, not Hugh and Gundreda) for the then earl of Norfolk was recorded as still holding the castle and manor of Bungay by service of a knight's fee to the earls of Warwick, *Calendar of Inquisitions post mortem* i, 240. How this conveyance was carried out is not easy to say, but the fact that after nearly a lifetime's litigation, Hugh Bigod, son of Gundreda, came to an agreement with his half-brother, Earl Roger Bigod, by which he surrendered his claim on large parts of the Bigod patrimony, and the earldom itself, in return for his homage and service, for the service of two knights and £30 of rents, in 1199, may have opened the way for a further agreement, by which Hugh (who was childless) ultimately surrendered or sold his reversion of the estate of Bungay to the earl after his mother's death.

CHAPTER 7

The Ideology of Civil War

THE DEBATE BETWEEN THE PARTIES

As the first year of the civil war in England closed, so we get at Hereford and Worcester a colourful but tragic glimpse of the complex motivation of the partisans. For the triumvirate of Robert of Gloucester, Miles of Gloucester and even Brian fitz Count, it was alienation from the centre of power that had ultimately caused them to turn against King Stephen. It should be emphasised that, at least at the beginning, they were rather *against* Stephen than *for* Mathilda. So far as Miles was concerned, it was always going to be uncertain how much the empress's rightful claims mattered to him. His seizure of Hereford in October 1139 was an early signal as to where his priorities lay: in the promotion of a regional hegemony which Stephen's indifference to him had made unattainable. Robert of Gloucester seems from the events of November 1139 to have been pursuing a number of private scores across England. His personal animus against Stephen and his lieutenant, Count Waleran, was what caused Worcester to be plundered and burned. Brian fitz Count is traditionally reckoned to have been the idealist amongst these three pillars of the Angevin cause.[1] But it is embarrassingly obvious that he did nothing to assist the foundering rebellion in the southwest during 1138 and 1139 until the day in October that Robert of Gloucester appeared before Wallingford and changed his mind.

All three men were effective and brave soldiers; all three took their commitment to the Angevin cause perfectly seriously, and two out of the three endured severe losses in pursuing it. But it is well to understand from the outset that their motives in supporting the empress were not straightforward and certainly not what we would call 'chivalrous'. Much the same was true for those lesser magnates who followed them. The brothers Robert and John fitz Harold had lands which lay squarely within the Vale of Gloucester and southern

---

1 Marjorie Chibnall in *The Empress Matilda* (Oxford, 1991), 84–5, 87 talks generously of his 'strong moral principles' and of few being as 'highminded' as Brian. While I would agree that his conduct after 1139 was laudably steadfast, too little account is taken of his inaction before 1139.

March. To support the king and resist Earl Robert and Miles would be to invite dispossession, so they cut their links with their former protectors, the king and the count of Meulan. It was very necessary for them to respect the menace represented by the greater magnates who were their neighbours.[2] About the only people who might be regarded as routinely idealistic in their selection of a cause to fight for were those tenants who followed the king or the empress behind their lords' banners. They were at least honouring a contract of loyalty from which they had benefited. But this sort of ideal was not the disinterested zeal of a royalist or Angevin partisan; whatever debate they had in his household, in the end, their lord had made that decision for his men.

Why, therefore, was there so much contemporary literature projecting an ideology of dissidence by the Angevin party? One of the more remarkable aspects of the civil war of Stephen's reign is how articulate were the respective parties in their rivalry: battle and siege were not the only ways in which they fought. The level of education and literacy amongst the higher aristocracy had much to do with this. They were brought up in the households of successive Norman kings who set a high value on literacy, particularly Henry. The 'palace school' of clerks and young aristocrats which itinerated with the king was one way in which learning permeated the life of the court, but we find that tutors and schools also played their part. Robert II of Leicester, one of the Beaumont twins, was claimed to have spent some of his youth studying under the learned Abbot Faricius at Abingdon. We know the name of the clerk Ranulf, canon of the minster of Warwick, who was tutor of the young Roger, Earl Robert's cousin, who became earl of Warwick in 1119. We have certain evidence for the literacy of a good number of Stephen's magnates: Count Waleran of Meulan, Earl Robert of Leicester, Earl Roger of Warwick, Roger, the son of Miles of Gloucester and, perhaps most notably, Earl Robert of Gloucester.[3] But even the magnate who was illiterate had the resources to join in intellectual debate. Brian fitz Count of Wallingford, although an intimate of King Henry, did not acquire the skills of reading. Yet he did have clerks in his household who were able to read to him and write for him and, in the example of his prose which has been preserved, we find a blunt and forceful intellect which was able to express itself clearly, if not elegantly.[4]

2 For this dynamic in aristocratic society, see D. Crouch, 'From Stenton to McFarlane: models of society in the twelfth and thirteenth centuries', *TRHS*, 6th ser., no. 5 (1995), 194–7.
3 For ideas of literacy as general amongst Anglo-Norman court culture and twelfth-century aristocrats, see H.G. Richardson and G.O. Sayles, *The Governance of Medieval England* (Edinburgh, 1963), 273; F. Barlow, *William Rufus* (London, 1983), 18–22; M.T. Clanchy, *From Memory to Written Record* (2nd edn., London, 1991), 186–97; C.S. Jaeger, *The Origins of Courtliness: Civilising Trends and the Formation of Courtly Ideals, 939–1210* (Philadelphia, 1985), 216–23. For the literacy of the twins, Waleran and Robert, see D. Crouch, *The Beaumont Twins: The Roots and Branches of Power in the Twelfth Century* (Cambridge, 1986), 207–11; for the clerical *magister* of Roger of Warwick, Cartulary of St Mary, Warwick, PRO, E164/22, fo. 2r. Roger of Hereford is recorded as himself reading the charters of Worcester cathedral, *The Cartulary of Worcester Cathedral Priory*, ed. R.R. Darlington (Pipe Roll Society, lxxvi, 1968) 29. On the literacy of Robert of Gloucester, William of Malmesbury, *De gestis regum Anglorum*, ed. W. Stubbs (2 vols, Rolls Series, 1887–9) ii, 521; *HN*, 23.
4 *LCGF*, 61.

The debate between the parties can be traced from the sources, and it is clear that it did not properly begin until several years into the reign. The only person wishing to argue Mathilda's corner in December 1135 was Mathilda herself. By Christmas 1135, virtually the entire Anglo-Norman realm was united against her. Even Baldwin de Redvers and Robert of Bampton, the West Country rebels of late spring 1136, were not fighting for her: Baldwin was in pursuit of the shrievalty of Devon and Robert was protesting against the peremptory loss – for whatever reason – of his manor of Uffculme to Glastonbury abbey and its titular abbot, Bishop Henry of Winchester. There could be no dialogue at the time of the succession, as there was no partner in it.

Nevertheless, the earliest years of the reign did generate some items on the intellectual agenda. There was the matter of the oath of 1127, from which the royalists claimed they had been released by the dying King Henry, and which features retrospectively both in William of Malmesbury's account of Earl Robert of Gloucester's internal debate and in a letter of Gilbert Foliot. As we have seen in an earlier chapter, Richard of Hexham described King David's actions when he seized Northumberland around Christmas 1135, compelling the barons of the region to honour the oath that they had sworn to the empress. Angevin supporters realised from the very beginning that the fact of the oath was something that the royalists could not comfortably explain away, and those who later seceded to the empress could use it as a badge of virtue that they had returned and adhered to it. Later on, those who were to swear fidelity to her in the summer of 1141 when Stephen was in captivity, found that their later return to allegiance to the king left them vulnerable to charges of perjury, a fact that Brian fitz Count was very keen to broadcast. Oaths might have been broken, but there was a price to pay for doing it in a society which had a high ideal of loyalty.[5]

Secondly, there was the legal argument, and in this context most particularly, that a woman could succeed her father as lawful heir. Although we do not find a counter-argument to this in royalist sources, it must have been brought up by them, or the Angevins would not have been so determined to put Mathilda's legitimate case. Arguing against female succession was a weak point in the royalist brief (many women had been heirs of earls and barons since the Conquest), so we find Stephen's proctors before Pope Innocent attempting to prove that the empress was born from an illegitimate union, and that her mother Queen Mathilda (II) had been snatched from the cloister in order to marry her to King Henry.

The papal Curia heard Stephen's case that he be confirmed as king in the first months of 1136, but so far as we can know, the pope heard only arguments and testimonials which presented his nearness in blood to the late king, his lineage, and which dwelt on the civil disorder which made his rapid coronation necessary. The ethical argument seems to have really begun, if at any

5 H.W.C. Davis, 'Henry of Blois and Brian fitz Count', *EHR*, 25 (1910), 302–3.

time, in the household of Robert of Gloucester in Normandy after the departure of Stephen for England in November 1137. Earl Robert's nature, as befitted a prominent royal justice, was to ponder the merits of any case before deciding his course of action. The exact status of his homage to King Stephen at Oxford in April 1136 was one point on which he ruminated. By the time William of Malmesbury got to hear his story from the earl himself (which would have been at the very end of 1139, or maybe not until 1140) the earl had decided that his homage to Stephen had only been conditional, until Stephen proved that he was an unsuitable king.[6] Another point was the idea of female succession, and we have the remarkable evidence that Earl Robert had referred to the biblical book of Numbers for validation of that point. In Chapter 27 God did indeed sanction female inheritance in cases where there were no sons, but that was not the chapter the earl quoted, although Gilbert Foliot pretended it was. The earl had quoted Chapter 36, which stated that women might well inherit, but if they did, they should not marry outside their tribe: surely a hit against the Angevin marriage of 1126, which he had (apparently) promoted?[7]

The broader arguments about the rights and wrongs of Stephen and Mathilda's claims fan out from what was being discussed and debated in the spring of 1138 around Earl Robert. The debate developed further in the episcopal halls and papal chambers of 1139, and arguments were thrown about, like an exchange of lances, between the baronial parties in the long and unresolved stalemate after 1141. There is an argument that the *Historia Novella* itself is simply an extension of the household deliberations of Earl Robert and his advisers into a wider intellectual arena.

In the end, of course, verbal argument settled little; it was the results of battles and sieges which were decisive. But the deliberations and debates (and also the arguments of the royal advocates at Winchester in August 1138) do indicate that the Anglo-Norman ruling class was now finding it impossible not to intellectualise its internal conflicts. Such an attitude of mind looks forward to the debates of successive generations about inheritance, royal power and representative consultation in the reigns of John and Henry III. The civil war which began in Normandy in 1138 and in England in 1139 was a traumatic event, but those who took the field in it did not leave their moral sensibilities behind when they joined in. We cannot really understand what was happening in Stephen's reign if we do not appreciate the intensity, passion and need for self-justification which possessed the chiefs of the warring parties. It is evidence that the men who fought the war were handicapped by scruples. They needed to justify themselves, and in due course it was their scrupulousness, as revealed by their rival ideologies, which would bring them to make peace.

6 *HN*, 17–18, 22–4.
7 *LCGF*, 61–2. See on this, D. Crouch, 'Robert of Gloucester and the daughter of Zelophehad', *Journal of Medieval History*, 11 (1985), 227–43.

THE IDEOLOGY OF THE 'TENURIAL CRISIS'

Over the years, there have been a number of models put forward to explain why it was that people were quite so willing to go to war both with passion and a degree of rationality in Stephen's reign. In the 1960s we find a revisionist view of the civil war emerging which explained the polarising of the political nation as a reaction to the over-dominant kingship of the Norman monarchy. The barons were characterised as having been driven to resist a regime which stifled their legitimate expectations. Nowhere was this baronial resistance so evident as in their natural desire to pass on their estates intact to their children, with no interference from kings. In the unfortunate words of Ralph Davis, 'That was what the barons fought for in Stephen's reign, and that is what they won.'[8]

One should always be wary of sub-Marxian determinist theories of society, which suggest that events can be completely explained as the action of invisible socio-economic forces. For historians who prefer to work from empirical observation, such theories tend to bring out their aggressive streak. The alleged 'tenurial crisis' of Stephen's reign is just such a red rag.[9] It began its life among the legal historians, and it remains very much a unicorn inhabiting their highly theoretical province. For Davis, the starting point for his theory was Professor Samuel Thorne's radical speculation on the nature of inheritance and ideas of property in the eleventh and twelfth centuries, published in 1959. Challenging the assumptions of the generations of Maitland and Stenton, Professor Thorne believed that firm rules of family inheritance were a relatively late development in English society. He particularly noted that the Crown's insistence that, on a tenant-in-chief's death, his estates pass into royal possession (seisin) until granted on to the heir, was a real obstacle to automatic hereditability.[10]

This is a controversy which is still thrashing the undergrowth in the forest of legal historical debate, but it was Davis's gloss on Thorne's theorising which generated the ideas of a 'tenurial crisis' of Stephen's reign. The resolution of laws of inheritance was believed to have occurred in the first half of Henry II's reign, therefore it followed for Davis that inheritance was a big issue in Stephen's reign and that the crisis had been brewing before Henry I died. Here his logic depended also on the work of Sir Richard Southern who

8 R.H.C. Davis, 'What happened in Stephen's reign, 1135–54', *History*, xlix (1964), 1–12, quotation p. 12.
9 The phrase 'tenurial crisis' was coined by Professor J.C. Holt in his article, 'Politics and property in early medieval England', *Past and Present*, no. 57 (1972), 3–52, note particularly 'the tenurial crisis of the Anglo-Norman period' (p. 44). His intention was to demonstrate the instability inherent in English politics due to uncertainties in succession to acquired and inherited lands by sons (particularly in succession to England and Normandy), see idem, 'Rejoinder', *Past and Present*, no. 65 (1974), 127–8, but the phrase has since been used (under the influence of Edmund King) as a shorthand term for what is in fact the Davis thesis. Professor Holt himself noted (*pace* Southern) that it was not inheritance that was in question in Henry I's reign, but how much the heir paid for it, ibid., 135.
10 S.E. Thorne, 'English feudalism and estates in land', *Cambridge Law Journal* (1959), 193–209, repr. idem, *Essays in English Legal History* (London, 1985), 13–29.

(also influenced by Thorne) suggested that Henry I manipulated his baronage by playing on the uncertainties in succession law, and allotting inheritance to his favoured candidates.[11] Until he died, Davis maintained his stand that the number of magnates dispossessed by Henry I because of uncertainties in succession law, roaming the wilderness with a grudge, predetermined that the civil war would happen whatever Stephen did.[12]

It should already be obvious from my own explanation of the civil war that I do not subscribe to any such view, even though there are some historians who still do. Marjorie Chibnall, in her study of the Empress Mathilda, advocates the idea that underneath the rhetoric of Brian fitz Count and Gilbert Foliot's correspondence is an abiding concern for inheritance rights, especially those of women, and that their concern for such rights determined the men of their party to rebel.[13] But apart from a concern for the empress's rights – which was not entirely selfless – I have not found it possible to detect such a prominent concern amongst contemporaries for inheritance within their own families or social group.

The men who precipitated civil war in England were not dispossessed of their estates, nor were they under any threat of dispossession; far from it, the triumvirate of 1139 was made up of men who had done very well out of Henry I's reign, and the gains they had made were explicitly confirmed to them by Stephen. As for succession, Miles of Gloucester and Earl Robert had an embarrassment of adult sons, and Brian fitz Count was childless; the question of daughters inheriting was not a major issue for them (although Miles of Gloucester's daughter-in-law, Cecilia, certainly had brought great wealth with her). None of them had much in the way of a reasonable complaint against Stephen, other than that he was making further preferment for them impossible and therefore imperilling their credibility as good lords to their men. Civil war was not inevitable in 1135. Stephen was, on the surface of things, a successful enough king of England until the summer of 1139, whatever went wrong in Wales and Normandy. He handled the Scottish problem well, and even the supposed explosion against him in Wales in 1135 on Henry I's death, said to be inevitable, turns out on examination to be an illusion; the Welsh did not begin to move against the Marchers until six months after the old king's death. No concern about inheritance customs pre-programmed men to defect from Stephen. There was never any inevitability about the civil war of 1139, any more than there was about the civil war of 1642; in both cases it is the

11 R.W. Southern, 'The place of Henry I in English History', repr. in *Medieval Humanism and Other Studies* (Oxford, 1970), 206–33, see esp. p. 223.
12 In the third edition of his *King Stephen* (London, 1990), Davis reprinted as Appendix IV (pp. 150–53) an updated 'state of the debate' article about the 'tenurial crisis', which described the conflicting claims to the same estates as having '. . . made the civil war of Stephen's reign virtually inevitable, fuelled it once it had begun and made the establishment of peace extremely difficult' (p. 151) and later talked of the hereditary disputes 'which *in 1135* had made civil war inevitable' (p. 153) my italics.
13 Chibnall, *Matilda*, 85–7; the influence of Southern's work on Henry I's interference with inheritance is apparent in her thinking here, as it was earlier in OV ii, pp. xxxvi–xxxvii.

remote influence of Hegelian deterministic thinking which has made historians think that there was.

However, Davis's belief in an ideological conflict over inheritance between king and barons in the middle of the twelfth century has been influential, and the debate it began has been very fruitful in a number of areas, not least the close analysis of succession custom and practice by several historians. But it has to be said that Davis's theoretical ideology of mid-twelfth-century baronial dissidence over property rights is no longer tenable. The Thorne thesis on the weakness of heritability and ideas of property may well have some life in it still, but the recent analysis of inheritance language in eleventh- and twelfth-century England by John Hudson has conclusively supported J.C. Holt's view that hereditability by sons was the norm in Henry I's reign, and a practice not resisted by the king, except occasionally in the understandable case of treason by the father and where custom allowed him latitude.[14] That being the case, we cannot look to a desire to reform inheritance custom as the motivating force for rebellion in Stephen's reign.

THE IDEOLOGY OF KINSHIP AND 'PATRIARCHAL' POLITICS

A recent contribution to the debate about the ideology of the Angevin party revolves around family and kin. Katharine Keats-Rohan has put forward a detailed argument which proposes that the line of division in 1138–39 between factions in the aristocracy followed a fundamental fault line in the English aristocracy. The fissure was between those aristocrats who entered England as part of the entourage of Bretons deriving from the east of Brittany and those who derived from the west. She went further, seeing the former group as naturally allied with Normans from the west of the duchy. Her somewhat startling conclusion is that: 'The civil war of Stephen's reign was . . . the logical result of a process that had been set in motion by two marriages around the year 1000' (she refers to the marriages of the brothers Count Alan III of Brittany and Count Eudo of Penthièvre, which produced rival lineages inside the Breton aristocracy, which fought their grudge out within England under Stephen).[15] Dr Keats-Rohan's theory is not unrelated to that of Davis. Both scholars see fear of dispossession as a motivating force in the partisanship of the aristocracy, but Dr Keats-Rohan goes rather further in the almost mystical weight she allows to kin-allegiance and its continued vitality from one generation to another.

That family and networks of patronage influenced an individual's political decision-making in Stephen's reign is a truism, and in the case of siblings as

14 J.G.H. Hudson, *Land, Law and Lordship in Anglo-Norman England* (Oxford, 1994), chs. 3–4, which builds on previous work by J.C. Holt, 'Politics and property', 3–52, and his presidential addresses, idem, 'Feudal society and the family in early medieval England', *TRHS*, 5th ser., 32–35 (1982–85), *passim*.
15 K.S.B. Keats-Rohan, 'The Bretons and Normans of England, 1066–1154: the family, the fief and the feudal monarchy', *Nottingham Medieval Studies*, xxxvi (1992), 42–78, quotation from p. 78.

close as the Beaumont twins, there is no doubting it. The half-brothers, Earl Ranulf II of Chester and William de Roumare, also worked closely together. Reginald de Warenne was the mainstay of the estate administration of his elder brother, Earl William III, before 1147.[16] But there are examples of siblings falling out with each other, as Bishop Rotrou of Evreux did with his brother, Earl Roger of Warwick, in the 1140s over possession of the family minster of Warwick, a case which went as far as Rome.[17] It is notorious that the king himself and his brother, Bishop Henry, did not see eye to eye on many issues. So it is unwise to base arguments about motivation on kinship without more supporting evidence. One of the key figures in the Keats-Rohan thesis is Brian fitz Count, the illegitimate son of Count Alan IV (Fergeant) of Brittany. Brian is the best-documented character of Stephen's reign, as far as self-justification for his actions is concerned; and for me it is highly significant that he never once mentions his Bretonness as an explanation for his actions, only his oath to Mathilda and his filial feelings for her father, who brought him up and endowed him with lands and wealth.

As Judith Green has now pointed out in an extensive review of the Keats-Rohan theory, the appearance of Breton and western Norman dominance in those lining up behind the empress is simply because of the accident of the southwest being colonised in the Conquest period by Count Brian of Brittany and his supporters and Count Robert of Mortain and his followers.[18] The formation of the Angevin party in 1138–39, as I have demonstrated above, has far more to do with the regional affinity of that most obviously un-Breton of magnates, Robert of Gloucester. Since his adherents were partly based in the southwest, it is hardly surprising to find a Breton and west Norman element in it, but it is pushing things very hard indeed to attempt to tie Earl Robert himself and Miles of Gloucester into such a deterministic political model of behaviour as Dr Keats-Rohan suggests. The dynamic of their exercise of power was essentially a regional one: they intended to dominate their own self-defined areas of the country. In this dynamic it was not so much kinship that mattered in choosing sides, it was where you lived. This regionalist imperative will be pursued in greater detail in Chapter 9.

However – as with the earlier theory of the 'tenurial crisis' – it would not do to dismiss the dynamic of kinship as having nothing to offer the student of Stephen's civil war. As later chapters look further into the course of the war, it will soon become clear that kinship was an imperative which *did* play an overt role in the policies of certain magnates. I want to draw particular attention

16 P. Dalton, 'Aiming at the impossible: Ranulf II of Chester and Lincolnshire in the reign of Stephen', in *The Earldom of Chester and its Charters*, ed. A.T. Thacker (Journal of the Chester Archaeological Society, 71, 1991), 109–34 *passim*. For Reginald and Earl William, see references in Brit. Libr. Harley charter 57 E 32; *EYC* viii, 92–3 (which name Reginald as the earl's principal justice in Norfolk).

17 *Papsturkunden in England*, ed. W. Holtzmann (3 vols, Berlin, 1930–52) i, 256.

18 J.A. Green, 'Family matters: family and the formation of the empress's party in south-west England', in *Family Trees and the Roots of Politics: The Prosopography of Britain and France from the Tenth to the Twelfth Century*, ed. K.S.B. Keats-Rohan (Woodbridge, 1997), 147–64.

to the example of Gilbert, earl of Pembroke, and his behaviour during the period 1141–48, when it becomes apparent that he was operating something which can be called 'patriarchal politics', acting to protect the landed endowment of a number of branches of his family. It was because he wished to favour his immediate kin that some parts of the realm – and Stephen's digestion – were badly troubled by him.

But granting this, I would never go so far as to say that kin-politics could actually explain the civil war, only that it helps to account for some episodes within it. My chosen example is the domino-fall of events in 1146 which led to the defection of the loyalist Earl Gilbert from the king's court. In that year, Earl Ranulf of Chester had badly miscalculated his standing at King Stephen's court, and ended up in prison at Stamford (see Chapter 10). A consequence of this was the subsequent fate of Earl Ranulf's nephew, Earl Gilbert of Hertford. Earl Gilbert, son of Earl Ranulf's sister, had offered himself and his castles as security for his uncle's release.[19] For whatever reason, King Stephen called in the security, held on to Gilbert and took his castles. At this, Gilbert took himself off to Earl Ranulf and joined him in making havoc in the north midlands. But the story does not end there, for as well as Earl Ranulf, Gilbert of Hertford had another uncle, his father's younger brother, Earl Gilbert of Pembroke, and the sequence of events affected this uncle too. Gilbert of Pembroke had been a close supporter of King Stephen from the beginning of the reign (apart from a brief period of several months in the summer of 1141 when Stephen was in captivity). He had been well rewarded, and by 1147 he had secured a wide spread of estates. Observing that his nephew's castles in England were being held by the king, Gilbert went to his royal master and asked that they be handed over to him, for the reason (according to the *Gesta Stephani*) 'that they were his by hereditary right [*iure hereditario*]'. The king's abrupt refusal of what Gilbert thought of as his right sent the earl into immediate rebellion.[20]

It is not necessary to pursue what happened to Earl Gilbert in rebellion. What is important is to return to the reason the *Gesta Stephani* gave for his rebellion: 'hereditary right'. The words used in the *Gesta* should not be defined too closely. Earl Gilbert was not claiming, I think, that his nephew's forfeiture had made him the next in line to the earldom of Hertford and the Clare estates in Kent, Suffolk and elsewhere. If he had been, he would have been indulging in a cynical opportunism which conflicts with what we otherwise know of uncle and nephew, that they were firm allies in the political upheaval of Stephen's reign. Cynical, because the nephew had younger brothers who would have had to be disinherited before the uncle could succeed. 'Hereditary right' here means something different from what it might be assumed to have meant from its occurrence in a charter or lawbook.

19 A charter of Stephen given at Stamford and dated 1146 by Davis has indeed as witnesses, amongst others, Ranulf of Chester, Earl Gilbert of Pembroke, his nephew Earl Gilbert of Hertford, and his brothers Baldwin and Walter, *Regesta*, iii, no. 494.
20 *GS*, 201–3.

A survey of Gilbert's career between 1136 and 1147 gives one clue. Gilbert began the reign as an ally of Stephen's lieutenant in Normandy, Waleran of Meulan. He married around this time Waleran's sister, Isabel. This connection probably brought him the estates of his two uncles, Roger, lord of Bienfaite and Orbec in Normandy, and Walter, lord of Striguil in the March of Wales. In 1138, he was one of Count Waleran's connections who was raised to an earldom, in his case, Pembroke, King Stephen's imperilled lordship in west Wales. He obtained also the confiscated lordship of Pevensey in Sussex, when the L'Aigle family defected to Geoffrey of Anjou around 1139. In 1141 he fought for Stephen at Lincoln, but in the summer of 1141 defected briefly to the Angevins along with the earls of Essex and Oxford. Despite this and despite the secession of his patron, Waleran, to the Angevins, Gilbert's career continued to flourish after 1141. The author of the *Gesta* makes much of the king's generosity to Gilbert, putting this pained lament in the king's mouth after Gilbert's fall from grace:

> It is wrong that the man to whom I have granted such great and varied wealth, whom I took when he was a poor knight and raised in honour to the dignity of an earldom, on whom again and again I have bestowed possessions in lavish abundance, according to his own heart's desire, it is wrong that he should now appear to be taking up arms so suddenly and so rashly and aiding the cause of my enemies against me.[21]

Clearly from this, Earl Gilbert's rocketing fortunes were a marvel amongst his contemporaries. The king, it appears, had allowed him to name the price of his support, and Gilbert had scribbled a high figure on the blank cheque. The demand that finally had been one demand too many was that he be handed his nephew's earldom and castles. The reason why this had been too much for the king may be found in what Gilbert had already asked for and got between 1141 and 1147. Every time a major honor in England of one of Gilbert's close relatives had been confiscated by the king, or otherwise come into the king's hands, Earl Gilbert had been there asking for it. In this way he had secured the earldom of Buckingham, the Giffard lands in England, when Earl Walter, his first cousin, had chosen to retreat to Normandy after 1141 and make peace with the Angevin conquerors. When his brother-in-law, William de Montfichet of Essex, died soon after 1137 he secured the Montfichet lands with the wardship of another nephew and namesake, Gilbert de Montfichet.[22] So when in 1147 he asserted 'hereditary right' and demanded the keeping of his other nephew's earldom of Hertford, he was doing no more than he had been doing for the past ten years: gathering together the lands his close kin had forfeited through political mistakes and death into his own protection, as patriarch of his family.[23]

---

21 *GS*, 203.
22 D. Crouch, 'The March and the Welsh kings', in *The Anarchy of King Stephen's Reign*, ed. E. King (Oxford, 1994), 275n, details the evidence for these transfers and grants.
23 It might be suggested that Earl Gilbert's military campaign in west Wales in 1145 was designed as much to regain his dead brother's lordship of Ceredigion as to secure the earldom of Pembroke.

Earl Gilbert's was not, however, an isolated example of patriarchal politics in Stephen's reign. At Oxford in July 1141 William de Beauchamp, former sheriff of Worcester, negotiated terms with the empress for his transfer of allegiance away from the captive King Stephen's embattled party. As part of the deal, the empress promised him the lands of his kin who continued to fight against her, and who could not or had not paid to regain her favour, unless there were any closer relatives fighting on her side (see Chapter 9).[24] Explicitly offered here to William de Beauchamp is precisely what Earl Gilbert was to demand of Stephen, five or six years later. The same claim of family on lands that might otherwise be alienated. We glimpse further possible examples. One that comes to mind is that of John Marshal, who appears in control of Newbury in 1152, the demesne of his late brother-in-law, the count of Perche.[25]

There were variants, too, on the same theme. Some of them are decidedly odd, as when Count Waleran of Meulan left England in 1141 and transferred his allegiance to the Angevin side. When he went he explicitly confided the oversight of his earldom of Worcester to his twin brother, the earl of Leicester, even though the earl was still a royalist. The lieutenancy of a royalist over the government of an Angevin-held county in the west midlands is a striking instance of the way that political faction and party did not necessarily coincide in Stephen's reign. Another variant is what went on in the Angevin-dominated Welsh March. Here two royalist earls held lordships isolated by surrounding Angevin supporters: Roger, earl of Warwick held Gower, and Gilbert of Pembroke held Striguil (Chepstow). Both lordships are found after 1138 being superintended by the earls' younger brothers: Henry du Neubourg in Gower, and Walter fitz Gilbert in Striguil.[26]

From this evidence the preservation of family interests and assets was clearly a major motive underlying the politics of Stephen's reign. This should be no real surprise, of course. The family machinations of the Beaumonts were identified by and known to a much earlier generation of scholars. The family identities and politics of the Clares and the Mandevilles were explored by John Horace Round before the turn of the century.[27] This dynamic was not by any means the only problem Stephen had to face during his reign. The existence of Mathilda remained the worst of his problems. But I think that many of Stephen's difficulties can be traced to this source, and it ought, I think, to have been an avoidable problem. From all the evidence it seems that he neither

---

24 *Regesta* iii, no. 68: '. . . *Et item dedi ei et concessi terras et hereditates suorum proximorum parentum qui contra me fuerint in werra mea et mecum finem facere non poterunt, nisi de sua parentela propinquiore michi in ipsa werra servierit.*'
25 D. Crouch, *William Marshal: Court, Career and Chivalry in the Angevin Empire, c.1147–1219* (London, 1990), 1–4.
26 Crouch, 'March and the Welsh Kings', 280–1. My student, Richard Dace, has pointed out to me the instance of the Cahaignes brothers, Hugh and William, who apparently chose different sides and rearranged possession of their widespread estates so that each brother was able to protect the Cahaignes inheritance in the area of the kingdom dominated by the party each nominally espoused, R. Dace, 'The Rise of the Banneret' (unpublished Leeds MPhil, 1998), 43–4.
27 J.H. Round, 'The family of Clare', *Archaeological Journal*, lvi (1899), 232–4.

understood the complex networks of claims of land and family amongst the top 300 of his subjects, nor could he see, as his uncle had seen, how they might become nets to trap and channel his magnates. Dr Keats-Rohan would take a determinist view of the influence of kinship on the politics of Stephen's reign. I would see kinship as yet another area of policy which he mishandled.

CHAPTER 8

Lincoln

STALEMATE AND PEACE TALKS, 1140

Earl Robert of Gloucester seems to have understood the general mood of frustration infecting the English aristocracy in 1140, and it would be surprising had he not, for he had reacted savagely against the same malaise. It gave him some limited room for manoeuvre in his efforts to extend himself outside the Severn valley, where the king had so effectively contained him and his supporters. That the empress's cause was now stalemated in the southern March must have become clear to him soon enough, and there was no doubting that Stephen had both the energy and the means to keep him and his supporters penned into the southwest and the March. There had been no major surge of magnates into the Empress Mathilda's camp since the previous autumn. Many regional barons even on the fringes of his area of domination, in Devon, Wiltshire and Herefordshire, were keeping stubbornly neutral. In the summer of 1140 – when a lull fell on what had already been an energetic campaigning season – it was open to Earl Robert (after nearly a year in England) either to negotiate, or to gamble on a military adventure and hope for the same luck that had brought him and the empress safely from Normandy to Bristol.

Stephen, for his part, was at last willing to consider negotiation. In February 1140 (helped possibly by his brother, Theobald) he had successfully brought to a close the negotiations for the marriage between his eldest son, Eustace, now a fourteen-year old, and Constance, the young sister of Louis VII of France. The young couple were formally betrothed in France, in the presence of Queen Mathilda, and they returned with her to England, Constance receiving a huge cash sum and the town of Cambridge as her dowry.[1] The marriage

---

1 For the marriage JW iii, 284; HH, 720. For Constance's control of Cambridge see her grants to the nuns of St Radegund in 1153 × 54, A. Gray, *The Priory of St Radegund, Cambridge* (Cambridge Antiquarian Society, 1898), 75, the original charter being Cambridge, Jesus College, ms. Caryl 1, Gray 3(a). Y. Sassier, *Louis VII* (Paris, 1991), 98 makes the point that Count Theobald, Eustace's uncle, might have promoted the marriage (under discussion since 1138).

must have reassured the king that the future lay with his dynasty and given him the confidence to talk to his enemies. It may be no accident, therefore, that in August 1140 a conference was arranged between the warring parties at Bath in Somerset, with Stephen represented by his queen and Archbishop Theobald. It was to Queen Mathilda that the king routinely entrusted delicate negotiations; it was she who had negotiated the peace with David of Scotland, which still survived despite the appearance of the empress in England. Earl Robert and the senior barons of the empress's party represented Mathilda. The king seems once again to have been responding to the advice of his brother, Bishop Henry, who had set up the talks.[2]

Although unsuccessful, the Bath peace conference was significant. The one account we have of it, from William of Malmesbury, tells us that a good deal of talking took place which occupied much of August and even perhaps some of September. Although we do not know what they were, terms were discussed which seem to have struck both parties as at least possible grounds for an agreement. Unfortunately, the royalist negotiators did not think them advantageous enough to the king and so did not agree to pursue them. But there was enough that was promising in them for Bishop Henry in September to cross to France to discuss them further with King Louis VII and Count Theobald. The fact that the French court was consulted is our only clue as to the nature of the proposed settlement. King Louis could have been involved for two reasons: that the settlement affected the interests of his sister, Constance, or that they involved the settlement of Normandy, of which he was nominal overlord. The Norman question would also have affected Count Theobald, whose concern it was to keep the duchy out of the hands of the Angevins.

In view of the proposals which were brought to the table in later peace conferences, we may therefore be seeing the first discussions which suggested that King Stephen sacrifice his ambitions to leave the Anglo-Norman realm intact to his son, Eustace. Whether it was discussed in 1140 that he should resign England or Normandy, or both realms, to the empress's heir is not possible to say, but it is the likeliest projection of the proposals for peace which Bishop Henry brought to him in London at the end of November. Certainly, two years later, two of the principals in the Angevin party took it as a matter of course that they were fighting for the rights of the young Henry Plantagenet as much as for those of his mother.[3] Stephen considered the proposals, and then (although they were allegedly acceptable to the empress) he rejected them, and the war recommenced. In the event, he may well have wished he had accepted the agreement offered him by the Angevin party in the autumn of 1140.

---

2 *HN*, 44–5.
3 The agreement between Earls Robert of Gloucester and Miles of Hereford, which Patterson plausibly dates to the summer of 1142, two years after these events, assumes that the war is between King Stephen and the empress '*et Henricum filium imperatricis*'. This implies that it was already then assumed that the war was as much for the rights of the young heir as for the empress, *Earldom of Gloucester Charters*, ed. R.B. Patterson (Oxford, 1973), 96.

PUBLIC ORDER AND THE BATTLE OF LINCOLN, FEBRUARY 1141

We approach now what was the defining event of Stephen's reign, his cata-strophic defeat and capture at Lincoln on 2 February 1141. Until the defeat, he remained in control of the bulk of his kingdom and his court while the number of Angevin adherents remained small. It is true that he was unable yet to defeat the empress's party, and indeed he may have been experiencing some financial difficulties as a result of the pressures of war on his treasury.[4] But in 1140 the rebellion had been successfully confined to an area not much larger than it had been at the end of the campaigning season in 1138, before Earl Robert and the empress arrived. There was a good chance that the fortunes of war might yet permit Stephen to seize sufficient castles to make the empress's cause untenable in England, or even allow him to fight that dangerous but potentially decisive set battle which would destroy the empress's field army (a perilous option some believed that he had been courting in Devon in January 1140). It must have been that optimism which had decided him against peace terms before Christmas 1140. After Lincoln, Stephen's chances of victory evaporated for good and the balance of support tipped away from him – first towards neutralism and then towards the Angevin cause.

While the king was engaged in containing the empress's party in the south-ern March and lower Severn valley, the rest of the kingdom was not immune to disorder. As long as Stephen had maintained the structure of monarchy he had inherited from his uncle, conservatism and vested interests would have reinforced the image of the kingdom of England as a realm of peace, law and due administrative process. He had begun to distort this image in 1138 with some unprecedented reforms in local government and by distancing himself from King Henry's curial bishops and new men. In fact, of course, England had never been quite as domestically tranquil in Henry's reign as common belief had it.[5] Local outbreaks had occurred and the king's representatives had to act to impose peace and a settlement. For instance, we know that in Leices-tershire, because of the dominance of a curial earl in the 1120s, the estates of the see of Lincoln and the earldom of Chester had been seized by the earl of Leicester through measures which look likely to have been extra-legal – 'by force and arms' as later legal records would put it.

But such seizures can be interpreted as negotiating ploys in local rivalries and are not symptoms of the slippage of public order into outright disorder. Settlements were sought and achieved, in the case of the Leicester–Lincoln dispute, by the king's direct intervention; and favourable settlements were

4 Such is one contemporary view, for which see HH, 724. Modern commentators are less sure, and point both to the fact that Stephen was able to continue to fund his campaigns and had the potential to raise large sums on credit, see H.A. Cronne, *The Reign of Stephen: Anarchy in England, 1135–54* (London, 1970), 233–6; J.A. Green, 'Financing Stephen's war', *ANS* xiv, ed. M. Chibnall (Woodbridge, 1991), 105–8.
5 For comments about the ambiguity of Henry I's reputation as a strong king see M.T. Clanchy, *England and its Rulers, 1066–1272* (Fontana, 1983), 73–5; overconcentration on Henry's undoubted centralising and administrative achievements (as Southern and Hollister demonstrate) can obscure the desperate political uncertainties of his reign.

what the magnates who precipitated these local crises wanted. The king himself might act decisively against suspect local magnates to redress the balance
of power in the localities. So between 1124 and 1130 the earl of Warwick had
lost a substantial fraction of his Warwickshire estates to the royal officer,
Geoffrey de Clinton, and his castle of Oakham in Rutland and lordship of
Gower in the March to the king (with only minimal compensation offered in
the royal forest at Sutton Chase). In Essex, the baron William de Mandeville
had endured considerable losses in the first years of Henry's reign, which
reduced him from dominance in the county to relative unimportance, and the
Bigods had lost ground in East Anglia to the Aubigné family of Buckenham
on the death of Hugh's father, Roger, in 1107.[6]

So, when we consider the first years of Stephen's reign it is not always
obvious whether what we are seeing is a new level of disorder, or simply a
continuation in the accepted way of doing business in King Henry's reign,
by deliberately precipitating a cycle of crisis, mediation and settlement. For
instance, after Stephen succeeded to the throne, the problem in Warwickshire
left him by his uncle – the hostility between Earl Roger and the Clinton
family – erupted in 1137 with depredations by the earl on Clinton estates and
a blockade of Clinton castles. But, in 1138, Henry, bishop of Winchester,
Robert, the earl's elder brother, and the earl of Warenne, acting as royal
mediators, heard the earl's complaints and arranged a settlement by which the
young Geoffrey II de Clinton acknowledged the earl's overlordship and was
betrothed to the earl's infant daughter, thus concluding a permanent settlement which ultimately left the Clintons as firm allies of the earl. It is all too
tempting (under historiographical pressure) to describe this sort of incident as
incipient 'anarchy' when it was in fact no more than one way of handling local
situations which had become intolerable: not so much 'private warfare' as
'armed negotiation'.[7]

Looked at in this light, the strategies of Robert of Bampton over Uffculme
and Baldwin de Redvers over Exeter in 1136 may not have been quite so crass
after all. What those magnates were undoubtedly expecting was a process
of mediation over their complaints which never came, and it did not come
because they forgot that the new king could not yet afford to countenance
apparent breaches in his peace. Stephen had become king on a public order
ticket, and he had to seem to be quite as austere and controlling as his uncle

6 For the Leicestershire disputes in Henry's reign, E. King, 'Mountsorrel and its Region in King
Stephen's Reign', Huntingdon Library Quarterly, xliv (1980), 3–6; D. Crouch, 'Earls and bishops
in twelfth-century Leicestershire', *Nottingham Medieval Studies*, xxxvii (1993), 11–14. For Warwickshire, D. Crouch, 'Geoffrey de Clinton and Roger earl of Warwick: new men and magnates
in the reign of Henry I', *Bulletin of the Institute of Historical Research*, liv (1982), 115–19; D. Crouch,
'The local influence of the Earls of Warwick, 1088–1242: a study in decline and resourcefulness',
Midland History, 21 (1996), 5–6. For the Mandevilles and Essex, C. Warren Hollister, 'The misfortunes of the Mandevilles', *History*, 58 (1973), 18–28. For the Bigods' losses, through a marriage
forced on them by the king during a minority, see Wareham 'The motives and politics of the
Bigod family, c.1066–1177', *ANS* xvii, ed. C. Harper-Bill (Woodbridge, 1994), 231.
7 For the idea of early twelfth-century magnate violence followed by adjudication, J.G.H. Hudson,
The Formation of the English Common Law (London, 1996), 108–9.

was reputed to have been. In May 1140, the trouble with Hugh Bigod over Bungay might be seen as just another such incident: an armed demonstration followed by brief confrontation and then formal settlement. But by 1140, any such attempt at a public showdown with a rival or with the king could not ignore the fact that there was in the kingdom a conflict going on which was of quite a different order – an open war of succession. All local difficulties then automatically became more serious, because they exerted pressure on a king with few resources and little time to spare. Every act of local rivalry and violence was sucked into the process of the war, and, of course, if reconciliation was impossible, there was now an alternative court to appeal to, as Bishop Nigel of Ely had already appealed to the empress.

As a result, from 1140 onwards, there was no politically neutral violence, and all violent actions tended to undermine Stephen's position. So we must say that public disorder was becoming more serious and the fabric of the state was beginning to tear in the aftermath of the failed settlement of the kingdom of November 1140. To maintain his credibility, the king had no choice but to take as an act against him any disorder in his kingdom outside the war zone in the Marches. At this point – and it is significantly well into the reign – the ambiguous figure of Earl Ranulf II of Chester becomes important. Apart from the trouble with the Scots, the north of England and the north midlands have played little part so far in this study. Robert of Gloucester's connections were few in the northern March and midlands, so there was little reason why there should be trouble for Stephen there. William fitz Alan was a connection of his in the northern March, but the campaigns of 1138 had dislodged him. Earl Ranulf had married Mathilda, a daughter of the earl of Gloucester late in King Henry's reign, and this connection was one that had some potential to cause Stephen trouble, even though Earl Ranulf showed little sign of sympathy with his father-in-law's cause in 1139 or 1140, something which had much annoyed Earl Robert, as William of Malmesbury, a good source, tells us.[8]

Before Christmas 1140 Earl Ranulf seized the castle of Lincoln. John of Hexham believed that he had done so as part of a wider dispute with Henry of Scotland, earl of Northumbria and Huntingdon, over Ranulf's supposed rights to Carlisle and Cumberland. A plot by Ranulf to kidnap Earl Henry is said to have come to the queen's attention, and she arranged for the king to provide a heavy escort for Earl Henry back to Scotland. How a dispute between the two earls on the subject of Cumberland could lead to the seizure of Lincoln is something that John fails to explain, other than to suggest that it was an attempt to pay back the king for thwarting his plot.[9] Sir James Holt has pointed out that Ranulf's claims on Carlisle and Cumberland were never Ranulf's patrimony, as John of Hexham claimed, and that what claim he had there was weak.[10] This being so, it is probable that John was stitching together rumours about Earl Ranulf into what he thought to be a likely story.

8 *HN*, 46, 47.
9 JH, 306.
10 J.C. Holt, 'Politics and property in early medieval England', *Past and Present*, no. 57 (1972), 51–2.

Recent historians have looked instead to Ranulf's local ambitions – and those of his half-brother, William de Roumare – in Lincolnshire as a more convincing explanation of the seizure of Lincoln.[11] It is worth noting that King Stephen's reaction to the seizure of Lincoln was the same as his reaction the previous May to Hugh Bigod's armed demonstration in Suffolk: he marched to meet the dissident magnates at Lincoln and negotiated a settlement, leaving the two brothers in peaceful control of the castle, having (one has to assume) allowed the justice of their claims, which certainly included the keeping of Lincoln castle.[12] Then, this time, for whatever reason (and no writer is willing to give us one) the king had second thoughts about resigning control over Lincoln to Ranulf. Secret messages from the bishop and citizens of Lincoln reached him in London at his Christmas court with information that the earl of Chester had settled peacefully in the city, and was vulnerable to attack, and the king acted. Stephen seems to have been suddenly very keen to retract what he had done at Lincoln the previous month. The best explanation is that he suddenly realised that too much had been given away, and that such generosity simply tempted other ambitious magnates to exploit his time of weakness.

How generous had he been? From the chronicle record, we only hear of him having given away Lincoln castle and certain unspecified 'honors'. But there is a better indication. This is the surviving text of a treaty between the king and Earl Ranulf which A.L. Poole believed dated to December 1140 and was a list of the very demands the earl had put to the king at Lincoln, and which the king had accepted. Davis and Cronne, in their great edition of Stephen's acts, believed that the agreement belonged to 1146 because it referred to lands in Normandy which the earl had lost. However, it is quite likely that the Angevin advance in Normandy had already swallowed up Ranulf's ancestral lands in the Bessin by the autumn of 1140, and there is nothing else in the agreement which stands against the 1140 dating. Indeed, the fact that the agreement included the grant of lands confiscated from Earl Robert of Gloucester in Grimsby positively screams of a date when Earl Ranulf was still perceived to be an unqualified opponent of the empress and her half-brother (see Appendix I to this chapter). If we accept this (and there is other good evidence in a writ of Earl Ranulf himself that we should) then the king's concessions to Ranulf in December 1140 had been remarkably, astonishingly, generous: the constableship of Lincoln and its two keeps till the king allowed Ranulf's claim to the southern Yorkshire honor of Tickhill or Blyth

11 P. Dalton, 'Ranulf II earl of Chester and Lincolnshire in the reign of Stephen', in *The Earldom of Chester and its Charters*, ed. A.T. Thacker (Chester Archaeological Society, 71, 1991), 109–32, esp. 109–10; idem, 'The armed neutrality of Ranulf II earl of Chester in King Stephen's reign', *ANS*, xiv, ed. M. Chibnall (Woodbridge, 1992), 39–59, esp. 42–3.

12 *HN*, 46. *Liber Eliensis*, 320–1, gives an independent and contemporary account of the battle of Lincoln; it states that the king had delivered the castle of Lincoln to Ranulf for keeping. The colourful account of the seizure of Lincoln castle by OV vi, 538–40 differs from that of Malmesbury, for he shows no knowledge of the king's visit there before Christmas or of the agreement between the king, Ranulf and William.

(which Stephen had earlier granted to the count of Eu[13]); the castle and honor of Belvoir on the Lincolnshire–Rutland border; the royal soke of Grantham in Kesteven (which the Tancarvilles had forfeited earlier in the reign); Newcastle-under-Lyme in Staffordshire; the royal soke of Rothley in Leicestershire (some of which Ranulf already held); the river-port of Torksey on the Trent in Lincolnshire and much of the coastal port of Grimsby; the town of Derby and a number of other Derbyshire estates, and, finally, the honor of Lancaster, with other northern lands that had belonged to Roger the Poitevin, count of La Marche at the beginning of the reign of Henry I.[14]

What Stephen had done was to create for Earl Ranulf a great corridor of power and influence from Cheshire across the north midlands and into southern Lincolnshire. When he had to return to face his magnates at his Christmas court, it would be very surprising had the king not found an uproar! The earl of Leicester, for all his recent royal grants in Herefordshire, would have found his rival of Chester occupying new castles and estates in an arc around his honor of Leicester: Belvoir was an uncomfortable neighbour to his northeast, and the soke of Rothley comprised much of the Soar valley north of Leicester. As we have seen, the two earls were already engaged in intense local rivalry in just that area. The cession of Derby to Ranulf had given the earl a keystone fortress between his old centre of Chester and his new centre of Lincoln. Other earls had equal cause to be outraged. There was an earl of Lincoln in the person of William d'Aubigné, whose earldom was now a joke. Alan, earl of Richmond (lord of Boston) and Gilbert de Gant his nephew (lord of Folkingham) were other Lincolnshire magnates with good cause to be alarmed, and Earl Henry of Northumbria might very well have been deeply annoyed and apprehensive at this new rival in the north (hence the story which John of Hexham tells of his fear of capture by Ranulf). Hardly any wonder that the author of the *Gesta* believed that Earl Ranulf ultimately came by all but a third of the kingdom by seizing this opportunity.[15]

The king's abrupt about-turn over Earl Ranulf's demands in the north is very likely to be testimony to the outrage of his advisers, and a dawning realisation that he had badly misjudged the situation at Lincoln. Hence, with his usual energy, he attempted rapidly to undo the harm he had done to his cause (with the assistance of another outraged local magnate, the bishop of Lincoln). He arrived outside Lincoln unexpectedly during the latter half of the Christmas season (that is between 1 January and 6 January). The city and bishop welcomed him, and the earl of Chester's garrison in the castle was too small to oppose him for long, for how could the earl have expected so abrupt a reversal of royal policy? Earl Ranulf escaped over the walls by night, and the

---

13 *Rotuli Curiae Regis*, ed. F. Palgrave (2 vols, Record Commission, 1835) ii, 162. Stephen's apparent willingness to contemplate negotiating away Tickhill, the possession of a supporter of his, would be because Count Henry of Eu had died earlier in 1140, and there is reason to believe that his heir, Count John, was a minor at the time of succession. This gave the king some leeway in negotiation – a marriage, for instance, might have satisfied the Chester claim.
14 *Regesta* iii, no. 178.
15 *GS*, 184.

king seems to have allowed his brother and their wives to leave peacefully after him.[16]

The king ordered other simultaneous attacks. John of Hexham records an undated surprise attack by Earl Alan of Richmond and Cornwall on the castle of '*Galclint*', which can be most obviously identified with that same castle of Belvoir which had been another of Earl Ranulf's recent gains (see Appendix II to this chapter). The logic of the map is that the seizure of Belvoir would mean that Ranulf had also lost Grantham, five miles to the east of the castle. Earl Alan then apparently moved further north, garrisoning Howden and Ripon for the king before returning to rejoin Stephen in Lincoln, a move to impress those engaged in the contested election of the new archbishop of York at the time. He also brought into the royal army a number of Yorkshire barons whom he and Earl William of York must have mobilised to increase the forces available to the king at Lincoln.[17]

Earl Ranulf was quick to call foul, and indeed he may well have had a right to be outraged in his turn. He had apparently met with the king peacefully, aired his numerous claims and been generously treated, with the resulting decisions of the king entrusted to a document. Within a fortnight, he found that the king had reversed all his decisions and that his lands across the north midlands were under attack. His response was equally decisive, an appeal to his father-in-law, Earl Robert of Gloucester. This brought a large army of Angevin supporters (including the stalwarts, Miles of Gloucester, Brian fitz Count and Baldwin de Redvers) and Welsh mercenaries to meet him in the Trent valley. Here for a month he based himself around his old castle of Donington and his new castle of Derby, from where he could counter further attacks from up the Trent valley or from Leicester. A charter of his at this time finds him encamped at Barrow-on-Soar, Leicestershire, doubtless prepared to counter any threat from Leicester and Belvoir, in company with his father-in-law and his wife. Nonetheless, despite the suddenly partisan nature of the conflict, it is very significant that a Lincolnshire landowner in 1141 recorded the resulting mêlée as 'the conflict between King Stephen and Ranulf earl of Chester'. To one contemporary onlooker, it seems that the battle of Lincoln was more to do with the baffled ambitions of a great northern earl than the struggle for the throne of England.[18]

The large army that Chester and Gloucester were able to assemble moved on to the relief of the beleaguered castle on 1 February 1141, and approached

16 HH, 724. JH, 307 notes that the king seized back Lincoln early in January. He also notes that William de Roumare, Ranulf's brother, escaped (or was released by) the king to join his brother, as no doubt also were the wives of the two earls. This is not incompatible with the statement in GS, 120 that William, his wife and Countess Mathilda of Chester were abandoned by Ranulf in the castle.

17 The list of those captured with the king on 2 February given in JH, 308 has a distinct Yorkshire bias.

18 F.M. Stenton, *The First Century of English Feudalism, 1066–1166* (2nd edn., Oxford, 1960), 243, notes a charter of Simon Tuschet dated '*in anno quo commissum est prelium inter regem Stephanum et comitem Cestrie Ranulphum*'.

the city of Lincoln up the Fosse Way, arriving on the banks of the river Witham to the south of it early in the morning of Sunday 2 February, the Feast of the Purification of the Blessed Virgin Mary. All the contemporary historians of the battle note the date, and since they were clerics it is hardly likely that they would miss the significance of the day. The Feast of the Purification (or Candlemas) was a turning point of the liturgical year, the day on which the church turns away from the triumphs and pomps of the season of the Incarnation, and looks toward the penitential season of Lent and the Passion beyond. Hardly a day of good omen on which to begin a battle to settle the fortunes of a kingdom, as Orderic observed, and many people advised the king not to fight that day, although some for more practical military reasons. The author of the *Gesta*, Orderic Vitalis and Henry of Huntingdon were quick to note other gloomy portents. At the early morning mass, around seven o'clock, while the king was receiving a large candle, lit and blessed by the bishop for the candle-lit procession into the cathedral in the dawn light, the candle broke, fell and was extinguished. Although the *Gesta* says that the king quickly joined the halves together in his hand and had it relit, the accident was later interpreted as foretelling the temporary loss of his kingdom.[19]

The morning found his enemies crossing the Witham to the west of the city and the king had the opportunity he desired of risking everything on the chances of a pitched battle with his chief rivals.[20] The glittering prospect of ending the rebellion at a stroke, and the confidence born of the military success he himself had enjoyed since the beginning of his reign, are enough to explain what happened next. The royal army descended the hill of Lincoln and advanced to do battle.[21] Henry of Huntingdon describes lavish pre-battle harangues to hearten each army, but we may reasonably doubt that these happened, and his reports were no more than rhetorical exercises. There was no time for such set-piece speeches to have been made. Although the king had with him his military household and a Flemish mercenary force under William of Ypres, and several of his chief magnates and their households (including Count Waleran of Meulan, Earl William de Warenne, Earl Simon of Northampton, Earl William of York, Count Alan of Richmond, Gilbert de Clare and Hugh Bigod), he was most decidedly outnumbered in infantry, despite the services of the city militia of Lincoln. Earls Robert and Ranulf, on the other hand, had spent the several weeks around Derby in building up a formidable force. They had brought into England the military households (*teuloedd*) and

---

19 *GS*, 110–12, whose interpretation is rather more upbeat than that of OV vi, 544 and HH, 732, who also notes that the pyx containing the host crashed to the ground in the bishop's presence during mass.

20 As Edmund King points out, 'Introduction', in *The Anarchy of King Stephen's Reign*, ed. E. King (Oxford, 1994), 21, William of Malmesbury also believed that the earl of Gloucester was ready by this time to gamble all on the result of one battle (see *HN*, 47–8).

21 Contemporary accounts of the battle are in HH, 724–38; OV vi, 542–4; *GS*, 110–14; JH, 307–8; *HN*, 47–9, and a neglected but independent account in *Liber Eliensis*, 320–1. Of the modern treatments of the battle, the most exhaustive and detailed is in J. Bradbury, *Stephen and Matilda* (Stroud, 1996), 90–8.

levies of the Welsh kings, Morgan ab Owain of Glamorgan and Cadwaladr ap Gruffudd of Gwynedd.[22] This gave them a decided edge in light infantry, and they also had a notable force of knights of their own, some being the 'disinherited', presumably those knights who had followed their lords and found themselves on the wrong side in the recent battles in Normandy, and the southwest of England.

In the event it was numbers which counted. An advance force of horse and foot sent to hinder the enemy as it forded the river was driven off, and its flight was followed up by a swift advance of the enemy on the main body of the royal army.[23] Chroniclers are divided as to how useful the Welsh were to the earls in the attack, but even if they had not stood up to the counter-charge of the Fleming and Breton infantry (led by Count Alan and either Earl William of York or William of Ypres) the Welsh still occupied the attention of forces that could be ill-spared. When the rebel earls' main forces followed them into the battle the royalist first line was driven in and scattered, and many later blamed the earls of York and Richmond for giving up the fight too soon. In the chaos, the rebel earls' forces were able to surround the king and his household. The royalist army rapidly broke up and the earls with the king's army, seeing that all was lost, made their escape and left the king himself surrounded by his enemies, unable to flee because he and his men had dismounted to fight. And so a brief and bitter struggle raged around him on some anonymous hillock below the walls of Lincoln, until his bodyguard was cut down or surrendered, and the king was left isolated with a few companions, laying about him with an axe, and when that broke, his sword. His steady bravery daunted his enemies (and caused Robert de Torigny to burst into celebratory verse at such a royal performance: 'Oh, if a hundred such men had been there, they would have carried the field!').[24] At the end, his enemies felled him with a rock hurled at his helmet, and a knight of the earl of Gloucester's household, William de Cahaignes, had the distinction of seizing him around the neck, shouting 'Here everybody! Here! I've got the king!'[25]

---

22 For the Welsh in the army, see D. Crouch, 'The March and the Welsh Kings', in *The Anarchy of King Stephen's Reign*, ed. E. King (Oxford, 1994), 277–8. *Liber Eliensis*, 321 mentions King Morgan as the leading Welsh magnate present, OV vi, 536 mentions as present Cadwaladr ap Gruffudd ap Cynan, joint-king of Gwynedd with his elder brother, Owain ap Gruffudd. The 'Maredudd' brother of Cadwaladr he also notes may have been Madog *ap Maredudd*, king of Powys (Cadwaladr's brother-in-law), but equally likely might have been a mistake for Maredudd ap Cadwaladr ap Gruffudd (Cadwaladr's eldest son).
23 This initial headlong confrontation at the ford may be what William of Malmesbury calls the 'joust' (*justa*) which the royalists lost, *HN*, 48–9.
24 RT, 141.
25 HH, 738. The identity of this William de Cahaignes is disputed, Greenway (HH, 738–9n) identifies him as a son of Hugh de Cahaignes, sheriff of Northamptonshire in 1130, but this is only conjecture. It is known that Hugh's elder brother, Ralph, lord of Tarrant Keynes, had a younger son called William. This William fitz Ralph de Cahaignes would fit the identity of the captor of Stephen, being the right age to be a *miles strenuus* and also being a Dorset landowner within the area dominated by Earl Robert of Gloucester (and as Chibnall notes, OV vi, 543n, son of a baron of the Norman Bessin, where the earl was also dominant and from which he drew

The disaster was all but complete. Whatever Earl Ranulf of Chester's original intentions, he had opened the way for the final victory of the empress in the war of succession. The fact that the king's household that day included numerous barons (Gilbert de Gant, Baldwin fitz Gilbert, Bernard de Bailleul, Roger de Mowbray, Richard de Courcy, William Fossard and William Peverel of Nottingham) meant that many of the king's significant supporters in the north also fell into Angevin hands. But the main prize was the king himself. After staying overnight in plundered Lincoln, he was escorted south to meet the empress at Gloucester in an interview that took place a week after the battle, and after discussion, he was sent on to the earl of Gloucester's principal castle of Bristol, there to be kept under guard, and eventually put in chains.[26] It remained only to the earl of Gloucester and his sister to manage her transition to the throne, and contain the remaining danger from Queen Mathilda and the surviving royalist earls.

APPENDIX 1 – THE DATING OF *REGESTA* III, NO. 178

A.L. Poole, *From Domesday Book to Magna Carta* (2nd edn., Oxford, 1955), 141 and n. argued for a date of 1140 for this important charter, seeing it as the actual agreement made between King Stephen and Earl Ranulf at Lincoln in November 1140. As we have seen, Cronne and Davis argued instead for a date in 1146, during the later negotiations between Stephen and Ranulf. Subsequent studies which have dealt with R178 have agreed with the editors of the *Regesta* rather than Poole. G. White, 'King Stephen, Duke Henry and Ranulf de Gernons, Earl of Chester', *EHR*, 91 (1976), 555–6 gave a major reassessment of the significance of this charter and much enhanced what we know of the estates it mentioned, but does not argue with the dating of the text in *Regesta*, nor does P. Dalton, '*In neutro latere*: the armed neutrality of Ranulf II Earl of Chester in King Stephen's reign', *ANS*, xiv, ed. M. Chibnall (Woodbridge, 1992), 46–7 although he is willing to believe that the 1140 and 1146 grants were much the same. Professor Edmund King has come nearest to readopting the 1140 date, on the basis of the match between the chroniclers' accounts of the dealings of Stephen with Earl Ranulf in that year, and those grants that R178 records (E. King, 'The foundation of Pipewell abbey, Northamptonshire', *HSJ*, 2 (1990), 171n).

To deal with the arguments against a date of 1140. First, the charter's reference to Ranulf's lost Norman lands: we find by this point in the struggle for the duchy that the Angevins had subdued the Hièmois and Bessin as early

---

many of his knights). The Philip de Cahaignes who was a tenant of the earl was likely to have been this William's brother. Davis, *Stephen*, 50n seems to assume that William also was a tenant of Gloucester, but in fact he held his lands first of his father and then his elder brother. Nonetheless, the fact that OV vi, 544 and JH, 308 record that the king surrendered to the earl of Gloucester is some evidence that Cahaignes was in the earl's household. For the Cahaignes see R. Dace, 'Towards the Banneret' (unpublished MPhil thesis, Leeds, 1997), 43–4, 46, 109–10.
26 HH, 738; *GS*, 114; *HN*, 50; JW iii, 292.

as the end of 1138. These were the provinces where many of Ranulf's Norman possessions were, and their fall to Count Geoffrey (although fighting continued there till the end of 1140, when Fontenay-le-Marmion surrendered) therefore supports 1140 not 1146, see RT, 136, 139. Second, the apparent dispossession of the count of Eu (who is not suspected of abandoning Stephen in 1140) of Tickhill in *Regesta* iii, no. 178 – which would stand against a 1140 date – is negated by the fact that the king did not, in fact, give Tickhill to Ranulf but pledged a tower of Lincoln to him until his claim on the castle was resolved. JH, 308 notes that Tickhill held out against Earl Ranulf long after the battle of Lincoln, so he never had possession of it in November 1140. The fact that Ranulf is granted the younger Roger de Bully's 'honor of Blyth' (of which honor Tickhill was the chief castle) can be accounted for by the fact that de Bully had held only a portion of the whole honor, and it was doubtless only that portion which Ranulf was being allowed (or why mention de Bully at all?) On the division of the honor of Tickhill-Blyth in Henry I's reign, see M. Chibnall, 'Robert de Bellême and the castle of Tickhill', *Droit privé et institutions régionales: Études historiques offertes à Jean Yver* (Paris, 1976), 152–4.

Another argument for a 1140 date for R.178 is an unpublished writ of Earl Ranulf II of Chester, dated at Barrow-on-Soar, Leics, addressed to his constable of Derby and witnessed by Earl Robert of Gloucester and Mathilda, his daughter, Ranulf's wife. The most likely date for this writ has to be during the January 1141 campaign, and it shows Ranulf already in possession of Derby, see Cartulary of Berkeley of Wymondham, Brit. Libr., ms Harley 265, fo. 82r. The attestation of Countess Mathilda to the writ does not invalidate the date, as we know that William de Roumare, as well as Ranulf, escaped the siege of Lincoln, and what we know of Stephen's record would rule out his holding the countesses prisoner while letting their husbands go.

APPENDIX II – ENCORE LE CHÂTEAU DE 'GALCLINT'

For the details of *Galclint*, see JH, 306, 308. A careful consideration of the evidence relating to the John of Hexham passages is to be found in E. King, 'The parish of Warter and the castle of Galchlin', *Yorkshire Archaeological Journal*, 52 (1980), 49–58, esp. 55–8, 'Appendix. The castle of Galchlin'. Professor King looks at the interpretations of the editors of the text, James Raine (1864) and Thomas Arnold (1885). Raine believed the place to be probably in Lincolnshire, while Arnold opted for Yorkshire, and simply on the grounds of place name similarity decided that it was Gilling (Castle) in the Howardian hills of the North Riding. Later scholars more aware of the niceties of the interpretation of place names went looking for occurrences of the name *Galclint* (Professor King points out that one manuscript of John of Hexham calls it *Galchlin*) or something like it. Sir Frank Stenton suggested to Sir Charles Clay a place called *Galklynt* in the thirteenth century, which is now Gaultney Wood in the parish of Rushton, Northamptonshire, between Kettering and Market Harborough (*EYC* iv, 90n.). The problem with this is that neither Gaultney nor Rushton have any immediate relevance to any of the named characters, and the place has no remains of any castle: strange when one thinks how important a castle this *Galclint* seems to have been.

R.H.C. Davis, as we know, suggested in 1967 the simple solution that *Galclint/Galchlin* is no more than an alternative name for Belvoir, the castle of William d'Aubigné Brito, taking Raine's point of a century before that it was most likely a Lincolnshire place name (*King Stephen* (3rd edn., London, 1990), 47n). Professor King accepts the logic of such a suggestion, especially as Belvoir was undeniably an object of desire to Earl Ranulf, but points out that Earl Alan of Richmond had no obvious claim on the place which would lead him to fight Ranulf for it. However, if one accepts the point that Earl Alan was acting at *Galclint* as a royal castellan, taking it and defending it in Stephen's interests rather than his own, then Professor King's objection evaporates. The strongest identifying evidence with Belvoir is that the castle had been garrisoned by 'William d' Aubigné and his men' whom Earl Ranulf had ejected before Count Alan took the place back. King, 'Parish of Warter', 55n, followed by P. Dalton, *Conquest, Anarchy and Lordship: Yorkshire 1066–1154* (Cambridge, 1994), 162, interprets this passage as saying that Earl Alan had driven William d'Aubigné out of *Galclint*, but the passage is not so specific and on a more faithful interpretation of the ablative absolute reads 'Earl Alan . . . possessed the castle with its great treasure, William d'Aubigné *having been* dislodged [from it] with his men'. It does not quite follow that d'Aubigné had been driven out by Earl Alan; a third party might have done that; a third party such as Earl Ranulf, after King Stephen had given him Belvoir in his grant of November 1140.

There have been further subsequent attempts to identify *Galclint* with Yorkshire, one assumes because of the association of the story with Earl Alan, lord of Richmond and thus a great Yorkshire magnate. Professor King diffidently suggested Gildersdale, a place name in the parish of Warter in the East Riding over which parish there was a known struggle between William de Roumare and William, earl of York. But this would depend on a remarkable error being made by John of Hexham in writing William de *Albanih* for William de *Romara* in his passage relating to *Galclint* in 1140. It would also stretch toponymic credulity that a known twelfth-century place name form of *Gildusdal'* ('valley of the gild-house') could become *Galclint*! Professor King is not the only one to bring forward a suggestion based on John of Hexham's alleged misdrafting of a personal name. Dr Dalton's attempted identification (1994) of *Galclint* with a place name near Willerby in East Yorkshire on the grounds of John of Hexham's William de *Albanih* being really the Yorkshire magnate William de *Albamarla* is once again special pleading, for John invariably calls him *Willelmus comes Eboraci* or *comes Eboracensis* in a number of other references before and after the *Galclint* incident, (JH, 164–5). The fact that earthworks near Willerby might be fortifications is neither here nor there. Most large parishes in England can show a range of earthworks of various dates and purposes.

I therefore follow the reasoning of R.H.C. Davis on the identification of *Galclint* with Belvoir, and William as William d'Aubigné Brito.

CHAPTER 9

Lords and Order

As the king was left to ponder his mistakes in Bristol Castle in February 1141, the country might look towards the prospect of a new monarch and (hopefully) a recovered peace. It was everyone's perception that, by 1141, England had ceased to be a peaceful land. We know that to call the state that it had fallen into 'anarchy' is to make an unnecessary judgement on medieval society: its members desired order, law and moral behaviour. So if we discard the idea of anarchy, what sort of England are we describing in 1141? Even in civil war, there was order of a sort, so much is clear, and if it did not depend on the king it depended on the lords of the land. What makes Stephen's reign different from the reigns that preceded and followed it, is that the perception of who it was that was responsible for public order shifted to the regional magnates away from the king – on whose ultimate responsibility everyone would once have agreed, even if they did not agree on the way he carried it out. The territorial magnates' position of power in society had been generally recognised in previous reigns, but only in that it was understood that they (and the ecclesiastical magnates) were the appropriate people for the king to associate with himself in power. Magnates should help and advise the king, not be little kings in their own regions. So, if we abandon the idea of an 'anarchic' England, we are nonetheless left with the idea of England as a land where the balance of secular power had moved away from the king and towards his magnates.

When did this occur? Was there any point between 1135 and 1141 when England crossed the line from a king-dominated country to a magnate-dominated country? There is an answer, although it may not be as precise as one would like. There was no breakdown in public order or the perception of the dominance of kingship in England during the first years of Stephen's reign, as we have seen. Even in 1138, when Robert of Gloucester's allies were attempting to dispute the southwest with the king, there were only a few small areas outside the March where the king did not exert authority. But overall royal control of the nation did not survive 1139, and we have had a glimpse of the way that it collapsed in what was going on in the lower Severn valley in October and November of that year. The problem of unrestrainable magnate power had begun before the end of 1139 and had gone beyond the king's ability to reverse it by the end of 1140. The king may himself have recognised the fact in his willingness to take the dangerous gamble of a pitched battle, when his chief enemies appeared together in front of him in arms.

The turning point for the aristocracy was the arrival of Robert of Gloucester and the empress on the south coast in September 1139. The empress gave dissident magnates an ideology to use to justify their actions, and an alternative court in which to pursue their ambitions (although it is doubtful whether the prizes there for her magnates were worth much of a struggle before 1141). Robert of Gloucester, the first great dissident of the reign, used this licence unsparingly in pursuit of his aim to put his half-sister on the throne, and keep himself at her right hand. Because of Earl Robert and his methods, others took the same course. Miles of Gloucester was the most notorious of these, but Earl Ranulf of Chester ultimately did the same, even if under provocation.

Earl Robert was also the first to demonstrate how a magnate could declare independence of the restrained political order that Stephen had inherited from Henry's reign. As we have seen, a fair number of magnates had already used their ability to act with force, in order to register what they believed to be a rightful protest against unfair treatment within the existing order. Robert of Bampton, Baldwin de Redvers and Miles de Beauchamp (and probably John Marshal) had done so at various times, but to no good effect. Earl Roger of Warwick, Hugh Bigod and (briefly) Earl Ranulf of Chester had done so to their temporary benefit. What Earl Robert of Gloucester did in the aftermath of his arrival in the southwest was a quite different order of magnate behaviour, and provides a benchmark in the political topography of the reign.

KINGS, ARISTOCRACIES AND ORDER IN ENGLAND AND NORMANDY

We need, at this point, to get something of a 'magnate's-eye view' of Anglo-Norman society. How did these two hundred or so great men see their world, their relationship with their prince, and their place in the political order which, if they wished, they could so easily disrupt? Few now would agree with John Le Patourel's view of the realm of the Norman king-dukes as an integrated whole, with administrative procedures in exchequer and chancery which had caused the duchy of Normandy and the kingdom of England to converge in their development to form one political unit. Certainly his view of the aristocracies of England and Normandy as one social group which spanned the Channel at the comital, baronial and knightly levels cannot be sustained. Recent studies have pointed rather to the very local nature of Norman and English society, a localism that was the magnates' accomplice in Stephen's reign.[1] It

1 For the developed Le Patourel thesis, see *The Norman Empire* (Oxford, 1976), 190–207. This has been comprehensively reassessed in D.R. Bates, 'Normandy and England after 1066', *EHR*, 104 (1989), 853–61; idem, 'The rise and fall of Normandy c.911–1204', in *England and Normandy in the Middle Ages*, ed. D.R. Bates and A. Curry (London, 1994), 19–35; J.A. Green, 'Unity and

has even been suggested that in any case a large number of the lesser English landowners were derived from families which had survived the Conquest and which had no French connections by descent, so could hardly be expected to cherish links with a homeland that was not theirs.[2]

However, as Le Patourel noticed, the most influential group in society, the greatest of the magnates, most assuredly did have an Anglo-Norman view of things. Although it could be suggested that they might have operated schizophrenically (Normans when in Normandy, English when in England) they did, nonetheless, help staple kingdom and duchy together into a community of interest. The likes of Ranulf II of Chester, for instance, worked in a broad political landscape: his interests extended in a great sweep from the borders of Gwynedd across the west midlands of England, spanned the Channel and dominated lower Normandy at the Breton border. To operate efficiently in his world, it was not just necessary that he know the ins and outs of the English royal court; he had to maintain a good intelligence of what was happening in the very different worlds of the warrior-kings of north Wales and the Franco-Breton mêlée of the duchy of Brittany (his grandson and namesake was to become duke there). It is no surprise, therefore, to find that Earl Ranulf's behaviour in Stephen's reign betrays a highly developed strategic vision of his world. This vision lifted his eyes into the stratosphere of ambition in the 1140s: the domination of the Trent valley and Lincolnshire, the extension of his great county franchise of Cheshire into Lancashire, and the invention of a county of the Avranchin for himself, commanding the peninsula of the Cotentin.[3]

Because there were such men whose interests spanned the Channel – and by Stephen's reign there had been such men for three generations – we must take seriously the idea that the structure of aristocratic society in Normandy might be interlinked with the structure in England. Recent research has tended to point out the structural differences between Norman and English aristocratic society. We know that the Norman magnate was comparatively lightly burdened with military service, and lightly burdened also with the customary obligations that went along with it: a Norman knight's fee might be anything between three or five times as large as an English one. We know that the honors of Norman magnates were concentrated in territorial blocks, and across most of the duchy were generally not intermeshed with the lands of other magnates;

---

disunity in the Anglo-Norman state', *Historical Research*, 62 (1989), 128–33; and regarding his views on an aristocratic community, D. Crouch, 'Normans and Anglo-Normans: a divided aristocracy?', in *England and Normandy in the Middle Ages*, ed. Bates and Curry, 51–67.

2 For the post-Conquest survival of significant numbers of lesser English landowners, C.P. Lewis, 'Domesday jurors', *HSJ*, 5 (1993), 17–29; A. Williams, *The English and the Norman Conquest* (Woodbridge, 1995), 71–97, 198–210.

3 For the direction of Earl Ranulf's ambitions in England, see J.A. Green, 'Earl Ranulf II and Lancashire', in *The Earldom of Chester and its Charters*, ed. A.T. Thacker, Journal of the Chester Archaeological Society, 71 (1991), 97–108; P. Dalton, 'Aiming at the impossible: Ranulf II of Chester and Lincolnshire in the reign of Stephen', in ibid., 109–34. For his Norman ambition to achieve a county of the Avranchin, see the charter he extorted from Duke Henry in 1153, *Regesta* iii, no. 180.

this had been so for over a century before the reign of Stephen. Across the Grand Caux, central Normandy and down to the Breton border, investigation has revealed a singularly coherent socio-political map. Honors like those of Eu, Aumale, Longueville, Tancarville, Pont Audemer, Evreux, Montfort-sur-Risle, Beaumont, Breteuil, Pacy-sur-Eure, L'Aigle, Grandmesnil, Mortain and St-Jacques-sur-Beuvron lay across the Norman countryside like a pattern of feudal paving slabs: each abutting the other, each weighted to the ground with one or more castles.[4]

In Normandy magnates knew where they were powerful, and their exclusive local positions of dominance had been established by generations of jostling and rivalry. Norman society was therefore more magnate-dominated but also (paradoxically) more stable, for each Norman magnate knew the boundaries where his sphere of local influence ended and that of another began. They could protect their own effectively, and should war break out, its effects were limited. The same could not be said when the same magnates crossed over to their English honors. In England, the great honors were by no means as geographically coherent as in Normandy, partly because of the haphazard way that the first Norman kings granted out lands as their influence spread north and west through England. This was compounded by the way that the dispersed pattern of estates of some pre-Conquest English landowners was perpetuated by their grant in one unit to a French successor. Here and there, arbitrary action by the first or second King William erected castellanries on the Norman pattern: good examples can be found in Sussex (Arundel, Hastings, Pevensey and Lewes) and in the north (Holderness, Conisbrough, Blyth, and Harterness, for instance). In Cheshire and Lancashire there survived large territorial units from the early days of the Conquest where administration and justice had been completely delegated to one magnate. But elsewhere the situation was by no means clear-cut. Great honors like Leicester, Warwick, Huntingdon-Northampton, Stafford, Tutbury, Gloucester, Bedford, Eye, Clare and Pleshey tended to have a concentrated core of estates, usually around a castle or great house, but even here they might be interpenetrated by the estates of other

---

4 For the honors of Upper Normandy, S. Deck, 'Le comté d'Eu sous les ducs', *Annales de Normandie*, 4 (1954), 100–16; J. Le Maho, 'L'apparition des seigneuries châtelaines dans le Grand-Caux à l'époque ducale, *Archéologie Médiévale*, 6 (1976), 5–148; for central Normandy, D. Crouch, *The Beaumont Twins: The Roots and Branches of Power in the Twelfth Century* (Cambridge, 1986), 72–3, 101–14, 121–3; for L'Aigle, K. Thompson, 'The Lords of L'Aigle: ambition and insecurity on the borders of Normandy', *ANS* xviii, ed. C. Harper-Bill (Woodbridge, 1995), 181. For lower Normandy, J. Boussard, 'Le comté de Mortain au xie siècle', *Le Moyen Âge*, 58 (1952), 253–79. For the Norman frontier and its honors, see generally, D. Power, 'What did the frontier of Angevin Normandy comprise?', *ANS*, xvii, ed. C. Harper-Bill (Woodbridge, 1995), 181–201; J.A. Green, 'Lords of the Norman Vexin', in *War and Government in the Middle Ages*, ed. J. Gillingham and J.C. Holt (Woodbridge, 1994), 47–63; K. Thompson, 'Family and influence to the south of Normandy in the eleventh century: the lordship of Bellême', *Journal of Medieval History*, 11 (1985) 215–26. For observations about the formation of Norman honors, D.R. Bates, *Normandy before 1066* (London, 1982), 99–106, 111–21. For the Norman honors generally, see F.M. Powicke, *The Loss of Normandy* (Manchester, 1913), 331–58. For the comparative largeness in value of the Norman knight's fee, Crouch, *Beaumont Twins*, 121–2; T.K. Keefe, *Feudal Assessments and the Political Community under Henry II and his Sons* (Berkeley, CA, 1983), 95–6.

magnates, or by those of the Church, and all had detached outliers, often quite valuable demesne assets, which, being detached, were vulnerable to their enemies.[5]

This structural difference between England and Normandy must be borne in mind when we look at the way that public disorder developed in England after 1139. Those great Norman magnates who were also great English magnates might well apply to their new territorial dilemma in troubled England what might be to them the obvious answer: to tidy up the socio-political map so that it resembled more closely the convenient pattern they knew in Normandy. They wanted to know what their boundaries were, and in knowing them, defend them. This also would account for the early resort to castle-building. A castle – under its lord's fluttering banner – was the recognisable sign of lordship in the landscape, as well as the means to defend lordship effectively, but before Stephen's reign castles fortified with a degree of science and expense were not numerous in England.[6] The annalist of Winchester, writing of 1138, says that 'there was no-one of any consequence or influence in England who did not build or possess himself of a castle'.[7] The Worcester chronicler, writing retrospectively of the breakdown of public order from his standpoint around 1140 saw the rich as being out for themselves, and castles as part of the cycle of oppression: 'The wealthy magnates of the kingdom, already flushed with riches, keep no order, so that the poor are godlessly oppressed. They take account of only themselves and their dependents. They fill their castles and towns with life's necessities, and garrison them in force with arms.'[8] The Peterborough monk who finished off the Anglo-Saxon Chronicle – looking back on the later 1130s from the last years of the reign – talked in similar terms of castles as being the way that the magnates imposed themselves on the localities and defied the king, and their provision and construction as one of the most obnoxious ways in which the poor were oppressed.[9]

5 On the various shapes of the English honor and how they came to be that way, see P. Sawyer, '1066–1086: a tenurial revolution', in *Domesday Book. A Reassessment*, ed. P. Sawyer (London, 1983), 71–85; R. Fleming, 'Domesday Book and the tenurial revolution', *ANS*, ix, ed. R.A. Brown (Woodbridge, 1986), 87–102; eadem, *Kings and Lords in Conquest England* (Cambridge, 1991), ch. 6; and especially now, J.A. Green, *The Aristocracy of Norman England* (Cambridge, 1997), ch. 2.
6 For studies emphasising this social and symbolic dimension of the twelfth-century castle see D. Crouch, *The Image of Aristocracy in Britain, 1000–1300* (London, 1992), 260–4; C. Coulson, 'Castles of the Anarchy', in *The Anarchy of Stephen's Reign*, ed. E. King (Oxford, 1994), 81. For the relatively small number of castles built in England after the Conquest period, and the possible limited extent of building in Stephen's reign, R. Eales, 'Royal power and castles in Norman England', in *Ideals and Practice of Medieval Knighthood*, iii, ed. C. Harper-Bill and R. Harvey (Woodbridge, 1990), 55–63.
7 *Annales de Wintonia*, 51.
8 JW iii, 216 (my translation).
9 *ASC, s.a.* 1137. The resentment of contemporaries against the building of new castles is no less evident in RT, 177, who (somehow) produced a figure of 'over 1,115' castles built since the death of Henry I. There is no biblical source for Torigny's mysterious number, and it is not likely that it was derived from any government record (as he wrote in Normandy not England). The number does however break down to one thousand, one hundred, one ten and five units (in Latin terms four different digits, MCXV); a number which might have been systematically selected simply to express a large quantity.

But it would be to misunderstand the conditions of the reign to deduce from these passages that castles were the cause of the civil disorder. They were not that, they were simply the visible and resented expression of the idea of magnate lordship and authority which did cause the breakdown. To contemporaries castles were the embodiment and expression of what they hated: the dark conjunction of power and licence, in a word, 'tyranny'.[10] The appearance of new and resented fortifications was routinely complained of in earlier times when public order collapsed, as Charles Coulson points out. Therefore the castle – particularly the so-called 'adulterine' castle – does not deserve quite the attention it has had so far in the historiography of Stephen's reign: it was a dangerous symptom of disorder, not its cause.[11]

So when they finally threw off Stephen's authority and went to war, the dissident magnates went to war with their neighbours as much as with the king, for it was their neighbours (of whatever party) who stood between them and the one tried and tested means of establishing security of which they knew. Some English scholars have recently explored the French parallels in the English situation after 1139, and cross-comparisons between English and French social development in the twelfth century can only be welcomed. But there are dangers if we try to read into English conditions the overarching models developed by French historiography, such as that developed by the regional school of Duby and Bonnassie, for instance, which has produced the idea of a 'feudal mutation' at the beginning of the eleventh century when the Carolingian model of kingship crashed and the violent local powers of competing barons and knights replaced it.[12] The dangers lie in producing yet another determinist social imperative for what happened in Stephen's reign. Paul Dalton, in his study of Stephen's Yorkshire, suggests some possible comparison between his area of study and what was happening in the Mâconnais

10 See the views of E. King, 'The Anarchy of Stephen's reign', 134–5, note especially his quotation (p. 135) of a letter of Pope Innocent II of 1140 concerning the losses of the Lincoln diocese, that 'the magnates of the land . . . led on by their sins have been transformed into tyrants, and they oppress churchmen with unaccustomed exactions', for the text of this see *The Registrum Antiquissimum of the Cathedral Church of Lincoln*, i, ed. C.W. Foster (Lincoln, Rec. Soc., xxvii, 1931), 239–40. For the exploration of the concept of 'tyranny' by John of Salisbury, who honed his idea of it in Stephen's reign, see C.J. Nederman, 'The changing face of tyranny: the reign of King Stephen in John of Salisbury's political thought', *Nottingham Medieval Studies*, 33 (1989), 1–20, esp. p. 15.
11 Coulson, 'Castles of the Anarchy', 68–9. See in particular Dr Coulson's judgement that 'organized warfare and consequential disorder . . . not castles were the problem of the anarchy', ibid., 91. Dr Coulson disposes of the myth that the new castles of Stephen's reign were built in defiance of the king's right to license fortifications. The word 'adulterine' applied to them by modern scholars as if in condemnation of Stephen's failure to control them, he sees as simply colluding with the contemporary 'castle-polemic' of the clergy, ibid., 72–3.
12 For recent critiques, C. Wickham, 'Mutations et révolutions aux environs de l'an mil', *Médiévales*, 21 (1991), 27–38 (pointing out the existence of an aristocratic order in the Carolingian world, an aspect also examined by J. Nelson, 'Ninth-century knighthood: the evidence of Nithard', in *Studies in Medieval History Presented to R. Allen Brown*, ed. C. Harper-Bill and others (Woodbridge, 1989), 255–66; D. Barthélemy, 'La mutation féodale a-t-elle eu lieu? Note critique', *Annales*, xlvii (1992), 767–77; idem, 'Debate: the feudal revolution', *Past and Present*, no. 152 (1996), 196–205.

in the eleventh century. His argument derived from the takeover of royal assets and prerogatives by the earl of York after 1138, and the earl's subordination of the lesser magnates of the North and East Ridings to his will. He looked also at the way that some of the lesser Yorkshire aristocracy seized their opportunities to assert their own interests against both king and earl; finding in the space of a decade the sort of double devolution of power and social confusion that Duby suggested for the Mâconnais over an entire century.[13]

Duby's model is deceptive, however, if it is applied to twelfth-century England. To follow it involves subscribing to a view of the military aristocracy as self-promoting agents of anarchy that reaches back ultimately to Montesquieu through Bloch, and that presupposes a natural rivalry between crown and aristocracy which had a definite beginning at a point where the 'feudal order' triumphed over monarchy (see Introduction for this). Furthermore, it takes no account of the English experience of aristocratic consent to strong, administrative kingship; nor is there any recognition of a situation where the aristocracy had for a long period transferred much of its competitive political jostling to the royal curia. For all William of Aumale's regional ambitions, he was not operating in the sort of political vacuum that Duby's counts of Mâcon are suggested to have exploited. He was addressed by royal writs and seems to have conscientiously (and, of course, profitably) discharged his lieutenancy in Yorkshire on the king's behalf. William was most likely drawing on his experience as count of Aumale when he was earl of York. Norman counts also in general operated within the structures laid down by their duke, as English magnates operated within the king's. We should remember at this point that Norman aristocrats had been brought into the same centralising movement in Normandy – at great labour and expense – as they had been in England by the three dukes who were also kings of England.[14]

If we are to consider modern French models of aristocratic behaviour, we might do better to look at the '*ordre seigneuriale*' of Dominique Barthélemy (which gives this chapter its title). Barthélemy refuses to subscribe to the traditional viewpoint when looking at the relations between king and aristocracy, looking down from the top at the 'dislocation' caused by the competing magnates. Adopting that viewpoint would lead one to see magnates as agents of anarchy working against the legitimate monarchical system. He prefers to view society on a more truly local level, and sees there 'concentration' of

13 P. Dalton, *Conquest, Anarchy and Lordship: Yorkshire 1066–1154* (Cambridge, 1994), 185–6, citing G. Duby, 'The nobility in the eleventh- and twelfth-century Mâconnais', in *Lordship and Community in Medieval Europe*, ed. F.L. Cheyette (New York, 1975), 137–55, the 1953 master thesis being, of course, idem, *La société aux xi° et xiii° siècles dans la région mâconnaise* (2nd edn., repr., École des Hautes Études, 1982). See also idem, 'Lineage, nobility and knighthood: the Mâconnais in the twelfth century – a revision', in *The Chivalrous Society*, trans. C. Postan (London, 1977), 59–80.
14 On the relationship between the centralising Duke Henry I and his Norman aristocracy, see Le Patourel, *Norman Empire*, 157–9; J.A. Green, 'King Henry I and the aristocracy of Normandy', in *La 'France Anglaise' au Moyen Âge* (Actes du 111° Congrès National des Sociétés Savantes, Poitiers, 1986), 161–73.

power and influence in the hands of the effective local lords. It was by working with these lords that some of the princes – those who 'stood the shock' of the great burst of castle-building in the eleventh century – and the later Capetian kings of France created a coherent political order.[15] His picture of regional aristocracies as co-operative with strong lordship, and as substantially in favour of arrangements to limit local disorder and promote peace, accords far better with what we know of Anglo-Norman magnates' behaviour, and fits a world where both in England and ultimately in France, Angevin and Capetian monarchies established a social hegemony by working with their aristocracies, not in spite of them. This being so, the ground lost by King Stephen in England after 1139 is all the more astonishing and regrettable.

HONORS, AFFINITIES AND REGIONAL POWER

Partly because of their Norman experience, and partly because of their irrepressible ambitions, English magnates had shown before Stephen's reign a desire to define and control particular areas of the kingdom, and demonstrated a willingness to negotiate or edge out any potential rival in those areas. We have seen this already in what Earl Robert of Leicester achieved in Henry's reign in northwest Leicestershire. This was local rivalry for local ends, and although it was rough-house behaviour, it was as far as things seem to have gone in terms of regional ambition in King Henry's reign in England. There was, however, a further stage in that rivalry, and that was when regional competition began to polarise lesser, independent landowners into groups under the leadership of one greater magnate, who would employ them to enhance his local domination. Later medieval historians call such groups 'affinities' (see Appendix I to this chapter).

In view of what has just been said about the duchy, this is something we catch sight of in Normandy before we find it in England. Robert of Leicester's brother, Waleran of Meulan, gives the first recognisable example of a great affinity in the process of being raised and extended in Stephen's reign. During the campaigns of 1136 and 1137 in Normandy, the count attracted into his household several minor Norman magnates of the Vexin, Lieuvin and Evreçin. This affinity survived until the count's final fall from power in 1153. Waleran also attracted into his household his own capable 'new men', men such as Alan de Neuville, whom he employed as his butler in return for an annual stipend; Ralph de Beaumont, later Henry II's physician, and Philip de Harcourt, later bishop of Bayeux. Alan went on to enter the Angevin royal household and become chief forester of England for King Henry II.[16] It was the importance and quality of this retinue which caused Geoffrey and Henry Plantagenet

---

15 D. Barthélemy, *L'ordre seigneurial, xie–xiie siècle* (Paris, 1990), 37–51, esp. 46. We might point out here the similar and earlier comments of Richard Mortimer, cautioning against a top-down view of twelfth-century society, see 'Land and service: the tenants of the honour of Clare', *ANS*, viii, ed. R.A. Brown (Woodbridge, 1986), 177–97.
16 Crouch, *Beaumont Twins*, 35–7, 155.

to be so circumspect in their treatment of the count despite their suspicions of him. Its existence was, as has been said, evidence of an aristocracy that had lost confidence in ducal government, and had looked to great magnates to fill the gap.[17]

But before the arrival of the empress, the same process can be seen happening in England. The trend betrays something of the essential frailty of public order in England, despite the best efforts of King Henry and his predecessors. It did not take much in the way of uncertainty before magnates were seen to be a better bet for local security than the king. Admittedly, both instances I will cite were in the Marches, where magnates had always been more independent. The first example is when Robert of Gloucester's defiance of King Stephen brought his Marcher affinity into the open when it revolted in his absence in the summer of 1138. The names of those who revolted are listed by Robert de Torigny and Orderic Vitalis, and show some common features: some were former *curiales* (such as Eustace and William fitz John); others are known to have allied with him through some formal link of fealty (such as Morgan ab Owain and Geoffrey Talbot); William fitz Alan had married into the Gloucester family; Walchelin Maminot and William Peverel were Kentish landholders, where Earl Robert had dominated until 1138; Ralph Louvel and William de Mohun were Somerset landholders, where Earl Robert was the dominant magnate.[18] Taken together they amount to an 'affinity' with a regional orientation, and, as an affinity, they present a good example of how dangerous such associations could be, when cut loose by their master to assert his local power by force, rather than by menace and manipulation. At this point, rough-house became open season.

A second example followed the establishment of Henry of Scotland as earl of Northumbria in April 1139. The northern English affinity Earl Henry formed was not called upon to be as warlike as Robert of Gloucester's, but it was no less formidable for all that. Although, as we have seen, the lesser magnates of Northumberland were left free by the treaty of Durham to refuse allegiance to Henry, there is plenty of evidence that several did not, such as Ralph de Merlay (and his successor, Roger), lord of Morpeth, and Robert Bertram, lord of Mitford (who acted as Earl Henry's sheriff). Before 1141, Gilbert d'Umfraville, lord of Prudhoe, had become Earl Henry's constable, and there were other lesser lords who followed where they led. There was some contact with the new earl of Northumbria's retinue from old friends of his father with extensive holdings outside Northumberland (who had nonetheless fought against him at Northallerton). Robert de Brus, lord of Harterness, makes frequent appearances in the numerous surviving charters of Earl Henry.

---

17 Note on this Orderic's continuous laments that Normandy had lost its 'protector' or 'ruler' (*rector*) after 1135, OV vi, 454, 456, 458.
18 D. Crouch, 'The March and the Welsh Kings', in *The Anarchy of King Stephen's Reign*, ed. E. King (Oxford, 1994), 276n. For Earl Robert's position in Kent before 1139, see R. Eales, 'Local loyalties in Norman England: Kent in Stephen's reign', *ANS*, viii, ed. R.A. Brown (Woodbridge, 1986), 91–2. See also above, p. 32.

Others, like Walter de Bolbec and Bernard de Bailleul, appear in his *curia*, albeit infrequently. Eustace fitz John had been committed to the Scottish cause even before the Standard, and makes a strong appearance with Earl Henry after 1139, although he also set his sights on alliance with Ranulf of Chester. Even those of these men who held land in Northumberland were not bound to do homage to Earl Henry, and others of them held their lands principally to the south of his earldom (like Brus, fitz John, Bolbec and Bailleul), but the logic of associating themselves for safety and advancement with a dominant magnate brought them into his affinity nonetheless.[19] So here in the north we see the same political processes at work as in the southwest.

THE CONSEQUENCES OF POLITICAL INSECURITY AND THE POLITICAL ORDER

The parading of open political affinities such as this (and there were perhaps others already in the process of formation which cannot be adequately documented) need not necessarily amount to public disorder: were that the case, England in the fourteenth century would have been rather more 'anarchic' than Stephen's England! But it does amount to a significant move towards the devolution of power; it shows, as I have said, that there had been a collapse of confidence in Stephen's rulership. Early twelfth-century society was so organised as to recognise, and even sanction, the local hegemony of the magnate. When the centralising tendency of Anglo-Norman kingship faltered, it was hardly to be wondered at that power should descend to the local level. That process became irreversible in Stephen's reign when Earl Robert of Gloucester took over the direction of affairs in the southwest in person in the winter of 1139–40. His methods were simple and had a brutal territorial logic. King Stephen had immediately confiscated all his lands which were within his reach as soon as Earl Robert's defection had become known to him: we have seen that Earl Robert's holdings at Grimsby were used by the king as part of his settlement with Ranulf of Chester in November 1140. Earl Robert's Kentish estates were kept in royal hands, although apparently in late 1141, his Kentish tenants were able to reach him and pay him some money for his support in captivity.[20]

19 See on this, J.A. Green, 'Anglo-Scottish relations, 1066–1174', in *England and her Neighbours, 1066–1453: Essays in Honour of Pierre Chaplais*, ed. M. Jones and M. Vale (London, 1989), 67; eadem, 'Aristocratic loyalties in the northern frontier of England, *c.*1100–1174', in *England in the Twelfth Century*, ed. D. Williams (Woodbridge, 1990), 97–9; Dalton, *Conquest, Anarchy and Lordship*, 206–8; idem, 'Eustace fitz John and the politics of Anglo-Norman England: the rise and survival of a twelfth-century royal servant', *Speculum*, 71 (1996), 370–2. We might note also the association of the Percy family with Earl Henry, for Alan de Percy, son of William, makes grants for the soul of the earl and his father, King David 'his lord', see *Cartularium abbathiae de Whiteby*, ed. J.C. Atkinson (2 vols, Surtees Soc., 1879–81) i, 58–59, 59–60, 174 (his brother, Geoffrey de Percy, attests an act of Earl Henry dated 1147, *Regesta Regum Scottorum* i, 159). Significant acts of Earl Henry that illustrate the early extent of his following are to be found in Archives départementales de l'Eure et Loire H1419 (Jedburgh, 1139 × 42), *Regesta Regum Scottorum* i, 138–9 (Selkirk, 1139 × 42), 145 (Huntingdon, 1139 × 41), 146–7 (Newcastle-upon-Tyne, 1141). They include all the magnates mentioned here.
20 *Regesta* iii, no. 178; *HN*, 66–7.

Earl Robert did to others indiscriminately what had been done to him with due legality (he had after all defied the king), and from 1139 he began a policy which was in the end followed by many of the magnates in the civil war. He simply took and acquired outlying estates of rivals which came within the area which he had set out in his mind as his own, and in addition he imposed his own levies in cash and services on all whom he had brought under his power. More than that, he arrogated to himself what had formerly been royal pre- rogatives. William of Malmesbury says that it was Earl Robert who conferred the status of earl of Cornwall on his half-brother, Reginald, and what right have we to question William of Malmesbury's reporting of events (however much we may doubt his interpretation of them)? The recent find of a large hoard of silver pennies at Box in Wiltshire (1994) has revealed for the first time that Earl Robert had also taken a further significant step in coining pennies in his own name. Interestingly, he had the pennies stamped with a lion, already the recognised symbol of the Angevin dynasty (and which after 1154 became the royal arms of England), but they were nonetheless issued under the name of 'Earl Robert'.

In recent years, local studies have much enhanced our knowledge of the methods of magnates in their localities in Stephen's reign. Robert of Glouces- ter's activities in the West Country occasionally surface in the records. One of his first targets had been his rival at court, Earl Robert of Leicester. Robert of Leicester's lands were principally in a compact block in the central midlands within a quadilateral defined by Nuneaton, Loughborough, Melton Mowbray and Market Harborough. There were substantial and lucrative outliers, of which some were easy to defend from his enemies (like Brackley in Northampton- shire) but others were not. Particularly exposed was his town of Bungay in Suffolk, and as we have seen, Hugh Bigod had abstracted this valuable estate from him in the summer of 1140. Also exposed, and very desirable as a seaport to communicate with Normandy, was another large Leicester outlier, the town and hinterland of Wareham in Dorset. Much of Wareham town, and its collegiate church (but not the castle), had been inherited by Earl Robert from his father, the great count of Meulan, and along with it went several demesne manors in the vicinity. The dean of Wareham in 1139, Adam of Ely, was a Beaumont clerk and nominee. By the end of 1141 Wareham and the sur- rounding Beaumont estates had come into Earl Robert of Gloucester's hands, and the town and castle became the principal Angevin base on the south coast. Adam of Ely resigned himself to serving a new master (he became one of the principal writing officers of the Gloucester household) and it became a Glouces- ter objective to make sure that what they had taken was not returned to its rightful owner. In *c.*1148, with the marriage of Robert of Leicester's daughter, Hawise, to the new Earl William of Gloucester, the ambition was fulfilled when much of the Leicester holding in Dorset was given with her to William as her marriage-portion. In this way, one of the major disseisins of Stephen's reign became – in effect – permanent (regardless of the fact that it was dressed up as an enfeoffment).[21] As we have seen, Earl Robert also reconciled himself to the loss of Bungay by exchanging his claim on it with his cousin Earl Roger of Warwick for the service of two knights in the midlands some time before 1153.

This gives us a clue as to the major reason for local instability in Stephen's reign after 1139: legal title to land was being temporarily overruled by the military logic of territorial domination. The chief victims of this were those who could best afford it, the great magnates of the land, who lost valuable demesne assets. It may have been that they were big enough men to take fringe losses, but the tenants of their outlying estates might have to pay the full cost if the new intruding lord had his own men to reward, or if they were persistent in their allegiance. These were the real 'disinherited' of Stephen's reign. Other potential victims were the ecclesiastical magnates and the monastic houses under royal patronage. For instance, Earl Robert of Gloucester had as little reason to love Bishop Henry of Winchester as he had to love Robert of Leicester. So it is no surprise to discover that after 1139 he picked off from Bishop Henry's abbey of Glastonbury the Wiltshire manor of Damerham which adjoined his centre of Cranborne in Dorset. This was an asset which in the end had to be returned, but it was all part of the logic of local hegemony. Damerham could be added to Earl Robert's demesne centre and forest of Cranborne to make a bigger and yet more profitable block of land.[22] These glimpses of Robert of Gloucester's local activities in the southwest of England after his return add something to our understanding of the meaning of the author of the *Gesta Stephani* (who lived literally in the middle of all this) when he wrote of the heyday of the earl's power:

> And the earl and his supporters fared successfully and joyously after this, made the kingdom subject to them far and wide, demolished with spirit and valour castles belonging to the king's men, in unchecked triumph built others for their more effectual subjugation, and without any resistance from anyone put almost half of England, from sea to sea, under their own laws and ordinances. This lordship of his the earl very greatly adorned by restoring peace and quietness everywhere, except that in building his castles he exacted forced labour from all and whenever he had to fight the enemy, demanded everyone's help either by sending knights or by paying scutage.[23]

Considering the author was a royalist, this would seem to be a compliment (although he, as a royalist, would not concede that the earl's peace between the Bristol and English Channels was anything more than 'a shadow of peace'). What he implies is that the earl did not victimise the small people within his

21 See on this, Crouch, *Beaumont Twins*, 46 and n, 85 and n, 152–3.
22 For Damerham's confiscation 'in werra' (after 1139), see N.E. Stacy 'Henry of Blois and the lordship of Glastonbury', *EHR*, 114 (1999), 21. For Cranborne as Gloucester demesne under Earl Robert, *Earldom of Gloucester Charters*, ed. Patterson, 147, 177.
23 *GS*, 148–50.

region, other than to levy labour on the peasantry. And indeed, from our limited evidence, he seems to have only picked on those of his own size.

Earl Robert's able second, Miles of Gloucester, adopted his neighbour's methods with enthusiasm. His intention was to control Herefordshire and the region around Gloucester itself, where he controlled the castle. He most likely had the empress's permission to acquire the city of Hereford, an acquisition he had made early in 1140. He was granted the title of earl there the next year, after the victory at Lincoln. But there were other assets which he coveted, and which his Angevin allegiance gave him the excuse simply to take. Gloucester abbey – although a house which had no post-Conquest founder, and if anything, a royal abbey – was acknowledging Miles's son, Roger, as its advocate (that is, its formal protector with rights of wardship and hospitality) by 1144, as it had most likely also acknowledged Miles (who had died in 1143).[24] Another of Miles's notable victims was the earl of Warwick. The earldom had its core in the valley of the Warwickshire Avon and along the northern scarp of the Cotswold hills but, like the earldom of Leicester, it had valuable demesne outliers, and two were situated in the Severn valley near Gloucester.[25] One was the manor of Hempsted, just outside the southern walls of Gloucester. The other, and far greater Warwick demesne asset, was the town and castle of Lydney, on the southern edge of the forest of Dean, of which Miles had acquired the keepership from Mathilda on his defection in 1139.

Lydney had come into the hands of Baderon, lord of Monmouth, before 1144, when Monmouth priory had a confirmation of his grant of Lydney church from Bishop Robert de Béthune. Baderon is known to have been one of those lesser magnates who entered the affinity of the earls of Hereford during the civil war, so it would seem to be through Miles's influence that he obtained rights in Lydney.[26] Miles perhaps realised that it was easier to confuse the matter of right to an estate if you not merely took it, but then passed it on to a third party as an enfeoffment (we will see later how the Church was quite often the preferred third party in such cases). In this case, the theft was so flagrant that Lydney had to be surrendered, but the grant of the church by the intruder caused much trouble later on. The fitz Osberns had used the

24 *Historia et cartularium monasterii sancti Petri de Gloucestria*, ed. W.H. Hart (3 vols, Rolls Series, 1863–7) i, 311, talks in 1144 of Roger '*ipsius ecclesie beati Petri advocatus*' conceding a settlement between the abbey and Walter of Clifford, and providing the land to facilitate it. For what the right of advocacy might involve in twelfth-century England, Crouch, *Image of Aristocracy*, 327–34.
25 For the earldom of Warwick and its Gloucestershire demesne (granted by William Rufus to Earl Henry I out of the former fitz Osbern lands) see D. Crouch, 'The local influence of the earls of Warwick, 1088–1242: a study in decline and resourcefulness', *Midland History*, 21 (1996), 15–16n.
26 *Chartes anciennes du prieuré de Monmouth en Angleterre*, ed. P. Marchegay (Les Roches-Baritaud, 1879), 28. Baderon's association with Miles cannot be proved from his few charters, although Baderon was one of the chief followers of Miles's son, Roger. But the fact that Baderon had already granted Lydney church to Monmouth priory less than a year after Earl Miles's death is indication enough that it was to Miles he owed the estate, and not Roger. Baderon is one of those listed as being in the empress's party in 1141 by Brian fitz Count, H.W.C. Davis, 'Henry of Blois and Brian fitz Count', *EHR*, 25 (1910), 303.

churches of Lydney to add to their Norman abbey of Lyre's English endowment. In 1158, as a result of the tenure by the Monmouths, Bishop Alfred of
Worcester as papal judge-delegate concluded a settlement by which Lyre and
Monmouth priory's mother house of Saumur exchanged tithes to buy off the
priory's claims on Lydney.

Miles may also have plagued the Warwicks over their manor of Hempsted
outside Gloucester's south walls. It came to the Warwicks (as had Lydney) out
of the former estates of William fitz Osbern in the reign of Rufus, but had been
promptly granted on to Walter of Gloucester before 1095 in return for knight
service. In September 1141 we find that Miles of Gloucester conveyed the
manor of Hempsted in the presence of the empress and Earl Robert of Gloucester to the refugee Augustinian canons of Llanthony, whom Miles had generously settled at Gloucester around 1136 when political conditions around their
Welsh priory became too uncertain. It was about that time that many former
royalist magnates (including Earl Roger of Warwick) capitulated to the empress.
No mention of any Warwick overlordship of Hempsted is recorded in Miles's
grant, nor any acknowledgement that service and a relief was owed for it,
only the pointed claim that his father had held it before him. It was not until
Henry II's reign that the earl of Warwick's rights in Hempsted were acknowledged and his consent secured in return for lodging and a relief payment.[27]

If Angevin supporters alone had been making the most of their opportunities in the localities, things would have been bad enough, but royalists were
also using the same methods. It is only fair to point out that if Miles was
victimising his neighbours around Gloucester, his own supporters and friends
were themselves being victimised. Miles's hospitality at Gloucester to the
refugee canons of Llanthony, fleeing the disturbed conditions in upper Gwent,
has already been mentioned. Canon David Walker has demonstrated how
Miles generously provided lands and rents in Gloucester for one Ralph fitz
Pichard, a citizen of Winchester who had been deprived of his property and
expelled as a refugee from the city for his support of the Angevin cause in
1141.[28] Such, indeed, was the pernicious logic which followed on from the
great land-swap which the war of succession had set in motion. We have
already looked at the extravagant regional claims of Earl Ranulf of Chester,

---

27 Cartulary of Llanthony, PRO, C115/K2/6683, fos. 24v, 35r. Earl William of Warwick (earl
after 1153) conceded Hempsted to Llanthony Secunda, while maintaining the claim to two *hospitia*
(not released by the earls till a concord of 1236). For Earl Miles's grant, see edition in D. Walker,
'Charters of the earldom of Hereford, 1095–1210', in *Camden Miscellany*, xxii (1964), 13–14. For
the Warwicks' rights in Hempsted, D. Walker, 'Hospitium: a feudal service of hospitality', *Transactions of the Bristol and Gloucestershire Archaeological Society*, 76 (1957), 48–61, the charters are
printed, 58–61.
28 D. Walker, 'Ralph son of Pichard', *Bulletin of the Institute of Historical Research*, xxxiii (1960),
195–202, esp. 197–8. One might also note in the same class of deprivation the case reconstructed
by M. Cheney where Earl Reginald of Cornwall lost an estate in the diocese of Salisbury during
Stephen's reign and an intruding clerk was appointed to its church, whom the earl attempted to
oust after 1154, '"Possessio/proprietas" in ecclesiastical courts in mid-twelfth century England',
in *Law and Government in Medieval England and Normandy*, ed. G. Garnett and J. Hudson (Cambridge, 1994), 250–1.

placed before King Stephen in November 1140 and temporarily conceded by him. The ruthless regional logic in them is very clear. Earl Ranulf was more or less staking a claim to control the Trent valley as far as the port of Torksey.

An even better example, because it concerns a royalist whose loyalties were unquestioned throughout the reign, is that of William of Aumale, earl of York. Earl William's career has been comprehensively explored by Paul Dalton. William was an early enthusiast for Stephen and did him good service in his northern campaigns, most notably on the battlefield of the Standard in 1138. For this service, William – already count of Aumale in Normandy – was given the second comital style of 'earl of York' by the king, presumably in the autumn of 1138. As with Count Waleran of Meulan in Worcestershire, William acquired much of the royal demesne assets in his new county for his support and this included the city and castle of York and some at least of the royal forest, as well as some significant royal estates (such as the manors of Great Driffield and Warter) and sokes such as that of Falsgrave on the Yorkshire coast, within which he founded the castle and port that came to be known as Scarborough). Using this and his new position he attracted into a new affinity a significant number of the minor magnates of the North and East Ridings of Yorkshire (such as Eustace fitz John, Robert de Stuteville, Adam de Brus and William Fossard) and acquired there a hegemony. He then used the hegemony for his own territorial advantage, and in the 1140s took over by force the possessions of Gilbert de Gant around Hunmanby and Bridlington on the coast of Yorkshire, and put pressure on the Mowbrays, south of York.[29] It seems not to have disturbed him at all that the Gants were also royalists, and that Gilbert's uncle, Robert de Gant (dean of York after 1147) was King Stephen's chancellor for most of his reign. We should not therefore be surprised to find another of those key texts relating to the devolution of power in Stephen's reign associated with Earl William of York, when William of Newburgh assessed him (from the other side of Henry II's reign) as 'more truly the king beyond the Humber than King Stephen'.[30]

LIONS AND JACKALS

So far I have been suggesting that the magnates were capable of maintaining order at the local level in England. In the case of some of them, such as Henry of Northumbria, Robert of Gloucester, Ranulf of Chester, Miles of Gloucester, Robert of Leicester and William of York, that seems to be the case, once they had targeted and mastered their local rivals. But the local efforts of such

29 Dalton, *Conquest, Anarchy and Lordship*, 152–95; idem, 'William earl of York and royal authority in Yorkshire in the reign of Stephen', *HSJ*, 2 (1990), 155–65; idem, 'The origins of Scarborough', in *Medieval Scarborough: Studies in Trade and Civic Life*, ed. D. Crouch and T. Pearson, forthcoming. Dr Dalton's argument concerning the extension of Earl William's control over hundred and wapentake centres is not adopted here. I have some doubts whether we can be quite as certain of the extent of wapentake and hundreds and the location of their centres in the twelfth century as Dr Dalton assumes we can be (he cites such takeovers as 'probable' or 'almost certain').
30 WN, 103.

great men were uneven, and there were other magnates who had neither the resources nor (probably) the ability to establish peace in their lands. So there occurred fault lines of public disorder in England, which were particularly unstable in regions where the influence of King Stephen and his Angevin enemies met. In such areas there were great opportunities for the unprincipled lesser magnate, and great troubles for innocent bystanders such as the villagers, townspeople and clergy who had to endure the troubles caused by long-term local insecurity.

Complaints of the unhealthy consequences of disorder begin in the chronicles during our key period of 1139–40. The passages are famous, but bear repeating simply because of the way they illustrate the conditions we are analysing. Henry of Huntingdon talks (when writing of Christmas 1139) of there being '. . . no peace in the realm, but through murder, burning, and pillage everything was being destroyed, everywhere the sound of war, with lamentation and terror' and in a Jeremiad talks of lords themselves being disturbed in their castles, priests and churches harmed, and good faith a thing of the past.[31] In his description of the state of England in 1140 (written only a few years later) William of Malmesbury composed a long aside. Like others, he sighed over the sudden prominence of castles and the menacing exactions of their garrisons, and like Henry of Huntingdon, lamented the particularly shocking fact that priests and the refuge of churchyards were no longer safe. Not even excommunication by the legate influenced the evil-doers. Most tellingly, he compared the tranquillity lately under King Henry with what England suffered under Stephen. It was the common perception now that Stephen had lost in a few years what Henry had gained in a reign of three and a half decades. Malmesbury rather spoiled the effect by his concluding remarks that, 'Meanwhile Robert earl of Gloucester behaved with restraint and avoided nothing more carefully than even a slight loss of men to gain a battle.'[32] The author of the *Gesta Stephani* writes, too, of late 1139 that 'not only they [that is, Brian fitz Count and Miles of Gloucester] but also a number of others who formerly were allied to the king by faith and oath now broke the bond of peace and concord and attacked him without restraint, and raging with all manner of savagery in different parts of England they were wickedly committing everywhere the most grievous or criminal things they could think of'.[33] He, being a royalist, puts the blame for the breakdown on the king's enemies, but his implication needs to be noted that the breakdown of order was limited to the region where the king's enemies were.

There is no reason to doubt the reality of the descriptions of these historians of this time of chaos, although one should remember that the chaos was limited in location to the fault lines of loyalty, and limited also in time, until the new order of castle-based magnate power was established. We might also say that the most unpredictable and unscrupulous agents of disorder were not

31 HH, 725.
32 *HN*, 40–1.
33 *GS*, 90.

the great magnates, but the lesser barons and mercenary captains who were their satellites. A good example of this would be John fitz Gilbert, otherwise known as John Marshal, lord of Hamstead Marshall in Berkshire, where he had a fortified manor house. John fitz Gilbert had been a low-ranking but assiduous courtier of Henry I, and was one of those lesser household officers who (like William Martel and Hugh Bigod) embraced the new regime of Stephen even before the great magnates had made up their mind. Like Martel and Bigod he was generously rewarded. He received the keeping of the great royal castle in northern Wiltshire, Marlborough, on the road between London and Bristol. This linked with his own modest estate lower down the Kennett valley towards Newbury to make him, for the first time, a landowner of consequence enough to look like a magnate. Another gift to him by the king was the castle of Ludgershall, on the road between Marlborough and Salisbury. Together, the three castles surrounded and defined for him a potential sphere of influence on the Wiltshire downs.[34]

John fitz Gilbert attended on the king with great faithfulness until the summer of 1138, and then he disappears from royal charters. No writer names him as one of the supporters of Robert of Gloucester who defied the king in summer 1138, but it is at least known that when the advance guard of the empress landed in Dorset in August 1139, the king was engaged in a siege of Marlborough. Contemporaries betray, as we have seen, some confusion as to who exactly it was that John was supporting in the campaigns of 1139–40, and the truth might well be that – like Ranulf of Chester – he was using his position to negotiate even further concessions from the beleaguered king. But he stood on shifting ground, being right on the border between the royalist and Angevin parties, and liable to attack from both. So, when Robert fitz Hubert, a prominent and vicious Flemish mercenary captain and a cousin of the king's mercenary, William of Ypres, working for Robert of Gloucester (a fact that William of Malmesbury fails to mention), decided to work for himself and seized Devizes castle from its royal garrison in March 1140, John had to do something. Devizes was immediately to the west of his own sphere of influence, and when fitz Hubert drove his ex-master's son, William, from the gate of the castle with insults, John fitz Gilbert realised he had a ruthless rival and neighbour about to attempt the same political game as he must have contemplated. Guessing that fitz Hubert would want to seize Marlborough to make himself secure in the region, he enticed him into attempting a surprise attack, and trapped the would-be entrappers. John handed fitz Hubert over to Earl Robert for execution at the gates of Devizes, an object lesson for those who would disturb the earl's peace. The castle surrendered itself for a cash payment to the king, as a result.[35]

Since William of Malmesbury thought that John fitz Gilbert was working for the empress during this episode, and John of Worcester thought he was

---

34 For his life and career, see D. Crouch, *William Marshal: Court, Career and Chivalry in the Angevin Empire, c.1147–1219* (London, 1990), 1–4.
35 Accounts of this famous episode are in *GS*, 104–8; *HN*, 43–4; JW iii, 284–90.

working for the king, we see quite how confused things were in the public mind during this period of political drift. We may well conclude that the only sure thing is that John – like Robert fitz Hubert – was working for himself. As an instance of this, we find that John of Worcester portrays John, the royalist, handing fitz Hubert over to Robert of Gloucester for a large sum of money and then acting on his behalf to negotiate with Devizes and hang the mercenary captain when it would not surrender to him. But this drift did not continue. In 1141, when the empress triumphed, John fitz Gilbert joined her side and remained constant to the Angevin cause thereafter until the very end of the reign. Indeed, as we will see, he was the indirect and accidental cause of the final settlement which brought King Henry II, the empress's son, to the throne of England.

In the meantime, John fitz Gilbert pursued his own agenda, set out by the triangle of territory marked out by his three castles of Marlborough, Ludgershall and Hamstead Marshall. He improved his castles and built more, massively refortifying Hamstead and building a forward post at Newbury down the Kennett, a large estate he obtained somehow from the absentee lord, the count of Perche. But he must have taken losses elsewhere.[36] Like most significant English landowners his lands were scattered across several counties and some estates must have been beyond his control; when he sold his large manor of Nettlecombe in Somerset to the Ralegh family just after the end of Stephen's reign, it may have been because he was sanctioning a loss he had sustained in the 1140s. There were compensations; it seems that he picked up a demesne estate in Herefordshire from an alliance made within the Angevin party.[37] Others suffered through John's need to establish himself in north Wiltshire. Within his self-defined area of lordship were the estates of several monasteries, and Abingdon abbey looked on him as one of their chief persecutors in Stephen's reign, extorting goods and castlework services from the monks' tenants, as the monks complained to the pope at Auxerre in 1147.[38]

36 For the building works at Hamstead, see D.J. Bonney and C.J. Dunn, 'Earthwork castles and settlement at Hamstead Marshall, Berkshire', in *From Cornwall to Caithness: Some Aspects of British Field Archaeology*, ed. M. Bowden and others (B.A.R., British Series, 209, 1989), 173–82. For the counts of Perche and Newbury, see S. Painter, *William Marshal*, (Baltimore, 1933), 271–2; D.A. Carpenter, *The Minority of Henry III* (London, 1990), 92. John may have laid claim to Newbury because the sister of his second wife, Sibyl of Salisbury (whom he married *c*.1145) was dowager countess of Perche, regarding it as fair game as being loosely family land (see below p. 259 for more on this).
37 The manor of Upleadon, Herefordshire, was in his hands in the 1160s, *Herefordshire Domesday*, *c.1160–70*, ed. V.H. Galbraith and J. Tait (Pipe Roll Society, new ser., xxv, 1950), p. 57. It is not known who granted it to the family or when, other than that John had a pardon for Danegeld in Herefordshire in 1156, *Pipe Roll of 2 Henry II*, p. 51. In 1242 Upleadon was noted as held by the Templars from the honor of Newbury of the grant of Earl William Marshal (John's son), *The Book of Fees commonly called the Testa de Nevill* (3 vols, P.R.O., 1920–31) ii, p. 808, which is some indication that it was an acquisition by John in Stephen's reign, for it was John who built the castle of Newbury early in the 1150s (see below). There is no account for Herefordshire in the 1130 pipe roll, so we have no way to check if he was a landowner in the shire in Henry's reign.
38 *Chronicon monasterii de Abingdon* ed. J. Stevenson (2 vols, Rolls Series, 1858) ii, 200. Abingdon had a large number of vulnerable estates in the Kintbury and Rowbury hundreds of Berkshire, which were well within John's reach.

But he suffered too, for to his immediate south was the expanding lordship of Earl Patrick of Salisbury who, in the mid-1140s, forced him into subjection to his own dominance after a local war. The fact that, at the time, both were of the Angevin party seems to have been a matter of little importance to their local skirmish of ambition. There was no ideology in the local politics of Wiltshire, as there was none elsewhere in England. The civil war on the ground came to be about survival and individual ambition.

Another very good instance of a local lesser landowner who attempted to play off the greater magnates for his own benefit is William de Launay (*de Alneto*). He was a substantial tenant of the earl of Leicester, with a concentration of estates to the east of Nuneaton, spanning Watling Street and in the rugged Charnwood area of Leicestershire. William occupied the very edge of chaos in the midlands. To the southwest of him Earl Ranulf of Chester was duelling with Robert Marmion for control of Coventry. On the east, Earl Ranulf was in a close contest with Robert of Leicester for the mastery of the Soar valley and Mountsorrel castle. For whatever reason, William de Launay chose the same path to security as his betters, and attempted to define his own territory. We do not know precisely what his adventuring led him to do, although we do know that he employed knights from the Warwickshire landed families, some of whom died in his service. What we do know is that when, in the last years of Stephen's reign, the earls of Leicester and Chester finally came to terms, one of their principal concerns was William de Launay. He had built a castle at Ravenstone in Charnwood, and the earls agreed that it was to be destroyed. They also agreed that neither would support William against the other (clearly his favourite tactic in furthering his own interests). We know that the earl of Leicester had (by 1155) deprived William of at least some of his lands, although an accommodation must have been reached between the earl and the Launay family in the end, for William's son, Hugh, became a chief counsellor to Robert III of Leicester in the early 1160s, before he succeeded the old earl, his father.[39]

A final example of the way that the succession crisis of 1139–40 transformed social behaviour is that of Eustace fitz John. He had already become an important Yorkshire magnate, and (by his first marriage) castellan of Alnwick in Northumberland, through the favour of King Henry before 1135. We have seen that early in Stephen's reign he decided to join his brother and other old *curiales* in opposition to the king. For him, the obvious ally was King David of Scotland, whom he would have known well from his days at Henry's court and who had ambitions to extend his influence south to the Humber, as we have seen. He crossed over to King David's allegiance in 1138, and despite the

---

39 For reconstructions of the Launay affair, based on the document printed by F.M. Stenton, *The First Century of English Feudalism, 1066–1166* (2nd edn., Oxford, 1960), 286–8, see H.A. Cronne, 'Ranulf des Gernons, earl of Chester, 1129–53', *TRHS*, 4th ser., xx (1937), 132; Crouch, *Beaumont Twins*, 80–1. For the Marmion–Chester conflict over Coventry (dating to the mid-1140s), see R.H.C. Davis, 'An unknown Coventry charter', *EHR*, 86 (1971), 533–47.

reverse of the Standard, Eustace stayed with the Scottish royal family, and until the mid-1140s was frequently to be found in company with King David and his son, Earl Henry. But around the year 1144, he successfully opened a new avenue to advancement when Earl Ranulf of Chester bought his allegiance with the succession to the barony of the late constable of Chester (whose sister he had married a decade or so earlier). The charter creating Eustace constable still survives and includes the curious clause that Eustace would be from then onwards the earl's 'constable and supreme counsellor after me above all the nobles and barons of my land'. It reads as if the earl was buying in Eustace as his future chief of staff and political manager, on the basis of his proven survival skills in the treacherous political world of the 1130s and 1140s. Eustace's allegiance to Earl Ranulf quite possibly brought further rewards, and Dr Dalton suggests that the earl used his influence to secure estates for Eustace in Yorkshire and marriages for his daughters. At the same time, Eustace was cultivating a productive and mutually beneficial relationship with the third of the great magnates of the north, Earl William of York, without which he could not have been as active as he was in the county.[40]

Such case studies as those of John fitz Gilbert, William de Launay and Eustace fitz John give us a further insight into the fluid political world that King Stephen and Robert of Gloucester created in England between Arundel in 1139 and Lincoln in 1141. It was not anarchic, because it had its own territorial and political logic. The chief players were the king and the greater magnates, those with the resources and base of power to create new regional affinities. These great men took great losses with their gains, and in some ways may be considered those who paid most dearly for the civil war (although that is not to minimise the sufferings of the defenceless poor and the clergy). But in their struggles they could create brand-new opportunities for their followers – and those whom they wished to be their followers – sometimes deliberately, sometimes despite themselves. The lesser magnates and the knights they employed reaped the real benefits of the civil war, unless, like Robert fitz Hubert and William de Launay, they got in the way of the greater predators who were fighting around them. It must be said that the Launays and the Marshals and others of that sort (as for instance Baderon of Monmouth, Geoffrey Talbot, Gilbert de Lacy, Josce de Dinan, and others whom we have yet to meet, such as Robert fitz Harding of Bristol and Arnold du Bois) do have an unfortunate resemblance to jackals slinking round the feet of greater beasts.

---

40 For Eustace's career in Stephen's reign, see the analysis by P. Dalton, 'Eustace fitz John and the politics of Anglo-Norman England: the rise and survival of a twelfth-century royal servant', *Speculum*, 71 (1996), 359–79. For his charter of enfeoffment with the constableship of Chester, see *Charters of the Anglo-Norman Earls of Chester, c.1071–1237*, ed. G. Barraclough (Record Society of Lancashire and Cheshire, cxxvi, 1988), 85–7 (a charter of the earl concerning Haltonshire implies that the constable's honor had been in the earl's hands for some time before he conveyed it to Eustace, ibid., 79–80).

APPENDIX – THE 'AFFINITY' IN THE TWELFTH CENTURY

Nobody will perhaps thank me for introducing a new construct into the debate about society in the twelfth century, or rather, applying a later medievalist's construct to earlier medieval society. There will be those who point out that the Latin word *affinitas* meant in the twelfth century something other than I want its English derivative to mean. In general, the word is used of degrees of relationship within families, and can be translated as 'kinship' or 'cousinship' (see for instance, William of Poitiers, *Histoire de Guillaume le Conquérant*, ed. and trans. R. Foreville (Classiques de l'Histoire de France au Moyen Âge, Paris, 1952), 142, where two Spanish kings look for a marriage alliance with the Conqueror to enhance their kingdom '*hac . . . affinitate*'). There will be others who point out that the twelfth-century 'affinity' cannot resemble that of two centuries later, as society then was more formally structured and there were far more opportunities in patronage in office-holding, through local government and magnate households. They may well also point out that twelfth-century society had one major feature which had all but disappeared by the fourteenth century: the honor. Even in Henry II's reign, the honor, its lord and its court were still an important feature in law and local politics.

However, the honor and the affinity should be seen as overlapping, not opposing concepts. Studies of honors have revealed that there were substantial tenants who took no apparent part in their lords' courts or affairs. There were others who held land of several lords and followed one rather than another. Recent studies have found that the following of a lord had also an 'extra-feudal' dimension: that is, there were men who were linked to a magnate through common interest, not formal ties of homage in return for land held. It happened then that the active following of a magnate would contain followers tied exclusively to him by substantial tenures, and others who also had links to other magnates but who opted to follow him. Marriage alliance with daughters was a further form of link between greater magnates and lesser, and although this often involved the transfer of land to the bride's family (as opposed to cash) the new son-in-law or brother-in-law could hardly be talked of as a member of the magnate's honorial baronage. But there would also be followers who were tied to them by simple pragmatic local alliances, and by no links of landholding, and others again who chose to follow them as household officers with no apparent landholding link. That is why the term 'affinity' is needed. The 'honor' does not accurately describe what was the basis of the power of a magnate; it was often more than simply 'feudal'.

As for the word 'affinity', we do at least find one unequivocal use of the word in the later medieval sense in the writings of that twelfth-century man Gerald of Wales, who talks of the barons of Pembrokeshire in 1203 as linked to him both by blood *and* by *affinitas* (*De iure et statu Meneuensis ecclesiae*, in *Opera* iii, ed. J.S. Brewer (Rolls Series, 1863), 313). His use of *affinitas* to supplement the concept of blood ties shows an appreciation that the word might be used in a broader political context. There were also current twelfth-century Latin terms which encompass something of what we mean by 'affinity'. Magnates' clerks occasionally talk of the *ditio* (obedience) or the *potestas* (power) of their lord. When they do, they appear to mean more than just those tied to their lords by formal homage and fealty (or they would use established words like *honor*, *feodum* or *baronia*); they mean the area where their lords were powerful, without any qualification deriving from landholding (see on this, E. King, 'The Anarchy of Stephen's reign', *TRHS*, 5th ser., 34 (1984), 133–4).

CHAPTER 10

The Failure of the Empress

As we have now surveyed the problems the war between Stephen and Mathilda in England was beginning to cause, we can perhaps see how her army's victory at Lincoln in February 1141 might have been regarded with relief. The author of the *Gesta* knew many to whom it seemed 'the dawning of a new day' and who expected a quick return to domestic peace in England to follow, while William of Malmesbury describes England as breathing a 'sigh of relief'.[1] Indeed, the battle triggered a rapid collapse of Stephen's support in some areas. Earl Alan of Richmond escaped the battlefield, but was soon after invited to a meeting by Ranulf of Chester, then treacherously arrested and imprisoned. After this, Alan's party in Cornwall collapsed so rapidly that Earl Reginald, the empress's half-brother, was able by March to leave it secure and attend personally on her. In Wiltshire, Hervey de Léon, Stephen's earl there since 1140, was driven from his base at Devizes by a coalition of local people affronted by his attempts to exert an effective lordship over the shire. In Bedfordshire, Earl Hugh, brother of Waleran of Meulan, surrendered Bedford to his local rival, Miles de Beauchamp, and, like Hervey, left the country to avoid the complete wreck of the royalist party.[2]

FROM LINCOLN TO LONDON

The months between February and September 1141 ought, therefore, to have been a time of triumph and reconstruction, but the empress's army and her advisers were cautious in taking advantage of the fact that they had the king in their power, and that little apparently stood in the way of Mathilda's taking up residence at Westminster and organising her coronation as first queen regnant of England. It would seem that they feared that the great victory of Lincoln was not quite as decisive as it appeared. Although Stephen was her prisoner, many of the great royalist magnates had escaped the field, and showed

1 *GS*, 114, see also comments, ibid., 120; HN, 64, '. . . *ad libertatem respirandum*'.
2 For all these dismal developments, *GS*, 116 is the main source. For Alan of Richmond's capture, see further, JH, 308.

surprisingly little immediate inclination to submit after the battle. There was also the other Mathilda, Stephen's queen, already now a woman with a formidable reputation as negotiator and leader in the field. Because she was still active in the southeast, the royalist party did not collapse, and the Angevin party had to move slowly and carefully to build on what Lincoln had won for it.

The first move of the Angevin party after Lincoln was to concentrate on Gloucester, where there was a council of leaders with the empress a week after the victory. On 17 February, a fortnight after Lincoln, the empress, her court and her military household began to move slowly southeastwards to Cirencester, a former royalist town which submitted to her promptly. But the empress's eyes were set on a much bigger acquisition: the city of Winchester, still the home of the royal treasury and jewel-house. Envoys were soon passing between her court at Cirencester, and that of the legate, the bishop of Winchester, who was cautiously accommodating to his brother's captors. The empress herself refers to a face-to-face interview which the two had on 23 February at the nunnery of Wherwell, where the road from Marlborough crossed the Test on its way to Winchester. It would seem that she pressed on to take up residence there some eight miles from Winchester until an agreement about her reception in the city was concluded.[3] Outside the city on the downs between Wherwell and Winchester, on a very wet and grey Sunday, 2 March 1141, the empress and her chief supporters again met Bishop Henry of Winchester, and this time received his allegiance. The bishop received in return some enhanced privileges over ecclesiastical appointments and a promise of admission to her council.

The speed of Bishop Henry's submission to his imprisoned brother's rival astonished and clearly shocked many, but it may well be that (as a brother) he felt he could be more use to Stephen at the empress's court, than beseiged by her in a castle; keeping open avenues of communication was always the trademark of his politics. But there must also have been a degree of resentment against the king for the way he had been edged out of the centre of policy-making over the past five years. William of Malmesbury reports a statement which the bishop made in council a month later, in which he gave as his principal motives for defection his brother's failure to maintain domestic peace and his abuses of Church property and appointments. There is some reason to believe this, for we know how Stephen had turned his back on his brother's policies of negotiation for one of confrontation in 1137, and contemporaries believed that this had rankled in his brother Henry's mind.[4]

3 *Regesta* iii, no. 343, '. . . *die dominica intrantis Quadragesime, qua venit contra me et locutus est mecum apud Warewell', que precessit diem Lune qua idem prelatus et cives Wintonienses honorifice in ecclesia et urbe Wintoniensi me receperunt'*. The Sunday referred to cannot be the first Sunday in Lent (16 February) because we know that she was still in Gloucester then, so we must assume that a vaguer meaning of '*that* Sunday at the beginning of Lent' is intended rather than '*the* Sunday at the beginning of Lent', and therefore the second Sunday of Lent is likely to be the one she meant (23 February).
4 JW iii, 294; *HN*, 50–1. OV vi, 546; HH, 738; JH, 309 all remark on the speed of Henry's capitulation, without attempting to explain it, but *HN*, 52–4 gives William of Malmesbury's

On the next day, a Monday, Mathilda made her first significant step towards coronation when she was received in procession by a large number of prelates headed by Bishop Henry, and the city fathers, led by William de Pont de l'Arche, who was a royal chamberlain, castellan of Winchester, and also sheriff of Hampshire. The lesser clergy of the city, the monastic convents and a great crowd of magnates and laity crowded behind them and in significant splendour the empress was escorted into the city of Winchester – till then the great royalist bastion against the Angevin-dominated West Country. She entered the cathedral supported by the legate on her right, and the bishop of St David's (her late mother's chaplain) on the left.[5] Later – doubtless in state in the royal palace – she appears to have publicly declared what her more enthusiastic advisers must have now decided was her *de facto* status, by issuing a charter in favour of Bishop Henry's abbey of Glastonbury in which her clerk described her as 'the Empress Mathilda, daughter of King Henry *and queen of the English*'.[6] There was actually no reason why she should not declare herself queen before her coronation, for some supporters of Stephen (notably the Londoners) had acclaimed him king before he actually ascended the throne, but it seems that if she and her closest advisers did play with the title 'queen' in the euphoria following Lincoln, she soon drew back from the claim, and opted instead after a discussion with the bishops to be described as 'lady of the English', until she received anointing. It may be that Bishop Henry or Archbishop Theobald had asserted some control over her pretensions, in order to establish a presence at the court and secure more respect for the Church's part in the process of queen-making.[7]

---

report of Bishop Henry's statement made at Winchester on 8 April 1141. *GS*, 118 talks of the bishop's indecision at this point, but is more willing to believe that he was trying to be of assistance to his imprisoned brother.

5 For the empress's reception in Winchester, see chiefly *HN*, 50–1; JW iii, 294, but Brian fitz Count indicates that William de Pont de l'Arche formally headed the delegation of citizens in 1141, see H.W.C. Davis, 'Henry of Blois and Brian fitz Count', *EHR*, 25 (1910), 302. See also *Regesta* iii, no. 897, where the empress addresses a writ (dating between 3 March and 8 April 1141) concerning land in Hampshire to Bishop Henry and '*Willelmo camerario de Pont*' *et omnibus baronibus de Hantescira*', which indicates that William was holding the shrievalty, as suggested by J.A. Green, *English Sheriffs to 1154* (HMSO, 1990), 44.

6 *Regesta* iii, no. 343. The charter exists in a cartulary copy, but seems unexceptionable. Although Dr Chibnall suggests that *regina Anglorum* was copied down in error for *domina Anglorum*, it has to be borne in mind that *domina* was an unfamiliar style and therefore a copyist would be unlikely to confuse it, besides which the two words are very unlike in formation and difficult to confuse. Another alleged charter of hers of Feb x May 1141 uses the same style, and was issued at Reading, perhaps en route to Winchester or on the subsequent journey from Winchester to Oxford, ibid., no. 699. But doubts about the genuineness of this last charter are raised by the editors and also in M. Chibnall, 'The charters of the Empress Matilda', in *Law and Government in the Middle Ages: Essays in Honour of Sir James Holt*, ed. G. Garnett and J. Hudson (Cambridge, 1994), 279. There are features about no. 699 that hint that a genuine charter does lie behind the text, particularly the witness list, but its use of the style *regina* cannot be trusted as an original feature.

7 Chibnall, *The Empress Matilda* (Oxford, 1991), 102; Chibnall, 'Charters of the Empress Matilda', 277–80, consider the style '*domina Anglorum*'. The existence of a second seal of hers with the style, '*Matildis imperatrix Rome et regina Anglie*', is known only from antiquaries' sketches, *Matilda*, 103–4, but *GS*, 118 backs up the evidence of *Regesta* iii, no. 343 in depicting the assembly at Winchester

The results of the empress's first move had been most gratifying, and those who were hesitant seem to have been influenced by it. With the legate now in her party, the archbishop of Canterbury was isolated. He did not hurry to Winchester – perhaps he felt that he would be overshadowed at that delicate moment of negotiation by being in the legate's own see and city, a place where he would not have been able to raise his metropolitical cross in his own province.[8] The empress had removed herself westwards to Wilton, the royal nunnery just beyond Salisbury, when the archbishop found her, some few days after her departure from Winchester. But he came only to negotiate, not to offer his allegiance. He wanted leave to meet the king at Bristol. When it was given, he and many other bishops (with some magnates) rode off to meet the king. Stephen himself gave them his permission to offer their allegiance to the empress, who was to celebrate Easter at Oxford.

We might expect that the empress's Easter court of 30 March 1141 would have been as significant as that of Stephen six years before, but it was not particularly well attended. The chance to hold it there may have been taken up at short notice because the castellan and sheriff of Oxford, Robert d'Oilly, one of Stephen's constables, had decided to switch allegiance, 'without compulsion' as the *Gesta* puts it in disgust. To assert herself in another former royalist bastion must have been the empress's chief object.[9] Those of Mathilda's charters which can be firmly attributed to the Easter court at Oxford show that she continued to be accompanied by her core of faithful magnates, the earl of Gloucester, Miles of Gloucester, Robert fitz Roy (another of her half-brothers) the refugee bishop of Ely and Brian fitz Count. William of Malmesbury implies that no summons was issued to call the magnates to her court, but on the contrary, that the court was dismissed for the festival.[10]

---

hailing her as '*domina et regina*' in March 1141, and in saying that 'she gloried in being called' *regina*. William of Malmesbury scrupulously calls Mathilda '*domina*' at this time, but also notes that the legatine council of Winchester accepted her as '*Anglie Normannieque domina*' on 8 April 1141, so we may suggest a period of debate and doubt about her style until the Church council resolved it, *HN*, 52–4. J.O. Prestwich, 'The treason of Geoffrey de Mandeville', *EHR*, 103 (1988) 311, appears to consider it possible that the empress did use a new seal in which she was styled '*regina Anglie*' briefly at Westminster in anticipation of her coronation.
8 The Fourth Lateran Council (1215) c.5, did not permit even the patriarch of Constantinople (second in precedence after the pope) the right to have his cross carried before him in the presence of a legate, and claims this was the ancient practice. It would seem from this that a legate's presence had already been long recognised as overriding lesser jurisdictions and privileges, *Constitutiones concilii quarti Lateranensis una cum commentariis glossatorum*, ed. A García y García (Monumenta Iuris Canonici, Series A: Corpus Glossatorum, 2, 1981), 52. English practice is obscure, but we can at least point to the resentment of the archbishop of York in 1164 about the papal prohibition on having his cross carried before him when he was within the province of Canterbury, see *Councils and Synods with Other Documents relating to the English Church*, ii, *1066–1204*, ed. D. Whitelock, M. Brett and C.N.L. Brooke (Oxford, 1981), 904–5.
9 Robert was sheriff of Oxfordshire in 1130 and was addressed by Stephen in a writ of 1136 concerning royal demesne at Garsington in the shire, which formed part of the sheriff's farm in 1130, *Regesta* iii, no. 642, which makes it likely that he continued to hold office uninterrupted till 1141. JW iii, 294 talks of him as 'one of the magnates' and of his holding the castle of Oxford; GS, 116 calls him '*ciuitatis Oxenefordiae sub rege praeceptor*'. See also J.A. Green, *The Government of England under Henry I* (Cambridge, 1986), 264–5 and eadem, *English Sheriffs to 1154* (HMSO, 1990), 70.
10 *HN*, 51.

Nonetheless, those few charters that were issued at this time do show the empress staking new claims on the kingdom. One addresses her people of Buckinghamshire and Northamptonshire – the first time they would have acknowledged her claims – and was issued in favour of a priory, Luffield, under the protection of the royalist Earl Robert of Leicester. Most significant of all is another addressed to the barons of the exchequer (whose seat was still presumably in the city of Winchester) granting the canons of St Frideswide in Oxford a quittance on a sum owed for the farm of the town. As Dr Chibnall says, the empress was already beginning to put some body in her claim to authority over the kingdom.[11]

Her next step would have to be to secure the acquiescence of London. The Londoners appreciated this too, especially as Bishop Henry had taken care to let them know that they were expected to show their faces at her court. The paranoia in the city after news of the defeat at Lincoln had reached it is colourfully recollected by a canon of St Paul's who wrote of the disorders which accompanied the translation of the body of the city's then patron, St Erconwald, from the crypt of the cathedral into the upper church a fortnight after the battle. A mob rapidly collected when the doors of the crypt were found barred, and suspecting a conspiracy, they caused a riot, through which the holy corpse had to be forced, and rapidly buried under a flagstone to protect it.[12] The nervous city (amongst whose leaders we can discern pro-Angevin

11 *Regesta* iii, nos. 571, 628; Chibnall, 'Charters of the Empress Matilda', 287. The exchequer was in Winchester in Henry I's reign, E.J. Kealey, *Roger of Salisbury, Viceroy of England* (London, 1972), 44; Green, *Government of Henry I*, 43–4, but how long it stayed there in Stephen's reign is unknown, although there is a good argument that Stephen's difficulties after the civil war had begun led him to shift it to Westminster, see K. Yoshitake, 'The exchequer in the reign of Stephen', *EHR*, 103 (1988), 958–9; J.A. Green, 'Financing Stephen's war' *ANS* xiv, ed. M. Chibnall (Woodbridge, 1991), 110–11. The pipe roll of 1156 mentions the 'houses of the exchequer' in the London account, *PR 2–4 Hen II*, 4. The evidence of Richard fitz Nigel, *Dialogus de Scaccario*, ed. C. Johnson, rev. F.E. Carter and D.E. Greenway (Oxford, 1983), 12, is that the sacrist of Westminster in 1170 was already claiming perquisites from his connection with the exchequer session as 'ancient right', see R.L. Poole, *The Exchequer in the Twelfth Century* (Oxford, 1912), 79 (curiously it was in 1170 that the exchequer sat again at Winchester, see J.H. Round, 'A glimpse of the young king's court', in *Feudal England* (London, 1895), 503–8). The evidence of R.628, the empress's eagerness to secure Winchester, and the importance of the chamberlain, William de Pont de l'Arche, in the city are, however, pretty good evidence that the exchequer still remained at Winchester in 1141. One might also note that the presence of curial magnates and officers as landholders in the city in the survey of 1148 had lessened since 1110, see M. Biddle and D.J. Keene, 'Winchester in the eleventh and twelfth centuries', in *Winchester Studies* i, *Winchester in the Early Middle Ages*, ed. F. Barlow, M. Biddle, O. von Fielitzen and D.J. Keene (Oxford, 1976), 490.
12 Cambridge, Corpus Christi College, ms 161 (*vita et miracula sancti Erkenwaldi Londoniensis episcopi*), fo. 43v. I owe this reference to my wife, Mrs Linda Crouch; a translation is to be found in *The Saint of London: the Life and Miracles of St Erkenwald*, ed. and trans. E.G. Whatley (New York, 1989), 153. J.H. Round, *Geoffrey de Mandeville: A Study of the Anarchy* (London, 1892), 81, also makes the point about unrest in the city of London, pointing to the evidence of the death of the elder Aubrey de Vere, Stephen's chamberlain, at the hands of a royalist mob, apparently roaming the streets following the declaration for the empress of the earl of Essex, his son-in-law, on 15 May 1141, for which see Matthew Paris, *Chronica Majora*, ed. H.R. Luard (7 vols, Rolls Series, 1875–85) ii, 174 (dated inaccurately, as Round argued, to 1140).

and royalist factions in conflict[13]) was therefore easily persuaded to send a delegation to attend the council of Winchester of 7–9 April, where the Church offered its formal recognition of the empress as 'lady of England'. The delegation (apparently including the prominent patrician, sometime city sheriff, and associate of Earl Robert of Gloucester, Osbert Huitdeniers) duly appeared on the last day of the council and represented itself as speaking for the 'commonalty' or 'commune' of the city.[14] According to William of Malmesbury (who was in a good position to know) the Londoners did not come meekly, the royalists amongst them were keen to act as ambassadors for those magnates who still held aloof from the empress, and they made so bold as to ask for the king's release from prison. They also brought with them a clerk of Queen Mathilda, called Christian, who took the opportunity to hand over a statement drawn up by the royalist leaders and the queen, also calling for the king's release, on the grounds that no lord could be held prisoner by those who were his sworn men. They seem to have been trying to turn the argument of oath-keeping back on the empress and her supporters. The delegation was dismissed, with little encouragement, and indeed with notice of excommunication against William Martel, the king's steward, and other loyalists. The Londoners departed unhappily for their troubled and divided city, leaving no-one in any doubt of their dissatisfaction, and did not resume negotiations with the empress for two months.[15]

The unwillingness of the greater magnates to submit to the empress is remarkable, even Earl Ranulf of Chester avoided her court until July. The only significant (and unsurprising) addition to her entourage before midsummer was King David of Scotland, who travelled south to meet her for the conversations with the Londoners at St Albans (taking in Durham on the

---

13 The *Annales Plymptonienses*, in *Anglo-Normannische Geschichtsquellen*, ed. Liebermann, 28, says of June 1141 that 'a plot was set afoot in the city of London by the citizens, one faction (the more respectable) worked on the empress's behalf, the other faction opposed her'.

14 Brian fitz Count puts Osbert Huitdeniers at the head of the Londoners in his notice of their temporary adherence to the empress in 1141, H.W.C. Davis, 'Brian fitz Count and Henry of Blois', 302. The empress addressed him *c.*June 1141 as sheriff, or justiciar, of London, and some time before June rewarded him with 20*li* rents in land, *Regesta* iii, nos. 275, 529. For a study of his importance, Round, *Geoffrey de Mandeville*, 374–5. Osbert may have been chosen as intermediary because he held land in Kent from Earl Robert of Gloucester, amongst the Gloucester fees in Kent which had been created before 1135, *Red Book* i, 189. He also held rents amongst his London estates which were in the soke of the earl of Gloucester, *Cartulary of St Mary Clerkenwell*, ed. W.O. Halsall (Camden Society, 3rd ser., lxxi, 1949), 12. After King Stephen's release, Osbert may well have taken refuge in the earl's household, where he appears in 1142 and 1146, see *Earldom of Gloucester Charters*, ed. Patterson, 34, 95, 170. Osbert may therefore be suggested to have been the head of the pro-Angevin faction within the city patriciate, one of those against whom the royalist city faction was directing the London mob. The fact that Thomas Becket served in Osbert's household as a clerk from *c.*1143–45 might explain how it was that Becket could in 1170 address a fulsome eulogy of Earl Robert to his son, Bishop Roger of Worcester, see *Materials for the History of Thomas Becket, Archbishop of Canterbury*, ed. J.C. Robertson (7 vols, Rolls Series, 1875–85) *epistolae*, no. 648. On Osbert and Becket, see F. Barlow, *Thomas Becket* (London, 1986), 26–7. For some observations on the commune of London and its rulers see S. Reynolds, 'The rulers of London in the twelfth century', *History*, 57 (1972), 337–57, esp. 342–3.

15 *HN*, 54–6.

way, where he installed his chancellor as keeper of the vacant bishopric in his niece's name).[16] Welcome though his support must have been, his absence until April 1141 could hardly have endeared the king to his niece. He had scrupulously honoured his treaty with King Stephen and offered the Angevin cause no support until well after the royalist defeat at Lincoln. A charter issued by the empress at the beginning of May in her court held at Reading shows no more magnates in attendance on her than would have been found the previous year: her loyalist half-brothers and their Marcher associates.[17] But the identity of the beneficiary at least shows that a drift to the empress was continuing. He was William Mauduit, an ambitious former chamberlain of the king, whose modest estates were to be found between Northampton and Rockingham, except for the estate of Hanslope, just across the Buckinghamshire border. Mauduit had appeared before the empress offering a hundred marks 'as a relief payment' so that he could continue to enjoy the soke of Barrowden in Rutland, previously granted by Henry I to his father-in-law and predecessor, Michael of Hanslope (or Hamslape).[18] As with the defection of Robert d'Oilly, this was the opportunistic ship-jumping of a minor magnate and *curialis*, one of those lesser men with most to lose from a miscalculation in continuing for too long to support the captive king. The bigger men were still, it seems, standing back without committing themselves to the empress, although whether through loyalty or through calculation is difficult to say.

The breakthrough the empress needed did not occur till mid-June 1141, when a second conference was arranged between herself and the Londoners at St Albans, to which she came after a long stay at her new headquarters of Oxford.[19] This further extension of her lordship is marked by her issuing of a writ dated at St Albans in favour of Miles of Gloucester, addressed to the justices and sheriff of Middlesex and her faithful people of Westminster, and another (undated) addressed to Osbert Huitdeniers and the justices of London ordering Bishop Henry of Winchester to be repossessed of his deanship and properties of St Martin-le-Grand.[20] She then moved down into the Thames valley and took up residence at the royal hall of Westminster. The queen and her party had by now evacuated London and moved south across the river into Kent, rather than withdraw to the less secure county of Essex, which had

16 *HN*, 56. JH, 309 says that King David did not set out for the south until after Ascension (8 May) and William of Malmesbury has him with Mathilda on her entry into Westminster before midsummer (24 June): *GS*, 120 implies that the king was at her court before her move towards London. For Earl Ranulf's tardiness, ibid., 59.
17 A point made by A.L. Poole, *From Domesday Book to Magna Carta* (2nd edn., Oxford, 1955), 142n.
18 *Regesta* iii, no. 581, see discussion in H.W.C. Davis, 'Some documents of the Anarchy', in *Essays in History presented to Reginald Lane Poole*, ed. Davis (Oxford, 1927), 183. For William Mauduit (II) and his family see *The Beauchamp Cartulary*, ed. E. Mason, (P.R. Soc., new ser., xliii, 1980), xxvi–xxix. For a discussion of Mauduit's other acquisitions during the reign of Stephen, notably the royal manor of Great Bowden, Leics., where he appears to have founded the town of Market Harborough, see D. Crouch, 'The origins of Market Harborough', *The Harborough Historian* no. 7 (1988), 4–5.
19 *HN*, 58 refers to Oxford as her '*statiua mansio*' in 1141, for her conference at St Albans, JW iii, 294.
20 *Regesta* iii, nos. 392, 529.

worse communications with her native Boulogne. The royalist party did not fade away, however: with the queen were William of Ypres and his Flemings and several earls and barons. It also seems that a royal garrison at Windsor still blocked off the approach to London from the west, hence the need for the empress to travel to the city across the Chilterns.[21] Waleran of Meulan was still at this time continuing the fight for the king, despite the worsening situation in Normandy. There is evidence (see below) that he had stationed himself in force at his city of Worcester, and his hostile presence in the royalist-dominated central midlands might well account for the reluctance of the other magnates to commit themselves to the empress, and for the hesitant lingering of the Angevin army at Oxford.

With the empress's arrival at Westminster in mid-June came the first important defections: notably Hugh Bigod, Aubrey de Vere and Earl Geoffrey de Mandeville, all three formerly close adherents of Stephen and all three with large interests in Essex and Suffolk. Of the three, the defection of Earl Geoffrey was the most significant, but also the most understandable. Thanks to the literary efforts of John Horace Round, the name of Geoffrey de Mandeville is now inextricably linked with the struggles between Stephen and Mathilda, and he and his like have long been taken as exemplars of the 'anarchic feudal spirit' which reduced England to chaos in 1141. But when you look past the (admittedly fascinating) evidence of the series of charters which Geoffrey obtained successively from the rivals for the crown, there is very little that was notable so far about his participation in the war between 1139 and 1141. Geoffrey had – since succeeding his disgraced father as a minor some time around 1116 – been working to restore his family's standing. Under Stephen he had achieved much. By 1141, he had recovered the custody of the Tower of London and several large demesne manors in Essex, which his father had forfeited in the previous reign. At some time in the middle of 1140, Stephen had selected him for elevation to the earldom of Essex, a sign that the king saw Geoffrey as the key character in the maintenance of royal control over the county, so close to the capital and so important to the security of the southeast.[22]

Despite his local importance, however, Earl Geoffrey did not occupy a particularly dominant place at Stephen's court, and is far less prominent in the

21 For the queen's party in the summer of 1141, see HH, 738, which mentions the adherence of the *Kentenses* under William of Ypres, and OV vi, 546 mentions Count Waleran, his half-brother, Earl William de Warenne, and Earl Simon of Northampton *aliique plures*, as staying loyal after Lincoln, and implies that Robert of Leicester, too, stayed loyal, ibid., 548. According to *Liber Eliensis*, 323 William d'Aubigné, earl of Arundel, remained loyal, and he is not to be found in Brian fitz Count's list of Mathilda's adherents in 1141. Furthermore, it is a fair assumption that Earl William of York made no attempt to temporise with the Angevins, despite the nearby power of Ranulf of Chester and Henry of Northumbria. The suggestion that Windsor resisted the empress is made by Chibnall, *Matilda*, 102, and would explain why she was confined to the upper Thames valley throughout the first half of 1141. William Martel was apparently active and troublesome to Bishop Henry throughout this period in garrison at Sherborne, as suggested by R.H.C. Davis, *King Stephen* (3rd edn., London, 1990), 54n.
22 *Regesta* iii, no. 273, and see C.W. Hollister, 'The misfortunes of the Mandevilles', *History*, lviii (1973), 18–28.

record before 1141 than Hugh Bigod. But when the royalist cause began to collapse after the battle of Lincoln (at which Geoffrey did not fight) his power in a region which the empress needed to penetrate to secure London brought him to the political foreground. Geoffrey's control of the Tower gave him great influence in the city. If he stayed loyal to the queen, the royalist party in the city would remain dominant, and so the London delegation might well go to Winchester in March and defy the empress to her face. But when Geoffrey wavered, the Angevin support in the city (as represented by Osbert Huitdeniers and his associates) could swing London over to the empress. This seems to be what happened in mid-May 1141 when Earl Geoffrey garrisoned the Tower; Queen Mathilda retired across the Thames out of the city, and Geoffrey's father-in-law, the aged Aubrey de Vere, was caught and killed by a (probably royalist) mob in a city street. It was doubtless Geoffrey's change of side that brought the Londoners to St Albans to submit to the empress in June, and which brought his brother-in-law and ally, the younger Aubrey de Vere, count of Guines by marriage, over to the empress with him. It would also seem to have swung Earl Gilbert of Pembroke over to the Angevin side, Earl Gilbert being a first cousin of Earl Geoffrey: the three turncoat earls are found operating together at the empress's court when it retired to Oxford in June.[23]

Geoffrey's decision was a pragmatic one and – since several others of Stephen's loyalists had already gone over to the empress by June 1141 – hardly to be condemned, especially as Earl Gilbert of Pembroke, who crossed over at much the same time, had as many favours to be grateful for from the imprisoned king. The same might very well be said of Hugh Bigod, who had much to thank Stephen for, since the time when he had been one of the first to rally to the new king in December 1135. All that could really be laid as charge against Earl Geoffrey de Mandeville in his conduct in June 1141 was that he had held the young Constance of France, wife of Eustace, the king's son, in the Tower against her will, and not allowed her to join her mother-in-law, Queen Mathilda, when she retired into Kent.[24] This was a charge that would – in due course – be held over him by Stephen (who refused to make war on women), but in the context of June 1141 the act was hardly one to be harshly condemned.

Earl Geoffrey's reward from the empress was considerable, and was delivered to him at Westminster when her court reached there. His paternal estate was confirmed to him complete, along with the earldom of Essex and there were substantial additions to what he had obtained from Stephen: the *hereditary* keeping of the Tower and the river-fort of Ravenger between the Tower and London bridge was the least of it. He acquired the market towns of Newport and Maldon, which would find him 100*li* in rents, taken from part of a much larger sum which King Stephen had made over to his brother,

23 *Regesta* iii, no. 634.
24 WN i, 44, 45. William of Newburgh was writing over sixty years after the event, but there must be some earlier source behind his story; his treatment of Stephen's reign elsewhere offers much information independent of the main chronicles.

Count Theobald, when they had come to an accord in 1137. He was also to have the knight service of an honor of twenty fees, the core of which was the fee of the late Hasculf de Tany. The most considerable acquisitions were jurisdictional, for Geoffrey was given hereditary possession of the shrievalty; a justiciarship of Essex (with jurisdiction over all crown pleas); a complete quittance on any debts owed to the exchequer by him from before the day he did homage to the empress, and an immunity from forest law in that heavily forested county. The end result was that Geoffrey was to hold Essex much as William of Aumale already held Yorkshire, exercising all the royal prerogatives in return only for the accustomed farms of the county.[25]

So in June 1141, the empress could be confident that London's principal fortress was held in her interest.[26] The chief magnates of Essex and Suffolk had recognised the inevitable and submitted to her. A pro-Angevin faction of the city fathers, led by Osbert Huitdeniers, appeared to have obtained the ascendancy over the volatile population of the crowded city (which may by this date have been between 100,000 and 200,000 people).[27] She entered Westminster with an impressive entourage; her West Country and Marcher loyalists were with her for the expected climax of her struggle for the throne, and two of them, William de Mohun and Baldwin de Redvers, were now ornamented with the style of earl. She also brought in her entourage a new bishop for London, Robert de Sigillo, once a senior royal clerk, who had retired into her father's abbey of Reading. In successfully nominating a bishop for the see, she exerted yet another prerogative of royalty and since he was a Cluniac of good reputation, avoided offending Henry of Winchester.[28]

But having done so well on her first day at Westminster, she appears then to have become reckless under the intoxication of growing good fortune. Chroniclers indeed tell us that her behaviour following the battle of Lincoln had become less and less gracious. They may have been biased in their reports through an inability to accept that any woman had the intellect and disposition to fulfil the role normally filled by males in their society. But if that were so, then it is surprising that such a bias is not evident in their treatment of Stephen's queen, Mathilda, who had been acting as an increasingly independent political force since 1138, and had been exercising leadership of Stephen's party since February. The author of the *Gesta*, who had no reason to love the

25 *Regesta* iii, no. 274. This important charter survives now only in fragments and in antiquaries' transcripts, for a consideration of its authenticity or that of its lost exemplar, J.O. Prestwich, 'The treason of Geoffrey de Mandeville', *EHR*, 103 (1988), 311–12.
26 London's other considerable fortress, Montfichet's Tower just southwest of St Paul's cathedral in the later Blackfriars precinct, was also in friendly baronial hands, for its castellan, William de Montfichet, had died soon after 1138 and his heir, Gilbert, was in wardship to his uncle, Earl Gilbert of Pembroke, another new adherent of the empress.
27 For some interesting questions about London's medieval population density (which on the basis of land values seems to have reached similar peaks in 1300 and 1600 (about 200,000), see D.J. Keene, *Cheapside before the Great Fire* (Economic and Social Research Council, 1985), 19–20.
28 For an indication of the empress's court at Westminster in June 1141, see *Regesta* iii, nos. 274, 911; JW iii, 296 talks of 'many bishops and magnates' travelling with her to London. For the nomination and election of Robert as bishop of London, JW iii, 296.

empress, talks of her insults to those who had joined her cause after Lincoln, her refusal to take advice even from her uncle, her half-brother and the legate, and her insensitive annulments of Stephen's grants in favour of her own people. William of Malmesbury, who had every reason to support her, mentions none of this, but does acknowledge that she antagonised the legate to the point where he left her court.[29] Although it is true that Bishop Henry was apt to take offence (as his brother found out to his cost) she should have been particularly on her guard to avoid alienating the legate in the sensitive circumstances of 1141. John of Hexham, whose allegiance to either party is less clear, but who was sympathetic to David of Scotland, tellingly repeats the stories of the empress's poor judgement, her insults to her followers, and comments in particular on her inability to take her uncle's advice and her declared intentions to act barbarously towards the captive King Stephen.[30]

If we balance these hostile comments against the evidence of the pragmatically cautious progress of the empress towards Westminster (as revealed by the charters), we can glimpse a divided court in the period from February to June 1141. The tension arose from the fact that the empress was increasingly keen to demonstrate her independence in council in opposition to her more cautious advisers, who were less convinced than she was of the inevitability of her coronation. The friction led to more and more dissent and stress around her, for her advisers were restrained by custom from answering her in the vigorous way she was employing to them, and it became harder and harder to restrain her. The explosion came in the days after her arrival at Westminster, when the empress would no longer be contained. The chroniclers give a pretty coherent account of how it happened. In the expectation of magnanimity at such a time, the empress was petitioned by several suppliants. She was asked again by the queen's envoys for the release of her husband; the legate asked for his nephew, Eustace, to receive his father's lands if he could not follow him as king; and the Londoners petitioned hopefully for confirmations of some privileges. The empress would have none of these, and in response made intolerable financial demands on the city's representatives. By doing this she crushed the fragile acquiescence of the Londoners to her impending reception and coronation, and so played into the hands of the royalist faction in the city. Messengers apparently informed Queen Mathilda in Kent of the breakdown of negotiations, and her army was moved up to the Thames across from the city. The royalist leaders eagerly embraced an alliance with her and repudiated the empress. The mob was mobilised again by the ringing of bells across the city, and on 24 June 1141 it poured in arms through the city gate, along the Strand and towards the royal palace of Westminster, causing the

---

29 *GS*, 120; *HN*, 57.
30 JH, 309–10. John's story of her threats to humiliate the captive king are borne out by Henry of Huntingdon's story that after her expulsion from Westminster by the queen and the Londoners, she had him placed in shackles ('*in compedibus*') HH, 740. Chibnall, *Matilda*, 97, 104–5, 204–5, gives a well-balanced and considered verdict on criticism of the empress, in the context of the difficulties that her time placed on a woman with independent political ambitions.

empress and her court (including Geoffrey de Mandeville) to take to their horses, leaving their dinner and baggage behind them as they fled for the safety of Oxford: the Angevin sympathisers in the city had just had time to warn her of the sudden reversal of the city's mood.[31]

THE RELEASE OF KING STEPHEN

It is unlikely that the empress's party would have seen its humiliation at the hands of the Londoners as in any way an irreversible defeat. That it saw it as a humiliation is certain, however, because the empress and her advisers exerted themselves to assemble a court and army at Oxford in July sufficient in size and prestige to erase the incident from memory. She was determined now to impress with her generosity. In gratitude for his assistance in extricating her from London, the empress raised Miles of Gloucester to the earldom of Hereford on 25 July.[32] The extent of the assembly of ecclesiastical and lay magnates at Oxford is known from a series of the empress's charters (some fourteen) and may be compared with the evidence of the list of magnates who did homage to the empress before she fell out with the legate in 1141, as given by Brian fitz Count in his letter to Bishop Henry. She had with her at Oxford the archbishop of Canterbury, the bishops of St David's, Ely, London and Lincoln, the king of Scotland, eight earls (possibly nine, if Warwick were also there) Gloucester, Hereford, Cornwall, Devon, Pembroke, Norfolk, Essex and Guines, and well over a score of magnates of greater or lesser degree. Also present were a number of barons from Anjou and Maine, led by Juhel de Mayenne, who would seem to have arrived at Oxford at that time as reinforcements sent by her husband, Count Geoffrey. But there were a further eight bishops, four earls and thirteen barons known to have adhered to her party who might have been at Oxford, unrecorded by the witness lists to the Oxford charters.[33]

31 The main accounts are in HN, 56–7; GS, 120–6; JW iii, 296. On the date of the Londoners' move against her, Chibnall, *Matilda*, 105n. JW iii, 298 says that the empress passed through Oxford in June to Gloucester, where she stayed as guest of Miles of Gloucester, but thence returned to Oxford in July. J.H. Round, *Geoffrey de Mandeville*, 116–18, suggests on the basis of late evidence that Earl Geoffrey escaped the ensuing siege of the Tower by the Londoners by taking hostage the new pro-Angevin bishop of London, and having deceived the mob as to his allegiance, rode to Oxford with him.
32 The exorcism of a defeat or humiliation by the calling of a great court to reassert lordship was practised by other contemporary lords, Waleran of Meulan, for instance, attempted to counterbalance his reverses at the hands of Henry II by a great court in 1155, see D. Crouch, *The Beaumont Twins: The Roots and Branches of Power in the Twelfth Century* (Cambridge, 1986), 74–7, and see below. For the promotion of Miles, JW iii, 298.
33 Her charters edited in *Regesta* iii, nos. 68, 275, 328, 377, 393, 629–31, 634, 646–8, 791, 899 (which can be assigned to July × September 1141 with reasonable confidence) give most of these names, and they must be balanced against the list of those who adhered to her during the course of the summer of 1141 given in H.W.C. Davis, 'Henry of Blois and Brian fitz Count', *EHR*, 25 (1910), 302. This adds to the list the bishops of Hereford, Worcester, Bath, Exeter, Chichester, Chester, Carlisle and Norwich, the earls of Chester, Lincoln, Somerset and Warwick, and a further thirteen barons. Some at least of these must have been at Oxford or Winchester with the empress. The earl of Warwick's presence at Oxford is possible, because it is known that his

The assembly was impressive, it demonstrated that the empress still commanded the loyalty of Essex, Bedfordshire and Suffolk, as well as her heartland in the southern Marches, and indeed further new adherents were still arriving. The empress welcomed to Oxford with the promise of great gifts William de Beauchamp of Elmley, Waleran of Meulan's sheriff of Worcestershire, who – seeing no hope in the continued fight and realising that his neighbour (and Waleran's cousin), the earl of Warwick, had already defected to the empress – had abandoned his lord, the count, and arrived in Oxford with a number of Worcestershire knights as refugees. Although he arrived a refugee, his arrival was still a great propaganda coup against Robert of Gloucester's arch-rival, the count of Meulan, who was holding out against the empress in Worcestershire at this time, as is evident from the charter's references to the losses Beauchamp had incurred by his defection, and to the fact that his relatives were still fighting for the count's party![34]

One great man who was not with her at Oxford was the legate, the bishop of Winchester. Contemporary chroniclers tell us that Bishop Henry had rapidly distanced himself from the empress after the debacle of Westminster, as indeed they tell us that he had already fallen out with her before June 1141. The sources differ as to how the break occurred, but several ideas were current. The monk of Gloucester who continued the Worcester chronicle (a man who tells us that his source for the climactic events of 1141 was no less than Miles, earl of Hereford) believed that the bishop had been insulted by the empress's disdain for his plea that his nephew, Eustace, be allowed to succeed to his father's 'county' (presumably that of Mortain, since he would have had Boulogne from his mother), and that when the Londoners had made their dramatic intervention in June, he slipped away to Winchester to 'mind his counsel and his reputation'. William of Malmesbury, who also had many friends in high places, tells much the same story, and believed that the legate had requested both Boulogne and Mortain for his nephew. He also thought

---

son-in-law and chief tenant, Geoffrey de Clinton (II) of Kenilworth, was there with the empress, see *Regesta* iii, no. 629. If we accept that the empress's writ addressed to him in favour of Thurstin de Montfort was issued on 3 March 1141 at Winchester, then Earl Roger had defected to the empress immediately after Lincoln, ibid. no. 597. It should be noted that Earl Roger's younger brother crossed to Normandy before the summer to enter Count Geoffrey's household, see below, p. 192.
34 *Regesta* iii, no. 68. See my comments on this charter in *Beaumont Twins*, 50–1. I differ from the interpretation of Chibnall, *Matilda*, 107, who follows the idea of Davis, *Stephen*, 155–6, that William de Beauchamp's bitter resentment of his 'forced' subordination to Waleran in 1138 motivated his change of side in 1141 and that he hoped to replace the count at Worcester. Were that the case, it is difficult to see how he could have reconciled himself (as he did) to Waleran's continued possession of the earldom of Worcester until 1153. Dr Chibnall sees evidence of William's bitterness in the provision of the charter which safeguarded William's position in Worcestershire: that the empress would not allow Waleran to make fine with her. Another interpretation would be that this was simply politic. The negative interpretation of *Regesta* iii, no. 68 depends on a twentieth-century assumption that a minor baron such as William de Beauchamp would necessarily have resented his 'subordination' to one of Europe's grandest aristocrats, with all the new opportunities and status it brought (including a marriage which brought his family into close cousinship with the kings of France and the counts of Vermandois). See further on this below, p. 193.

that the empress intended to award these counties to others (which in the case of Boulogne would have been deeply improper, since it belonged by rights to Queen Mathilda). The legate was supposed by his account to have left London for Guildford and there secretly met the queen, his sister-in-law, and promised to undertake the freeing of King Stephen. Even if he had not changed sides at this point, he had lifted the excommunications against the royalist magnates, and is said to have talked openly of his suspicions of the empress, and condemned her for her misjudgements and failure to keep her promises to him. The author of the *Gesta* did not think there was much more to the rift than the empress's failure to treat Bishop Henry with the respect he required and was owed, but he did believe that he was already colluding with the queen before the debacle at Westminster, and suspected him, too, of collusion with the Londoners. The *Gesta* also reports a meeting (in London, after the empress's flight) between the queen and the legate, at which Bishop Henry offered her his support in getting Stephen released.[35]

The empress's court at Oxford was therefore literally the critical point for her ambitions to rule England as queen. She and her advisers must secure what progress they had made and recover the ground that they had lost. One way in which this was attempted was by offering (or promising) extraordinarily generous terms to the new adherents from the southeast of England or the midlands. William de Beauchamp (as we have seen) although only a minor baron, did represent a weakening of the hard core of royalist support in the central midlands, so he was promised a hereditary position as powerful in Worcestershire as any sheriff had ever enjoyed in England, with no subordination to any magnate with a comital style, indeed, he would have been as powerful as any earl. A new, enhanced charter was offered to Earl Geoffrey de Mandeville, with extensions of his singular privileges out of Essex and into neighbouring Middlesex and London and Hertfordshire, where he was given the shrievalties and also the title of 'justiciar'. He was also given the Norman and English honors of his maternal grandfather, Eudo Dapifer, which had been kept in royal hands for the past twenty years. He was left free to build castles wherever he wished, and given the empress's aid in extorting the castle of Bishop's Stortford from the bishop and chapter of London. His eldest son, Arnulf, a bastard, was given enough lands to raise him to baronial status and his hereditary right to them (always a matter of uncertainty with bastards) put beyond question. The charter also swore that the empress and her husband would never make an agreement with the Londoners without Earl Geoffrey's consent, 'for they are his mortal enemies'. Those who were his friends were, by contrast, to have the empress's favour, and a list of them and their claims was added, including twenty pounds per annum to be offered to Osbert Huitdeniers, now it seems a refugee from the city which had excluded both him and Earl Geoffrey. Numerous guarantors were named so as to reassure Earl Geoffrey: his fellow earls, other barons and the remoter assurances of the

35 JW iii, 296; *HN*, 57–8; *GS*, 120, 120–4.

count of Anjou, his son and heir, and even the king of France, if he could be persuaded to concern himself in the case. The empress's urgency in this matter demonstrated how weak was her hand in negotiating with Earl Geoffrey, and, indeed, he had reverted to his allegiance to Stephen within a month (see below).[36]

The offer of concessions such as these had other consequences. Earl Geoffrey de Mandeville had been raised to the status of a 'super-earl' with privileges wider than those which the earls of Gloucester and Hereford formally enjoyed under the empress, and greater than those asked for by Ranulf of Chester and William of York. England had seen nothing like this since the ducal grandeur of Aethelred's ealdormen, no wonder that the *Gesta* says of Geoffrey after this that 'everywhere . . . he took the king's place and was listened to more eagerly than the king'.[37] Incentives such as those offered to Geoffrey de Mandeville meant that other local earls had to be compensated and protected, so these in turn bred further concessions. Count Aubrey de Vere of Guines, Earl Geoffrey's brother-in-law, who was a lesser magnate of Essex and Suffolk, was awarded an English earldom, although since Essex already had an earl – and Suffolk might have been considered to look to Hugh Bigod as earl – Aubrey was given the choice of five possible titles (Cambridge, Oxford, Wiltshire, Berkshire and Dorset). Despite the fact that he did not own so much as an acre of land there, he ultimately chose Oxford (presumably because in July 1141 it was firmly in Angevin hands and he could be sure that his comital prerogative of the third penny of the profits of justice would be paid over). He had all his paternal inheritance confirmed to him, and (like Earl Geoffrey) a blanket exemption from forest pleas on all his lands. As with the Essex grants, Aubrey secured considerable new assets: the castle of Colchester, the honor of William

---

36 *Regesta* iii, no. 275. The dating of this charter has been the subject of long debate. I adopt here the position on it of R.H.C. Davis, 'Geoffrey de Mandeville reconsidered', *EHR*, 79 (1964), 299–307, as revised in *From Alfred the Great to Stephen*, ed. Davis (London, 1991), 203–19 (and developed by idem, 'Comment', *EHR*, 103 (1988), 313–17; 'A final comment', ibid., 967–8; 'Last words on Geoffrey de Mandeville', *EHR*, 105, 671–2; *Stephen*, 157–60), who disputed Round's idea that R.275 was the empress's (later) bribe to win back Geoffrey from Stephen's side in 1142, and saw it as the second part of the empress's transactions with Geoffrey in the summer of 1141. Davis pointed out that if R.275 was granted at Oxford in spring 1142 (as Round suggested), with its apparatus of pledges and in a public assembly, it could not have been kept secret till 1143. We would also have to believe that Geoffrey was planning to defect to her at a time when her cause was at one of its lowest points. The compatibility of the persons named in R.275 with the empress's other charters of July × August 1141 is remarkably close. Davis's reasoning of 1964 was challenged by J.O. Prestwich, 'The treason of Geoffrey de Mandeville', 288–312, in 1988 on the basis that the numerous guarantors inserted in R.275, whose names indicated a 1141 date to Davis, need not actually have been present, and that the prominence in it given to Geoffrey of Anjou's rights in England reflected the circumstances of 1142, when Robert of Gloucester was sent abroad to negotiate his involvement in the English wars. While it may be admitted that there is nothing absolutely decisive for July 1141 in Davis's reasoning as he presented it, there is equally nothing that proves Mr Prestwich's case beyond doubt. For myself, I find the appearance of Earl Gilbert of Pembroke as a guarantor for Geoffrey in R.275 incomprehensible in the circumstances of 1142, and that evidence, along with the balance of likelihood and arguments in Davis's favour, decides me in favour of a date of July 1141, see also the comments in Chibnall, *Matilda*, 108–11.
37 *GS*, 160.

d'Avranches[38], and the subordination to him of the fee of the lesser Essex baron, William de Helion. His relatives were to share in his good fortune: his younger brother, Geoffrey de Vere, was to have the fee of the late Geoffrey Talbot (who had died in 1140); another brother, Robert, was to have an honor of equal value, and a third, the clerk William de Vere (later to be bishop of Hereford), was promised the chancellorship when William Giffard (the brother of John fitz Gilbert) should surrender it (but he never got it).[39] Like the empress's second charter to Geoffrey de Mandeville, this charter had an elaborate apparatus of pledges and guarantors, and the count of Anjou and the king of France were likewise to be asked to endorse it.[40]

The empress had done her best to erase the humiliation of Westminster by a display of power and by grants of startling generosity; and we would be even more startled, perhaps, could we but know what she had offered to her other new adherents, Hugh Bigod, earl of Norfolk, and Gilbert fitz Gilbert, earl of Pembroke. Her next move must be to assert herself by a military demonstration, and her victim had to be Bishop Henry, who had abandoned her at Westminster and returned to Winchester. She needed to curb and control the legate, and regain the city he had delivered to her in March, and had now taken away again. It seems that she moved southwest from Oxford to Devizes to gather support for her next great enterprise, and here she must have been delighted by what was the greatest stroke against the royalists since the king was captured: Count Waleran of Meulan, long Stephen's mainstay, sought her out and offered his submission. Although he was still resisting the empress in July when she was at Oxford, news of the danger to his estates by Angevin advances in Normandy had reached him, and he knew that he could not stay any longer in England. We only know of this meeting through charter evidence, but even that bland medium does not disguise that the empress was not gracious to the count. She issued two surviving charters as a consequence of their interview, both were directed to the abbey of Bordesley which Count Waleran had founded in 1139 on royal demesne land in Worcestershire. The charters declare that the empress was in fact the abbey's founder, and the unspoken assumption behind them is that Waleran's earldom of Worcester was to be suppressed and his grants there annulled or transferred (as in the case of Bordesley abbey) to royal patronage.[41]

---

38 That is, a part of the barony of Folkestone, which he claimed by right of his wife's grandmother, Emma, whose niece had married William d'Avranches and taken part of the barony away with her, see *Complete Peerage* x, 200n
39 For Aubrey's brothers, see charters in P. Morant, *A History of Essex* (2 vols in 3, London, 1768) ii, 506n; *Cartularium prioratus de Colne*, ed. J.L. Fisher (Colchester, 1946), 25; *Chronicon monasterii de Abingdon* ii, 59. For a biography of William, see J. Barrow, 'A twelfth-century bishop and literary patron: William de Vere', *Viator*, xviii (1987), 175–89.
40 *Regesta* iii, 634.
41 For Waleran's appearance with the empress at Devizes, see *Regesta* iii, nos. 115–16. The dating of both charters is similar as they feature Miles as earl of Hereford (which he became on 25 July 1141) and note that Robert earl of Gloucester was present (which means that they must have been issued before his move to Winchester, at the latest 12 August 1141). The charters could not have been issued after Earl Robert's release, because Count Waleran was back in Normandy by

Heartened, she then turned to the problem of the bishop of Winchester. William of Malmesbury talks of her sending her half-brother, the earl of Gloucester, with a small force to find out how things stood in the city, but he returned when he found the situation past negotiation. The bishop was shut up in his formidable castle-palace of Wolvesey, set in the southeastern corner of the city screened from the rest of the city behind the precincts of the cathedral and the abbey of St Mary. He had recently extended and fortified Wolvesey using materials he had quarried from the old royal palace.[42] The empress responded by moving with her court and usual escort of loyalist magnates south to Winchester. She arrived in the city around 12 August 1141, the earl of Gloucester having preceded her by some days – according to the Gloucester continuator – to seize and prepare the royal castle on the opposite side of the city. The empress took up residence in the castle, not (apparently) immediately deploying her army for the siege of Wolvesey. William of Malmesbury says that she summoned the bishop to meet her at the castle 'perhaps meaning him no harm', and that is by no means unlikely for she did not come with a large army. It would have been far better for her had Bishop Henry humbly submitted once again; rather that than besiege a papal legate in his own palace! But the bishop did not comply, and stalled while he sent envoys out to ask for aid. He and his men were blockaded in his palace by troops stationed in the neighbouring cathedral and abbey.[43]

Within a few weeks, the queen, Bishop Henry's sister-in-law, responded and she and a formidable army moved to blockade those who were blockading the legate, and a curious double siege developed in mid-September. Once more the empress was in a most difficult situation, and it is hard to say whether it was because she moved too hastily and unprepared from Oxford to Winchester, or whether it was because she genuinely thought she could talk the legate round, or it may even be that she reckoned that her court at Oxford had demonstrated that most of the kingdom was on her side, so there was no danger. But all her calculations were wrong: the bishop resisted; the earls of Essex and Pembroke abandoned the empress and moved directly from

November 1141, and he did not return to England thereafter, see on this Crouch, *Beaumont Twins*, 50–1, see also comments in E. King, 'Waleran, count of Meulan earl of Worcester, 1104–1166', in *Tradition and Change: Essays in Honour of M. Chibnall*, ed. D. Greenway *et al.* (Cambridge, 1985), 170n; Chibnall, *Matilda*, 112–13.

42 *HN*, 58. For Bishop Henry's activities at Wolvesey in 1138, Gerald of Wales, *Vita sancti Remigii*, in *Opera* vii, ed. J.S. Brewer and others (Rolls Series, 181) 295; *Annales de Wintonia*, 51. For the site and history of the palace, M. Biddle and D.J. Keene, 'Winchester in the eleventh and twelfth centuries', in *Winchester Studies* iii, *Winchester in the Eleventh and Twelfth Centuries*, ed. M. Biddle and D.J. Keene (Oxford, 1976), 323–8.

43 *HN*, 58–9. *GS*, 126 says that she came with 'a well-equipped force' and 'a very large retinue' and gathered an even greater force for the siege of Wolvesey, but the list the author gives is no more than those West Country and Marcher magnates who were the core of her support, with the addition of Ranulf of Chester whose arrival, according to *HN*, 59, was 'late and ineffective', and who seems from the account of JH, 310 to have gone over to the royalists, along with many others, the hapless Roger of Warwick perhaps being another. Chibnall, *Matilda*, 113, plausibly reconciles the discrepancy in accounts of the size of the empress's army by suggesting mass defections as the siege became more desperate.

Oxford to rejoin Queen Mathilda (and with them would have gone the other magnates of Essex and Suffolk).[44] The empress's household at Winchester was heavily outnumbered by the queen's relieving force which could not be prevented from throwing a cordon round the city and blockading it off from any supplies, while it provisioned and reinforced Wolvesey (the earl of Northampton is known to have led a force into it in support of the bishop). A most grave situation developed as the empress's blockade of the royalists in August turned into a royalist blockade of the empress in September.

The decisive point was reached in the second week of September, when a hostile column under William of Ypres moved round the north of Winchester and having burned Andover, moved south to the river Test at Wherwell, with the obvious intention of encircling Winchester and cutting the empress off from Oxford, Gloucester and Bristol. Although the citizens of Winchester rallied to her and their leader, William de Pont de l'Arche, remained firm, the powerful and well-armed militia of the city of London was moving on their city, and the bishop's garrison at Wolvesey was anything but quiet, indeed, they forced back the empress's men who were stationed in St Mary's abbey, and set the place alight. John of Hexham reports Ranulf of Chester 'fearing treachery' as one of those who defected to the queen as the situation worsened for the besieged.[45]

Earl Robert of Gloucester, commanding the siege of Wolvesey from the cathedral next to the abbey, had little choice but to gather up his sister and abandon Winchester on Sunday 14 September. He honourably stationed himself in the rearguard, to resist the forceful onset of the royalist army which suddenly descended on them as they emerged from the city gate. The empress's escort was able to keep together for an eight-mile pursuit to the Test at Stockbridge, but there it became clear that there was to be no escape: Earl Miles of Hereford and King David of Scotland and their households were driven apart from the earl of Gloucester and had to ride for their lives. There was just time to hustle the empress off across the river with a small escort commanded by Brian fitz Count and (or) Earl Reginald of Cornwall to race to Devizes and safety, while the earl of Gloucester vainly attempted to hold up the pursuit. Another small force under Robert of Okehampton, Geoffrey Boterel, the brother of Earl Alan of Richmond, and John Marshal, had already been despatched to secure supplies, but had been trapped by William of Ypres' knights at Wherwell abbey, which they hastily fortified. There they were besieged in the church, and forced out by fire, all except for John, who held on despite the flames until his pursuers gave him up for dead. He emerged free but badly wounded, one eye blinded by molten lead which had dripped on him from the roof, but it seems that his desperate action had prevented

---

44 *Liber Eliensis*, 323, places the earls of Warenne, Arundel, Geoffrey de Mandeville, Earl Gilbert 'and other powerful helpers' with Queen Mathilda's forces at Winchester. *HN*, 67 confirms that Earl Gilbert fought with the royalists, and indeed captured the pro-Angevin magnate, William of Salisbury.
45 JH, 310.

William of Ypres' pincer movement closing, and so allowed the empress to get away – riding astride like a man for more speed, much to her enemies' amusement. Earl Robert was not so fortunate, he was trapped by his enemies while defending the bridge, and taken prisoner by Earl William of Warenne. Other magnates had fallen into royalist hands, Earl Gilbert of Pembroke had captured William, sheriff and castellan of Salisbury and William of Ypres had seized Humphrey de Bohun.[46]

The French language has a word, *bouleversement*, which alone expresses quite how radical a turnabout the empress's fortunes had received. As she had entered Winchester in August, she had the king in prison and still apparently enjoyed a large body of support, and she had had the recent satisfaction of receiving the submission of the man who had done more than any other to thwart her ambitions in Normandy and England for the past five years, Waleran of Meulan. A month later, she was escorted exhausted back into the castle of Devizes by the barons and knights charged to hustle her away from danger. Her brother and chief adviser was a prisoner and her army was scattered or captive. The king of Scotland, a fugitive, had barely escaped capture by bribing those royalist knights who came near to taking him to let him go, and it was said that David Olifard, his godson and a member of the royalist army, had smuggled him away rather than let him be captured and dishonoured. He did not attempt to rejoin his niece, but made his way back north with those few followers he could gather up from the wreck of the Angevin army. Earl Miles of Hereford eventually toiled into Gloucester castle several days after the battle, having lost his horse and arms, and having walked a good fifty miles on his own. A similarly dejected John Marshal limped into his castle of Ludgershall.[47] There was very little left that the empress could do but negotiate her one surviving asset, the captive king. To many people an exchange of the king and the earl of Gloucester was a fit and satisfactory resolution to the impossible situation of having the anointed king in prison: for what could have been done with him if the empress had been crowned queen?

Contemporaries (even hostile ones) were delighted that the king, imprisoned as an act of God's judgement on his folly, was now to be liberated by an obvious act of God's mercy.[48] The twelfth century had no concept of abdication, which would have seemed theological nonsense and indeed had never (so far

46 The principal accounts of the siege and rout of Winchester are, *HN*, 59–60, 67; *GS*, 126–34; JW iii, 298–302; HH, 740; JH, 310–11. For an excellent modern synthesis see J. Bradbury, *Stephen and Matilda* (Stroud, 1996), 108–12. For a recent account of the rout itself see R. Hill, 'The battle of Stockbridge', in *Studies presented to R. Allen Brown*, ed. C. Harper-Bill and others (Woodbridge, 1989), 173–7. The *Annales de Waverleia*, 229 and JW iii, 298, talk of the empress arriving and Robert of Gloucester beginning the siege on 1 August (but that may refer to his earlier reconnaissance of the city). *HN*, 61 talks of the empress arriving a few days before the Assumption (15 August). JW iii, 300 says the siege occupied seven weeks before 14 September.
47 For the escape of Miles of Hereford, JW iii, 302; for that of John Marshal, *History of William Marshal*, ed. A. Holden and D. Crouch, trans. S. Gregory (3 vols, Anglo-Norman Text Society, forthcoming) i, 212ff. For the fate of King David, *GS*, 134; JH, 311.
48 HH, 740.

as we know) been discussed in 1141. One suggestion (stemming from his wife) was that the king, once released, should leave England and dedicate his life to God either in a monastery or in the Holy Land. Another possible solution, apparently discussed at one point by the earl of Gloucester's household, was to bundle the king off to Ireland and keep him there. This would at least have dealt with the anomaly of what to do with a man indelibly anointed by the Church, who had lost his quasi-sacerdotal royal function, yet remained marked out from amongst his fellows.[49]

The negotiations were not straightforward, and Robert of Gloucester had nearly two months at Rochester castle to demonstrate he was the equal of King Stephen in graciousness and equanimity in captivity. Before he falls silent, the continuator of the Worcester chronicle reports a scheme said to have been discussed between Queen Mathilda and Countess Mabel of Gloucester, that the king be restored to his throne, and that Earl Robert would become a sort of justiciar under him. How Angevin claims were to be accommodated under such a scheme is not revealed, but the idea was no simple rumour, for William of Malmesbury also discussed it and treated it as an attempt to bribe the earl into changing sides. Yet if the royalist negotiators knew their man at all, the scheme was hardly likely to have been quite so crude as that. What it does indicate is that some people at least thought that the wider problems of the realm could be settled during the discussion, rather than both sides returning to arms, just as if Lincoln and Winchester had never happened. The continuator concluded his story (and his historical work) by describing Earl Robert's rejection of the scheme because it would not gain the empress's consent, and so the war began again, as he ruefully concludes and as also does the *Gesta*, which also regrets the lost opportunity, though its author saw no other choice at the time.[50] All that was decided in the end was the terms of the exchange, which were as elaborate as anything the Cold War spawned. It involved the queen herself and one of her sons travelling to Bristol to be kept as hostage for the king, while the king travelled to Winchester on 1 November 1141 to release Earl Robert (who had been moved there). The earl returned in his turn to release the queen, leaving his heir, William, until she returned safe from Bristol. William of Malmesbury records the intriguing fact that the king and the earl had some time at the cross-over point

---

49 For the suggestion that the king become either *monachus* or *peregrinus* were he released, see JW iii, 296. For the Irish option, *HN*, 68. The sacramental nature of the anointing within coronation was accepted at this time, see P. Schramm, *A History of the English Coronation*, trans. L.G. Wickham-Legge (Oxford, 1937), 6–8. The consequences of sacramental anointing were a persistent anxiety to the laity, and the anxiety comes out in later medieval confusion as to the status of those who had received extreme unction and yet survived: the evidence of episcopal capitularies from the early thirteenth century is that popular belief was that – as consecrated to God – they should abstain from sex and eating meat, and not go about barefoot, like the regular religious, see W. Maskell, *Monumenta Ritualia Ecclesiae Anglicanae* (2nd edn., 3 vols, Oxford, 1882) i, pp. cclxxxv–cclxvii.
50 JW iii, 304; *GS*, 136. *HN*, 61, 68, 70, also notes that the earl was adamant that he would make no negotiation unless the empress consented to it.

in Winchester to exchange a few apparently friendly words, in which the earl protested that his opposition to Stephen was nothing personal but a stand on principle.[51]

In retrospect, the end of 1141 marked the end of the empress's chance of military victory. Even with the king in her hands, it is remarkable how hard she found it to break out of her West Country heartland. From February till June very few magnates took the step of entering her camp. It was only when people perceived that she was on the very point of coronation that defections began in earnest, and when that chance evaporated she could hold on to them for little more than a month. She had seen Geoffrey de Mandeville and his East Anglian allies first extort exorbitant terms for their adherence, and then turn their backs upon her and rejoin Queen Mathilda. Earl Ranulf of Chester had first assisted in the king's capture, then disappeared about his own business in the north. He appeared briefly in Oxford in July, followed the empress to Winchester, and then he, too, disappeared as soon as the situation became dangerous. The record of her uncle, King David, was little better. When the year is put in long view the empress could only trust those three men who had first embraced her cause together in 1139: Earl Robert, Earl Miles and Brian fitz Count. The other major magnates preferred to be uncommitted. Whether they did so through feelings of loyalty to King Stephen, discomfort with the idea of the empress (or dissatisfaction with her conduct) or simple neutralism is difficult to say. I would decide for neutralism, because the astonishing incentives needed to stir up magnates to join her show that their own advantage remained uppermost in their minds. What is clear is that no military victory was possible for the empress unless the uncommitted magnates could be persuaded to adopt her cause, and with all her considerable advantages, she had failed to do that in 1141. Of course, the symptoms predicting eventual success were not all that much more hopeful for the king. Although Queen Mathilda had maintained herself in the field against the empress, and fought a skilful campaign (which included an element of propaganda) her chief mainstay had been a mercenary general. The best that could be said is that the majority of magnates preferred to see Stephen on the throne rather than the empress, but few would exert themselves or endanger themselves to keep him there.

51 *HN*, 61–2, 67–70.

CHAPTER 11

The Failure of King Stephen

Just as the empress had attempted to erase the embarrassment of the retreat from Westminster in June by a great court at Oxford a month later, so now the newly released King Stephen attempted to cancel out his nine-month captivity by a stage-managed reaffirmation of his kingship. A Church council was rapidly summoned by the legate for 7 December 1141 at Westminster. Here the king appeared and assumed his place among his subjects as if there had been no period of captivity. They were still 'his men' as if they had not – most of them – sworn loyalty to the empress the previous summer. But he did seek the Church's condemnation of those of his subjects who had turned against him and remained against him, despite the support of a bull of Pope Innocent on 1136. The legate also had his chance to vindicate the behaviour of himself and the Church in general over the previous year. He called for the excommunication of all Angevin supporters except for the empress herself.[1] Once the king had reasserted before the bishops his legitimate right to rule, he needed to demonstrate it before the rest of the world. The obvious occasion would be the coming Christmas, and a large court was indeed assembled at Canterbury, appropriate as being in the heart of loyalist Kent which had served him so well the preceding year. On Christmas Day 1141, the king was solemnly crowned by the archbishop, and in a gesture as much symbolic as appropriate, Queen Mathilda also appeared in the church wearing a gold crown on her head.[2]

But if the idea was that the king was to be seen by all renewed in his kingship, from the king's point of view as he looked down from his throne, the same old faces of compromised aristocrats surrounded him on every side. The Canterbury court has also left us with a further survival: yet another charter addressed to Earl Geoffrey de Mandeville. By this, the earl had confirmed to him by the king all the extraordinary grants and jurisdictions in Essex, Hertfordshire, Middlesex and London that he had extorted from the

---

1 *Annales de Wavereleia*, 229; *HN*, 62–4.
2 GC i, 123–4.

empress at Oxford the previous July. One of the few major concessions he did not secure this time was his exemption from forest law. However politic this confirmation was (and there is evidence in the charter that Queen Mathilda had promised him such a confirmation in writing, no doubt to secure him to her side at Winchester in July or August) the king could hardly fail to reflect on the dubious way that Mandeville had improved his position at his expense. Indeed, there was to be no new start in 1142.[3]

THE LOSS OF NORMANDY, 1141–44

Something that could never be reversed after 1141 was the damage done to Stephen's position in Normandy. It is true that the royalist party in the duchy was already crumbling in 1140, but until then there was always the possibility that the king or the count of Meulan might have reversed the decline, as they had done three times between 1136 and 1139. At the end of 1140, the king's sympathisers still withstood the count of Anjou in the Cotentin and the central Norman plain; the count of Blois and the king of France were still Stephen's active allies, and these advantages might still have been built upon with the commitment of time and resources. But matters were already well adrift by the time of the battle of Lincoln. It is remarkable how little apparent contact there was by 1141 between King Stephen's court and Normandy. Few Norman bishops appeared before the king in England, and Count Waleran remained firmly on the English side of the Channel after Easter 1139. Here we see into the heart of Stephen's failure: neither he nor his advisers had the ability to rise above the task immediately in front of them. There was no world-view in the context of which Stephen could compose a strategy to meet his circumstances. Had there been, Stephen would not have lightly abandoned Normandy. He assuredly did not want to lose Normandy, but he never grasped that by directing his chief energies towards the duchy he would have partly solved his English problem. Had he stayed there in 1138, Robert of Gloucester and the empress would never have dared open a personal campaign in England against him, and he could have operated effectively against Anjou with his then allies, Count Theobald and Louis VII. In the event he could not rise above his fear of King David and pro-Angevin conspiracy amongst the English aristocracy.

By the beginning of 1141, it was probably already too late to find the resources to stem the decline of Stephen's party in the duchy. The news of the king's capture was the signal for those with any political sensitivity to start looking for terms from Count Geoffrey. Geoffrey was in a good position to exploit the sudden turn of events. The end of 1140 had found him in control of most of the Hièmois as far north as the ducal citadel of Falaise, not, as yet, seriously threatened and under the control of the baron, Robert Marmion.

---

3 *Regesta* iii, no. 276. The intriguing clause '. . . *Et preterea quicquid carta regine testatur ei dedi et concessi*', which has so confused the chronology of the Mandeville grants, is most easily explained as a general reference back to the queen's provisional confirmation of Mandeville's gains granted him in July 1141, on his defection to her army.

Indeed, so frustrated had the count become that he sent a column north around Falaise to punish Robert by destroying his ancestral castle of Fontenay-le-Marmion, which was north down the Orne valley towards Caen. Caen and Bayeux had been delivered to him by Robert of Gloucester in 1139. But, as yet, Count Geoffrey had made no impact on the Lieuvin and the Evreçin, and the castles of Bonsmoulins and Moulins-la-Marche still closed his way on to the plain of the Ouche. But there were problems behind the front line. Earl Robert of Leicester had (it appears) fallen out with Richer de L'Aigle, castellan of Bonsmoulins, and his mercenaries had kidnapped Richer in September, keeping him in prison in his chief Norman castle of Breteuil. This antagonised Richer's uncle, Count Rotrou of Perche, who held Moulins-la-Marche, and who retaliated in October by trapping and capturing Robert's mercenary captain, Robert Poard. Even so, Richer did not escape Leicester's custody until March 1141.[4] Internal difficulties were therefore causing havoc in the royalist camp, and we may put this down as much to the destabilisation and insecurity caused by the deep salient the Angevins had established in the duchy as to local rivalries.

After the rebellion of Earl Ranulf of Chester and the Lincoln campaign of January–February 1141, Count Geoffrey made significant advances. Earl Ranulf's defection meant that he had a new and powerful ally in the Avranchin. As the news of the king's capture paralysed many former royalists in England, so it also heartened the Angevin sympathisers in Normandy and disheartened the supporters of Stephen. Orderic tells us that the Norman magnates responded (as they had responded in 1136) by gathering for a conference. The gathering was held outside the duchy early in March at Mortagne, one of the chief fortresses of the count of Perche. Archbishop Hugh of Rouen was present as chairman of the discussions and it was he who presented a solution to Stephen's elder brother, Count Theobald of Blois: that Theobald himself should lay claim to the kingdom of England and the duchy of Normandy. Count Theobald declined the offer, being deterred by the difficulty of the undertaking. Instead, he said he was prepared to resign his claims on England (*regium ius*) to Geoffrey of Anjou, providing that he hand over Tours (an Angevin conquest from Blois) and obtain the release of Stephen from prison.[5] If these terms were ever put to Geoffrey, he never seriously entertained them. But, as we have seen, the idea that he had acquired a direct interest in the settlement of England had penetrated people's minds by July 1141, when we find the need for his consent and support written into the treaties between the empress and the earls of Essex and Oxford.[6]

Earl Robert of Leicester was present at this meeting, and (recognising the beginning of the end for Stephen's cause in Normandy) he used the occasion to begin negotiating a way out of the impasse for himself and his twin brother. News would by now have reached him of the surrender of Oxford and

4 OV vi, 546–8.
5 OV vi, 548.
6 *Regesta* iii, nos. 275, 634.

Winchester to the empress, and his younger brother, Hugh's, surrender of Bedford. Earl Robert first sought and obtained peace from Count Rotrou, which he secured by releasing Richer from his prison at Breteuil. He then contacted Count Geoffrey and made a truce on his own and his brother's behalf until Waleran should arrive in Normandy to come to terms with Count Geoffrey. But by then the situation had escaped his control, and the Angevin forces began to press forward out of their salient in the Hièmois towards the Seine valley, meeting little opposition. The border castles of Verneuil and Nonancourt, on the Norman march towards Blois-Chartres capitulated to the Angevins without a fight. The city of Lisieux was surrendered to Count Geoffrey around Easter (30 March) by its aged and sick bishop, John, formerly justiciar under Henry I.[7] Truce or not, Angevin forces occupied Count Waleran's town and sea port of Pont Audemer around this time, and they may have established their forward lines along the Risle valley rather than as yet attempt the capture of the southern Roumois, for Robert de Torigny (who was then living in the Roumois in the abbey of Bec-Hellouin) records that the district did not surrender till rather later in the year. Robert du Neubourg, the lord of Le Neubourg and cousin and ally of Waleran of Meulan appeared at this time from England to join his old friend, Count Geoffrey. We find that the count committed Pont Audemer, and perhaps other lands of Waleran, to Robert's keeping until the count should himself arrive.[8]

As we have seen, Waleran still held on in England for a few more months, despite the desperate situation in Normandy. It was not until early August 1141 that he met the empress at Devizes. After that painful interview it is unlikely that he stayed long at her court, and as she moved off to deal with Bishop Henry of Winchester, so Waleran travelled south to cross to Normandy. There is every reason to believe that he received a very warm welcome indeed at the court of Count Geoffrey (which he would have reached late in August or early in September) and a description of that welcome makes up much of Robert's annal for 1141:

> Count Waleran of Meulan, who surpassed all the magnates of Normandy in castles, revenues and allies, made an agreement with Count Geoffrey of Anjou, and the castle of Montfort [sur-Risle] was conceded to him which he had held since King Henry died. And so all the *Rothomagenses* submitted to that noble prince – not the citizens of Rouen, but those people who lived between the river Seine and the river Risle.[9]

Count Geoffrey was willing to extend a welcome to Waleran, because the count's adherence brought over the greatest individual Norman magnate, and

7 OV vi, 550 says Lisieux surrendered in the last week of Lent (16–22 March 1141) but RT, 142 says it surrendered during the octave of Easter (31 March–6 April).
8 For Robert du Neubourg's enfeoffment in Pont Audemer by 'the lord of Normandy', recorded in an agreement between him and Count Waleran in the winter of 1141–42, see D. Crouch, 'A Norman *conventio* and bonds of lordship in the middle ages', in *Law and Government in Medieval England and Normandy*, ed. G. Garnett and J. Hudson (Cambridge, 1994), 304, 322.
9 RT, 142.

with him the peaceful adherence of his allies, as indeed Robert de Torigny tells us. So there was no fuss made about Waleran's continued enjoyment of Montfort, the castle and honor between Pont Audemer and Brionne which was, in fact, the lordship of Waleran's own dispossessed nephew, Robert de Montfort, whose father had been deprived for joining in Waleran's unsuccessful 1123 rebellion against King Henry. Its possession gave Waleran complete control of the Lower Risle valley.

We also know that Count Geoffrey must have frustrated his wife's attempt to repossess Worcester and Waleran's English earldom in August. By the end of September the arrival of the dreadful news of the defeat at Winchester meant that Waleran's adherence was all the more important, and he must not be given an excuse to change sides once again. In the end, Waleran lost very little by going over to Count Geoffrey, just those of his English estates which were within range of King Stephen's wrath against his former ally. In fact, in the end, Waleran gained a wife, for during the winter of 1141–42 he was granted in marriage Agnes, elder sister of Simon, the young count of Evreux, and along with her some revenues and estates across the Seine near Lillebonne Unfortunately for Waleran's brother, Count Geoffrey could not be prevailed on to be so sympathetic to the earl of Leicester, who had returned to England and maintained his allegiance to Stephen. Earl Robert's great Norman lordship of Breteuil was confiscated and entrusted to his enemy, William III de Breteuil-Pacy, and his castle of Pont St-Pierre to his other rival, Roger de Tosny.[10]

One of the oddest things about the next few years is the degree of patience and deliberation with which Count Geoffrey set about reducing Normandy to obedience. It was to be fully three years before he was complete master of the duchy. Each year he set himself a Norman objective, and with calculation and deliberation set about achieving it. It is less odd when you take into account the slow progress of his campaign before his breakthrough of 1141, the fact that he had a troubled principality of his own to rule and administer, and that the political world of northern France was in perpetual turmoil. Count Geoffrey therefore rationed himself severely in his indulgence in his Norman ambitions. We see this in 1142 when he deliberately turned his back on the temptation of a quick strike at Rouen. The campaign of 1142 was intended to secure only what had been achieved in central Normandy, by securing his rear. To do that he moved westwards from captured Falaise and concentrated on reducing the castles towards the Breton border.

We are well informed of his summer campaign of 1142, because William of Malmesbury's interest in Robert of Gloucester led him to describe what happened in the duchy when Earl Robert crossed over to meet the count of Anjou and solicit material asistance for the cause of the empress in England. Earl Robert crossed over a little after midsummer (24 June 1142) and found

---

10 For the terms of Waleran's settlement with Geoffrey of Anjou, D. Crouch, *The Beaumont Twins: The Roots and Branches of Power in the Twelfth Century* (Cambridge, 1986), 52–3 and for the confiscation of Breteuil, ibid., 55. Estates he is known to have lost after 1141 were Lessness, Kent (granted on to Richard de Lucy) and Stanford-on-Avon, Northants.

the count in central Normandy, willing to join him for a council of war at Caen. Geoffrey was perfectly clear that he was not going to be distracted by English affairs while so much remained to be done in Normandy, and over the next month or so, the earl was tugged along with the Angevin army as it systematically reduced the fortresses of the Bessin as far as the river Vire and the borders of the Cotentin. Then the count moved south and reduced the four castles of Stephen's county of Mortain, and so brought the Avranchin into his obedience. By this time it was September, and the count drew the campaign deliberately to a close, leaving those who still resisted in the Cotentin to be dealt with next year. Earl Robert, disappointed, had to cross back to England with only token reinforcements and the symbolic presence of the nine-year-old boy, Henry, Count Geoffrey's eldest son and heir, to show off so as to encourage the Angevin cause in England.[11]

Count Geoffrey's objective for 1143 was to secure Normandy from the Atlantic to the Seine. He spent the summer in finishing off the conquest of the Cotentin, by the reduction of the fortress of Cherbourg. His armies also secured central Normandy up to the Seine, with the surrender of the ducal fortress of Vaudreuil on the lower Iton. As with the previous year, he achieved more perhaps than he had set out to secure when he received the voluntary submission of the magnates of the Pays de Caux (north of the Seine estuary), led by Earl Walter Giffard. Earl Walter – like Waleran of Meulan – had abandoned his lands in England to save his greater lands in Normandy.[12] All that was left to Stephen in Normandy by the end of 1143 was the region of the Roumois north of the Seine around Rouen, and the Pays de Talou, the border region between the rivers Béthune and Bresle, where the counts of Eu and Aumale and the earl of Warenne had still not submitted.

The climactic campaign for Normandy was clearly going to be that of 1144, and Count Geoffrey collected together a great army for the blockading and capture of Rouen in January. As far as we know, King Stephen was able or willing to do little to save the city. It seems that he had put Earl William de Warenne in command of his surviving Norman allies, and the final redoubt was to be the ducal castle of Arques, a great promontory fort which commanded the port of Dieppe, and ensured communications with England. But Stephen had no plan to take up command of the defence of Rouen himself. Count Geoffrey orchestrated a brief and effective campaign to overawe the

11 *HN*, 72–4; RT, 143. Torigny says that the people of the Cotentin (*Constantinienses*) as well as the people of the Avranchin (*Abrincatenses*) surrendered to Geoffrey in 1142, but records that castles were still resisting in the Cotentin the next year. It seems most likely that Geoffrey's objective in 1142 was the Bessin and Avranchin, and he received the voluntary surrender of those in the Cotentin who saw the writing on the wall.

12 RT, 145. Robert de Torigny records the surrender of Verneuil in 1143, whereas Orderic records its surrender in the spring of 1141, OV vi, 550: it is difficult to reconcile these conflicting notices. Earl Walter Giffard is absent from accounts of the English wars in 1141, and he may have moved to Normandy by then, if not before. As it transpired, his English lands were confiscated by Stephen after 1142, but were entrusted to the wardship of his first cousin, Earl Gilbert of Pembroke, for the evidence for this see D. Crouch, 'The March and the Welsh kings', in *The Anarchy of King Stephen's Reign*, ed. E. King (Oxford, 1994), 275n.

city, which he wished to capture with as little loss and in as much triumph as possible. Rather than assault it directly across the river – a very difficult undertaking – he set Waleran of Meulan before Christmas to pillage the suburb of Emendreville to the south of the Seine bridge. He was to destroy its great church of St-Sever, giving warning to Rouen of the horrors which awaited it should the city not surrender when summoned. It seems that the citizens had broken down the fortified bridge of Rouen, to impede any southern approach.[13]

A few weeks later, Count Geoffrey himself took the main army upriver to cross at the bridge of Vernon a day or two after the feast of St Hilary (13 January). Vernon was held for him by its lord, William, younger brother of the redoubtable Baldwin de Redvers. Count Geoffrey marched downriver – giving the city time to fret, worry and consider its response – and established a fortified camp on the heights of La Trinité du Mont on (probably) 19 January 1144, in the midst of a gale worse than anyone could remember. Here he was informed by the city that it would surrender, and on 20 January he was received as lord in solemn procession by the citizens and was welcomed by the archbishop into the cathedral of St Mary. The day was wet and it was in a heavy storm that he went into the city, but it apparently blew itself out, uncannily, at noon. The Tower of Rouen, beset by the tempest of war rather than nature, would not surrender, however. A formal siege began on 25 January and despite an intense bombardment by engines the Earl Warenne's garrison did not submit until 23 April, and then only because of a deficiency of food.[14] Since it is from the point of the surrender of the Tower of Rouen that Robert de Torigny begins to call Geoffrey duke of Normandy, it may be that he received investiture by the archbishop as duke immediately afterwards.[15]

Geoffrey of Anjou's leisurely conquest of Normandy was as much the product of circumstances as of strategy. No-one but the odd, isolated and recalcitrant Anglo-Norman magnate was willing to try to stop him. King Stephen, as we have seen, was obsessed by the need to secure England, and we may well believe that if Normandy entered much into his ideas between 1141 and 1144, it was simply the further objective which would follow on from his final defeat of his enemies in England. The wider situation in northern France also shielded Geoffrey from external intervention. Count Theobald of Blois, the prince he had most need to fear, had publicly disavowed any interest in

---

13 RT, 151 records its repair by Duke Geoffrey in 1145.

14 RT, 147–8; *Chronicon Rotomagense* in *RHF* xii, 785. Torigny gives the feast of Fabian and Sebastian (20 January) as the date of the city's surrender, the Rouen chronicle gives 14 kalends February (19 January). A reasonable reconciliation would be that the process of negotiation and surrender covered two days.

15 RT, 148, see also *Chronicon S. Michaelis in Periculo Maris*, in *RHF* xii, 773, '. . . *reddita est turris Rotomagensis Gaufredo comiti Andegavensi et exinde factus est comes Normanniae*'. For the Norman ducal investiture, see D. Crouch, *The Image of Aristocracy in Britain, 1000–1300* (London, 1992), 184–6, 193, 201–2. There seem to be some grounds to believe that many credited Geoffrey with the title of duke before 1144. Seemingly genuine charters of his wife to Godstow abbey dated to 1143 talk of him as 'my husband Geoffrey duke of the Normans and count of Anjou', *Regesta* iii, nos. 370–1, and a charter of William count of Ponthieu dated to September 1143 likewise refers to Geoffrey as duke, C.H. Haskins, *Norman Institutions* (New York, 1918), 130n.

Normandy in 1141, and never did intervene in the duchy again until his death in 1152. This, in turn, had much to do with the policies of the young king Louis VII, who was beginning to make his own mark on French politics. Following his father's death in 1137 Louis had continued to work with Theobald of Blois and Ralph of Vermandois, his father's chief counsellors in his latter days.[16] Both these great magnates had an interest in supporting King Stephen: Theobald for family reasons, and Count Ralph because he was the uncle of Waleran of Meulan. The pro-Stephen policy of the Capetians was still active in 1140, when Louis VII's sister, Constance, was married to Eustace, Stephen's son, and when Louis was drawn into the discussions over a possible peace settlement later in the year.

The disaster of Lincoln had its effect on the Capetian court. In July 1141, as we have seen, it was known to the empress that King Louis had expressed some interest in the Angevin pacification of England, and might be applied to for assistance in arbitration. This shift in the king's mind would very likely explain why, as early as March 1141, Count Theobald would not take up the claim to the Anglo-Norman realm, and shifted his position in the meeting at Mortagne from resistance to the Angevins, to negotiation with them. But Count Theobald did not like the way that the balance of forces in northern France had shifted. By June 1141 Theobald's differences with the king of France had become public, when he refused to accompany Louis on his campaign against Toulouse. The situation between the former allies became very bad the next year, when Theobald also fell out with his former ally, Ralph of Vermandois, who divorced his first wife, Theobald's niece, in order to marry one of the heiresses of Aquitaine. Theobald found himself engaged in a war with Louis VII for control of his county of Champagne which lasted fitfully from June 1142 to the end of 1143.[17] This conflict, involving the king in physical warfare with Count Theobald and moral warfare with St Bernard of Clairvaux and the pope, ruled out any intervention in Norman affairs from Blois or Paris.

It was only in the last phases of the Angevin conquest of Normandy that Louis VII was able to exert any influence on Geoffrey of Anjou. During the siege of Rouen, the distinguished Crusader and former ally of Stephen, Count Rotrou of Perche, had died fighting for the Angevins. His sons were still minors, and King Louis's immediate concern was to establish his right to wardship of the strategic county of Perche, between Normandy and Blois-Chartres. Northern French custom allowed him to take possession of the county and the widow, Countess Hawise (who was incidentally an Englishwoman and the daughter of Walter, sheriff of Salisbury). The marriage of Countess Hawise to Louis's younger brother, Robert, allowed Robert to assume the titles of Count of Perche and lord of Bellême until the young heir of Perche came of age. This adroit move weakened Count Theobald's influence (as Perche and

16 Y. Sassier, *Louis VII* (Paris, 1991), 56–8.
17 Sassier, *Louis VII*, 104–5, 107–26.

Blois-Chartres had been long-term allies) and placed a Capetian prince as a new power along the southern borders of Normandy. Elsewhere, King Louis intervened directly in the final battles for Normandy in the Pays de Talou. He led an army to assist the reduction of Henry I's newly built fortress of Neufchâtel-en-Bray, north of Rouen, and the castle of Lyons-la-Forêt, then held by Hugh de Gournay, the leading magnate of the Norman Vexin. Along with Louis came Geoffrey's brother-in-law, Count Thierry of Flanders, another former ally of King Stephen.[18] So when the last areas of Normandy began to capitulate in the summer of 1144, it was not Geoffrey's achievement alone, but one sanctioned by his overlord, the king. We have the later evidence of Abbot Suger that King Louis formally acknowledged Geoffrey as duke, and it must have been during this campaign that the solemn recognition was given to his elevation.[19] Louis was able to profit from this friendship and assistance by the cession to him of the castle of Gisors, a Norman enclave in the French Vexin. Gisors was to form the basis for a claim to the whole of this area, up to the valley of the Andelle, which was conceded to Louis later when his support was needed for the investiture of the young Henry Plantagenet as duke.[20]

Duke Geoffrey's systematic conquest of Normandy owed quite a bit to good fortune, but it would be unfair to deny that it also revealed in him a degree of good judgement. He was doubtless wise to refuse any distractions in England. There was every reason why he, like Stephen, should concentrate on Normandy. Normandy was the key to security for him too. If Geoffrey had crossed the Channel and become drawn into England's political and military mess Anjou would have been open to attack, and the Norman aristocracy was not safe to trust on its own as yet.[21] We should also note Geoffrey's ability to temporise and dissemble while he was still exposed to threat. Robert de Torigny observed of the duke's dealings with his Norman magnates that Geoffrey had only accommodated them for the time being, while he needed their assistance.[22] The same might be said of Geoffrey's alertness to the wider situation in northern France, and in particular of his knowledge of when it became wise to include Louis VII in his campaigns and how to use that for his benefit at minimal cost.

Following the assimilation of Normandy, the new duke devoted his time to the consolidation of his position. There is plenty of evidence of calculation and even-handedness in his policies. He kept Waleran of Meulan happy by

18 RT, 148–9.
19 Suger wrote to Louis VII early in 1150 referring to 'the count of Anjou, *whom you made duke of Normandy*', *RHF* xv, 522.
20 Arques was the last stronghold of Stephen in Normandy, and was held by a Flemish mercenary, William le Moine, on the king's behalf until William was killed by a random arrow while walking on the keep in the summer of 1145, RT, 150. For Louis's acquisition of Gisors, JM, 72, 215. For the cession of the Norman Vexin *c.*1151, see J.A. Green, 'Lords of the Norman Vexin', in *War and Government in the Middle Ages*, ed. J. Gillingham and J.C. Holt (Woodbridge, 1994), 47–61.
21 See the comments of GC i, 123.
22 RT, 179

appointing Robert du Neubourg, Waleran's first cousin and councillor, as one of his chief justices. Waleran and Robert made a remarkable political pact in the winter of 1141–42 to consolidate their future relationship, a pact by which Waleran retained Robert for a very handsome annual sum and some major land grants.[23] The bishopric of Bayeux became vacant in 1142 on the premature death of Bishop Richard, Robert of Gloucester's illegitimate son. Duke Geoffrey's choice as replacement could not have made Earl Robert happy, for he nominated Philip de Harcourt, Waleran's cousin and long-time clerical protégé.[24] Since most of Robert of Gloucester's Norman estates were concentrated in the diocese of Bayeux, we see evidence that Duke Geoffrey wanted it to be understood that he owed nothing to the earl. Waleran's brother-in-law, William Louvel, lord of Ivry and Bréval, also benefited. Before 1147 Duke Geoffrey appointed him as justiciar in the border region of Verneuil and Nonancourt.[25]

The only Norman magnate who can be proved to have exerted any great weight with Duke Geoffrey was Count Waleran of Meulan. The evidence surviving for his six-year rule over Normandy can tell us that Earl William de Roumare of Lincoln, William, count of Ponthieu, and his son Count John of Alençon were on occasion found at Geoffrey's court, but not how often and what influence they wielded.[26] Duke Geoffrey seems to have relied mainly on a small group of Norman *curiales* in his rule of the duchy: the lesser magnates, Reginald de St Valèry, Robert du Neubourg (already mentioned), William de Vernon, and the justices, Engelger and Alexander de Bohun, Richard de la Haie and Robert de Courcy. These followed him around the duchy in much the same way as he associated with a small group of Angevin *curiales* when south of Normandy: Guy de Sablé, Payn and Geoffrey de Clairvaux, Pepin and Goscelin de Tours, the despenser, and the brothers Geoffrey and Hugh de Clères, the seneschal. Quite often we find these Angevin *curiales* in Normandy, and even in England in the summer of 1141, liaising with the empress. Once we find their Norman equivalents in Maine at Saumur with Duke Geoffrey.[27]

Geoffrey's six-year rule as duke of Normandy and count of Anjou was remarkably successful. The duke had a shrewd appreciation of the strengths

---

23 Robert du Neubourg was a leading attestor of Duke Geoffrey's acts, and is addressed by some of them before 1147 as a ducal justice, *Regesta* iii, nos. 55–6, 779. Haskins, *Norman Institutions*, 147, would like to believe that Robert occupied the post of seneschal of Normandy under Duke Geoffrey as he was later to do under Henry II, but firm evidence is lacking, and the two known Norman seneschals of Duke Geoffrey were Reginald de St-Valèry and Robert de Courcy (who had previously been a seneschal of Henry I), *Regesta* iii, pp. xxxv–xxxvi. Despite his place in the ducal administration, Robert is found frequently in Meulan acts of the mid-1140s, and in *c*.1147 was acting as a justice of Count Waleran at Brionne, Crouch, *Beaumont Twins*, 160–1. For Robert's treaty with Count Waleran in early 1142, see Crouch, 'A Norman *conventio*', 299–306, 321–3.
24 RT, 145.
25 *Regesta* iii, no. 283.
26 The exception may be that William, lord of Néhou (Manche) and Vernon (Eure), was the brother-in-law of Earl William de Roumare (and brother of the Angevin loyalist, Baldwin de Redvers, earl of Devon) which looks like one possible strong family grouping at the ducal court. For the family links, see *Charters of the Redvers Family*, ed. Bearman, 4, 5, 17.
27 *Regesta* iii, no. 443.

and weaknesses of his situation. He knew precisely how far he could press his claims with a reasonable expectation of success. Consolidation of his control of the duchy was his principal aim, and it was achieved. In that respect it is instructive to find that a major theme in his forty or so surviving acts as duke is the sworn inquest to establish rights: he was determined that the duchy, once his, should be put in good order.[28] The Church in Normandy may have antagonised him by its slowness to abandon Stephen. Bishop Arnulf of Lisieux still acknowledged Stephen as rightful ruler in 1142 – although Geoffrey fully controlled his diocese at the time – and Archbishop Hugh of Rouen was still recognising Stephen in 1143.[29] So it is not surprising to find that another area in which he invested much energy was in his attempts to monitor and control episcopal elections. We know of this particularly in the case of the unlicensed and unnominated election of Arnulf, archdeacon of Séez, to succeed his uncle Bishop John of Lisieux during the 1141 campaign, before Geoffrey could intervene. He also became involved in a disputed election to Séez in 1144, where the chapter had the peculiar distinction (with Carlisle) of being made up of Augustinian canons. The chapter had wanted an Augustinian bishop and appealed against having a secular clerk placed over them by the duke. In both cases he backed down – though not before drawing the fire of Bernard of Clairvaux – but seems to have at least established his right to nominate.[30]

In all these actions we see another manifestation of that remorseless patience exhibited in his military campaigns between 1136 and 1144. Whether through limited imagination or rigid realism, he was not going to attempt more than he could reasonably achieve – but he would not let go of what he must achieve. For this reason England meant little to him, or at least he would not allow it to mean anything to him until he had a reasonable chance of securing it. It may well be that he had long suspected or decided that England was a task for the next generation of his family – hence his decision to send the boy Henry to live at Bristol under his uncle's tuition in 1142. In retrospect, one is rather driven to the conclusion that the Anglo-Norman aristocracy had made a serious error when they rejected Count Geoffrey as their king-consort in 1135.

THE RECAPTURE OF OXFORD (DECEMBER 1142)

The empress had been able to hold on to few of the trophies of 1141, and in the next few years she took further losses. Winchester, sacked and humiliated, returned to Stephen's obedience. We know that one at least of its leading citizens and Angevin supporters, Ralph fitz Pichard, left the place as a refugee and settled in Gloucester.[31] The other great Angevin acquisition had been

28 *Regesta* iii, nos. 55–57, 665, 726.
29 Haskins, *Norman Institutions*, 130n.
30 *The Letters of Arnulf of Lisieux*, ed. F. Barlow (Camden Soc., 3rd ser., lxi, 1939), pp. xix–xx, 4–5. For a discussion, M. Chibnall, *The Empress Matilda* (Oxford, 1991), 139–40.
31 D. Walker, 'Ralph son of Pichard', *Bulletin of the Institute of Historical Research*, xxxiii (1960), 195–202.

Oxford. With Oxford went control of the upper Thames valley. This was most inconvenient for King Stephen since the town linked neatly with the otherwise isolated fortress of Brian fitz Count at Wallingford to form a rebel salient in the southern midlands. If Oxford could be recaptured by the king, the military situation would be restored more or less to where it had been before the battle of Lincoln, although some territorial losses (such as that of Cornwall to Earl Reginald and Devon to Earl Baldwin) could not be easily reversed, and indeed never were.

There was perhaps another loss that had to be made good before the return of Oxford could be attempted. Let us not forget, as broad-brush treatments of kingdoms and regions can too often forget, that we deal here with people of flesh, blood and feelings. The posturing of the Canterbury court of Christmas 1141 is proof enough that King Stephen and Queen Mathilda felt that their prestige had been seriously damaged by the king's nine-month captivity, even though the rout of Winchester had damaged the empress more.[32] All commentators agree that the king had conducted himself with nobility on the field of Lincoln and in captivity at Bristol. But at what cost? The king's long illness in the spring of 1142 tells us vividly what the cost was. There is very little evidence of the king's movements between Christmas and Easter, and none of any actions he took. Things were so quiet that William of Malmesbury assumed that Lent had been agreed as a time of formal truce between the parties. At the end of Lent, there was a breakthrough in the north, when William Peverel regained Nottingham while the empress's castellan, William Paynel, had travelled south to consult with his mistress. The king and queen travelled north to York together immediately after Easter (19 April 1142) to consolidate this coup. Around this time, the king was formally reconciled with Earl Ranulf of Chester (who may indeed have been behind the recovery of Nottingham for the royalist cause). There is some reason to believe, as we have seen, that Ranulf may never have seen himself in the past year as actually *at war* with the king, but simply asserting his rights.[33] Military games had been announced in the city, with the earls of York and Richmond leading either side, but the king cancelled them. John of Hexham writes of the king's urgent desire to avenge his injuries and restore his prestige. The games would presumably

32 It is worth noting that Earl Henry of Northumbria dated a perambulation '. . . *die veneris crastino Ascensionis Domini anno scilicet secundo quo Stephanus rex Anglie captus est*' (viz. 29 May 1142) *Regesta Regum Scottorum* i, 157, which is a solid illustration of quite how large a milestone Lincoln remained in people's consciousness.

33 *ASC, s.a.* 1141 [1142] implies that this happened when Stephen was in the north in 1142, and this might be linked to the belief expressed in JH, 310 that Ranulf had changed sides (like a prototype Stanley at Bosworth) during the sieges of Winchester in 1141. See the discussion on this in P. Dalton, '*In neutro latere*: The armed neutrality of Ranulf II Earl of Chester in King Stephen's reign', *ANS*, xiv, ed. M. Chibnall (Woodbridge, 1992), 50–1, who points out that Ranulf's castles of Briquessart and Vire in Normandy were seized by Earl Robert and Count Geoffrey in the summer of 1142, which they would hardly have done had he still been an adherent of the empress, as R.H.C. Davis, 'King Stephen and the Earl of Chester revised', in *From Alfred the Great to Stephen* (London, 1991), 216–7 and H.A. Cronne, 'Ranulf des Gernons, Earl of Chester, 1129–53', *TRHS*, 4th ser., xx (1937), 122–5 argue.

have been a distraction from the gathering of the great army which would do all these things. However, the expected campaign fizzled out. While progressing across the northern midlands the king fell into illness, and languished at Northampton until after Whitsun (7 June). His grand army was sent home.[34]

William of Malmesbury caught the optimistic expectation of the empress's party that the king might die. But it takes very little to believe that the king's illness was only partly physical. Not much had happened since Christmas 1141. The author of the *Gesta* talks of the king's 'torpor' which paralysed the royalist party until the summer of 1142.[35] It is well within the realms of possibility that Stephen, like any man in his mid-forties, no longer had the mental resilience that could shrug off prolonged stress. It would have been harder for him in that the accepted norms of behaviour in his time demanded of a king that he be perpetually cheerful, affable and unemotional. He had survived a very stressful and anxious year, but I would suggest that he had not survived it without cost to himself. Lack of energy and purpose in the once purposeful, bouts of illness and lassitude, all are reactions to extreme stress, even in those who survive it. The six-month period after his release seems to have been Stephen's nadir of emotional exhaustion, when he had to rebuild his life and expectations.

Unfortunately for the empress, she was not able to take much advantage of all this confusion. She was on the defensive, without the resources to capitalise on the king's lassitude, even had she wished. The *Gesta* tells us that her military men were perfectly well aware of the fact that Oxford would be the king's first objective, and that they attempted to meet the threat. William of Malmesbury tells us that the town itself had been massively fortified with embankments under the earl of Gloucester's personal direction. Henry I's hall at Woodstock was fortified to command one route from the north. Strategic sites were selected for the erection of outposts to ensure communications with the Angevin heartland to the west. A temporary castle was erected at the great royal hundredal centre of Bampton, by strengthening the bank that surrounded the ancient minster church there, and using the stone tower of the cruciform church on the south of the circuit as a sort of keep. Fortifying Bampton helped to make the links with the west more secure (a scheme doubtless linked to a new castle raised next to the abbey at Cirencester even further west). Just to the south at Radcot the strategic bridge over the Thames was also fortified. Bampton and Radcot between them closed communications up and down the Thames. The empress, too, was busy rallying her party. Letters – and troops of cavalry – issued forth in every direction, to support friends and intimidate enemies.[36] In the comparative investment of resources and prestige, the defence

---

34 *HN*, 71; JH, 311–12. A charter of the king recalls a grant made to Arrouaise 'in my illness at Northampton', *Regesta* iii, no. 25.
35 *GS*, 138: the word '*torpor*' used by the *Gesta* of the period after Christmas 1141 is complemented by the word '*modestia*' used by William of Malmesbury, *HN*, 70.
36 *GS*, 138; *HN*, 74. For the hundred, town and minster of Bampton and the site of Radcot bridge, *VCH Oxfordshire* xiii, 1–2, 12, 22.

of Oxford was to be her Stalingrad: a final redoubt from which retreat would signal the beginning of the end for her cause.

A council was summoned to meet the empress at Devizes on 14 June 1142, a time when the king's recovery would have become known and his preparations for war revealed. An earlier 'secret' council had been held there in March. It had pretty soon become known that the earlier meeting had recommended that the empress's husband, the count of Anjou, be asked to come to England to rally the cause. The June council reaffirmed this, but learned that the count would negotiate with no-one but the earl of Gloucester. So to Normandy he was sent, despite the desperation of the hour. He crossed from his own port of Wareham a day or two after midsummer (24 June 1142) taking with him hostages from the less secure of the empress's adherents.[37] In Normandy, as we have seen, he did far more for Count Geoffrey by his presence than the count would do for him in England. He returned with a substantial force of knights in October and the empress's eldest son, but without the count of Anjou. By then the situation had become quite as desperate as the empress's council had feared it would become. Earl Robert had not been the only one to cross the Channel in June 1142, so also had Queen Mathilda. She can be found holding court at Lens on 23 June 1142, perhaps doing the same as the earl for his party, raising troops, money and support abroad.[38]

The king had fully recovered his sense of purpose and his vigour by August 1142. He summoned an army and with his former energy and ability, appeared at the end of summer, perhaps in August, before the key port of Wareham in Dorset. He drove out its commander, William, the earl of Gloucester's eldest son – a young man of just over twenty at this time – and seized both town and castle, thus cutting off the earl from any easy return to England. From Dorset the king led a chevauchée unexpectedly into Gloucestershire. Cirencester fell into his hands with ease, and he then moved rapidly eastwards upon Oxford, seizing the defensive forts at Bampton and Radcot on the way. The king had come quite the other way to that which had been expected. He arrived opposite the town on the west bank of the river Thames on 26 September 1142. He chose his time well. The hereditary castellan, Robert d'Oilly, had died a fortnight before and was now lying in a grave in Eynsham abbey and (from accounts of the subsequent siege) he had not been replaced in office. Oxford was garrisoned only by the empress's military household, which bravely or foolishly turned out to dispute his crossing of the river. The king and his bodyguard surprised them by somehow finding a passage across the network of watercourses to south and west of the town. One source even suggests the king and his men swam at one point. Their quick onset caused a panic among the outnumbered defenders. The king's men swarmed through the gates on the heels of the retreating garrison. The town was set alight. The royal army put the castle, at the town's western end, under close blockade.

37 *HN*, 71–2.
38 *Regesta* iii, no. 26.

Once again, the empress had been trapped by a royalist army's all too rapid movement.[39]

This time matters were even more desperate than they had been at Winchester a year before. There was no earl of Gloucester or earl of Hereford to mastermind her escape and protect it with a rearguard action. The empress was trapped in the castle with only a small force to protect her, and the king himself and a large army outside. The siege continued remorselessly until December 1142, the king being 'more keen to capture her than take the town', as John of Hexham said.[40] There was no hesitation this time in the assault, as there had been at Arundel three years before: the king wanted her in captivity. Siege engines battered the castle and a strict blockade closed it from the rest of the world for two and a half months. There was little prospect of relief. The king's camp was sited within the powerful defences of the town of Oxford, and the Angevin sympathisers gathered at Wallingford were impotent to reach him. Earl Robert of Gloucester had returned from Normandy around the end of October and regained Wareham after a three-week siege, but he was unwilling or unable to do more than re-establish a presence in Dorset. After the fall of Wareham, he busied himself in securing the Isle of Purbeck, obtaining control of fortifications on the Isle of Portland and at Lulworth. It was not until the beginning of December that Earl Robert began to mass a relief column at the eastern outpost of his party at recaptured Cirencester.[41]

Earl Robert's reluctance to move to the rescue of his lady the empress till the end of the year is revealing. He had poured treasure and lives into her cause for years, so we have to assume that he did not want her captured. So it must be that the Angevin cause was really on the ropes in the second half of 1142, and Earl Robert found on his return that his party was completely demoralised. It ought to be noted that William of Malmesbury said that the earl took hostages from his principal allies before he had left for Normandy. This was because Malmesbury said that he had already learned to distrust their commitment the previous year. The idea was that hostages would make them keener to stand by the empress once he had left.[42] Such a strategy does not say much for the earl's perception of his allies' commitment before he left. Now

39 *GS*, 140–2; *HN*, 73–4; GC i, 124. For the castle and topography of medieval Oxford, H.E. Salter, *Medieval Oxford* (Oxford Historical Society, 100, 1936), 29, 66–89; *VCH Oxfordshire* iv, 296–9.

40 JH, 317. For the duration of the siege from Michaelmas into Advent, see HH, 742. *GS*, 142 reckoned the siege as lasting three months, although it could only have been two-and-a-half months according to the other evidence.

41 *HN*, 76 has the earl preparing a relief column at Cirencester after the beginning of Advent (in early December). GC i, 124 has the siege of Wareham occupying three weeks, which (with the other military activities in Dorset) would project the earl's arrival in England back to the end of October or beginning of November.

42 *HN*, 72. R.B. Patterson, *Earldom of Gloucester Charters* (Oxford, 1973), 96, identifies the *conventio* between Earl Robert and Earl Miles as one of these pledges of allegiance secured in June–July 1142. I would go along with this suggestion, especially as the treaty binds the countess of Gloucester to support Earl Miles (only necessary if she were about to become the leader of the Gloucester party in her husband's absence). The treaty significantly requires Earl Miles of Hereford to surrender his son Mahel.

he was back he must have found his cause in collapse. The earl's furious activity in Dorset, a hundred miles from the trapped empress, would then make sense as part of a wider campaign to inspire confidence in his shattered party. William of Malmesbury believed that the earl was indeed too weak to confront the king directly, but suggested that, by campaigning in Dorset, he hoped to draw King Stephen south away from the siege of Oxford. If that were Earl Robert's intention, it would seem to have been a pretty forlorn hope in the circumstances.[43] The only other possibility – and it has to rely on a cynicism which is not much in evidence elsewhere in his career – is that the earl was willing still to count on the king's generosity to his female opponents. Since he had her eldest son and heir with him in his army, he may have felt that the Angevin cause would have survived her imprisonment. But this sort of cold calculation does not seem very likely. In the event, the empress pulled off yet another of her great escapes (the fourth, as the *Gesta Stephani* wryly notes). Early on a snowy mid-December night, with an escort of three to five knights (accounts vary) all muffled in white cloaks, she fled the castle of Oxford through a postern gate and crossed the ice of the frozen Thames just below the western castle walls. She and her knights hurried on foot across the river meadows and frozen water courses south of Oseney to the Abingdon road, and eventually the protection of the abbey there, six miles to the south. Somewhere on the road she swore that if she ever got away safely she would found a Cistercian abbey as a gesture of thanks to God, a promise fulfilled in Normandy ten years later. From Abingdon the empress made good her escape to her friends at Wallingford the next day. Oxford castle surrendered once she was safely away, and, in a characteristic gesture, the king allowed the brave garrison easy terms.[44]

NEUTRALISM, MISJUDGEMENT AND STALEMATE (1143)

As the year 1143 opened, the king still seemed to believe that a victory over his enemies might be there to be grasped. The fall of Oxford, in whose defence the empress and Earl Robert had invested so much of their prestige, was what J.H. Round rightly called the 'final blow' to her cause.[45] It is not going too far to say that it was the end of her hopes of securing the throne for herself. The Oxford disaster demonstrated that her party was too weak even to motivate itself to rescue her from imprisonment; in the end she had to arrange her own escape from danger. So, on the face of things, King Stephen

43 *HN*, 75–6.
44 For the empress's escape see the accounts in *GS*, 144–5; *HN*, 76–7. JH, 317, HH, 742 and GC i, 124–5, give the detail of the white cloaks. The account in *ASC*, *s.a.* 1141 [1142] describes her being let down by ropes from the walls (but this would seem to be an echo of St Paul's night-time escape from Damascus, let down from the walls in a basket, Acts 10: 25). The end of the siege appears to have happened in mid-December, perhaps the second or third week, as the chroniclers note that Christmas followed soon after her escape, HH, 742 dates her escape '. . . *non procul a Natali*'. For the empress's vow to found an abbey if she escaped, see below p. 283 and n.
45 J.H. Round, *Geoffrey de Mandeville: A Study of the Anarchy* (London, 1892), 200.

had restored his position in England considerably since the previous year. He had re-established the front line with the empress's party in the southwest. With the adherence of the earls of Chester, Leicester and Warwick, he was in nominal control of the central midlands and northwest. The earls of Richmond and York still maintained his power in Yorkshire.[46] King David and his son, Earl Henry, were remarkably quiescent in the far north. We find also that Stephen was still able to exert himself in remote Staffordshire and Shropshire in the mid-1140s, so his kingship was by no means moribund in the Welsh Marches either.

Oxford was the king's once again, and he erected it into a powerful bastion of the royalist cause, placing it under the control of the capable local loyalist, William de Chesney, who had been a prominent leader (with his brother Roger) in the royal army at Winchester in 1141.[47] Chesney became the latest example of one of Stephen's regional governors. His position in 1143 paralleled that of William of Ypres in Kent, Henry de Tracy in Somerset and Devon, or William Martel in Dorset at Sherborne. Chesney was conceded control over the castle and borough of Oxford (describing himself on one occasion as its 'alderman'). He was also given in his own right the important castle and town of Deddington (which closed the northern approach to Oxford).[48] The king asserted himself determinedly in the recaptured shire. Chesney was given at least temporary keeping of the confiscated estates of Robert d'Oilly, the former castellan and Oxfordshire's most considerable magnate, who had defected to Mathilda too hastily in 1141 and died at Eynsham abbey a fortnight before the king captured the town of Oxford in September 1142. His son and heir, Henry d'Oilly, took refuge at the empress's court.[49] In

---

46 Note a writ of June 1143 directed to Stephen's officers in Yorkshire and Nottinghamshire, *Regesta* iii, no. 109.

47 *GS*, 130. A charter of December 1142 × June 1143 addresses the king's justice, sheriff and officers of Oxfordshire, *Regesta* iii, no. 855. The shrievalty of Oxfordshire was filled by one Azor in the 1140s, who would seem to have acted as nominee of Chesney, see J.A. Green, *English Sheriffs to 1154* (HMSO, 1990), 70. I differ from the broad dating of the editors of this act to 1140 × 43, because the attestation of Earl Geoffrey de Mandeville and the address to the royal officers in Oxfordshire must date it to a time after the recovery of Oxford, as also does the grant it records to Turgis of Avranches within the royal estate of Woodstock. A possible alternative date of late 1140 × Feb. 1141 (when Geoffrey was an earl and Oxford still the king's) is unlikely.

48 For William de Chesney (not to be confused with King Stephen's long-time servant, William de Chesney 'of Norwich'), a younger son of the Domesday Oxfordshire landowner, Roger de Chesney, see studies of the family in H.E. Salter, 'The family of Chesney', in *Cartulary of the Abbey of Eynsham*, ed. Salter (2 vols, Oxford Historical Society, 49, 51, 1907–8) i, 411–23; H.M. Colvin, *A History of Deddington* (London, 1963), 19–20; A. Morey and C.N.L. Brooke, *Gilbert Foliot and his Letters* (Cambridge, 1965), 32–6, 50. The study of him in H.A. Cronne, *The Reign of Stephen: Anarchy in England, 1135–54* (London, 1970), 150, confuses the two unrelated Chesney families.

49 E. Amt, *The Accession of Henry II in England: Royal Government Restored, 1149–1159* (Woodbridge, 1993), 48. In ibid., 52–3, Dr Amt argues against the grant of the Oilly honour to Chesney on the basis that only one Oilly manor, Watlington (and of course the castle of Oxford) can be found in Chesney's hands. However, the terms in which Chesney confirmed the church there to Oseney priory are telling. Archbishop Theobald talks of the church 'which Robert d'Oilly and Henry his son, and after them William de Chesney, conceded the priory *quando in manu sua regis Stephani auctoritate et donatione devolvetur*', A. Saltman, *Theobald, Archbishop of*

the course of 1143, the king would assume control over Buckingham and its shire, when Earl Walter Giffard declared his hand, and joined the party of Geoffrey of Anjou in Normandy. The fall of Oxford to the king had therefore delivered the southern midlands back into his hands with the exception of Bedford, whose castellans stayed aloof from the king until forced into submission early in 1146.[50]

The Angevin party was once again contained along the line of the Cotswolds. Further south in Wiltshire and Dorset, lines were less clearly drawn. William Martel dominated the north of Dorset from Roger of Salisbury's great stone fortress of Sherborne (which the *Gesta* famously described as 'the single key to the whole kingdom') but Sherborne was countered by the earl of Gloucester's garrisons at Dorchester, Wimborne and Corfe, and the Angevin anchor post of Wareham in the south.[51] In Wiltshire, Walter, son of Edward of Salisbury, the castellan and sheriff, had joined the Angevin party before Winchester in 1141, and with John Marshal at Marlborough and Humphrey de Bohun at Trowbridge, the northern fringe of Wiltshire was closed to the king. His most considerable asset within the county was the powerful castle the bishop of Winchester had built at Downton, five miles south of Salisbury on the Hampshire border.[52] Stephen's military objectives in 1143 were therefore to challenge the empress's partisans in Wiltshire and Dorset, and to move royal control westward through the counties to link up with his beleaguered allies still holding out in Somerset. This was a reasonable plan, and if he had succeeded, there would have been the chance of trapping the empress a fifth time, as her centre at Devizes would then have been dangerously exposed.

Canterbury (London, 1955), 415. She argues instead that Chesney obtained from the king several former Oxfordshire estates of William fitz Osbern that had come into royal demesne, and had illegally and opportunistically seized Watlington because the Oilly family had obtained it long ago as a fitz Osbern tenancy. But I would argue that the archbishop's words cannot bear that interpretation, and it seems unlikely that the fitz Osbern estates in Oxfordshire would be still remembered as a unit by the 1140s. The transfer of the castle of Oxford to Chesney from the Oilly family would – with the Watlington example – indicate a confiscation of some or all of the honor.
50 For the Giffard control over the town of Buckingham see *VCH Buckinghamshire* iii, 480 and *Facsimiles of Charters in Oxford Muniment Rooms*, ed. H.E. Salter (Oxford, 1929), no. 44. That this control included the castle is indicated by a Giffard charter of the 1150s dated '. . . *Apud Buckingham*' in Cartulary of Missenden, BL ms Harley 3688, fo. 95v. The Giffard honours were granted to his cousin, Earl Gilbert of Pembroke (see above), but the precise fate of the castle of Buckingham in the 1140s is unknown. But note that *Regesta* iii, no. 487 implies that Buckingham, Bedford, Leighton Buzzard and Aylesbury were all answering to the king's officers in 1146. *GS*, 184 indeed mentions the surrender of Bedford to the king early in 1146.
51 For the Gloucester garrisons in Dorset, see the slightly misleading list in *Annales de Wintonia*, 51 (which purportedly deals with 1138, but in fact reflects later military circumstances).
52 The king's position in Wiltshire was weakened when the king's earl in the county, Hervey de Léon, was blockaded in Devizes by his *comprovinciales* (who can be guessed to have been led by the Salisbury family) and driven out probably after the battle of Lincoln, *GS*, 108, 116. W(alter) of Salisbury was an adherent of the empress and acting as her joint justice in Wiltshire with John Marshal before the battle of Winchester, in which William, his son, was captured by Earl Gilbert of Hertford, *HN*, 67; *Regesta* iii, no. 791 (the editors identify *W. de Salesb'* as 'William', but were that the case Salisbury would have been lost to the Angevins when he was captured in September. 'W.' is more likely to be Walter, sheriff for Stephen in 1140, *Regesta* iii, no. 684). For the castle at Downton, fortified around 1138 by Bishop Henry, see *Annales de Wintonia*, 51.

But Stephen's campaign was not just a matter of councils of war and coloured lines across maps. Neutralism had long been a problem for both sides. We have seen how extravagant were the inducements that the empress had to offer the eastern earls in order to stir them to stay on her side through the summer of 1141. There were more signs of trouble in the symptoms of military exhaustion in the campaigns of 1142. Earl Robert of Gloucester had found it difficult to generate sufficient enthusiasm to move to the empress's relief at Oxford. But William of Malmesbury also tells us that there was a general idea that some members of the king's army in the town had deliberately allowed the empress's escape, by relaxing the pickets around Oxford castle. We will come back to these symptoms, which herald the onset of the exhaustion and lethargy which eventually undermines any civil war, when both sides come to realise that, ultimately, they are all losers.

The king moved south in force probably some time after Easter (4 April 1143). He began by a ferocious assault on the Gloucester fortress of Wareham, which was the southern flank of the Angevin party. But he found that Earl Robert had not neglected to strengthen and reinforce the castle, and his attack failed. After laying waste the surrounding country, the king moved north to muster a large army at the nunnery of Wilton, just west of Salisbury, which was fortified as a base of operations and thus (with Downton) cut the approaches to the city. In co-operation with his brother, Bishop Henry, the king's intention was apparently to contain and eventually reduce the garrison of the castle of Old Sarum and humiliate its castellan, Walter, son of Edward of Salisbury, who was now the chief Angevin supporter in Wiltshire. Once Salisbury fell, the road would be clear for a vigorous campaign to link up with the surviving royalists in Somerset. Such a reverse would weaken the rebellion to the point where it had been at the beginning, five years before. But this time it was the king's turn to be humiliated. Despite the appearance of many allies at Wilton, including the bishop of Winchester, the king's army was surprised by Earl Robert of Gloucester's forces. As Gervase of Canterbury tells the story, the earl made a surprise attack as the sun was setting on 1 July 1143 and the king's household was settling down for the night. The king and his brother were able to slip away under cover of darkness, but his army was dispersed and his baggage lost. His close friend and steward, William Martel, was captured as he covered the king's retreat from the burning monastery.[53]

As with the empress's defeat at Oxford, the king's humiliation at Wilton had deeper consequences than the occasion itself would appear to have merited. The *Gesta Stephani* dates from this battle the complete collapse of the royalist cause in the southwest. For its Bath-based author, Wilton marked the point where the earl of Gloucester finally established his dominion from the Severn estuary to the English Channel. Henry de Tracy chose this time to end his isolated campaign in Somerset 'until the king was stronger in those

53 *GS*, 144–8; GC i, 125–6; *Annales de Waverleia*, 229.

regions'. The king surrendered Sherborne – and any remaining influence in Dorset – in order to gain the release of Martel. Dominance in Dorset passed to Stephen de Mandeville, lord of the honour of Erlestoke in Wiltshire (and brother of Geoffrey de Mandeville, lord of Marshwood in Dorset). He was a friend and lieutenant of Baldwin de Redvers, earl of Devon and friendly also with Robert of Gloucester.[54] The earl of Gloucester now even had some hope of penetrating Hampshire, because William de Pont de l'Arche, the leader of the men of Winchester, fell out with the bishop and fortified his castle of Portchester. Earl Robert sent the Flemish captain, Robert fitz Hildebrand, to join with William and force a new salient to outflank the king in the south. Fortunately for the king, William and the Fleming soon fell out. Robert fitz Hildebrand seized the castle and offered an alliance with the royalists. But even after this relief, Stephen's influence now stopped west of the Test valley, and Winchester was the king's frontier fortress. To the west of Winchester was a realm which had largely come under the effective rule of the earl of Gloucester, a realm whose peace was his sole concern, and King Stephen would not trespass there again until the very end of the reign.[55]

Stephen crowned a disastrous year by a very serious political error. He chose September 1143 to move against Geoffrey de Mandeville, earl of Essex. Precisely why he should do so at that time is very difficult to say. William of Newburgh, sixty years after the event, suggested – implausibly – that it was because the earl had detained the king's daughter-in-law, Constance of France, in the Tower when the queen withdrew from London in 1141, and had concealed his anger for two years until it was safe to act.[56] A more obvious possibility is the destabilising effect on the royal court of the power and influence Earl Geoffrey accumulated in London, Middlesex, Hertford and Essex during 1141. As a monopoliser of royal patronage, Earl Geoffrey was now in the same relationship to the king as Waleran of Meulan had been before 1141. It may simply be that Geoffrey was a natural focus for suspicion and envy at court, and the coup against him was as inevitable as the falling-out between Waleran of Meulan and Robert of Gloucester had been in 1138, or the conspiracy by Waleran and his cronies against Roger of Salisbury the next year. Contemporaries speculated that Earl Geoffrey had been conspiring against

54 Stephen de Mandeville's activities in the shire in 1144 are noted by GS, 168–70. He was not related to the earl of Essex in any way. He had formerly shared Baldwin de Redvers' exile and fought with him in the Cotentin (where he had considerable estates) in the late 1130s, OV vi, 510. See for his lands, R. Bearman, 'Baldwin de Redvers: some aspects of a baronial career in the reign of Stephen', ANS xviii, ed. C. Harper-Bill (Woodbridge, 1996), 34–5. He attested as first of Earl Baldwin's lay tenants in a charter at Exeter in 1143 × 44, and again in 1146, *Charters of the Redvers Family*, ed. Bearman, 74–5, 76–7. He also witnessed *ex parte* Earl Robert of Gloucester in 1146 at Devizes, *Regesta* iii, no. 58. In 1147 he went on the Second Crusade with Earl Baldwin, never to return, for which see, *Wulfric of Haselbury*, ed. Bell, 119.
55 GS, 148–52.
56 WN i, 44–5. R.H.C. Davis, *King Stephen* (3rd edn., London, 1990), 58, 77, gives this story more credence than it deserves. If it explains anything, it is that people of the time found the arrest quite unaccountable.

Stephen in the same way that they speculated as to whether Bishop Roger of Salisbury had been involved in treachery before his arrest.[57]

The author of the *Gesta* writes of Geoffrey de Mandeville in very warm terms, praising his judgement and military abilities. As we have seen, a long-term historical debate has established that his behaviour between 1135 and 1143 was loyal and serviceable to the king, rather than contingent and acquisitive, which agrees with what the *Gesta* has to say. There was his brief defection to the Angevin party in the summer of 1141, when he went over with the earls of Pembroke and Oxford, but he returned rapidly to his allegiance as soon as he realised the incompetence of the empress. But the *Gesta*'s author significantly adds that 'everywhere in the kingdom he took the king's place and in all transactions was listened to more eagerly than the king and received more obedience when he gave orders'. From this observation he goes on to talk of the enmity Geoffrey inspired in the king's intimates and the common gossip that he was plotting to establish the empress on the throne. But common gossip was all that these suspicions were, fanned, no doubt, by envy. Geoffrey seems to have been quite oblivious to these suspicions, or at least behaved as if he were, until he was confronted with the accusations when he came unescorted into the king's presence at St Albans soon after Michaelmas (29 September) 1143. His first reaction was apparently incredulous amusement, which soon changed to anger when he was seized at the door of the king's hall as he was leaving.[58]

The pattern set by the arrest of Roger of Salisbury was repeated. Geoffrey was taken under confinement to London, where a threat was made to hang him at the gates of the Tower unless it surrendered to the king. Geoffrey had little choice, and his ancestral castles of Pleshey and Saffron Walden in Essex were also duly instructed to surrender to royal officers. It seems that King Stephen used Geoffey de Mandeville's local rival, Earl William of Arundel, to seize his Middlesex estates and his *curialis*, Turgis d'Avranches, to seize some of Mandeville's Essex lands.[59] If Stephen, by then releasing Geoffrey, thought that the affair was at an end, he was deluding himself. Perhaps Stephen was unimaginative enough to believe that a magnate without castles was powerless to hurt him. The king had also not calculated on the damage that his prestige had suffered after the fiasco of Wilton and the shallowness of his support in his own kingdom. So Geoffrey de Mandeville put himself at the head of those inclined to dispute Stephen's control in East Anglia, and gathered

---

57 HH, 742 believed that Stephen had to arrest Geoffrey because Geoffrey was conspiring against him, and force of circumstances excused the breach of due legal process.

58 GS, 160, see also the details of the arrest preserved in *Historia fundationis Coenobii sancti Jacobi apostoli de Waldena*, in *Monasticon* iv, 142. The date for the St Albans council '*post festum sancti Michaelis*' is given by the London chronicle source, *De Antiquis Legibus Liber*, ed. T. Stapleton (Camden Soc., old ser., 34, 1846), 197.

59 GS, 162. Ibid., 176 tells us that Stephen's *curialis*, Turgis of Avranches, was awarded the keeping of Saffron Walden. *Waltham Chronicle*, 78, describes William of Arundel's seizure of Geoffrey's estates near Waltham.

a formidable force. He did not, however, declare for the empress. All sources suggest that he was doing nothing more than proving to Stephen the mistake he had made in attacking him. Geoffrey was making an incontrovertible argument that the prudent course for the king would be to restore his castles.

Earl Geoffrey chose to fight his campaign in the wet wilderness of the great fens between Huntingdon, Peterborough, Wisbech and Cambridge, well to the north of his Essex estates. He could work here in alliance with another of Stephen's former close allies, Earl Hugh Bigod, who had not returned to Stephen's court after he had abandoned the empress in the summer of 1141. But, as Round pointed out, he could have relied on a whole network of support from his numerous relatives, his illegitimate eldest son, Arnulf, who acted as his stipendiary commander, and his brother-in-law, William de Saye, for certain, and perhaps also the Clares and the Veres. But Geoffrey was well able to carry on campaigns to the south too, retaliating against Earl William of Arundel at Waltham for his trespasses against the Mandeville estates in north Middlesex.[60] Geoffrey's forces were able to break their way into the king's town of Cambridge, and helped themselves undisturbed to its riches, even pillaging the parish churches. He took advantage of those great East Anglian monasteries that he could reach. The fenland monasteries of Ramsey and Ely were occupied and looted. Ramsey apparently was seized in December 1143 and in view of the date of the papal instruction from Rome to excommunicate Geoffrey for seizing Ely and the neighbouring castle of Aldreth (late May 1144), Ely and Fordham must have been seized about the same time, as the earl skilfully created a whole internal network of fortified posts at significant dry spots, such as Benwick at the crossing of the Nene north of Ramsey abbey.

The monasteries were fortified to fill the place of Earl Geoffrey's lost castles. For instance, Ramsey abbey's outer gate became the keep of a makeshift castle within its precinct. Geoffrey was duly excommunicated by the Church. Taking no account of this, he made the Cambridgeshire fenland his own private domain, and ruled over it – or rather plundered and wasted it – for as long as nine months. The Ramsey chronicle talks of his distributing the abbey demesne estates to his knights in place of wages. The Waltham chronicle mentions his use of Flemish mercenaries in his Essex chevauchée.[61] An attempt by the king to contain Geoffrey's activities in the midwinter season of 1143–44 was easily evaded, and all that Stephen was able to do was to place temporary garrisons around the fen country to try to control Geoffrey's movements. But in the end, it was fate rather than the king's calculations that ended Geoffrey's year-long career as a rebel. Stephen had placed a powerful fort at Burwell to blockade another of Geoffrey's bases at Fordham abbey, on the southeastern edge of the Cambridgeshire fen country near Newmarket. Burwell was an ambitious structure with massive embankments and the excavated remains

60 *Waltham Chronicle*, 78–80.
61 *Waltham Chronicle*, 80.

show the beginnings at least of a large stone tower-keep.[62] It therefore attracted Earl Geoffrey's attention. While commanding a siege of the unfinished castle, probably at the end of August 1144, Geoffrey de Mandeville received a head wound from a stray arrow after he had taken off his helmet in the heat of the day. It became infected and a month later, on 26 September 1144, he died, while around him his clerks were frantically drawing up charters to make effective restitution for the sins he had confessed on his deathbed.[63] His excommunicate body was received by the London Templars, but they did not dare give it burial until Pope Alexander III allowed him posthumous absolution twenty years later, in 1163![64]

The rebellion of Geoffrey de Mandeville makes a colourful and compelling story, which probably explains why its wider significance is sometimes overlooked. There is little hint at all that Earl Geoffrey attempted to work in the empress's interests during his rebellion in 1143–44, despite the suspicions of the chroniclers that he had been contemplating defection in September. The Ramsey chronicler alone says that he favoured the empress's interests, but implies that Geoffrey's chief aim was rather to thwart the king, and indeed it was the king's friends and interests he particularly targeted and plundered. But, as we have seen several times already, to attack the king was not necessarily to be working for the empress. Since the very beginning of the reign, magnates like Robert of Bampton and Baldwin de Redvers had been taking arms to protest at their own complaints, not at the treatment of the empress. Geoffrey de Mandeville was acting no differently from his predecessors in dissidence.

The sources of the time reflect this complexity of motivation. The Waltham chronicler, who knew Geoffrey personally, writes only good things about him, both as a man and as a Christian. Although Geoffrey did burn the town of Waltham, he was, it seems, distressed that the property of the church (which he had patronised) was damaged in the attack.[65] For all that Ramsey abbey had every reason to demonise and despise Earl Geoffrey, its chronicle does not blacken him in everything. In fact it captures something of the man's quandary. The chronicler hints at the earl's embarrassment that he was forced to live like a common robber. The dispossessed former abbot, Walter, sought him out in late spring 1144, on his return from Rome. As a result of his interview with the earl, Abbot Walter was allowed to resume the headship of his community, but Geoffrey and his men would not leave the part of the precinct which they had fortified. So the abbot valiantly attempted in person to burn down their encampment around the precinct gatehouse with a flaming

---

62 J. Bradbury, *Stephen and Matilda* (Stroud, 1996), 115–16.
63 *Waltham Chronicle*, 80 mentions that he languished forty days after his wound at Burwell.
64 *GS*, 164–6; GC i, 128–9; HH, 744–6; *Liber Eliensis*, 328–9; *Chronicon abbatiae Ramesiensis*, ed. W. Dunn Macray (Rolls Series, 1886), 327–34. The best account of Geoffrey's fenland rebellion is still to be found in Round, *Geoffrey de Mandeville*, 209–26, which admirably reconciles the diverse contemporary and near-contemporary sources. The recent study by Bradbury, *Stephen and Matilda*, 130–2 is valuable as being free of anti-Mandeville prejudice.
65 *Waltham Chronicle*, 78–80.

torch. Earl Geoffrey nevertheless allowed him to come and go in peace (after the fires were put out). He was – it seems – tense and nervous with the abbot in private interviews; willing to offer dates to withdraw from Ramsey on more than one occasion. Yet he could not fulfil his promises of course, for he was as trapped by circumstances as were the monks of Ramsey. Still, he remembered his promises as he was confessed on his deathbed, when his clerks took down his instructions to his son and chief captain, Arnulf, to quit the abbey as partial restitution for his sins.[66]

This is, perhaps, the key point to make about the civil war in its fifth year. By now everybody was trapped into a cycle of distrust and violence, whether they liked it or not. Geoffrey de Mandeville, apparently, did not like it. This was hardly surprising, since he had devoted the many years of his political life before his forced rebellion to public service. He was not fighting for the empress in 1143, but for his own survival. The empress's stock was now so low that magnates like Geoffrey de Mandeville and Hugh Bigod might well defy the king by 1144 without much reference to her cause. There was not much material help to be expected from the empress if the battle was to be fought in East Anglia in any case. So by 1144 we have reached the point when the partisan impetus which was behind the civil war was grinding to a halt. The empress Mathilda was discredited and her party could no longer be motivated on her behalf. The king's prestige also had been damaged, and the Wilton campaign must have convinced everyone that he was now unable to resolve the military situation in his favour. The war had set hard into stalemate. Neutralism and self-preservation had developed into the guiding principles of the English magnates.

---

66 *Chronicon abbatiae Ramesiensis*, 332, which states that Arnulf did reluctantly leave. HH, 746 says, however, that Arnulf did not abandon Ramsey immediately, and only gave it up after his capture by the king's men. As we have seen, the Ramsey precinct was only partially fortified, and Arnulf might have claimed to have fulfilled his instructions if he had moved his men from the claustral buildings while still garrisoning the gatehouse-keep. Arnulf and his younger legitimate brother, Geoffrey (III) de Mandeville found refuge at least temporarily in Wiltshire, where the empress found Arnulf land to support himself and recognised the younger Geoffrey as earl of Essex, see *Regesta* iii, no. 43 and comments in Chibnall, *Matilda*, 125. Arnulf later went abroad, presumably joining the Second Crusade.

CHAPTER 12

The End of the Civil War

The last disaster for the empress in 1143 was the untimely death of Miles, earl of Hereford. One of his household knights accidentally pierced him in the chest with an arrow while attempting to hit a deer while out hunting on Christmas Eve.[1] In some ways, this death is as significant as the rebellion of Geoffrey de Mandeville – not so much because it removed a trusted and close adviser from the empress's side (although that was serious enough) but because it brought forward a new and forbidding political talent, Miles's son, Earl Roger. Earl Roger was a pragmatic young man, who had been closely engaged in the war alongside his father. But he had apparently developed during this period an insouciant attitude to the claims of the party which his father had supported in a more wholehearted way. Earl Roger's actions from 1144 onwards reveal a man who had assessed the situation of the civil war as being incapable of resolution. His strategy was therefore to seek to avoid battle and maintain his property and influence in any way that he could. It was the likes of Earl Roger who were the principals in negotiating what R.H.C. Davis memorably called the 'magnates' peace'.

EARL ROBERT AND THE FIGHT FOR GLOUCESTER, 1144–47

While Earl Robert of Gloucester was still active, there was little chance of the war simply petering out in non-aggression pacts. Even so, by 1144 the earl and the empress found their ability to engage the king had been sadly undermined. They did not have the strength to assault a major fortress like Winchester, and even their local allies in the West Country could not be relied on. A good illustration of this is the miniature war that began in Wiltshire in 1144 between two Angevin supporters, John Marshal and Patrick of Salisbury. John Marshal had been identified with the empress's cause since 1140, although his behaviour before then had been less committed. Nonetheless, he had proved himself something of a hero in the disastrous retreat from

---

1 *GS*, 160; GC i, 126; JH, 315.

Winchester in 1141, and had served the cause as well as himself by converting the north Wiltshire downs into an Angevin stronghold. He had a triangle of castles at Marlborough, Ludgershall and Hamstead Marshall which closed off the direct approach to Bristol from the royalist centres in Berkshire. John Marshal had converted the area into a miniature principality, employing mercenary knights and paying them by levying payments on surrounding abbeys and other churches (and also, one assumes, surrounding landowners who needed his protection). Excommunication made not the slightest difference to him. Clergy were summoned to his courts 'as though he had the power of a bishop'. In this way he served his own profit and prestige simultaneously.[2]

John Marshal was doing in small scale in the Kennet valley no more than greater men did with whole shires or regions, men like Robert of Gloucester in the West Country and Geoffrey de Mandeville in the fenlands. But the morality of such private enterprise was very much relative, and the bigger perpetrators of the culture of plundering could very well turn on the lesser practitioners as disturbers of the peace. This is what happened to John Marshal. The chief magnates of Wiltshire were the descendants of Edward of Salisbury, the Domesday sheriff, an Englishman who had integrated by marriage into the Norman aristocracy.[3] The Salisbury family lands dominated the south of the shire, and for long stretches of time Edward's son, Walter, was sheriff and local justice of Wiltshire in the reigns of Rufus and Henry I. Humphrey de Bohun, a royal constable, was introduced into Wiltshire and settled at the castle of Trowbridge as part of a marriage alliance with the Salisbury family. Bishop Roger of Salisbury would have eclipsed Walter within Wiltshire in Henry I's reign, and indeed during his episcopate it was the treasurer, William de Pont de l'Arche, who held the shrievalty. But by 1139 Walter must have obtained control of Salisbury castle as a result of the bishop's fall. It has been suggested above that Walter and John Marshal acted together when the king miscalculated and imposed an earl on the shire in 1140 with a brief to rule it from Devizes. Both men were justices in the shire for the empress in 1141, and both remained in her party after Winchester.

In 1144, the aged Walter of Salisbury's heir was his younger surviving son, Patrick (the elder, William, died the previous year). It was almost certainly in 1144 that the empress decided to strengthen her party after the expulsion of the king from Wiltshire by creating Patrick earl of Wiltshire.[4] Earl Patrick's

---

2 D. Crouch, *William Marshal: Court, Career and Chivalry in the Angevin Empire*, 1–3.

3 For Edward's possible English, or mixed, descent, see J.A. Green, *The Aristocracy of Norman England* (Cambridge, 1997), 61–2.

4 For the date of the creation of the earldom, R.H.C. Davis, *King Stephen* (3rd edn., London, 1990), 137, which establishes that he was earl before 1147. It can be assumed that he would not have been created earl while his elder brother, William, was still alive and castellan of Salisbury. William died after a severe illness in 1143, *GS*, 148. The (admittedly late) evidence of the *History of William Marshal* is that Patrick was already earl when he fell out with John Marshal in 1144–45. S. Painter, *William Marshal* (Baltimore, 1933), 12 (followed by M. Chibnall, *The Empress Matilda* (Oxford, 1991), 126) speculates that John Marshal brought Earl Patrick into the empress's camp, but the indications are that the Salisbury family had abandoned Stephen since 1140 and never returned to his party thereafter.

response was only partly what his mistress (residing in Wiltshire at Devizes) would have wanted. John Marshal, colourfully described as 'the offspring of hell and root of all evil', was remarked upon by the author of the *Gesta* as being very active in 1144 in extending his grip on Wiltshire.[5] The new earl responded by opening up a vigorous campaign against his supposed colleague, John Marshal. The only justification could have been to bring John to heel or destroy him as an independent castellan. The memoir of John Marshal's son records that Patrick became 'too hot a neighbour' and that John was forced to make peace. There is some evidence that a treaty of sorts was reached between Earl Patrick and John, with the possible mediation of Earl Robert of Gloucester. John divorced his wife of many years, the mother of his two sons, and married Earl Patrick's sister, Sibyl, early in 1145.[6] John's ex-wife, Adelina, was remarried to a certain Stephen Gay, a widower who was the earl of Gloucester's uncle, the brother of his mother. It is from this that we can suggest the earl's likely involvement in settling the business.[7] The Marshal's remarriage at least brought some consolation. As part of the settlement, he acquired through his wife the Salisbury family manor of Mildenhall, in Wiltshire, which neighboured the Marshal castle of Marlborough.[8] It had perhaps already fallen into Marshal hands: it may even have been the original cause of the difficulties between the two families.

The earl of Gloucester must have found the Wiltshire problem yet another major burden to bear. It revealed how fragile was the superstructure of his party, and how shallow the foundations. The earl's reach was very limited in his last years in command of the empress's party. Most of the determined action of those years took place along the Cotswolds and in the upper Thames valley; the only places where the earl himself could exert direct military control. The objective of the earl's party was Oxford and that of the king's party

5 *GS*, 168. A letter of Gilbert Foliot to the bishop of Salisbury dated 1144 × 45 reveals that John Marshal (called 'John of Marlborough') was pillaging Wiltshire outside any control from Earl Patrick at that time, *LCGF*, 71–2.
6 This can be ascertained by the fact that her eldest son by this marriage, John Marshal (II), came of age in 1166, and her second son, William, in 1167. Since the age of majority in both cases would seem to have been twenty-one, then the marriage must have occurred around the beginning of 1145, see Crouch, *William Marshal*, 2.
7 For the remarriage see *Regesta* ii, no. 339. The Gai or Gait family held lands in Kirtlington hundred, north of Oxford, where Robert Gay (on the grounds of chronology, probably the elder brother of Stephen Gay) founded a Cistercian abbey at Oddington around 1137 (soon afterwards transferred to Thame), *The Thame Cartulary*, ed. H.E. Salter (Oxford Record Society, 25, 1947), 2, 4–5 '. . . *assensu et consensu comitis Gloecestrie*'. A charter of Stephen Gay's son, Philip, reveals that Stephen had held the manor of Northbrook, Oxfordshire, also in Kirtlington hundred, St John's College, Oxford, muns., XXI (1). The young Philip Gay was a member of the earl of Gloucester's military household at Bristol in 1138 and JW iii, 248–50 describes him as '. . . *quendam comitis cognatum Philippum Gai nuncupatum*'. If *cognatus* signifies that he was the earl's first cousin, then Stephen and Robert Gay were brothers of Earl Robert's mother, Henry I's mistress. The proximity of the Gay family's lands to Henry I's favoured residence of Woodstock explains the liaison between the king and one of its women. See on this, D. Crouch, 'Robert of Gloucester's mother and sexual politics in Norman Oxfordshire', *Historical Research*, lxxii (1999), 323–33.
8 N. Stacy, 'Henry of Blois and the lordship of Glastonbury', *EHR*, 114 (1999), 32–3.

was Gloucester. The principal military theatre of the next few years was on the routes between these two towns, some fifty miles apart. In 1144 Earl Robert sent William Peverel of Dover, his longtime adherent, to fortify a new castle at Cricklade on the Thames. It was a site chosen to interrupt communications with Malmesbury, which was still held by a royalist garrison. At the same time the earl raised siege works all around the town to blockade and reduce it. From Cricklade, William Peverel was able to harass the royalist troops in Oxfordshire and continue to keep a presence in the upper Thames valley, lost when the king swept aside the temporary forts at Bampton and Radcot in 1142.[9]

Earl Robert's aggression dragged the king into a narrow cockpit. Stephen led a relief column in force to Malmesbury, resupplying it and placing Walter de Pinkney as a commander. He took the opportunity to harry the garrisons of Earl Robert's siege works. So close did he come to taking the works at Tetbury, that Earl Robert and the new Earl Roger of Hereford were drawn into assembling the biggest force they could, drawing on their Welsh allies and the town militia of Bristol. They threatened to engage the king's army directly. At this, the royalist barons with the king urged him to break off the action immediately: the risks involved in a battle, they said, were too great. Whether they were right or wrong, their cautious attitude in the face of battle is significant. Pressure to avoid open battle from the magnates with armies of either party was to be a common occurrence from now on until the end of the reign. Stephen went off instead to retaliate for the affront of Cricklade by assaulting and taking Earl Roger of Hereford's castle of Winchcombe. This gave him the compensation of closing off a route into Oxfordshire across the Cotswolds and opening the possibility of a counterstrike at the earl of Hereford's chief fortress of Gloucester.[10]

The upper Thames campaign became an annual event for the next few years. In view of what was at stake for the Angevin party, this is hardly surprising. In 1145, Earl Robert pressed Malmesbury castle hard. In the course of the campaign, William Peverel was able to trap and imprison in Devizes the king's commander at Malmesbury, Walter de Pinkney. But even so, the castle would not surrender despite everything the empress could do in person to threaten and cajole Walter into ordering its garrison to open its gates. During the course of the year, a new governor was appointed to maintain and extend the Angevin aggression down the Thames to Oxford. Philip, a younger legitimate son of Earl Robert of Gloucester, was given command of both Cirencester and Cricklade by his aunt, the empress. Like Patrick of Salisbury, the young Philip (who could only have been barely twenty-one years of age) seems to have been awarded the title of earl (possibly of Oxford) to further his campaign and raise the young man's status. Philip's enthusiasm for the campaign had a devastating effect on the region, and its savagery was remembered

9 *GS*, 170.
10 *GS*, 172–4.

several years later by a Tewkesbury writer as an event traumatic enough to mark out the year 1145 from others.[11] Philip advanced his control downriver and built a new castle at Faringdon, on the hills above the site of the earlier Angevin castle of Radcot. From here Philip was able seriously to threaten the garrison of Oxford, causing William de Chesney to appeal for the king's help once again.[12]

Stephen arrived once more in Oxfordshire in the summer of 1145, and led his army to the siege of Faringdon. He had made a great effort to raise as impressive a force as possible: perhaps he remembered his magnates' refusal to fight the previous year. A large force of Londoners even appeared to add their support. The king prosecuted the siege heedless of casualties, and made daily assaults on the ramparts, despite the heavy cost. In the end, the commanders of the castle were so shaken by the ferocity of the assault that they secretly asked for terms, without even telling their men. The castle surrendered, and in doing so dealt a deep blow to the credibility of the earl of Gloucester and his son. Both the author of the *Gesta* and Henry of Huntingdon believed that the surrender of Faringdon was a significant achievement for the king. It swung the pendulum of prestige back towards Stephen and encouraged neutralism amongst the lesser magnates and knights of the region. It also gave the king reason to hope that he could actually seize the prize of Gloucester from Earl Roger of Hereford.[13]

An astonishing defector to the king at the end of 1145 was the defeated Philip, the son of Robert of Gloucester. He formally exchanged hostages with Stephen and received in return, as well he might, considerable gifts both in money and lands. The king apparently also extended Philip's power in the region by adding further castles (perhaps Malmesbury and Winchcombe) to create a southern Cotswold commandery for him. This alone should tell us something about the seriousness with which contemporaries regarded Earl Robert's crumbling campaign in the Thames valley. The earl had staked his prestige and all of his limited resources on the result of this campaign, and the end of 1146 revealed that he had lost. His son's change of side meant that the Angevin outposts of Cricklade and Cirencester, as well as Faringdon, had become a royalist enclave, and that the pressure on Malmesbury and Oxford was lifted. It also opened Brian fitz Count and Wallingford castle to a new phase of isolation and an even harsher siege, as the king's forces (including Ranulf of Chester) closed around it and trapped the garrison by new and

---

11 Cartulary of Tewkesbury, BL ms Cotton Cleopatra A vii, fo. 78v, a charter of 1151 × 57 which mentions a seisin dated '. . . *multo tempore antequam Philippus com[es] habuit castellum de Crichelade et de Cirencestre*'. The question of the county of which Philip was made earl is impossible to settle (Wiltshire and Gloucestershire were already titles held by others). I therefore diffidently suggest Oxfordshire, which was the object of his campaigns (Earl Aubrey de Vere of Oxford was then a royalist). However, it is just as likely that Philip was referred to as 'earl' by right of his father's dignity and of his being the grandson of a king, see D. Crouch, *The Image of Aristocracy in Britain, 1000–1300* (London, 1992), 68 and n.
12 *GS*, 176–80.
13 *GS*, 182–4; HH, 746.

ambitious siegeworks at nearby Crowmarsh Giffard, across the Thames. Young Philip was anything but diffident in his efforts to support his new party, and was as active against his former friends as he had been against his former enemies. He obtained the castle of Miserden from Robert Musard by laying an ambush outside the gates until Musard simply walked unsuspecting into it. Miserden was in the Cotswolds only six miles from Gloucester, now exposed enough to become the king's objective.[14]

The reaction of Earl Robert and the empress to this disheartening turn of events was to reopen the peace negotiations last attempted during the time in October 1141 when the king and the earl had both been in captivity. A formal safe conduct was issued for the participants. But the severe disruption of the times can be seen in the fact that Earl Reginald of Cornwall, travelling to the meeting of the king and the empress at some unknown location, was waylaid by his nephew, Philip, and held captive until the king got to hear of the outrage and insisted on the earl's release. The face-to-face discussions were, as it happened, fruitless. The author of the *Gesta* simply describes the sides taking up unyielding positions. The king, probably assessing his position at least in regard to Gloucester as a very strong one, would make no concessions as regards his kingship and, one assumes, the prospects of his heir, Eustace. The empress, for her part, seems to have been keen to establish that the royal title was rightly hers, something that Stephen would not concede. The discussions therefore broke down.[15]

But it was very significant that the sides did go so far as to talk in 1146. The author of the *Gesta* describes complete confusion and dislocation in Gloucestershire, where the earls of Gloucester and Hereford were now wholly on the defensive. Philip, the earl of Gloucester's son, was pressing hard on the Vale of the Severn. Flemish mercenaries, like the Caudry brothers, were preying ruthlessly on the lands of the abbey of Gloucester and on their neighbours. The earl of Hereford himself seems to have decided that the end was in sight for his control of Gloucester if he did not move to protect himself in whatever way he could. Throwing any morality of partisanship aside, he decided that the only way to preserve himself was to do what everyone else was doing. The earl therefore set his brother, Walter, lord of Abergavenny, to arrest their own ally and relative, Roger of Berkeley, Gloucestershire's most significant magnate.[16] Roger of Berkeley held the important castles of Dursley and

---

14 HH, 748; *GS*, 184–6; GC i, 129–30. Philip's military activities around Miserden (only six miles southeast of Gloucester) and Berkeley, almost on the Severn estuary, would indicate that the king had made over command of the royal garrisons in Malmesbury and Winchcombe to him.

15 *GS*, 186.

16 For evidence of Walter of Hereford's inheritance in 1143 of the fees his father had acquired from Brian fitz Count, see *Regesta* iii, no. 314 (confirming to him the lordship of Grosmont, *c*.1153) and PRO C56/20 (Confirmation Roll of 4 Hen. VII), m. 29 (confirming a grant to Llanthony Secunda Brian fitz Count had made in the lordship of Abergavenny). He also enjoyed possession of Alvington, Gloucs, in his brother's lifetime, D. Walker, 'Charters of the earldom of Hereford, 1095–1210', in *Camden Miscellany*, xxii (1964), 41–2.

Berkeley itself, which between them controlled the roads between Gloucester and Malmesbury and Gloucester and Bristol. Roger was taken, stripped and chained, and hung in front of one of his castle gates until the garrison surrendered. He was then placed in prison.[17] Nothing better demonstrates the paralysis afflicting the Angevin party in 1146 than this pragmatic and sordid incident. Earl Roger of Hereford signalled to everyone that while the emergency continued his first priority was his own interest. The empress would have of him only what he chose to give.

The year 1147 saw no resolution of the continuing military mess in the vicinity of Gloucester. The early part of the year may have brought some relief for the region as Philip, the earl's son, and a number of greater and lesser magnates of both parties, responded to the enthusiasm of the moment for a new crusade in Palestine. Louis VII held a great international gathering of princes and magnates to hear the crusade preached at Étampes on 16 February 1147. Many of the participants adjourned and reassembled at Vézelay on 13 April to assume the cross, and then to move on to Paris for the Easter court (20 April) where the pope joined the great religious festivities. King Louis left Paris for the final muster at Worms, on the Rhine, on 15 June 1147.[18] It is likely that Philip of Gloucester quit England to join a number of other Anglo-Norman magnates assembled in the Île de France well before April.[19] Nor was he alone of his party in joining the large Anglo-Norman contingent, which included both royalist and Angevin supporters. Baldwin de Redvers, earl of Devon, with his brother-in-arms, Stephen de Mandeville, lord of Erlestoke, and Arnulf de Mandeville, the son of the late Geoffrey de Mandeville, also left the country and crossed to France. They joined a contingent headed by the Angevin supporters, Waleran, count of Meulan and Bishop Arnulf of Lisieux, but also including King Stephen's friend and loyalist, William (III) earl of Warenne.

Although Philip, the earl's son, had left England, never to return, other troubles soon descended on Gloucestershire. Henry fitz Empress, fourteen years of age in March 1147, arrived in England (perhaps in or just after February) without permission and having duped a small band of mercenaries into joining his expedition, failing to tell them he had no money to pay them. What the boy thought he was doing is hard to say, but he must have heard that his mother's cause was failing fast, and this was his attempt to do something about it in person. He had spent a considerable time with his mother and his uncle in England after being fostered into Earl Robert's household in autumn 1142. Opinions differ as to when his father had summoned him back across the Channel. Gervase of Canterbury says that the young Henry had spent four years in England (that is, till the end of 1146) but then contradicted

17 *GS*, 190.
18 OD, 12–16; RT, 152.
19 RT, 154 says that Henry fitz Empress returned from England to Normandy at the end of May 1147, and it seems that Henry had not encountered Philip when he attacked his castles in the West Country.

himself by suggesting that Duke Geoffrey had asked for his return once Normandy was conquered and Anjou settled (that is, 1144). The latter suggestion is more likely, as we know that he was in England with his mother at Devizes at the beginning of the year, but with his father at Angers in March 1144, where he subscribed a diploma to the abbey of Tournus.[20]

Henry's expedition had its comical aspects. His small mercenary force was not able to match the expectations that had momentarily elevated the spirits of his party. The knights he brought performed poorly – as they well might since they had not been paid when they were hired, but were fighting in anticipation of reward. Henry led them against Cricklade and the nearby fort of Purton, in Wiltshire; now apparently without Philip as castellan. His little force ran away when it met determined opposition, and many of his soldiers simply abandoned the adolescent captain. Henry was left severely embarrassed both for money and by his men. He was able to secure and maintain himself in some castles, although we do not know which ones, and the men to whom he had entrusted them needed money. He had interviews with his uncle and his mother, but neither of them would bail him out of his difficulty. In the end, we are told by the author of the *Gesta* that he applied to King Stephen for help, and the king sent him money sufficient to pay off his men and take himself back home to Normandy. It seems a crazy story, but Stephen did things even more generous than that, so we cannot discount it. Henry obligingly returned across the Channel; which may have been the king's chief hope in paying him off. We find Henry receiving a rapturous reception from the monastic community at Bec-Hellouin on 29 May 1147, soon after his landing.[21]

The earl of Gloucester prepared himself for a further summer campaign in 1147, after this opéra-bouffe distraction, which did not seem to have amused him at all. He shifted his attention to Hampshire, for the first time in four years. His party maintained a castle which represented a toehold in the north of the shire at a place the author of the *Gesta* called *Lidelea*, which has been identified with a place name *Beddelie*, or Barley Pound Castle, within the cathedral-priory of Winchester's manor of Crondall, in Hampshire, near Farnham.[22] It had been taken from the bishop of Winchester some time before by an associate of Brian fitz Count, and the bishop had tried to contain the damage by having his military men raise siege castles in the neighbourhood (two have been identified at Bentley and Powderham close by). The earl's intention was to muster as formidable a force as he could and relieve *Beddelie*. Unfortunately for his plan, the bishop warned the king and Stephen's arrival with a much larger force drove the earl away in something resembling a rout.

20 GC i, 131, For a discussion see A.L. Poole, 'Henry Plantagenet's early visits to England', *EHR*, 47 (1932), 447–51, esp. p. 450, and comments in Chibnall, *Matilda*, 144–5.
21 *GS*, 204–6; RT, 154. *Regesta* iii, no. 43 reveals the young Henry at Devizes with his mother and his uncles Earl Robert and Robert of Okehampton at some time in the course of his campaign.
22 P.A. Stamper, *Excavations of a mid twelfth-century siege castle at Bentley, Hampshire* (1979).

Alas, this undistinguished sally was the last campaign of the great warrior-earl. Although he retired to Bristol and began reassembling an army to renew the campaign, in the autumn he became ill and feverish. On 31 October he died and he was buried in the priory church of St James, which he had founded in more tranquil days as a cell of Tewkesbury abbey in Bristol in 1129 in the castle barton (or demesne park).[23]

It would not be too far short of the truth to suggest that the death of Earl Robert of Gloucester marked the effective end of the civil war. It is true that I have argued that the campaign of 1144 exhausted the Angevin party and prevented any further major initiatives. Earl Robert was still, however, the great man who provided the soul and energy for the movement. He fought on till the end, even though his reach was limited by 1147. The way in which the author of the *Gesta* insinuated that the earl had died unconfessed and without making reparation for his sins tells us quite how much the royalists feared him: they did not like to think of a man making a good end who had done so much to damage the king. A good end was the property of a good man. After he was gone, the empress's party was unable to do more than attempt to maintain itself. There was to be no co-ordinated strategy against the king in future, because there was no longer a leader with the personal force of will to energise and dominate the rest. It was not until 1153, when Henry fitz Empress reappeared in England as duke of Normandy and Aquitaine, that the war once more was taken forward by a directing will.

Earl Robert had his faults. He was obsessive in his distaste for Stephen, which hampered any possible diplomatic solution to the civil war. His strategy for contesting the war was really no more than mass-dispossession of those he disagreed with who were within his military reach. Yet he was also a man who earned the respect of those ambitious and egotistical noblemen who were his fellow barons. He was one of the few magnates who was able effortlessly to command others. He was brave, intelligent and dogged, and the full measure of his ability is that he was irreplaceable as a leader. History has been kind to him. He commissioned William of Malmesbury, one of the most accomplished writers of his day, as his apologist. Malmesbury's talented pen portrayed Robert of Gloucester as a noble and disinterested warrior, fully and selflessly committed to his half-sister's cause. It is only within the past generation that some shade has been added to his glowing portrait. Robert's posthumous reputation also benefited from the fact that his side did ultimately win the war, and the victorious Angevin dynasty rewarded his memory by promoting him as one of the heroic servants of its cause. William fitz Stephen, Becket's biographer, said that in 1170 Henry II verbally attacked Earl Robert's son, Bishop Roger of Worcester, by contrasting his behaviour with the paragon of loyalty who was his father.[24] It would be churlish to say that Earl Robert did not deserve some measure of his posthumous reputation, my only

23 *Annales de Margan*, 14, gives the date of death as 31 October. *GS*, 210; *GC* i, 131, give details of the death which are of debatable worth; Gervase dates the death of the earl to 1 November.
24 William fitz Stephen, *Vita sancti Thome*, in *Materials for the History of Thomas Becket* iii, 104–5.

qualification of it would be that, as an Angevin partisan, Earl Robert was more against Stephen than for the empress.[25]

STEPHEN, HIS NEW MEN AND HIS EARLS, 1142–47

We have already seen quite how influential over the king were his intimate court advisers in 1143, in the affair of Earl Geoffrey de Mandeville. This group emerges as the principal influence on his decision-making after his release in November 1141. It has several times been noticed that after 1141 the dominance of the great magnates at his court ended.[26] It was not that occasional magnates did not attend upon him. Earl William d'Aubigné of Arundel, Earl Simon de Senlis of Northampton and (up till 1147) Earl Gilbert of Pembroke were constant companions. But gone after 1143 were the sort of domineering aristocratic advisers who influenced his strategy – there were no more Walerans. There must have been a feeling that such great men were unsafe to rely on, especially after the way that some earls who were once very close to Stephen (like Hugh Bigod, Aubrey de Vere, Gilbert of Pembroke, and Geoffrey de Mandeville) had wavered in the summer of 1141 and crossed over to the empress, however briefly. So Stephen abandoned the strategy of his uncle, which after his fashion he had been consciously following until 1141. He no longer attempted to use his most useful and capable magnates in the business of government, but turned wholly to what for King Henry had always been his second string: his own personal creations, his 'new men'.

The king may occasionally have been very blunt in his message to magnates who were formerly close to him. It has been suggested that when he set up William de Chesney as regional governor of Oxfordshire in 1142, he did so in part by depriving Earl Robert of Leicester. Robert of Leicester was Count Waleran of Meulan's twin and had returned to England after losing his Norman estates. Howard Colvin suggested that Robert had been given the important town and castle of Deddington in Oxfordshire in Henry I's reign, but that in 1142 this was reclaimed and allotted to William de Chesney, who kept it at the king's will till he died.[27] If this were the case, it does explain why it was that after so much sacrifice and commitment, Robert of Leicester was rarely to be found even in the remote neighbourhood of the royal court after 1141. We have also seen the treatment meted out to Earl Geoffrey de Mandeville of Essex in 1143, which was met without Robert of Leicester's patience and apparent equanimity.

---

25 See my reasoning for this judgement in D. Crouch, 'Robert of Gloucester and the daughter of Zelophehad', *Journal of Medieval History*, 11 (1985), 227–43.

26 Davis, *Stephen*, 65–7, puts the change down to the king's disenchantment with his experience of Waleran of Meulan in particular. K.J. Stringer, *The Reign of Stephen*, (London, 1993), 56, suggests that the magnates had rejected Stephen as being a failure as a national leader.

27 H.M. Colvin, *A History of Deddington* (London, 1963), 19. Colvin's deduction is based on the facts that Deddington was rated as thirty-six hides in 1086 (the only thirty-six-hide estate in Oxfordshire at the Domesday inquest) and that Earl Robert of Leicester had an exemption for thirty-six hides in the Oxfordshire account of 1130.

The characters who were dominant at court after 1142 were a small, although not exclusive, body of Stephen's *curiales*. There were about seventeen names which can be picked out from Stephen's later charters. The leaders were William of Ypres, William Martel, the steward, Robert de Vere and Henry of Essex, successive constables, Richard de Lucy and Richard de Canville (who shared with William de Chesney the keeping of Oxfordshire).[28] But these men, for all their loyalty and evident capacity, could by no means counterbalance the weight of the greater magnates, and indeed overreliance on them was as isolating and dangerous as favouring any aristocratic clique had been. It is doubtless these men whom the chroniclers mean when they talk of Stephen's counsellors urging him to one more self-defeating act of confiscation against a magnate perceived as a danger to him.[29]

Stephen's relations with the supposedly royalist earls between 1143 and 1147 were mercurial, to say the least. We have already dealt with his peremptory demands on Geoffrey de Mandeville, earl of Essex, and their dramatic (and surely unexpected) consequences. Associated with Earl Geoffrey in his retaliatory action against the king was Earl Hugh Bigod of Norfolk, Stephen's oldest ally, but another defector to the empress in the 1141 campaigns. It is impossible to pin down what precisely Earl Hugh had done after the empress's defeat. There is certainly no evidence that he stayed with her after the debacle of Winchester; on the other hand there is no evidence that he reverted to an active allegiance to the king, as had Geoffrey de Mandeville, Earl Aubrey and Earl Gilbert of Pembroke. He may very well have pursued the same tactic as Earl Robert of Leicester: returned to his estates and minded his own interests. When Earl Geoffrey began his fenland campaign at the end of 1143, we are told that Earl Hugh allied with him, but what use the alliance was to Geoffrey is hard to say: the Bigod estates and castles were concentrated on the coastal flank of Suffolk, well away from Geoffrey's military operations. Hugh was certainly active against the king early in 1145 when, thinking the king was too deeply involved in his Gloucestershire campaigns to touch him, he plundered the king's Suffolk manors. This brought about powerful and unexpected retaliation from the king in person, and the building of new castles to contain the Bigod aggression.[30]

But if it is suggested that Earl Hugh was a major irritant to the king, it is hard then to account for the fact that he remained largely untroubled on his

---

28 The others were Turgis d'Avranches (till 1145), constable, Fulk d'Oilly, brother of the late Robert d'Oilly, Richard de Montacute, Henry de Neufmarché, Adam de Beaunay, Hugh des Essarts, Warner de Lusors, Roger de Fresnay, Robert de Valdari, William de Chesney of Oxford and Baldwin fitz Gilbert, the only one amongst them who came near the status of magnate, having the barony of Bourne, Lincs.

29 Doubtless these are '*omnes primi*' who urged the king to act against Earl Ranulf in 1146, and those '*persuadentes*' who urged him to act against Earl Gilbert, *GS*, 194, 202. They would also fit the description of '*qui se familiariori dilectione regi coniunctius*' who were antagonistic to Geoffrey de Mandeville in 1143, *GS*, 160–2.

30 *GS*, 166, 179.

Suffolk estates until the very end of the reign, and beyond. Other than refusing to recognise the comital title that the empress had given Hugh, the king did not try to dispossess him.[31] Norfolk was solidly royalist, and much of Suffolk was in the personal demesne of the king. It would have been far, far easier for the king to crush Hugh Bigod than it was for him to crush Robert of Gloucester. The point may well be that the king had decided that Earl Hugh was never going to embrace the Angevin cause actively, and all that had to be done with him was to tolerate him and contain his defiant exuberance. He had to be dealt with like a bumptious adolescent; he was a dissident but not a rebel. In October 1148, for instance, Earl Hugh thumbed his nose at the king by acting as protector of Archbishop Theobald on his landing in England at his port of Gosford. He entertained him in lavish style and with great respect at his chief castle of Framlingham while the archbishop reasserted his control over the English Church.[32] But the fact that the quarrel between Archbishop Theobald and King Stephen was settled during the archbishop's residence at Framlingham could indicate that Earl Hugh had acted as an honest broker between the spiritual and temporal powers, allowing ambassadors between the two to meet under his protection. He was not therefore an unqualified nuisance to King Stephen.

Another earl whose relations with the king were uneasy after 1141 was Gilbert fitz Gilbert, earl of Pembroke. Earl Gilbert had defected to the empress with Geoffrey de Mandeville in 1141, but changed sides to help the queen before September. He was apparently welcomed back at the court after the king's release. He was not as lukewarm in his attachment to the royalist cause as were the earls of Leicester and Norfolk. Indeed, in 1143 he was highly favoured with a grant of the wardship of the earldom of Buckingham forfeited by Walter Giffard on his defection to Geoffrey of Anjou.[33] Yet even Earl Gilbert had problems which must have stemmed from the king's distrust of any great magnate. In 1145 the earl took the most unusual step of quitting the court, and England, and travelling by way of Angevin Worcester through the heart of Wales and into his Marcher earldom of Pembroke. Here he stayed and was very active against the royal house of Deheubarth for over a year. He was able to reverse some of the native Welsh gains in west Wales and recaptured Carmarthen.[34] But it is doubtful whether his expedition was the result of Stephen's initiative: the king actively discouraged warfare in the Marches of Wales. It is more likely that Earl Gilbert went into temporary exile when he found his ambitions frustrated at court.

31 Davis, *Stephen*, 138–9.
32 GC i, 136; A. Saltman, *Theobald, Archbishop of Canterbury* (London, 1955), 30.
33 This grant can be worked out from Earl Gilbert's known control of a couple of Giffard manors in this period, see *The Norfolk Portion of the Cartulary of the Priory of St Pancras of Lewes*, ed. J.H. Bullock (Norfolk Record Society, 12, 1939), 17 (Shouldham); *Reading Abbey Cartularies* i, 209–10 (Chelsfield).
34 *Cartulary of Worcester Cathedral Priory*, ed. Darlington, 134–6 shows that his route to and from Wales was through Angevin-held Worcester (the possession of his brother-in-law, Waleran of Meulan). For his activities in Deheubarth, *Brut*, *s.a.* 1145, 1146.

Earl Gilbert's eventual fate demonstrated that no great magnate was sure of Stephen's goodwill after 1141. As the *Gesta* tells the story, Gilbert did not act with any great discretion; whether this was through foolhardiness, desperation or misjudged ambition is now impossible to say. He was faced with a difficult situation early in 1147. His nephew and namesake, Gilbert de Clare, earl of Hertford, had sided with Earl Ranulf of Chester in his dispute with King Stephen. The king had seized the Clare castles in Suffolk and Kent because Gilbert de Clare had acted as hostage for his uncle, Earl Ranulf, and Earl Ranulf had gone back on his pledges. King Stephen was undoubtedly within his rights in seizing Gilbert de Clare's castles, but there were complaints that he had kept Gilbert unnecessarily long in prison. There was also an expectation that the king would exercise some charity in the situation.

This was probably why Earl Gilbert of Pembroke went to the king and asked him to entrust the Clare castles to him 'by hereditary right' (as the *Gesta* mysteriously says).[35] When the king civilly refused as this was not to his advantage at the time, the earl withdrew and did as so many magnates had previously done when crossed. Gilbert went off intending to fortify his castles against the king. But the king was expecting him to do just that. His advisers seem to have warned him of the probable outcome of refusal, and so he struck first, seizing three of Earl Gilbert's castles and trapping the earl in a fourth, Pevensey in the west of Sussex (which the earl had as a gift from King Stephen after Richer de l'Aigle had forfeited it in 1141).[36] The earl of Pembroke surrendered to the king's mercy, was reconciled, and died soon after. His career is yet another variant on what we have seen of Stephen's volatile relations with nominally loyalist magnates. It is also a variant in being one of Stephen's successes. The succession of the earl's under-age son, Richard fitz Gilbert, meant that the earl of Pembroke ceased to be a problem to Stephen and considerably reduced the danger from the Clare dynasty.

KING STEPHEN AND EARL RANULF OF CHESTER, 1144–47

The final and most instructive example of quite how detached from the king royalist magnates might be after 1141 is that of Earl Ranulf of Chester. Earl Ranulf had an admittedly checkered career as a supporter of Stephen. No-one could forget that he had been responsible for the king's humiliation at Lincoln.[37] His return to the king's allegiance at Winchester in September 1141 could hardly have cancelled the king's resentment at what Ranulf had put him through. Yet despite all that, the earl of Chester did assist in maintaining the royal ascendancy in the north of England for the next five years or so. He did

---

35 For a similar request in 1141 from William de Beauchamp of Worcester to the empress, that he should have the keeping of his relatives' confiscated lands while they were on opposite sides, see *Regesta* iii, no. 68.
36 *GS*, 200–4.
37 *GS*, 184 refers to the 'cruelty and treachery' of 1141 of which Ranulf had to be conscious in coming humbly before the king in 1146.

so passively, simply by not supporting the empress. Ranulf's nominal support of Stephen prevented any northwards movement of the Angevin sphere beyond Herefordshire and Worcestershire. But Ranulf was by preference, as Paul Dalton points out, a neutralist. Passive support was all that Stephen could expect from him, and that only so long as his great gains in the Trent valley were respected. In the meantime, Ranulf was anything but passive in his relations with neighbouring magnates.

After Stephen's release, Earl Ranulf was still in control of Belvoir castle, Lincoln and Derby. He was still the dominant magnate in the northwest of England, and wanted to be more dominant than he was in Warwickshire, Leicestershire and Lincolnshire. It was because of his local ambitions that we hear so much of him between 1141 and 1146. Even though he was so far from the places where chroniclers were at work, his local activities were too outrageous and aggressive to leave no trace even in the thin primary sources for the north and midlands. The author of the *Gesta* lived far away in the southwest of the kingdom, but in 1144 he heard that '. . . the earl of Chester afflicted the whole of the north with an unending persecution'. What was the nature of this 'persecution'? There is evidence in 1144 that Ranulf launched local campaigns on several fronts. He was indiscriminate in his targets. The *Gesta* remarks on his attacks on the 'king's barons' near him.[38] He was out to maintain his ascendancy and weaken potential rivals. He had clearly targeted Robert Marmion, lord of Tamworth, as one obstacle. The southern pole of Ranulf's central midland estates was the castle and borough of Coventry, where he shared local power with the Benedictine cathedral chapter. Coventry was surrounded by a tight group of Chester estates – however, it was detached from the rest of the earl's dominion and some distance from the earl's Trent valley castles of Mountsorrel and Donington.[39] Coventry was therefore exposed, and Robert Marmion's lordship sat right across the routes to the city from Ranulf's other key castles of Newcastle-under-Lyme and Derby. The fact that the Marmions were consistent royalists and had held out for the king even in his cause's dark night of 1141, made little difference to the nominal royalist, Earl Ranulf.[40] He persecuted them as readily as the Salisbury family persecuted John Marshal in Angevin Wiltshire (see above).

Local warfare broke out between Earl Ranulf and Robert Marmion early in 1144. As with the contemporary violence in East Anglia between Geoffrey de Mandeville and the king, the Church suffered. Marmion successfully seized the cathedral-priory of Coventry in August 1144. He fortified the precinct in order to blockade the earl's castle. On the approach of the earl and a large

---

38 *GS*, 166–8.
39 For the spread of Chester estates outside Cheshire, see C.P. Lewis, 'The formation of the honor of Chester, 1066–1100', in *The Earldom of Chester and its Charters*, ed. Thacker (Journal of the Chester Archaelogical Society, 71, 1991), 41–57.
40 The empress had granted Tamworth to William de Beauchamp of Elmley in the summer of 1141. This was a speculative grant in that the Marmions must still have held it for the king at the time, *Regesta* iii, no. 68.

force to relieve the castle, Marmion seems to have gone forward to scout the enemy's strength, but he took a fall from his horse and broke his leg. While he was struggling on the ground, a Chester foot-soldier ran up and decapitated him. The Marmion–Chester conflict did not end with this stroke, however. Robert Marmion's son, also called Robert, continued the fight. The younger Robert maintained himself in Coventry and northern Warwickshire until Earl Ranulf conceded control of the borough (but not the castle) to him at some time between 1144 and 1146.[41] There are some hints that the warfare affected a wide area of the Arden region. Hugh fitz Richard, sometime sheriff and leading tenant of the earl of Warwick, with a house at Amington, south of Tamworth, dated one of his charters in the 1140s 'in the year when the earl of Chester captured me while out hunting'.[42]

There was trouble involving Ranulf further to the north. John of Hexham records that around the same time that Geoffrey de Mandeville had fortified Ramsey abbey, Earl Ranulf and Gilbert de Gant were harrassing Earl William of York in the East Riding of Yorkshire. Gilbert de Gant was lord of Hunmanby and Filey and advocate of the large Augustinian priory at Bridlington, which his father, Walter, had founded. Earl Ranulf was related to Gilbert by marriage, having married him to a niece while he had him in captivity after the battle of Lincoln. From this it would seem that late in 1143, or in the first half of 1144, Ranulf had marched north and joined with Gilbert in defence of his interests against the aggressions of William of Aumale.[43] Paul Dalton gives good reason to believe that Gilbert's holdings in the north of the East Riding were an obstacle to the extension of his control over coastal Yorkshire. Earl William's decisive answer was to seize the priory precinct at Bridlington, and fortify some or all of it in the same way that Geoffrey de Mandeville had fortified Ramsey abbey and Robert Marmion had fortified Coventry cathedral.[44]

These rumours of widespread local conflict between Earl Ranulf and his neighbours early in 1144 would account for Henry of Huntingdon's otherwise mysterious account of King Stephen's siege of Lincoln in 1144. Henry records the erecting of large siege works against Lincoln castle 'which the earl of

41 For the struggle, see HH, 744, with additional details in WN i, 47. I have largely followed the reconstruction of the local warfare in R.H.C. Davis, 'An unknown Coventry charter', *EHR* 86 (1971), 533–47 repr. in *From Alfred the Great to Stephen*, 221–33; see also G. White, 'Were the Midlands "wasted" during Stephen's reign?' *Midland History*, 10 (1985), 36–8. The continued presence of the earl's constable or castellan, Ivo of Alspath, at Coventry, indicates that the earl kept the castle: it is not mentioned in the surviving treaty between Earl Ranulf and the Marmions. For Ivo, brother of the earl's despencer, see D. Crouch, 'The administration of the Norman earldom', in *The Earldom of Chester and its Charters*, ed. A.T. Thacker (Journal of Chester Archaeological Society, 71, 1991), 78, 93–4.

42 For Hugh and his family, D. Crouch, 'The local influence of the earls of Warwick, 1088–1242: A study in decline and resourcefulness', *Midland History*, 21 (1996), 5, 7, 18. For his arrest by the earl, Cartulary of Reading, Brit Libr. ms Harley 1708, fo. 123v. For his possession of Amington, Warws, Bodl. Libr. mss Dugdale 13, p. 15; 15, p. 77.

43 JH, 315.

44 P. Dalton, *Conquest, Anarchy and Lordship: Yorkshire 1066–1154* (Cambridge, 1994), 65–6, for the significance of Bridlington (I do not follow him in his placing of the '*Galclint*' episode within the East Riding, for which see above pp. 144–5).

Chester held by force', and also records the collapse of a bank or tunnel which killed large numbers of the king's engineers. Following this disaster the king broke off the attack.[45] We need not doubt Henry's account – he was, after all, a good source for what happened at Lincoln, being an archdeacon of the diocese. The aggressions of the earl of Chester in the midlands and in Yorkshire against his fellow royalist magnates are enough to account for the king's launching of a strike against him. Stephen's siege of Lincoln in 1144 can be understood as a warning to Earl Ranulf that he had gone too far and that he was endangering the possessions he had won from the king four years earlier. Henry of Huntingdon later mentions a pact (*concordia*) which had been reached between king and earl at some time before 1146.[46] This would indicate that the king's warning strike at Lincoln had brought Ranulf to realise that he had gone too far. He would seem to have made a formal settlement. Ranulf's submission would doubtless have once again eased relations while the king concentrated on weakening the Angevin cause in the south.

But the accord between the earl of Chester and the king renewed in 1144 was only a temporary convenience. Earl Ranulf's eventual come-uppance was perhaps more predictable than that meted out to Geoffrey de Mandeville and Bishop Roger of Salisbury in their days. Yet the earl seems to have been just as oblivious to its approach as Mandeville had been. Or, if he were not oblivious, then the number of distractions caused by his overstretched interests had hidden the danger. One particular danger close to home was that represented by the power of the kingdom of Gwynedd. In 1141, Ranulf had been in alliance with the royal brothers Owain and Cadwaladr ap Gruffudd, who had assisted his army at Lincoln. By 1146, Cadwaladr and Owain had fallen out and Ranulf had taken the part of the younger brother, now in exile at his court. This was bad judgement, for it was Owain who had the real power of the two. He demonstrated this by crossing the river Clwyd in force and seizing the region of Tegeingl, on the borders of Cheshire.

Ranulf joined the king's army for his renewed assault on Wallingford in the summer of 1146, after the collapse of the Angevin campaign in the upper Thames valley. His sudden solicitude for the king's fortunes was regarded with suspicion in the royalist camp, and rightly so. He had been out for his own advantage since the beginning of the war. I have called it neutralism here; to the author of the *Gesta* it was 'fickleness' or 'inconsistency'.[47] Ranulf was quite clearly alarmed by the Welsh danger, and according to the author of the *Gesta*, lamented openly at court about 'the uncivilised horde of the Welsh' who were pillaging his lands in the March and besieging his castles and towns. He wanted the king to intervene in person, and offered cash subsidies to recruit a sufficient force to secure the border. The king was apparently all for this new adventure. But his intimates saw their opportunity and warned him

45 HH, 744.
46 HH, 748. I argue elsewhere that the *concordia* mentioned here is not the document represented by *Regesta* iii, no, 178 (see above, pp. 143–4).
47 GS, 184.

that the earl was plotting to get him into the remote border region and do away with him: '. . . it was reckless and excessively rash for the king to be willing to enter the earldom of the man who had appropriated from him a very large part of the kingdom'. Instead the king was persuaded that now was the time to arrest Ranulf and extort from him the hostages for good behaviour that would keep him in line in future. At Northampton the earl was confronted with demands for pledges and hostages before the relief campaign could be taken further. When he refused to negotiate, the suspicions of the king were confirmed, and Ranulf was promptly arrested and gaoled until he co-operated.

It was all richly ironic. Ranulf, of all men, had every interest in keeping Stephen on the throne. Stephen's kingship had given him unparalleled opportunities for local ambition and advancement. He had no intention of doing away with the king in some damp and forested Welsh valley. Yet at the point when he most needed Stephen, the consequences of his neutralism caught up with him. His lack of commitment to the king's cause, and well-known local aggression looked all too much like the diffidence and double-dealing that masks the potential traitor. So he fell victim to his many enemies at court, and suffered the fate of Geoffrey de Mandeville. Undoubtedly, he deserved his fate more than had Geoffrey, yet he was not guilty of what he had been charged with. But the king had his way and many of Ranulf's castles were surrendered, notably Lincoln and Coventry. The king seems to have got away with his stratagem too. It would seem that at this time he took over the defence of Warwickshire, garrisoning the castle of Warwick as well. The earl of Chester lost his hold on the Trent valley and we can suggest that he found himself also at war with the earl of Leicester, who forced him also to surrender his castle of Mountsorrel and give up control of Charnwood. But the king's gains have to be balanced against the fact that Earl Ranulf was from now onwards bound to be a firm adherent of the empress.

PART THREE

Settling the Kingdom, 1147–1154

CHAPTER 13

War, Peace and the Magnates, 1147–1152

Mutual exhaustion can resolve civil wars. Sooner or later, the accumulated human loss and material damage begin to put the conflict into a new perspective. Is it all worth the effort? Is any principle the excuse for such waste? Are there better ways of resolving the difficulty? This point was reached quite quickly in the wars of Stephen's reign. This may be a tribute to the shallowness of the ideological veneer the leaders put on the conflict. Ideas of loyalty and right heredity made for a thin sort of gloss when it was clear to everybody that individual and dynastic gain was really at issue. The gloss became almost a transparent membrane when it was stretched to cover the squabbling and greed of the magnates and opportunists who fought the wars in the field. With no great depth of conviction, the roots of partisan warfare could not supply enough hatred to keep the war flourishing and spreading.

As early as the autumn of 1139 it could be argued (and has been above, p. 109) that Queen Adeliza had invited the empress to Arundel in the hope of brokering a peace. And within a year of the empress's landing, the king – still in control of most of his kingdom – had allowed a long and elaborate conference at Bath between his ambassadors and those of the empress, in the hope of an acceptable settlement (see p. 134). Although unsuccessful, this conference was followed by other negotiations in the various and changing circumstances of the autumn of 1141 and of 1146.

As early as 1141, the dead weight of neutralism amongst the magnates was putting a drag on the most energetic plans of the leaders of either party (see the end of Chapter 9). By 1144 neutralism and self-preservation were everywhere predominant, as we see in the behaviour of Geoffrey de Mandeville, Hugh Bigod and Earl Roger of Hereford. By 1147 the internal divisions of the king's party had become so open as to frustrate any further decisive campaigning. No real surprise then that in the course of 1148 the frustration was recognised when the magnates ceased to listen to Devizes and Westminster, and began to manage their own relations with little reference to partisan objectives.

This malaise was clear to the people of the time. Before the end of Stephen's reign, William of Newburgh, who had come to adulthood in the Yorkshire priory from which he took his name, wrote his own retrospective on this period.

> At first it seemed the kingdom of England was to be cut in two, some supporting the king, others the empress; but neither king nor empress was in control of their supporters, for each depended from day to day on their people's military efforts. Neither could curb or dictate to their party, and both appeased their supporters, denying them nothing, in case they withdrew their support.

In such circumstances, Newburgh said, partisan warfare could not be maintained, but there was plenty of scope for individual magnates to reap the benefits of constant insecurity.[1] More than anything else, the death of Earl Robert of Gloucester assisted the breakdown of party. This was partly because his personal prestige and fearsome reputation had kept his allies committed to his campaigns; they would not lightly cross him. But it was also because his son, Earl William, was nowhere near as committed as Robert had been to the war against Stephen.

THE TREATIES OF 1148–49

Magnates in the 1140s were already adept at making peace; quite as adept as they were at breaking it. It was part of aristocratic life to harass your neighbours in pursuit of an objective; bring the struggle to the edge of violence (or across it) and then make a deal with a greater or lesser degree of compromise.[2] This deal was often called by contemporary scribes (in Latin) a *conventio* (a 'coming together' or 'agreement'). There is plenty of evidence from the reign of Henry I that even then magnates were already in the habit of negotiating complex issues (over property and rights) and coming to agreements – which were often written down.[3] This pragmatic habit was part of a wider European practice of formally negotiating difficulties, often with the assistance of the Church. To indicate how widespread this was, treaty-making is as evident amongst the Welsh in the eleventh century as amongst their contemporaries in central France. No surprise then that in his difficulties with his Welsh magnate

---

1 WN i, 69.
2 See for an essay on this, D. Crouch, 'Earls and bishops in twelfth-century Leicestershire', *Nottingham Medieval Studies*, xxxvii (1993), 9–20.
3 See on this, M. Chibnall, 'Anglo–French relations in the work of Orderic Vitalis', in *Documenting the Past: Essays in Honour of G.P. Cuttino*, ed. J.S. Hamilton and P.J. Bradley (Woodbridge, 1989), 16–17; E. King, 'Dispute settlement in Anglo-Norman England', *ANS* xiv, ed. M. Chibnall (Woodbridge, 1992), 115–30; D. Crouch, 'A Norman *conventio* and bonds of lordship in the middle ages', in *Law and Government in Medieval England and Normandy*, ed. G. Garnett and J. Hudson (Cambridge, 1994), 306–10. For the antiquity of the written settlement in western Europe, and its Roman roots, see A.J. Kosto, 'The *convenientia* in the early middle ages', *Medieval Studies*, 60 (1998), 1–54.

neighbours in Glamorgan in 1136, Earl Robert of Gloucester chose to seek a conference or conferences, which led to a number of written agreements to re-establish local peace.[4]

It was a natural extension of this process in time of civil conflict, for the magnates to take it beyond the sphere of local property and rights, and into the stratosphere of regional and national politics. We find that Earl Robert of Gloucester sought to bolster his relations with fellow Angevin supporters by written agreements, without reference to the empress. In the summer of 1142, just before he left for Normandy, he negotiated and sealed a solemn commitment (called both a *conventio* and an 'alliance of love', *confederatio amoris*) with one of the other leaders of his party, Earl Miles of Hereford. It may have been one of several such agreements; Earl Robert had good cause to worry about the commitment of his fellow partisans at the time.[5] This Gloucester–Hereford treaty is revealing in its terms. Earl Robert knew his neighbour and appreciated Miles's desire for security and self-aggrandisement, so he promised him exactly what he wanted: to maintain Miles in the lands that he had by right and those that he had acquired (*conquisita*) so far through his adherence to the empress. He would help Miles obtain those things which he claimed were his by right, but which he did not yet have. He also promised that Miles would have his military help if anyone attempted to take anything away from him, and that he would never temporise with those who were Miles's enemies (unless Miles was willing to let him). In this way, the two magnates carved up the southern March of Wales and the West Country. Neither of them appears to have consulted the empress as to what they were doing, for her consent and participation are not noted.

As I have said, this document of 1142 was pragmatic (and there are others with which to compare it in the first half of Stephen's reign).[6] The Gloucester–Hereford agreement of the summer of 1142 spends most of its time talking about the relationship between the earls. It has very little to say about the ideological struggle between king and empress in which they were engaged, other than that they intended to 'be as one' ('*ad unum opus erit*') in fighting it; a strikingly ambiguous endorsement. The ambiguity is the key. This document and others like it give us a more subtle perspective on the war than that of the chroniclers. The treaties preserve more of the nuances of politics in a

4 Rice Merrick, *Morganniae Archaiographia*, ed. B. Ll. James (South Wales Rec. Soc, no. 1, 1983), 39–40. See comments in D. Crouch, 'The slow death of kingship in Glamorgan, 1067–1158', *Morgannwg: Transactions of the Glamorgan History Society*, xxix (1985), 34.
5 See above, p. 203n. For the date of the *confederatio amoris*, see R.H.C. Davis, 'Treaty between William earl of Gloucester and Roger earl of Hereford', in *A Medieval Miscellany for Davis Mary Stenton* (Pipe Roll Society, new ser., xxxvi, 1960), 142.
6 For instance, the Warwick–Clinton *conventio* of 1138; the Meulan–Neubourg *conventio* of 1142; the Chester–Marmion *conventio* of 1144. Professor King, like J.H. Round, would include within this group the agreements early in the reign between the king and the magnates who came over to his side, which Round called 'treaties between equal powers'. As I have said, I do not share Round's belief that Stephen was so weak or prodigal in the first years of his reign as to need to concede such agreements.

complicated and shifting struggle, when the only anchor to which a magnate could chain himself was the needs of himself and his dependents. The king and the empress received what surplus attention and resources the magnates had left to offer. Looked at through this sort of lens, the neutralism we have already mentioned is perfectly understandable. The thing that distinguished one magnate from another is the relative weight each gave to the interests of self and of party. By this measure Earl Robert of Gloucester and Brian fitz Count were better partisans than Miles of Hereford; they put more of themselves into the war. But despite that, all three had this in common: they were fighting and competing for their own interests in difficult circumstances.

From this *conventio* of 1142 between two magnates of the same party, it is instructive to move on to those made after Earl Robert's death in 1147, when we find a sudden flurry of surviving *conventiones* – some within the same party, others between magnates of opposing parties. As has been said, what they all reveal is a pronounced neutralism. Three earls – Gloucester, Hereford and Leicester – seem to have moved almost simultaneously, once Earl Robert had died, to secure the peace of the midlands and southern March. The participation of one of the earls is significant. Earl Robert of Leicester was by 1147 achieving military and political dominance of the central midlands, and exerted control over Worcester on the Severn as his brother's lieutenant. Earl Robert was still nonetheless a nominal royalist, and appears with the king's army as late as 1153.[7] But long before 1148 the war had come to the point where local needs cancelled out party allegiance. We have already seen the way two Angevin magnates, John Marshal and Earl Patrick of Salisbury, fought out their personal struggle for dominance in Wiltshire in the years 1144–45.[8] To find an Angevin and a royalist earl negotiating a peace treaty in 1147–48 is no surprise at all.

There was a strong political need for the new earl of Gloucester, of all earls, to seek peace. Earl William was politically weaker than his father. His widowed mother retained and exercised claims on the bulk of her father's lands in Glamorgan and Gwent, which William only ruled by her courtesy.[9] Earl William – a man in his late twenties – did not inherit his father's ascendancy over the senior Angevin magnates, which passed to the older and decidedly more formidable Earl Roger of Hereford.[10] It may therefore have been Earl William who was the first of the three earls to move to the conference table: circumstances which seem to have caused the author of the *Gesta* to stigmatise William on taking up his earldom as 'a peaceable man, more fond of staying at

---

7 See D. Crouch, *The Beaumont Twins: The Roots and Branches of Power in the Twelfth Century* (Cambridge, 1986), 79–85.

8 See above, pp. 213–15.

9 See the evidence of Countess Mabel's grants in her own right and jointly with Earl William relating to her honors of Glamorgan and Gwynllwg, *Earldom of Gloucester Charters*, ed. Patterson, 49, 88–9, 152, 171–2.

10 D. Crouch, 'The March and the Welsh kings', in *The Anarchy of King Stephen's Reign*, ed. E. King (Oxford, 1994), 281–3.

home than fighting'.[11] He and his mother, Countess Mabel, can be found within months of Earl Robert's death, making peace with the bishop of Salisbury, a dogged and undaunted opponent, over their continued possession of Sherborne (and the episcopal lands in Dorset), surrendered to Earl Robert by King Stephen in the campaigning of 1143. Although the earl and countess kept the castle, they recognised that the possession was not perpetual, and returned the bulk of the bishop's lands and rights.[12]

We can tie this Gloucester–Salisbury *conventio* in with Gloucester's others with the earls of Leicester and Hereford. A text of the Gloucester–Leicester treaty of 1147–48 does not now survive, but its terms can be reconstructed and it, too, must have related to past Gloucester territorial aggression in Dorset. The other of Earl William's principal castles in Dorset was that at Wareham, which his father had abstracted by force from the king and the earl of Leicester in 1139. Earl William found (or was presented with) a simple and ingenious solution to the Wareham problem before the end of 1148. He was to marry Hawise, eldest daughter of Earl Robert of Leicester, a girl in her early twenties. A father would normally present to the young couple a customary marriage-gift of cash or land. So Earl Robert gave with Hawise some of the large Leicester estate in Dorset, including Wareham; the same estate that Earl William was already holding by force.[13] In this way the Leicester–Gloucester rivalry was peacefully solved. The rough date of the marriage is established by the fact that in a charter dated January 1148 Earl William was still clearly unmarried,[14] but in his treaty with the earl of Hereford, reached before March 1149 (see below) William was acting also with the earl of Leicester. We could therefore suggest with a degree of plausibility that the union between the two families had been celebrated during the summer or autumn of 1148, maybe even as early as the spring of that year.

At much the same time the earl of Hereford was brought into the web of negotiations between Gloucester and Leicester. Between the time of the departure of the empress for Normandy in February 1148 and March 1149 at the latest, the earl of Gloucester renewed his father's treaty with the earl of

---

11 *GS*, 210. Potter prefers a more derisive translation of '*uir mollis et thalamorum magis quam militiae appetitor*', a slant which to my mind does not tally with the mildly approving things which the author goes on to say about Earl William's ('one-off') military success in front of Castle Cary. Earl William in fact had a long experience of leadership in war since his first appearance in arms at the seige of Bristol ten years earlier.

12 For the document and its dating, *Earldom of Gloucester Charters*, ed. Patterson, 155–6. Earl William was in fact resident in Dorset at Wareham in January 1148, ibid., 161, 162. For comments on Bishop Joscelin's strategies to recover his diocese's rights, see E. King, 'The Anarchy of Stephen's reign', *TRHS*, 5th ser., 34 (1984), 139–40.

13 For the transfer of estates from Leicester to Gloucester, see Crouch, *Beaumont Twins*, 85 and nn.

14 *Earldom of Gloucester Charters*, ed. Patterson, 161, a charter of Earl William to Tewkesbury abbey dated 11 January 1148 which commemorates the souls of his father, mother, and all his relatives, but mentions no wife. Hawise explicitly refers to the manor of Pimperne in Dorset as her '*liberum maritagium*' which she had from her father, in one of her own charters, *Earldom of Gloucester Charters*, ed. Patterson, 72–3.

Hereford.[15] The text of this second-generation *confederatio amoris* survives. On the surface, it looks much like the treaty reached between their fathers, especially as Earl Roger admits that Earl William is still his lord (presumably for his castle of Gloucester), but there are several signs that the balance of power had now tipped heavily towards Hereford. This time, the earl of Hereford offers no son as hostage. The long list of pledges for each earl also tells its story. Standing by Earl Roger were almost all the minor magnates of Herefordshire and the southern March, alongside Earl William stood only his own knights.[16] This treaty also tells us that Earl William was already bound to Earl Robert of Leicester in another agreement he had with the earl of Hereford (which had preceded the Gloucester–Hereford treaty).

Alongside these treaties, which belong to a flurry of negotiation in the southern March and midlands in 1148, we must place certain others involving Earl Robert of Leicester. These record his dealings with a fourth earl, Ranulf of Chester. By 1148 Earl Robert had already reached a treaty with Ranulf over their respective claims to the Charnwood area of Leicestershire. They did so, as the document strikingly says '. . . in the fields between Leicester and Mountsorrel' (their respective fortresses in the area).[17] The document records an open-air conference on the border between their spheres of influence, the sort of Marcher encounter normally orchestrated between rival princes. It tells you that by 1148 'rival princes' were exactly what the great English earls were. Further striking testimony to the independence of these two earls is the final treaty that Ranulf went on to make with Robert of Leicester. It has never been possible to date this Leicester–Chester *conventio* precisely, but it has to date to a time after December 1148, when Robert de Chesney was consecrated bishop of Lincoln, and the most likely circumstances for its composition are the hostilities in the Trent valley of the autumn of 1149 (see Appendix to this chapter). Its manifest intention was the same as the Gloucester–Hereford *conventio*, to limit warfare between its principals and agree to work against a third party, in this case a rogue baron on the Leicestershire–Warwick border.[18]

So we see from the English Channel coast at Wareham, through Dorset and into the Severn valley, and further north across the midlands to the Trent valley, a network of alliances which inhibited warfare had been formulated by

15 Since the treaty mentions only Henry fitz Empress's claims to England, it must have been issued after the empress quit England in mid-February 1148, and Davis points out that the treaty must have been sealed before the death of William of Berkeley (who had been succeeded in his lands by 9 March 1149), 'Treaty between William earl of Gloucester and Roger earl of Hereford', 144.

16 *Earldom of Gloucester Charters*, 97.

17 E. King, 'Mountsorrel and its region in King Stephen's reign', *Huntingdon Library Quarterly*, xliv (1980), 3–4, finds this interpretation of an outdoor conference between two great magnates 'implausible', yet if this were so, the idea of two kings like Richard the Lionheart and Philip II discussing their affairs, one on a boat on the Seine the other on horseback on the bank, as they did in January 1199, would be even more absurd.

18 For a translation and text, F.M. Stenton, *The First Century of English Feudalism, 1066–1166* (2nd edn., Oxford, 1960), 250–3, 286–8; another edition of the text is to be found in *Charters of the Earls of Chester*, 123–5.

the end of 1149. The network set up in 1148 might well have stretched rather wider than the bishop and earls of whom we know. There is the interesting and little-noted fact that after 1148, William de Chesney, the royalist governor of Oxford, appears at the court of the Angevin supporter, Earl Roger of Hereford, on more than one occasion. Chesney might have been acting under the influence of Robert of Leicester, his powerful neighbour to the north.[19] The king and the empress clearly had no part in this peace-making; it was private enterprise amongst openly neutralist magnates on either side. Warfare was thus eliminated in that cockpit ravaged so cruelly right up to the previous year by the king and the earl of Gloucester: the borders of Wiltshire, the Cotswolds and the Severn valley. Eliminated, that is, except for those magnates of whom Earl Roger disapproved, such as his Herefordshire rival, Gilbert de Lacy, against whom the Gloucester–Hereford treaty is specifically directed, as also is another treaty that Earl Roger made, with his brother-in-law, William de Briouze.[20] This was, in fact, the 'magnates' peace' described so memorably by R.H.C. Davis, although he placed its outbreak rather later than I do, around 1150. When it came it signalled the effective end of the war. For how can there be a war when the principal partisans of one side will not fight the other?

THE DEPARTURE OF THE EMPRESS AND THE CAUSE OF DUKE HENRY, 1148–50

A sort of peace was settling into place before the end of 1148, and like a blanket of snow over rocks, it transformed the situation in England. The empress did not stay in England longer than four months after the death of Robert of Gloucester. So rapid a departure does more than hint that she felt that there was little hope that her party would rally to continue the struggle. She sat isolated in Devizes with only her military household to depend upon. She could only expect the magnates of the region to rally to her if she was in danger of capture by the king, and it may well have worried her (thinking back to her entrapment at Oxford) that they might not turn out for her even then. The bishop of Salisbury for one seems to have sensed her weakness and that the time was right to attempt to reclaim the castle where she had quartered herself and her household since her expulsion from Oxford in 1142. As early as November 1146 the bishop's agents had obtained from the pope a bull recognising his claim to Potterne Canning and the castle of Devizes, and a threat of excommunication against those who detained it. Still the empress hung on, and she appears to have attempted to negotiate with the bishop by

19 Walker, 'Earldom of Hereford charters', 25, 28. It is worth observing that Robert de Chesney, archdeacon of Leicester before 1147, was the brother of William. Archdeacon Robert was promoted to the see of Lincoln after Bishop Alexander's death in 1147, and seems to have had a working political relationship with the earl of Leicester, see Crouch, *Beaumont Twins*, 82.
20 Hereford D & C Archives, no. 790.

offering compensation elsewhere.[21] It is unlikely that she would ever have entertained the possibility of vacating Devizes and giving it back to the bishop had she still felt sure of her support (certainly her son never did more than promise a future restoration of the castle). But the energy of the bishop against her is a good indication that people knew her cause was failing even before Robert of Gloucester died, and that they believed that there was every chance she might soon give up and return to her husband.

The capitulation came early in 1148 (probably mid-February at the approach of Lent) when the empress quit Devizes and crossed to Normandy. It is some measure of how her fortunes had declined that only one source mentioned her departure: the clerk writing at Canterbury whom Gervase of Canterbury later used for his source. The author of the *Gesta*, John of Hexham and Henry of Huntingdon all overlooked her departure. The nearest they come to noticing it is their unexplained assumption that the empress's eldest son, Henry, was the new dynastic hope of the Angevin party. The Canterbury source ventures an explanation why the empress left: that she was 'worn down by the trials of the English hostilities . . . preferring to retire to the haven of her husband's protection than endure so many troubles in England'.[22] Whether this is the opinion of Gervase or of his contemporary source, it rings true. The empress had been presiding over a sagging cause for over five years, watching the gradual progress of the king's armies and allies up the Thames and across the Cotswolds, observing Robert of Gloucester's influence shrink. Even had she known that the king's cause was as badly hampered as her own by self-interested magnates, she could hardly pretend that her cause had done anything other than collapse since 1142. After November 1147 her influence was confined to very little more than the reach of the garrison of Devizes. No wonder that she packed up and left England less than four months after her half-brother's death. That she left disheartened is indicated by her departure from active politics after 1148. She entered upon a retirement in Normandy in the vicinity of Rouen, living principally across the Seine at the palace-priory of Bec at Le Pré. She had permanently settled there by March 1149 and she was to spend most of the rest of her twenty years of life there; not entirely disconnected from political life, but more of an observer than an actor.[23]

The Empress Mathilda left the active pursuit of her cause not to her husband, but to her son, Henry Plantagenet. He had been associated with her dynastic claim since probably 1140, when he was a boy of only seven. He had more than once been in England as a visible reminder that the line of Henry I lived on now in a male grandson since his father had sent him to live at Bristol late in 1142. He had stayed with his uncle in England until early in 1144, and, aged fourteen, had returned again to fight a mad little campaign early in 1147.

---

21 King, 'Anarchy of King Stephen's reign', 139–40; M. Chibnall, *The Empress Matilda* (Oxford, 1991), 148; *Sarum Charters and Documents*, ed. W. Rich-Jones and W. Dunn McCray (Rolls Series, 1891), 12–13.
22 GC i, 133, '*imperatrix . . . ante quadragesimam in Normanniam transfretavit*'.
23 For the empress's retirement and future role, Chibnall, *Matilda*, 148–9, 151ff.

When his mother effectively resigned her claim by quitting the struggle in February 1148 it would have been automatic for the English magnates who had favoured her cause to adopt Henry as the new dynastic figurehead. Indeed, it is quite conceivable that the empress could have sent them word before she left that it was her will that Henry now be regarded as claimant. It is worth noting that Earl William of Gloucester in mid-1148 swore to assist Roger of Hereford against all men 'saving the person of their lord Henry'.[24] Moreover, when Gilbert Foliot was consecrated bishop of Hereford in September 1148 at Arras he swore fealty to Henry, rather than King Stephen, Duke Geoffrey or the empress.[25]

Whatever the circumstances of the changeover, there was an element of calculation in the change of direction in the Angevin cause. Marjorie Chibnall points to the presence of Duke Geoffrey, the empress and their sons all together in Rouen in October 1148. A relaunch of the Angevin cause may have been discussed there.[26] Duke Geoffrey was not an old man but he was plagued by ill-health, and his eldest son was approaching the age of sixteen, the age of majority in much of northern France. It was time for Henry to take up the part of a man. The family's decision appears to have been that Henry must return once more to England. It is unlikely that a renewal of the military campaign against Stephen was contemplated.[27] It may well be that Duke Geoffrey planned only that some public recognition be staged of Henry's new status as the rightful heir to his grandfather's throne. Henry's sixteenth birthday was the obvious point to do so. As a young warrior, he must receive arms to signal his passage to manhood. As the claimant to the kingdom of England, it would be best if the ritual could be performed there rather than in France. If Henry were to receive them in the Angevin heartland of England, only the late Earl Robert of Gloucester, his uncle, could have acted as president of the rite of passage into adulthood. So Henry must go to the north, and to his venerable great-uncle, King David of Scotland, who would deliver to him the attributes of noble manhood.

On 13 April 1149 the young Henry was already in England and holding court at his mother's old stronghold at Devizes in Wiltshire. He may have been there some little time, for he had been able to summon to his court the earls of Cornwall, Gloucester, Hereford and Salisbury, and the barons Humphrey de Bohun, John fitz Gilbert, Roger of Berkeley, Elias Giffard and William de Beauchamp of Worcester. On that day he came to an agreement with the bishop of Salisbury about the castle of Devizes. Praising the bishop's

---

24 *Earldom of Gloucester Charters*, ed. Patterson, 97.
25 *Historia Pontificalis*, 44; Chibnall, *Matilda*, 147.
26 Chibnall, *Matilda*, 153.
27 J.W. Leedom, 'The English settlement of 1153', *History*, 65 (1980), 350–1, interprets the decision to send Henry to England in 1149 differently, as an attempt to stave off imminent military collapse. This is a possible argument, but it does not take into account the fact that Duke Henry's progress around England in 1149–50 was not in any sense a military success. Why then did not the Angevin cause collapse in England? My argument is that Stephen was not as strong as Leedom assumes and that Henry had other reasons to be in England than military.

'good will' he thanked him for allowing him to maintain himself at the castle 'which I keep in my possession still, because of my great necessity'. In compensation, he recognised the validity of the bishop's claim, and returned to him the hundredal manor of Canning in which the castle lay.[28]

Henry's brief appearance in the west of England as a promising young adult, and the relative peace that now reigned there as a result of the empress's departure the year before, seems to have been a tonic to the Angevin cause. However weak he was militarily, Henry seems to have convinced people that the future lay with him, not his mother, or the discredited King Stephen, nor Stephen's son, Count Eustace. It was around this time that the author of the *Gesta*, long a royalist and still based in royalist Bath, at last decided that the future was not with Stephen's dynasty and, in his account of Henry's appearance in the West Country in the spring of 1149, calls him 'the right heir of England'.[29] His change of mind is not surprising if we remember the actions of that other long-time royalist at this time, Robert of Leicester, who was happily temporising with the Angevin party in expectation of an Angevin future.

From Wiltshire Henry made an apparently peaceful progress north under the escort of the earl of Hereford and other West Country magnates, and with an entourage of young noblemen of his age who wished to receive arms alongside him. He had reached Carlisle by the feast of Pentecost (22 May 1149).[30] John of Hexham tells us that the young Henry was received by his great-uncle at his court with great honour. In the festivities that followed King David, his son, the earl of Northumbria, and Earl Ranulf of Chester, presided over Henry's investiture with the belt (and sword) of knighthood. It may be at this point that he began to use the ducal title, for Bishop Arnulf of Lisieux wrote from Normandy around this time to urge his friend, the new bishop of Lincoln, to 'favour as much as you can the cause of *our duke*, to whom due right of succession owes the rule of your realm'.[31] At the same court, Earl Ranulf and Henry of Northumbria settled their long-standing quarrel, and Ranulf's claim to overlordship of northern Lancashire was recognised by the Scots, while he recognised their claims on Cumbria and did homage to King David. Part of the terms of the agreement was a future marriage between one of Ranulf's sons and one of Earl Henry's daughters.[32]

The court at Carlisle in May 1149 was clearly meant to inaugurate a new episode in the fortunes of the Angevin party. It was a carefully crafted

28 *Regesta* iii, no. 795, cf. also nos. 420, 666.

29 *GS*, 214.

30 Coincidentally, or not, Archbishop Theobald of Canterbury appears on 26 January 1149 in the west midlands, at Worcester, ostensibly in attendance at the deathbed of Bishop Simon. It is worth noting that it would not have been beyond the bounds of possibility for him to have moved to meet the young duke at Devizes, or loitered in the west to greet him on his way north to Carlisle, A. Saltman, *Theobald, Archbishop of Canterbury* (London, 1955), 546.

31 *Letters of Arnulf of Lisieux*, ed. Barlow, 7; see comments in M. Chibnall, 'Normandy', in *The Anarchy of King Stephen's Reign*, ed. E. King (Oxford, 1994), 106–7. JH, 323 calls Henry '*tyro . . . dux Normanniae*' immediately after talking of his knighting.

32 JH, 322–3; HH, 754; Green, 'Earl Ranulf II and Lancashire', in *The Earldom of Chester and its Charters*, ed. A.T. Thacker (Journal of the Chester Archaeological Society, 71, 1991), 106.

propaganda event. Both John of Hexham and Henry of Huntingdon portray it as such. The *Gesta Stephani*, on the other hand, represents it as a preliminary to an assault on York, giving the episode a misleading appearance of the beginning of a major campaign, and the renewal of the war.[33] The *Gesta's* interpretation is by no means uncontestable. The *Gesta* says that Stephen moved north to York in order to pre-empt an Angevin assault on the city. The citizens had warned him of the approach of the Scots and Henry's supporters.[34] Henry of Huntingdon tells the story differently. By his account King Stephen moved north and encamped at York throughout August, *in case* the Scots launched an assault on York. But King David kept to his lands and eventually moved off back north. John of Hexham talks of a planned muster at Lancaster which was to follow the festivities at Carlisle, after which the assembled force would 'march on King Stephen', but Earl Ranulf failed to appear so the Scots went home and Henry returned south. He mentions no attack planned on York and, like Henry of Huntingdon, implies that Stephen was in the north of England before York was in any danger.[35]

Rather than a flexing of military muscle in the north, Henry Plantagenet's appearance at Carlisle is best interpreted as a symbolic event. Henry received the blessing of his most powerful relative and political ally, King David, who presided over his passage into manhood. If, indeed, King Stephen was in York as late as August to counter fears of a Scottish invasion, then the discussions and public events associated with the delivery of arms at the end of May went on well into the summer. If we accept what John of Hexham says about a muster of forces at Lancaster after Carlisle, it might be interpreted as a further stage in the festivities: one of a series of assemblies and military games, somewhat like those prolonged festivities and tournaments which accompanied the coronation of the young Philip II of France in 1179. When the fun and the posturing were over, Henry Plantagenet took himself off back to the south with the earl of Hereford as his escort, and (not without adventure) reached Bristol after evading the patrols of Count Eustace which were hoping to waylay him in the lanes of Gloucestershire.[36]

Henry seems to have had no other intention in travelling south than to return home to Normandy, but he did not do so immediately. If he was not in England to fight a war, King Stephen certainly thought he was. After shadowing Henry from York, Stephen had him pursued into the southwest. Count Eustace, Stephen's son, was sent to take up quarters in Oxford with a force of knights. He led his troops into the old campaigning grounds of the Thames valley where his father and Philip of Gloucester had done so much to damage Earl Robert in the years from 1144 to 1147. There was a brief campaign,

---

33 R.H.C. Davis, *King Stephen* (3rd edn., London, 1990), 104–5, follows the *Gesta's* interpretation; the more recent interpretation by Bradbury, *Stephen and Matilda* (Stroud, 1996), 145, is circumspect.
34 *GS*, 216.
35 JH, 323.
36 *GS*, 216–18; JH 323.

the high point of which was the narrow escape of Henry Plantagenet from capture by Eustace at Dursley. Thereafter, Eustace's troops ranged across north Wiltshire and the Cotswolds, but seem to have accomplished little by it other than dashing here and there and unsettling the established garrisons in Devizes, Marlborough and Gloucester. Rather more damage was done when King Stephen himself appeared from York by way of London (and perhaps Bedford) and joined his son in the west.[37] Their combined forces turned south with a more concentrated fury upon Marlborough, Devizes and, eventually, Salisbury. The evident intention was to destroy the hold of the allied Marshal and Salisbury families on that troubled county.

Whether he wanted it or not, Henry was now engaged in a campaign in the southwest of England. Like Robert of Gloucester before him, his main ally was the neutralism of the royalist magnates. Stephen was only able to maintain the fight where he, his son, or his immediate officers were. There were no significant magnates who could be trusted to carry the war to the enemy unless the king himself was there to urge them on. But Henry could count on the self-interest of his own allies. While Stephen concentrated his military household in the south in an attempt to reopen the fight for Bristol and Gloucester, Earl Ranulf of Chester in his rear happily renewed his own fight to regain Lincoln, lost to him in 1146. The fortunes of Henry were doubtless of only limited interest to him. But, by attacking Lincoln and pressing hard on the garrison, he forced Stephen to give up his campaign in Wiltshire after only a few weeks and move to the relief of the city. The late autumn of 1149 then saw a stubborn and inconclusive campaign develop in the Trent valley, as the king attempted to push westward from Lincoln and contain Ranulf within his patrimony, which he eventually did by the fortification of a certain unnamed castle.[38]

While the king was lured away north, other areas of the kingdom were troubled. Hugh Bigod and the Beauchamp family of Bedford were harried by Count Eustace in case they, too, took advantage of the king's engagement in the north. Henry Plantagenet and his allies continued the shadow-boxing, gathering their forces against Stephen's military governor in Somerset and Devon, Henry de Tracy. Their campaign had little effect other than economic, for Tracy kept his head down and he and his men retreated to his castles. But in the meantime Count Eustace dashed across the southern midlands, hoping to seize Devizes while Henry fitz Empress was in Devon. Eustace's single-mindedness in pursuit of his cousin is notable, no wonder that John of Hexham speculated, 'There was between [Henry] and Eustace, the son of King Stephen, a contest of arms, for they were rivals for the same crown'.[39] Eustace was

37 According to evidence given in the county court of Norfolk and Suffolk in 1150, the previous year the king had been at the siege of Bedford where the besiegers had plotted to assassinate him, *English Lawsuits from William I to Richard I*, ed. R.C. van Caenegem (2 vols, Selden Soc., 106–7, 1990–1) i, 289.
38 *GS*, 216–18, 220.
39 JH, 323.

foiled when Henry's column of knights appeared while he was in the process of forcing the outworks of Devizes, and he retreated hastily, having no resources for a full-scale battle. It was now the middle of winter and both sides abandoned the field. Henry's advisers in England persuaded him that he had done enough and should return to Normandy. He left at the beginning of January 1150 and rejoined his father. Whatever plans he was contemplating, he would not return to England for over three years.[40]

STEPHEN, COUNT EUSTACE AND THE CHURCH

While the royalist and the Angevin parties were reeling about England like two punch-drunk prizefighters, another more significant battle was being fought outside the ring. Eustace, Stephen's eldest son, had come of age in the summer of 1147 when he was twenty-one (the age which was to become the customary age of majority in England later in the century). His father himself performed the ceremony of girding with arms, and conferred on his son the county and honor of Boulogne which had belonged to Eustace's mother.[41] Presumably Queen Mathilda had sanctioned this transfer of her patrimony. Eustace was, by the partial account of the *Gesta*, a promising young man. He was said to be skilled both as politician and warrior, and the campaigning of 1148 had demonstrated his energy and courage at the very least. Although young, he would fearlessly lead troops against magnates of formidable reputation and experience, such as Ranulf of Chester and Roger of Hereford. Eustace was a trusted aide to his father, and it can be seen how the king used him as an alter ego to campaign in the southwest and the eastern counties while he went north.[42] With Eustace, rather than his magnates or even his *curiales*, the king could be sure of total commitment.

For the king's part, he not unnaturally wished his son to succeed him on the throne. Perhaps unwisely, Stephen may have allowed negotiations back in 1140 which hinted that he might not insist that Eustace should receive all the Anglo-Norman realm as he himself had inherited it in 1135. Thereafter, Eustace might never be entirely assured of his future kingdom in this world. This insecurity might very well account for the frenetic energy of his 1149 campaigns, when he had Henry fitz Empress at the metaphorical point of his lance. To dispose of Henry was to dispose of his main rival. As we have seen, John of Hexham believed that there was indeed a particular animosity and rivalry between the two young men over the throne they both thought to be theirs by right.

Once Eustace was of age, King Stephen began what moves he could make to secure his son's succession. The surest way to do this was by arranging Eustace's coronation as king in Stephen's own lifetime. The coronation of the heir in the lifetime of the father was a venerable practice belonging to an

---

40 *GS*, 222–4; GC i, 42; RT, 161.
41 *GS*, 208.
42 A point made by *GS*, 208.

earlier age when the royal dignity was held to be shared among the family. It was an attitude still to be found in Wales, where kingship was divisible between siblings, as Owain and Cadwaladr ap Gruffudd ap Cynan demonstrated after 1137. It had recently been seen in France too, where the young Louis VII was crowned at Reims by no less a person than Pope Innocent II in 1131, six years before the death of his father, Louis VI. It would be seen again in the next generation, for Louis VII was still alive (if ailing) when his young son, Philip II, was crowned in 1179.[43] True, coronation of the heir had not been an English practice (the concept of the 'atheling', or king-designate, made it unnecessary in pre-Conquest times). But when Stephen asked for Eustace to be crowned as joint-king he was asking something the Church could grant, if it so wished. Unfortunately for him, the Church had no wish to oblige him in the matter.

The papacy had been a great support to Stephen. It was Innocent II's decision early in 1136 to accept Stephen's declaration that public order in England depended on his coronation that had made Stephen's accession difficult to challenge. Later, when the representatives of the empress attempted to argue the legitimacy of Stephen's claim at the Lateran Council in 1139, Pope Innocent had once more stood by Stephen. But the death of Innocent in 1143 changed papal policy to England at the Curia. The new pope, Celestine II, lasted less than a year on the throne of St Peter. As a cardinal, Celestine had opposed Innocent's laissez-faire attitude to English affairs. He did not last long as pope, but in his brief reign of about six months (September 1143 to March 1144) he did make one significant pronouncement. John of Salisbury records that Celestine wrote to Archbishop Theobald of Canterbury pronouncing that there should be no change (*innovatio*) concerning the crown of England, because it was under dispute and its transfer had been (apparently) irregular. His declaration was confirmed by his two successors.[44] What this appears to have meant was that Stephen should continue to be recognised as king by the Curia. This may sound positive for Stephen, but it did not commit the pope to anything more than maintaining Stephen as king and left as an open question whether he could be admitted to be a rightful king. Archbishop Theobald certainly took this tack. Celestine's mandate was his excuse for not agreeing to Stephen's request to crown Eustace.

Precisely when the request for Eustace's coronation had been made at Canterbury and Rome is difficult to say, but it is a question of some importance. If we knew when the issue became a critical one for King Stephen, we would know when it was that he (like the empress in her turn) saw the beginning of the end. John of Salisbury and John of Hexham both say that when Henry Murdac achieved recognition as archbishop of York from the king, that is in January 1151, the archbishop promised to get the pope to agree to Stephen's request. He was at Rome at Easter (8 April 1151), but accounts differ as to the

---

43 Suger, *Vita Ludovici Grossi regis*, ed. H. Waquet (Paris, 1964), 268; RT, 287.
44 *Historia Pontificalis*, 85–6.

degree of his success there. John of Salisbury says Henry Murdac achieved nothing at the Curia, but John of Hexham says that the pope was willing to recognise Eustace as 'true heir to the kingdom' (which does not necessarily mean that he was willing to permit Eustace's coronation at that time).[45]

The chronology of the decision to get Eustace crowned can therefore be calculated back from this manoeuvre of January–April 1151. What we know of it implies that the king had already tried, and failed, to get the pope to allow his son to be crowned some time before 1151. An approach to the pope would presumably have been after a direct approach to Archbishop Theobald had failed and an appeal had been made to the Curia (as John of Salisbury implies). Professor Cronne associated the scheme with Bishop Henry of Winchester's embassy to Rome to work for reconciliation in the dispute over the acceptance of the pope's nominee for the archbishopric of York, Henry Murdac. This mission has been recently dated to the winter of 1149–50 and Stephen's olive branch to Eugenius III sent with that embassy might well have been his willingness to accept Murdac.[46] The turnabout over Murdac in 1149–50 would explain why it was that a year later Archbishop Henry was willing to take up the cause of Eustace at Rome, as a trade-off. If this were so, the plan to get Eustace crowned followed on from the campaign between Henry and Eustace in the West Country in 1149.[47] Henry's assumption of the title of 'duke' during this campaign would have been another spur to try to exalt Eustace higher than the rank of count. The chronology tells us that Stephen had assessed Henry's first adult tour of England to be a very damaging political coup against him, despite its lack of any military impact.

THE FIGHT FOR NORMANDY, 1150–52

Since Count Eustace and his father had been unable to overpower Henry fitz Empress in England, and since warfare in England tended to run aground on the shoals of neutralism anyway, an alternative was to attempt to carry the war to the Angevins in France. Henry had returned to his father, Duke Geoffrey, in January 1150. The return of King Louis VII from the Second Crusade in late autumn 1149 had brought the period of peaceful relations between the Capetians and Angevins to an end, and so opened up new opportunities for Stephen. Duke Geoffrey's aggressive incursions into Poitou, in pursuit of one of his fractious Angevin subjects, caused the problem. Poitou had come under Louis's lordship through his marriage to Eleanor of Aquitaine,

---

45 *Historia Pontificalis*, 83; JH, 325–6.
46 H.A. Cronne, *The Reign of Stephen: Anarchy in England, 1135–54* (London, 1970), 60, fails to date Bishop Henry's mission, but its date is usefully considered in *English Episcopal Acta* viii, *Winchester*, ed. Franklin, p. xlvi. A letter of Bishop Henry's seeking safe passage through Flanders and northern France shows he must have planned the first stage of his journey before the return of Louis VII in November 1149, *RHF* xv, 494–5.
47 Saltman, *Theobald*, 30, also opts for the end of 1149 as the time when the idea of the coronation of Eustace was floated, but he gives no reason.

and the rebel in question, Giraud Bellay, castellan of Montreuil-Bellay, appealed to Louis, as to his lord, for protection. He might reasonably expect to get it, as he was Louis's seneschal for Poitou. But Duke Geoffrey continued to assault Montreuil despite Louis's order to withdraw into Anjou.[48] Since Louis had no intention of overlooking this insult, there was plenty of scope for the renewal of the alliance between Stephen and the French.

The hard winter of 1149–50 saw preparations for a major confrontation between Duke Geoffrey and King Louis. As part of it, the duke resigned Normandy to the keeping of Henry fitz Empress after his return from England in January 1150.[49] According to the indirect evidence of Robert of Torigny, Geoffrey even laid down the ducal style he had used since 1144 and resumed the title of 'count of Anjou'.[50] Envoys arrived in France from King Stephen offering an alliance and military assistance. We know of them in part because Arnulf of Lisieux wrote to Abbot Suger of St-Denis early in 1150 suggesting that he delay as far as he could Louis's reply to the envoys of the king of England while he awaited results from his own mission to the courts of Count Geoffrey and Duke Henry.[51] The identity of at least one, and perhaps two, of those envoys is clear. Bishop Henry, the king's brother, took in the region of Paris on his way to Rome. A sequence of letters shows him planning to enter France through Flanders and Vermandois in the early autumn of 1149. There is some evidence that he was accompanied as far as the borders of Flanders by no less a person than his sister-in-law, Queen Mathilda.[52] There were clearly some talks between the bishop, Abbot Suger and King Louis at the end of 1149 or beginning of 1150, and then Bishop Henry moved on south, leaving behind one of his unnamed intimates accredited to continue the discussions. He also left with Suger a very flattering letter addressed to him by King Stephen, promising to safeguard the lands of the abbey of St-Denis which were in his power, and look to the abbey's lands 'still in the power of my enemies'.[53] A formal alliance (*foedus*) between Louis VII and Stephen was soon in negotiation. Suger was not in favour of it, indeed he wrote to Count

---

48 RT, 159, 160. Y. Sassier, *Louis VII* (Paris, 1991), 217–21; Chibnall, *Matilda*, 153–4 glosses over the difficulties of chronology of the Norman campaigns of 1150–51, eadem, 'Normandy', 109–10 gives a clearer treatment. For Montreuil-Bellay, its siege and its lords, J. Chartrou, *L'Anjou de 1109 à 1151* (Paris, 1928), 69–74.

49 Geoffrey was by this time prey to bouts of chronic illness, see his letters to Suger of *c*.1148, *RHF*, xv, 493–4, 494. It might be justifiable to trace this back to the severe leg injury he received in the campaign of 1136 in Normandy, OV vi, 472–4. Robert Hemerichs has recently suggested that the transfer of lordship in Normandy to Henry was designed to forestall Capetian demands for Henry to do homage for Normandy to Louis VII, as no ruling duke had yet done so, 'The siege of Montreuil-Bellay', in *The Anglo-Norman Anonymous*, 17 (1999), 8. However, Henry did so nonetheless in 1151.

50 RT, 161, Geoffrey is called consistently '*comes Andegavensis*' by Robert after the resignation, and Bishop Arnulf of Lisieux distinguishes between *Duke* Henry and *Count* Geoffrey early in 1150, *Letters of Arnulf of Lisieux*, 9.

51 *Letters of Arnulf of Liseiux*, 9.

52 Queen Mathilda issued a charter at Steenvorde (*Osinforth*) on the borders of Boulogne and Flanders between 1148 and 1152, a visit to her ancestral county in 1149–50 is the most likely period for this, see below, p. 261n.

53 *RHF* xv, 520.

Geoffrey at the beginning of 1150 frankly warning him, 'We advise your Nobility that you should work hard and long both through your friends and through your confidants to seek the love and peace of the lord king [Louis] while it can still be sought, and while as yet he has opened no treaty with your enemies!'.[54]

In the end no major campaign occurred in 1150, partly because the dying Abbot Suger threw his moral weight in the balance on the side of peace. Stephen's blandishments seem to have been wasted on him. The appalling harshness of that terrible winter in England and northern France, and the famine that followed in the spring and early summer, must also have had something to do with the truce that held for most of the year in both countries. That winter, great rivers froze so that men could cross them on horseback, and snow and ice lay thick on the ground from Christmas until April. The growing season came late, too late for the poor. Starving vagrants besieged monasteries seeking alms. For once, forces greater than kings and princes laid waste the land, and war withered away with the frostbitten crops.[55]

However, King Stephen's planned alliance with the French did come to fruition in 1151. King Louis ignored Anjou and Poitou and concentrated his forces on Normandy. His main assault was in the north, where he had negotiated the support of the count of Ponthieu the previous year, and where the county of Boulogne was, of course, still held for Stephen. With the assistance of his brother-in-law, the king, Count Eustace began a campaign in Upper Normandy. Moving from the Beauvaisis, Eustace penetrated the Pays de Bray north of Rouen and seized the formidable fortress of Neufchâtel, which Henry I had built at great expense. From Neufchâtel, Eustace moved to the coast to assault Arques. His intention was clearly to close in on the capital from the north. In the meantime, Count Waleran of Meulan, whose influence controlled the Seine valley from Poissy downriver to the eastern borders of Normandy, allowed Louis unhindered access through the Vexin and Méresais. Waleran had begun to feel the cold wind of Angevin disfavour after accompanying Louis VII to Palestine, and so he was opening up new avenues of advancement.[56] On the south of Normandy, Count Geoffrey and his ally, the count of Alençon, campaigned against Robert, count of Dreux and the Perche, the brother of Louis VII. Count Robert was able to deal some heavy blows against Geoffrey, penetrating into Normandy as far as Séez.[57]

The king of France, concentrating on the main objective, had massed his forces for the stroke down the Seine which would seize Rouen. A great army was assembled in the Mantois, ready to punch through into the duchy, where Duke Henry was lying low and doing his best to avoid battle. Then in August 1151, King Louis fell ill at Paris before he could join his great army. A truce

54 *RHF* xv, 520–1. See a reconstruction of this diplomatic activity by Sassier, *Louis VII*, 219–21.
55 For the horrors of the winter of 1149–50 in England and northern France, see RT, 160; GC i, 142–3; *Annales de Wintonia*, 54; *Chronicon S. Stephani Cadomensis*, in *RHF*, xii, 780.
56 Crouch, *Beaumont Twins*, 69–71.
57 RT, 161–2.

was sought, and with the king still prostrate, peace was eventually agreed despite the earlier eagerness for war. The fall of Montreuil-Bellay to the Angevins had removed the principal *casus belli* by the summer in any case. Duke Henry travelled with his father to Paris. Although Geoffrey refused to release Giraud Bellay, he did compromise so far as to consent to his son's homage to the king and the confirmation of the Norman Vexin to Louis. The father and son are reported as returning congratulating themselves. Duke Henry hurried back to Normandy, instructing that his nobles attend a great assembly at Lisieux on 14 September where plans would be discussed for an invasion of England and renewal of the war there. Duke Henry had clearly realised that the best way to avoid war in the duchy was to take the war to Stephen in England. His father in the meanwhile had returned to Anjou where he caught a fever (allegedly from taking a plunge in a cold river) and died after a short illness on 7 September, not yet an old man.[58]

The illness of Louis VII had temporarily dashed the hopes of Stephen and Eustace. But Count Geoffrey's death redeemed the situation for them. Instead of leaving his father to contain Louis VII while he took the fight back to England, Duke Henry now had to stay on the Continent and secure his ancestral realm of Anjou and the Touraine. He had many potential problems in doing this, although no major internal ones. Normandy had already accepted him as duke, and Anjou likewise welcomed him. He was at Le Mans briefly for his father's funeral but did not arrive to take formal possession of the county till November, holding a council of his Angevin barons and receiving their fealty.[59] The delay in crossing into Anjou indicates that Henry anticipated little difficulty from his nobility there.[60] Henry's problems in northern France were mostly to do with his neighbours, who were anxious to undermine the Norman–Angevin condominium his father had patiently constructed. It was these external powers – whether Stephen of England or Louis VII of France or Theobald of Blois – which were willing and able to exploit rival claims to his inheritance, whether by promoting Count Eustace's claims to Normandy or the emerging discontent of Henry's own younger brother, Geoffrey fitz Empress, to whom their father had left four castle-lordships concentrated in the Touraine.[61]

In 1152 these external forces combined to threaten Duke Henry's continued enjoyment of Normandy and Anjou. The eventual military catharsis which must resolve this was inevitable in the charged political atmosphere of northern France, but Henry himself helped it along. In March 1152, Louis VII secured the annulment of his marriage to Eleanor, the heir to the duchy of Aquitaine. The annulment was granted on the grounds of consanguinity, they were both descended (within the prohibited seventh degree of kinship) from

58 RT, 162–3; *Chroniques des comtes d'Anjou*, 72.
59 RT, 163; *GS*, 224; *Regesta* iii, nos. 440, 776.
60 RT, 163–4.
61 WN i, 113 names three of the great demesne castles of the south and east of the county of Anjou: Chinon, Loudun and Mirebeau.

King Robert of France. Other reasons for ending the marriage were suspected. It was said by John of Salisbury that Eleanor and her uncle, the prince of Antioch, had fallen out with Louis while they were being entertained in his city in Syria in 1149, and that the prince had denounced their marriage as uncanonical. On their return from the East, Pope Eugenius III is said to have worked hard to establish a reconciliation between the feuding royal pair while they were staying with him at Tusculum, and confirmed their marriage publicly.[62] But the reconciliation was temporary. The real problem must have lain in the personalities of the couple, and the scandal attached to their public hostilities may have been the true reason for having the marriage voided. For Louis the scandal of continuing the marriage outweighed the scandal of ending it. It is impossible to know which partner's passions provided the impetus for the final break. French curial sources piously point to the king's discomfort in being in breach of the Church's rules on marriage.[63] However, if consanguinity had been the only problem, Louis could have lived with it; he went on to marry two other women related to him more closely than Eleanor, as Yves Sassier points out. It was believed later, in Angevin England, that Eleanor herself had skilfully contrived the annulment and that it was she who engineered the prompt remarriage to Duke Henry.[64]

Duke Henry must have learned at first hand of the marital difficulties of the king and queen of France in the summer of 1151 in Paris when he came with his father to offer his homage for Normandy. After the annulment, Eleanor retired hastily (and allegedly in some peril) to Poitou and there – most unconventionally according to contemporary mores – she and the young duke of Normandy themselves negotiated a marriage (ignoring the rights of King Louis, their overlord) which was blessed at the cathedral of Poitiers on 18 May 1152. Whether this was true or not, by simply entering a church, Henry had acquired claims to a third of France, and most importantly in strategic terms, the county of Poitou, which neighboured Anjou on the south. He had also made impossible any peaceful relationship with the king of France and the count of Blois-Chartres, who were both now at a decided military and strategic disadvantage against Henry, and could hardly ignore the danger.[65]

Duke Henry had still been contemplating renewal of his mother's fight for England in the spring of 1152. His uncle, Earl Reginald of Cornwall, had sailed to Normandy in Lent to advise him and the Norman nobility of the English situation at a further council at Lisieux on 6 April 1152. Despite the marriage to Eleanor, the duke still moved to Barfleur in June to supervise preparations for an invasion fleet. But by this time a great alliance was in

62 *Historia Pontificalis*, 52–3, 61.
63 *Historia gloriosi Ludovici regis*, in *RHF* xvi, 172.
64 GC i, 149. Gervase's ironic comments on the marital difficulties of Louis after the goings-on at Antioch, '. . . which it were far better to keep quiet about' are good evidence of the contemporary perception of pragmatism that lay behind the divorce, particularly his satirical '. . . Surprise! Louis suddenly decided to work for an annulment on the grounds of consanguinity!'.
65 For accounts of the remarriage of Eleanor and its importance, Chibnall, *Matilda*, 155–6; W.L. Warren, *Henry II* (London, 1973), 42–5; Sassier, *Louis VII*, 229–43.

motion against him. Count Eustace had been in England for his mother's death and funeral in April–May 1152, having lost Neufchâtel by the truce of 1151, but still lived in hopes of a renewed campaign. Now his chance had come to renew the war with an even better hope of success. To further their joint cause, Louis VII handed over to Eustace control of some border fortresses, doubtless the castles of the Norman Vexin he had held since 1144.[66] To the south and east of the duchy, Louis could count on the support of his brother, Robert of Dreux, and Eustace's first cousin, Henry of Blois, the new count of Champagne (Stephen's brother, Theobald, having died at the beginning of 1152). Within the Angevin realms, Louis could now count on Geoffrey fitz Empress, who laid claim to Anjou and took the field against his brother.[67]

The young duke of Normandy and Aquitaine found himself involved in a very difficult war on several fronts. Robert of Torigny was convinced that it was his enemies' intention to deprive him of his lands and carve them up between them. The first casualty of the war was Duke Henry's invasion of England. On 16 July 1152 he abandoned Barfleur and his preparations and, moving fast out of the Cotentin, rapidly deployed his forces to east and south. Neufchâtel was again under siege, and again fell to the French, this time by a trick. Duke Henry seems to have spent August garrisoning castles and containing the French, being ostentatiously unwilling to fight his lord, the king, in the field. The king, for his part, withdrew beyond the frontier, to Chaumont, while Duke Henry fortified the line of the Andelle and punished the barons of the Vexin who were fighting for Louis, in connivance with Waleran of Meulan. In mid-August Louis looped south and crossed the Seine at Meulan – undoubtedly at Waleran's invitation – and punched through the Norman defences south of the Seine. In a rapid response, Duke Henry rode for Pacy-sur-Eure, and alarmed King Louis into retreating. Then, following up his advantage, the duke beat up the borders of the county of Dreux and returned to Normandy to crush his own vassal, Richer de L'Aigle, who had jumped too quickly on the Capetian bandwagon. Richer had to give hostages and saw his castle of Bonsmoulins, which he had been given by King Stephen in 1137, burned.[68]

At this point, Duke Henry clearly felt that he was free to retrieve the damage his brother was doing in Anjou, and at the end of August moved south. He did not meet much resistance. He rapidly reduced the fortress of Montsoreau, whose lord, William, had taken Geoffrey's part. He then harried Geoffrey fiercely until he sought to make peace. Although the duke's absence allowed the count of Dreux to make serious and brutal inroads on the borders of southern Normandy, besiege Nonancourt, and assault Tillières and Verneuil,

---

66 *GS*, 226.
67 RT, 165. The claims of Geoffrey fitz Empress against his brother appear (from later sources) to have been derived from the alleged legacy of Anjou to Geoffrey by their father on his deathbed, to be fulfilled when Henry conquered England, WN i, 112–13. See on this Warren, *Henry II*, 45–6. It might equally well be that in 1152 Geoffrey found himself under threat in what little he already held in Anjou and that his was a defensive reaction.
68 RT, 165–6, 169–70.

the risk proved worth taking. To have made peace with Geoffrey fitz Empress reduced the war to one front only, along the southeastern borders of the duchy. King Louis and Robert of Dreux seem indeed to have been troubled by the turn of events. A truce was negotiated during the autumn, and Duke Henry daringly returned to his preparations for an expedition to England. He could not go with the forces he had previously assembled – they were needed for the defence of Normandy – but he could go himself. He may have calculated, as the *Gesta* suggests, that his departure for England would force another enemy to quit the attempt on Normandy, Count Eustace. In the second week of January 1153, leaving the military forces of the duchy under the command of his reconciled brother, Geoffrey, Henry found his window of opportunity and, despite stormy weather, crossed the Channel with his uncle, Earl Reginald, and a small but experienced force of knights, and landed on the south coast, most likely at or near Southampton.[69] It was to be the last campaign of the reign.

APPENDIX – THE DATE OF THE CHESTER–LEICESTER *CONVENTIO*

Sir Frank Stenton established the parameters of the date of this most important treaty from internal evidence. It must have been drafted after (presumably several months after) the consecration of Robert de Chesney, bishop of Lincoln on 19 December 1148, for Bishop Robert acted as a guarantor of the treaty. It must belong to the period before the death of Earl Ranulf on 16 December 1153. Other than that, Stenton was cautious about narrowing the date (see F.M. Stenton, *The First Century of English Feudalism*, 1066–1166, 253n). R.H.C. Davis and Edmund King and others (including myself) have since shared Stenton's cautious approach to the dating. But Geoffrey Barraclough, in the notes to his edition of Ranulf's charters, did attempt to narrow the options. He made the useful point that the phrase *ligius dominus* which Ranulf used to allude to Duke Henry could be more appropriate to a time after May 1149 and the court at Carlisle. Otherwise, his argument rested on dating the *conventio* to the political circumstances of February–March 1153 when both Ranulf and Robert would have been anxious to limit the conflict while both earls judged how the land lay between King Stephen and Duke Henry while the duke approached Leicester from the west (*Charters of the Earls of Chester*, 125–6).

Barraclough looked to external evidence to narrow the date of the *conventio*. However, his argument for 1153 as the probable date could just as well apply to other periods when it was in the interest of both earls to limit the damage

---

69 *GS*, 230. GC i, 151 has the duke landing in England on the feast of the Epiphany 1153, that is 6 January. RT, 171 has him landing within the week after the Epiphany. HH, 763 gives no date, but talks of the stormy season of the crossing. A writ of Duke Henry dated at Southampton before he took the title of Aquitaine (that is, before April 1153) must have been issued on or soon after his first arrival in England, *Cartulaire de Afflighem*, ed. E. de Marneffe, in *Analectes pour servir à l'histoire ecclésiastique de la Belgique*, iie section, *série des cartulaires et des documents étendus*, pt. 2 (Louvain, 1896), 149–51.

that the war might do to their lands. Another likely period in which to locate it would then be the autumn of 1149. Earl Ranulf was at that time engaged in a struggle to regain his influence in Lincolnshire, while the king was pressing hard upon his possessions and strongholds in the Trent valley. For several reasons, the 1149 date is preferable to one in 1153. Firstly, there is the fact that Earl Robert of Derby, the ally of Earl Ranulf in this document, was in conflict with Duke Henry in May–June 1153 (*GS*, 234) and one would have thought that Earl Ranulf – in high favour – would have protected his myrmidon from the duke. Secondly, there is the documentary context. The *conventio* refers to an earlier charter by which Earl Ranulf surrendered the castle of Mount-sorrel to Earl Robert, for his homage (Stenton, *First Century*, 285–6). This Mountsorrel charter has not been satisfactorily dated by any scholar, but it must date to the time when Earl Gilbert de Clare of Hertford (a witness) was sheltering with Ranulf after his dispute with Stephen in 1147–48. Earl Gilbert had returned to Stephen's court by 1149 (*Regesta* iii, no. 169). The Mountsorrel charter in turn refers to another, earlier charter, this time concerning land at Charley near Mountsorrel which can be dated to the period 1145–47 and is the record of a border conference between Earl Ranulf and Earl Robert 'in the fields between Leicester and Mountsorrel' (*Charters of the Earls of Chester*, 82–3).

The sequence of the three documents is clear, and the dates which can be assigned to the two earlier ones span the period 1145–48. It makes sense to suggest then that the third and greatest of them, the Chester–Leicester *conventio*, is closer to 1148 than 1153, and the autumn of 1149 becomes the best possible suggestion. The reason why autumn 1149 is a good suggestion is because the whole emphasis of the *conventio* is on limiting damage to either earl's interests at a time when both men were being pressed. Earl Robert, a royalist, must support King Stephen, but the treaty offers him a way of doing so without being too aggressive. He could argue that Earl Ranulf was his lord and although King Stephen was his 'liege lord', Robert had every right to limit the military commitment in knights or castles which he could be asked to make against Ranulf. The arc of territory that the two earls were discussing is a line which defines Earl Robert's interests as Leicestershire up to the southern hills above the Trent, but secures communications in the Trent valley as far as the strategic castle of Belvoir to Earl Ranulf. At a time when Ranulf was under pressure from the king at Lincoln, this would be the very area (particularly the key castle of Donnington) which Ranulf would wish to protect from Robert's potential aggression. I have therefore made here the Chester–Leicester *conventio* a document of the campaigns of 1149. I think that the balance of likelihood makes this the most justifiable date, though I would be wrong to suggest that the date of 1149 is as yet conclusively proved.

CHAPTER 14

The Solution

What Duke Henry's real intention in England was in 1153 is difficult to assess, but we can make some reasonable hypotheses. Euphoria may be assumed to have been part of the equation. He had recently confronted and temporarily mastered Louis VII. He had survived a co-ordinated assault on his domain by several of his enemies. He had acquired a second duchy by marriage. In that sort of mood, it might have seemed inevitable that England must fall into his hands. God was clearly with him. In his early years as king, Henry was to favour the bold, grand campaign, whether in 1159 against Toulouse or in 1165 against Gwynedd. Neither campaign was a particular success for him. But they may be later echoes of what he thought he was doing in 1153. Duke Henry may have been determined simply to give the tree an almighty shove, and see what fell out. Yet calculation must have informed his decision too. He knew that if he was in England, and Normandy was untroubled in its loyalty to him, then at least one of his enemies must follow him back across the Channel. Count Eustace had to hope for a personal victory over Henry in order to secure his chance of the English throne. Duke Henry must also have been well aware of the mood among the Angevin magnates; his uncle, Reginald of Cornwall, had been with him in Normandy in 1152. His own experience in England had been very recent, and his knowledge both of the country and of his party there was good. So, whether he was euphoric from recent successes, or whether he was possessed by the optimism of youth and self-confidence, he must have assessed as good his chances of coming away from England with something to his benefit.

In the period when the duke was struggling to master the situation in northern France, his party had not prospered in England. The years 1150 and 1151 had been quiet, for a variety of reasons. Famine and economic exhaustion had stilled conflict in 1150, and the next year had seen only desultory campaigning, perhaps because Stephen was for once distracted by affairs across the Channel and expending resources on his son's campaign in Normandy. The only known major campaign in England in those two years was fought over possession of Worcester (for the chronology of these, see Appendix). In itself, the fight for Worcester tells us a good deal about the state of the parties. The city and most of the shire of Worcester was still the possession of Count Waleran of Meulan, but for all practical purposes his interests there were delegated to his sheriff, William de Beauchamp, the only major secular magnate in the county. Waleran's twin brother, the nominally royalist earl of Leicester, had some responsibility for oversight of his brother's sheriff, but distance must have made this difficult for the earl. William de Beauchamp seems to have had liberty to make his own arrangements for the security of his area.[1] The nearest major royal outposts were some considerable distance away, at Warwick – where the earl had been dispossessed of his castle by a royal garrison some years previously – and across the Cotswolds in the upper Thames valley. Although the county was exposed, there was therefore little obvious danger to Worcester. The fact that Angevin and royalist magnates could operate jointly in its government tells us that the war had passed it by. The county seems to have been largely peaceful for most of Stephen's reign after 1141, so much so that there was a scheme mooted that Archbishop Theobald should retire to the diocese or its close vicinity when he was in conflict with King Stephen in 1148. He did, in fact, make a stay in Worcester in January 1149, visiting the deathbed of its bishop, Simon.[2]

It was the death of Bishop Simon that may have been the trigger for Stephen's attempted intervention in the shire. We know from a disgruntled letter of Bishop Gilbert Foliot of Hereford that the dying bishop had confided the keeping of the diocese to the archdeacon of Worcester, instead of himself. He was therefore concerned in the aftermath, if only to prove how much better things would have been had he been put in charge. A chronicle fragment from Evesham abbey for 1149 tells of growing tension between the abbey and William de Beauchamp, who trespassed within the precincts and imposed a levy on the abbey. The abbot went out to confront him and excommunicated William and his armed retinue as they sat on their horses looking at him. The abbot's own tenants took to arms and raided the Beauchamp castle of Elmley, killing one of William's knights, who was consequently refused burial. The men of Evesham were able to overthrow the sheriff's temporary fortification placed by the bridge of the town, presumably to control and tax trade.[3]

The situation in Worcestershire grew even more scandalous the next year and became more than a matter of a local sheriff exerting himself to raise funds from the local church. Bishop Gilbert's letters show the two magnates, Earl Roger of Hereford and William de Beauchamp, making free with the right of sanctuary in the diocese in the summer of 1150 by seizing and ransoming knights who had 'taken refuge' in the precincts of Leominster

---

1 D. Crouch, *The Beaumont Twins: The Roots and Branches of Power in The Twelfth Century* (Cambridge, 1986), 174; E. King, 'Waleran, count of Meulan, earl of Worcester, 1104–1166', in *Tradition and Change: Essays in Honour of M. Chibnall*, ed. D. Greenway and others (Cambridge, 1985), 173–4.
2 A. Saltman, *Theobald Archbishop of Canterbury* (London, 1955), 546; *LCGF*, 115–16.
3 *Chronicon abbatiae de Evesham*, ed. W. Dunn Macray (Rolls Series, 1863), 99–100.

priory and Evesham abbey. This was a significant extension of the earl of Hereford's military activity eastwards out of Herefordshire, a county which he had already mastered. Since four of the knights concerned belonged to Gilbert de Lacy, we may suggest that Earl Roger was extending his power into the Severn valley in pursuit of his old enemy. But since the earl of Hereford self-righteously appealed his case to the archbishop of Canterbury, we might suggest that he saw himself as enforcing public order in alliance with his friend, the excommunicate sheriff, William de Beauchamp, with whom, as Bishop Gilbert said, 'he agrees in all things'.[4] It could be that the king felt obliged to enter the county in force to impose his will at a time when the earl of Hereford was apparently opening a new front against him, and at a time when the shire was in disarray. The king's action seems to have been rather more brutal than the situation required. His enemies might reasonably, if piously, claim to have been engaging in police actions to support public order. The king, on the other hand, entered the county like an invading power, and committed its city to flames.[5] His unsophisticated intention seems to have been to solve the problem of Worcester by crushing William de Beauchamp.

The limited success of King Stephen in Worcestershire in 1150 persuaded him that it was worthwhile renewing the campaign in 1151. Again his object-ive was to secure Worcester. The *Gesta* reveals that the situation within the city had become more complicated since the previous year. Its author talks of Beauchamp as having been seized and imprisoned by 'the knights of the count of Meulan' who had taken control of the castle. They now were apparently in control of Worcester. Who were these men? They would seem to have been followers of the count who had fallen out with their master's lieutenant in the county, presumably because his policies and alliance with Earl Roger were not to their taste. We know the name of their leader, a Norman knight of the count called Ralph de Manneville.[6] Then, bizarrely, Earl Roger chose to attempt to get his friend released by approaching the king to gain his support in a siege of the castle, going so far as to entice the king by the proposal of a formal alliance with him. The *Gesta* shows the earl as simultaneously urging Duke Henry to come to England to assist his cause, and hints that the earl had no preference for either solution.

4 *LCGF*, 127–35, esp. 131. For another reference to the alliance between Earl Roger and William de Beauchamp, see *GS*, 228 saying of William that he '. . . favoured in all things the earl of Hereford'. William, and Walter his brother, attest a number of charters of Earl Roger, one dating to before March 1148, see D. Walker, 'Charters of the earldom of Hereford, 1095–1210', in *Camden Miscellany*, xxii (1964), 41–2. From this it would seem that the Beauchamp–Hereford alliance predated – and was independent of – that between Hereford and Leicester.
5 HH, 754.
6 *Annales de Theokesberia*, 47 says under 1151 that 'Ralph de *Mandevilla* captured William de Beauchamp'. A prominent tenant family of the count of Meulan was indeed the Mannevilles, and a Ralph de Manneville was a frequent witness to Waleran's charters, holding rents from his master at Charlton Marshall in Dorset (Crouch, *Beaumont Twins*, 157n). It would seem from this that Ralph was the head of a faction of the count's supporters enfeoffed in Worcestershire which had arrested William and confined him.

The wary king – now in secret alliance with the leader of the enemy group of magnates – proceeded to the siege of Worcester with some determination, investing time and money in raising siege works around the castle, which lay on the south side of the cathedral precinct, on a steep slope above the Severn. But the king's siege was frustrated – not by the earl of Hereford, but by his nominal friend, the earl of Leicester. Henry of Huntingdon reports as a well-known fact that Earl Robert deployed his influence and cunning to frustrate the conduct of the siege, after the king had left it to his officers to pursue it in his absence. As Professor King notes, this appearance of Count Waleran's brother overturning the siege works at Worcester gives us some idea as to who it was who had persuaded the knights of the count of Meulan to seize William de Beauchamp.[7] The end result was the surrender of the castle of Worcester to Earl Roger on terms which included, one assumes, the release of William de Beauchamp.[8]

The complications and convolutions of the Worcester campaigns of 1150–51 give us an insight into the situation of the parties in those latter years when Stephen was principally preoccupied with plotting for the succession of his son, Eustace, and deploying him in creating a Norman front. Local affinities and alliances made nonsense of party. The only reliable assumption was that magnates would seek to keep their interests intact, and extend them where they safely could. The Beauchamp–Hereford alliance was an axis by which Earl Roger rolled his power further eastward into the middle Severn valley. Its disadvantageous effects on the interests of the count of Meulan, who was of the same party as both men, weighed as nothing in the balance of their ambition. The earl of Leicester, who was not of their party, acted against both of them, but also against the king, his principal, in order to safeguard his brother's county. Yet Leicester was also allied with Hereford, or at least had been a couple of years previously. From all their perspectives, Worcestershire in 1151 was a tiresome and troublesome gaming board which could never be conclusively won. No wonder that Earl Roger was urgent in his messages to Duke Henry to return. There was no hope of resolution in Stephen, nor in the unaided efforts of individual magnates, even the greatest of them (which Earl Roger could now fairly claim to be). Any hope there now was lay in the young Duke Henry. And there, unknown to him, lay the golden key to his coming triumph: he could offer hope to the exhausted.

Count Eustace could not spark the imagination of the magnates in the same way as his cousin. But Stephen did not give up hoping that the royal charisma could be called down on to his son.[9] The beginning of 1152 saw his last attempt to impose the idea of Eustace's succession on the country. A great council was called at London after Easter (30 March) where Stephen mustered as many earls and barons as he could. They were required to swear allegiance

7 HH, 756; King, 'Waleran, count of Meulan', 174.
8 *GS*, 230.
9 GC i, 150 actually puts the situation in terms much like those.

to Eustace, and did so.[10] But Stephen had good reason to remember how the barons of England had sworn allegiance to the empress and then ignored her claims when her father died. So the demand was put to the archbishop of Canterbury and the other bishops that they anoint Eustace without further delay. The archbishop had held a legateship from the pope since 1150, and could conceivably have proceeded to a coronation on his own authority. But the bishops, led by Archbishop Theobald, insisted that the pope had forbidden Eustace's coronation (apparently citing the pronouncement of Celestine II, which had been confirmed by his successors). Doubtless, the bishops thought that the issue had been settled by the archbishop's first refusal in 1149, and the king's renewed insistence caught them by surprise. The bishops present were put under house arrest and their temporal possessions threatened with confiscation unless they complied. The archbishop fled to the quays, pursued by a party of royal household knights, hailed a ferry-boat to take him across the Thames, rode south to Dover, and so crossed the Channel into temporary exile in Flanders. The exile was not a long one, probably because the king's anger was directed more towards Rome than Canterbury, and Theobald had returned by August.[11]

The year 1152 was shaping up to be a dismal one for Stephen. He manfully soldiered on. This time he scraped together the resources and the enthusiasm for a renewed Thames valley campaign. He had returned to the old battlefields of 1142–45, but not to the old enemies. The retirement and death of Brian fitz Count, probably in 1150, may have persuaded him that the time had come again when he might seize the enclave of Wallingford. But his objectives were wider than one fortress. John fitz Gilbert came under his onslaught once more. John had created a new forward post at Newbury in Berkshire, a possession of his cousin, the count of Perche. The king first encamped at Reading, and outraged local sensibilities by fortifying the abbey precinct as a forward base.[12] Then he moved west to Newbury. The castle was besieged, and in the biography of John fitz Gilbert's son, William, then a boy of about five years, we catch a glimpse of the king in this, his last campaign to suppress his enemies. William was used by his father as a hostage for good faith when he negotiated a truce with the king, ostensibly so that he could consult with the castellan of Newbury about surrender. Instead, John resupplied the castle and abandoned his little son to the king's mercy. William Marshal's childhood memories of this traumatic incident in his young life were later retold to his household, and they were transmitted by his sons and followers to his biographer, working in the 1220s. The sort of king the boy remembered was a man of energy and determination, committed to the task

10 The great council at London and the submission of the magnates to Eustace is mentioned by *Annales de Waverleia*, 234 (which places it before Queen Mathilda's death in May). The date of the octave of Easter for the archbishop's arrest is given by *Compendium vitae Theobaldi*, in *PL* 150, cols. 733–4.
11 HH, 758; GC i, 150–1; see the account in Saltman, *Theobald*, 37–9.
12 RT, 174.

in hand, but not so committed that he would take a small boy's life. Little William was (all unwitting) threatened with several fearful deaths in the face of the garrison. But he prattled cheerily to his captors, and the garrison ignored him, for their lord had said that he had 'the hammers and anvil' to make more and better sons. The siege had to be prosecuted to the end. King Stephen ignored his more ruthless advisers, who would have had the boy executed for his father's bad faith, and carried him about with him as his page for a year. William records a priceless memory of being with the king (a distinguished man now approaching the age of sixty) in his flower-strewn royal tent in the siege camp, playing a child's game of knights, with straw dolls.[13]

There was some reason for the king's abstracted sentimentality at this time. It was – despite the apparent heartlessness of John fitz Gilbert towards his son – no part of the twelfth-century ideal of manhood that fathers be brutal to their children and unloving to their wives. It may be that John fitz Gilbert was willing to abandon William to the king's mercy precisely because he knew that Stephen was kindness itself to women and children. In good time, William Marshal would prove himself an affectionate and beloved father to his own children. In this, Stephen himself may have been an influence, showing how patriarchal dignity was not compromised by open affection. When Stephen began the siege of Newbury, he was a recent widower. Queen Mathilda had died on 3 May 1152 at Castle Hedingham in Essex, at the shining new comital palace of Earl Aubrey de Vere, whose countess was her friend and former lady-in-waiting. If the king's charter dated at Hedingham, which confirms the queen's grant of the hospital she had founded next to the Tower of London to the priory of Holy Trinity, was issued at her deathbed, then both the king and Count Eustace were present when she died. We know from the records of Aldgate priory that she survived for three or four days after her illness was diagnosed as mortal, for the prior of Aldgate was her confessor and was summoned into Essex to assist in the administration of the last rites.[14] The queen's body was taken south to London and then on into Kent where she was laid to rest in the sanctuary of the new royal Cluniac abbey at Faversham; an abbey built in 1147 to be Stephen's version of Henry I's great dynastic statement at Reading.

Queen Mathilda had been a great queen. She had been a regent, a diplomat and even a war leader for her husband, and had been accomplished in all she did. King Stephen won his freedom in 1141 only because she refused to give up in the face of what looked like defeat. In the latter years of the reign, after 1147, she had based herself at Canterbury, frequently residing at the monastery of St Augustine outside the city wall. It seems that in this, she was following

---

13 For this see, *History of William Marshal*, ed. Holden and others, i, ll.658ff. D. Crouch, *William Marshal: Court, Career and Chivalry in the Angevin Empire, c.1147–1219* (London, 1990), 16–18. Other evidence of the siege of Newbury is a note of a charter of Stephen to Bermondsey priory '. . . *apud Neueberia in obsidione*', *Regesta* iii, no. 89. It corroborates one aspect of the Marshal story by confirming that Earl William of Arundel was with the king's army in the siege.
14 *Regesta* iii, no. 505; *Cartulary of Holy Trinity, Aldgate*, 232.

the same model of pious queenship as her namesake the empress, also living in seclusion within monastic walls near Rouen, while keeping an eye on worldly business. From St Augustine's the queen personally supervised the building and endowment of Faversham abbey, seven miles west of Canterbury on the Roman road towards London.[15] But she had not confined herself within the walls, in fact she allegedly found the monks of St Augustine unsociable (because they kept strict silence), and summoned priest-monks from the cathedral to say mass in her chapel. There is some evidence that she travelled to Flanders in 1150 to support the negotiations with King Louis.[16] She was with her husband in London for the great church council of 1151 and had attended the general council in London in early April 1152.[17] It was on a social visit to Hedingham to Euphemia, countess of Oxford, a close friend (probably following on from the council in London), that she became ill and died.[18] That her death must have deeply affected Stephen is quite certain, and although he may have recovered from the emotional shock, what he could not replace was the queen's steadfastness of purpose and her steady judgement, faculties which gave him a certain independence of other members of his family. It is not unlikely that it was she who was pressing Stephen to get their son, Eustace, crowned king; the subject was not raised again after her death and the succession of their second son, William, to the crown never even reached the agenda. Her loss may have brought the king closer to his brother, Bishop Henry, with all that implied for a negotiated end to the succession dispute, for Bishop Henry begins to appear at the top table once again in the penultimate year of the reign.

But in the aftermath of the queen's death in 1152, King Stephen was still vigorously pursuing a military solution. It is possible that the vigour he displayed at this time – when the *Gesta* was pleased to note that 'he had the upper hand everywhere and did everything in the kingdom as he wished' – may have been a result of his need to find solace in activity.[19] If so, the castle of Newbury and its captured garrison were sacrifices to a king's unhappiness.

15 GC i, 39. Faversham abbey was dedicated under the name of St Saviour and founded by a colony of monks from Bermondsey in November 1148, but the foundation charter (*Regesta* iii, no. 300) reveals that the queen and king had been preparing the ground in Kent for some time before then, the queen exchanging her land at Lillechurch, Kent, with William of Ypres to secure the endowment. The queen would also have needed to come to an arrangement with the monks of St Augustine, her hosts, for they held the rectory of the churches of Faversham, *Regesta* iii, no. 157. After 1148, the queen added to the endowment her manor of Tring, Bucks (ibid., no. 301).
16 A charter of hers, granting her abbey of Coggeshall freedom from tolls at Dover and in her Continental ports of Boulogne and Wissant, was issued at *Osinforth*, which can be identified with Steenvorde on the border between her county of Boulogne and the county of Flanders, PRO, C56/52, m. 3, a version printed in R.H.C. Davis, *King Stephen* (3rd edn., 1990), 167. It dates to a time after the investiture of her son, Eustace, as count, and it would match the diplomatic circumstances of the winter of 1149–50 when we know that her brother-in-law, Bishop Henry, travelled by that route to the French court (see above, p. 248).
17 *Regesta* iii, no. 185; *Compendium Vitae Theobaldi*, in *PL* 150, col. 734.
18 A charter of Countess Euphemia granted 100s. of land to Colne priory at Ickleton, Cambs, for the souls of Stephen and Mathilda 'who gave me the said manor in free marriage', *Cartularium prioratus de Colne*, ed. L. Fisher (Colchester, 1946), 29–30. Ickleton was a member of the queen's honor of Boulogne.
19 *GS*, 226.

From Newbury – which would now defend his rear from any Angevin assault from Wiltshire – the king circled north to Wallingford. Brian fitz Count had died in or soon before 1150, and the great castle he had defended against repeated royal attacks since 1139 was now returned to his widow, Mathilda. The castellan of the place in 1151 was William Boterel, a Breton relative of the late Brian. It may be that Mathilda of Wallingford had already retreated to a nunnery by 1152. Later sources indicate she died a professed religious.[20]

The king's siege of Wallingford continued remorselessly through the second half of 1152, and this time he could not be distracted by counter-campaigns: the events of 1151 around Worcester reveal that there was no unity of purpose to be found in the Angevin party that would have supported a column of troops large enough to secure the relief of the fortress. Stephen's army was in any case remarkably large, including a formidable contingent from the city of London. Earl Roger attempted what he could, but was driven off from Wallingford with ease.[21] As we have seen, Earl Reginald of Cornwall, the duke's uncle, had crossed to Normandy at the beginning of the year. He had attended the duke's council at Lisieux in April 1152 to urge him to intervene in England, and it seems that he remained at his side. Earl Roger of Hereford and the garrison of Wallingford in the meantime addressed their own urgent appeals to the duke to come to England immediately.[22] Doubtless, Roger now realised that the Angevin party could only be resuscitated and directed if the golden youth himself came to England. As we have seen, Duke Henry did listen to his allies' appeals, and cutting through a jungle of distractions and dangers, crossed to England in January 1153. He did not come with an armada. His little fleet of thirty-six ships carried only a modest army, William of Newburgh talks of only 140 knights and 3,000 footsoldiers.[23] But that was not important. The most important thing was that he had himself come. As we shall see, that itself was the deciding factor in the critical year of 1153.

THE CAMPAIGN OF 1153

The chronicle accounts tell us that after landing the duke went straight on to the attack, and led his little army north to Malmesbury.[24] We ought to assume

20 On Brian's death, K.S.B. Keats-Rohan, 'The devolution of the honour of Wallingford, 1066–1148', *Oxoniensia*, liv (1989), 315; M. Chibnall, *The Empress Matilda* (Oxford, 1991), 149–50. For William Boterel as castellan of Wallingford at this time, *Regesta* iii, no. 88.
21 *GS*, 226.
22 HH, 760; *GS*, 228.
23 WN i, 88. RT, 171, gives the number of ships. HH, 762 talks only of his bringing only a small force, but *GS*, 230 talks on the contrary of Henry bringing a 'vast army' (*immensum agmen*) of knights and infantry. The *Gesta*'s assessment is unlikely, considering the problems the duke left in Normandy, and also does not tally with the size of the fleet given by Robert de Torigny. The author goes out of his way to detail the murderous and profane exploits of part of Henry's force, a force of 500 foreign mercenaries, who plundered Malmesbury and were sent home by the duke to avoid further scandal, *GS*, 230–2, and it may be that the author wished to inflate the size of the duke's army so that the loss of the mercenaries would not seem so critical.
24 HH, 762, notes he besieged Malmesbury 'disdaining delay' ('*mora maxime perosa*'). *GS*, 230 has the duke proceeding to Malmesbury 'without delay' ('*adempta dilatione*').

from this that the assault on Malmesbury happened in late January 1153. But before the assault he may have first moved to Devizes, where he held a court at which he welcomed Earl Ranulf of Chester. By now the ducal entourage had acquired most of the loyalist Angevin earls: Salisbury, Gloucester, Hereford and Lincoln. Earl Ranulf was issued with a charter of confirmation of breath-taking generosity. It conceded him a large part of the Trent valley, added the county of Stafford and created for him a county of Avranches in Normandy. If the charter had ever been implemented Ranulf would have been the most powerful man in England. The profligacy more than hints that the duke was prepared to promise anything at this time to secure military support, and the man who accepted such gifts would have been a fool if he ever thought he would be left in peace to enjoy them.[25]

The duke's first serious military venture since landing had to be a glowing success. His choice of Malmesbury shows that beleaguered Wallingford was then very much on his mind. The road from Gloucester into the Thames valley could be opened by seizing the royal fortress there. As it happened, the duke was to be disappointed. Stephen moved rapidly to confront the Angevin force and the castle of Malmesbury proved stubborn in its resistance. The town of Malmesbury soon fell – and was ruthlessly plundered by the duke's mercenaries – but the castle (one of Roger of Salisbury's expensive stone fortresses) proved impossible to storm. The duke was therefore forced to attempt to starve the garrison. This allowed the king, warned by the commander, one Jordan, to bring up his army through sleet and rain to relieve the castle. The accounts of the subsequent events differ, but both have the armies of king and duke in bitter weather (Huntingdon talks of a gale-driven rainstorm) confronting each other across a river near the town. Henry of Huntingdon has the royal army so dispirited by the weather that it broke off the impending battle, the king returning to London. The castle surrendered when the relief column disappeared so abruptly and disappointingly.[26] The author of the *Gesta* has a different and more telling explanation. He believed that neither army was willing to fight, in part because of the winter famine which made sustenance in the field difficult, but also in part because the king,

> . . . noticed that some of his leading barons were very casual in their service and had already sent envoys by stealth and made a compact with the duke.[27]

This was something new. The king had had several years to get used to the fact that many of his magnates could not be trusted to pursue any interests but their own, but we must presume that he would not have called upon such men to form the strength of the field army that had been besieging Wallingford,

25 *Regesta* iii, no. 180. It is worth suggesting that Henry was duplicating his father's strategy in Normandy in 1141–44.
26 HH, 762–4. For a recent account of the siege see J. Bradbury, *Stephen and Matilda* (Stroud, 1996), 159–60.
27 *GS*, 234.

and which he had led to the relief of Malmesbury.[28] But what happened before Malmesbury was different from neutralism – it was defeatism amongst those who were formerly his most loyal allies. Stephen was right to be depressed, he was contemplating new and very treacherous territory.

Following the surrender of Malmesbury, the *Gesta* tells us that the duke 'gave his army some rest because it had been harassed by a toilsome siege and greatly weakened by danger of starvation'.[29] This would imply that he went into winter quarters, although no source tells us where. What we do know, however, is that he was active over the next couple of months further south, in Hampshire. Although no chronicle source mentions it, at some time in February or March Henry received the submission of the wealthy port of Southampton, if not its castle. The town was a significant acquisition. At the time it was one of the chief entry points into England of the wine trade. Its fathers had clearly decided that the great continental power represented by the duke had more to offer them than the king. In garrison there the duke could threaten Winchester and unsettle all the south coast. There was even more to encourage Henry while he was there. A charter issued at Southampton gives the first creaks of the wheels of a bandwagon moving in his train. The charter is attested by Joscelin of Louvain, the brother of the late Queen Adeliza, and castellan of Arundel.[30] Joscelin was lord of the barony of Petworth in Sussex, and a tenant and close ally of Adeliza's widower, Earl William d'Aubigné of Arundel. Earl William was a hitherto staunch ally of King Stephen and had been in his army at Newbury, Wallingford and Cirencester, yet here we find his brother-in-law joining the duke's entourage after the retreat from Malmesbury. It must be that Joscelin was sent to represent his lord and cover Earl William's back in case the duke ultimately triumphed. This rather confirms what the *Gesta* had said about Stephen's reasons for withdrawing from Malmesbury. The main concern for both the earl and for Joscelin was the continued enjoyment by Earl William of the late queen dowager's honor of Arundel, which he held only by the favour of King Stephen. Since the earl and the late queen had provided for the landless Joscelin out of Arundel, Earl William's concerns were Joscelin's too. A settlement of land claims once the conflict had been settled was beginning to be feared by the more forward-thinking magnates.[31] Duke Henry must have been only too pleased to receive worried new adherents like this, but William of Newburgh and Gervase of

---

28 *Regesta* iii, no. 192, dated at Cirencester, has (with reason) been taken by Davis as being issued by the king *en route* to Malmesbury (GC i, 152, mentions that the king spent the night before his attack on Malmesbury at Cirencester). If so, it reveals that the king had the loyalist earls of Arundel and Northampton in his entourage at this point, as well as his usual *familiares*.
29 GS, 234.
30 *Cartulaire de Afflighem*, ed. Marneffe, pt 2, 149–51. The charter was issued before Duke Henry added Aquitaine to his style (which he did in April 1153). However, it appears that the bishop of Winchester still had control of the castle of Southampton in November 1153, *Regesta* iii, no. 272.
31 *Regesta* iii, no. 568 is a charter issued by Duke Henry (after April 1153) confirming to Joscelin the honor of Petworth granted him by his sister, Queen Adeliza, out of her dower lands of Arundel. Joscelin must have gone to Duke Henry concerned that the duke would reclaim his sister's dower lands, which she had by royal grant for life from Henry I. The title to Arundel of

Canterbury believed (and attestation lists confirm) that most of those who flocked to join him after landing were old Angevin loyalists.[32]

The second datable appearance of Duke Henry in 1153 was also in Hampshire, at Stockbridge, the crossing of the river Test where, in 1141, the empress had narrowly avoided capture and Earl Robert of Gloucester had been taken by his enemies. On 9 April we find the duke there at a most intriguing meeting. The event is known from a *conventio*, drawn up either there or soon after, between the duke and Joscelin, bishop of Salisbury. The bishop was still pursuing his claim to Devizes. He and the duke came to an interim settlement at Stockbridge whereby Henry was to keep the castle of Devizes for three years. Significant in itself, the *conventio* is even more significant in the list of guarantors and witnesses it lists. The Angevin earls of Gloucester, Cornwall and Salisbury, as well as John fitz Gilbert and Robert de Dunstanville, were present to support the duke. But the key characters in the negotiation were Archbishop Theobald, Bishop Henry of Winchester and the bishops of Bath and Chichester.[33] The presence of the bishops does not imply their recognition of the duke, but it indicates that the months of apparent inactivity after Malmesbury can now be explained. The duke had secured Southampton, and the whole of England (as Henry of Huntingdon poetically says) was shaken by his arrival in a way that it had not been in 1147 and 1149. Stephen had already realised this, and we can assume with confidence that the discussion 'on the causeway of Stockbridge' was about more than Devizes; it was a Marcher conference where the king's ecclesiastical ambassadors were exploring the ground for negotiation between the parties. The presence of Bishop Henry also indicates that, with the death of the queen and in the absence of any influential magnate group, the king had turned to his brother as counsellor.

Whatever the result of the discussions at Stockbridge, the duke moved northwards out of Hampshire and we next find him deploying all his resources to celebrate Easter in royal style in the Angevin heartland of the lower Severn valley. Easter that year was on 19 April. We find the duke at Stockbridge ten days before, and the logic of R.H.C. Davis's reconstruction of his movements was that, travelling by way of his old home at Bristol, he chose to spend the holy festival at the ancient crown-wearing palace of Gloucester, dignifying the splendour of the occasion by assuming the *de uxore* title of 'duke of Aquitaine'.[34] The Bristol and Gloucester ducal acts reveal that his

---

Earl William, her second husband, was vulnerable. It would seem that Joscelin therefore went to the duke to negotiate his brother-in-law's title. Clearly, he was ultimately successful.

32 GC i, 152; WN i, 89.

33 *Regesta* iii, no. 796.

34 Davis's argument (*Stephen*, 115–17) is based on the reconstruction of Duke Henry's itinerary in Z.N. and C.N.L. Brooke, 'Henry, duke of Normandy and Aquitaine', *EHR*, 61 (1946), 86–8. The logic relies on the fact that on his charters issued at Bristol Henry is 'duke of Normandy and count of Anjou', *Regesta* iii, nos. 126, 309, 438 but on those issued at Gloucester, he is 'duke of Normandy *and Aquitaine* and count of Anjou', ibid., nos. 193, 339, 363a–b, 364, 840, 901. The idea that Duke Henry spent Easter at Gloucester depends on the pattern of Henry I's crown-wearings. The next date we can attach to his itinerary is his stay at Leicester at Whitsuntide (7 June 1153).

entourage was still not drawing in many new members. The magnates in general remained cautious about accepting him. However, at Bristol one significant face appears. Robert de Breteuil, the adult son of Earl Robert of Leicester, appeared before the duke (perhaps as his father's emissary) and was received with great glee, as it seems from the duke's prompt return to him of those Norman honors which the recently dead William de Pacy had enjoyed at Earl Robert's expense after 1141.[35] Earl Robert himself, attended by his seneschal, Arnold du Bois, followed his ambassadors and is found at the court at Gloucester which was held immediately after that at Bristol.[36] The significance of the declaration of the earl of Leicester for the duke was long remembered, and Gervase of Canterbury noted that after the fall of Malmesbury 'the noble earl, Robert of Leicester, began to favour the duke's side and for some time to supply his wants'.[37] But, nonetheless, the Gloucester charters reveal that, apart from the Leicester affinity, no other notable defectors had crossed over to Henry. The duke still had to rely on the earls of Hereford, Chester, Gloucester and Cornwall. The former three were in any case already formally allied to Robert of Leicester, so his crossing into the Angevin camp was a well-prepared move in other respects too. Leicester merely completed the presentation set of Angevin-inclined earls. No support had come from Scotland, which the deaths of Henry of Northumbria in July 1152 and the illness and death of King David in May 1153 had neutralised.[38]

From Gloucester the duke headed up the Severn valley with his court and across the midlands.[39] His intentions are difficult to assess. It may be, as Davis suggested, that the duke and king had agreed (perhaps at Stockbridge) that each should keep to a different part of the kingdom for a period of truce between them. But the duke certainly did not feel that he was unable to use

35 *Regesta* iii, no. 438. For the deprivation and restoration of the Norman honours of Earl Robert, see Crouch, *Beaumont Twins*, 55, 86–7. There is some question as to whether Earl Robert joined Duke Henry at Bristol or later at Gloucester. The charter to Robert de Breteuil is attested by Reginald de Bordigny and Geoffrey l'Abbé, both household officers of the earl. But they, like the earl's son, may have preceded the earl himself as envoys. For the chronology, see observations in J.C. Holt, '1153: the treaty of Winchester', in *The Anarchy of King Stephen's Reign*, ed. E. King (Oxford, 1994), 310 and n., which disputes but fails to disprove the priority of R. 438. J.W. Leedom, 'The English settlement of 1153', *History* 65 (1980), 354, argues that Robert of Leicester had rebelled against Stephen in 1151 and had been his opponent since then, but this theory is not easy to reconcile with the language of the chroniclers.
36 *Regesta* iii, no. 840.
37 GC i, 152–3. W.L. Warren, *Henry II* (London, 1973), 50, says that Robert's defection brought thirty castles into the duke's hands, but Gervase does not link this transfer of loyalties directly to Earl Robert and is simply commenting on what he believed to be a mass defection to the duke at this time.
38 See the cautionary remarks of G. White, 'The end of Stephen's reign', *History*, lxxv (1990), 7–8, about the extent of defections.
39 The only source for his itinerary is *GS*, 234–6. Davis's treatment of his itinerary, based on that of the Brookes, reverses the order of *GS*, which places Henry at Tutbury after seizing Warwick. I follow *GS* by placing him first in the Warwick/Leicester area, then at Tutbury with a rapid march across country to Bedford, where he ended up before attempting Stamford. There is really no reason why Henry should not have begun his midlands itinerary till late May, and there is as much room for a long siege of Tutbury after the Pentecost court at Leicester as there is before it.

what forces he had to improve his position. It would seem that the duke made first for the town of Leicester, where he stayed for the feast of Pentecost (7 June 1153) in the impressive new hall that Earl Robert had built within his castle by the Soar. It was modelled on the royal hall of Westminster and, like Westminster, had nearby a prestigious dynastic *Eigenkirk*, in this case a great new Augustinian abbey, in its own faubourg outside the north gate, the wealthiest and largest of its order in England. It was commenced around 1139 when Earl Robert and his brother were at the height of their influence at Stephen's court.[40]

It was probably on this occasion that the duke confirmed to the father the Norman honors which had been handed over to Robert de Breteuil at Bristol in April. There was one addition to the concessions, which in its way was a telling one. The duke was asked now to confirm the exchange of fees made between Earl Robert and his cousin, the earl of Warwick, some years previously. There had been a treaty between the two magnates by which the earl of Leicester gave to the earl of Warwick fees of his in Warwickshire, receiving in return an equal number of fees in or close to Leicestershire. The idea had been to rationalise the grouping of their estates by mutually surrendering outliers.[41] In itself this was a symptom of the territorial imperative during the earlier disorders of the reign, but there is a wider significance in the concern the earl of Leicester was showing in 1153 to gain retrospective consent from Duke Henry. Like Joscelin of Louvain, the earl was expecting a future enquiry into irregular land transactions done in Stephen's reign, and was – like Joscelin – asking for insurance cover. He had swapped knights' fees held in chief with a neighbour, without the consent of their overlord, and was now attempting to make his threatened situation secure. It is by this that we know that the more forward-thinking magnates were already in the spring of 1153 visualising and discussing the future shape of a peace settlement, before even the peace conference had begun![42]

Two local operations were directed from Leicester. Earl Robert was, it seems, in communication with his half-sister, Gundreda, countess of Warwick (daughter of his stepfather William II of Warenne). The Warwicks had been dispossessed of their great castle at Warwick, which had been garrisoned by Stephen's household knights. Earl Roger, her husband, was at the royal court in the southeast of England in the summer of 1153. In his absence,

40 The date of Duke Henry's stay at Leicester in 1153 is established by his retrospective reference in one of his charters, issued at Warwick, which confirms to the bishop of Lichfield all his assarts from the earliest times 'up to the time when I was at Leicester at Pentecost in the year of the Incarnation 1153', *Regesta* iii, no. 459. For the large and singular hall of Leicester castle built in the second half of Stephen's reign, N.W. Alcock and R.J. Buckley, 'Leicester castle: the great hall', *Mediaeval Archaeology*, xxxi (1987), 73–9. For the abbey of Leicester, traditionally believed founded in 1143, but redated to 1139, D. Crouch, 'The foundation of Leicester abbey and other problems', *Midland History*, xi (1987), 1–13.

41 *Regesta* iii, no. 439; Crouch, *Beaumont Twins*, 86.

42 We see a similar example in the way that Robert fitz Harding of Bristol and Roger of Berkeley resolved their dispute over Berkeley by a marriage alliance between Maurice, Robert's son, and Roger's daughter (see Appendix II). This Berkeley agreement was drawn up at Bristol before Duke Henry, but cannot be dated closely.

Countess Gundreda was able to trick the garrison of Warwick into surrendering to a party of Duke Henry's supporters (possibly led by the duke himself). Unfortunately for her, when the news was brought to Stephen's court, on 12 June 1153, her husband collapsed with shock and died.[43] The *Gesta* implicates Earl Robert of Leicester as the man who induced Duke Henry to march into Staffordshire to beseige Tutbury, the chief fortress of Robert de Ferrers, earl of Derby, the son of that Earl Robert who had so distinguished himself in Stephen's service in 1138. The second Earl Robert de Ferrers was a confirmed neutralist. He attended Stephen's court in 1141 and 1146, but there is little sign of his having exerted himself for either party in the years between 1138 and 1153.[44] All that can be said is that at the time of the Leicester–Chester treaty (which I have dated to 1149) he was closely allied to Earl Ranulf of Chester. This would not be surprising. Earl Robert used the title of 'Derby' and if he did so for a reason it was only by courtesy of Ranulf, who was the actual possessor of the town. But between 1149 and 1153 the two earls had fallen out, and even if they were not now enemies, Ranulf made no attempt to persuade Duke Henry not to attack Tutbury when Robert of Leicester urged the duke to crush him. So the attack was duly made and after a significant period of resistance the earl made his submission. As a demonstration of new Angevin authority in the north midlands, it was a most effective exercise.[45] Duke Henry's campaigning began to gather momentum as repeated success demonstrated that few were willing to resist him, at least in the midlands. After the fall of Tutbury, he led a rapid march across country and appeared in force in front of Bedford, his purpose being, perhaps, no more than to punish the town that had humiliated the earl of Leicester's brother, Hugh, in 1141. Without bothering to proceed to a siege of the royal castle, the duke had the town plundered and burned. The duke's midlands campaign was chiefly being fought in the interests of his two great allies, Leicester and Chester. We hear how the duke 'many times' during the summer of 1153 promoted Earl Ranulf's interests (as much as Earl Robert's).

Whatever truce had been agreed between the king and the duke had expired by the beginning of August 1153, for it was at this time that the duke marshalled his forces and moved south to the relief of Wallingford. The duke was intent on breaking the blockade by destroying the substantial counter-castle that King Stephen had caused to be constructed opposite Wallingford across the river Thames at Crowmarsh Gifford. Here success eluded him. Stephen's

---

43 *GS*, 234; RT, 172. *Regesta* iii, no. 459 is a charter of Duke Henry dated at Warwick at a time after the duke had spent Whitsun at Leicester, and is assigned by Cronne and Davis to the time of the Angevin seizure of Warwick. Although it is possible that Henry visited Warwick from his base at Leicester at that time, it is possible also that he was there later, in the unaccounted time while King Stephen was at Woodstock after Christmas 1153.

44 *Regesta* iii, nos. 276, 494. Davis, *Stephen*, 136, followed by G. White, 'The end of Stephen's reign', *History*, lxxv (1990), 8, suggests that Robert de Ferrers had been alarmed by the scale of grants to Earl Ranulf.

45 *GS*, 234.

experienced garrison successfully ambushed and routed the impetuous assault made by the Angevin army. So Duke Henry was forced into a blockade and dug in, knowing that Stephen would be sure to retaliate in force, and that soon. King Stephen was all set to fight one of his more successful campaigns. A force of three hundred knights was sent to augment his garrison at Oxford and isolate the ducal army, which it did by raiding and wasting the vicinity. The duke, realising the danger, struck back against the royalist commander, William de Chesney, the governor of Oxford, ambushing and routing both him and the king's *familiares*, Richard de Lucy and William Martel, as they were going about their ruthless business.[46] By this time – early August 1153 – the king had mustered all those magnates who were willing to support him and brought up to Wallingford an impressive force, which is reported to have considerably outnumbered that of the duke. The situation was better than Stephen could have dared hope; he had isolated and trapped the duke and his army, and all that was now needed was the final coup. But his army refused to fight.[47]

A decade of neutralism and, latterly, open evasiveness, had come to the point where a dissident baronage had turned on both principals in the succession conflict. Both the duke and the king were outraged – or said they were. But it was 'the leading men of each army' who were now in charge of the situation. The magnates of either army knew each others' minds and were united now in thinking that any battle that would be fought would achieve nothing, other than destroying more lives and harvests to the impoverishment of the kingdom. So they proceeded to organise a peace conference on the spot. The king and duke were presented with a joint demand from their armies and asked to meet in person to discuss terms and dates. The armies then demolished the castle at Crowmarsh and simply packed up and went home.

One can but admire the way that these twelfth-century men conducted themselves, and the distaste for purposeless war exhibited by trained warriors.[48] Not everyone was inclined to praise them for their forcible peace-making. Henry of Huntingdon – who did not always see the best in his neighbours – was convinced that the only motive the magnates had was to stop one or other of the contenders coming out on top, so they could continue to play one off against the other.[49] But, as we have seen, Joscelin of Louvain, William of Arundel and Robert of Leicester's actions before Wallingford betray a sense of the end-game: that the magnates of both sides were indeed looking for a solution and not a continuation. It is more than ironic that Gervase of Canterbury puts into the mouth of Earl William of Arundel the speech representing Stephen's magnates' desire for peace. Earl William might well have been

---

46 RT, 174 reports this incident and says that the duke charged his own men that they were not to plunder the country, but stop the king's men doing so, and protect the peasants from them.
47 *GS*, 236–8.
48 *GS*, 238.
49 HH, 766.

concerned to bring an end to the kin-strife of the war – as he said he was – but that would have been because his brother-in-law was in the duke's camp negotiating for the earl's future prosperity![50]

Count Eustace, the king's son, was contemplating a most unsatisfactory end-game too. He had carried on a personal confrontation with the young duke, his cousin, since attempting to ambush and (probably) murder him at Dursley in 1149. He had pursued him to Normandy in 1151 and 1152, but had failed every time to bring Henry down. So now, breaking off from his father's army, he led his household into a frustrated personal campaign without much apparent purpose other than to demonstrate his wrath. He based himself at his town of Cambridge, and made for the abbey of Bury St Edmunds where he was received politely, but his demand for funds was refused. So he laid waste the abbey's lands on 10 August 1153, and returned to the castle of Cambridge. There, sitting down for his dinner – provided by the food looted from Bury – the young man of not yet thirty had a seizure of some kind as he took the first mouthful, and died a week later in great pain. This was naturally taken as a testimony to the power of St Edmund to defend his monks. Eustace's body was taken to Faversham and laid with his mother, the late queen, in the great choir which was built as a mausoleum for his family.[51]

THE PEACE SETTLEMENT OF 1153

What happened next was a classic *conventio*, a protracted series of negotiations between intermediaries to produce a lasting settlement of the succession dispute. It was given real force firstly by the deep-seated conviction of the magnates that the time had come to stop fighting, but also by God's open demonstration through the sudden death of the dissident Count Eustace that the time had indeed come for peace. The negotiations had begun, after a fashion, even before the confrontation at Wallingford early in August. The meeting at Stockbridge in April 1153, with the appearance before the duke of Archbishop Theobald and Bishop Henry of Winchester, shows every symptom of having been a delegation from the king to the duke looking for means to facilitate his negotiated departure from the realm. The apparent four months of truce that followed may have stemmed from the bishops' initial work there. The interim had proved that the magnates wanted peace as much as the prelates did. So ground work had already been done before Wallingford. The face-to-face discussions of King Stephen and Duke Henry (across a stream

50 GC i, 154. White, 'End of Stephen's reign', 7, makes the point that William d'Aubigné was besides one of Stephen's earls whose comital title the duke recognised after he became king.
51 GC i, 155; *GS*, 238; HH, 768; RT, 176; John of Salisbury, *Policraticus*, ed. C.C.I. Webb (2 vols, Oxford, 1909) ii, 394–5. For a study of Eustace's end see, T. Callahan Jr., 'Sinners and saintly retribution: the timely death of King Stephen's son Eustace, 1153', *Studia Monastica*, 18 (1976), 109–17, who concludes that foul play was involved. I favour the food poisoning theory myself (1152–53 seems to have experienced the outbreak of quite a potent bacterial infection, judging by the number of prominent deaths in the period). Earl Simon of Northampton, who had also been at Wallingford, died of the same affliction in the same week as Eustace, HH, 768.

feeding into the Thames) before the break-up of the rival camps in early August would not have been more than an authorisation for the delegates to proceed with some vague idea of what the king and duke were agreed upon as a starting position.

But although talks were under way, the war continued in a desultory fashion. After the break-up of his army, the duke turned north and besieged Stamford, another royal centre, which submitted on terms some time early in September after a siege of several weeks. Charters reveal that the earl of Chester was still with him, but few other magnates; he was mostly surrounded by his household.[52] The king at this time was unable to come to Stamford's assistance. He was using this period of truce between the two principals to exert himself in neutral ground, East Anglia, where he had decided on one final attempt to crush that irritating mosquito of his reign, Earl Hugh Bigod. One can quite understand the king's feelings.[53] The duke was aware of what was going on, and, according to William of Newburgh, he made an attempt to campaign into Suffolk after the fall of Stamford. Like Southampton, the port of Ipswich had been persuaded by events that now was the time to declare for the Angevin dynasty and had welcomed Hugh Bigod within its walls, so the king put the town under close siege. Ipswich was unlucky, and fell to the avenging Stephen (although whether Hugh was taken with it is unknown). The duke retired to the safety of the midlands.[54] The duke was still active in the interests of Earl Ranulf, taking his part against William Peverel of Nottingham, with whom Ranulf had waged a personal feud since 1146. The apparent cause of the animosity was Ranulf's belief that Peverel had attempted to poison him while at a banquet as his guest, as a consequence of which the earl was severely ill and three of his household died.[55] The poisoning had no doubt more to do with poor food hygiene than Machiavellian politics, but this was an age that believed sudden death was evidence of the unnatural intervention of either God or man.

Despite the continuance of the war, it was almost as if king and duke were setting sieges just to keep themselves occupied. There was a distinct feeling of reconciliation even while they were campaigning. While attempting to reduce the castle of Stamford, the duke was assisting Earl Ranulf of Chester in his compensation of the bishop and chapter of Lincoln for the damage he had done their estates in the past years.[56] Like his fellow magnates, the earl must

---

52 HH, 768; RT, 174. *Regesta* iii, no. 492 is dated 'Monday the eve of St Giles at the siege of Stamford' (that is 31 August 1153), cf. also ibid., no. 81.
53 *GS*, 234–6.
54 HH, 768; WN i, 89.
55 *GS*, 236; HH, 768. The feud is mentioned in the grants Duke Henry made to Ranulf in spring 1153, which included '. . . the castle and borough of Nottingham and whatever I had in Nottingham, in fee and heredity to [Earl Ranulf] and his heirs . . . and all the fee of William Peverel wherever it may be, unless William should come before me and plead in my court concerning [his] plundering and treachery . . .', *Regesta* iii, no. 180.
56 *Regesta* iii, no. 492. This was a process he had begun before Archbishop Theobald at Crowmarsh while the confrontation with the king was still going on, ibid., no. 491. In another act the earl gave the chapter the church of Repton, also as compensation, *Charters of the Earls of Chester*, 116.

have been contemplating the certainty of extensive and protracted claims against him in the near future. In what must have been an atmosphere of excitement as well as apprehension, the work of peace-making was proceeding. The work was carried out by a commission of sorts. Archbishop Theobald and Bishop Henry worked with the king. There were others involved, as we have reference to the *internuncii* (intermediaries) who communicated the duke's wishes, but no source names them, or says whether they were laymen or ecclesiastics.[57] The work of negotiation took several months and was not complete until the end of November, by which time the military campaigning had simply died away. It seems that the negotiators were thorough. The lost life of St Osyth which contained autobiographical notes by William de Vere, brother of Earl Aubrey of Oxford and canon of St Osyth, preserved in the extracts of the antiquary Leland, records a 'day of peace and concord' when Stephen's second son, Count William of Boulogne and Warenne, met the duke at Colchester in the presence of Archbishop Theobald. He was presumably there to discuss the terms of the settlement as they affected Count William and this excursion into Essex presumably had happened under safe conduct before the assembly of the great council at Winchester which was to publicise them.[58]

The king and the duke met once again at Winchester on 6 November 1153. The assembly is best interpreted not as a 'peace conference' but a royal council brought together to witness the duke's homage to King Stephen after the agreement of terms for their future relationship. To view it as a conference between equal powers would have seemed to both principals demeaning to the kingship of Stephen and therefore the future kingship of Henry fitz Empress. Henry had already demonstrated a remarkably high idea of respect for the dignity of kingship in his refusal in the French campaigns of 1151–52 to engage directly in battle with Louis VII. It should also be remembered that what was to be done at Winchester in November 1153 was exactly what Henry had already done in his homage to Louis at Paris in August 1151; he had made formal submission to an overlord to gain a greater end.

If what happened at Winchester was not a 'peace conference' neither was the later document that records the meeting a 'peace treaty'. From the way that Sir James Holt has recently and carefully analysed it, it is best described as the

---

It seems that the earl may have gone on from the duke's army to Lincoln itself, for he dates a charter there which must belong to a time after the settlement between duke and king, ibid., 106–7. Barraclough, ibid., 119, appears to interpret the Stamford charter as paving the way for Ranulf's surrender of his claims on Lincoln. Although by no means impossible, this interpretation overlooks the fact that Duke Henry's 1153 otherwise generous confirmation charter to Ranulf at Devizes studiously fails to mention Lincoln at all, which implies that Ranulf's claims on the city were already defunct.

57 HH, 770. *GS*, 240 mentions the bishop of Winchester as the principal negotiator for the king. White, 'End of Stephen's reign', 11, suggests plausibly that Earl Reginald of Cornwall would have been the duke's principal negotiator; the earl's importance in the spring and summer of 1154 goes some way to support this suggestion.

58 *Leland's Itinerary in England and Wales*, ed. L. Toulmin Smith (6 vols, London, 1906–10) v, 171.

document describes itself, a 'charter' or, to paraphrase Sir Charles Clay's words, 'the king's notification of a settlement'.[59] The document itself was not written and sealed until the next month, by which time duke and king had moved on amicably to Westminster for Christmas. The written settlement as we have it tells us a number of things which had occurred at Winchester. Firstly, and perhaps most importantly, Duke Henry had been designated Stephen's successor and heir. He and his heirs (he now had a son, William) had been given England.[60] Following this, the duke had done homage to King Stephen as his lord, and sworn surety by an oath that he would be faithful to the king, and maintain his life and honour with all his might 'according to the agreements (*conventiones*) debated between us'.[61] The king for his part swore to maintain Henry as if he were his son. As for Stephen's real son, William of Boulogne, the peace settlement goes into elaborate detail as to how his station in life was to be exalted and maintained in default of his succession to the throne. For this, William did the duke homage. Homage or an oath of good faith was also given by the followers of the duke to the king, and the followers of the king to the duke. The valiant garrison of Wallingford – seemingly regarded as an Angevin SAS – agreed to do homage now to the king and give hostages for its future conduct, while the garrisons of the king's castles and citizens of his towns did homage to the duke. The king's faithful servant, Richard de Lucy, took charge of the Tower of London and Windsor castle, giving his son as hostage to the duke that he would surrender them on Stephen's death. Lincoln and Oxford were given over to two of the duke's household, to hold as guarantees of the king's good faith. The bishop of Winchester likewise would surrender the castles of Winchester and Southampton to the duke if the king broke his agreement. All the archbishops, bishops and abbots of England were to do homage to the duke at the king's command, as would all who later became bishops and abbots.[62]

Although very informative, the settlement sealed at Westminster in December 1153 is rather selective as to what it records as happening at Winchester, over a month before.[63] Like any set of good minutes, it records only what was to the advantage of the meeting to have recorded. Nevertheless, those resolutions which were not recorded at Westminster later were still regarded as part of a settlement. Henry of Huntingdon regarded at least one of the unrecorded

---

59 J.C. Holt, '1153: the treaty of Winchester', in *The Anarchy of King Stephen's Reign*, ed. E. King (Oxford, 1994), 293–5. I offer the word 'settlement' here as the Westminster document refers to itself in its later clauses as a *pactio*, as well as a *carta*.

60 It is worth emphasising here Professor Holt's point that this clause was a recognition by the duke that the king's title to England was genuine 'You cannot make a man your lawful heir without appearing as his lawful ancestor', Holt, '1153: the treaty of Winchester', 312.

61 *Regesta* iii, no. 272. The '*conventiones . . . prolocutas*' would seem to allude to the discussions carried out on behalf of king and duke between August and November.

62 In considering what the Westminster text says it is worth noting GC i, 156. Gervase's report of the Winchester council is very close to what the preamble of the Westminster text says (and may even have been drawn from it).

63 I follow in this assumption, Holt, '1153: the treaty of Winchester', 296–7, although Professor Holt does not consider the writ evidence included here.

resolutions (that about demolishing adulterine castles) as part of the *concordia* between duke and king.[64] Chroniclers and several significant writs issued at this time give a coherent idea of what those unrecorded resolutions at Winchester were. The contemporary chroniclers who offer us an insight into what was actually discussed at Winchester are Robert de Torigny and the author of the *Gesta Stephani*.[65] The latter was probably himself at Winchester (if he was Bishop Robert of Bath, or one of his immediate staff) and Robert de Torigny may have acquired his detailed and accurate information from any number of contacts: Earl Robert of Leicester was at Bec-Hellouin (where Torigny was still prior, until he became abbot of Mont St-Michel in May 1154) well within a year of the Winchester court. Bec still had close contacts with the Empress Mathilda (who was living at the Bec priory of Le Pré, not far away from the mother house) and with the household of Archbishop Theobald.[66]

The first major topic of discussion at Winchester which did not make the written agreement was that topic which we know had been keenly discussed in some magnate households since at least April, and probably long before: what to do with the lands which had been expropriated during the crisis of 1139–40, to the disinheritance of others. This was a major issue not because the disinherited were woeful and impoverished people petitioning frantically for the return of their lands filched by more powerful neighbours, but because most of the *exhereditati* were either the great church dignitaries or the great magnates themselves, who had lost their outlying estates to their colleagues' need for territorial security. Neither king nor duke could ignore such a lobby, and there is some evidence that the duke, at least, took the problem very seriously. By the time he reached Leicester in June 1153 the duke had welcomed into his entourage Gilbert de Lacy.[67] Since 1139, Gilbert de Lacy had been doggedly pursuing the Lacy inheritance to which he had a claim through his mother, and as a result had been forcibly excluded from Herefordshire by Earl Roger of Hereford and in 1150 was being harried in Worcestershire by the earl.[68] The fact that Duke Henry had ostentatiously welcomed him into his household early in 1153 was a signal to all who looked for peace, and a challenge to Earl Roger – one of the most aggressive disinheritors of others in the realm, yet one of the chief supporters of the duke's own party. The

---

64 HH, 772.

65 Ralph de Diceto, writing from the other side of Henry II's reign, gives a long (and eruditely expressed) list of the measures allegedly adopted at Winchester. These include the basic ones derived (it seems) from Torigny, but also a number of others, and two of them at least have some contemporary confirmation: the intention to improve the coinage, and the repatriation of Flemish mercenaries. There is nothing to confirm his other clauses (governance of the clergy, action against simony, restoration of agriculture and trade, and reform of sheriffs and their corrupt practices), *Opera Historica*, i, 296–7.

66 For Robert of Leicester at Bec-Hellouin in 1154, see his charter dated there, *Select Documents of the English Lands of the Abbey of Bec*, ed. M. Chibnall (Camden Soc., 3rd ser., lxxiii, 1951), 12; Crouch, *Beaumont Twins*, 88. Earl Robert is known to have been at Winchester in November 1153 from the accidental survival of a writ-charter he issued there, BL, Additional charter 47384.

67 *Regesta* iii, nos. 104, 140.

68 See above, pp. 256–7.

message had by then already been understood, and we find both Earl William of Arundel and Earl Robert of Leicester conscious of the consequences of a general restoration.

Robert de Torigny tells us of the Winchester meeting that 'it was sworn that the property forcibly taken by interlopers should be returned to its former, lawful owners, whose property it had been in the time of King Henry the Great'. The *Gesta* merely says that the assembly wanted 'the disinherited (*exheredati*) restored to their own'.[69] The account by Torigny seems near to what was actually decided. This we know from a writ issued by Duke Henry actually at Winchester soon after the court in which the settlement was proclaimed. It ordered his cousin, Earl William of Gloucester, to reseise Bishop Henry of Winchester and the abbey of Glastonbury in the manor of Siston, Gloucestershire 'to hold it as well and as peacefully as ever they held it on the day on which King Henry was alive and dead' (see also Appendix II).[70] This writ is conclusive proof that Robert de Torigny was correctly reporting the Winchester resolution about restoration of property, including the defining date of 1 December 1135 as the point from which the status quo would be assessed.[71] Bishop Henry, whose hand was heavy on the negotiation of the settlement clearly did not wait long before using it to his advantage. As we see from this, which is the earliest known writ commanding a restoration, the process was engineered by the bishops and great magnates on their own behalf, whoever else was to benefit.[72]

Another unminuted resolution proclaimed at the Winchester court in November 1153 was (according to Torigny) 'that the castles built since the death of King Henry be demolished'; he adds that there were more than 1,115 of

69 RT, 177, *GS*, 240.

70 Text printed in R.B. Patterson, 'An un-edited charter of Henry fitz Empress and Earl William of Gloucester's comital status', *EHR*, 87 (1972), 755, and see comments on dating in D. Crouch, 'Earl William of Gloucester and the end of the Anarchy: new evidence relating to the honor of Eudo Dapifer', *EHR*, 103 (1988), 71–2. Compare also a writ of Stephen to the same Earl William commanding that the monks of Glastonbury be free of toll at Bristol, which, since it is dated at Windsor, may have been issued during the royal-ducal visit there in late November 1153, see below and *Regesta* iii, no. 344.

71 Holt, '1153: the treaty of Winchester', 302–3, ponders whether the terminal date was only a gloss composed by Torigny, but the Glastonbury writ indicates otherwise. This being so, Holt's idea that the 1153 settlement intended simply to maintain tenures that had been granted and inherited before that date seems unlikely, and the reconstitution of the tenurial situation in 1135 was indeed the ideal that was formulated by Archbishop Theobald, Bishop Henry and their committee. That Henry II intended this too is indicated by his coronation charter, as Holt quotes it. The idea of using a royal death as a point of establishing legal ownership is prefigured in the 1136 charter to the Church, which uses the death of the Conqueror as a reference point, *Regesta* iii, no. 271. Henry I's death was a natural point of reference to establish right, and it is interesting to see that Earl Henry of Northumbria and his father, King David of Scotland, were using it in just that way in charters to Tynemouth priory and various individuals, one as early as 1141, *Regesta Regum Scottorum* i, 146–7, 151–2.

72 Davis, *Stephen*, 120, claims great things for this clause, seeing it as the resolution of an ideological struggle between king and aristocracy, and as signalling the origins of private property in England, since it assured heirs of their rightful succession. This is claiming far too much for what was a pragmatic resolution to a problem caused by the territorial logic of civil war. See above pp. 125–7.

them![73] The *Gesta* simply records that 'the new castles were to be demolished' (omitting the binding date clause). Again, an early writ is known to have survived which commands just this. It was issued at Windsor before the end of November 1153, as the joint royal and ducal entourage travelled up to London after the Winchester court had ended. It is again a writ of the duke, and this time it commands Earl Patrick of Salisbury to demolish fortifications he had raised within the cathedral precinct of Old Sarum to extend Salisbury castle.[74] Once again we see the duke enthusiastic and active in pursuit of the settlement, even though he was acting against his own long-standing partisan.

Sir James Holt suggests that these two clauses were left out of the written settlement sealed at Westminster, precisely because they were so confrontational with the magnates.[75] He believes that this was the reason why they were not formally enacted. Holt may be right, but it seems that there was at least some initial effort made before the end of November 1153 to enforce these contentious terms, in an immediate flurry of acts directed by the duke to his own men to do just that. Two administrative orders survive, and we must assume that there were many more that did not. Perhaps by the time the court got to London the king and the duke were being urged by a restive baronage to slow down, or it may be that the king became reluctant to continue a policy that was beginning to cost his intimate followers much of their accumulated rewards for their loyalty.[76] Yet the enforcements did continue, if selectively. We are told that at Dunstable in January 1154 Duke Henry complained that the king was not pursuing the demolition of castles as enthusiastically as he was.[77] The clause about restoration was not suspended either.

---

73 Robert de Torigny's figure is enormously inflated, careful modern estimates suggest that the number of 'adulterine' castles of Stephen's reign did not even reach 100, C. Coulson, 'Castles of the Anarchy', in *The Anarchy of King Stephen's Reign*, ed. E. King (Oxford, 1994), 69–70. JH, 331 also refers to the destruction of castles built since Henry I had died. Diceto, *Opera Historica* i, 297, repeats the same figure as Torigny.

74 A text of this writ does not survive, but a digest of it is printed in R. Benson and H. Hatcher, *Old and New Sarum* (Salisbury, 1843), 32, from a document then existing in the cathedral archive but now lost. Issued at Windsor under the name of the duke it is dated 18 Stephen, which places it between 1 December 1152 to 30 November 1153. In terms of the known itinerary of duke and king after Winchester, it would appear to have been issued en route to London and the joint Westminster court. Stephen's acts were regularly dated by his regnal year up to 1139, although only very rarely thereafter and Henry of Huntingdon continued to use Stephen's regnal years as the basis for his chronology until the end of his *History*. The use of the regnal year is no cause to doubt the authenticity of this lost act; *GS*, 240 does say that before he left England the duke 'destroyed very many castles that harmed the kingdom'.

75 Holt, '1153: The treaty of Winchester', 297.

76 *Regesta* iii, no. 177 is a charter of 1153–54 by which King Stephen granted William de Chesney of Suffolk, his justice in East Anglia, a hundred and a half in Norfolk as compensation for the manor of Mileham which (Davis suggests) had been restored to the fitz Alan family as a result of the Winchester settlement. Abbot Hamelin of Gloucester, originally a royal abbey whose advocacy was usurped by the earls of Hereford, seems to have been panicked at this time into approaching the king at Windsor in November 1153 for a confirmation of his abbacy, the nomination for which he had probably received in 1148 from Earl Roger of Hereford, *Regesta* iii, no. 358. He may also have sought a royal protection for himself and his abbey's possessions, ibid. no. 359.

77 HH, 772.

There were too many good reasons to pursue it. It would not just benefit the
'disinherited'. It would very much benefit Duke Henry himself in the long
run, and might be of advantage to him in the short term too. Anyone who
had received grants out of the royal demesne since 1135 from the king or the
empress was very vulnerable to the process of recovery – as people had realised long before Winchester. It has been suggested that reclamations of royal
demesne had been attempted during the period of the empress's ascendancy
over the captive Stephen in 1141. Henry did not wait very long to execute its
full force against his enemies. Count Waleran of Meulan was probably the
first to suffer a major confiscation. His honor in England, the earldom of
Worcester, was taken back into demesne perhaps as early as November 1153
when the settlement was decided at Winchester. We know from Torigny that
in the late autumn of 1153 Waleran's nephew, Robert de Montfort, was employed as a ducal agent to arrest him in Normandy and confiscate the honor
of Montfort-sur-Risle which he had obtained from Stephen in 1136. Well
before Stephen's death, all that was left to Waleran in England was his small
ancestral estate in Dorset, and the king and the duke had both been immediate
beneficiaries.[78] But what happened against Waleran was opportunistic. The
enormous grants made to Earl Ranulf of Chester early in 1153 out of royal
demesne were still in his possession on the day he died, in December of that
year. But Ranulf's death provided the duke with his chance to impose the terms
of Winchester and his under-age son, Earl Hugh II, did not succeed to them.[79]

King Stephen and Duke Henry's joint progress from Winchester to Windsor and to London in November and early December 1153 was a unique and
reportedly sumptuous event. We hear of the cheering of huge crowds of
common people, great processional receptions, solemn and packed assemblies. There was in England the emotional, and half-incredulous, feeling of
release which comes with the final realisation that there is at last peace.[80] Fate,
too, conspired to remove some of the most wilful propagators of war in the
past fifteen years. Earl Simon de Senlis of Northampton had died within a few
days of Count Eustace, in August. Earl Ranulf II of Chester had retired to the
provinces before the conference at Winchester and was taken ill probably at
Rocester abbey on the road from Newcastle-under-Lyme to Derby. He made
one more stage of his journey, to his house at Gresley, near Burton in Derbyshire, early in December 1153. There he made a suitably penitent end, attended
by the bishop of Coventry, the abbot of Grimsby and several abbots and
priors of surrounding houses. After confession, he made – as was customary –
numerous grants in restitution to churches he had exploited during the past
years, including the abbeys of Chester and Burton and Trentham and Minting

78 Crouch, *Beaumont Twins*, 74–5.
79 In one of his deathbed acts, Earl Ranulf made a grant out of the revenues of Staffordshire, which had been granted him at Devizes early in 1153, *Charters of the Earls of Chester*, ed. Barraclough, 133.
80 Generally, HH, 770–2

priories.[81] His under-age son, Hugh, succeeded only to what his father had held in 1135: all Ranulf's great gains in Lincolnshire, Staffordshire, the Trent valley and Lancashire returned to the king or to his rivals. Ranulf's death was clearly a glowing opportunity to put into practice what had been decided at Winchester, and not one that the duke and king were inclined to miss.

After the Christmas court at Westminster, which promulgated a written and edited version of the settlement made earlier, at Winchester, the king and duke separated. The king seems to have undertaken a spot of peaceful hunting at his lodge of Woodstock (rather more heavily fortified now than it had been at the beginning of the reign) but it is not known where the duke went. The king was attended by a small group of his closest *familiares*, including Richard de Lucy, Richard de Canville and William de Chesney, and Roger de Clare, the new earl of Hertford (Earl Gilbert did not survive 1152).[82] His excursion into Oxfordshire in early January 1154 has something of a holiday air. The joint court reassembled at nearby Oxford on 13 January 1154, and here the English magnates did homage, as they had undertaken to do, to Duke Henry, reserving their loyalty to King Stephen.

After the break-up of the great court at Oxford, the royal and ducal households moved across the southern midlands to the royal palace-priory of Dunstable, where we find the king surrounded by his customary *familiares*, and the duke by his, with the earls of Hereford, Gloucester and Cornwall in attendance. Each issued a number of interesting writs which are relevant to the continuing endeavours to secure peace. One is a charter of the king confirming an earlier charter of the duke to Bristol abbey. Another is a grant by Duke Henry of the fee of Eudo dapifer in England and Normandy to Robert, the infant son of Earl William of Gloucester (and grandson of Robert II of Leicester).[83] The charters tell us that the joint government instituted at Winchester (or rather, as the king put it, the promise that 'I will manage the business of the kingdom with the counsel of the duke') was being operated. Formerly sovereign acts of the duke were now being submitted for the king's confirmation. The king, for his part, was sharing the distribution of patronage with the duke; the honor of Eudo dapifer lay mostly in the counties of Kent and Essex, where the king had complete control. The duke could not have offered that particular piece of patronage to the Gloucesters without Stephen's consent. At the same time, the grant to Earl William's son and heir,

---

81 *Charters of the Earls of Chester*, ed. Barraclough, 48–9, 130–1, 132–3. The story that he died of poisoning administered at Nottingham by William Peverel is a garbled version by Gervase of Canterbury of the contemporary accusation reported by the *Gesta* that Peverel was alleged to have attempted to poison him the previous year, *GS*, 236; *GC* i, 155. It might be noted that the direction of Ranulf's travel during his illness was apparently *towards* Nottingham, not away from it. RT, 183 reports the disinheritance of William Peverel in 1155 for the poisoning of Ranulf, but in fact King Henry II was then executing a judgement made against Peverel for public crimes as early as April 1153 at Devizes.

82 Davis dates several acts issued at Woodstock to this time, *Regesta* iii, nos. 239a, 242, 864–5.

83 *Regesta* iii, nos. 126–7; D. Crouch, 'William, earl of Gloucester and the end of the Anarchy', 69–70.

rather than the earl himself, showed that the duke was heeding the king's possible prejudices against the son of his old enemy, Robert of Gloucester, by making the grant to the grandson. Another significant act issued at Dunstable was that by the duke in favour of Stephen's household intimate, Richard de Canville. It assured Richard's wife, Milicent, 'at the request and instruction of King Stephen' of her continued enjoyment of Stanton Harcourt, Oxfordshire, which Milicent enjoyed as a marriage gift from the late Queen Adeliza out of former royal demesne.[84] Richard and King Stephen were making sure that his title to the land was secure in case the duke might later attempt to reclaim it as former demesne alienated since 1135.

However, not all was well in the relationship between King Stephen and Duke Henry in January 1154. Henry of Huntingdon reports that at Dunstable the royal pair had a mild altercation over the way the king was implementing the settlement terms. Duke Henry challenged the king for being selective in demolishing the adulterine castles of his supporters. But at least this reference reveals that many castles built since 1135 had indeed been dismantled, and it seems that the duke was able to be philosophical about the king's failure to pursue the project with his own energy, preferring to maintain good relations than back out of the settlement.[85] The need to keep up good relations was pressing, because the duke must soon return to Normandy and his other French dominions, from which he had been absent now for over a year. So, any political differences were kept hidden, and it seems from the evidence of surviving writs that the stay at Dunstable was generally productive.

From Dunstable, the king and duke moved south to Canterbury, by way of St Albans and London, the king having given the duke his leave to depart the realm. The joint entourage was received at Christ Church cathedral by a vast crowd and by a solemn procession of the monks, and Stephen and Henry remained in Kent for most of the rest of the duke's stay in England. The stay at Canterbury was broken during Lent (probably early in March) by a move to Dover, for a conference with Count Thierry of Flanders and his wife (Countess Sybil was Duke Henry's aunt). Although nothing is directly known about the content of the talks, it would have been unlikely had they not been discussing the future relationship between England and Flanders when Henry had succeeded, and the situation with regard to the king of France. Count Thierry had extensive diplomatic contacts, both with the Empire and with Paris, and the settlement of the succession to England on Duke Henry gave him the opportunity to bring the prospective new king into his web of alliances. His relationship with the duke had been poor until very recently, for he had supported Louis's campaign against Normandy in July 1153.[86] It is little wonder he was more than eager to cross the Channel only seven months later

---

84 *Regesta* iii, no. 140, a further charter to that effect was issued soon afterwards at St Albans, ibid. no. 140a.
85 HH, 772.
86 RT, 175.

for a 'border conference' at Dover, the place where traditionally the kings of England and counts of Flanders had met.[87]

Gervase of Canterbury gives some later hint that the negotiations at Dover concerned the Flemings who had flooded into England during Stephen's reign. He reports a conspiracy amongst the Flemings of Kent to murder Duke Henry as he returned to Canterbury. Gervase would have been well aware that the Flemish count, William of Ypres, Stephen's principal military commander during the 1130s and 1140s, was based in Kent, where he still acted as royal military governor despite advancing age and blindness. Since these Flemings 'feared equally peace and the duke', it would seem that Gervase believed the Dover talks had been in part about evicting Flemish mercenaries from England.[88] Nothing came of the alleged conspiracy, says Gervase, as the conspirators were thrown into disarray when the king's son, Count William of Boulogne, who knew of the plot, fell from his horse on the Roman road across Barham Down south of Canterbury, and broke his leg badly.[89] Conspiracy or not – and Richard Eales believes it an unlikely story – Duke Henry left Canterbury for Rochester, and from there passed on to take ship at London for Normandy, to which he must have returned in mid-March.[90] At Rochester, the duke paused to confirm to 'his close and beloved friend' Bishop Walter of Coventry, the grant of a mint at Lichfield as made him by King Stephen. We may therefore suspect that the tales of treachery were no more than the excitability of an excitable age – co-operation in government was continuing up till the moment of the duke's departure, and there is nothing to sustain Lewis Warren's view that Henry retired to Normandy as a matter of prudence in the face of threat.[91]

DUKE HENRY IN NORMANDY

The duke would seem to have landed at Eu, a port on the northern border of his duchy, and a charter issued there indicates that he had brought over with him his uncle, Earl Reginald of Cornwall. The strange thing (to a modern

87 For Thierry's personal appearances at the court of Louis VII and of Frederick Barbarossa in the late 1140s and early 1150s see T. de Hemptinne and M. Parisse, 'Thierry d'Alsace, comte de Flandre: biographie et actes', *Annales de l'Est*, 43 (1991), 92–5. It was in Flanders, a neutral power, that Archbishop Theobald had sought refuge in exile in both 1148–49 and again in 1152.
88 Diceto, *Opera Historica* i, 297, a late source for the 1153 settlement, includes a clause that 'many of the Flemings' were to be repatriated.
89 GC i, 188. R. Eales, 'Local loyalties in Stephen's reign: Kent', *ANS*, viii, ed. R.A. Brown (Woodbridge, 1985), suggests plausibly that another topic of negotiation at Dover might have been the assurance of the peaceful succession of Count William, the king's son, to Boulogne. The report of the same incident in WN i, 91, mentions only the dangerous fall and fracture, and says nothing of a conspiracy.
90 RT, 179 says he returned 'around Easter' (viz. 4 April).
91 *Regesta* iii, no. 459, Warren, *Henry II*, 53. We might also note that the Templars sought from the king early in the summer of 1154 a general confirmation of the lands they were seised of from him on 4 April 1154, *Regesta* iii, no. 866. This indicates that the Templars shared a continuing expectation that the agreement of 1153 would hold, and were seeking reassurance that their land and privileges would not be challenged by Stephen's successor.

eye) is that although the earl was in his entourage, Reginald is named in the charter as 'the one who maintains my position in this and in my other business in England' and who, indeed, was responsible for the assignment of the grant.[92] Earl Reginald's importance in the Angevin cause in the final years of the reign has been observed elsewhere. He was in Normandy with his nephew early in 1152 and probably crossed to England with him in January 1153. Thereafter, Earl Reginald appeared with Duke Henry at several points on the duke's itinerary around the kingdom. It would seem from this that he crossed back to Normandy with the duke, and there is evidence that Earl Robert of Leicester did so too, for we find him in central Normandy on two occasions early in 1154. Why it should be that two of the most capable and powerful magnates involved in the Angevin cause should disappear to Normandy at that critical moment is hard to explain, especially as one of them is named explicitly as the duke's English lieutenant in his absence, and another of them would become his chief justiciar early in 1155.

The fact that the earls of Cornwall and Leicester left England to accompany the duke to Normandy in March 1154 is worth pondering. It assuredly tells us some important things. It tells us that – despite Henry of Huntingdon and Gervase of Canterbury's talk of problems between king and duke – Henry was, in fact, very confident about the security of the settlement when he left: how otherwise would he dare take his chief supporters with him? The Rochester writ tells us that both sides were still jointly at work in the business of the kingdom when he left, and that prospects were good for future co-operation. In due course, Henry's supreme confidence at the point of succession, when King Stephen died in October, tells us the same. He did not hurry back, because he saw no point in doing so. To him in March 1154, England was a problem temporarily solved (especially now that Ranulf of Chester was dead). Duke Henry, after all, had likewise sailed away confidently from an as yet unsettled Normandy in January 1153 to seek a greater end; now he had done the same to England. For that reason, he was quite content to take the two greatest of his English supporters abroad with him, or at least to allow them to follow the will o' the wisp of his court. Earl Reginald's responsibility for England may have been left undefined in March 1153, odd though this may seem to the modern managerial mentality. Graeme White points out that, in any case, the duke may have left no alternative government behind him in England for the earl to preside over, and also notices that King Stephen's writ was now running again in the Angevin heartland of the southwest. What then was there for Reginald to do but keep a watching brief for his nephew? He was still in Normandy in the summer of 1154, attending the duke at his court at Rouen, where we find the earl of Gloucester in attendance also.[93] For

---

92 *Regesta* iii, no. 709.
93 *Regesta* iii, no. 49. See comments in White, 'End of Stephen's reign', 17. Reginald's long stay in Normandy in 1154 would account for the surprised observation by E. Amt, *The Accession of Henry II in England: Royal Government Restored, 1149–1159* (Woodbridge, 1993), 20, that the earl was absent from King Stephen's court during the critical period after Henry's departure.

his part, Earl Robert of Leicester had other good reasons to be in Normandy. He had his great Norman honors of Breteuil, Pacy-sur-Eure and Pont-St-Pierre to recover after they had been for nearly thirteen years in the hands of William de Breteuil-Pacy, his wife's cousin. The earl would also be influenced by the current sad state of affairs of his brother, Count Waleran of Meulan.

Count Waleran was the greatest single magnate in Normandy, and that position had allowed him to survive 1141 with – if anything – an enhanced position of landed power. Duke Geoffrey had allowed him to continue to enjoy what he held of the gift of King Stephen: the honor of Montfort-sur-Risle, wardship of the county of Evreux and control of the viscounty and city of Evreux. Count Waleran's formal alliance with his cousin, Robert du Neubourg, in the winter of 1141–42 had extended his power at court by adding to his affinity the emerging leader of the Norman magnates attached to the Angevin administration and court. Waleran did not limit his possibilities of further advancement by courting the Angevins. Geoffrey of Anjou had given him in marriage Agnes, elder sister of the under-age Count Simon of Evreux, along with custody of his lands. Although this alliance was only intended by Geoffrey to give him a few estates in the Pays de Caux, Waleran enhanced the value of the marriage by assiduous attentions to King Louis VII in the later 1140s. He joined the Second Crusade as one of the leaders of the Anglo-Norman contingent. When he returned from Normandy he was deep in Louis's counsels. This brought major benefits. The counts of Evreux enjoyed the possession of a major lordship at Gournay-sur-Marne east of Paris. This had come into Waleran's hands as part of his wife's marriage-portion by 1149 (although the surviving marriage contract from 1141–42 does not mention it). Louis was even more generous a few years later. On the death of Waleran's uncle, Count Ralph of Vermandois, in 1152, the wardship of the under-age heir, Ralph II, was awarded to him. This gave Waleran nominal control of much of northern France from the Seine basin to the borders of Flanders. Hardly surprising that the count was absent from Duke Henry's side at the time of the French incursions into Normandy of 1150–52, and indeed that the bridges of the Seine under his control at Mantes and Meulan were open to King Louis's armies.[94]

A description of Count Waleran's systematic overthrow in Normandy in 1153–54 makes up much of what Robert de Torigny has to say of the period of Duke Henry's absence in England. In its way, the disgrace of Count Waleran in Normandy was as significant as the settlement of Winchester was in England. Like Winchester, the fall of Waleran marked the end of the period when the magnates could use the wars of succession as levers to jack up their own power and wealth. There were earlier hints that a reckoning was in preparation. The Empress Mathilda had little reason to love Waleran, and she went out of her way to hinder the foundation of a Cistercian abbey that the count had vowed to build on his safe return from the Holy Land in 1149. Waleran

94 Crouch, *Beaumont Twins*, 66–9, 71–4,

had wanted to use an estate near Lillebonne for the abbey, called Le Valasse, which adjoined a parcel of ducal demesne. A long and involved wrangle then occurred between Waleran and the empress, who also had a vow to found an abbey to fulfil (made, it was claimed, on her successful escape from Oxford in 1142). In 1150 Waleran attempted to install a colony from his abbey at Bordesley in Worcestershire, while the empress promoted a foundation from her favoured ducal house of Mortemer. By 1152, the tangle was such that Archbishop Hugh of Rouen was invited to settle the business. He suggested combining the vows and endowments and erecting Le Valasse as a daughter house of Mortemer. A rather poignant and defeated letter of Count Waleran survives by which he surrendered his endowment to the empress. The empress's intervention and Waleran's rout tells us that he was in trouble in the early 1150s.[95]

At the end of 1153 Waleran was brought to book by the Angevin rulers of Normandy. It was done with some artfulness. The agent chosen was his nephew, Robert de Montfort. Robert had good reason to act against his uncle, who had connived at his father's continued imprisonment after the death of King Henry, who had originally imprisoned him. King Stephen had kept Hugh de Montfort in custody, and Waleran had continued to enjoy the escheated honor of Montfort by royal gift. The honor of Montfort-sur-Risle lay between the count's honors of Pont Audemer on the coast and Beaumont-le-Roger inland. Control of Montfort had given Waleran the entire line of the Risle valley downriver of the forest of Breteuil. Waleran kept the young Robert for some years amongst the wards in his household but by 1153 Robert was at large with a grievance. As Christmas approached in 1153, and as news of Duke Henry's triumph filtered across the Channel to Normandy, Count Waleran rode, a little too trustingly, to an interview with his truculent nephew near the town of Bernay, on the western border of Waleran's honor of Beaumont. In the course of the interview Waleran was captured and then borne off some eight miles to the castle of Orbec, which Robert de Montfort must have been holding as a ducal agent.[96] The count's household and barons hurled a frantic and unsuccessful assault against Orbec. When it failed, Waleran bought his freedom by the surrender of Montfort to Robert. No doubt he

95 My account of this foundation in *Beaumont Twins*, 69–71, is corrected as to chronology by Chibnall, *Matilda*, 184–5; eadem, 'Normandy', in *The Anarchy of King Stephen's Reign*, ed. E. King (Oxford, 1994), 112–13. Dr Chibnall also stands up vigorously for the probity of the empress's motives. For Waleran's letter of surrender, Rouen, archives départementales de la Seine Maritime 18 H, fonds du Valasse, carton 5, translated in Crouch, *Beaumont Twins*, 70–1. I remain unconvinced that the empress was justified in her actions over Le Valasse. As heir to Henry I she might contest any monastic foundation by a ducal tenant-in-chief in Normandy as a matter of course. However, her only reasons for her actions over Le Valasse were political; she was not defending the ducal demesne around Lillebonne, for Waleran was attempting to plant an abbey on his own lands. Dr Chibnall's argument that the site Waleran selected was a politically sensitive one seems difficult to sustain – if Waleran wished to threaten the passage of the Seine to Rouen, he had a castle at Vatteville on the left bank which was a far bigger threat than any abbey. I believe that the troubles over Le Valasse were a side-effect of the policy of the empress and her son to undermine Waleran; that they had good reason to act against him is another matter.
96 The castle of Orbec had been a possession of the royalist Earl Gilbert fitz Gilbert of Pembroke before 1141, and must have been confiscated by Duke Geoffrey when central Normandy fell.

calculated that he might be able to regain Montfort by siege at his leisure, and in the new year he raised two siege castles to blockade the tower there. But again he miscalculated; his nephew was able to break the siege and drive off Waleran with humiliating ease.[97]

By the time Duke Henry returned to Normandy at the end of March 1154, the count of Meulan was a spent and broken force. As Robert de Torigny says, the duke 'began to reassume his demesne rights, little by little and with care, which his father had conceded for a time to the Norman magnates in his time of difficulty'.[98] So in Normandy in early 1154 we see a parallel process of settlement to what had happened in England the previous year. Exploitation of faction was no longer possible, so grants made at a time of weakness could be safely recalled. As in England, the restoration of royal demesne rights was one of the first priorities. As the biggest offender in that regard, Count Waleran was made to fall hardest. Once he was beaten and humiliated, lesser men had little choice but to conform. The duke's good fortune was that Count Waleran's defeat was accomplished before he had even returned from England. He was also lucky that Normandy had suffered less than might have been feared from his absence. At the end of July 1153 King Louis VII, with the strong support of Count Thierry of Flanders, had massed an army and moved down the Seine to Vernon, the castle and fortified bridge on the Norman border. But the castle resisted, and eventually the king and count retired under a face-saving formula, that the banner of Flanders be raised by Richard, son of William de Vernon, over the keep, which was confided to Goel fitz Baudrey, a baron of the Norman Vexin with a castle at Baudemont near Vernon on the Epte, who held fees of some sort from both the king and Richard. A strangely feeble attempt by Louis in September on Verneuil, a ducal castle on the frontier of the Avre, was equally unsuccessful.[99] Though there are other reports of disorder along the Norman frontier no sustained and supported assault was made on the duchy during Duke Henry's long stay in England.

Duke Henry could therefore pass through Normandy and on south into Aquitaine to quell some disturbances. He returned to Normandy in June 1154. Around the beginning of August he met the king of France and came to a settlement of their dispute over the Vexin. The king returned to the duke the castles of Vernon – demilitarised the previous year – and Neufmarché on the Epte on the border of the Norman Vexin towards Beauvais. The duke paid over to the king 2,000 marks as compensation for his expense in taking and garrisoning the two castles. After this the duke had a relatively quiet year. At the beginning of October, he joined Louis in a campaign in the Norman Vexin to subdue Goscelin Crispin. In western Normandy a rebellion of Duke Henry's cousin, Richard, son of Earl Robert of Gloucester, for causes unknown, led to the siege of Richard's castle of Torigny-sur-Vire. And it was

97 RT, 177–8. For Hugh de Montfort's continued imprisonment after 1135, OV vi, 356. For this little war see Crouch, *Beaumont Twins*, 74–5.
98 RT, 179.
99 RT, 175.

during the siege of Torigny that the unexpected news reached the duke that King Stephen was dead and that the crown of England was undoubtedly his.[100]

THE END OF THE REIGN

The pattern of dating of the acts of King Stephen leads to a belief that (despite contemporary rumours of a Flemish plot in his household against Henry) the king went with the duke to London to see Henry and his household off on their voyage back to Normandy. The king then made a long stay in the city. It is interesting (and not quite profitless) to speculate what Stephen's feelings were at this point. Was he relieved, exultant, calculating or despondent? Commentators seem to believe that (foolishly or not) he felt exultant in experiencing the reality of kingship in an undivided kingdom for the first time in many years. The author of the *Gesta* notes in the brief conclusion to his work that after the duke left, the king reduced England to peace and took the whole kingdom into his hand and John of Hexham says much the same. Henry of Huntingdon observed that there was peace in England and 'for the first time' Stephen enjoyed the full glory of kingship. But he also believed that Stephen owed the credit for this to Duke Henry. William of Newburgh also takes up this theme; he comments of Stephen in 1154 that 'it was as if he began now to reign for the first time', and in his progress north was 'showing himself as if he were the new king'. He also believed that there were elements in the king's household which wanted to disrupt the settlement and bring the king and duke once more to blows. Gervase of Canterbury also considered that there were those around the king who wished to overturn the settlement, presumably because they feared that the eventual accession of the duke to the throne would not be to their advantage.[101] How trustworthy are these allegations of smouldering discontent and conspiracy?

Graeme White has pointed out that it is implicit in the Winchester settlement and the language of chroniclers (as for instance the account of the quarrel at Dunstable) that there was still a perception of two opposing sides in England after November 1153.[102] Such a perception indicates that underneath the temporary euphoria, the kingdom remained taut of nerve over the future of the settlement. Yet the evidence of tension and conspiracy theory is hardly to be wondered at after fifteen years of almost continuous conflict, and the contrasting evidence of the immediate reconstruction of a political community of the whole kingdom is solid and revealing. For William of Newburgh, the Winchester settlement had purified Stephen of his tyrannical usurpation, and had endowed his kingship with justice.[103] Newburgh's expression may have been flowery, but his simple argument is that after the settlement it was generally felt that none of the Angevin party might lawfully oppose the king.

---

100 RT, 178–81.
101 *GS*, 240; HH, 772–4; GC i, 158; WN i, 91, 94.
102 White, 'End of Stephen's reign', 12.
103 WN i, 91.

The sober evidence of 1154 charter attestations, and the retrospective evidence of the early pipe rolls of Henry II's reign, indicate that the Angevin earls not only accepted Stephen's right to intervene in their lands, but were content to attend his court. Earl Hugh Bigod returned to his former master's court at London, complete with comital style awarded him by the empress, and it was as if he had never been away.[104] Eustace fitz John, the great rebel of 1138 and then the myrmidon of Ranulf of Chester, appears reconciled to Stephen at the royal court at York in August 1154, having already made moves to secure the succession of his son to the many estates he had accumulated since 1135.[105] Earl Patrick of Salisbury was not only with the king at St Albans at some time in 1154, we also know through the evidence of the 1156 pipe roll that the earl had paid the county farm of Wiltshire at the royal exchequer at Michaelmas 1154, a month before Stephen died.[106]

These solid indicators of restoration in 1154 are more reliable than the rumours of chroniclers, who (like modern journalists) looked for a story with an edge. It has been customary to play down John of Hexham's very positive picture of an England in Stephen's last year where lawlessness ebbed and foreign mercenaries left the country and 'justice and peace everywhere returned to the kingdom', but to do so may be to fall for Angevin propagandists who preferred to give the full credit to their man.[107] The pattern of Stephen's acts in the last year of his reign shows him issuing charters for areas where he had had no influence since 1139.[108] How happily this national reconstruction would

104 *Regesta* iii, nos. 696, 896
105 *Regesta* iii, no. 664. Eustace had been at Earl Ranulf's deathbed, but probably before then had come to an independent accommodation with Duke Henry, the duke confirming to Eustace's son, William de Vescy, his rights in England and Normandy, *Regesta* iii, no. 912 and see comments in Holt, '1153: the treaty of Winchester', 301, and P. Dalton, 'Eustace fitz John and the politics of Anglo-Norman England: the rise and survival of a twelfth-century royal servant', *Speculum*, 71 (1996), 379–80, who points out that Eustace's brother, William, had been appointed a ducal justice in Normandy, so assisting the relationship.
106 *Pipe Roll of 2 Henry II*, 56; G. White, 'King Stephen, Duke Henry and Ranulf de Gernons, earl of Chester', *EHR*, xci (1976), 565; idem, 'End of Stephen's reign', 19 and n. The Stixwould charter witnessed by Earl Patrick at St Albans appears to date from after December 1153, as it places Earl Ranulf amongst the dead with Countess Lucy and William de Roumare. Amt, *Accession of Henry II*, 121, suggests that Patrick actually accounted in 1154 at an Angevin exchequer in the West Country. This is an argument worth considering, especially as others have suggested with some reason that such a body existed, see K. Yoshitake, 'Exchequer in the reign of Stephen', *EHR*, 103 (1988), 958. However, Yoshitake himself assumes that the Wiltshire farm paid in 1154 was paid at the king's exchequer, the reason presumably being the continuity in record-keeping it demonstrates. We might also note that there is little evidence of Duke Henry having left behind him in England any administration capable of collecting and recording debts and payments, and that the terms of the Winchester settlement imply in any case that he should have supported the king's government not maintained his own.
107 JH, 331. WN i, 94 is also willing to give Stephen credit for destroying castles. I would contest Leedom and Holt's view that Stephen was a spent force in 1153–54, J.W. Leedom, 'The English settlement of 1153', *History*, 65 (1980), 347–64; Holt, '1153: the treaty of Winchester', 307, '. . . Stephen was on the way out and had been for some time'.
108 *Regesta* iii, no. 344, a writ concerning Earl William of Gloucester and lands in Bristol issued at Windsor, probably en route to London in November 1153. Cf. also ibid., nos. 127, 358, 358–9, 360 (which I would date to Stephen's court at Oxford in January 1154).

have gone on had the king lived longer is not a question for an historian, but it has a certain relevance. In the summer of 1154 King Stephen remained an active man, outwardly hale despite his domestic tragedies of the last year. The former dissident magnates had decided to accommodate themselves to his rule, and reconstruction of the central structures of Henry I's reign was already under way. A key development was now that the magnates had accepted that there was no dynastic competitor to whom to appeal in the event of any dispute with the king. The Winchester settlement had convinced the political community that Duke Henry and King Stephen were genuinely reconciled. The deaths of Count Eustace, Earl Simon of Northampton and Earl Ranulf of Chester eliminated some of the men who might have been tempted to challenge the settlement by appealing over the king to the duke. The great earls of Leicester and Cornwall had confidently chosen to leave England to settle itself, and had taken advantage of the opportunities at the ducal court in Normandy. In this situation it is very likely that England would have completed its process of political restoration even had Stephen lived on to the end of the 1150s – there were still outside enemies enough for him to have exerted his military talents with profit. As later with Henry II, it is likely that Stephen would by 1155 have been inevitably drawn to the Welsh and Scottish Marches to restore the political balance in Britain towards the king of England, an ambition which both the duke and the Marcher magnates themselves would have supported.

It follows that we must ask how autonomous King Stephen's policy-making was in 1154. He and the duke had ample time between November 1153 and March 1154 to discuss a mutual agenda for the future and there are some good indications (apart from the Winchester settlement itself) that duke and king had embarked on a joint policy in 1154. After all, the assurance of a joint policy would help to account for Duke Henry's confident departure in March 1154. King Stephen's northern progress in the summer of 1154, his high-profile siege and capture of Drax, and his great court at York show a dawning agenda. The king was going to continue to enforce Winchester where he could. The restoration of Drax to its original lords, the Paynels, was a blunt signal to the likes of Count William le Gros of Aumale that the old game was up. Stephen had given Drax to Robert de Gant in marriage, after the disinheritance of the sons of William Paynel who had supported the empress. Now, under Duke Henry's influence, he duly restored the honor to the Paynels, except the marriage portion that went with the Gant marriage. One of Gant's followers, Philip de Colleville, resisted from Drax castle, only to be crushed. Stephen's decisive action was taken despite one of the Gants being his chancellor.[109] When Henry II campaigned in England the next year, it is surely no accident that he, too, marched north to York and that the count of Aumale was forced to give up the royal demesne which he had been enjoying as

---

109 For the siege of Drax, south of York, and the issues associated with it, WN i, 94; Davis, *Stephen*, 122; Holt, '1153: the treaty of Winchester', 306n.

military governor of Yorkshire.[110] Henry II in 1155 may well have been carrying out the second part of a campaign planned by himself and Stephen in 1154. Beyond Yorkshire and the Tees was the expanded realm of the king of Scotland, and this, too, Henry II curbed in 1157. In the nature of things Stephen would also have been drawn to campaign here had he lived, simply because the Scots were overstretched and were ruled by an under-age king.

Graeme White's question as to what a successful Stephen in charge of a peaceful and prosperous England in 1160 would have done about the question of succession is as intriguing as it is unanswerable. We must confine ourselves to the reality that the king did not survive 1154. In October, Stephen moved to Dover for a second meeting with Count Thierry of Flanders. As with the spring meeting, we have no idea what the two rulers were discussing, although Boulogne and the expulsion of mercenaries (mentioned by John of Hexham as happening at this time) could have been on the agenda. Following the count's departure Stephen was suddenly seized with a painful bowel disorder which, by Gervase of Canterbury's description, was accompanied by internal bleeding.[111] It rapidly became clear that he would not survive, and the king's friend and his late wife's confessor, Prior Ralph of Holy Trinity, Aldgate, was among those summoned to Dover to assist in the rites of his passage. Almost certainly the deathbed was presided over by Archbishop Theobald, for he took responsibility for communicating the news to Duke Henry and administering the kingdom in the interregnum. King Stephen passed his last days at Dover priory (doubtless the '*curia monachorum*' referred to by Gervase of Canterbury), and died there on 25 October 1154.

From Dover the royal body was carried westwards to Stephen's abbey at Faversham, where the Cluniac monks were obliged to celebrate the royal exequies for the third time in three years; no doubt the archbishop of Canterbury presided, although no source mentions that he did. The monks of Faversham were hopefully more charitable to the king's memory than their ironic contemporary at Winchester who noted his death and consigned him 'to the place to which his merits entitled him'.[112] It is the best evidence for Stephen's success in containing and curbing disorder during 1154 that there were no outbreaks after his death, although Gervase of Canterbury preferred to give the credit to God and Archbishop Theobald. After the funeral, the archbishop moved with his court to London and there the chronicle of Battle Abbey portrays him awaiting the arrival of the duke in a city packed with magnates assembled from all over the country. The archbishop's retinue was

---

110 Warren, *Henry II*, 60 and n, which makes the important point that Henry II held the whip hand over Count William, for he had it in his power to restore to William his Norman county of Aumale.

111 *Liber Eliensis*, 371, says he died of dysentery.

112 *Annales de Wintonia*, 55. The royal burials at Faversham apparently took place in an unusually long choir, presumably designed for the accommodation of appropriate tombs, and the consequent liturgy; see B. Philip, *Excavations at Faversham, 1965* (Kent Archaeological Research Group, 1968), 7–17. My thanks to Professor Larry Hoey and Dr Heather Tanner for discussing this point.

sheltering Stephen's intimate, Richard de Lucy, whose source of employment and influence had just been buried at Faversham. Like him, England waited peacefully, but expectantly, for the arrival of its new young king, who did not reach Westminster for his coronation until 19 December.[113]

APPENDIX I – THE DATE OF THE WORCESTER CAMPAIGNS, 1150–51

Henry of Huntingdon (HH, 754–6) records two campaigns against Worcester, one in 1150, when Stephen took and plundered the city, but could not (or did not bother to) take the castle. Another was in 1151, when Stephen made a serious attempt to blockade and take the castle. The *Gesta*, on the other hand, records only one attack on Worcester (*GS*, 229), which appears from its mention of the assault on the castle to be the second of those mentioned by Huntingdon. The two accounts are not incompatible, and it could be suggested that the *Gesta* overlooked the first attack as no more than a plundering mission in the Severn valley, but focused on the second because of its more important political consequences. A further point raised by Davis in his comments on the *Gesta*'s account is the date at which the attacks occurred. The *Gesta* deals with the Worcester campaign simultaneously in its text with the renewed assault on Wallingford, which we know to have occurred in 1152. Davis therefore suggested redating Henry of Huntingdon's two attacks on Worcester to 1151 and 1152. The only recent treatment of the Worcester campaigns is by Edmund King ('Waleran count of Meulan', 173–4) who prefers to retain Huntingdon's chronology and refers to Davis's suggestion as to the date as only raising uncertainty, and does not in the end find sufficient evidence to decide one way or another.

In deciding which chronology to follow here, I have agreed with Professor King. I believe that the *Gesta* is conflating several events, careless of chronology. It is something which the author does elsewhere: as, for instance, in his account of Eustace in Normandy in 1151–52. There is some supporting evidence for Huntingdon's chronology. The Annals of Tewkesbury (a house in the diocese of Worcester) record the burning of Worcester under the year 1150, and although they record nothing concerning the city in 1151 they do mention the capture of William de Beauchamp in that year by one Ralph de Manneville – a known household intimate of Waleran of Meulan (*Annales de Theokesberia*, 47). Though late in compilation, the annals have independent value, and can be taken as confirmation of Henry of Huntingdon's chronology. The Evesham chronicle's record of rising tension in the diocese in 1149 would also indicate that there was trouble brewing which peaked in 1150 (*Chronicon de Evesham*, 99–100). There is some further evidence to take into account: this is the vacancy in the see of Worcester. The letters of Gilbert Foliot inform us of some considerable violence within the diocese of Worcester

113 GC i, 159–60; RT, 181; WN i, 95; HH, 774; *Cartulary of Holy Trinity, Aldgate*, 232; *The Chronicle of Battle Abbey*, ed. E. Searle (Oxford, 1980), 152.

during 1150 on the part of William de Beauchamp and Earl Roger of Hereford, which led to William's excommunication. As explained above, this would indicate that the vacancy was used by these two magnates as an excuse to increase their hegemony in the area, and would explain also why King Stephen suddenly became interested in relatively remote Worcestershire, seeing a chance to exert control within a 'long-lost' county (*LCGF*, 127–35).

APPENDIX II – WHAT HAPPENED AT SISTON, 1138–53

In the past ten years the manor of Siston in Gloucestershire has become a very significant place in the understanding of what was happening in Stephen's reign. This is largely due to the documentation that the contest for its possession generated. The whole problem has recently been highlighted (and much that was obscure explained) in an article published by N.E. Stacy. As Dr Stacy reconstructs its history, Siston was a possession of the first family of Berkeley, which held it in 1086. It was a manor which was rather vulnerable to powerful neighbours, adjoining the earl of Gloucester's manor of Kingswood on the west and the abbey of Glastonbury's manor of Pucklechurch on the northeast. In Henry I's reign it came into the hands of a Berkeley family widow, Racendis, as dower land (remote estates were often designated as dower or marriage-portion land). In the years between 1126 and 1138 Racendis was inspired or led to promise the estate of Siston to Glastonbury and its aggressive new abbot, Henry of Blois. In 1138 King Stephen was prevailed upon by his brother to confirm the abbey's right to Siston as being its ancient possession (Stacy, 'Henry of Blois', 11–13). What that ancient right was is difficult to know, but Dr Stacy suggests 'imaginative work in the scriptorium'. To suggest forgery and deceit may be overly cynical. Siston could very well have been an ancient satellite of Pucklechurch plundered by laymen in past centuries but not forgotten by the monks, as Dr Stacy acknowledges (ibid., p. 11). Be that as it may, there was no doubt that in 1135 the Berkeley occupation of Siston had been long and uncontested. At some time between 1138 and 1153 Siston was taken from Glastonbury. There could have been a number of perpetrators of the disseisin. The earl of Gloucester must have been involved in some capacity; he was overlord of the Berkeleys for two fees and his younger son, Philip, married Roger of Berkeley's niece (*GS*, 190). I suggested some time ago that he simply took Siston and added it to his demesne at Kingswood (Crouch, 'Earl William of Gloucester and the end of the Anarchy', 71–2). This now looks unlikely. It seems much more likely that the case of Siston was brought before the earl's honor court during the period of his ascendancy in the west (1139–47) when he put the region under his own law, and the abbey was duly disseised in favour of the Berkeleys.

Siston reappears in the record in 1153 in two documents related to the settlement of Winchester. The first was drawn up before Duke Henry at Bristol at some time in 1153, after he took the title of Aquitaine in April but before the Winchester settlement. It was a treaty between the Bristol merchant and financial agent, Robert fitz Harding, and Roger of Berkeley. Fitz Harding had acquired the castle and farm of Berkeley early in 1153 from Duke Henry despite Roger of Berkeley's rights there (*Regesta* iii, no. 309). The settlement of their difficulties was framed around the marriage of his son Maurice to the daughter of Roger of Berkeley, but it also looked forward to a further marriage between Roger's male heir and one of fitz Harding's daughters. If this were to happen Roger '. . . should give in dower to Robert's daughter the manor of Siston near Bristol, which is of Roger's inheritance' (*Descriptive Catalogue of the Charters and Muniments at Berkeley Castle*, ed. I.H. Jeayes (Bristol, 1892), 4–6). This does not prove that the Berkeleys had recovered Siston, indeed the conditional nature of the grant may imply otherwise, but they certainly were maintaining their claim to it, and also its status as nominated dower land within their honor.

The second document mentioning Siston in 1153 is that writ which has already been mentioned, by which Earl William of Gloucester was abruptly ordered by Duke Henry at Winchester in November 1153 to reseise Glastonbury abbey with the manor. This tells us that the abbey had indeed been disseised of Siston since 1138. We may guess, as Dr Stacy has guessed, that it was the Berkeleys who had taken it back. This is perfectly possible, but the earlier marriage agreement raises some doubts. There is, for instance, another possible scenario. This is that Siston was given to Philip of Gloucester with his Berkeley wife as a *maritagium* grant. After his death in 1148, Philip's widow would have continued to enjoy it in her own right. This would explain why the fitz Harding–Berkeley marriage treaty places the grant of Siston to the Berkeley heir's wife as dower in the future: the family was waiting for it to revert back. It would also explain why Earl William of Gloucester was ordered to restore Siston to Glastonbury, as the guardian of his brother's widow as much as the Berkeleys' overlord. In the end the Berkeleys reclaimed it, but at the cost of doing homage to the abbey of Glastonbury for it (Stacy, 'Henry of Blois', 13–14).

Although we cannot fully elucidate what was happening at Siston there is no doubt that the fight to possess it tells us some important things about Stephen's reign. The first is that it was sometimes the Church which was the hunter, and not the hunted. Another point is that as early as November 1153 Duke Henry was perfectly capable of throwing over his West Country supporters if it was in his interest, whether the supporter was the earl of Gloucester or Roger of Berkeley. A third point to make is that – as we saw earlier with Bungay in Suffolk – the upheavals caused by the territorial transfers of 1139–41 were complex and long-lasting, and the eventual settlement did not always favour the disinherited, despite the promises of Winchester.

PART FOUR

The Impact of Stephen's Reign

CHAPTER 15

The Church

In considering the Church in Stephen's reign we must consider well what we mean by the word 'Church'. Aside from theological considerations about the term, there was a contemporary perception of there being a distinct unit of the catholic Church focused in England. This observation has to be qualified, however, for in the reign of King Henry, as Martin Brett has observed, the claims of the archbishops of the two English provinces of Canterbury and York extended beyond the boundaries of the lands of the king of the English into Wales and Scotland, and even Ireland. Furthermore, the close association of the English and Norman episcopates brought Norman bishops (notably the archbishop of Rouen) into English councils.[1] But, indistinct around the edges or not, since there was some perception of the English Church in contemporary discourse, we should expect to find that the kings treated it as a body with which they could negotiate. This is indeed what we find in the reigns of both Henry and Stephen.

When we talk of an 'English Church' which had a voice, we generally mean the episcopal hierarchy and the prelates (secular and regular) who had some attachment to the court. Its closeness to the king gave the hierarchy some representative function for the institution itself: the curial bishops and abbots could speak for the *Christianitas Angliae* or *Ecclesia Anglicana*. There was undoubtedly some collegial feeling amongst these men apart from their common consecration and their confraternity in prayer. It would have been expressed by their group identity in the royal council (they generally attest first, as a group, in the more solemn royal acts) and formed in their debates in church councils. At times the curial hierarchy (or a large part of it, English and Norman) could meet as a delegation to treat with the king, their lord. It happened in 1136, 1139, 1141, 1150 and in 1152. On four of the five occasions the king sought them out because he wanted the Church's support in matters relating to the succession (either his own, or that of his son, Eustace).

---

1 M. Brett, *The English Church under Henry I* (Oxford, 1975), 6–33.

It was only in 1139, in the aftermath of the arrest of Roger of Salisbury, that the debate between king and Church touched on matters other than dynastic. It was here that the hierarchy demonstrated that it could be anything but united and collegial. There was a serious division amongst the bishops as to how far the king might treat them like any other subject in so far as their secular possessions were concerned. In the end, the majority of bishops took the king's part, under the leadership of the archbishop of Rouen, a Cluniac monk who had presumably less attachment to secular property than a worldly bishop such as Roger of Salisbury. The division between secular and regular clergy amongst the bishops is of significance. The fact was that the debate of 1139 showed that the collegiality of bishops did not necessarily translate into unanimity. There was no single mind at the head of the English Church.[2]

DID STEPHEN HAVE A POLICY TOWARDS THE CHURCH?

The king undoubtedly perceived the 'Church' as a body with which he might negotiate, and it was a body which was critical in his succession to the throne. This perception of the Church as a political force might be seen as one effect in England of Gregorianism, where the papacy's tendency to develop policies hostile to royal power filtered down into the consciousness of national churches, which found themselves suddenly (and often reluctantly) at odds with their offended monarchs. This had happened in England, and the reign of King Henry had seen significant concessions over investiture, and there were some clear examples of papal intervention and influence in English church affairs: the transfer and creation of sees, arbitration and the award of the pallium to archbishops.[3]

The king's perception that he was dealing with a body which had its own agenda, and which (if it wished) could further his own ends, is an important one. But it does not follow from this that the king formulated 'policies' relating to the Church (as is often said). In general we can say that Stephen had needs rather than objectives, and that his overriding need was to keep himself on the throne. To do that he had to maintain what control he had over the Church, and if this amounts to a 'policy', that was his policy. Nor does it follow that the Church in England itself had something that amounted to a 'policy' in relation to royal power. The bishops and abbots of England at the beginning of Stephen's reign were in no position to agree on any agenda relating to the royal power which had appointed most of them to their positions; they were too far compromised by the act of patronage that made them prelates. The Church's 'policy' may have amounted only to an ecclesiastical push when it felt a royal shove. It was only when the king pushed his own agenda too far that the Church found itself forced into conflict, and then the dispute usually centred around a stand-off between the king and a particular

---

2 C. Harper-Bill, *The Anglo-Norman Church* (Bangor, 1992), 33–4, drawing particular attention to the disruptiveness of the Canterbury–York dispute.
3 Brett, *The English Church under Henry I*, 57–62.

individual, like William de St Calais, Ranulf Flambard or Anselm of Canterbury. It is surely significant that when this happened, these men found only a limited degree of support from their colleagues.

But much of the historiography of Stephen's reign relating to the Church is framed around the idea of policies. Isabel Megaw's pioneering work on Stephen's early years is entitled 'The ecclesiastical policy of Stephen, 1135–39' and portrays a king initially eager to secure an alliance with the Church in order to legitimate his succession and avoid the stigma of perjury, and then very keen to get out of the consequences of his generosity. The arrest of the bishops in 1139 was to her 'a sudden reversal of policy' and an abnegation of the former alliance in the changed circumstances of impending war, when Bishop Roger's faction began to look dangerous.[4] Can Stephen's seeking of the Church's support be called something as sophisticated as a 'policy'? If it can, then it was a policy at a very low level. Stephen wished to use the Church to maintain himself, and was willing to trade with the hierarchy. What he could trade was his royal prerogative, as it had been handed on to him by King Henry. The maintenance of their traditional rights was the only policy towards the Church that can be discerned in the reigns of Stephen or his royal predecessors.

Work on Stephen's reign after Megaw has undermined the view that the idea of trading with the Church was even Stephen's. Cronne and Davis's view was that Bishop Henry of Winchester masterminded Stephen's succession, and this breaks down Megaw's case that the lay power was negotiating with the spiritual over the succession. In fact, by this view, the second most prominent churchman in England, the bishop of Winchester, was manipulating his colleagues in the hierarchy into assenting to his brother's succession as king, which hardly speaks of any unanimity of Gelasian feeling amongst the bishops. To Cronne and Davis, the ecclesiastical policy being executed in Stephen's reign was Henry's, within a Cluniac ideology of co-operation with the lay power and conversion of it to Gregorian ideals.[5] The importance of Bishop Henry in his brother's reign is indisputable, but, as we have seen, his influence on the king was considerably less than Cronne and Davis believed.

To talk of King Stephen's ecclesiastical 'policy' can lead to an unnecessarily negative view of the king's achievements. His need for revenue and patronage led him to try to maintain the prerogatives which he inherited from his uncle. He was not systematic in this, and his reign is marked by a failure to exercise a consistent royal control of ecclesiastical appointments. In this he was quite unlike his uncle. However, this lack of systematic pursuit of one aspect of his prerogative was not a failure of a royal policy, rather it was the result of both the disruptions of a national conflict and Stephen's genuine willingness to allow a degree of freedom to ecclesiastical communities to select their own

4 I. Megaw, 'The ecclesiastical policy of Stephen, 1135–39', *Essays in British and Irish History in Honour of J.E. Todd*, ed. H.A. Cronne and others (London, 1949), 24–45.
5 H.A. Cronne, *The Reign of Stephen: Anarchy in England, 1135–54* (London, 1970), 122–9; H.W.C. Davis, *King Stephen* (3rd edn., London, 1996), 17–18.

nominees. Stephen did not surrender his traditional rights over the Church, he simply had neither the time nor the inclination to enforce them systematically.

Rather than considering the ecclesiastical policies in Stephen's reign to have been a failure (a view which depends on a high idea of royal ambition to control the Church) we could turn the debate on its head and talk instead of a period of relatively fruitful co-operation between king and hierarchy. As several historians have pointed out, the bishops were strikingly reluctant to defy Stephen right up to the end of the reign.[6] It was only under the pressure of the hostile papacy of Eugenius III and the growing lay support for Duke Henry that they eventually shifted their ground. Almost up till the end Archbishop Theobald was anything but intransigent towards his king, despite their several disputes. And at the end Theobald seems to have acted as faithful pastor to the king, his lord, confessing him and burying him.

THE SIGNIFICANCE OF THE OXFORD CHARTER OF 1136

Professor Barlow's point that Stephen had to struggle with the inheritance of the aggressive exploitation of the Church by Henry I echoes what has already been said about the way Henry's ideology of strong kingship overshadowed Stephen's efforts in other areas.[7] But whereas Stephen tried to maintain that aura of overbearing kingship in lay matters (and stumbled), in ecclesiastical matters he tried to put Henry's legacy aside. Things happened so quickly in December 1135 that one can hardly talk of a trade-off between Stephen and the Church over the succession: consent following on from concession. What appears to have happened at Winchester in mid-month was a close conference between the 'king-elect', the archbishop of Canterbury and the bishops of Winchester and Salisbury, which ended in the archbishop laying aside his scruples over the oath of 1127, and agreeing to anoint Stephen. Undoubtedly, the subject of what Stephen would do as king in ecclesiastical matters would have been of concern to the bishops, but we know that the issue which was most pressed at the time was the allegedly imminent descent of the kingdom into disorder.[8]

The significant meeting between king and Church, and the one that set the tone for the whole reign, was the council at Oxford, which happened within the Easter court of 1136. It was at this meeting that the text issued by the new king to 'Holy Church' was agreed. Here we will find a policy if anywhere. What we find was a significant moderation of the king's insistence on his traditional rights over the Church; but only a moderation, not a renunciation. The draughtsmen of the charter begin by making much of what he owed already to the Church. Stephen had been elected – like a bishop – by his clergy and people; he had been consecrated by Archbishop William, who was papal legate in England, and confirmed in his kingship by the pope. Stephen then

6 K.J. Stringer, *The Reign of Stephen* (London, 1993), 62.
7 F. Barlow, *The English Church, 1066–1154* (London, 1979), 91–2.
8 Above, pp. 52–3.

pledged himself never to accept money in return for a Church appointment, or allow it to be done. He resigned to the bishops jurisdiction over the incumbents of churches and over clerks in orders. He also gave up any claim to intervene in a bishop's right to 'the distribution of the goods of the Church'. Other than that, he set the death of William the Conqueror (in 1087) as the point of definition as to what the Church's possessions were, unless he should himself allow otherwise. He resigned any claim on the developing custom amongst beneficed clergymen of making last testaments, and promised to take account of the Church's views on the disposal of the estate of a clergyman who died suddenly, without a testament. The king affirmed that he had the right to place vacant episcopal sees into the hands of guardians, but said that he would appoint clergy as guardians, or, failing that, 'upstanding men of the diocese'. He promised finally that he would rein in sheriffs in their exactions in murdrum fines and pleas on the Church. This seems of a piece with an earlier clause by which the king reversed his uncle's extension of forest exactions on the Church. The archbishops of Canterbury and Rouen, and twelve English, Welsh and Norman bishops witnessed this charter.[9]

It has to be said that from this evidence the king made only modest promises to the Church at Easter 1136, although (as we have seen in Chapter 2) he may initially have offered more. He had enjoyed several very successful months as king by March, and there was little need to show a generosity verging on weakness.[10] The charter gave up nothing of his traditional rights, and the concessions which he made were undemanding ones. In fact they reflect what the Church had been quietly discussing in England since the council of Westminster in 1125.[11] Like any respectable twelfth-century king, Stephen foreswore simony, and his main concessions were over what seem to have been newer causes of friction – the developing Church courts administering their own ecclesiastical law, and the emerging custom of the testamentary disposition of moveable goods before death.[12] As far as Church courts went, Stephen was doing no more than the Conqueror had done, when he admitted that there could be such a thing as ecclesiastical (or 'episcopal') jurisdiction.[13] Although Stephen distanced himself from King Henry's shameless exploitation of vacant

9 *Regesta* iii, no. 271. There are a number of parallels to the concessions of this charter with the demands of the canons of the legatine council of Westminster of 1125, which in turn reflected the agenda of the Lateran Council of 1123, Brett, *English Church under Henry I*, 43.
10 Here I differ from the verdict of the editors of *Councils & Synods with other Documents relating to the English Church* i, ed. D. Whitelock, M. Brett and C.N.L. Brooke (Oxford, 1981), 762, who see both the 1135 and the 1136 charter as signs of 'insecurity' in the succession. I would only apply that word to the earlier document. John of Ford, *Life of Wulfric of Haselbury*, ed. Bell, 117, has Wulfric charging Stephen, while still count, to protect the Church when he was king. This shows some general contemporary perception that Stephen as a king was thought to be favourable to the Church.
11 Cronne, *Stephen*, 125; *Councils & Synods* i, 738–41, esp. cc. 2, 4.
12 For a case where the testamentary disposition of a layman in Henry I's reign came before a bishop (of Bath), his archdeacons and men of the neighbourhood, see *English Lawsuits*, ed. van Caenegem i, no. 226.
13 M. Chibnall, *Anglo-Norman England, 1066–1166* (Oxford, 1986), 192–4, 197–201; J.G.H. Hudson, *The Formation of the English Common Law* (London, 1996), 48–50.

sees, he allowed himself the possibility of appointing lay guardians over dioceses providing that they lived within them and were respectable (*probi*) men. As with his distribution of the spoils of office to lay people, Stephen was by no means as profligate in his concessions to the Church as he was once pictured as being. The Oxford charter to the Church makes conciliatory noises but keeps promises to a minimum. Stephen's Church 'policy' in 1136 was a reasonable maintenance of his traditional rights, and reasonable concessions in the new circumstances of his own time.

Despite William of Malmesbury's complaints that the king's promises (such as they were) were worthless immediately after their issue, there is good reason to believe that the king did make an effort to hold to his opening manifesto.[14] It may have helped that his promises were so modest. He was still maintaining his pledges about newly afforested church land in the later 1140s (see Chapter 2). As promised, he also appointed clerics to custody of vacant sees, although since one such beneficiary was his brother, Henry, who was given Hyde abbey in 1136, the see of Exeter briefly in 1137, Canterbury between 1137 and 1138 and Salisbury in 1139–40, his generosity there may have been tempered by needs for patronage and conciliation. When Stephen was in captivity in 1141, Bishop Henry stipulated in his discussion with the empress that she should resign her claim to appoint to bishoprics and abbacies. He may have done so, not so much to advance the autonomy of the Church when the king was out of action, but to safeguard a gain for the Church which had already been made.[15]

ELECTIONS AND APPOINTMENTS

In the notices that we have for the reign which mention vacancies in sees and houses under the king's control, there is good evidence that the king was often content to withdraw from the process after 1136. Communities were willing to encourage him in this by agreeing to requests to pay a fine in order to have free elections, although this skirted the borders of the dark land of simony. If the views of any individuals were heeded, then appointments seem to have been made more with an eye to the legate, to the individual chapters, and occasionally to other powerful figures within England and within the Church, such as St Bernard. But the process of appointments could be so complex as to leave the modern historian guessing as to which was the dominant influence. An example is the appointment to Battle abbey in 1138. The papal legate in England, Alberic of Ostia, began the process by obliging Abbot Warner of St Martin of Battle to retire. In the choice of the new abbot, the king sought the counsel of the queen and the magnates. The fact that the name approved was the brother of Richard de Lucy, who was already emerging as one of the

14 *HN*, 20, which accuses not so much the king as his advisers, of simoniacal appointments, looting and alienation of ecclesiastical property and bad appointments.
15 *HN*, 50–1.

king's leading *curiales*, and kinsman of Abbot Geoffrey of St Albans (another royal favourite), shows that in this case the king heeded his own courtiers. But he must also have satisfied the legate who had concerned himself with the abbey's affairs. The Battle Chronicle stresses Walter de Lucy's learning and practical wisdom, that is, his suitability for office.[16]

It is quite difficult to find appointments in which the king took a direct interest. His clerical brother was already well taken care of when he became king. Although Stephen has been criticised for not nominating Henry to Canterbury, there were pressing and practical reasons why he should not to do so. He did endow Bishop Henry further, with the deanship of the college of St Martin-le-Grand in London and with the custody of vacant benefices, as we have seen. One clear example of purposeful royal intervention must have been the election in 1138 of Stephen's son, Gervase, while still a young man in his early twenties to the abbacy of Westminster. Abbot Gervase was undoubtedly favoured by his father. There is evidence that the king tilted the scales of justice in his son's favour in his dispute over possessions in London with Colchester abbey. The abbot may also have been able to influence the king, his father, and Bishop Henry, his uncle, to support the abbey's bid to have Edward the Confessor canonised.[17] But, as Emma Mason has noted, the abbey of Westminster was not overwhelmed by royal generosity under its rule by a king's bastard, indeed it later found that it had to make good by forgery the relative dearth of charters it had from Stephen.[18] Glastonbury abbey did far better for royal privileges under its rule by the king's brother. Yet Gervase was an efficient and energetic abbot, and (despite later accusations) promoted good housekeeping around the convent, built improvements and did what he could to mitigate the bad effects of his father's reign on the abbey lands. His was not a bad appointment.[19]

The king seems to have been content to let elections, or at least nominations, happen and simply confirm the results, if they were not complicated by any external influences. This applies to sees and royal abbeys alike. For instance, Exeter had a new bishop in 1138, before Stephen's kingship was

16 *Chronicle of Battle Abbey*, 140–2; JW iii, 262. There must have been a similar mixture of influences which obtained for Alice, sister of Payn fitz John the *curialis*, the abbey of Barking in 1136 × 37, *Regesta* iii, no. 32.
17 H.G. Richardson and G.O. Sayles, *The Governance of Medieval England* (Edinburgh, 1963), 414.
18 For Gervase's promotion, JW iii, 262; *Westminster Abbey Charters*, ed. Mason, 12. For the tussle between Westminster and Colchester abbeys over the possession of St Mary Woolchurch (or Newchurch) based on contradictory grants to Colchester by Eudo dapifer and to Westminster by a priest called Aelward, see *Cartularium monasterii sancti Johannis de Colecestria*, ed. S.A. Moore (2 vols, Roxburghe Club, 1897) i, 3, 6, 13, 15, 18, 50, 82; Cartulary of Westminster, Brit. Libr., ms Cott. Faustina A iii, fos. 57r, 64r–v, 76r, 165r–v. See also J.H. Round, 'The early charters of St John's abbey, Colchester', *EHR* 16 (1901), 721–30; *Regesta* ii, nos. 677, 1096, 1204; iii, no. 930. Colchester's title was stronger than Westminster's, but Gervase was able nonetheless to secure possession by a writ of his father. For Westminster's forgeries of Stephen's acts (six forgeries out of seventeen) see *Westminster Abbey Charters*, ed. Mason, 62–8.
19 B. Harvey, 'Abbot Gervase de Blois and the fee farms of Westminster abbey', *Bulletin of the Institute of Historical Research*, xl (1967), 127–41; *Westminster Abbey Charters*, ed. Mason, 16–17.

disputed in England and when he was still unchallenged in power. The new bishop, Robert, was nephew to his predecessor and already archdeacon in the diocese, so the likelihood is that he was the chapter nominee accepted, and not contested, by Stephen.[20] Similarly, when Bishop Roger of Salisbury died in December 1139 the two royal abbeys which he had held in commendation, Malmesbury and Abbotsbury, were promptly allowed their own regular abbots elected from amongst their communities. Malmesbury abbey paid a fine for its right to appoint, and there was a prompt allegation that this payment was simoniacal (the first of many such cases in the reign). As a result, the king was taken to task by his brother, the legate. But Malmesbury's historian, William, refused to see the payment as in any way improper, despite his personal feelings about the king.[21] Also in 1139, Stephen had heeded the lobbying of Miles, the powerful sheriff of Gloucester, when he furthered the nomination of the Cluniac, Gilbert Foliot, to the abbacy of Gloucester. Gilbert was well connected in court circles, being the son of the seneschal of David of Scotland in England and cousin of Miles of Gloucester, so his might be seen as a candidacy that arose from both local and court connections. Does Stephen's distance from appointments amount to a significant weakening of royal rights? In Henry's reign, that king, too, had found it politic to listen to local opinion, and in 1131 he had consulted his local officers and magnates before appointing Robert de Béthune as bishop of Hereford, after a three-year vacancy.[22]

If we are looking for a national fixer of appointments, we find it not in the king, but in his brother. Bishop Henry was principally a nepotist, although he seems to have worked to find places for promising fellow Cluniacs where he could. His first major act of patronage was the appointment to Bath in 1136 of his fellow Cluniac, Robert of Lewes. However, Robert was not only a Cluniac but was the bishop's household familiar; he had been Bishop Henry's viceger-ent in his administration of Glastonbury abbey. Another Cluniac, and kinsman, one Robert, was appointed to Winchcombe in 1138.[23] In 1141, the bishop per-suaded another able Cluniac, one Peter, formerly prior of La Charité-sur-Loire, to take up the abbacy of Malmesbury.[24] In 1140, Henry was very busy look-ing to find a suitable position for his nephew and namesake, Henry de Sully, son of his elder brother, Count William. His first attempt was to place Henry in the vacant bishopric of Salisbury, after Roger's death. This failed when the magnates of the court, particularly Waleran of Meulan, opposed Henry with the rival candidacy of Philip de Harcourt, Waleran's cousin and protégé. Bishop Henry was defeated at this time of Beaumont ascendancy, and so withdrew in

20 *English Episcopal Acta* xi, *Exeter, 1046–1184*, ed. F. Barlow (British Academy, 1996), pp. xxxiv–xxxv.
21 JW iii, 280; *HN*, 40.
22 Brett, *English Church under Henry I*, 104–5; *English Episcopal Acta* vii, *Hereford 1079–1234*, ed. J. Barrow (Oxford, 1993), pp. xxxvi–xxxviii. The appointment of Abbot Reginald of Evesham, Gilbert Foliot's uncle and Miles of Gloucester's kinsman, in 1129, would seem to be another such instance of local lobbying, *Chronicon de Evesham*, 98–9.
23 JW iii, 240.
24 JW iii, 292.

anger, while the king attempted to appease him by offering Henry the abbacy of the great Norman ducal house of Fécamp, vacant since 1138.[25] Bishop Henry did not by any means rest easy with this defeat. When the chapter of York's elected candidate for archbishop in 1141, Waltheof of Kirkham, withdrew, Henry de Sully was promoted for nomination by Bishop Henry. But the nomination failed because (like his uncle) Henry de Sully wanted to hold his see in plurality with an abbey, and the pope refused him permission.[26] As far as Salisbury was concerned, Bishop Henry also persisted, and obtained the election of his archdeacon, Joscelin de Bohun, as bishop in 1142, after Philip's withdrawal.[27] Even after the loss of his legateship, Bishop Henry's influence remained strong. So, in 1147, through his influence at Rome, he engineered the promotion of another former household familiar of his, Hilary, to the see of Chichester (after previously urging him on the chapter of York to replace St William).[28] It is difficult to know whether it was Henry or the king who promoted their nephew, Hugh, to be abbot first of St Benet Hulme and then of Chertsey, but it is most likely that it was the bishop, since Hugh was moved into his diocese at Chertsey in 1149.[29]

But these examples aside, many elections simply happened, and were allowed to happen quickly, providing the communities were willing to pay a fine for the privilege. The free election in 1152 to the see of London of Richard de Beaumeis II, archdeacon of Middlesex, the chapter candidate, cost the chapter 500*li*.[30] The election by his chapter of the anti-Semite William Turbe, prior of Norwich, to the see of Norwich in 1146 might be another such case. Since Prior William could not have been in any way in the king's favour, having led the opposition to his sheriff and justices in 1144 over their protection for the Jewish community in the city, one wonders what inducement the king was offered to accept him.[31] In London and Kent, where the king was strongest, he seems to have let many appointments be made 'freely' and quickly. So in January 1147, the favoured priory of Holy Trinity at Aldgate elected its subprior Ralph in succession to its late prior Norman after a vacancy of only six days.[32] At Canterbury in 1151, the great royal abbey of St Augustine proceeded likewise to elect Silvester, prior of the community in succession to its late abbot, Hugh, after (apparently) a short vacancy, but here the convent had

25 OV vi, 536; JW iii, 284.
26 JH, 306–7, which calls him, inaccurately, abbot of Caen. When he became legate, Archbishop Theobald also proved a nepotist, nominating his brother, Walter, already archdeacon of Canterbury, to the see of Rochester, traditionally dependent on Canterbury, A. Saltman, *Theobald: Archbishop of Canterbury* (London, 1955), 103–4.
27 JH, 302.
28 Saltman, *Theobald*, 101–2.
29 *Regesta* iii, nos. 169–73 concern Hugh's appointment to Chertsey and a subsequent surge of favours to the abbey.
30 Diceto i, p. xxv.
31 Thomas of Monmouth, *The Life and Miracles of St William of Norwich*, ed. A. Jessopp and M.R. James (Cambridge, 1896), p. xxi; *English Episcopal Acta* vi, *Norwich, 1070–1214*, ed. Harper-Bill (British Academy, 1990), pp. xxxiii–xxxiv.
32 *Cartulary of Holy Trinity, Aldgate*, 231–2.

cautiously offered the king 500 marks for the privilege before the vacancy had begun.[33] Outside the southeast, royal monasteries could aspire to complete liberty. In 1148, rather than let their promoted abbot, Gilbert, hold the abbey in plurality with the see of Hereford, the monks of Gloucester elected as new abbot their prior, Hamelin, after only a three-week vacancy.[34] It is therefore very difficult to talk of Stephen losing influence over the Church in the context of appointments, for he never aspired to much in the way of influence, so to that extent he kept to his promise of 1136. He did not, however, let the Church elect for free, even if he let it elect freely.

On the rare occasions when Stephen did attempt to act, the results appear to justify his caution. The appointment of Theobald to Canterbury is likely to have been the only occasion when he exerted himself, and even then it was only, perhaps, to act as referee between court factions. The need for caution is most evident in the vacancy at York following the death of Archbishop Thurstan in 1140. Here at first the chapter of the cathedral appears to have moved quickly to a free election and produced the name of Waltheof, then Augustinian prior of the house of Kirkham, in the Derwent valley not far from York. Waltheof was an aristocrat, the son of the first Earl Simon de Senlis of Northampton, and stepson of King David of Scotland. Being descended through his mother, Mathilda, from the ancient earls of Northumbria he was very much a weighty local candidate. But his election was set aside or resigned, not least because William de Aumale, the earl of York, appears to have compromised his candidature by seeking a simoniacal gift for his support.[35] As we have seen, the attempt of the legate to intrude his nephew, Henry de Sully, ran aground on the opposition of Innocent II. So in January 1141 a third attempt was made, and this time the chapter elected its treasurer, William fitz Herbert, who was also a nephew of Bishop Henry, through a half-sister, Emma, who had married Count Herbert of Maine. The earl of York directed the chapter to elect William, 'speaking in the king's place'; but whether he was entirely solicitous for William as his own or the king's candidate is unclear. The pope later heard complaints that money had changed hands between the earl and William (perhaps another of those contentious fines for a free election). The earl was remorselessly supportive of the royal candidate, and intervened by arresting and confining a leading opponent of the election. The archbishop-elect was received at Lincoln by the king, just before the fateful battle that made him a prisoner. His episcopate was to be as unhappy as the circumstances of his election predicted.[36]

---

33 *Annals of St Augustine*, 82; Saltman, *Theobald*, 72–3. The monks of Thorney elected successive abbots from their community in 1151 and 1154, obtaining on each occasion a charter of Stephen (perhaps in the manner of a receipt for their fine?), *Regesta* iii, nos. 895–6.

34 *Historia et Cartularium de Gloucestria*, ed. Hart i, 19.

35 *Vita sancti Waldeui*, in *Acta Sanctorum*, August I (Paris, 1867), Bk 2, cc. 29–30. See also, D. Nicholl, *Thurstan Archbishop of York, 1114–1140* (York, 1964), 244–5; D. Baker, 'Legend and reality: the case of Waldef of Melrose', in *Studies in Church History*, 12, *Church, Society and Politics*, ed. D. Baker (Oxford, 1975), 59–82, esp. 75–6.

36 JH, 306–7.

It was hardly surprising that the progress of the civil war would add obstacles to the king's ability to make appointments, especially in those sees which passed out of his military control. But the dioceses of Hereford and Bangor offer two notable and surprising examples of the way bishops could be made in Stephen's reign, without Stephen's nomination and outside his area of power but nonetheless with Stephen's involvement. In December 1139, the 'clergy and people' of Bangor (for which we might well read, the king of Gwynedd and the episcopal community) elected one Meurig (Maurice) as bishop. Meurig went to Theobald of Canterbury for consecration, but on the way met Stephen at Worcester where the bishops of Hereford and Chichester presented him and told the king 'that he [Meurig] was worthy to be canonically elected to the episcopate'. Here, after some debate, Meurig was persuaded to swear fealty to King Stephen although he held no lands in England.[37]

The election of Gilbert Foliot to the see of Hereford in 1148 is also very instructive. Bishop Robert de Béthune died at Reims in April 1148 just after the end of the great council held under the presidency of Pope Eugenius III. Archbishop Theobald was at Reims and arranged with the pope for the almost immediate provision of Gilbert Foliot, abbot of Gloucester and one of his entourage at Reims, to the see of Hereford. The choice was a good one: Gilbert was a Cluniac monk and had been established in the region of the diocese of Hereford since 1139, when Miles of Gloucester had promoted his candidacy to the king for the headship of the royal abbey of Gloucester in the neighbouring diocese of Worcester. Under Gilbert, indeed, Gloucester abbey had acquired a dependent priory of St Guthlac in the city of Hereford. Gilbert's abbacy had been distinguished by his energy and competence. He was therefore a good candidate on several counts, and with papal approval was consecrated at St-Omer in Flanders by Archbishop Theobald in September 1148. In this way the vacancy at Hereford was short and a bishop was found without reference to the king, but instead provided by the legate and the apostolic see.[38] Consultation with the lay power over the 'election' to Hereford did occur, if only as consent after the choice. John of Salisbury believed that Henry fitz Empress had consented to Gilbert's elevation, as he 'then controlled election to this see'. Yet the duke was strangely insistent by this account that he would only confirm the election if Gilbert swore to do homage to him. Henry's reported reason was that the Church recognised only one lord of England, and that was King Stephen. So, despite the intrusion of papal and Angevin power in the appointment of Gilbert Foliot, it seems that the king's rights were not quite extinguished. Far from it, as it eventually turned out. Duke Henry's suspicions were justified for, despite his own personal opinions, on his return to England Bishop Gilbert swore his loyalty to the king. He was defended in this by Archbishop Theobald, who said that a bishop had no right to refuse fealty 'to the prince approved by the papacy'.[39] So dioceses outside the king's immediate

37 JW iii, 278.
38 A. Morey and C.N.L. Brooke, *Gilbert Foliot and his Letters* (Cambridge, 1965), 96–7.
39 *HP*, 47–9.

control might acknowledge his kingship and rights too, even if their bishop was appointed by a roundabout route.

Stephen did not attempt to use high preferment as rewards for royal clerks, and as we have seen, it seems to have been his brother, as legate, who attempted to push relatives and friends into sees and abbacies. In this vacuum, magnates, Welsh and English cathedral chapters, the distant papacy, and the not-so-distant legate, operated as active nominators in the king's stead. The king became a passive collector of the requisite fines for election. But was he ill-advised to do this? As Christopher Holdsworth has pointed out, in leaving the appointment of bishops to the Church Stephen may have given up the ultimate patronage desired by the clerks of his chapel, but it did produce a very respectable and not undistinguished bench.[40] Perhaps he was not wrong to do it. Curial bishops like Roger of Salisbury and Nigel of Ely, or even Henry of Winchester, were hardly good advertisements for the regime operated by King Henry before him. Was it better for Stephen to have pastoral, prayerful and intellectual bishops, or the passionate and political type furthered by his uncle? The consequences of Henry II's promotion of the intensely political animal, Thomas Becket, to Canterbury might stand as a sermon on King Stephen's prudence.

CHURCH COURTS

It may well be that the overall political insecurities in England after 1138 acted as a dampener on tensions between king and bishops. The issue of ecclesiastical jurisdiction was raised in 1135–36 and the king was prevailed upon to confirm to the bishops the right to judge clerks in orders and cases involving Church goods. This is a debate which surfaces in 1138 when a *cause célèbre* arose over the intrusion into the church of Luton of an alleged layman by the earl of Gloucester. Bishop Alexander of Lincoln had great difficulty in getting the offending person to answer in his court, even with the king's support, because the intruder claimed that it was a lay, feudal tenure.[41] He would hardly have tried this tack if it was not by then understood that lay and ecclesiastical courts were separating in jurisdiction. The problem with the evidence is that the Luton case is far clearer in its significance than others which have survived.

There is some evidence that recognisable Church courts were active and occasionally effective in their dioceses, even without the sort of papal mandate that settled the Durham question in 1143. A letter of 1150 from Bishop Gilbert Foliot to Gilbert de Lacy reveals that following a writ from Stephen, the bishop had pursued Earl Roger of Hereford over a case of sanctuary-breaking. The bishop had heard the plea, but on appeal by the earl to Archbishop Theobald (presumably as papal legate) the case had been adjourned to Theobald's court. The case seems to show a hierarchy of Church courts in operation which were

---

40 C.J. Holdsworth, 'The Church', in *The Anarchy of King Stephen's Reign*, ed. E. King (Oxford, 1994), 212–13.
41 *English Lawsuits*, ed. van Caenegem, i, 249–50.

responsive to both king and pope, even if they could not do much. Bishop Gilbert did at least promote ecclesiastical justice, and in 1153 is found employing a clerk who was a specialist in Roman law.[42]

The foundation of the abbey of Biddlesden on the border of Northamptonshire and Buckinghamshire is another case in point. The land on which the Cistercian monastery was founded in 1147 had been taken from the minor Buckinghamshire baron, Robert of Meppershall by his lord, Earl Robert of Leicester, for his refusal to answer a military summons, as the abbey's foundation chronicle tells us. The earl granted the land on to his steward, but since they regarded the tenure as likely to be dubious, the steward and the earl persuaded the Leicestershire Cistercians of Garendon to take on the land and colonise it as a daughter house. Robert of Meppershall did not give up without a struggle, and he sought to implead the monks. His case came to trial in 1151 in an assembly at St Albans made up of the bishop of Lincoln, five of his archdeacons and numerous other clergy; an ecclesiastical court of the synodical sort, the same sort to which (notoriously) the Jews of Norwich were summoned to answer for the death of the boy, William, in 1144. Robert of Meppershall relinquished his claim to the land (when the earl paid him ten marks, as the monks later stated) and received further confirmation in a charter of King Stephen.[43]

On the other hand possible proceedings in an ecclesiastical court were sometimes ignored. When the monks of Battle fell out with the archbishop of Canterbury over the right of wreck at Dengemarsh, the archbishop pursued the monks in the royal court, which adjourned the case to the abbot's own (secular) court. Then there is the case of the claim of the churches of St Aldate and St Edward in Oxford, of which the bishop of Lincoln claimed a share against St Frideswide's priory at some time after 1148. King Stephen brusquely ordered the bishop that the claim could not be heard anywhere except in the court *coram rege*, that is before the king himself, because the case involved churches in his gift. Yet the case was plainly an ecclesiastical one under the provisions of 1136.[44] Finally, there is evidence that plaintiffs might attempt to suit themselves where they pleaded in ecclesiastical causes. Refusing to plead their liberties against the bishop of Chichester in synod in 1148 – presumably because it was too like being judged by the bishop himself – the monks of Battle took their case to the court *coram rege* at St Albans. The king referred the parties to a later court at London, where only the plaintiffs appeared and the bishop sent excuses. The king judged the abbey to be in the right on a matter of exemption from episcopal oversight, presumably because it was a royal foundation with a banlieu granted by the Conqueror.[45]

42 *LCGF*, 132–3, 145.
43 For the development of these courts see C. Morris, 'From synod to consistory: the bishops' courts in England, 1150–1250', 115–23. For the cases cited, see Cartulary of Biddlesden, Brit Libr ms. Harley 4714, fos. 1r, 2r–v; *English Episcopal Acta* i, *Lincoln 1067–1185*, ed. D.M. Smith (British Academy, 1980), 56–7; *English Lawsuits*, ed. van Caenegem, i, 266–7, 43–7.
44 *Chronicle of Battle Abbey*, 142–4; *Regesta* iii, no. 650.
45 *Chronicle of Battle Abbey*, 149–53.

In general, it would seem that there was not always too firm an idea of what ecclesiastical cases were; where they should be tried in Stephen's reign; and who was ultimately responsible for seeing that it should be done. Stephen seems to have at least begun by believing that it was his prerogative to ensure that justice was done in ecclesiastical cases as much as in lay. At some time in the first years of his reign he directed a writ to the archdeacon of Canterbury ordering that right be done to St Augustine's abbey in a plea concerning a church, in the same way that he might have directed a writ to one of his sheriffs.[46] This lack of definition as to where ecclesiastical causes ended and lay causes began – and where the king fitted into the whole picture – is nowhere more evident than in 1139, when the bishops of Salisbury, Lincoln and Ely and others were deprived, and two of them imprisoned, by verdict of the king's court, with results we have seen above. Despite the sacred nature of the episcopal office, most of the bishops bowed in council to the argument put forward by the king's attorneys that the lay courts had jurisdiction over bishops in their character as tenants of royal fees and lands. As a result of all this vagueness and contention, Stephen's ability to keep to the promise made in 1136 was not too difficult. But that there was nonetheless some developing tension can be seen by what was said in the synod of Norwich when John the sheriff denied its jurisdiction over the Jews: 'They declared unanimously that a manifest outrage was being done to God and christian law, and they advised that it should be straightway vindicated with rigorous ecclesiastical justice.'[47] But the culmination of that feeling was left for Henry II to deal with.

STEPHEN AND THE PAPACY

Stephen's relationship with the papacy was much more involved than that of his uncle. King Henry was able to keep the pope at a distance. But even Henry had occasionally to accommodate himself to the presence of a papal legate in England, notably John of Crema in 1125–26. Stephen had a legate to deal with in England for a large part of his reign. Archbishop William de Corbeil of Canterbury held a legateship till his death in 1136. The Cluniac cardinal, Alberic bishop of Ostia, was sent into England and Scotland as legate from the apostolic see in 1138–39. In 1139 Bishop Henry of Winchester revealed that he had a commission as legate from Innocent II, and proceeded to lord it over his fellow bishops until 1143. In the spring of 1145 another legate, Cardinal Imar of Tusculum arrived as legate from the Curia. He made only a brief stay in England but was very active while he was present. After 1150, Archbishop Theobald himself held a legateship from Eugenius III which was renewed at the pope's death and held by Theobald till his own death in 1161. Stephen's views on such direct contact with the papacy are difficult to work out. Until 1144 he was very much reliant on the support of successive

---

46 *Regesta* iii, no. 159.
47 *Life of St William of Norwich*, 46–7.

popes. It is perhaps significant that by 1150 he was sufficiently exasperated with Eugenius III to deny entry into England to the papal legate to the Irish Church, Cardinal John Paparone. Paparone was sent back to the Curia and only permitted to pass through England when he undertook to do no harm to England as he passed through, and after he had been ordained a cardinal-priest. His previous status as cardinal-deacon would have been intolerable to Archbishop Theobald, who had shown himself very sensitive to the awkward questions of status which rose when the metropolitan bishop was confronted by a papal representative who was ranked in the hierarchy above all other bishops; he went out of his way to avoid Bishop Henry of Winchester while he was legate and fell into conflict with him after his commission lapsed.[48]

Stephen must have disliked the way that the papacy, either directly or through legates, began to make active interventions in elections. The first was as early as 1137, when in the Canterbury vacancy John de Sées was provided by Innocent II to the see of Rochester.[49] Although Stephen did not hold strong views on appointments, he could hardly have welcomed the constraints that papal interventions put on the process. Such controls caused him some of the more embarrassing problems of his reign. As we have seen, when the king and his brother tried to get Henry de Sully consecrated as archbishop of York in 1141, their attempt foundered on Pope Innocent's refusal to let Henry hold Fécamp in plurality with York. This may have been an indirect swipe at Henry of Blois, who was concurrently legate, bishop of Winchester, abbot of Glastonbury and dean of St Martin-le-Grand in London.

The York elections after 1140 must have seemed like a miniature Purgatory to the king and his brother. Although they may have thought that William fitz Herbert was safely consecrated in 1141, the pope persisted in denying William his pallium, the strip of lamb's wool which was papal recognition that a bishop was of metropolitical status. This arose out of the allegations of simoniacal dealings between William and the king, which Bishop Henry referred to the Curia at Rome in 1142, where the case was expensively held over until 1143, and eventually decided by the swearing of an oath to clear William. He was finally consecrated to York in October 1143 by the legate in his cathedral of Winchester, but then compromised himself by failing to go to receive the pallium brought to England for him by the legate, Imar, in 1145. William appears to have forgotten, being distracted by less important matters 'as was usual with him'.[50] As a consequence he opened himself to the active opposition of that European busybody, St Bernard of Clairvaux.

Bernard had been alerted to something irregular in William's election as early as 1141. His source would undoubtedly have been the two large Cistercian communities in the diocese of York, who would – in their pharisaic way – have interpreted any chapter fine for a free election as simony. By 1143 Bernard had already decided that Archbishop William was a corrupt man and a disgrace

48 JH, 319. On Stephen's legates, Saltman, *Theobald*, 133–7.
49 Barlow, *English Church*, 95 and n.
50 JH, 313, 315, 317.

309

to Christendom and was agitating at the holy see for his removal. His pressure was, in the end, to produce the candidature of his old friend and English protégé, Henry Murdac, former monk of Clairvaux and later abbot of Fountains. The case was dragged to Rome again in 1146 as Archbishop William sought his pallium, only to find that at Paris in 1147 Pope Eugenius was happy to force him to stand down, and order a new election, which produced the name of Henry Murdac. Murdac's arrival in the diocese of York as archbishop in 1148 forced a schism which lasted in effect till 1152, and led to anathemas flying between Murdac and the chapter in a most unseemly way. In the course of the affair, the abbey of Fountains was burned down. Stephen had little to do with all this, but he did accept the papal action. He needed Murdac to influence St Bernard and the pope over his plans to get Eustace crowned.[51]

Durham was another diocese where heavy-handed papal intervention was experienced. Here there was a vacancy in the see on the death of Bishop Geoffrey Rufus in 1141. This triggered a prolonged struggle over the see in which King David was deeply involved. Most of the diocese was by 1141 under Scottish control, or rather, the control of King David's son, the earl of Northumbria, based at Newcastle-upon-Tyne. William Cumin, archdeacon of Worcester, and since 1136 the Scottish king's chancellor, was the king's choice to succeed. Passing south to join his niece, the king refused to allow Bishop Geoffrey's body to be buried until the city received Cumin, and once Cumin was installed, he confided the wardship of the diocese to him. The king said that he was acting on the empress's behalf.[52] Despite the high-handedness of King David, the choice of Cumin was not outrageous, he had been a clerk and student of the late bishop so his choice might even be said to have been sensitive. Unfortunately, Cumin's behaviour at Durham thereafter was anything but sensitive. He fell out with the established powers of the archdeacon and the cathedral chapter, who took their complaints to the pope. By papal mandate an election was held at mid-Lent in 1143 in York minster, which produced the name of William de St-Barbe, then dean of York. St-Barbe was consecrated in June at Winchester by Henry of Blois, and Cumin was excommunicated. This sparked further trouble as Cumin, with the support of Earl Henry of Northumbria and Earl Alan of Richmond, plundered the diocese and garrisoned the cathedral priory. The situation was not resolved until 1144, when the death of his nephew and heir disheartened Cumin and brought him to terms.[53] In the wrangles over Durham we see that the lay power initially attempted to assert

---

51 For Bernard and Murdac, and the limited role of Stephen in this affair, see C. Holdsworth, 'St Bernard and England', *ANS* viii, ed. R.A. Brown (Woodbridge, 1986), 138–53 *passim*.

52 JH, 309. It is worth noting that RH, 157 describes David in 1138 as rather more assertive towards Durham, demanding that Bishop Geoffrey Rufus accept him as his overlord and re-nounce Stephen, G.W.S. Barrow, 'The Scots and the north of England', in *The Anarchy of King Stephen's Reign*, ed. E. King (Oxford, 1994), 246–7.

53 JH, 313–14, 316–17. A. Young, *William Cumin: Border Politics and the Bishopric of Durham, 1141–1144* (Borthwick Paper, 54, 1979) *passim*; idem, 'The bishopric of Durham in Stephen's reign', in *Anglo-Norman Durham*, ed. D. Rollason and others (Woodbridge, 1994), 353–68, esp. 357–9.

the right of custody and nomination, although this time it was the empress (through her uncle) who was asserting it. But when the situation became unmanageable, papal arbitration was sought for a final settlement. It would seem that here, secular confusions reinforced an existing drift to look to the apostolic see for firm decisions.

Appeals to the holy see had begun before Henry I died, and the practice was intensified in Stephen's reign. There were many notable cases. Bishop Alexander of Lincoln gained the support of Pope Innocent in 1139 in his struggle to recover Newark castle from Earl Robert of Leicester. In 1144 Bishop Rotrou of Evreux went to Rome to get the minster of Warwick, which his brother Earl Roger had taken back, returned to him. We have seen how the candidates for York wore a hollow path travelling to and fro to Rome between 1142 and 1150. Bishop Nigel of Ely travelled to Rome in his difficulties with King Stephen in 1144; no wonder his chapter retained a proctor in Rome, one Richard.[54] These are only some of the major cases. The king's attitude to Rome must by then have become distinctly jaundiced as the intruding juridiction of the papacy compromised his rule in England. The king attempted to stop Archbishop Theobald leaving the realm in 1148 to attend the great council at Reims, a further sign of frustration which would explode into royal anger over Eugenius's failure to acknowledge Eustace's right to a coronation.

MONASTICISM AND SOCIETY

There were many great changes in religious life while Stephen was king, but few had anything to do with the fact that Stephen was king. For instance, the reign saw further moves towards the deterioration of the ancient pastoral structure of the Church in Wales and England. The old mother churches or minsters continued to decay or were converted into regular priories, while a developing network of localised village or town churches, with small tithe-paying flocks, replaced them. The number of secular, as well as regular, clergy continued to expand, as education and opportunity allowed more and poorer men to take orders. Church discipline continued to tighten on clergy and laity alike, particularly in matters relating to sexual and marital relations. Despite the civil disorders of the reign, churches great and small continued to be rebuilt ambitiously in stone. A great crusade fired Europe with a temporary enthusiasm in the years 1147–49, and many English and Normans alike were inspired to join Louis VII on the road to Antioch. Others took ship to join the crusade to free Portugal from the Moors, and they assisted in the seizure of Lisbon, whose first bishop was, as a result, an Englishman. But all these things happened with no reference to Stephen; they would have happened just the same had he not been king and they had no significant effect on the course of his reign and the nature of his government.

54 *Liber Eliensis*, 350.

But one great ecclesiastical development did have a particular effect on England and a direct effect on Stephen and his aristocracy: the expansion in the monastic orders. It was a major movement with significant consequences, both political and economic. The statistics are impressive. According to Christopher Holdsworth's recent calculations, over 170 houses were founded in England and Wales in Stephen's reign, considerably more than the number of castles now believed to have been built in the same period. There were over double the number of monasteries in England in 1154 that there had been in 1135.[55] These houses, great and small, were generally the result of aristocratic patronage, although the king, the queen and the empress themselves contributed to the total, as we have seen. As we will see in the next chapter, the fact that this amount of enthusiasm could be sustained in Stephen's reign, and such foundations advanced, tells us a lot about the state of the country. Disruption of the civil order was never so severe that religious men could not accumulate estates, build large churches in stone and travel around the country. Edmund King's recent study of the involved business of founding Pipewell abbey in the county of Northampton in the 1140s is a good example of the way that difficulties in competing jurisdictions and local rivalries could be triumphantly overcome by determined but ordinary men.[56]

The political relevance of these foundations appears in the motives of their founders. Probably most were the result of simple spiritual aspirations. Their founders wished to promote prayer for their souls and those of their families, and a monastery was the best way to do it. Some intended that one day they would retire into the house they had founded, to die in the habit of a professed religious. Thus, before his death in 1168, Robert, earl of Leicester was received as a canon into the Augustinian abbey of Leicester he had founded around 1139. His widow, Countess Amice, left the world immediately on his death to become a nun in the priory they had begun founding before the end of Stephen's reign, which had settled at Nuneaton before 1160. A number of well-known characters of Stephen's reign ended their days in the cloister: Earl Roger of Hereford died at Gloucester abbey in 1155, Waleran of Meulan died a Benedictine at Les Préaux in Normandy in 1166 and Brian fitz Count may have ended his days at Reading around 1151. Richard de Lucy retired to the Augustinians of Lessness in Kent in 1179, to be a canon for a few months before he died. Count Henry and his son Count John of Eu also ended their days as Augustinian canons of the abbey of Eu, where they died in 1140 and 1170 respectively.[57]

55 Holdsworth, 'The Church', 216–17.
56 E. King, 'The foundation of Pipewell abbey, Northamptonshire', *HSJ*, 2 (1990), 167–77.
57 For Earl Roger, *Historia et Cartularium de Gloucestria*, ed. Hart i, 88–9; for Waleran, Amice and Robert, D. Crouch, *The Beaumont Twins: The Roots and Branches of Power in the Twelfth Century* (Cambridge, 1986), 78–9, 95–6; for the Eus, D. Crouch, *The Image of Aristocracy in Britain, 1000–1300* (London, 1992), 321; for Brian, M. Chibnall, *The Empress Matilda* (Oxford, 1991), 149 (Reading seems to me the most likely place of retirement for Brian for reasons of emotional ties to the old king and of patronage, though no source actually says so); for Richard de Lucy, E.M. Amt, 'Richard de Lucy, Henry II's justiciar', *Medieval Prosopography*, 9 (1985), 82.

Politics came into the trend for monastic expansion when the monasteries were founded as a political statement. Waleran of Meulan and his twin brother, the earl of Leicester, embarked on two major projects in 1138–39. To mark his arrival as earl of Worcester in 1138, Waleran founded a large Cistercian abbey in the forest of Feckenham in Worcestershire. In that same year or the next, Earl Robert promoted a lavish 'twin' foundation of Augustinians in his comital town. Both these great men had a point to make, both to their shires and to themselves. In Waleran's case, as we have seen, politics complicated his statement. First the empress in 1141, and then her son, Henry II, around 1153, moved to make Bordesley their own, because it had been founded on land which had been royal demesne. Other lords founded or repaired monasteries in reparation for damage they had done to the Church during the wars: Welbeck abbey and Stone priory were partly penitential foundations. Lincoln and Chichester cathedrals were given grants by the earls of Chester and Arundel respectively, because of the damage done them.[58]

More contentious still was the practice of using monastic foundations in the battle for regional control. Earl Robert of Leicester is found using the Cistercians both of Garendon and Biddlesden in just this way: granting them contentious parcels of land, in order to give himself a continuing, if indirect, control over land which was being challenged. Edmund King has explored how the foundation of Garendon abbey by the earl of Leicester in 1133 assisted his long-term aims to secure the Charnwood area of Leicestershire against the earl of Chester. Garendon was actually founded on an estate abstracted somehow from a Chester tenant.[59] As we have seen, the same ploy was dusted down and used by the earl and his seneschal when they wished to deprive Robert of Meppershall of the estate of which the earl had deprived him at Biddlesden in the 1140s. Less contentious, and a recent suggestion by Paul Dalton, is that some monasteries were founded as part of the process of pacifying regional struggles. The foundation by William of Aumale of the Augustinian house of Thornton in Lincolnshire in 1139 looks to be a promising example of this sort of monastic valentine card. Count William associated with himself in the foundation Earl Simon II de Senlis, and their mutual rival, Earl Henry of Northumbria. Dr Dalton reasonably associates the enterprise with the peace talks at Durham in that year.[60] Some detailed work on the dynamics of monastic foundations in Stephen's reign is to be hoped for in the near future.

---

58 Holdsworth, 'The Church', 227 and n.
59 E. King, 'Mountsorrel and its region in King Stephen's reign', *Huntingdon Library Quarterly*, xliv (1980), 5–6.
60 P. Dalton, 'Politics, patronage and peace: the foundation and endowment of religious houses in northern England in the reign of Stephen', abstracted in *Anglo-Norman Anonymous*, 16 (1998), 3–4. There may be some earlier Norman parallels to this suggested process in the way that competing magnates in the Roumois had helped to found Bec-Hellouin, and the way that another group of border magnates had founded St-Evroult in the mid-eleventh century: both were powerful statements of a desire for public peace and order at a disturbed time.

THE SPIRITUALITY OF THE KING AND QUEEN

Only a limited amount can be said about Stephen's spiritual life but something should be, as it was the more important part of the life of any intelligent twelfth-century man and it should be a part of posterity's treatment of him. Like any other wealthy man of his age, spiritual advice and theological conversation was always available to Stephen. There was a strong clerical element in any great lay entourage. We know, for instance, that the king's friend, Waleran of Meulan, organised his four chaplains so that they alternated in pairs in periods of residence in his travelling retinue.[61] In Waleran's household, as in others, the offices of chaplain and clerk were distinguished from each other. Men occupying the offices are consistently called by their assigned title. This may echo a distinction of function: chaplains saying the office and celebrating the mass within the household chapel, and clerks (often placed below them in charter witness lists) being scribes and administrators. Even so, anyone close to a great magnate might find himself being delegated to deal with the administration of estates or of justice, and that applied to clerks and lay people indifferently.[62]

The lay duties of clerks must have been even more demanding for clergy in the households of kings. This may account for the lack of differentiation between whether a man was a 'king's clerk' or a 'king's chaplain'; in *c.*1136 Gilbert de Cimmay is referred to as 'clerk and chaplain of the king'.[63] The clerk Alexander is called also 'the king's chaplain' on another occasion.[64] They were all perceived as deriving from the king's chapel, and as being his familiar clerks. It may be also that the lack of distinction as to whether a man was a royal clerk or chaplain could have been because neither the king nor the queen used their household clergy consistently in a pastoral or spiritual capacity. It is notable that the king apparently formed no close relationship with any of his household clerks. None was marked out for any great promotion. One only was promoted to the bench of bishops, and he was the king's nephew; a stall in the collegiate church of St Martin-le-Grand or in various secular cathedral chapters was the most to which the others could look forward.[65]

The spirituality of twelfth-century laymen was focused on their attendance at the mass. In Stephen's household it would have been said daily either by a chaplain or by a visiting prelate. Regular witness of the offering of the mass was already regarded as an aid to salvation. Part of the appeal of the Cluniac

61 'Nor was he [Waleran] ever happy with less than four chaplains, of whom two accompanied him wherever he went; the others stayed at home to celebrate divine office', *Chronicon Valassense*, ed. F. Sommènil (Rouen, 1868), 11.
62 The Church was beginning to frown on the practice of clerks becoming administrators for lay magnates. Clerks in the major orders were prohibited from undertaking duties as reeves or collectors for lay people by the canons of the Council of London of 1143, *Councils & Synods*, 803. Nonetheless, there are many known instances of this canon being flouted.
63 *Gesta abbatum monasterii sancti Albani* ed. H.T. Riley (3 vols, Rolls Series, 1867–9) i, 114.
64 *Regesta* iii, p. xi.
65 An exception would be William fitz Herbert, consecrated to York in 1141, who – then being treasurer of York – is called 'my chaplain' in 1136 by the king, *Regesta* iii, no. 979.

houses for aristocrats in the early twelfth century was the heavier emphasis they placed on elaborate liturgy than other Benedictine communities. It is doubt-less for this reason that pious and earnest queens, like Mathilda of Boulogne and the empress, settled for long periods within conventual precincts, as the former did at St Augustine's Canterbury and the latter did at Le Pré near Rouen. We see this preoccupation with the mass within the court circle – William of Ypres is said to have asked the cathedral priory of Rochester to say a daily mass in honour of the Virgin.[66] Since the mass was such a part of the lives of Stephen, his queen and his court, any irregularity or incident in its performance was noted and interpreted ominously. It was the point where heaven met earth and where Christ appeared on the altar, so it was for them a time when such messages might be expected. Thus in Stephen's coronation mass the aged Archbishop William forgot to give the kiss of peace to the clergy in the sanctuary before the offertory which preceded the eucharistic prayer, and this omission was later interpreted as a sign of unrest to come in the new reign.[67] The most dramatic turning point of Stephen's reign was the breaking of a candle in his hand as he participated in the processional mass for the Presentation (Candlemas) on 2 February 1141 before he rode off to lose the battle of Lincoln. In that same mass the pyx for the host crashed to the floor of its own accord as a further sign of ill omen and the upset of the natural order. John of Hexham is full of such stories, and illustrates the outrageous tyranny of Count Eustace over the clergy of York in 1148 by his prohibition of the saying of mass in the city.[68]

But as well as participating in corporate devotion, Stephen and his queen can be found in search of a more personal holiness. The Church had been encouraging penitents to make their private confession to priests since at least the eighth century, and the practice had certainly spread to the laity long before the eleventh century.[69] A deathbed confession was a feature of the last days of Queen Margaret of Scotland in 1096 as was also the presence in her life of priests to whom she customarily turned for counsel. King Henry I had particular clerical friends who might have fulfilled a similar role. In the second half of his reign Aethelwulf, Augustinian prior of Nostell and (after 1133) bishop of Carlisle, was Henry's accustomed 'spiritual director' (if we can call the position by that modern name). Robert de Torigny described Aethelwulf as the man 'to whom the king was accustomed to confess his sins', which hints at a formally recognised role outside the household clerks.[70] The liking

---

66 Gerald of Wales, *Speculum Ecclesiae*, in *Opera* iv, 202, see S.E. Roper, *Medieval English Benedictine Liturgy* (London, 1993), 47.

67 JH, 287.

68 JH, 324. In a similar way stories were told of Duke Henry, who, according to John, took it into his head to enter into a church he was passing after his landing in England, and walked straight into the arms of the priest who was just commencing the offering of the kiss of peace, JH, 325.

69 For the antiquity of lay confession, M. Dudley, 'The Christian tradition', in *Confession and Absolution*, ed. M. Dudley and G. Rowell (London, 1990), 56–9.

70 RT, 123.

for Augustinian confessors is evident in other contemporary royal house-holds. Louis VI and Louis VII (at least at the beginning of his reign) turned to successive abbots of St-Victor of Paris for spiritual counsel.[71]

Queen Mathilda made regular confession, the hearing of which was deleg-ated by Archbishop Theobald to Ralph, canon, subprior and then (after 1147) prior of Holy Trinity, Aldgate. This Augustinian priory had a very good reputation for the austerity and faithfulness of its community and it had been partly founded by the earlier Queen Mathilda, the first wife of Henry I, who had died in 1118. The first prior, Norman, was well known for his rigid dis-cipline both as regards himself and his canons, and his mixture of charisma and eccentricity brought him and his house a degree of fame. The king and queen had clearly been taken with the community perhaps as far back as Henry's reign, when they were still count and countess of Boulogne. The queen chose the priory for the burial of her infant children Baldwin and Mathilda in 1137, having them laid in the sanctuary on either side of the high altar. Ralph dutifully confessed her at her death in Essex in 1152, being summoned three days before her end 'because he was the father of her confessions by licence and commission of Archbishop Theobald'. He was also present with Arch-bishop Theobald at the death of the king at Dover priory in 1154, so it seems likely that he had some commission to confess the king too as Theobald's delegate; we do not know whether any others had such a licence.[72]

The king and queen's liking for holy men is clear elsewhere, and again it seems to have predated their coronation. Stephen is said to have gone to visit the redoubtable rustic prophet, Wulfric, in the company of his brother, Bishop Henry, at some time between 1129 and 1133. Doubtless, Stephen and Henry were on the road between the bishop's city of Winchester and his castle of Taunton in Somerset: Wulfric's hermitage at Haselbury was near Yeovil on the bishop's route into the west. Since Wulfric hailed Stephen as the future king, Stephen can only have been impressed, and on a later occasion is said to have made his confession to Wulfric at some time after his release from captivity in 1141 (but he is only likely to have campaigned so far west in the campaigns of 1142–43). The saint is said to have stirred the king by a refer-ence to an obscure cause of the king's anxiety about the state of his soul. We remember here the chronicler's account of his public agonies after Lincoln, swearing that his sins had reduced him to the state of captivity.[73] It is alleged that the king in penance offered his face to Wulfric to be spat on and slapped hard. Some years earlier the king had sent his wife to see Wulfric, and there is a record of her visit to him, probably in 1136 while the siege of Exeter was going on. True to form, he upbraided the queen for her humiliation of a Somerset noblewoman at her court at Corfe earlier in the year.[74] The evidence

71 For the early Capetian confessors, G. Minois, *Le confesseur du roi* (Paris, 1988), 127–45.
72 *Cartulary of Holy Trinity, Aldgate*, 231–2.
73 *GS*, 112.
74 *Life of Wulfric of Haselbury*, ed. Bell, 108–9, 117–18. The queen's visit to Wulfric is said to have occurred well before 1141 – and before 1139 too, as Corfe fell to the Angevins in that year – and

indicates that it was Stephen who helped to bring Wulfric into vogue and to the notice of his uncle, King Henry, before 1133 (for Wulfric's prophecy of the king's death in Normandy was brought to Henry's attention by courtiers). The queen had her own clientele of holy people, and gave an acre in Faversham for an eremitical nun called Helmid to build a cell next to the cemetery of the church of St Mary.[75]

Stephen's search for holiness may have taken him to Savigny in his Norman county of Mortain, a community founded in the wilderness by the itinerant preacher and occasional hermit, St Vitalis. Stephen was count of Mortain for several years before Vitalis's death in 1119. We do not know if they ever met, although the degree to which Stephen and his wife were drawn to the re-formed monasticism of Savigny argues that he at least had fallen under the influence of its founder (Mathilda and Stephen married six years after Vitalis's death). Stephen founded an abbey at Furness in Lancashire as a colony of Savigny in 1127 and others at Buckfast in Devon and Longvilliers near Montreuil in 1135/6. The queen herself founded another Savignac house at Coggeshall on land of her inheritance in Essex at some time in the 1140s.[76] This was a substantial investment in a particular form of monasticism and it is interesting to see that Stephen was not drawn to the parallel movement of reformed Benedictinism represented by Cîteaux. This investment in Savigny may explain something of the perception that the king was not sympathetic to the Cistercians in his troubles with Henry Murdac over the see of York. However, the queen and he lavishly patronised (and attempted to refound) the Cistercian abbey of Clairmarais in the same county, so the perception was not entirely accurate.[77]

As a warrior, as well as a king, Stephen found much also to admire in the order of the Temple. But in this case, it would seem that his wife, and not he, was the driving force. It was Queen Mathilda who inspired the foundation of preceptories at Cressing Temple in Essex in 1137 and at Temple Cowley in Oxfordshire *c.*1139. The flow of grants and confirmations continued throughout the reign.[78] The king usually appears in these foundations as confirming the grants made by his wife. Nonetheless, the fact that numbers of his friends and courtiers also favoured the Templars tells us that he was perceived as a leading patron of the Temple.[79] In the case of Stephen, his sponsorship of the

---

at a time just after a section of the nobility had been cool to the new king. This would indicate the period between the coronation and the fall of Exeter, to which the queen might have been travelling if she sought out Wulfric on the road into Devon from Corfe.

75 *Regesta* iii, no. 157.
76 B. Poulle, 'Savigny and England', in *England and Normandy in the Middle Ages*, ed. D.R. Bates and A. Curry (London, 1994), 159–65.
77 Ralph of Coggeshall, *Chronicon Anglicanum*, ed. J. Stevenson (Rolls Series, 1875), 11; *Regesta* iii, nos. 194–200.
78 *Regesta* iii, nos. 843–53, 855–66.
79 Notable patrons of the Temple in England and Normandy included the king's early friend, Waleran of Meulan, Waleran's brother-in-law, Earl Gilbert of Pembroke, and the *curiales*, William Martel, Richard de Lucy and Turgis d'Avranches.

Templars may represent a dim echo of the call that took his father twice to the Holy Land. For the queen, the motivation may have been more complex. She was a dauntless and decisive woman, accustomed to command. If she could not lead the knights of Christ against the enemies of the Church, she could at least provision them. It may be no accident that Queen Mathilda in 1141 suggested that a solution to the dilemma of what to do with her captive and dispossessed husband was to send him to Palestine; she must have intended to accompany him.

Elsewhere, we find that Stephen and his queen were generous to the Cluniac community. Since the queen's father had ended his days at the Cluniac house of Romilly, and her mother was buried at Bermondsey, and since Stephen's mother had also been devoted to the abbey, the embracing of the Cluniac order is no surprise. They were second- or third-generation Cluny supporters. Stephen made several grants to Bermondsey priory, and when he and his wife began to plan their dynastic burial church at Faversham in the mid-1140s, it was to the Cluniacs of Bermondsey they turned for a colony to found the new abbey, consecrated in 1148. From this it appears that Stephen had been impressed by his uncle's similar foundation at Reading, and it seems as though Faversham should be regarded as Stephen's statement as to what he regarded as the proper form of monastic community for a king (rather than a count) to turn to for liturgical commemoration.

It is difficult to penetrate the spiritual world of the twelfth-century layman, but in Stephen's case we can go some way. His religious outlook would have been formed long before he was king, and as a child it would have been formed under the influence of the exceptionally pious and domineering princess who was his mother. Whatever influence the secularity of King Henry's court had on his character, he retained a serious concern with matters religious. His mother and his uncle made Stephen in many ways a conventional magnate in his church patronage: he responded to the intellectual earnestness of the Augustinians and the liturgical majesty of the Cluniacs in the way his uncle had. It is no surprise to find that at the end, he and his wife went to the former for absolution and the latter for commemoration. There is, nonetheless, evidence of a certain spiritual restlessness in Stephen which we glimpse in other magnates of his generation. The Beaumont twins, as much as he himself, sought out holy men in the woods and deserts of their estates, and offered them support. Conscious through their personal penitential regime of the distance between them and their God, magnates of their generation looked to associate with those who were further on the road to salvation. So, before 1135, Stephen had turned to Savigny and to Wulfric of Haselbury and perhaps to others of whom we know nothing, seeking forgiveness and reassurance. Unlike Waleran of Meulan, there is some evidence in his actions that Stephen had by 1135 taken to heart what he had heard preached. Time and again, whether before Oxford, Ludlow and Lincoln, or in his treatment of his rivals, of women or of his hostages, Stephen showed that he understood something of what had been preached in Galilee a thousand years before. Stephen shows himself to have been one of the most prominent early propagators of the Christian and ethical knighthood preached in the next reign by his namesake, Stephen de Fougères, bishop of Rennes. We find in Stephen's personal behaviour a more noble man than his royal predecessor and successor, and that perhaps is the fairest judgement that can be made upon him.

CHAPTER 16

The Nation

Stephen has been most condemned by generations of historians for the dam-age his reign did to the 'state' of England. Since Stubbs, historians have seen the reign of Henry I as a time when the centralising apparatus focused on the English king grew more defined, noticeable and resented. This belief could perhaps be disputed, but if so discussion would centre on the degree to which such developing royal control was effective, rather than on whether it actually occurred.[1] Since Stubbs also, Stephen has been seen as a king who imperilled or even reversed this move towards the effective government of England as a stable political unit. Indeed, contemporaries said as much, as did Gilbert Foliot with heavy irony in around 1144:

> Who was it that has made a fool of England? My answer is that it is that wretched ruler (whoever *he* might be!) in whom abound so many perjuries, murders, arsons, crimes, sorrows and treacheries. How is it that he who has debased the kingdom, dishonoured the episcopate and laid deep shame not just on us but on those who come after us may keep himself unaffected? Believe me, the inheritance into which he rushed at the beginning, will be anything but blessed at the end![2]

This is itself ironic, as we have seen, because it was Stephen's initial desire very much to be seen as a king in the mould of his uncle: offering strong rule and ensuring civil tranquillity. That indeed was his manifesto for election to kingship. Stephen's good intentions foundered on his own inability to carry through his policy and to find trustworthy advisers who could have done it for him. But despite that, England survived as a nation with a distinct iden-tity. Much of what Henry had achieved in the administration of royal, as opposed to communal, justice survived into the reign of Henry II. Stephen's local administration was undoubtedly battered and undermined by the war-fare and dislocation of his reign, yet not uniformly throughout the kingdom,

1 J.A. Green, *The Government of England under Henry I* (Cambridge, 1986), 216–19.
2 *LCGF*, 63–4.

and again it proved possible to restore the structure once circumstances allowed. It will be the argument of this chapter that King Henry survived as king long enough for what he established to become deeply embedded in people's consciousness of how kingship should be exercised. As a king he was so successful that he extinguished any other pattern of kingship, not least because the ramshackle Capetian kingdom of France was so woeful in comparison in everything but dignity. No-one could look at the embattled palace at Paris under Louis VI and see there anything resembling the authority and wealth of Westminster under Henry. That was both King Stephen's good fortune and his misfortune.

ENGLAND AND ITS EMPIRE

Despite ideas in recent scholarship of borders being permeable regions rather than boundaries, the idea of what and where was England was consolidating in the early twelfth century. England as an entity, as the kingdom of the 'English', had been established in the consciousness of its neighbours and its own people since the tenth century and perhaps earlier. *Anglia* could be personified in poetry and in history, and contemporaries did both. The king also could address charters generally to his subjects of England and talk of England as a place where he had rights and authority.[3] Nonetheless, it was equally true that not all the English were ruled directly by the king of the English. *Angli* lived in the Welsh and Scottish Marches on both sides of where the border was understood to be.[4] So the perception of England as the kingdom of all the English – of a narrow nationality – was still far in the future.

Yet King Henry had given this evolving idea some definition in his development of central institutions. The 1130 pipe roll could be said to have defined a momentary England, not least because it demonstrated where the king had sufficient power for his representatives to collect revenue and for his justices to operate in the local courts. According to this document (even though it is regrettably incomplete) England included Northumberland, Westmoreland and Carlisle in the north and all the shires along the Welsh border – in other words, something resembling the England we know today.[5] The exceptions

3 For England's early days, P. Wormald, 'Bede, the *Bretwaldas* and the origins of the *Gens Anglorum*', in *Ideal and Reality in Frankish and Anglo-Saxon Society*, ed. P. Wormald and others (Oxford, 1983), 99–129. For the development of its nationhood, see J. Campbell, 'The late Anglo-Saxon state: a maximum view', *Proceedings of the British Academy*, 87 (1994), 47–50.
4 A charter of Earl Robert of Gloucester (*c.*1147) addresses his sheriff and all his men of Glamorgan '. . . *Francis, Anglis et Gualensibus*', *Earldom of Gloucester Charters*, ed. Patterson, 114. Earl Henry of Northumbria, in an act concerning Melrose and his Scottish lands referred to his men '. . . *Francis et Anglis totius regni Scotie*', *Regesta Regum Scottorum* i, 157.
5 G.W.S. Barrow, 'The Scots and the north of England', in *The Anarchy of King Stephen's Reign*, ed. E. King (Oxford, 1994), 232–4, 237–9 sounds a note of wise caution about where England ended and Scotland began, and about 'Scottish' attitudes to England. Nonetheless, his argument relies too much on the eleventh-century circumstances of Domesday Book and the eleventh-century dynastic heritage of the northern earls and the Scottish royal family, without taking sufficient account of the impact of Henry I on the north.

are that it also included Pembroke and its shire, because the king's officers there tendered an account, and it did not include Cheshire, for its officers answered directly to their earl. Of Cheshire, it was said at the end of the twelfth century that it 'answers in its assemblies more to the sword of its prince than the crown of the king', but it was understood by the same writer that this was only because the king allowed it to be so.[6]

Is there any evidence that this idea of the extent of England was in any way challenged by Stephen's reign? The Empress Mathilda thought not. In 1141 she talked of 'the Christian folk of England' *'Christianitas Anglie'* some of whom acknowledged her power; the fact that many of them did not does not alter the perception behind it that there was a theoretical England with its own integrity. Others thought so too. The same perception is found in 1153, when Stephen's settlement with Duke Henry says that he will exercise his royal justice in the 'whole kingdom of England', of which part was the duke's, and part was his.[7] The compiler of the Plympton annal for 1141, who seems to have been drawing on a local and contemporary source, noted that Lincoln delivered to the empress the *'status regni'*, that is, the 'full extent of the realm'.[8] Writers have recently given due weight to the ambitions of the Scottish royal family to gain control of Carlisle, Northumberland and County Durham, and even to exert themselves further south, in Yorkshire. A good deal of consideration has also been given to the historical circumstances that impelled the Scots kings to look south: shared allegiances of Anglo-Scottish barons and ancient dynastic claims.[9] Indeed, Geoffrey Barrow has said that it was by no means a 'foregone conclusion' that the contested areas of northern England would have ended the twelfth century as part of England or Scotland.[10] But less attention has been paid to the indications that despite these circumstances, the northern lands were still regarded as the lands of the king of England.

Here in the north, I would suggest that King Henry's activities had had more effect than is allowed by Professor Barrow's remark. Henry had been effective in the north, further developing his elder brother's work. It was Henry, not a king of Scots, who had fortified Carlisle and created its diocese. It was Henry also who had been the patron and mentor of the young David of Scotland, establishing a relationship of dependence. There was a military confrontation between Kings David and Stephen. It was fierce but brief: a short campaign in 1135–36 and a more dangerous outbreak in 1138. But for all practical purposes war between the Scots and English ended in 1139 and

6 *Liber Luciani de laude Cestrie*, ed. M.V. Taylor (Rec. Soc. of Lancashire and Cheshire, lxiv, 1912), 61.
7 *Regesta* iii, nos. 272, 275.
8 *Annales Plymptonienses*, 28, see also above p. 85n (Chapter 5).
9 See recently, J.A. Green, 'Aristocratic loyalties in the northern frontier of England, *c.*1100–1174', in *England in the Twelfth Century*, ed. D. Williams (Woodbridge, 1990), 83–100; Barrow, 'The Scots and the north of England', in *The Anarchy of King Stephen's Reign*, ed. E. King (Oxford, 1994), 231–53; P. Dalton, 'Scottish influence on Durham, 1066–1214', in *Anglo-Norman Durham, 1093–1193*, ed. D. Rollason, M. Harvey and M. Prestwich (Woodbridge, 1994), 339–52.
10 Barrow, 'The Scots and the north of England', 250–1, returning to the argument made in idem, *The Kingdom of the Scots* (London, 1973), 139–61.

ended in Stephen's favour. One could hardly call a campaign King David's embarrassing journey south to the empress in the course of her few triumphant months in 1141. There was only a brief outbreak in 1149 when Duke Henry came north to receive arms from his uncle, but that seems to have been more accidental than intended.[11] The Scottish acquisition of England's northern counties was anything but the result of successful military campaigning and in fact depended very much on King Stephen's good will until the reverse of 1141.

King David and his son, Henry of Northumbria, based their control over the northern shires on two agreements with Stephen, treaties of 1136 and 1139. The terms of the treaty sworn at Durham on 9 April 1139 gave Northumberland to Henry of Scotland, but the loyalty of its barons to the king of England was excepted. Bamburgh and Newcastle, the possessions of the bishop of Durham and the enclave of Hexhamshire were excluded from the agreement. Stephen still regarded the barons of Northumberland after 1139 as his men and Henry of Scotland accepted that Northumberland would retain the laws and customs it knew in the previous reign. As earl of Northumbria, Henry, though son of the king of Scotland, was an English earl, in the same way as he would have been as earl of Huntingdon. On occasion his acts reflect that fact. In charters to various individuals in Northumberland and County Durham, Earl Henry granted or confirmed to them land or rights as on the day when King Henry died or when King Henry was alive, phrasing which indicates that those counties were regarded as part of a continuing English, not a Scots, polity.[12] It has been recently pointed out that the coinage of the north of England issued from Carlisle, Bamburgh and Newcastle retained the name of Stephen well into the 1140s, when the local issues of King David and Earl Henry superseded it, as local issues also did in Yorkshire.[13] When King David handed over Durham to William Cumin in 1141 he did so as a representative of the empress, not on his own account. It is true that Earl Henry made free with Newcastle-upon-Tyne and judging by the pattern of the dating of his acts, made his base there in northern England, which was more than was agreed in 1139. Still, the same accusation of self-aggrandisement has been made against his southern neighbour, Earl William of York, and there is no suggestion that he was attempting to remove Yorkshire from the kingdom of England.

The tenuous nature of the Scottish hold on the north is alluded to by later sources. Both William of Newburgh and Roger of Howden repeat a story (not given by any contemporary) that in 1149 King David manoeuvred Duke Henry into a promise that he would allow the Scots to continue to hold the northern shires in perpetuity when he became king.[14] Both these northern chroniclers recognised in this way that Scottish possession depended not on

11 See above, pp. 241–3.
12 *Regesta Regum Scottorum* i, 146–7, 149.
13 M. Blackburn, 'Coinage and currency', in *The Anarchy of Stephen's Reign*, ed. E. King (Oxford, 1994), 192–3
14 WN i, 70; Roger of Howden, *Chronica* i, 211.

right but on royal good will, and portray David as playing a desperate hand in 1149. When Henry became king, the good will was withdrawn, whatever promises had been made. Once Henry II had settled Yorkshire, Malcolm IV was instructed in 1157 to surrender Carlisle, Cumberland and Northumberland, and did so promptly in return for the earldom of Huntingdon his father and grandfather had held till 1141. The abruptness of the surrender might have something to do with King Malcolm's relative weakness against Henry II, but it might just as well reflect the unchallenged perception established by Henry I, that England went as far north as Berwick, and included Carlisle.

England's western border against the Welsh was stable throughout the reign of Stephen, as it had been since the time of Gruffudd ap Llywelyn, the king of all the Welsh who had been Earl Harold's great foe and who had died in 1063. For the most part the border still reflected the line supposedly drawn by the great Offa in the eighth century. This stability says more about the diverse ambitions of the separately weak Welsh kings, than the strength and direction showed by Stephen. As we have seen, his indifference to Wales was one of Stephen's greatest blind spots: it put the English at a disadvantage in Wales for a century. The great victories of the Welsh kings in the period 1136–38 may have destabilised the Marcher lordships within that boundary, but at least they did not affect England directly. There was a nervousness about the triumphant Welsh and what they might do after 1136. John Gillingham points to at least one English writer who saw evidence in the popularity of the Arthurian legend of a Welsh plot to regain what they had lost in Britain.[15] But more dangerous than Arthur was the support which the *teuloedd* (military households) of the Welsh kings offered to the Angevin party's armies. The Welsh came to England as mercenaries and not as conquerors.

Stephen's reign had a much more serious effect on the relationship between England and Normandy. In recent years historians have been unanimous in seeing serious long-term damage done by Stephen to the *regnum* represented by the kingdom of England and duchy of Normandy. By unceasing effort and expense between 1106 and 1135 Henry I had managed to impose some order and meaning on this *regnum*. The advantages of the political order he had imposed were clear both to Church and magnates, and their determination that the link between England and Normandy should continue was what decided the succession of Normandy was to go to Stephen in December 1135.

John le Patourel entitled his study of England and Normandy in Stephen's reign 'the End', meaning that it was the end of the ascendancy established by Henry over not just the Anglo-Norman lands but over their neighbours in Britain and France. His contention was that, despite Henry II's language of continuity and reconstruction, he never did resurrect the 'Norman Empire' of his grandfather, but created something new 'on its ruins', a condominium with a different hub and different priorities, focused more on Anjou and its

15 J. Gillingham, 'The context and purposes of Geoffrey of Monmouth's *History of the Kings of Britain*', *ANS*, 13 (1991), 112–18.

interests, a place where the Norman–English link was less important, and provincial autonomy more characteristic.[16] In broad terms it is difficult to disagree with this analysis. In Normandy between 1144 and 1154 the leading Anglo-Norman magnates generally had to choose on which side of the Channel to operate. There were exceptions, but for the most part those landowners who chose England had to quit Normandy and suffer the loss of their lands: this was especially true of the earls of Leicester, Pembroke, Chester, Surrey and York, all of whom sustained great loss of property. When the link of lordship was re-established under Henry II, the Anglo-Norman axis had lost much of its importance, and the formerly important bond between kingdom and duchy which existed at the top of the aristocracy was no longer a key fact of unity. It had given a chance for other cross-border links, such as those of the Franco-Norman magnates (the counts of Perche, Alençon, Evreux and Meulan, and the lords of L'Aigle, Bréval, and the Norman Vexin) to pull Normandy in a different direction, towards the Capetians.[17] One direct consequence of Stephen's failure to take Normandy seriously was that it allowed a fissure to open up that would eventually cause the duchy to break off, like a piece of pack ice, and drift towards Paris.

EARLS AND GOVERNORS

Professor Warren identified the most significant change in administration in Stephen's reign as being the downgrading of government from the centre at the expense of the promotion of regional officers.[18] He was referring to Stephen's move – first identified by Ralph Davis – to create earls with the ability to exercise a mediated royal authority in their shires. As we have seen, this move can be first detected in late 1138, and such earls were still being created by the king in 1140 (at Hereford). It obviously impressed contemporaries, because the empress was forced to follow his lead in order to satisfy her own supporters, and William of Malmesbury for one mentions it as an (unwelcome) trend he had noted in Stephen's kingship, and relates it to the political insecurity caused by the expected and imminent defection of Robert of Gloucester.[19] The earldoms of Worcester and York, as we have seen, were specifically given former royal possessions, demesne and forest. Worcester gives an example of the earl taking over the collection of Danegeld and Leicester and York give some evidence of the earls assuming the right to coin money.

R.H.C. Davis analysed a number of the new earls' charters and found evidence from them that the office of sheriff had been subordinated to the earls. This was perhaps the most surprising and daring innovation of all. The king's

16 J. Le Patourel, *The Norman Empire* (Oxford, 1976), 109–17.
17 D. Crouch, 'Normans and Anglo-Normans: a divided aristocracy?', in *England and Normandy in the Middle Ages*, ed. D.R. Bates and A. Curry (London, 1994), 50–67.
18 W.L. Warren, *The Governance of Norman and Angevin England, 1086–1272* (London, 1987), 92–4, a point developed by K.J. Stringer, *The Reign of Stephen* (London, 1993), 52–5.
19 *HN*, 23.

reeve in the shires had been the key agent of royal authority in the localities. However much this officer was compromised by association with local magnates, or by his own local interests, he nonetheless stood accountable in the end before his royal master. The only exception had been the border shires of Wales, and that only briefly in the Conquest period. Only Cheshire had retained the formal subordination of sheriff to earl in Henry I's reign. The earls greatly valued their new privilege, and some, such as Robert of Leicester, gave the office to their own trusted estate administrators. Until 1155, Leicestershire was entrusted to his seneschal and the son of his former butler, Geoffrey L'Abbé.

As was said in Chapter 5, the king and his advisers were imaginative in their reform. In thus formally tying magnates into the governmental stucture they were following no obvious precedent, other than the Conqueror's emergency measures of 1071. There was certainly little relation to the linked offices of *comes* and *vicecomes* as they were to be found in the various realms of northern France. It is difficult to be sure that William of Malmesbury was right to relate the creation of administrative earls to the defection of Robert of Gloucester. The creations seem, if anything, to have followed on from the northern campaign of 1138 and the defeat of the Scots. There is an argument that Henry of Northumbria was himself intended to be just such an earl, after the peace was made. It may be that the new sort of earl was the response of the king and his advisers to the belief that the localities needed firmer control in 1138.

The experiment of decentralisation to territorial earls was brief. Stephen must have discovered how little it was in his interest before the battle of Lincoln. After Lincoln there appears a revised strategy which depended this time on (for want of a better label) regional military governors. As with the administrative earls, the idea may have dawned gradually on the king. Henry de Tracy's activities in the exposed royalist salient in Somerset after 1139 may have been one source of the idea, as indeed may the highly effective commandery of Brian fitz Count in the Thames valley on the other side. I would suggest that the strategy became a conscious one in 1141–42 with the establishment of William of Ypres in Kent, and William de Chesney in Oxford after its fall to the king. Chesney replaced the former castellan of Oxford, the late Robert d'Oilly, in his office and estates, but he was clearly a greater man than that. The citizens of Oxford took to calling him their 'alderman' but he was also sheriff of Oxfordshire. The chronicles depict him in command of troops of cavalry enforcing the royalist presence in the county and we find him also negotiating with neighbouring powers, notably the Angevin earl, Roger of Hereford, in the later 1140s. Since Abbot Gilbert Foliot was William's nephew we have some glimpse of him at work in Oxfordshire and the Cotswolds in the 1140s: imposing a payment of fifteen marks (10*li*) on the estates of Gloucester abbey within his reach, and receiving not just the money but a stinging rebuke for his harsh conduct towards the Church and the poor.[20] In the final campaign of 1153 we find Chesney receiving command of an army sent into

20 *LCGF*, 54–5.

Oxfordshire in order to harass Duke Henry. The fact that one brother, Reginald, received the abbacy of Evesham and another brother, Robert, achieved the see of Lincoln in 1148, tells us that he commanded great local influence, sufficient to win relatives the nominations of harassed chapters of great churches. He married a member of the Lucy family, which shows him extending his connections amongst the king's familiars.[21]

Although we have less detail about their activities, we can suggest that a similar wide-ranging authority was conceded to William of Ypres in Kent, probably from 1141 onwards; to William Martel in Dorset and Wiltshire between 1141 and 1143; to Philip of Gloucester in the Cotswolds around Cricklade and Cirencester in 1146–47; and to Richard de Lucy in Essex and Middlesex, after the fall of Earl Geoffrey de Mandeville in 1143. William of Ypres appears as the farmer of the bulk of royal demesne in Kent in 1154, including the royal holdings in Canterbury and Hove. It is likely that the queen had placed him in power there during the emergency of 1141, supporting her kinsman, Faramus of Boulogne, who remained castellan of the key fortress of Dover, which she had seized from Robert of Gloucester in 1138. As a sign of his authority William had permission to found a Cistercian abbey at Boxley, a royal manor. The church of Canterbury was particularly irked by his power and rather absurdly referred to his rule of Kent as a tyranny.[22] Although Kent was not a frontier area, the placing of a powerful regional governor there had advantages, not least in securing the passage between London, Boulogne and Flanders. William de Chesney and William of Ypres and their like show the responsiveness of Stephen to changing circumstances in his reign. They demonstrate that he was aware of the weaknesses of the administrative earldoms and was innovative enough to revise the scheme, employing *curiales* who were more closely tied to him than the earls. It was a step back towards centralisation and away from regionalism.

STEPHEN'S EXCHEQUER

The fate of the English exchequer under Stephen has been of special interest to historians. This was the body which produced the 1130 pipe roll. The document is a landmark in the history of the development of a national administration. As has been said already, the pipe roll in effect defines the king's view of England. The exchequer called in the local officers of the king to make and pay their accounts twice a year, with the final accounting session at Michaelmas (29 September). Of course it was not a complete picture; for historical reasons Cheshire did not feature on the roll in 1130 or after 1154. Carlisle and Northumberland are there in 1130, but do not appear in Henry II's rolls until 1158. The exchequer as an institution was the financial memory of the king's officers

---

21 E. Amt, *The Accession of Henry II in England: Royal Government Restored, 1149–1159* (Woodbridge, 1993), 51–4, see also above p. 222.
22 *Red Book* ii, 648–9; Eales, 'Local loyalties in Stephen's reign: Kent', *ANS*, viii, ed. R.A. Brown (Woodbridge, 1985), 100–1.

and its novelty had an impact nationally, in ways other than fiscal. The earl of Leicester had formed his own small-scale financial bureau in imitation of it well before 1135, clearly impressed at the way that central accounting could enhance his own administration. That impression was as strong elsewhere; I have suggested that Earl Ranulf II of Chester formed his own central financial office around the year 1140, and he would have done so because the royal exchequer was such a potent example of good estate-management practice.[23]

The fact that the utility and vitality of the exchequer were so much recognised amongst contemporaries guaranteed its survival, even through the messier parts of Stephen's reign. No pipe roll survives for an entire year of the reign of Stephen, but there is evidence that the exchequer continued nonetheless; it certainly survived until 1141. One of the charters of the empress to Geoffrey de Mandeville mentions the customary sheriff's farms of London, Middlesex, Hertford and Essex still being owed, somewhere. In the same year the empress addressed a writ in favour of the canons of Oseney to the barons of the exchequer, making a grant out of the farm of Oxford.[24] It seems unlikely that the exchequer had been much affected by the fall of Roger of Salisbury, despite what Bishop Roger's grandson was claiming in the reign of Henry II. The fact is that the skills and importance of the exchequer were far more widely understood and appreciated in society than in the small circle of Bishop Roger and his household, as the Leicester and Chester examples indicate. It should be noted that it was to Richard de Lucy, Stephen's new man, that Henry II turned when he looked for a layman to preside over his exchequer.[25]

Although we know that the exchequer and its procedures were still intact in 1141, it is far less clear what happened to the exchequer between 1141 and 1154, and what happened to the royal revenues in those counties of the north and west where King Stephen's officers were excluded. Kenji Yoshitake has considered the reasonable suggestion that the Angevin party set up its own shadowy office of receipt in the West Country during the 1140s. Although evidence is allusive, the pattern of payment in the exchequer of the 1150s gives some reason to accept this.[26] The best evidence for the continuation of the royal exchequer at Winchester or Westminster into Stephen's last year is the account rendered by Earl Patrick of Salisbury in the roll of 1155–56, which refers to a debt owing 'for the third year', that is, for the year before last.[27]

---

23 D. Crouch, *The Beaumont Twins: The Roots and Branches of Power in the Twelfth Century* (Cambridge, 1986), 163–6; Crouch, 'The administration of the Norman earldom', in *The Earldom of Chester and its Charters*, ed. A.T. Thacker (Journal of Chester Archaelogical Society, 71, 1991), 82, 88–9.
24 *Regesta* iii, nos. 275, 628. Cronne, *Stephen*, 227, makes the useful point that the canons did not use this writ but kept it in their archive, a possible indication that the session of the exchequer for which it was intended to be used in 1141 did not meet.
25 Amt, *Accession of Henry II*, 121.
26 K. Yoshitake, 'Exchequer in the reign of Stephen', 954–9.
27 *PR 2 Hen II*, 56. This is the view of K. Yoshitake, 'The Exchequer in the reign of Stephen', *EHR*, 103 (1988), 956–7. Amt, *Accession of Henry II*, 121, believes that Earl Patrick could not have owed a debt at Stephen's exchequer but suggests instead an Angevin one. But as we have seen above (p. 276) Patrick was one of the first to receive a writ from Stephen commanding a restoration in 1153, and his immediate involvement in the joint government of Stephen and Henry is likely.

That would have been the exchequer year September 1153 to September 1154. Earl Patrick had come to terms with Stephen in November 1153, and it seems that his debt for Wiltshire had become due – and had been unpaid – at an exchequer which met somewhere (probably at Westminster, where the king was) on 29 September 1154. Earl Patrick was one of an exceptional group of administrative survivors into Henry II's administration. As he retained his responsibility for Wiltshire well into the reign of Henry II, reference to this continuing debt survived until the resumption of the surviving sequence of pipe rolls in 1155–56. The Wiltshire reference, important though it is, cannot tell us much more than that a roll was made at Michaelmas 1154. It is still possible that the 1154 exchequer was a revival of the institution, rather than the last of the sequence of Stephen's exchequers of receipt.[28] But at least it attests to the continuation of the skills of the exchequer in England after 1141 and the continuation of the idea of the sheriff's farm of his county.

The early records of the exchequer of Henry II indicate that 'survival' is about as much as could have been expected of Stephen's exchequer. The abstracted references which are all we possess of the pipe roll of 1154–55 can be made to give a picture of decayed revenue and uncertainties in procedure which lasted until 1158.[29] Some of the twenty-four counties whose sheriffs answered the summons, especially Richard de Lucy's Essex, presented detailed accounts for the full year (which included Stephen's last months) but most did not. Some accounted only for nine months, the period after Henry II's coronation, which hints at the removal of some sheriffs at Stephen's death. However, the more complete accounts include Wiltshire and Herefordshire, where Stephen had no power before 1153, so the presentation of an account was a matter of the sheriff's aptitude and personal weight rather than which party his county had favoured. There are minimal accounts for Hertfordshire and Yorkshire as much as for Somerset. No doubt for this reason twenty-one new sheriffs were appointed in 1155. In Emilie Amt's judgement, full efficiency was not restored to the Crown's administration and collection of its finances until 1160.[30]

THE COINAGE

The central administration of the mints was another notable feature of Anglo-Norman England; a handsome legacy of pre-Conquest England. Coin dies

28 G. White, 'Continuity in government', in *The Anarchy of King Stephen's Reign*, ed. E. King (Oxford, 1994), 140 notes the evidence of *Regesta* iii, no. 993 which makes a grant in 1154 to St Peter's hospital out of the city farm of York. The grant was payable by the sheriff at Easter and Michaelmas. White suggests from this that the city farm was payable at the exchequer at Easter and Michaelmas 1154. However, the grant mentions those two terms for payment only with reference to the gift, not to the farm and makes no explicit mention of the exchequer at all.
29 G. White, 'Continuity in government', 139–40.
30 Amt, *Accession of Henry II*, 122–7. For the roll of 1154–55, *Red Book* ii, 648–58, Amt (p. 123) makes the point that the abstracts must miss out many items of revenue (and indeed the rubrics say as much). Even so, some counties are remarkably fuller in their abstracted form than others.

were issued from central workshops in London to sixty or seventy licensed moneyers throughout the land. Under Henry I the national currency was occasionally renewed in a general recoinage. No foreign currency was allowed to circulate in England; it was melted down and recoined at the ports of entry. There was an absolute royal monopoly on the coinage, which much enhanced the king's wealth. The quality of the sterling silver penny was tightly monitored, and under King Henry savage penalties were meted out to corrupt moneyers in an effort to maintain the silver standard of 92.5 per cent in the sterling penny of 21–22 grams weight. How did the coinage fare under Stephen? The fate of the mints under Stephen has long been an object of fascination to historians, although the evidence is highly technical and not always easy to interpret.[31]

After over thirty years of analysis and a number of sensational finds of hoards (notably at Coed-y-Wenallt in the north of Cardiff in 1980, at West Meon in Hampshire in 1992 and at Box in Wiltshire in 1994) what can be interpreted is interesting, if not entirely satisfying to a historian. As Mark Blackburn sketches the broad conclusions, we find that the relatively tight national administration operated by King Henry's officers survived into the first years of the reign of Stephen. He issued a comparable national coinage to that of Henry I as soon as he was settled on the throne (the issue known from its British Museum Catalogue listing as 'Stephen Type 1') although he greatly increased the number of mints, which Henry had restricted. With the arrival of the empress and the creation of an Angevin enclave by Robert of Gloucester, a national coinage collapsed. Pennies were issued in her name by her supporters in or after 1140 from known mints at Bristol, Cardiff, Oxford and Wareham, which circulated principally in the southwest of England. Alongside this, other unofficial issues circulated in the west, north and midlands. Some were struck from local imitations of Stephen's official dies, usually in Stephen's name. Others were private issues, mostly substandard in weight and silver content and only vaguely corresponding to the royal types.[32] Some of these were issued with nonsensical inscriptions like 'Pereric' (an issue associated with the period of Stephen's captivity) or innocuous-sounding but unattributable royal names like 'Henry' and 'William'.

However, in the southeast and East Anglia, Stephen's officers still kept some control and his official dies were used on the London side of the limestone belt, from the Wash down to Oxford and Sussex. These coins indicate that Stephen still had the power in the second half of his reign to order two recoinages: one in the late 1140s (Type 2) and another in the early 1150s (Type

31 The principal modern studies are in R.P. Mack, 'Stephen and the Anarchy, 1135–54', *British Numismatic Journal*, xxxv (1966), 38–112; M.M. Archibald, 'Coins', in *English Romanesque Art, 1066–1200* (Arts Council, 1984), 320–41; G.C. Boon, *Coins of the Anarchy, 1135–54* (Cardiff, 1988); J.A. Green, 'Financing Stephen's war', *ANS* xiv, ed. M. Chibnall (Woodbridge, 1991) 102–3; M. Blackburn, 'Coinage and currency', 145–205. For a valiant effort by an historian to use the mass of numismatic information to interpret the reign, see E. King, 'The Anarchy of Stephen's reign', *TRHS*, 5th ser., 34 (1984), 147–51.
32 Doubtless the rogue issues noticed by William of Malmesbury in 1140, *HN*, 42.

6). It was doubtless the continuance of a respectable official coinage in the region of London that inhibited the penetration of foreign coin into England. In that regard, Stephen maintained the rights of his ancestors over coinage.[33] The settlement of 1153 led to another recoinage, as Ralph de Diceto tells us.[34] A Stephen penny (Type 7) was issued which once more circulated nationally, and stayed current several years into Henry II's reign. The eccentric local issues were all suppressed, and Henry II inherited a coinage well on the way to restoration to what it had been before 1139.

The story that the coinage tells is the same as that of the chronicles. In itself this is an important fact to establish. We find from the coinage that the royal monopoly collapsed in the same areas in which the political geography of Stephen's reign would lead us to expect that it would. We find that even royalist earls and magnates outside the southeast became indifferent to the royal right to control the money supply – men such as Earl Robert of Leicester. Most dramatic is the number of magnates so indifferent to Stephen that they issued their own coinage in their own names.[35] The identifiable ones are such as you might expect: Earl Patrick of Salisbury, Earl Robert of Gloucester, and Earl Henry of Northumbria, and also barons on the fringe, like Robert de Stuteville, Eustace fitz John of Alnwick and Henry du Neubourg of Gower. The number includes a late York issue by one 'Bishop Henry' (presumably Archbishop Henry Murdac).[36] Perhaps most surprising is that Earl Robert of Gloucester might issue coins in his own name from a mint at Bristol within his half-sister's heartland of support in the West Country. Despite the deferential use of an Angevin lion on the obverse, the very fact of striking this issue was a challenge to the empress's known jealousy about her own rights and dues. This coin issue is an unsettling hint that the empress's party leaders did not always follow her direction even in matters known to be important to her.[37]

THE FOREST

Another legacy to Stephen from Henry's reign was the system of farms, fines and gelds by which the first three Norman kings had enriched themselves.

33 I follow Mark Blackburn's chronology in this much-disputed area, see Blackburn, 'Coinage and currency', 194–9, for his observation about the absence of foreign coin, ibid., 149.
34 *Opera Historica* i, 296–7.
35 Successive finds have invalidated Edmund King's suggestion that 'baronial issues' were struck by lesser magnates, not so closely tied to the party leaders, King, 'Anarchy of Stephen's reign', 151. In his 'Economic development in the early twelfth century', in *Progress and Problems in Medieval England: Essays in Honour of Edward Miller*, ed. R. Britnell and J. Hatcher (Cambridge, 1996), 16, Professor King sees the loss of central control of the coinage as 'anarchy'. For myself the continued deference to royalty shown by the irregular issues, even if only the royalty of Henry and William, rather contradicts this idea. People still knew who should have been in charge.
36 Blackburn, 'Coinage and currency', 184–6.
37 These were found in the Box hoard in 1994, I must thank Marion Archibald for allowing me to examine these and for discussing them with me. For the association of the lion device with Henry I and the Angevin comital family, see D. Crouch, *The Image of Aristocracy in Britain, 1000–1300* (London, 1992), 223–4.

As we have already seen, Stephen was occasionally profligate with the royal demesne assets when it suited him. Waleran of Meulan was able to acquire most of the royal assets in Worcestershire: the city itself, several royal manors, including the prized saltworks of Droitwich, and the forest of Feckenham all found their way into Waleran's hands. Presumably Waleran had these by grant along with the earldom.[38] William of Aumale seems likewise to have absorbed most of the royal assets in the east of Yorkshire, although it may be that he helped himself to more than was intended. The copyist of the 1155 roll was struck that no account could be presented of the royal manors in this huge shire, other than a few odd payments. Yorkshire saw an almost complete dislocation of royal demesne, which could in the end only be resolved by the confiscation of Earl William's gains. William of Ypres is found in 1155 in control of six of the great royal manors of Kent, including the royal share of Canterbury, but at least he was paying their farms. Stephen had been using his Kentish demesne for the purposes of patronage since the beginning of the reign: the manor of Lessness had been used to reward Waleran of Meulan before 1141, and was then transferred to Richard de Lucy.[39]

But despite this apparent surge of overgenerosity to his intimates, King Stephen was by no means as profligate as might appear. After all, as Judith Green points out, he was never without money to the end of his reign and it was not financial exhaustion that brought him to negotiate the succession in 1153.[40] The royal forests were by no means dismembered by Stephen. One of his most notorious and resented acts as a new king was to authorise in October 1136 a wide-ranging forest eyre which bore heavily on the magnates.[41] Henry I had increased the area of afforested land in England. The protests of the Church on this at least had been heard, when Stephen promised at Easter 1136, that he would not exact forest charges on any land of the Church within the forest his predecessor had created.[42] He also undertook at Easter to resign these rights to the kingdom at large, but by October this had slipped his mind, and he found it politic to exploit the forest as extensively as he did the elections to bishoprics and abbeys. David Crook's fascinating study of the forest in Nottinghamshire based on an inquest of 1155 reveals that Stephen or his officers actually increased the forest area in the shire during his reign.[43]

There are other indications of a surprisingly vital administration of the royal forest under Stephen. The fact that he did his best to maintain his promise of

38 Crouch, *Beaumont Twins*, 30 and n. Much of the Worcestershire demesne had been returned by September 1154, through the agency of the ruthless new sheriff, William Cumin, *Red Book* ii, 656.
39 *Red Book* ii, 648–9, 652; For Lessness, see Crouch, *Beaumont Twins*, 53 and n.
40 Green, 'Financing Stephen's war', 91.
41 HH, 708.
42 *Regesta* iii, no. 271. Almost immediately the king ordered an inquest in Herefordshire into his uncle's afforestations, in order to free the lands of Hereford cathedral; this may have been one of many such writs, ibid., no. 382, another is possibly represented by his quittance to York minster, ibid., no. 976.
43 D. Crook, 'The archbishopric of York and the extent of the forest in Nottinghamshire in the twelfth century', in *Law and Government in the Middle Ages: Essays in Honour of Sir James Holt*, ed., G. Garnett and J. Hudson (Cambridge, 1994), 325–38.

1136 to the Church helps us, because it generated the occasional charter of confirmation of exemption. Such acts show that a network of royal foresters was at work throughout his reign in those parts of England which acknowledged his rule. In 1143 he exempted Peterborough abbey from the inquest of his foresters in Northamptonshire in one of its assarts. In 1146 the king addressed Earl William of York and the foresters of Yorkshire in a writ in favour of the hospital of St Peter in York.[44] There survives an act of Stephen to Wenlock priory, which shows that between 1146 and 1148 the king still exercised an effective forest administration even in Shropshire, and that he insisted that his officers should not trouble the priory in its woodlands which lay within the area that King Henry had afforested.[45] A late grant of Stephen of the assart later called Hainault to Barking abbey refers to the pleas of assarts still being held in the forest of Essex in the last two years of his reign, nor is that the only evidence from the county. In December 1153, Stephen quit the abbey of Colchester of pleas of assarts and the forest in its double-hundred of Tendring in Essex and at much the same time quit the chapter of St Paul's of pleas in its assart of Runwell and the abbey of Holy Trinity of Caen at Felsted. The 1155 pipe roll contained a full account for the New Forest from Walter Waleran, its chief forester in Stephen's last year, and its abbreviator noted (if not copied) another for the forest of Windsor.[46]

TAXATION AND TENSERIES

If Stephen was exerting himself in his forest administration thoughout his reign in the areas where he could, we should perhaps credit him with a similar energy in his other demesne assets. Henry I had used the system of taxation known as the Danegeld to raise a regular revenue, amounting to 2,400*li* in 1130. He also found ways of raising money through other sources: the use of murdrum fines, feudal aids and aids levied on his boroughs. The other items were variable in the amount they brought into the king's treasury, and in 1130 only amounted to one-fifth the value of Danegeld. Danegeld had attractions in being an annual levy on the shires and hundreds which was more predictable in what it might bring in. Danegeld was unpopular: it was levied unevenly across the country and the king seems to have raised the rate as and when it suited him, and may even have lumped further exactions on counties he believed were not paying enough. Another reason for unpopularity was

44 *Regesta* iii, nos. 655, 992.
45 D.C. Cox, 'Two unpublished charters of King Stephen for Wenlock Priory', *Shropshire History and Archaeology*, lxvi (1989), 58–9.
46 *Red Book* ii, 649, 651. For the grant of Hainault, Cartulary of Ilford Hospital, Hatfield House, Marquess of Salisbury MS, Ilford Hospital 1/6, fo. 5v, a reference I owe to the generosity of Professor Nicholas Vincent. For Tendring, Felsted and Runwell, *Regesta* iii, nos. 137, 239, 239a, 565–6. Other such grants of exemption from pleas of assarts occur in Yorkshire, ibid. no. 561 (1135 × 54, probably 1135 × 40). The hierarchy of the forest administration of Essex under Stephen is revealed by *Regesta* iii, no. 41 which is a confirmation of the succession of Humphrey of Barrington to his father, Eustace, as keeper of Hatfield forest under the county's hereditary chief forester, William de Montfichet.

that the king issued blanket exemptions for exchequer officials and favoured courtiers, who in turn used their influence to extend it to their men. In 1130, for instance, King Henry had exempted the lands not just of Waleran of Meulan and his brother, but their principal servants and barons as well as at least one French monastic house with English lands under their patronage. He did the same too for his son, Robert of Gloucester. It may be, as Judith Green suggests, that the king was aware of the unpopularity of the tax, and there is a story that in 1130 he suspended its collection for seven years in gratitude for escaping a storm at sea.[47]

Henry of Huntingdon gives us some reason to believe that the royal officers were aware of the problem when Stephen came to the throne. Abolition of Danegeld was one of the proposed measures under discussion in January 1136, according to Huntingdon.[48] However, the proposal had been forgotten by Easter 1136, and there are scattered references that indicate that Stephen's administration was levying it at least until 1138. A charter of Waleran of Meulan dating to 1140 mentions that Worcester cathedral priory owed 'the king's geld, which is mine'.[49] This would imply that the king was levying Danegeld in Worcestershire up to the time when Waleran received the earldom of Worcester (in 1138). But the very nature of the reference indicates that the collection of Danegeld was being enfeebled by then, if it was given away to an earl to collect, whether in full or subcontracted in return for a farm.[50] Nonetheless, there are some hints that – as with control over the mints – the southeast was different, and that Danegeld continued to be levied there, where Stephen's sheriffs were most effective. So we find that the abbot of Westminster sought a writ from Stephen to compel his tenants (particularly the abbot of Chertsey) to pay the Danegeld they owed for their tenures. The writ also pardoned Westminster abbey for the surplus money taken from it for his Danegeld. Since the writ is attested by Henry of Essex, it probably dates to a time after 1145, which is the earliest firmly dateable appearance Henry makes in the king's service.[51] Other than that there is not much evidence. Blanket exemptions of religious institutions which mention Danegeld amongst the items tell us very little, other than implying that the king might one day consider levying it.[52] The abstracted notes of the roll for 1154–55 mention no Danegeld

47 For this see, JW iii, 202; J.A. Green, 'The last century of Danegeld', *EHR*, 96 (1981), 241–58; eadem, *The Government of England under Henry I* (Cambridge, 1986), 69–78. For the exemptions quoted, Crouch, *Beaumont Twins*, 25–6.
48 HH, 704.
49 H.W.C. Davis, 'Some documents of the Anarchy', in *Essays in History presented to Reginald Lane Poole*, ed. Davis (Oxford, 1927), 170–1.
50 A writ of Stephen to the justice and sheriff of Norfolk exempts Coxford priory from 12d danegeld, but cannot be assigned a narrow date, *Regesta* iii, no. 248.
51 *Regesta* iii, no. 934. The editors of the *Regesta* give the broad range 1135 × 54 for it.
52 This same objection applies to the case where Ralph Picot, sheriff of Kent, was accused in 1153 of levying a range of exactions (including Danegeld) on Elverton, a manor of Canterbury cathedral priory, *English Lawsuits from William I to Richard I*, ed. R.C. van Caenegem (2 vols, Selden Soc., 106–7, 1990–1), i, 296–7. We do not know if the later record of this case is making assumptions about what might have been, rather than what actually was, demanded of the monks.

payments, nonetheless the tax was levied by Henry II in 1155–56.[53] This either may mean that Stephen's sheriffs and exchequer were incapable of levying the geld in his last years, or that Stephen could have done, but chose not to. The fact that Henry *did* levy the tax in 1155–56 is some evidence, however, that Stephen had recently levied Danegeld on the part of England he had ruled. Henry II's administration restored this source of revenue suspiciously quickly.

As Edmund King has demonstrated, the most important indicator about the health of Stephen's centralised financial system was the degree to which it was usurped. This is nowhere more evident than in the collection of private taxes by individual magnates, the *tenseries* occasionally mentioned (with outrage) in ecclesiastical sources. Stephen must attract some blame here. We have already seen how the collection of the geld in Worcestershire was delegated to its earl in or soon after 1138. It is likely enough that the king might have consented to other favoured earls doing the same. What, then, was the difference if magnates, desperate for ready money to finance their fight for survival, chose to levy taxes on the regions where they could exert the menace of armed force on the inhabitants? The *tenserie* is mentioned in the famous description from Peterborough abbey of the nature of the disorder of Stephen's reign. Castles were built and garrisoned by 'devils and wicked men' and 'at regular intervals they levied a tax called *tenserie* upon the villages'.[54] Professor King describes examples of forced exactions of cash and services from all around the kingdom – for instance the local magnates of the diocese of Ely who enraged the bishop by demanding tenseries and services from his people.[55] Professor King sees this as the very stuff of Anarchy, and I suppose from Stephen's point of view it might have looked like that, but hardly from the point of view of the harassed baron. Fortunately we have the words of just such a harassed baron, Brian fitz Count, and from his point of view, imposing a tax on the merchants going to the bishop of Winchester's fair was all that lay between his men and starvation: 'in the narrow pass in which I find myself, I cannot collect an acre of corn from the land which [King Henry] gave me. How surprising then if I take from another what I and my men need to survive?'[56]

The Church might well complain under these irregular exactions, and it did so copiously. But the answer could be given to the Church's complaints, that in many cases where they were paying protection money to barons, they would in other circumstances have been paying it to the king. The real problem for the bishops and abbots of England was that the king was rapacious but at least regular in his demands, and the magnates were rapacious but irregular. Following the diatribe of the monk of Peterborough against the castellans who imposed themselves upon his abbey comes a less often quoted passage:

> During all these evil days, Abbot Martin governed his abbey with great energy for twenty and a half years and eight days. He provided everything

53 Green, 'Last century', 242.
54 *ASC, s.a.* 1137.
55 *Liber Eliensis*, 326–7. See generally, King, 'Anarchy of Stephen's reign', 135–8.
56 H.W.C. Davis, 'Henry of Blois and Brian fitz Count', 302.

necessary for the monks and the visitors and was liberal in alms-giving; he was careful to see the monks got their commons, and punctilious in holding commemoration feasts . . . he extended the church and set apart the income from various estates and also other moneys for the building costs . . . He recovered monastery property in the shape of lands which great men held by force . . . He admitted many monks and planted vineyards, and built many domestic buildings, and changed the site of the town to a better position than formerly.[57]

From this we find that, nineteen long winters or not, Abbot Martin of Peterborough (1134–54) rose above them. Despite tenseries he could find the food to feed not just monks, but guests; he could find money not just to rebuild his abbey and its domestic buildings, but to give to the poor; although a persecuted monk, he nonetheless knew how to overawe and intimidate the local magnates who sought to make him a victim; although the roads were disrupted, he could find a better site for the town which provided the market for his abbey, and successfully attract trade there.

From the evidence of Peterborough, times were hard and uncertain in Stephen's reign, but not so hard that an astute estate-manager could not still make money, exploit trade and raise crops.[58] We find the same elsewhere. When St Ailred was abbot of Revesby in Lincolnshire between 1143 and 1147 he was able to extend the new abbey with some success despite the fact (as his hagiographer says) that the country was 'reduced almost to a desert by the malice, slaughters and harryings of evil men'.[59] The sceptical assessment of the monastic evidence for disruption of life in English monasteries during Stephen's reign, which Thomas Callahan, Jr. carried out, is instructive. Some houses in the war zone suffered physical damage, others elsewhere suffered intermittent persecution but much of that was trivial and could have been suffered whether or not Stephen was king. Where damage is known to have occurred – and it is only recorded as being suffered by a small minority of chapters – nearly half the houses received compensation. Callahan's main point, however, is that the evidence for damage is outweighed by physical and documentary evidence of prosperity both in church and estate building. Whether or not the obstacles in the way of this were greater in Stephen's reign, prosperity and building were still possible.[60]

ROYAL JUSTICE

Stephen's reign now looks far less significant in the history of English law and justice than it once did. If we jettison the idea that many of Stephen's problems

---

57 *ASC, s.a.* 1137.
58 See comments by C.J. Holdsworth, 'The Church', in *The Anarchy of King Stephen's Reign*, ed. E. King (Oxford, 1994), 228–9.
59 Walter Daniel, *The Life of Ailred of Rievaulx*, ed. F.M. Powicke (London, 1950), 28.
60 T. Callahan, Jr. 'The impact of Anarchy on English monasticism, 1135–1154', *Albion* 6 (1974), 218–32.

arose from the insistence of the English magnates that they should be free to leave their lands to their children after them with no royal interference, then Stephen's reign no longer has a crisis, and becomes more 'normal'. By 'normal', I mean that it belongs in a continuing line of development and has no appearance of revolution. As with the history of Stephen's exchequer, we see the mechanisms of justice in his reign falter, if not seize up, but they do survive reasonably intact. Where justice and law are concerned we might even suggest that there was less to lose in England in Stephen's reign than there had been in administration.

King Henry's ideology of strong kingship had caused him to promote in the middle years of his reign the idea of touring royal justices (the eyre) drawn from his leading courtiers sitting in the shire and hundred courts.[61] These, in turn, had tutored the country at large – from Northumberland to Cornwall – in the idea that there were certain pleas 'of the crown' which ought to be reserved to the eyre, because they were offences against the king's peace (murder, assault, arson and rape). The private compilation of law from the first half of Henry's reign, the *Leges Henrici Primi*, shows an already well-developed idea that the king had a particular jurisdiction. King Henry had also, on occasion, sent out judicial writs: written orders to sheriffs or other individuals informing them that a case had come to his attention, and that he wished to see it settled without delay. So here again we see Henry promoting centralising tendencies in the basic functions of government. But how deep did the effects of this go? The argument might be made that most law in England and the Marches was still customary and communal, and where it was not communal it was seigneurial; it belonged to the honorial courts of the magnates. King Henry even increased the number of communal hundred courts under the hereditary jurisdiction of magnates, which rather argues against Henry having a conception that justice should be concentrated in royal hands. Offering patronage was clearly a higher priority. It is certain that both Henry and his subjects believed that the normal structures for establishing right and justice in the land did not belong to the king and could go on without him. It was simply the king's duty to ensure justice was done. The same was true in the next reign. Whether Stephen sent out justices and writs or not, courts still sat and justice was still done.[62]

King Stephen had respected the legacy of King Henry, and his officers were just as alert to the issue of crown pleas. One of his first acts as king was to examine the case of the murder in the first days of December 1135 of William Maltravers, keeper of the honor of Pontefract. Clearly Stephen believed it to be his prerogative, especially as the murder was that of a tenant-in-chief. In January 1136 he decided to pardon the murderers because the murder had

61 See sketch of these developments in W.L. Warren, *The Governance of Norman and Angevin England, 1086–1272* (London, 1987), 81–2.
62 For Henry I and the complicated state of justice in his reign, see the admirable surveys in Green, *Government of Henry I*, 95–117; M. Chibnall, *Anglo-Norman England, 1066–1166* (Oxford, 1986), 166–74.

happened between the time King Henry died and Stephen was anointed his successor, and so presumably his majesty could not be offended by it.[63] As with the exchequer, it is possible to find evidence which indicates that the routine established in Henry's reign survived well into the first years of Stephen. David Cox's discovery of a 1138 charter of Stephen to Wenlock priory gives us, in its unique provisions, a picture of business as usual in the local courts of Shropshire (although the place had been shaken by the recent siege of Shrewsbury). Stephen granted that:

> ... the church of St Milburga should send its steward or chief reeve (*magistralem seruientem*) to the usual county courts and my hundred courts, who there will hear my writs, and give judgement with my other judges. No other of its men need go there or reply to the courts, unless they are subject to a plea which touches my crown. Otherwise they need not go there for any plea, or reply there, unless the prior of Wenlock fails to do right to them in his court.[64]

From this we see that in one of the more exposed of the shires in the troubled year of 1138 – when Robert of Gloucester's affinity was disturbing the middle March – its landowners still expected the county and hundred courts to meet, the king's writs to be read by the sheriff's clerks, and pleas to be brought forward. This was so much so that the prior of Wenlock succeeded in persuading the king to narrow the summons to the court to his steward or a senior reeve, so that the obligation would not weigh so heavily on his tenants.

Another significant point about the Wenlock grant of 1138 is the reservation of crown pleas. This is something which the king continued to do till the end of his reign. In 1148, the king reserved 'all customs which pertain to my crown', in a grant to the Templars of a half-hundred in Essex.[65] In 1150, the king was still concerning himself closely in what went on in the shire courts within the parts of the kingdom which acknowledged him. In Norwich that year the joint court of Norfolk and Suffolk met in the bishop's garden. There was a large attendance of the men of the honors of Warenne, Framlingham and Eye, the bishops of Ely and Norwich, the abbots of Bury and St Benet, the sheriffs, and others. But as well as these local dignitaries there was also present a contingent of Stephen's *curiales* and the president of the whole assembly was William Martel, the king's steward. The assembly discussed a case of the previous year where knights of the abbey of Bury St Edmunds were accused of collaborating with the enemies of the king in Bedford in an attempt to assassinate him. The court had to decide whether the king's rights in this overrode the liberties of Bury, but apparently only pleas relating to treasure-trove and murder could do that.[66] The presence of a powerful group of royal justices at Norwich in 1150 seems to indicate that the centralising

63 See above, p. 40.
64 Cox, 'Two Charters of King Stephen', 56–8.
65 *Regesta* iii, no. 846.
66 *English Lawsuits*, ed. van Caenegem i, 288–91.

trend of royal interference was by no means absent in Stephen's reign, for all the crown's weakness in other respects. Indeed, in 1151, the canons of the Council of London complain that the pleas of the crown were weighing heavily on churches.[67]

Through the king's charters we catch occasional glimpses of royal justice in action even in the latter half of the reign, although the glimpses are few and far between. For instance, Nicholas Vincent has recently unearthed a charter of Stephen to Stratford Langthorne abbey which was issued from London and can be dated to a time between 1146 and 1150. There had been a complaint that the abbey did not have its rights in the royal manor of Havering-atte-Bower in Essex, and so the king confirmed 'those 10*li*-worth of land in my manor of Havering which Adam de Beaunay delivered them according to my writ by oath of the men of the village'. There had been a dispute, a writ, and inquisition by jury before a royal justice and a resolution propagated by a royal charter.[68] A similar procedure is also evident in Essex in a charter of a similar date, where the college of St Martin-le-Grand in London recovered a piece of moorland, after the sheriff (or under-sheriff) Maurice of Tilty held a jury of recognition in the hundred court of Maldon.[69]

Outside Essex and the southeast, we cannot be in any way confident that the concept of royal justice survived into the second half of the reign. But just as the control over the coinage survived in the southeast, to be revived generally before the end of the reign in the issue of a new national coinage, so did the idea of the royal judicial writ. We have already noted in Chapter 14 how the joint government of Henry and Stephen began issuing writs into Gloucestershire and Wiltshire commanding reseisin even as the duke and king travelled up from Winchester through Windsor to London. The first known recipients were the earls of Gloucester and Salisbury, long-term Angevin supporters. Neither was a man who had been politically active in the reign of Henry, but they began to experience what Henry's chancery had been able to do to intimidate magnates even before Stephen was dead.

67 *Councils & Synods with other Documents relating to the English Church* i, ed. D. Whitelock, M. Brett and C.N.L. Brooke (Oxford, 1981), 824.
68 Essex Record Office, ms D/DU 102/28. The attestation of Count Eustace dates it after 1146, and that of William of Ypres indicates a date before 1150, when his growing blindness led to his retirement to Kent. I must thank Professor Vincent for his generosity in providing a copy of the charter before publication.
69 *Regesta* iii, no. 547.

CHAPTER 17

Conclusion

At the beginning of this work I said that I would seek an explanation for the historical problems of the reign of Stephen through a study of the man himself. Having now seen him on his deathbed and committed his mortal remains to the monks of Faversham, what is there to say? I am happy to praise Stephen the man. There is no cause to belittle Stephen as a moral creature as a previous generation of historian has done.[1] As we have seen, there is every reason to believe that he was more deeply marked than many of his contemporaries by the ethics of the faith in which he had been brought up. If we start in his immediate circle, he had a happy and apparently chaste marriage and was supported by loyal sons. His queen and he seem to have been closer than a merely dutiful marriage called for: they clearly shared a spiritual outlook. Aldgate priory sources attest to the joint grief of king and queen at the early deaths of two of their children, and reveal a relationship of intense and pastoral friendship with its prior, Ralph. Stephen had produced one son, Gervase, from a relationship before his marriage. He acknowledged this son, had him educated and after his succession to the throne, granted him the abbacy of the royal *Eigenkirk* of Westminster. Even this aspect of his life was arranged decently. But Stephen did not promote Gervase unduly, to the extent that Henry I had lavishly furthered the clerical career of Henry of Blois.

Stephen was able to attract and maintain the loyalty of capable household intimates, intelligent men whose devotion to him is itself a testimony to his character. But again, in rewarding these men, Stephen was not wildly over-generous. Even his acknowledged intimate, William Martel, for whom he gave up Sherborne castle to buy his freedom, attained no great landed honor or earldom through Stephen. Richard de Lucy, the greatest of Stephen's new men, was given some royal estates and opportunities to enrich himself. Richard achieved the status of a minor magnate of Essex, no more. Only one of

---

1 GS, 220, shows Stephen in 1149 directing his army to burn not just crops, but also churches, across Wiltshire. It should be remembered from this that Stephen was a warrior of his age, and his age did not shrink from wasting whole regions in order to cripple a stubborn enemy.

340

Stephen's inner circle of new men was to betray him, Turgis d'Avranches in 1145. Stephen's record was considerably better than his uncle's in this regard. Taking the evidence that we have, we can confidently state Stephen to have been a brave, loyal, humble and often charming man, with a gift for assessing men and a capacity for striking up close relationships.

So where did the problem lie? Stephen's capacity to judge men was not matched by a capacity to judge situations. Decisive in battle and siege, Stephen could dither when faced with complex problems of policy. There seem to have been intellectual limitations which inhibited Stephen from any creative ability with the raw materials of politics. His record proves that he was unable to sustain any world-view, nor could he visualise the consequences of his actions for others. In Wales and Normandy he proved simply unable to grasp what the actions of the Welsh, the Marchers and the Angevins all meant. He did not notice what the deliberate alienation of his uncle's old cronies was doing before it was too late, and they had rallied around his arch-enemy, Robert of Gloucester. He seems to have been humble enough to have been impressed by men with apparently greater abilities than he acknowledged in himself, so he was taken in first by his brother and then by Count Waleran of Meulan. But both men had their limits, and by not appreciating this Stephen made a succession of errors. His retreat into the arms of his own household officers after 1141 might have seemed the obvious alternative, but showed poor judgement. He ought to have tried to understand better the mechanics of the old king's complex relationship with his magnates, whose co-operation gave his kingdom reality. Here, indeed, is the irony. Stephen was very anxious to be another Henry, and began by adhering closely to his understanding of his uncle's style of kingship. Yet he did not have Henry's breadth of mind and cool calculation, which was unfortunate for his subjects. So we must first blame Stephen the man for not being aware of his limitations, and then we must exonerate him, because ill-judged ambition is by no means an uncommon fault in humanity.

The kingship of Stephen is beginning to get a less hostile treatment from historians. Lewis Warren's reassessment (published in 1987) was a milestone in that regard. He gave due weight to Stephen's tenacious defence of his rights and raised doubts as to how insecure a hold Stephen had really had on his kingdom. 'He could count on the loyalty of the majority of his barons even in adversity. The civil war was intermittent and left much of the realm untroubled.'[2] The more extended treatment given here shows that this was not an unfair verdict. Within his personal limitations Stephen was a dogged, competent and conscientious king of England who spent eight years of his nineteen-year reign fighting a bitter war in a corner of his kingdom with a dynastic rival. Apart from one disastrous campaign, he limited the war to that corner, and after 1148 could be said to have expelled his rival, the empress, and achieved a dominant edge over his opponents, even if outright victory

2 W.L. Warren, *The Governance of Norman and Angevin England 1086–1272* (London, 1987), 91–2.

eluded him. Where he maintained his rule he was an effective king whom people dared not ignore. His is not the record of a failure or an incompetent.

Whatever misfortunes Stephen experienced in his reign, they were as nothing to the damage done to his posthumous reputation by being the first victim of modern scientific history. Stephen's misfortune was to be the successor of Henry I and the predecessor of Henry II, both the darlings of the school of Anglo-American constitutionalist and administrative historians who dominated the writing of history between the 1870s and the 1970s. Looked at down their noses through their particular spectacles, Stephen must seem a disappointment, although they generally allowed that he was an effective warrior. To them his reign seemed a blip in a clear line of development between the reign of Henry I and Henry II. For historiographical reasons going back to the eighteenth century, the blip became an 'anarchy' and Stephen the villain in a constitutional drama. But, as we have seen, Stephen was not trying to preserve a constitution between 1135 and 1154, he was trying to rule a kingdom. When his uncle's methods broke down, he tried his own: the regionalisation of power first through chartered earls and then through ad hoc military governors like William Martel, William de Chesney, Henry de Tracy, Philip of Gloucester and William of Ypres.

It is not in England that we find Stephen the failure, but in Wales and Normandy. Here indeed he proved inadequate, but, with the exception of the greatest of kings, who could have done better? Rather than compare Stephen's record to the success of King Henry I, we would do better to compare it to that of Louis VII of France. Louis VII had his military successes, but they were never decisive. Louis, too, attempted to rule two realms, the Capetian principality and the duchy of Aquitaine, and rapidly lost the latter to a rival. Louis, too, could do no more than contain his formidable rivals in key provinces, such as the Vexin and Vermandois, and in the end lost ground in both. Yet he is not considered such a failure as a king, probably because the reigns of his predecessor and (initially) his successor were not marked contrasts to his own. It is for the next generation of historians to start looking at Stephen and his reign more objectively, and judge them accordingly.

Select Bibliography

This bibliography does not include unprinted sources, which are cited in full in the notes when quoted. All printed sources used are listed here. The most frequently cited are noted in the text by abbreviations, which are listed in the front of the book. The section on secondary works lists only items which are cited more than once in the notes or which are particularly significant historiographically; a number of principal secondary works are also cited by abbreviation in the footnotes to the text.

PRINTED PRIMARY SOURCES

Annales de Theokesberia, in *Annales Monastici*, i, ed. H.R. Luard (Rolls Series, 1864).

Annales de Waverleia, in *Annales Monastici*, ii, ed. H.R. Luard (Rolls Series, 1865).

Annales de Wintonia, in *Annales Monastici*, ii, ed. H.R. Luard (Rolls Series, 1865).

Annales Monastici, ed. H.R. Luard (5 vols, Rolls Series, 1864–69).

Annales Plymptonienses, in *Ungedruckte Anglo-Normannische Geschichtsquellen*, ed. F. Liebermann (Strasbourg, 1879).

Bruges, Galbert of, *Passio Karoli comitis*, ed. R. Köpke (Monumenta Germaniae Historica, Scriptores, 12), 537–61.

Brut y Tywysogyon: Peniarth MS. 20 Version, ed. T. Jones (Cardiff, 1952).

Brut y Tywysogyon: Red Book of Hergest Version, ed. T. Jones (2nd edn., Cardiff, 1973).

Calendar of Charter Rolls preserved in the Public Record Office (6 vols, PRO, 1903–27).

Calendar of Documents preserved in France, i, *918–1206*, comp. J.H. Round (London, 1899).

Canterbury, Gervase of, *Opera Historica* (2 vols, Rolls Series, 1879–80).

Cartae et alia munimenta quae ad dominium de Glamorgancia pertinent, ed. G.T. Clark (6 vols, Talygarn, 1910).

Cartulaire de Afflighem, ed. E. de Marneffe, in *Analectes pour servir à l'histoire ecclésiastique de la Belgique*, iie section, *série des cartulaires et des documents étendus*, pt. 2 (Louvain, 1896).

Cartulaire général de Paris, ed. R. Lasteyerie (Paris, 1887).

Cartularium abbathiae de Whiteby, ed. J.C. Atkinson (2 vols, Surtees Soc., 1879–81).

Cartularium monasterii sancti Johannis baptiste de Colecestria, ed. S.A. Moore (2 vols, Roxburghe Club, 1897).

Cartularium prioratus de Colne, ed. L. Fisher (Colchester, 1946).

Charters of the Anglo-Norman Earls of Chester, c.1071–1237, ed. G. Barraclough (Record Society of Lancashire and Cheshire, cxxvi, 1988).

Charters of the Redvers Family and the Earldom of Devon, 1090–1217, ed. R. Bearman (Devon and Cornwall Record Society, new ser., 37, 1994).

Chartes anciennes du prieuré de Monmouth en Angleterre, ed. P. Marchegay (Les Roches-Baritaud, 1879).

Chartes de l'abbaye de Jumièges, ed. J.-J. Vernier (2 vols, Société des historiens de la Normandie, 1916).

Chronicles of the Reigns of Stephen, Henry II and Richard I, ed. R. Howlett (4 vols, Rolls Series, 1884–89).

Chronicon abbatiae de Evesham, ed. W. Dunn Macray (Rolls Series, 1863).

Chronicon abbatiae Ramesiensis, ed. W. Dunn Macray (Rolls Series, 1886).

Chronicon monasterii de Abingdon, ed. J. Stevenson (2 vols, Rolls Series, 1858).

Chronicon Rotomagense in *RHF* xii.

Chronicon S. Michaelis in Periculo Maris, in *RHF*, xii.

Chronicon S. Stephani Cadomensis, in *RHF*, xii.

Chronicon Valassense, ed. F. Somménil (Rouen, 1868).

Chroniques des ducs de Brabant, ed. E. de Dynk, i, pt. 1 (Brussels, 1854).

Coggeshall, Ralph of, *Chronicon Anglicanum*, ed. J. Stevenson (Rolls Series, 1875).

Compendium vitae Theobaldi, in *PL*, 150.

Councils & Synods with other Documents relating to the English Church i, ed. D. Whitelock, M. Brett and C.N.L. Brooke (Oxford, 1981).

Cox, D.C., 'Two unpublished charters of King Stephen for Wenlock priory', *Shropshire History and Archaeology*, lxvi (1989), 56–9.

Daniel, Walter, *The Life of Ailred of Rievaulx*, ed. F.M. Powicke (London, 1950).

De Antiquis Legibus Liber, ed. T. Stapleton (Camden Soc., old ser., 34. 1846).

Deuil, Odo de, *De Profectione Ludovici VII in Orientem*, ed. V.G. Berry (New York, 1948).

Dialogus de Scaccario and Constitutio Domus Regis, ed. C. Johnson (rev'd edn., Oxford, 1983).

Diceto, Ralph de, *Opera Historica*, ed. W. Stubbs (2 vols, Rolls Series, 1876).

Diplomatic Documents preserved in the Public Record Office, ed. P. Chaplais, i, *1101–1272* (HMSO, 1964).

Domerham, Adam of, *Historia de rebus gestis Glastoniensibus*, ed. T. Hearne (2 vols, London, 1727).

Dugdale W. and Dodsworth, R., *Monasticon Anglicanum*, ed. J. Caley and others (4 vols in 8, London, 1795–1815).

Earldom of Gloucester Charters, ed. R.B. Patterson (Oxford, 1973).

Early Yorkshire Charters, vols i–iii, ed. W. Farrer (Edinburgh, 1914–16); vols iv–xii, ed. C.T. Clay (Yorkshire Archaeological Society, Record Series, Extra Series, 1935–65).

English Episcopal Acta i, *Lincoln, 1067–1185*, ed. D. Smith (British Academy, 1980).

English Episcopal Acta vi, *Norwich, 1070–1214*, ed. C. Harper-Bill (British Academy, 1990).

English Episcopal Acta vii, *Hereford 1079–1234*, ed. J. Barrow (Oxford, 1993).

English Episcopal Acta viii, *Winchester, 1070–1204*, ed. M.J. Franklin (British Academy, 1993).

English Episcopal Acta xi, *Exeter, 1046–1184*, ed. F. Barlow (British Academy, 1996).

English Episcopal Acta xiv, *Coventry and Lichfield, 1072–1159*, ed. M.J. Franklin (British Academy, 1997).

English Lawsuits from William I to Richard I, ed. R.C. van Caenegem (2 vols, Selden Soc., 106–7, 1990–91).

Ernald, abbot of Bonneval, *Vita sancti Bernardi: Liber Secundus*, in *PL*, 185, cols. 301–2.

Facsimiles of Charters in Oxford Muniment Rooms, ed. H.E. Salter (Oxford, 1929).

Ford, John of, *The Life of Wulfric of Haselbury*, ed. M. Bell (Somerset Record Society, xlvii, 1933).

Gesta abbatum monasterii sancti Albani, ed. H.T. Riley (3 vols, Rolls Series, 1867–69).

Gesta Stephani, ed. K.R. Potter and R.H.C. Davis (Oxford, 1976).

Giry, A., *Histoire de la ville de Saint-Omer* (Paris, 1877).

Gray, A., *The Priory of St Radegund, Cambridge* (Cambridge Antiquarian Society, 1898).

Hemptinne, T. de and Parisse, M., 'Thierry d'Alsace, comte de Flandre: biographie et actes', *Annales de l'Est*, 43 (1991), 83–113.

Herefordshire Domesday, c.1160–70, ed. V.H. Galbraith and J. Tait (Pipe Roll Society, new ser., xxv, 1950).

Hexham, John of, *Symeonis Historia Regum Continuata per Johannem Hagustaldensem*, in *Historia Regum*, ed. T. Arnold, ii (Rolls Series, 1885).

Hexham, Richard of, *De Gestis Regis Stephani et de Bello Standardii*, in *Chronicles of the Reigns of Stephen etc*, ed. R. Howlett, iii (Rolls Series, 1886).

Histoire de Guillaume le Conquérant, ed. and trans. R. Foreville (Classiques de l'Histoire de France au Moyen Âge, Paris, 1952).

Historia et cartularium monasterii sancti Petri de Gloucestria, ed. W.H. Hart (3 vols, Rolls Series, 1863–67).

Historia gloriosi Ludovici regis, in *RHF*, xvi.

Historiola de primordiis episcopatus Somersetensis, in *Ecclesiastical Documents*, ed. J. Hunter (Camden Soc., old ser., viii, 1840).

Huntingdon, Henry of, *Historia Anglorum*, ed. D. Greenway (Oxford, 1996).

Jumièges, William of, *Gesta Normannorum Ducum*, ed. E.M.C. van Houts (2 vols, Oxford, 1992–95).

Leland's Itinerary in England and Wales, ed. L. Toulmin Smith (6 vols, London, 1906–10).

Liber Eliensis, ed. E.O. Blake (Camden Society, 3rd ser., xcii, 1962).

Liber Luciani de laude Cestrie, ed. M.V. Taylor (Rec. Soc. of Lancashire and Cheshire, lxiv, 1912).

Liber monasterii de Hyda, ed. E. Edwards (Rolls Series, 1866).

Magnum Rotulum Scaccarii vel Magnum Rotulum Pipae de Anno Tricesimo-primo Regni Henrici primi, ed. J. Hunter (Record Commission, 1833).

Malmesbury, William of, *Historia Novella*, ed. K.R. Potter (London, 1955).

Malmesbury, William of, *De gestis regum Anglorum*, ed. W. Stubbs (2 vols, Rolls Series, 1887–89).

Map, Walter, *De Nugis Curialium*, ed. and trans. M.R. James, rev. C.N.L. Brooke and R.A.B. Mynors (Oxford, 1983).

Marmoutier, John de, *Historia Gaufredi ducis*, in *Chroniques des comtes d'Anjou et des seigneurs d'Amboise*, ed. L. Halphen and R. Poupardin (Paris, 1913).

Materials for a History of Thomas Becket, ed. J.C. Robertson and J.B. Sheppard (7 vols, Rolls Series, 1875–85).

Merrick, Rice, *Morganniae Archaiographia*, ed. B. Ll. James (South Wales Rec. Soc, no. 1, 1983).

Monmouth, Thomas of, *The Life and Miracles of St William of Norwich*, ed. A. Jessopp and M.R. James (Cambridge, 1896).

Newburgh, William of, *De Rerum Anglicarum*, in *Chronicles of the Reigns of Stephen etc*, ed. R. Howlett, i–ii (Rolls Series, 1884–85).

Orderic Vitalis, *The Ecclesiastical History*, ed. M. Chibnall (6 vols, Oxford, 1969–80).

Patrologia Latina, ed. J.-P. Migne (221 vols, Paris, 1844–64).

Pipe Roll of 31 Henry I (see *Magnum Rotulum Scaccarii . . .*).

Reading Abbey Cartularies, ed. B. Kemp (2 vols, Camden Society, 4th ser., 31, 33, 1986–87).

Recueil de documents pour servir à l'histoire de Montreuil-sur-Mer, 1000–1464, ed. G. de Lhomel (Compiègne, 1907).

Recueil des chartes de l'abbaye de Cluny, ed. A. Bernard and A. Bruel (6 vols, Paris, 1876–1903).

Recueil des chartes de St-Nicaise de Meulan: prieuré de l'ordre du Bec, ed. E. Houth (Paris, 1924).

Recueil des historiens des Gaules et de la France, ed. M. Bouquet and others (24 vols, Paris, 1869–1904).

Regesta Regum Anglo-Normannorum, ed. H.W.C. Davis and others (4 vols, Oxford, 1913–69).

Regesta Regum Scottorum i, *The Acts of Malcolm IV*, ed. G.W.S. Barrow (Edinburgh, 1960).

Rievaulx, Ailred of, *Relatio de Standardo*, in *Chronicles of the Reigns of Stephen etc*, iii, ed. R. Howlett (Rolls Series, 1886).

Rotuli Curiae Regis, ed. F. Palgrave (2 vols, Record Commission, 1835).

Salisbury, John of, *Policraticus*, ed. C.C.I. Webb (2 vols, Oxford, 1909).

Sancti Gregorii magni expositio in librum primum regum, ed. P. Verbraken (Corpus Christianorum Series Latina, 144, 1963).

Sarum Charters and Documents, ed. W. Rich-Jones and W. Dunn McCray (Rolls Series, 1891).

Select Documents of the English Lands of the Abbey of Bec, ed. M. Chibnall (Camden Soc., 3rd ser., lxxiii, 1951).

Sir Christopher Hatton's Book of Seals, ed. L.C. Loyd and D.M. Stenton (Oxford, 1950).

Suger, *Vita Ludovici Grossi regis*, ed. H. Waquet (Paris, 1964).

The Book of Fees commonly called the Testa de Nevill (3 vols, P.R.O., 1920–31).

The Cartulary of Holy Trinity, Aldgate, ed. G.A.J. Hodgett (London Record Society, 7, 1971).

The Cartulary of St Michael's Mount, ed. P.L. Hull (Devon and Cornwall Record Society, new ser., 5, 1962).

The Cartulary of Worcester Cathedral Priory, ed. R.R. Darlington (Pipe Roll Society, lxxvi, 1968).

The Chronicle of Battle Abbey, ed. E. Searle (Oxford, 1980).

The Chronicle of John of Worcester, iii *The Annals from 1067 to 1140*, ed. P. McGurk (Oxford, 1998).

The Historia Pontificalis of John of Salisbury, ed. M. Chibnall (Oxford, 1986).

The Letters and Charters of Gilbert Foliot, ed. A. Morey and C.N.L. Brooke (Cambridge, 1967).

The Letters of Arnulf of Lisieux, ed. F. Barlow (Camden Soc., 3rd ser., lxi, 1939).

The Letters of Peter the Venerable, ed. G. Constable (2 vols, Cambridge, Mass., 1967).

The Life of Christina of Markyate: a twelfth-century recluse, ed. C.H. Talbot (Oxford, 1959).

The Murder of Charles the Good, trans. J.B. Ross (Columbia, 1967).

The Norfolk Portion of the Chartulary of the Priory of St Pancras of Lewes, ed. J.H. Bullock (Norfolk Record Society, 12, 1939).

The Peterborough Chronicle, ed. C. Clark (Oxford, 1970).

The Red Book of the Exchequer, ed. H. Hall (3 vols, Rolls Series, 1896).

The Registrum Antiquissimum of the Cathedral Church of Lincoln, ed. C.W. Foster and K. Major (10 vols, Lincoln Record Society, 1931–73).

The Thame Cartulary, ed. H.E. Salter (Oxford Record Society, 25, 1947).

The Waltham Chronicle, ed. and trans. L. Watkiss and M. Chibnall (Oxford, 1994).

Therouanne, Walter de, *Vita Karoli Comitis*, ed. R. Köpke (Monumenta Germaniae Historica, Scriptores, 12), 561–619.

Torigny, Robert de, *Chronica*, in *Chronicles of the Reigns of Stephen etc*, ed. R. Howlett, iv (Rolls Series, 1889).

Tournai, Herman of, *Liber de restauratione monasterii sancti Martini Tornacensis*, ed. G. Waitz (Monumenta Germaniae Historica, Scriptores, 14), 284–9.

Ungedruckte Anglo-Normannische Geschichtsquellen, ed. F. Liebermann (Strasbourg, 1879).

Wales, Gerald of, *De iure et statu Meneuensis ecclesiae*, in *Opera* iii, ed. J.S. Brewer (Rolls Series, 1863).

Wales, Gerald of, *Itinerarium Kambriae*, in *Opera* vi, ed. J.F. Dimock (RS, 1868).

Walker, D., 'Charters of the earldom of Hereford, 1095–1210', in *Camden Miscellany*, xxii (1964), 1–75.

Westminster Abbey Charters, ed. E. Mason (London Record Society, 25, 1988).

William fitz Stephen, *Vita sancti Thome*, in *Materials for a History of Thomas Becket*, iii, ed. J.C. Robertson (Rolls Series, 1877).

Worcester, John of, see *The Chronicle of John of Worcester . . .*

SECONDARY WORKS

Adams, G.B., *Councils and Courts in Anglo-Norman England* (repr. New York, 1965).

Alexander, J. *et al.* (eds), *English Romanesque Art, 1066–1200* (London, 1984).

Amt, E., *The Accession of Henry II in England: Royal Government Restored, 1149–1159* (Woodbridge, 1993).

Barlow, F., *The English Church, 1066–1154* (London, 1979).

Barrow, G.W.S., *The Anglo-Norman Era in Scottish History* (Oxford, 1980).

Barrow, G.W.S., *David I of Scotland, 1124–1153* (Reading, 1985).

Barrow, G.W.S., 'The Scots and the north of England', in *The Anarchy of King Stephen's Reign*, ed. E. King (Oxford, 1994), 231–53.

Barthélemy, D., *L'ordre seigneurial, xie–xiie siècle* (Paris, 1990).

Bates, D.R., *Normandy before 1066* (London, 1982).

Bates, D.R., 'Normandy and England after 1066', *EHR*, 104 (1989), 853–61.

Bates, D.R., 'The rise and fall of Normandy, *c.*911–1204', in *England and Normandy in the Middle Ages*, ed. D.R. Bates and A. Curry (London, 1994), 19–35.

Bates, D.R. and Curry, A. (eds), *England and Normandy in the Middle Ages* (London, 1994).

Bearman, R., 'Baldwin de Redvers: some aspects of a baronial career in the reign of Stephen', *ANS* xviii, ed. C. Harper-Bill (Woodbridge, 1996), 19–46.

Biddle, M., 'Seasonal festivals and residence: Winchester, Westminster and Gloucester in the tenth to twelfth centuries', *ANS*, viii, ed. R.A. Brown, (Woodbridge, 1985), 51–63.

Blackburn, M., 'Coinage and currency', in *The Anarchy of King Stephen's Reign*, ed. E. King (Oxford, 1994), 145–205.

Boon, G.C., *Coins of the Anarchy, 1135–54* (Cardiff, 1988).

Bradbury, J., 'The early years of the reign of Stephen', in *England in the Twelfth Century*, ed. D. Williams (Woodbridge, 1990), 17–30.

Bradbury, J., *Stephen and Matilda* (Stroud, 1996).

Brett, M., *The English Church under Henry I* (Oxford, 1975).

Bur, M., *Suger: Abbé de St-Denis, Régent de France* (Paris, 1991).

Cam, H., *Lawfinders and Lawmakers* (London, 1962).

Carpenter, D.A., *The Minority of Henry III* (London, 1990).

Chartrou, J., *L'Anjou de 1109 à 1151* (Paris, 1928).

Chibnall, M., 'Anglo-French relations in the work of Orderic Vitalis', in *Documenting the Past: Essays in Honour of G.P. Cuttino*, ed. J.S. Hamilton and P.J. Bradley (Woodbridge, 1989), 5–19.

Chibnall, M., *The Empress Matilda* (Oxford, 1991).

Chibnall, M., 'Normandy', in *The Anarchy of King Stephen's Reign*, ed. E. King (Oxford, 1994), 93–116.

Coplestone-Crow, B., 'Payn fitz John and Ludlow castle', *Transactions of the Shropshire Archaeological and Historical Society*, lxx (1995), 171–83.

Coulson, C., 'Castles of the Anarchy', in *The Anarchy of King Stephen's Reign*, ed. E. King (Oxford, 1994), 67–92.

Cronne, H.A., 'Ranulf des Gernons, earl of Chester, 1129–53', *TRHS*, 4th ser., xx (1937), 103–34.

Cronne, H.A., *The Reign of Stephen: Anarchy in England, 1135–54* (London, 1970).

Crook, D., 'The archbishopric of York and the extent of the forest in Nottinghamshire in the twelfth century', in *Law and Government in the Middle Ages: Essays in Honour of Sir James Holt*, ed. G. Garnett and J. Hudson (Cambridge, 1994), 325–38.

Crouch, D., 'Geoffrey de Clinton and Roger earl of Warwick: new men and magnates in the reign of Henry I', *Bulletin of the Institute of Historical Research*, lv (1982), 113–24.

Crouch, D., 'Robert of Gloucester and the daughter of Zelophehad', *Journal of Medieval History*, 11 (1985), 227–43.

Crouch, D., *The Beaumont Twins: The Roots and Branches of Power in the Twelfth Century* (Cambridge, 1986).

Crouch, D., *William Marshal: Court, Career and Chivalry in the Angevin Empire, c.1147–1219* (London, 1990).

Crouch, D., 'The administration of the Norman earldom', in *The Earldom of Chester and its Charters*, ed. A.T. Thacker (Journal of Chester Archaeological Society, 71, 1991), 69–95.

Crouch, D., *The Image of Aristocracy in Britain, 1000–1300* (London, 1992).

Crouch, D., 'Earls and bishops in twelfth-century Leicestershire', *Nottingham Medieval Studies*, xxxvii (1993), 9–20.

Crouch, D., 'Normans and Anglo-Normans: a divided aristocracy?' in *England and Normandy in the Middle Ages*, ed. D.R. Bates and A. Curry (London, 1994), 51–67.

Crouch, D., 'A Norman *conventio* and bonds of lordship in the middle ages', in *Law and Government in Medieval England and Normandy*, ed. G. Garnett and J. Hudson (Cambridge, 1994), 299–324.

Crouch, D., 'The March and the Welsh kings', in *The Anarchy of King Stephen's Reign*, ed. E. King (Oxford, 1994), 255–89.

Crouch, D., 'From Stenton to McFarlane: models of society in the twelfth and thirteenth centuries', *TRHS*, 6th ser., no. 5 (1995), 179–200.

Crouch, D., 'The local influence of the earls of Warwick, 1088–1242: a study in decline and resourcefulness', *Midland History*, 21 (1996), 1–22.

Dalton, P., 'William earl of York and royal authority in Yorkshire in the reign of Stephen', *HSJ*, 2 (1990), 155–65.

Dalton, P., 'Aiming at the impossible: Ranulf II of Chester and Lincolnshire in the reign of Stephen', in *The Earldom of Chester and its Charters*, ed. A.T. Thacker (Journal of the Chester Archaeological Society, 71, 1991), 109–34.

Dalton, P., 'Ranulf II earl of Chester and Lincolnshire in the reign of Stephen', in *The Earldom of Chester and its Charters*, ed. A.T. Thacker (Chester Archaeological Society, 71, 1991), 109–32.

Dalton, P., '*In neutro latere*: the armed neutrality of Ranulf II earl of Chester in King Stephen's reign', *ANS*, xiv, ed. M. Chibnall (Woodbridge, 1992), 39–59.

Dalton, P., *Conquest, Anarchy and Lordship: Yorkshire 1066–1154* (Cambridge, 1994),

Dalton, P., 'Eustace fitz John and the politics of Anglo-Norman England: the rise and survival of a twelfth-century royal servant', *Speculum*, 71 (1996), 358–83.

Davies, R.R., 'Henry I and Wales', in *Studies in Medieval History presented to R.H.C. Davis*, ed. H. Mayr-Harting and R.I. Moore (London, 1985), 132–47.

Davis, H.W.C., 'The Anarchy of Stephen's reign', *EHR*, 18 (1903), 630–41.

Davis, H.W.C., 'Henry of Blois and Brian fitz Count', *EHR*, 25 (1910), 297–303.

Davis, H.W.C., 'Some documents of the Anarchy', in *Essays in History presented to Reginald Lane Poole*, ed. Davis (Oxford, 1927), 170–1.

Davis, R.H.C., 'Treaty between William earl of Gloucester and Roger earl of Hereford', in *A Medieval Miscellany for Doris Mary Stenton* (Pipe Roll Society, new ser., xxxvi, 1960), 139–46.

Davis, R.H.C., 'What happened in Stephen's reign, 1135–54', *History*, xlix (1964), 1–12.

Davis, R.H.C., 'An unknown Coventry charter', *EHR*, 86 (1971), 533–47, repr. in *From Alfred the Great to Stephen*, (London, 1991) 221–33.

Davis, R.H.C., *King Stephen* (3rd edn., London, 1990).

Davis, R.H.C., 'The college of St Martin-le-Grand and the Anarchy', in *From Alfred the Great to Stephen* (London, 1991), 237–54.

Eales, R., 'Local loyalties in Stephen's reign: Kent', *ANS*, viii, ed. R.A. Brown (Woodbridge, 1985).

Finberg, H.P.R., 'Uffculme', in *Lucerna* (London, 1964), 212–21.

Fleming, R., 'Domesday Book and the tenurial revolution', *ANS*, ix, ed. R.A. Brown (Woodbridge, 1986), 87–102.

Fleming, R., *Kings and Lords in Conquest England* (Cambridge, 1991).

Garnett, G. and Hudson, J. (eds), *Law and Government in the Middle Ages: Essays in Honour of Sir James Holt* (Cambridge, 1994).

Gillingham, J., '1066 and the introduction of chivalry into England', in *Law and Government in the Middle Ages: Essays in Honour of Sir James Holt*, ed. G. Garnett and J. Hudson (Cambridge, 1994).

Gillingham, J. and Holt, J.C. (eds), *War and Government in the Middle Ages* (Woodbridge, 1994).

Green, J.A., 'The last century of Danegeld', *EHR* 96 (1981), 241–58.

Green, J.A., 'King Henry I and the aristocracy of Normandy', in *La 'France Anglaise' au Moyen Âge* (Actes du 111ᵉ Congrès National des Sociétés Savantes, Poitiers, 1986), 161–73.

Green, J.A., *The Government of England under Henry I* (Cambridge, 1986).

Green, J.A., 'Unity and disunity in the Anglo-Norman state', *Historical Research*, 62 (1989), 128–33.

Green, J.A., *English Sheriffs to 1154* (HMSO, 1990).

Green, J.A., 'Earl Ranulf II and Lancashire', in *The Earldom of Chester and its Charters*, ed. A.T. Thacker (Journal of the Chester Archaeological Society, 71, 1991), 97–108.

Green, J.A., 'Financing Stephen's war', *ANS*, xiv, ed. M. Chibnall (Woodbridge, 1991), 105–8.

Green, J.A., 'Lords of the Norman Vexin', in *War and Government in the Middle Ages*, ed. J. Gillingham and J.C. Holt (Woodbridge, 1994), 47–63.

Green, J.A., 'David I and Henry I', *Scottish Historical Review*, lxxv (1996), 1–19.

Green, J.A., 'Family matters: family and the formation of the empress's party in South-West England', in *Family Trees and the Roots of Politics: The Prosopography of Britain and France from the Tenth to the Twelfth Century*, ed. K.S.B. Keats-Rohan (Woodbridge, 1997), 147–64.

Green, J.A., *The Aristocracy of Norman England* (Cambridge, 1997).

Harper-Bill, C., *The Anglo-Norman Church* (Bangor, 1992).

Haskins, C.H., *Norman Institutions* (New York, 1918).

Helmerichs, R., 'King Stephen's Norman itinerary, 1137', *HSJ*, 5 (1995), 89–97.

Holdsworth, C.J., 'The Church', in *The Anarchy of King Stephen's Reign*, ed. E. King (Oxford, 1994), 207–30.

Hollister, C. Warren, 'The Anglo-Norman civil war, 1101', *EHR*, 88 (1973), 315–43.

Hollister, C. Warren, 'The misfortunes of the Mandevilles', *History*, 58 (1973), 18–28.

Hollister, C. Warren, 'The Anglo-Norman succession debate of 1126: prelude to Stephen's Anarchy', *Journal of Medieval History*, 1 (1975), 19–41.

Hollister, C. Warren, 'Royal acts of mutilation: the case against Henry I', *Albion*, 10 (1978), 330–40.

Hollister, C. Warren, 'Henry I and the invisible transformation of medieval England', in *Studies in Medieval History Presented to R.H.C. Davis*, ed. H. Mayr-Harting and R.I. Moore (London, 1985), 303–16.

Hollister, C. Warren, *Monarchy, Magnates and Institutions in the Anglo-Norman World* (London, 1986).

Hollister, C. Warren, 'Anglo-Norman political culture', in *Anglo-Norman Political Culture and the Twelfth-century Renaissance*, ed. C.W. Hollister (Woodbridge, 1997).

Hollister, C. Warren and Baldwin, J.W., 'The rise of administrative kingship: Henry I and Philip Augustus', *American Historical Review*, 83 (1978), 867–905.

Holt, J.C., 'Feudal society and the family in early medieval England', *TRHS*, 5th ser., 32 (1982), 193–212; 33 (1983), 193–220; 34 (1984), 1–25.

Holt, J.C., 'Politics and property in early medieval England', *Past and Present*, no. 57 (1972), 3–52, repr. in *Landlords, Peasants and Politics in Medieval England*, ed. T.H. Aston (Cambridge, 1987), 65–114.

Holt, J.C., 'Rejoinder', *Past and Present*, no. 65 (1974), 127–35; repr. in *Landlords, Peasants and Politics in Medieval England*, ed. T.H. Aston (Cambridge, 1987), 132–40.

Holt, J.C., '1153: the treaty of Winchester', in *The Anarchy of King Stephen's Reign*, ed. E. King (Oxford, 1994), 291–316.

Hudson, J.G.H., *Land, Law and Lordship in Anglo-Norman England* (Oxford, 1994).

Hudson, J.G.H., *The Formation of the English Common Law* (London, 1996).

Kantorowicz, E.H., *The King's Two Bodies: A Study in Medieval Political Theology* (Princeton, 1957).

Kealey, E.J., *Roger of Salisbury, Viceroy of England* (London, 1972).

Keats-Rohan, K.S.B. (ed.), *Family Trees and the Roots of Politics: The Prosopography of Britain and France from the Tenth to the Twelfth Century* (Woodbridge, 1997).

Keefe, T.K., *Feudal Assessments and the Political Community under Henry II and his Sons* (Berkeley, CA, 1983).

King, E., 'King Stephen and the Anglo-Norman aristocracy', *History*, lix (1974), 180–94.

King, E., 'Mountsorrel and its region in King Stephen's reign', *Huntingdon Library Quarterly*, xliv (1980), 1–10.

King, E., 'The parish of Warter and the castle of Galchlin', *Yorkshire Archaeological Journal*, 52 (1980), 49–58.

King, E., 'The Anarchy of Stephen's reign', *TRHS*, 5th ser., 34 (1984), 133–54.

King, E., 'Waleran, count of Meulan, earl of Worcester, 1104–1166', in *Tradition and Change: Essays in Honour of M. Chibnall*, ed. D. Greenway and others (Cambridge, 1985), 165–76.

King, E., 'Dispute settlement in Anglo-Norman England', *ANS*, xiv, ed. M. Chibnall (Woodbridge, 1992), 115–30.

King, E., 'The foundation of Pipewell abbey, Northamptonshire', *HSJ*, 2 (1990), 167–77.

King, E. (ed.), *The Anarchy of King Stephen's Reign* (Oxford, 1994).

Latimer, P., 'Grants of "totus comitatus" in twelfth-century England: their origins and meaning', *Bulletin of the Institute of Historical Research*, lix (1986), 137–45.

Leedom, J.W., 'William of Malmesbury and Robert of Gloucester reconsidered', *Albion*, 6 (1974), 251–63.

Leedom, J.W., 'The English settlement of 1153', *History*, 65 (1980), 347–64.

Lewis, C.P., 'The King and Eye: a study in Anglo-Norman politics', *EHR*, 104 (1989), 569–87.

Lewis, C.P., 'The formation of the honor of Chester, 1066–1100', in *The Earldom of Chester and its Charters*, ed. A. Thacker (Journal of the Chester Archaeological Society, 71, 1991), 41–57.

Leyser, K.J., 'The Anglo-Norman succession, 1120–1125', *ANS*, xiii, ed. M. Chibnall (Woodbridge, 1991), 224–41.

LoPrete, K.A., 'The Anglo-Norman card of Adela of Blois', *Albion*, 22 (1990), 569–90.

McKisack, M., 'London and the succession to the Crown in the Middle Ages', in *Studies in Medieval History presented to Frederick Maurice Powicke*, ed. R.W. Hunt and others (Oxford, 1948), 76–89.

Megaw, I., 'The ecclesiastical policy of Stephen, 1135–39', in *Essays in British and Irish History in Honour of J.E. Todd*, ed. H.A. Cronne and others (London, 1949), 24–45.

Morey A. and Brooke, C.N.L., *Gilbert Foliot and his letters* (Cambridge, 1965).

Mortimer, R., 'Land and service: the tenants of the honour of Clare', *ANS*, viii, ed. R.A. Brown (Woodbridge, 1986), 177–97.

Mayr-Harding, H. and Moore, R.I. (eds), *Studies in Medieval History Presented to R.H.C. Davies* (London, 1985).

Painter, S., *William Marshal* (Baltimore, 1933).

Parker, C.J.W., *The English Historical Tradition since 1850* (Edinburgh, 1990).

Patourel, J. Le, *The Norman Empire* (Oxford, 1976).

Patterson, R.B., 'William of Malmesbury's Robert of Gloucester: a re-evaluation of the *Historia Novella*', *American Historical Review*, 70 (1965), 983–97.

Patterson, R.B., 'Stephen's Shaftesbury charter: another case against William of Malmesbury', *Speculum*, 43 (1968), 487–92.

Poole, A.L., *From Domesday Book to Magna Carta* (2nd edn., Oxford, 1955).

Powicke, F.M., *The Loss of Normandy* (Manchester, 1913).

Prestwich, J.O., 'The treason of Geoffrey de Mandeville', *EHR*, 103 (1988), 283–312, 960–67.

Richardson, H.G. and Sayles, G.O., *The Governance of Medieval England* (Edinburgh, 1963).

Round, J.H., *Geoffrey de Mandeville: A Study of the Anarchy* (London, 1892).

Rowlands, I.W., 'The making of the March: aspects of the Norman settlement in Dyfed', *ANS*, iii, ed. R.A. Brown (Woodbridge, 1980), 142–57.

Saltman, A., *Theobald, Archbishop of Canterbury* (London, 1955).

Sassier, Y., *Louis VII* (Paris, 1991).

Sawyer, P., '1066–1086: a tenurial revolution', in *Domesday Book. A Reassessment*, ed. P. Sawyer (London, 1983), 71–85.

Sharpe, R., 'The prefaces of "Quadripartitus"', in *Law and Government in Medieval England and Normandy*, ed. G. Garnett and J. Hudson (Cambridge, 1994), 299–324.

Southern, R.W., 'The place of Henry I in English history' reprinted in *Medieval Humanism and Other Studies* (Oxford, 1970), 206–33.

Stacy, N.E., 'Henry of Blois and the lordship of Glastonbury', *EHR*, 114 (1999), 1–33.

Stenton, F.M., *The First Century of English Feudalism, 1066–1166* (2nd edn., Oxford, 1960).

Stringer, K.J., *The Reign of Stephen* (London, 1993).

Stubbs, W., *The Constitutional History of England* (3 vols, Oxford, 1874–8).

Thacker, A.T. (ed.), *The Earldom of Chester and its Charters* (Journal of the Chester Archaeological Society, 71, 1991).

Thompson, K., 'Family and influence to the south of Normandy in the eleventh century: the lordship of Bellême', *Journal of Medieval History*, 11 (1985), 215–26.

Thompson, K., 'William Talvas, count of Ponthieu and the politics of the Anglo-Norman realm', in *England and Normandy in the Middle Ages*, ed. D.R. Bates and A. Curry (London, 1994), 169–84.

Thompson, K., 'The lords of L'Aigle: ambition and insecurity on the borders of Normandy', *ANS*, xviii, ed. C. Harper-Bill (Woodbridge, 1995), 177–99.

Thompson, K., 'The formation of the county of Perche: the rise and fall of the house of Gouet', in *Family Trees and the Roots of Politics: The Prosopography of Britain and France from the Tenth to the Twelfth Century*, ed. K.S.B. Keats-Rohan (Woodbridge, 1997), 300–14.

Thorne, S.E., 'English feudalism and estates in land', *Cambridge Law Journal* (1959), 193–209, repr. idem, *Essays in English Legal History* (London, 1985), 13–29.

Walker, D., 'The "honours" of the earls of Hereford in the twelfth century', *Transactions of the Bristol and Gloucestershire Archaeological Society*, lxxix (1960), 174–211.

Walker, D., 'Miles of Gloucester, earl of Hereford', *Transactions of the Bristol and Gloucestershire Archaeological Society*, lxxvii (1958), 66–84.

Wareham, A., 'The motives and politics of the Bigod family, c.1066–1177', *ANS*, xvii, ed. C. Harper-Bill (Woodbridge, 1994), 223–42.

Warren, W.L., *The Governance of Norman and Angevin England, 1086–1272* (London, 1987).

White, G., 'King Stephen, Duke Henry and Ranulf de Gernons, earl of Chester', *EHR*, 91 (1976), 555–65.

White, G., 'Were the Midlands "wasted" during Stephen's reign?', *Midland History*, 10 (1985), 26–46.

White, G., 'The end of Stephen's reign', *History*, lxxv (1990), 3–22.

White, G., 'Continuity in government', in *The Anarchy of King Stephen's Reign*, ed. E. King (Oxford, 1994), 117–44.

White, G.H., 'King Stephen's earldoms', *TRHS*, 4th ser., xiii (1930), 51–82.

Wightman, W.E., *The Lacy Family in England and Normandy, 1066–1194* (Oxford, 1966).

Williams, D. (ed.), *England in the Twelfth Century* (Woodbridge, 1990).

Yoshitake, K., 'The Exchequer in the reign of Stephen', *EHR*, 103 (1988).

Yoshitake, K., 'The arrest of the bishops in 1139 and its consequences', *Journal of Medieval History*, 14 (1988), 97–114.

Maps

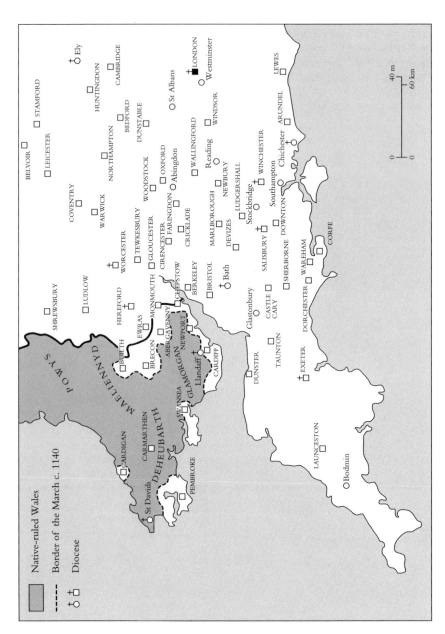

The March and southwest England in Stephen's reign

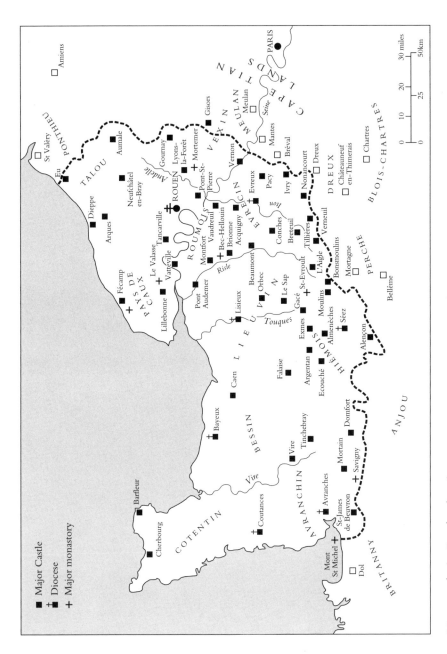

Legend:
- ■ Major Castle
- ✦ Diocese
- ✚ Major monastery

Normandy in Stephen's reign

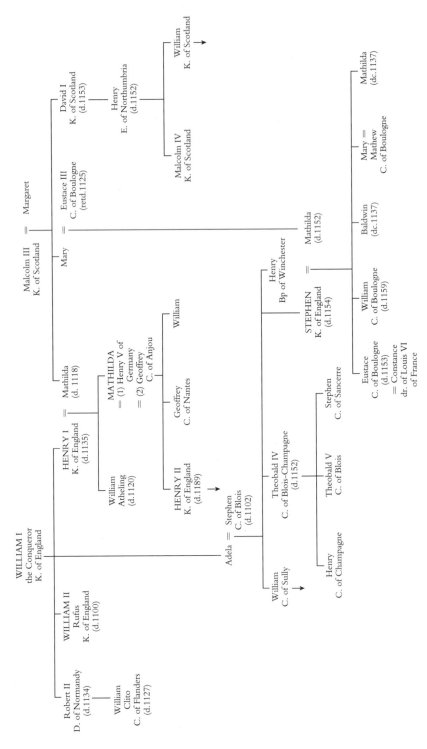

Genealogical table showing the connections of Stephen of Blois

Index

Guildford 181

Guines, county of 27 (count of, *see* Aubrey)

Guizot, François 3 and n

Gundreda, countess of Norfolk, second wife of Earl Hugh Bigod 120

Gundreda, daughter of Earl William II of Warenne, countess of Warwick 267–8

Guy, count of Ponthieu 27n

Guy de Sablé 198

Gwent 110, 236

Gwent, Upper 159

Gwlad Morgan (or Glamorgan), kingdom of 55, 56

Gwynedd, kingdom of 55, 56, 58, 148, 228, 255, 305

Gwynllwg, lordship of (in Gwent) 236n

Hainault, counts of (*see* Baldwin IV)

Hainault, wood in Essex 333 and n

Haltonshire 165n

Hamelin, abbot of Gloucester 276n, 304

Hampshire 208, 220, 264–5

Hamstead Marshall 162, 163 and n, 214

Hanslope 174 and n

Harold II, earl of Wessex and king of England 54, 324

Harptree 80

Harterness (Hartlepool), lordship of (*see* Robert de Brus) 149

Hasculf de Tany 177

Hastings, battle of 69

Hastings, lordship of 149

Hatfield, forest of 333n

Havering 339

Hawise, countess of Gloucester, wife of Earl William, daughter of Robert II of Leicester 156, 237 and n

Hawise, countess of Perche, wife of Count Rotrou III, daughter of Walter of Salisbury 163n, 196

Hayling Island 107n

Hedingham, castle of 260, 261

Helias de St-Saens 27

Helmerichs, Robert 248n

Helmid, anchorite of Faversham 317

Hempsted 158, 159 and n

Henry, abbot of Glastonbury (1126) bishop of Winchester (1129), son of Stephen-Henry, count of Blois 12–13, 28n, 54n, 58 and n, 94, 108, 114n, 136, 170 and n, 172, 175n, 178, 179, 189, 207, 214, 220, 316 (birth) 12, 13n (and Henry I) 12–13, 340 (and Glastonbury) 13–14, 46 and n, 157, 290–1, 301, 302 (and Winchester) 13–14, 183–5, 208 (character of) 13–14, 58, 178 (and Stephen) 36 and n, 45n, 51 and n, 52, 58, 68, 101, 102, 119, 128, 169, 181, 189, 261, 297, 298–301, 341 (his fall from royal favour) 73, 102 (and Canterbury) 63, 73, 91–3, 300, 301 (and Uffculme) 51n, 54n, 123 (diplomatic activity of) 47, 51, 63, 134, 180–1, 247 and n, 248, 261n, 265, 270 (and ecclesiastical appointments) 46 and n, 101, 119, 174, 177, 300–3, 304 (his legateship) 93, 100, 308, 309, 310 (his castles) 94n, 206, 264n (and the empress) 109, 110, 169–70, 180–1, 183–5, 300 (and 1153 settlement) 271–3

Henry, count of Champagne 252

Henry, count of Eu 99, 139n, 312

Henry, count of Louvain 89n

Henry, earl of Huntingdon and Northumbria, son of King David of Scotland 96, 175n, 200n, 205, 242, 275n, 313, 321n, 323 (homage to Stephen) 40 (earl of Huntingdon) 41, 323 (grants to) 41, 154 (and earldom of Northumbria) 41, 73, 89–90, 117n, 154–5, 310, 326 (and Stephen) 42, 90, 102, 323, 326 (invasions of England) 74, 82 (marriage of) 90 (and Ranulf of Chester) 137, 139, 242 (political affinity of) 154–5, 165 (and William Cumin) 310 (private coinage of) 323, 331 (death of) 266

Henry, earl of Warwick (his sons, Roger, Robert du Neubourg, Rotrou of Evreux, Henry du Neubourg of Gower) 65, 158n

Henry I, king of England (1100) duke of Normandy (1106) (his sons William Atheling, Robert of Gloucester,